South Africa
a country study

Federal Research Division
Library of Congress
Edited by
Rita M. Byrnes
Research Completed
May 1996

On the cover: Cape Town skyline against Table Mountain

Third Edition, First Printing, 1997.

Library of Congress Cataloging-in-Publication Data

South Africa : a country study / Federal Research Division,
  Library of Congress ; edited by Rita M. Byrnes. — 3d ed.
  [Rev. ed.]
      p. cm. — (Area handbook series, ISSN 1057–5294)
  (DA Pam ; 550–93)
      "Supersedes the 1981 edition of South Africa : a coun-
  try study, edited by Harold D. Nelson."—T.p. verso.
      "Research completed May 1996."
      Includes bibliographical references (pp. 421–483) and
  index.
      ISBN 0–8444-0796–8 (alk. paper)
      1. South Africa. I. Byrnes, Rita M., 1943– . II. Library
  of Congress. Federal Research Division. III. Series. IV.
  Series: DA Pam ; 550–93.
DT1719.S67 1997   96–48983
968—dc21   CIP

Headquarters, Department of the Army
DA Pam 550–93

For sale by the Superintendent of Documents, U.S. Government Printing Office
Washington, D.C. 20402

Foreword

This volume is one in a continuing series of books prepared by the Federal Research Division of the Library of Congress under the Country Studies/Area Handbook Program sponsored by the Department of the Army. The last two pages of this book list the other published studies.

Most books in the series deal with a particular foreign country, describing and analyzing its political, economic, social, and national security systems and institutions, and examining the interrelationships of those systems and the ways they are shaped by historical and cultural factors. Each study is written by a multidisciplinary team of social scientists. The authors seek to provide a basic understanding of the observed society, striving for a dynamic rather than a static portrayal. Particular attention is devoted to the people who make up the society, their origins, dominant beliefs and values, their common interests and the issues on which they are divided, the nature and extent of their involvement with national institutions, and their attitudes toward each other and toward their social system and political order.

The books represent the analysis of the authors and should not be construed as an expression of an official United States government position, policy, or decision. The authors have sought to adhere to accepted standards of scholarly objectivity. Corrections, additions, and suggestions for changes from readers will be welcomed for use in future editions.

Louis R. Mortimer
Chief
Federal Research Division
Library of Congress
Washington, DC 20540–4840

Acknowledgments

The authors wish to acknowledge the contributions of the writers of the 1981 edition of *South Africa: A Country Study,* edited by Harold D. Nelson. The authors also wish to thank numerous individuals in various government agencies and private institutions who generously shared their expertise and research materials in the production of this book. Thanks are due to R.T.K. Scully, Medical Assistance Programs (MAP) International; Harvey Leifert, Medical Education for South African Blacks (MESAB), Inc.; James B. Parks, American Federation of Labor-Congress of Industrial Organizations (AFL-CIO); Smaroula Georgina Stephens, United States Information Agency; and Witney Schneidman, Samuels International Associates. Valuable assistance was also provided by analysts Brenda Branaman, Ed Campbell, Joe Dickie, Simon Dodge, W. Fitzpatrick, Thomas Ofcansky, and Rachel Warner. Specialists at the International Labor Organization; Investor Responsibility Research Center; United States Department of Commerce, Bureau of the Census International Programs Center; and World Bank-International Monetary Fund Joint Library also helped the authors acquire recent information on South Africa. None of these individuals is responsible for the work of the authors, however.

Members of the diplomatic mission of South Africa provided valuable assistance despite the pressing demands of their country's political transition. Juan A. Henriquez, of the South African Embassy Public Affairs Office, deserves particular thanks; he and several other embassy officials took time to explain the often complex transition as it unfolded in their country. The views presented in this book do not necessarily agree with theirs, however.

Several employees of the Library of Congress made special efforts to acquire timely materials on South Africa for this volume. Afaf S. McGowan, of the African/Middle Eastern Acquisitions Section; M. Laverne Page, of the African-Middle Eastern Division; and Joseph Rowe, of the Federal Research Division, deserve particular mention.

The authors also wish to thank members of the Federal Research Division staff who contributed directly to the preparation of the manuscript. These people include Sandra W. Meditz, who reviewed all drafts and served as liaison with the sponsoring agency; Marilyn Majeska, who managed editing and book production; Andrea Merrill, who reviewed tables and maps; Barbara Edgerton and Izella Watson, who performed word processing and initial typesetting; and David P. Cabitto and Janie L. Gilchrist, who prepared the camera-ready copy. Thanks also to Helen C. Metz for proofreading almost-final copy.

Contributors to the preparation of this volume also included Mimi Cantwell, who edited chapters; Carolyn Hinton, who performed the prepublication editorial review; and Joan C. Cook, who compiled the index. Graphics were prepared by David P. Cabitto, who, along with the firm of Maryland Mapping and Graphics, prepared the final maps. Special thanks are owed to Sandra K. Ferrell, who designed the illustrations on the cover and the title page of the chapters.

Finally, the authors acknowledge the generosity of individuals who allowed their photographs to be used in this study. Particular thanks go to R.T.K. Scully for photographs taken during his extensive anthropological research and travels in South Africa.

Contents

List of Figures

Preface

South Africa's emergence from global isolation in the 1990s parallels its political and economic reorganization, as it works to eliminate vestiges of the notorious system of apartheid. That system provoked international condemnation and deprived society of much of its human potential, and coping with its legacies has complicated the process of establishing a new system based on nonracial norms. An interim constitution, first implemented in April 1994 to govern the political transition, is being replaced by a new constitution, intended to protect legal equality for individuals regardless of racial identity after 1999. The transition has just passed the halfway mark as this book goes to press, and this volume reflects the fact that many political and social issues remain unresolved.

This book replaces *South Africa: A Country Study*, also produced in a time of turmoil in 1981, as the country began to recognize some of the demands for broader political participation by all racial groups. Like its predecessor, this study is an attempt to treat in a concise and objective manner the dominant historical, social, economic, political, and national security aspects of contemporary South Africa. Sources of information included scholarly books, journal articles, and monographs; official reports of governments and international organizations; foreign and domestic newspapers; the authors' previous research and observations; and numerous periodicals. Chapter bibliographies appear at the end of the book; brief comments on particularly valuable sources appear at the end of each chapter.

Place-names follow the system adopted by the United States Board on Geographic Names (BGN), wherever possible. Nine new provinces have been designated to replace the four provinces and ten homelands of the apartheid era. Some other desigations—for historical landmarks, public holidays, as well as some public buildings and government offices—are still being changed in the mid-1990s in recognition of the country's new political dispensation. New names have been included as available. As of early 1997, the provincial capital of KwaZulu-Natal is still to be decided between Ulundi and Pietermaritzburg. The apartheid-era designation for the racial category known as "coloured" is retained in this volume for historical accuracy.

The country has eleven official languages, which include nine Bantu languages, selected to recognize the first language of almost all South Africans. The two previous official languages, Afrikaans and English, remain important, but the former no longer dominates the public media and is being phased out in some official contexts, such as military training. Some provincial legislatures are considering language policies to be incorporated into provincial constitutions in the late 1990s.

All measurements in this book rely on the metric system; a conversion table is provided to assist those readers who are unfamiliar with metric measurements (see table 1, Appendix). A glossary is also included to explain terms with which the reader may not be familiar. The use of the term *billion* follows the American system; for example, one billion means 1,000,000,000.

The body of the text reflects information available as of May 1996. Certain other portions of the text, however, have been updated: the Introduction concludes with a discussion of significant events that have occurred since the information cutoff date; the Country Profile and Chronology include updated information as available; and the Bibliography lists recently published sources thought to be particularly helpful to the reader.

Table A. Selected Acronyms and Contractions

Acronym or Contraction	Organization or Term
AAC	All-African Convention
Aasac	All-African Student Committee
ABSA	Amalgamated Banks of South Africa
ACDP	African Christian Democratic Party
ADB	African Development Bank
ADM	African Democratic Movement
AEC	Atomic Energy Corporation
AECI	African Explosives and Chemical Industries
AHI	Afrikaanse Handelsinstituut (Afrikaner Trade Institute)
AIDS	acquired immune deficiency syndrome
ALUSAF	Aluminum Corporation of South Africa
Amcor	African Metals Corporation
AMCP	African Moderates Congress Party
AME	African Methodist Episcopal Church
AMP	Africa Muslim Party
AMWU	African Mineworkers' Union
ANC	African National Congress
ANCWL	African National Congress Women's League
ANCYL	African National Congress Youth League
AOW	African Organisation for Women
APLA	Azanian People's Liberation Army
ARM	African Resistance Movement
Armscor	Armaments Corporation of South Africa
AVF	Afrikaner Volksfront
AVK	Afrikanervroue-Kenkrag (Akrikaner Women's Organisation)
AWB	Afrikaner Weerstandsbeweging (Afrikaner Resistance Movement)
Azanyu	Azanian National Youth Unity
BBB	Blanke Bevrydingsbeweging (White Protection Movement)
BCM	Black Consciousness Movement
BCMA	Black Consciousness Movement of Azania
BDF	Bophuthatswana Defence Force
BMATT	British Military Advisory Training Team
BOSS	Bureau of State Security
BPC	Black People's Convention
BWB	Boere Weerstandsbeweging (Boer Resistance Movement)
CAAA	Comprehensive Antiapartheid Act
CCI	Crime Combatting and Investigation Office
CDF	Ciskei Defence Force
CID	Criminal Investigation Department

Acronym or Contraction	Organization or Term
CITES	Convention on International Trade in Endangered Species of Wild Fauna and Flora
CNETU	Council of Non-European Trade Unions
Codesa	Convention for a Democratic South Africa
Cosag	Concerned South Africans Group
COSAS	Congress of South African Students
COSATU	Congress of South African Trade Unions
CP	Conservative Party
CPSA	Communist Party of South Africa
CSO	Central Selling Organisation
CYL	Congress Youth League (also ANCYL)
DBSA	Development Bank of Southern Africa
DCC	Defence Command Council
DP	Democratic Party
EAC	Economic Advisory Council
EC	European Community
ECC	End Conscription Campaign
EEC	European Economic Community
EEZ	Exclusive Economic Zone
Eskom	Electricity Supply Commission
EU	European Union
FAK	Federasie van Afrikaanse Kultuurvereniginge (Federation of Afrikaner Cultural Organisations)
FAWU	Food and Allied Workers' Union
FF	Freedom Front
FNLA	Frente Nacionale de Libertação de Angola (National Front for the Liberation of Angola)
Foskor	Phosphate Development Corporation
FP	Federal Party
FRELIMO	Frente de Libertação de Moçambique (Front for the Liberation of Mozambique)
FSAW	Federation of South African Women
FY	Fiscal Year
GDP	gross domestic product
Genmin	General Mining Corporation
GNP	gross national product
GST	general sales tax
HEU	highly enriched uranium
HNP	Herenigde Nasionale Party (Reunited National Party)
HNP	Herstigte Nasionale Party (Reconstituted National Party)
IBRD	International Bank for Reconstruction and Development
ICU	Industrial and Commercial Workers' Union of South Africa
IDA	International Development Association
IDC	Industrial Development Corporation

Table A. (Continued) Selected Acronyms and Contractions

Acronym or Contraction	Organization or Term
IDRC	International Development Research Centre
IEC	Independent Electoral Commission
IFC	International Finance Corporation
IFP	Inkatha Freedom Party
IMF	International Monetary Fund
IOC	International Olympic Committee
IP	Independent Party
Iscor	South African Iron and Steel Corporation
ISL	International Socialist League
JATS	Joint Air Training Scheme
JCI	Johannesburg Consolidated Investments
JMC	Joint Management Center
JMCC	Joint Military Coordinating Council
JSE	Johannesburg Stock Exchange
MARNET	Military Area Radio Network
MDM	Mass Democratic Movement
MF	Minority Front
MK	Umkhonto we Sizwe (Spear of the Nation)
MNR	Mozambican National Resistance (also Renamo)
MPLA	Movimento Popular de Libertação de Angola (Popular Movement for the Liberation of Angola)
NACOSA	National AIDS Convention of South Africa
Nactu	National Council of Trade Unions
NAFCOC	National African Federated Chamber of Commerce
NAM	Nonaligned Movement
NDM	National Democratic Movement
NEC	National Executive Committee
NEHAWU	National Education, Health, and Allied Workers' Union
NGK	Nederduitse Gereformeerde Kerk (Dutch Reformed Church)
NIA	National Intelligence Agency
NICC	National Intelligence Coordinating Committee
NIDR	National Institute for Defence Research
NP	National Party
NPKF	National Peacekeeping Force
NPP	National Peoples' Party
NPT	Nuclear Nonproliferation Treaty
NSMS	National Security Management System
NUM	National Union of Mineworkers
NUMSA	National Union of Metalworkers of South Africa
NUSAS	National Union of South African Students
NWC	National Working Committee
OAU	Organization of African Unity
OPEC	Organization of the Petroleum Exporting Countries

Table A. (Continued) Selected Acronyms and Contractions

Acronym or Contraction	Organization or Term
PAC	Pan-Africanist Congress
PASO	Pan-Africanist Students' Organisation
PFP	Progressive Federal Party
Popcru	Police and Prisons Civil Rights Union
PSA	Public Service Association
PTA	Preferential Trade Area for Eastern and Southern Africa
Putco	Public Utility Transport Corporation
PWV	Pretoria-Witwatersrand-Vereeniging
RDP	Reconstruction and Development Programme
Renamo	Resistencia Nacional Moçambicana (Mozambican National Resistance)
RFC	Royal Flying Corps
RSC	regional services council
SAA	South African Airways
SAA	South African Army
SAAC	South African Aviation Corps
SAAF	South African Air Force
SABC	South African Broadcasting Corporation
SACC	South African Council of Churches
SACCOLA	South African Employers' Consultative Committee on Labour Affairs
SACOB	South African Chamber of Business
SACP	South African Communist Party
SACTU	South African Congress of Trade Unions
SACU	Southern African Customs Union
SADC	Southern African Development Community
SADCC	Southern African Development Coordination Conference
SADF	South African Defence Force(s)
Safmarine	South African Marine Corporation
SAIC	South African Indian Congress
SAIRR	South African Institute of Race Relations
Samcor	South African Motor Corporation
SAMS	South African Medical Service
SAN	South African Navy
SANAC	South African Native Affairs Commission
SANDF	South African National Defence Force
SANLAM	South African National Life Assurance Company
Sansco	South African National Student Congress
SANTAM	South African National Trust Company
SAP	South African Party
SAP	South African Police
SAPA	South African Press Association
SAPS	South African Police Service
SAPU	South African Police Union

Table A. *(Continued) Selected Acronyms and Contractions*

Acronym or Contraction	Organization or Term
SARCC	South African Rail Commuter Corporation
SASO	South African Students' Organisation
SASOL	South African Coal, Oil, and Gas Corporation
SASS	South African Secret Service
Satour	South African Tourism Board
SATS	South African Transport Services
SDF	Seaward Defence Force
SEIFSA	Steel and Engineering Industries Federation of South Africa
Soekor	Southern Oil Exploration Corporation
Soweto	Southwestern Townships
SSC	State Security Council
SWAPO	South-West Africa People's Organisation
SWATF	South-West Africa Territorial Force
TEC	Transitional Executive Council
UDF	Union Defence Force(s)
UDF	United Democratic Front
UNESCO	United Nations Educational, Scientific, and Cultural Organization
UNHCR	United Nations High Commissioner for Refugees
UNITA	União Nacional para a Independência Total de Angola (National Union for the Total Independence of Angola)
UNOMOZ	United Nations Operation in Mozambique
UNOMSA	United Nations Observer Mission in South Africa
UP	United Party
Usco	Union Steel Company
UWUSA	United Workers Union of South Africa
VAT	value-added tax
VOC	Verenigde Oostindische Compagnie (Dutch East India Company)
WHO	World Health Organization
ZANU-PF	Zimbabwe African National Union-Patriotic Front
ZCC	Zion Christian Church

Table B. Chronology of Important Events

Period	Description
EARLY HISTORY	
ca. 50,000 B.C.	Date of archaeological remains of Homo sapiens in southern Africa.
ca. 25,000 B.C.	Earliest rock art paintings in southern Africa.
ca. 14,000 B.C.	Earliest archaeological evidence of San hunter-gatherers.
ca. 500 B.C.	Earliest archaeological evidence of sheep and cattle herding.
ca. A.D. 300	Archaeological evidence of Iron-Age settlements south of the Limpopo River.
FIFTEENTH CENTURY	
1488	Portuguese navigator Bartholomeu Dias rounds Cape of Good Hope. Khoisan-speaking herdsmen and hunters establish trade with Europeans.
1497	Portuguese navigator Vasco da Gama arrives at Cape of Good Hope en route to India.
SIXTEENTH CENTURY	Portuguese ships land at Table Bay; Bantu-speaking farmers and herdsmen establish trade with Europeans.
SEVENTEENTH CENTURY	
1652	First permanent Dutch settlement at Cape of Good Hope.
1658	Dutch import slaves from Angola and West Africa.
1659	Khoikhoi revolt against Dutch encroachment.
1663	European settlement at Saldanha Bay.
1673–77	Warfare between Khoikhoi and Dutch.
1688	French Huguenots begin to settle at Cape.
EIGHTEENTH CENTURY	
1713	Smallpox epidemic devastates Khoikhoi.
1779–81	Frontier warfare; Afrikaners defeat Xhosa.
1793	Frontier warfare: Xhosa defeat Afrikaners.
1795	Britain seizes control of the Cape.
1799	First of a series of Xhosa-British wars.
NINETEENTH CENTURY	
ca. 1800	Drought- and famine-produced upheaval in Natal.
1803–06	Dutch Batavian Republic controls Cape.
1806	Britain regains control over Cape.
1807	Britain ends its slave trade; British missionaries arrive in southern Africa.
1809	Pass laws enacted.
1810	Shaka defeats Buthelezi chiefdom.
1814	London Convention; Dutch formally cede Cape to British.
1815	Afrikaner rebellion against British rule at Slachters Nek.

Table B. (Continued) Chronology of Important Events

Period	Description
1816	Shaka assumes control over Zulu.
1817–28	*Mfecane* (or crushing); Zulu expansion, decade of upheaval.
1819	British defeat of Xhosa; expulsion of Africans between Great Fish and Keiskama rivers.
1824	First white settlement at Port Natal.
1828	Shaka assassinated, succeeded by Dingane.
	Mpondo repulse Zulu attacks; Zulu power wanes.
1828–34	Consolidation of Swazi kingdom under Sobhuza I, Sotho under Moshoeshoe I, Ndebele under Mzilikazi.
1834–35	British and colonial forces defeat Xhosa.
1834–38	Emancipation of slaves in Cape Colony after Britain abolishes slavery in its possessions.
1836–40	Great Trek begins: 6,000 Afrikaners migrate eastward from Cape Colony.
1838	Battle of Blood River on December 16 avenges Afrikaner deaths earlier that year.
1839	Voortrekker Republic of Natalia established.
1843	Britain annexes Natalia, renamed Natal.
1850	Last surviving San rock artists killed.
1852	Sand River Convention; Britain recognizes Transvaal as the independent Afrikaner South African Republic.
1854	Bloemfontein Convention; Britain recognizes Orange Free State as independent Afrikaner republic.
1856–57	Xhosa cattle sacrifices lead to famine.
1867	Diamonds discovered in Orange Free State and Kimberley.
1868	Britain annexes Sotho territory of Basutoland.
1870	Death of Sotho King Moshoeshoe I.
1872	Introduction of pass laws to control labor force in Kimberley diamond mines.
1873	Diamond diggers exceed 50,000.
1877	Britain annexes South African Republic, renamed Transvaal. Xhosa-Mfengu warfare.
1878	Britain claims Walvis Bay.
1879	Zulu defeat invading British force; British and colonial forces destroy Zulu army at Isandhlwana. Griqualand East annexed to Cape Colony.
1880	First Anglo-Boer War erupts. Cecil Rhodes establishes De Beers Consolidated Mines.
1881	Pretoria Convention recognizes Transvaal independence.
1883	Paul Kruger president of South African Republic.
1885	Cape-to-Kimberley railroad completed.
1886	Gold discovered at Witwatersrand; Johannesburg established.

Table B. (Continued) Chronology of Important Events

Period	Description
1890	Rhodes prime minister of Cape Colony.
1891	German headquarters established in South-West Africa.
1892	Property qualifications reduce coloured voters in Cape.
1894	Cape Colony annexes Mpondo territory.
1895–96	Unsuccessful Jameson Raid against Afrikaner dominance in Transvaal.
1897	Part of Zululand incorporated into British colony of Natal; King Solomon ka Dinizulu exiled.
1897–98	Rinderpest epidemic decimates livestock.
1899	South African (Anglo-Boer) War.
TWENTIETH CENTURY	
1900	Britain claims Transvaal (South African Republic).
1902 May	British victory; Peace Treaty of Vereeniging ends South African War.
1905–06	Last Zulu uprising against British.
1907	White miners strike against Chinese labor.
1909	British Parliament enacts the South Africa Act, proposed constitution of Union of South Africa.
1910	Self-governing Union of South Africa established within British Commonwealth.
1911	Legislation reserves skilled jobs for whites.
1912	Land Bank established to assist white farmers. South African Native National Congress (later African National Congress—ANC) formed.
1913	Natives Land Act limits black ownership to reserves.
1913–14	Campaign of civil disobedience led by Indian human rights activist Mohandas Gandhi.
1914	Government foils coup plot by Afrikaner military officers. South Africa invades German South-West Africa, Germans surrender.
1914–19	South Africa supports Allies in World War I.
1918	Founding of Afrikaner Broederbond.
1920	South Africa receives League of Nations mandate to administer former German colony, South-West Africa.
1921	Communist Party of South Africa established (later—after 1953—the South African Communist Party).
1922	Army quells miners' strike, killing 214.
1923	Natives Urban Areas Act authorizes segregation in urban areas. South African Indian Congress established. South African Native National Congress becomes African National Congress (ANC).
1925	Afrikaans recognized as South Africa's official language.
1927	Segregation compulsory in twenty-six urban areas.

Table B. (Continued) Chronology of Important Events

Period		Description
1929		National Party wins national elections.
1931		Britain's Statute of Westminster affirms autonomy of South African parliament.
1934		South African parliament enacts Status of Union Act claiming full sovereignty for South Africa.
1936		Black voting rights revoked in Cape; black land ownership expanded, but still restricted to 13 percent of land.
1939		Ossewabrandwag (Ox-wagon Guard) Afrikaner paramilitary group established.
1939–45		South Africa supports Allies in World War II.
1943		ANC Youth League formed. United Party wins general elections.
1946		Army quells gold mine strikes.
1947		South Africa rejects United Nations (UN) oversight in South-West Africa.
1948	May	National Party (NP) election victory based on racial issues.
	August	Government ends military training for blacks.
1949	January	Asian-Zulu clashes in Durban and Rand area.
	May	South Africa rejects UN concern over treatment of Indians.
	June	Prohibition of Mixed Marriages Act.
	December	Opening of Voortrekker Monument.
1950	April	South Africa severs judicial appeals channels to British Privy Council.
	May	Population Registration Act authorizes racial classification.
	June	Suppression of Communism Act bans anti-apartheid activities. Communist Party of South Africa disbands (reemerges in 1953 as South African Commnunist Party).
	July	International Court of Justice supports League of Nations oversight in South-West Africa. Group Areas Act authorizes residential segregation.
	August	South African Air Force assists UN in Korean war effort, flies 10,000 missions in three years. NP election victory in South-West Africa.
	December	South Africa rejects UN criticism of apartheid, reasserts claim to South-West Africa. Black political organizations unite to oppose apartheid.
1951	February	Britain blocks incorporation of Botswana, Lesotho, Swaziland into South Africa.
	May	Separate Representation of Voters Act separates voting lists for whites, coloureds.
	November	United States-South Africa military agreement under Mutual Defense Assistance Act.
	December	ANC leaders petition for direct parliamentary representation, end to apartheid. UN calls for South-West African independence. South Africa suspends participation in UN General Assembly.

Table B. (Continued) Chronology of Important Events

Period		Description
1952	March	South African Supreme Court invalidates removal of coloureds from voting lists.
	June	Passive resistance campaign by ANC and South African Indian Congress; 8,000 arrested.
	November	Interracial violence flares. Black Defiance Campaign leaders convicted of "statutory communism."
1953	October	Reservation of Separate Amenities Act strengthens apartheid in public places. Bantu Education Act limits black education. Communist Party of South Africa reactivated as South African Communist Party (SACP).
1954	August	South Africa proclaims South-West Africa a province.
1955	February	International condemnation of forcible resettlement of Sophiatown (most residents moved to area later named Soweto).
	April	South Africa quits United Nations Educational, Scientific, and Cultural Organization (UNESCO) after protests over apartheid.
	June	Congress of the People adopts Freedom Charter based on UN Universal Declaration of Human Rights; signers later charged with high treason.
1956	February	South Africa expels Soviet diplomats.
	March	Tomlinson Commission recommends formation of Bantustans in reserved areas.
	May	Industrial Conciliation Act reserves most skilled jobs for whites.
	December	Police arrest 156 for signing Freedom Charter.
1957	September	Forty die in Sotho-Zulu violence.
1958	April	Parliamentary elections increase NP majority.
1959	April	Pan-Africanist Congress established.
	June	Racial violence erupts in Durban, lasts several months.
	November	Queen Elizabeth II appoints Charles Swart governor general of South Africa.
1960	February	British Prime Minister Harold Macmillan's "Winds of Change" speech.
	March	Sharpeville protests over pass laws; at least sixty-seven deaths, several thousand arrested.
1961	January	UN Secretary General Dag Hammerskjöld visits South Africa, expresses racial concerns.
	March	Pretoria court acquits twenty-eight activists, including ANC leaders Nelson Mandela and Walter Sisulu.
	May	Republic of South Africa established on May 31, quits Commonwealth. Month-long police raids, 8,000 arrested.
	June	ANC establishes military wing, Umkhonto we Sizwe (Spear of the Nation); PAC establishes armed wing Poqo (blacks only).

Table B. (Continued) Chronology of Important Events

Period		Description
	November	UN General Assembly refuses to recognize South Africa.
	December	ANC leader Albert Luthuli receives Nobel Peace Prize. Nelson Mandela announces campaign of sabotage against government buildings.
1962	November	UN General Assembly calls for sanctions against South Africa. Nelson Mandela sentenced to five years in prison for inciting unrest, travelling abroad without a passport.
1963	May	Military wings of ANC, PAC banned.
		Newly established Organization of African Unity (OAU) charter condemns apartheid.
	August	UN voluntary embargo on arms shipments to South Africa. Libya joins Algeria and Egypt, prohibits South African overflights.
	October	Rivonia trial of ANC activists begins.
1964	January	Odendaal Commission recommends apartheid in South-West Africa.
	March	OAU funds liberation fighters in southern Africa.
	June	Eight ANC activists, including Nelson Mandela, sentenced to life in prison in Rivonia trial.
1966	June	Government snubs visiting United States Senator Robert Kennedy.
	September	Prime minister Verwoerd assassinated, succeeded by John Vorster. Bechuanaland independence from Britain as Botswana.
	October	Basutoland independence from Britain as Lesotho. UN General Assembly terminates South Africa's mandate to administer South-West Africa.
1967	May	Last British-appointed governor general and first president, Charles Swart, steps down.
	September	Malawi first black African state to establish diplomatic ties to South Africa.
	December	World's first heart transplant operation performed by South African surgeon, Dr. Christian Barnard, at Groote Schuur Hospital in Cape Town.
1968	September	Swaziland independence from Britain.
1969	May	Pan-Africanist Congress founder Robert Sobukwe released after nine years in prison.
	October	Herstigte (Reconstituted) National Party established by white extremist wing of NP.
	December	International Monetary Fund agrees to $35-an-ounce "floor" for South African gold.
1970	February	Black Homelands Citizenship Bill authorizes withdrawal of South African citizenship from blacks.
	May	International Olympic Committee (IOC) refuses recognition of South Africa (participation suspended since 1964).
1971	December	Zulu Prince Goodwill Zwelithini installed as king.

Table B. (Continued) Chronology of Important Events

Period		Description
1972		Black People's Convention founded to coordinate black consciousness movement role in politics. Afrikaner intellectuals protest against apartheid.
1973	November	Sixteen Arab countries implement OAU embargo against oil to South Africa.
1974		NP increases parliamentary majority in April elections. Coup in Portugal signals impending independence for colonies in Africa. UN General Assembly rejects South African participation.
1975	May	First television transmissions in South Africa.
	November	Reports of white South Africans killed in fighting in Angola.
1976	June	Worst racial violence in history in Soweto; 575 reported dead.
	August	Turnhalle Constitutional Conference sets Namibian (South-West African) independence December 1978 (subsequently postponed repeatedly until March 1990).
1977	January	Government acknowledges 2,000 South African troops in Angola.
	March	US corporations adopt Sullivan Principles to counter effects of apartheid.
	September	Black Consciousness leader Steve Biko dies in police detention; thousands attend funeral.
	November	UN mandatory embargo against arms shipments to South Africa. Pretoria adopts Total Strategy to counter internal and external threats.
1978		Ministry of Information scandal leads to Vorster resignation; succeeded by P. W. Botha.
1979		Government recognizes black labor unions.
1980	June	Largest conventional military assault since World War II on South-West Africa People's Organisation (SWAPO) bases in Angola.
1981	February	Asian, coloured populations win representation on President's Council.
1982	February	Labor activist Neil Aggett first white to die in police custody.
	March	NP expels extremist wing; Andries Treurnicht forms Conservative Party of South Africa.
1983	September	Parliament approves multiracial representation, excluding blacks.
	November	New constitution approved by whites-only referendum.
1984		Extension of UN sanctions barring military purchases from South Africa.
	March	Koeberg nuclear power station operational after 1982 sabotage. Nkomati Accord nonaggression pact with Mozambique.
	May	South Africa, Mozambique, Portugal agreement to build Cahora Bassa dam in Mozambique.
	August	Elections for tricameral parliament; escalating township unrest.

Table B. (Continued) Chronology of Important Events

Period		Description
	September	P. W. Botha named state president. Implementation of 1983 constitution establishing tricameral parliament.
	October	Anglican Bishop Desmond Tutu awarded Nobel Peace Prize.
1985	June	United States ban on computer, nuclear exports to South Africa for security forces. South African commando attacks on ANC in Botswana. First in a series of nationwide states of emergency.
	July	Britain blocks Commonwealth sanctions.
1986	January	President Botha opens Parliament with reference to "outdated concept of apartheid." Parliament repeals Pass Laws, Prohibition of Mixed Marriages Act.
	May	Military attacks on ANC in Botswana, Zambia, Zimbabwe.
	October	US Congress passes Comprehensive Antiapartheid Act (CAAA) over presidential veto. Mozambican President Samora Machel killed in plane crash in South Africa. Lesotho Highlands Water Project undertaken to provide water to South Africa. Dutch Reformed Church synod declares apartheid an error.
	November	United States bans direct US-South Africa air travel.
1987		United States bans new investments, bank loans to South Africa. National (white) elections name Conservative Party as parliamentary opposition. Mineworkers strike by 250,000.
1988	December	Angola-Namibia Accords signed in New York.
1989	January	Botha suffers stroke, Frederik W. (F. W.) de Klerk succeeds him as NP leader in February; as state president in August.
	February	Democratic Party established as alternative to ANC. UN Transitional Assistance Group (UNTAG) prepares for Namibian elections.
	July	President Botha, ANC leader Nelson Mandela meet for first talks in person.
	September	White, coloureds, Indians vote in parliamentary elections.
	October	Walter Sisulu and other activists released after 25 years in prison.
	November	Last South African troops withdraw from Namibia.
1990	February	Mandela released on February 11, after twenty-seven years in prison.
	March	Violent antigovernment demonstrations in Ciskei, Bophuthatswana.
	April	ANC exiles begin return to South Africa.
	July	First official meeting of Mandela and de Klerk.
	August	ANC declares end of armed struggle.
	October	Parliament repeals Reservation of Separate Amenities Act.

Table B. (Continued) Chronology of Important Events

Period		Description
1991	June	Repeal of Population Registration Act, Land Acts, Group Areas Act; and release of political prisoners.
	July	Most sanctions under US CAAA lifted. "Inkathagate" revelations of government funding for IFP. Nelson Mandela elected ANC president. IOC readmits South Africa.
	September	National Peace Accord agreement.
	December	Convention for a Democratic South Africa (Codesa) begins on December 20.
1992	January	Most European sanctions lifted; UN General Assembly ends restrictions on cultural, academic exchanges.
	March	Whites support political reforms in referendum.
	April	Arms manufacturing company, Denel, formed out of portion of Armaments Corporation of South Africa (Armscor) and subsidiaries.
	June	Kenyan president Moi visits, signals end of African boycott. ANC withdraws from Codesa because of IFP attack on Boipatong and sub-rosa support for IFP by police. Negotiations suspended.
	July	Mandela charges government with state terrorism before UN and OAU; fact-finding visit by UN envoy Cyrus Vance; arrival of UN observers.
	September	Ciskei Defence Force fires on ANC protesters; at least 29 deaths, 200 injured.
1993	March	Government proclaims nuclear weapons dismantled. Constitutional negotiations resume.
	April	SACP leader Chris Hani murdered by white radical. Death of ANC president Tambo.
	June	White radicals storm constitutional negotiations.
	July	President de Klerk, ANC leader Mandela visit US, jointly receive Liberty Medal. IFP, conservatives withdraw from constitutional negotiations.
	August	Political violence surges. US citizen Amy Biehl killed in township unrest. ANC acknowledges human rights' abuses in Angola, Tanzania.
	September	De Klerk, Mandela visit United States. Joint mission of ANC and South African Defence Forces (SADF) to United States to discuss military reorganization.
	October	Most UN sanctions lifted. Two whites sentenced to death for Hani murder.
	November	US CAAA repealed. Interim constitution signed by nineteen political parties, provides for 5-year Government of National Unity.
	December	Constitution of the Republic of South Africa ratified on December 22. Transitional Executive Council (TEC) established.
		De Klerk, Mandela receive Nobel Peace prize.

Table B. (Continued) Chronology of Important Events

Period		Description
1994	January	National Peacekeeping Force (NPKF) mobilized, disbanded in May. PAC suspends armed struggle, agrees to participate in national elections.
	February	South Africa formally relinquishes Walvis Bay to Namibia.
	March	TEC assumes control over Bophuthatswana after deaths in pre-election violence, and over Ciskei after police mutiny. Zulu demonstration erupts into violence at ANC headquarters (Shell House), Johannesburg; eight demonstrators killed. State of emergency in Natal, KwaZulu. Goldstone Commission report forces senior police suspensions.
	April	First democratic national elections held April 26–29 (April 27 first day of nationwide voting). Interim constitution implemented for five-year transition period on April 27. Violence subsides.
	May	Legislators elect Mandela president. Government announces Reconstruction and Development Programme. UN Security Council lifts arms embargo.
	June	South Africa joins Organization of African Unity, rejoins British Commonwealth of Nations, resumes participation in United Nations. British Military Advisory and Training Team assists military integration. Government proposes Truth and Reconciliation Commission to consider amnesty, compensation for human rights violations under apartheid.
	July	French president François Mitterrand first foreign head of state to visit. Resignation of Minister of Finance Derek Keys. South African Operation Mercy shipments to Rwanda. Mandela's first state visit (Mozambique).
	August	Mandela speech marking 100 days in office interrupted by labor unrest.
	September	New Air Force Headquarters opened in Pretoria. British Prime Minister's first address to South African parliament since 1960. Violent protests by coloureds against government racial bias.
	October	President Mandela on state visit to United States, addresses joint session of Congress. South African officials accept salary cuts to help fund development.
	November	Soweto forgives US$400 million unpaid rent, utility fees. South Africa hosts first conference in Africa on implementing Convention on Chemical Weapons.
	December	ANC conference reelects Mandela as president. South African Ambassador Franklin Sonn arrives in Washington.
1995	January	Death of Joe Slovo, minister of housing, former SACP leader.
	February	Constitutional Court sworn in by President Mandela. Mandela disavows reelection plans in 1999.

Table B. *(Continued)* Chronology of Important Events

Period		Description
	March	Winnie Mandela dismissed as deputy minister for arts, culture, science, and technology. Unification of two-tier exchange rate; financial rand abolished. Pretoria-Witwatersrand-Vereeniging (PWV) province renamed Gauteng (Place of Gold).
	June	Mandela claims responsibility for March 1994 Shell House shootings of IFP demonstrators. Constitutional Court abolishes death penalty.
	August	South Africa agrees to lease oil storage space to Iran.
	November	Archbishop Desmond Tutu named chair of Truth and Reconciliation Commission. Mandela denounces Nigeria's execution of human rights activists, including Ken Sarowiwa.
1996	January	Mandela initiates urgent peace talks in KwaZulu-Natal aimed at ending political violence and resuming IFP participation in Constitutional Assembly.
	April	First public hearing of Truth and Reconciliation Commission, in East London, April 15. White extremists sentenced to prison for 1994 bombings intended to derail national elections.
	May	Parliament approves draft final constitution. Constitutional Assembly Chair Cyril Ramaphosa resigns from parliament to join private sector.
	June	NP quits Government of National Unity to become official parliamentary opposition. Nearly 28,000 striking platinum mineworkers fired for defying court order to return to work.
	September	Former police colonel implicates former government and security officials in wide-ranging atrocities, illegal acts under apartheid.
	October	Former senior military officials (including a former minister of defense) acquitted of charges related to murders of antiapartheid activists.
	November	Free State provincial premier and Executive Committee resign following allegations of corruption and nepotism.
	December	President Mandela signs legislation approving final constitution, to be implemented in stages by 1999. South Africa announces plans to sever diplomatic ties with Republic of China (Taiwan) and to recognize People's Republic of China (Beijing), 1997.
1997	January	Five former policemen apply for amnesty before Truth and Reconciliation Commission for 1977 killing of Steve Biko.
	February	South Africa's first offshore oil field, south of Mossel Bay, begins production.
	March	South African Navy celebrates seventy-fifth anniversary in joint naval exercises with Argentina, Brazil, Uruguay. Deputy President Thabo Mbeki, in Zaire, urges rebel-government cease-fire.

Country Profile

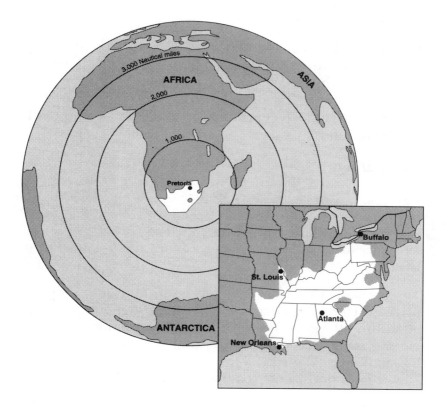

Country

Formal Name: Republic of South Africa.

Short Form: South Africa.

Term for National(s): South African(s).

Administrative Capital: Pretoria.

Legislative Capital: Cape Town.

Judicial Capital: Bloemfontein.

Independence: May 31, 1910, as Union of South Africa, self-governing British dominion; sovereignty recognized May 1, 1934, under Britain's Statute of Westminster. Republic of South Africa, May 31, 1961.

Public Holidays: New Year's Day (January 1), Human Rights Day (March 21), Good Friday, Family Day (Easter Monday), Freedom Day (April 27), Workers' Day (May 1), Ascension Day, Youth Day (June 16), Women's Day (August 9), Heritage Day (September 24), Day of Reconciliation (December 16), Christmas Day (December 25), and Day of Goodwill (December 26).

Geography

Size: South Africa occupies 1,227,200 square kilometers at the southern tip of Africa; seventh largest African country; twice the size of Texas. Coastline nearly 3,000 kilometers. Extraterritorial holdings: Prince Edward Island and Marion Island (Indian Ocean).

Topography: Interior highlands continuation of African plateau stretching north to Sahara, 1,200 meters average elevation. Plateau rises to Drakensberg Mountains (3,300 meters) south and east; Great Escarpment descends to coastal lowlands. Marginal coastal lowlands vary from eighty to 240 kilometers wide. Regular coastline, few natural harbors.

Climate: Variable; warm temperate climate overall; Mediterranean conditions far southwest; subtropical northeast; desert northwest. Moderating influence of ocean currents: East coast warmed by Agulhas current, west coast cooled by Benguela current. Dry, sunny winters (April–October), summer rains (November–March) except in southwest, where rainfall yearround; average annual rainfall 484 millimeters.

Time: 2 hours ahead of Greenwich Mean Time.

Society

Population: 41.2 million, 1995 estimate (1996 census not yet final). Annual population growth 2.2 percent. Fertility: 4.4 births per female; crude birth rate: 23.4 per 1,000; 12 percent of births to teenagers. Population to double in twenty-five years. Life expectancy: sixty-three years males, sixty-eight years females, marked racial differences. Crude death rate: 9.4 per 1,000. Median age 19.2, declining; 37 percent under age fifteen. Density 33.8 persons per square kilometer, uneven distribution; concentrations in KwaZulu-Natal (21 percent of population), Gauteng (17 percent), Eastern Cape (17 percent). Estimated urban population, 57 to 63 percent; rural, 37 to 43 percent. Major urban areas: Cape Town, 2.2 million; Johannesburg, 1.9 million; Durban, 1.1 million; Pretoria, 1.1 million; Port Elizabeth, 854,000. Ethnic heterogeneity: estimated 76 percent black Africans—Nguni (Zulu, Xhosa, Swazi, Ndebele), Sotho-Tswana, Venda, Tsonga-Shangaan, Khoisan; 13 percent whites—Afrikaners, British, other Europeans; 11 percent Asians and others. Government estimates at least 2 million foreign workers (1996).

Languages: Eleven official languages. Most widely used: isiZulu, isiXhosa, Afrikaans, English, and sePedi; also seSotho, seTswana, xiTsonga, siSwati, tshiVenda (luVenda), and isiNdebele. English important in commerce.

Religion: No government restrictions. Population 80 percent Christians, mostly Protestant. Of these, 8 million members of African Independent churches; 4 million, of Dutch Reformed churches. Traditional African beliefs remain important, especially in rural areas. Asians almost equally Hindu and Muslim; Islamic community growing rapidly.

Education and Literacy: Superior education system primarily served racial minority until 1990s. Nine years compulsory education universal after 1994; shortages of schools, teachers. Estimated 7.17 million primary pupils, 4.59 million secondary pupils; 20,780 primary and secondary schools, of which 20,303 government operated; 336,653 primary and secondary teachers. Adult literacy estimated 61 percent. Nineteen major universities, two correspondence; extensive vocational and technical training available.

Health: Health problems reflect racial, class differences. Physicians 1 per 1,200 people in wealthy areas (1 per 10,000 in poor, rural areas). Acquired immune deficiency syndrome

(AIDS): 10,351 reported cases (1996); human immunodeficiency virus (HIV) infection estimated close to 1 million. Infant mortality declining: 43.1 deaths first year per 1,000 live births (54.3 blacks, 7.3 whites). National health insurance system being phased in.

Economy

Character and Structure: Economy based on market-oriented, private enterprise, bolstered by state subsidies; traditionally strong public sector undergoing initial privatization. Industry and manufacturing crucial to growth. Government's five-year Reconstruction and Development Programme emphasizes public services, job creation to ameliorate most severe impacts of apartheid. Gross domestic product (GDP) estimated US$133.6 billion; US$3,010 per capita (1995). Major contributions to GDP: manufacturing, 25.2 percent; trade, 15.5; finance, 15.3; general government, 14.1; mining, 8.9. Economic growth, 3.1 percent (1996), predicted 2.5 percent (1997). Inflation, 8.7 percent (1995); 7.4 percent (1996).

Government budget: FY1997–98 proposed expenditures, R186.7 billion; revenues R162.0 billion; projected deficit R24.7 billion. Budget allocations: military, 5.7 percent; police, 7.0 percent; interest on government debt, 20.4 percent; education, 21.3 percent; allocations to provinces, 43.2 percent. Proposed relaxation of exchange controls, tax reductions in lower income brackets (1997).

Mining and Minerals: Mining based on unparalleled reserves: gold, diamonds, platinum, chromium, manganese, vanadium; also coal, iron ore, uranium, copper, silver, fluorspar, asbestos, limestone. Mineral concentrations greatest in Gauteng, Northern Province, Mpumalanga. One offshore oilfield, further exploration underway.

Manufacturing: Steel, steel products, chemicals, electronics, automobiles, textiles, paper, food processing. Strong growth in export-oriented manufacturing, increasing capacity utilization, mid-1990s. Substantial foreign investment. Factors favoring investment: broad technological base, highly trained managerial class, abundant labor supply, specialized financial institutions. Factors countering investment: abundance of unskilled, uneducated workers; crime, violence; labor militancy. Industrial interests protected by South African Chamber of Business (SACOB), Steel and Engineering Industries Federation of South Africa (SEIFSA), Afrikaner Trade Institute (Afrikaanse Handelsinstituut—AHI), National African Federated Chamber of Commerce (NAFCOC).

Agriculture, Forestry, and Fishing: Arable land roughly 11 percent of total, mostly eastern provinces, far southwest. Principal crops: cereals and grains, especially corn; wool; sugar; peanuts; tobacco; fruits and vegetables; affected by early 1990s periods of drought. Flourishing wine industry. Livestock, dairy farming. Government marketing boards being phased out. Land claims disputes arising out of apartheid era being adjudicated, could affect 30 percent of farm land. Small timber industry meets most domestic demand. Large commercial fishing industry exports more than 60 percent of catch.

Energy: Extensive coal reserves expected to last through most of twenty-first century; uranium plentiful. Limited hydroelectric potential, plans to import electric power from cooperative ventures in Lesotho, Mozambique. Imported petroleum, refined domestically. World leader in coal liquefaction to synthesize oil and gas; one nuclear power facility, plans for additional nuclear facilities after 2000.

Labor: Work force estimated 14.5 million (1995). Employment in manufacturing (16.6 percent), agriculture (12.2 percent), commerce and trade (11 percent), domestic service (8.5 percent), education (7.8 percent), mining (6.9 percent). Unemployment, 29–32 percent of formal work force. Job creation proceeding slowly. Looming shortage of skilled labor, oversupply of unskilled labor. Public-sector employment increasing, especially in provincial governments. At least 194 recognized trade unions; roughly 25 percent of labor force. Wage disparities among racial groups persist, especially in manufacturing.

Tourism: More than 4.6 million international arrivals (1995), including more than 3.4 million Africans; also British,

Germans; growing Asian interest. Well-developed tourism industry; key attractions Kruger National Park, Western Cape, Blue Train (Pretoria-Cape Town).

Foreign Economic Relations: Major exports: gold, precious metals, precious stones, base metals, textiles, chemicals, paper products, agricultural products. Increasing coal exports. Major imports: machinery, vehicles, petroleum products, chemicals, scientific instruments, base metals, textiles. Early 1990s growth in imports slowed in mid-1990s; exports rose steadily, but declining value of rand reduced impact on trade balance. Value of exports US$27.9 billion, value of imports US$27.1 billion (1995). Major trading partners: United States, Britain, Germany, Japan, Italy. Trade with United States: exports US$2.21 billion, imports US$2.75 billion (1995). Binational Commission with United States, binational chambers of commerce in other countries promote trade, investment. Southern African Customs Union with Botswana, Lesotho, Namibia, and Swaziland. Trade with other African countries: exports US$2.5 billion, imports US$664 million (1994). Major South African investments in Africa: tourism, telecommunications, railways, ports, breweries, mining. Pursuing stronger trade, investment ties to China, Japan, Singapore, India, Australia.

Currency: Rand (R)=100 cents. As of March 1, 1997, US$1=R4.66; conversely, R1=US21.4 cents, following uneven decline through 1996.

Fiscal Year: April 1 through March 31.

Transportation and Telecommunications

Transportation System: Government corporation, Transnet Ltd., embarking on privatization. Transnet divisions: Spoornet (railroads), Portnet (ports), Autonet (roads), Petronet (pipelines), South African Airways (SAA), PX (parcel delivery service).

Railroads: Well-developed rail network: 21,303 kilometers, almost all narrow-gauge (regional standard), 1.067–meter; 314 kilometers, 0.610–meter gauge. 18,241 kilometers electrified;

3,009 bridges; 625 stations. Reliance on steam power or steam-generated electricity; hauled 164 million tons of freight, 600 million intercity passengers, 1994. Urban commuter lines managed by South African Rail Commuter Corporation (SARCC); more than 2 million urban commuters daily.

Roads: Extensive national, provincial, and municipal road system: 5,943 kilometers freeways; 93,000 kilometers all-weather, paved roads; 130,000 kilometers unpaved, gravel or earth roads. More than 3.5 million passenger cars, 2.5 million commercial vehicles. Bus, private van service vital to urban commuters. World record accident fatality rates in urban areas.

Ports: Six major ports: Durban, Cape Town, Port Elizabeth, Richards Bay, East London, Saldanha Bay; secondary ports: Mossel Bay, Simonstown. First-class facilities and services. At least 104 million tons of cargo shipped and more than 16 million tons landed per year.

Civil Aviation: South African Airways (SAA) national carrier (forty-eight aircraft), increasing competition from smaller airlines. Nine major airports: three international—Johannesburg, Cape Town, and Durban; plus Bloemfontein, East London, Kimberley, Port Elizabeth, George, and Upington. Five runways more than 3,659 meters; ten runways 2,440 meters to 3,659 meters. In addition, at least 140 permanent surface runways and 250 landing strips, private and commercial use.

Pipelines: 931 kilometers crude oil; 1,748 kilometers other petroleum products; 322 kilometers natural gas.

Telecommunications: Advanced, modern system managed by Telkom SA Ltd., served racial minority until mid-1990s. Carrier-equipped, open-wire lines, coaxial cables, radio relay links, fiber optic cable, and radiocommunication stations. Key centers: Bloemfontein, Cape Town, Durban, Johannesburg, Port Elizabeth, and Pretoria. State-owned South African Broadcasting Corporation subject to independent review for political neutrality; increasing competition from independent stations. Radio service from fourteen amplitude modulation (AM) stations, 286 frequency modulation (FM) stations; near-universal access; estimated 7 million radios, not licensed. Government funds Channel Africa, 203 hours weekly broadcasts outside South Africa. At least 2.2 million televisions. Three main TV channels; English, Afrikaans, five African languages, Hindi, Tamil. M-Net (880,000 subscribers) broadcasts in above languages plus Hebrew, Greek, Portuguese. Three satellite earth stations. Telephones: more than 5.3 million (1996), priority on service to rural areas; cellular telephone service expanding rapidly.

Government and Politics

Political System: Federal state consisting of central government and nine provincial governments. Interim constitution: approved December 22, 1993, implemented April 27, 1994, intended to be in force until 1999, being replaced by final constitution in phases, 1997–99. Interim constitution provides for Government of National Unity: bicameral parliament includes 400-member National Assembly (popularly elected by party, list-system proportional representation based on universal suffrage at age eighteen), ninety-member Senate (indirectly elected by provincial legislators). President elected by parliament; deputy presidents named by parties winning 20 percent of popular vote (minimum two). Executive branch under interim constitution: president, Nelson Mandela (African National Congress—ANC), two deputy presidents— Thabo Mbeki (ANC) and Frederik Willem de Klerk (National Party—NP). President appointed twenty-eight cabinet ministers from parties with 5 percent of popular vote. Executive, legislative officials normally serve five-year terms. Final constitution drafted by Constitutional Assembly (both houses of parliament), 1996; replaces Government of National Unity with majoritarian rule: Party winning majority of popular vote names executive officials; also replaces Senate with National Council of Provinces: six permanent members indirectly elected by each provincial legislature; each province fills additional four seats on national council by rotation from provincial legislature. NP abandoned Government of National Unity, June 1996, to become parliamentary opposition. Status of KwaZulu-Natal unresolved. Parliamentary Volkstaat Council considering proposals for self-determination by proapartheid whites in separate *volkstaat.*

Major political parties: ANC, NP, Inkatha Freedom Party (IFP), Freedom Front (FF), Democratic Party (DP), Pan-Africanist Congress (PAC), African Christian Democratic Party (ACDP); several smaller parties. Next national elections scheduled 1999.

Administrative Divisions: Nine provinces, provisional boundaries subject to change by referendum. Provinces (and capitals): Eastern Cape (Bisho), Mpumalanga (Nelspruit), Gauteng (Johannesburg), KwaZulu-Natal (Ulundi or Pietermaritzburg), Northern Cape (Kimberley), Northern Province (Pietersburg), North-West Province (Mmabatho), Free State (Bloemfontein),Western Cape (Cape Town).

Provincial and local government: Nine provincial governments formed by list-system proportional representation. Provincial premier (executive) appoints Executive Council (cabinet) based on party strength; provincial assemblies, 30 to 100 legislators based on party strength. November 1995 elections for 688 metropolitan, town, and rural councils, except in KwaZulu-Natal (violence), areas of Western Cape (boundary disputes). Low voter turnout; ANC 66.3 percent, NP 16.2 percent, Freedom Front 5 percent. Western Cape elections, May 29, 1996; NP won control of all contested councils; ANC second. KwaZulu-Natal elections, June 26, 1996, IFP 44.5 percent, ANC 33.2 percent (concentration in urban areas). Provincial authority still being defined; provincial constitutions, once approved by Constitutional Court, could give provincial governments most responsibility for agriculture, education (except universities), health and welfare, housing, police, environmental affairs, language use, media, transportation, sports and recreation, tourism, urban and rural development, and role of traditional leaders. Status of *volkstaat* not yet determined.

Judicial System: Based on Roman-Dutch law, altered by British rule and post-independence constitutions. Interim constitution of 1993 empaneled eleven-judge Constitutional Court to rule on legislative constitutionality. Supreme Court: Appellate Division (Bloemfontein); six provincial division headquarters: Cape Town, Grahamstown, Kimberley, Bloemfontein, Pietermaritzburg, Pretoria; local divisions. Lower courts: district magistrates hear cases concerning lesser offenses. Judges or magistrates decide guilt or innocence; jury system abolished 1969. Penalties include corporal punishment (whipping). Death penalty abolished in 1995.

Foreign Affairs: Global diplomatic isolation ended in early 1990s. Foreign policy goals: independence from foreign interference; desire to balance friendships with powerful donor nations against loyalty to former antiapartheid allies; desire for close political ties to Africa, close economic ties to Asian "tigers."

International Memberships: Participation in United Nations restored, June 1994. Membership: British Commonwealth of Nations, International Labour Organisation, International Telecommunications Union, Multilateral Investment Guarantee Agency, Nonaligned Movement (NAM), Organization of African Unity (OAU), Southern African Customs Union (SACU), Southern African Development Community (SADC), Universal Postal Union, World Health Organization (WHO), World Intellectual Property Organization, World Meteorological Organization, World Trade Organization.

National Security

Armed Forces: Armed forces renamed South African National Defence Force (SANDF). Military reorganization in mid-1990s to integrate national armed services with former homeland and liberation forces. Active-duty forces (1996): 137,900. Army 118,000, of whom 4,000 women; air force 8,400, of whom 800 women; navy 5,500, of whom 350 women; medical service 6,000, of whom 2,000 women. Commandos 76,000. Reserves: approximately 474,700, of which army 453,000, air force 20,000, navy 1,700. Downsizing to reduce SANDF to 90,000 by 1999. Civilian minister of defense; president commander in chief. Conscription ended, 1994; voluntary service of two to six years, followed by ten-year part-time service (maximum sixty days training per two-year period). Military budget (R10.7

billion), less than 2 percent of GDP, 1997.

Police: 147,000: 110,000 active, 37,000 reserves (1997). Reorganized in 1994 as South African Police Service under minister for safety and security. President appoints national police commissioner, nine provincial police commissioners. Emphasis on ending violence, reducing crime, improving community relations, racial tolerance, decentralization of leadership, demilitarization of ranks and symbols. Vigilantism increasing in response to continued violence. Senior ranks still predominantly white; some racial biases persist. Police budget (R13.1 billion), 2.1 percent of GDP, 1997.

Prisons: 129,000 prisoners (1996), severe overcrowding, manpower shortages in prisons. More than 200 deaths in police custody (1995). Laws amended in 1995 to prohibit detention of children under eighteen in prisons.

National Reconciliation: Truth and Reconciliation Commission investigating human rights violations 1960–93. Hearings since early 1996 considering victim compensation, amnesty for most political crimes, to be completed in 1997 or 1998. Several senior security officials indicted for murders committed under apartheid; others implicated in testimony before commission. Government-appointed Human Rights Commission to investigate, assist aggrieved individuals seeking redress against government officials and others.

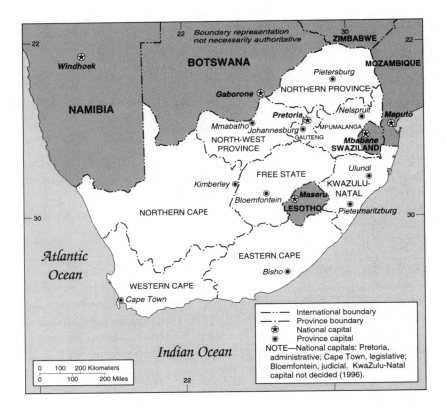

Figure 1. Administrative Divisions of South Africa, 1996

Introduction

DURING FOUR DAYS IN APRIL 1994, more than 19 million South Africans, roughly 91 percent of registered voters, went to the polls, most for the first time, and elected South Africa's first democratic government. The establishment of a government led by the African National Congress (ANC), under the presidency of Nelson Mandela, signaled emphatically the demise of apartheid and the return of South Africa from the pariah status it had occupied for decades to a respected place in the world community. The change was as swift as it was dramatic. Only five years earlier, in 1989, barely one-eighth as many voters (roughly 69 percent of an electorate restricted by law to members of the white, mixed-race "coloured," and Asian communities) had returned to power those who were committed to maintaining apartheid. The African majority was, until then, explicitly denied full citizenship rights on the basis of skin color. The ANC was an illegal organization, as it had been since April 1960. Nelson Mandela in 1989 was spending his twenty-sixth year in prison. The fact that South Africa went on to overturn the apartheid ideology and, in large part, apartheid practices between 1989 and 1994 was a stunning development, unforeseen by political forecasters and paralleling the overthrow of communism in Eastern Europe.

Yet the repudiation of apartheid did not mean the end of racial divisions. Although the electors voted in 1994 to end apartheid, they still cast their ballots largely along racial and ethnic lines. Most African voters supported the ANC, except in KwaZulu-Natal where Mangosuthu (Gatsha) Buthelezi's Inkatha Freedom Party (IFP) secured a majority of Zulu votes and won control of the newly established provincial government. Most whites—Afrikaners and English speakers alike—voted for F. W. de Klerk's newly antiapartheid National Party (NP), avoiding both the ANC and the Democratic Party (which in a previous form, as the Progressive Federal Party, had led the parliamentary fight to end apartheid). Coloured voters, largely concentrated in the Western Cape province, were concerned that their interests might be ignored by an African majority government. Hence, they voted for the NP, thereby ensuring that it won control of the Western Cape provincial government.

Nor did the repudiation of apartheid mean the end of the economic and social problems that have increasingly bedeviled South African society since the 1980s. Racially discriminatory policies enforced by successive governments throughout the twentieth century have left the African majority of the population in possession of only about 13 percent of the nation's land, and most of that of poor quality. Unable to achieve sustainable agricultural development, Africans continue, as they have for decades, to flock to cities. Urban migration, in turn, has created enormous squatter encampments, particularly in and around Gauteng. Most of these squatters, as well as nearly one-half of the adult African population nationwide, cannot find work within the formal sector of the economy. The results are widespread poverty, appalling living conditions, and an increasing incidence of crime. South Africa's per capita crime rate, overall, has exceeded that of almost any other country since 1992. The government has acknowledged the seriousness of the problem but has not been able to end the wave of crimes against persons and property that is fueled by lingering poverty.

Even for many South Africans who have jobs, economic conditions are difficult, as black wages remain low compared to those of white workers. Mandela's government said in 1995 that it could not afford to equalize pay scales across public-sector jobs in order to compensate for past discrimination. Given these circumstances, one of the most difficult tasks facing the new government is to balance the high expectations of its black supporters against economic realities. Initially, after the historic 1994 elections, President Mandela's personal charisma and the great respect in which he is held by most South Africans—both black and white—helped to ensure political stability. But Mandela has said that he would not remain in office after 1999, and the question of succession, therefore, lingers over many 1990s political debates about the future.

South Africa's contemporary problems have deep historical roots. Although human settlement in the subcontinent extends back thousands of years, racial conflict dates from the Dutch arrival at the Cape of Good Hope in 1652, when the Dutch East India Company established a resupply station at Cape Town for its fleets traveling between Holland and its empire in South and Southeast Asia. During the first 150 years of European control of the Cape, the company, a commercial operation, established some of the most enduring features of colonial society.

The company was not interested in expanding European settlement across Africa, but only in acquiring goods (fresh water, foodstuffs, replacement masts) to resupply its ships. When local Khoisan peoples refused to provide these goods on terms set by the company, the Europeans took up arms and drove most of the local population into the interior. In place of local producers, the company relied on a combination of European farmers (mostly former employees of the company) and imported African slave labor to work the land that had been seized from local residents.

When the European farmers (known as Boers) attempted to escape the monopolistic trading practices and autocratic rule of the company by moving into the interior, the company prohibited further expansion, ended the emigration of Europeans to the Cape, and expanded the use of slave labor. By the end of the eighteenth century, society in the Cape was marked by antagonism between the local white community (mostly descended from the same small group of seventeenth-century Dutch, French, and German settlers) and a largely disinterested and exploitative metropolitan ruler. The racial divide was reflected in the pattern of land ownership and the authoritarian structure of labor relations, based largely on slavery.

British acquisition of the Cape at the beginning of the nineteenth century accentuated divisions between local settlers and metropolitan rulers and widened the racial divide between whites and blacks. The British conquered the Cape largely to prevent it from falling into the hands of Napoleon, and thus to protect their only sea route to their empire in South Asia. Like the Dutch East India Company, the British were not interested in expanding settlement but wanted to keep down the expense of maintaining their strategic resupply station at Cape Town. Initially, they continued to import African slaves to meet the labor needs of white farmers, and they did not interfere with the farmers' harsh treatment of black workers. But the British also tried to prevent further white expansion in South Africa—with its attendant costs of greater levels of colonial government and the risk of wars with Africans—by closing the borders of the Cape and importing British settlers to create a loyal buffer in the east between expansionist Boers and densely settled African communities. Moreover, the British, influenced by strong humanitarian groups at home, took steps to eliminate the racially discriminatory features of colonial society, first by reforming the judicial system and punishing white farmers who assaulted black workers, and later by freeing all slaves throughout the British empire.

Desperate for more land and fearful of losing all of their black labor, many Boer families in the 1830s marched into the interior of South Africa on the Great Trek, skirting the densest African populations. These Voortrekkers, or trekkers, hoped to establish their own communities, free of British rule. Prevented by the British from establishing a republic on the Indian Ocean coast, where the British colony of Natal helped protect the sea route to India, the Boers formed two republics in the interior, the South African Republic (the region known as the Transvaal) and the Orange Free State. Both republics' economies were based on near-subsistence farming and hunting, and both limited political rights to white males. Thus, white settlement expanded across the region, but almost entirely into areas with few local inhabitants. The majority of black Africans still lived in their own autonomous societies.

The discovery of minerals in the late nineteenth century— diamonds in 1867 and gold in 1886—dramatically altered the economic and political structure of southern Africa. The growing mineral industry created ever-greater divisions between British and Boer, white and black, rich and poor. At the turn of the century, for the first time, South Africa had an extremely valuable resource that attracted foreign capital and large-scale immigration. Discoveries of gold and diamonds in South Africa exceeded those in any other part of the world, and more foreign capital had been invested in South Africa than in the rest of Africa combined. In the Transvaal, the site of the gold discoveries, the white population expanded eightfold, while hundreds of thousands of Africans sought work each year in the newly developed mines and cities of industrializing areas. Yet not all shared equally in this newfound wealth. Diamond and, in particular, gold mining industries required vast amounts of inexpensive labor in order to be profitable. To constrain the ability of African workers to bargain up their wages, and to ensure that they put up with onerous employment conditions, the British in the 1870s and 1880s conquered the still-independent African states in southern Africa, confiscated the bulk of the land and imposed cash taxation demands. In this way, they ensured that men who had chosen previously to work in the mines on their own terms were now forced to do so on employers' terms. In the new industrial cities, African workers were subjected to a bewildering array of discriminatory laws and practices, all enforced in order to keep workers cheap and pliable. In the much diminished rural areas, the wives and children of these migrant laborers had to survive in large part on the limited remittances sent back by their absent menfolk. In short, many of the discriminatory features so typical of twentieth-century South Africa—pass laws, urban ghettos, impoverished rural homelands, African migrant labor—were first established in the course of South Africa's industrial revolution.

But the discovery of minerals also exacerbated tensions between the British and the Boers. Gold had been discovered in the Transvaal, and that was beyond the reach of British rule. Yet the capital invested in the mines, and thus the ownership of the gold industry, was primarily British controlled. Lacking investment capital, the Boers found themselves excluded from ownership and thus from the profits generated in their midst. Indeed, most profits from the mines were reinvested in Europe and the Americas and did not contribute to the growth of additional industries in South Africa. The Boers sought to gain access to some of this wealth through taxation policies; these policies, however, incurred the wrath of the mine magnates and their supporters in England. The South African War, fought by the Boers and the British between 1899 and 1902, was primarily a struggle for the control of gold. Although the Boers lost the war, in large part they won the peace. The British realized that in order for the diamond and gold industries to be operated profitably, they had to have a local administration sympathetic to the financial and labor needs of mining. They also realized—given demographic trends at the time—that Boers would always constitute a majority of the white population. With these factors in mind, the British abandoned their wartime anti-Boer and pro-African rhetoric and negotiated a long-term political settlement that put the local white community in charge of a self-governing united South Africa.

The Union of South Africa, established on May 31, 1910, as a self-governing state within the British Empire, legislatively restricted political and property rights to whites at the expense of blacks. With the exception of a very small number of voters in the Cape Province and Natal, Africans were kept off electoral rolls throughout most of the country. By the terms of the Mines and Works Act (1911), only whites were permitted to hold skilled jobs in the mining industry. The Natives Land Act (1913) prohibited Africans from owning land in any part of

South Africa outside a small area (7.5 percent, expanded to 13 percent in the 1930s) set aside for their use. These laws ensured that Africans would have to seek jobs from white employers, that their jobs would be the lowest paid available, and that without the right to vote they could do little to change the laws that excluded them from the political process and relegated them to the bottom of the economy.

Two nationalist movements emerged in the aftermath of the formation of the union, one racially and ethnically exclusivist, the other much more disparate in its membership and aims. The Afrikaner nationalist movement, built around the National Party, appealed to Afrikaners (as they increasingly referred to themselves after the South African War), who were still bitter about their suffering in the war and frustrated by the poverty in which most of them lived. The black nationalist movement, led primarily by the African National Congress (formed in 1912), addressed the myriad injustices against black South Africans.

Although Afrikaner generals helped unite South Africa's first government, most Dutch speakers did not share in the fruits of victory. Much of their land had been confiscated by the British during the war and was not returned after it ended. The main source of employment, the mines, was owned by English speakers. Rural Afrikaners moving to the cities had neither capital nor marketable skills, and thus they found themselves competing with Africans for low-paid unskilled work. As a result, they often supported racially discriminatory legislation, such as the Mines and Works Act, that gave them privileged access to jobs solely on the basis of their color. But because Afrikaners wanted a greater share of the economy than they could earn as employees of English speakers, they pooled their funds and resources to establish banks, insurance companies, and other businesses in order to wrest a portion of the economy out of the control of English businessmen. A few Afrikaner leaders then led in the denunciation of the business community in increasingly extreme, anticapitalist, and anti-Semitic terms.

Afrikaner nationalists spoke of themselves as a chosen people, ordained by God to rule South Africa. They established their own cultural organizations and secret societies, and they argued that South Africa should be ruled in the interests of Afrikaners, rather than English businessmen or African workers. Throughout the 1920s, 1930s, and 1940s, the Afrikaner nationalist movement grew in popularity, fueled by fears of black competition for jobs, by antipathy toward the English-speaking mine magnates, by the memory of past suffering, and by the impact of World War II (especially massive black urbanization). In 1948, with the support of a majority of Afrikaners (who constituted about 60 percent of the white electorate), the NP won the election on its apartheid platform. Henceforth, South Africa was to be governed by a party that hoped to shape government policies to work in favor of whites, in general, and Afrikaners, in particular. Moreover, the NP denied that Africans, Asians, or coloureds could ever be citizens or full participants in the political process.

The black nationalist movement had no such success. For most blacks, lack of access to the vote meant that they could not organize an effective political party. Instead they had to rely on appeals, deputations, and petitions to the British government asking for equal treatment before the law. The British responded by pointing out that South Africa was now self-governing and that the petitioners had to make their case to the local white rulers. Although Africans, Asians, and coloureds shared common grievances, they were not united in their organizations or their aims. Physically separated and legally differentiated in practically every aspect of their lives, they formed separate organizations to represent their interests. Moreover, their leaders, with few exceptions, adopted accommodationist rather than confrontational tactics in dealing with the state. Failing to gain any real concessions from increasingly hard-line governments, none of the black political movements succeeded in building a solid mass following. Even the ANC had a membership of only a few thousand (out of an African population of about 8 million) in 1948.

With the introduction of apartheid, the NP extended and systematized many of the features of entrenched racial discrimination into a state policy of white supremacy. Every person resident in South Africa was legally assigned, largely on the basis of appearance, to one racial group—white, African, coloured, or Asian. South Africa was proclaimed to be a white man's country in which members of other racial groups would never receive full political rights. Africans were told that eventually they would achieve political independence in perhaps nine or ten homelands, carved out of the minuscule rural areas already allocated to them, areas that even a government commission in the 1950s had deemed totally inadequate to support the black population.

Coloureds and Asians, too, were to be excluded from South African politics. By law, all races were to have separate living areas and separate amenities; there was to be no mixing. Education was to be provided according to the roles that people were expected to play in society. In that regard, Hendrik F. Verwoerd, the leading ideologue of apartheid and prime minister of South Africa from 1958 until his assassination in 1966, stated that Africans would be "making a big mistake" if they thought that they would live "an adult life under a policy of equal rights." According to Verwoerd, there was no place for Africans "in the European community" (by which he meant South Africa) above the level of certain forms of labor.

Expecting considerable opposition to policies that would forever exclude the black majority from any role in national politics and from any job other than that of unskilled—and low-paid—laborer, the NP government greatly enlarged police powers. People campaigning to repeal or to modify any law would be presumed guilty of one of several crimes until they could prove their innocence. The government could "list," or ban, individuals, preventing them from attending public meetings, prohibiting them from belonging to certain organizations, and subjecting them to lengthy periods of house arrest.

The most draconian piece of security legislation, the Suppression of Communism Act (1950), adopted an extraordinarily broad and vague definition of communism—i.e., the aim to "bring about any political, industrial, social, or economic change within the Union by the promotion of disturbance or disorder." Also included under the act was anyone who encouraged "feelings of hostility between the European and the non-European races of the Union." This legislation enabled the police to label almost any opponent of apartheid as a supporter of the outlawed Communist Party of South Africa (reactivated in 1953 as the South African Communist Party—SACP).

Blacks rose up in protest against apartheid in the 1950s. Led by Nelson Mandela and Oliver Tambo, the ANC sought to broaden its base of support and to impede the implementation of apartheid by calling for mass noncompliance with the new laws. Working together with white, coloured, and Indian opponents of apartheid, the ANC encouraged people to burn their passes (identity documents, then required of all African males and soon to be required of all African females in South Africa).

The ANC also urged people to refuse to use the separate amenities (such as public toilets, park benches, and entrances to post offices) set aside for them, to use those intended for whites instead, and to boycott discriminatory employers and institutions. Such tactics, all of them purposely nonviolent, although not successful in changing NP policies, did attract large-scale support and won new members for the ANC.

In 1955 representatives of the ANC, as well as white, coloured, and Indian organizations opposed to apartheid, drafted a Freedom Charter as a basic statement of political principles. According to the charter, South Africa belonged to all who lived within its boundaries, regardless of race. The charter stated that no particular group of people should have special privileges, but that all should be treated equally before the law. It also stated that all who lived in South Africa should share in the country's wealth, an ambiguous statement sometimes interpreted by supporters of the ANC, and more frequently by its opponents, to mean a call for nationalization of private-sector enterprises.

The NP government dealt harshly with all those who opposed its policies. Tens of thousands were arrested for participating in public demonstrations and boycotts, hundreds of thousands were arrested each year for pass-law offenses, and many of the delegates who drew up the Freedom Charter were arrested and tried for treason in a trial that lasted nearly five years. Repression became harsher as opposition grew. In 1960 police at Sharpeville, a black township south of Johannesburg, fired into a crowd of Africans peacefully protesting against the pass laws, and killed sixty-seven. In the aftermath of the shooting, which attracted worldwide condemnation, the government banned the ANC, the Pan-Africanist Congress (PAC), and other organizations opposed to apartheid; withdrew from the British Commonwealth of Nations; and, after a referendum among white voters only, declared South Africa a republic.

During the 1960s, the implementation of apartheid and the repression of internal opposition continued despite growing world criticism of South Africa's racially discriminatory policies and police violence. Thousands of Africans, coloureds, and Asians (ultimately numbering about 3.5 million by the 1980s) were removed from white areas into the land set aside for other racial groups. Some of these areas, called black homelands, were readied for independence, even though they lacked the physical cohesiveness—Bophuthatswana, for example, consisted of some nineteen non-contiguous pieces of land—to make political or economic independence a viable or believable concept. None of the four homelands declared independent received any form of world recognition. The ANC and the PAC, banned from operating within South Africa, turned to violence in their struggle against apartheid—the former organization adopting a policy of bombing strategic targets such as police stations and power plants, the latter engaging in a program of terror against African chiefs and headmen, who were seen as collaborators with the government.

Verwoerd's government crushed this internal opposition. Leaders of the ANC and PAC within South Africa were tracked down, arrested, and charged with treason. Nelson Mandela was sentenced in 1964 to imprisonment for life. Oliver Tambo had already fled the country and led the ANC in exile. Despite growing international criticism, the government's success in capturing its enemies fueled an economic boom. Attracted by the apparent political stability of the country, and by rates of return on capital running as high as 15 to 20 percent annually, foreign investment in South Africa more than doubled between 1963 and 1972. Soaring immigration increased the white population by as much as 50 percent during the same period. Apartheid and economic growth seemed to work in tandem.

Yet a number of contradictory developments during the 1970s displayed the shaky foundations of the apartheid edifice. In 1973 wildcat strikes broke out on the Durban waterfront and then spread around the country. Because Africans were prohibited from establishing or belonging to trade unions, they had no organizational leaders to represent their concerns. Fearful of police repression, strikers chose not to identify publicly any of their leaders. Thus employers who considered negotiations had no worker representatives with whom to negotiate and none to hold responsible for upholding labor agreements. Several hundred thousand work hours were lost in labor actions in 1973. That same year, in a sign of growing world opposition to state-enforced racial discrimination, the United Nations (UN) declared apartheid "a crime against humanity," a motion that took on real meaning four years later, in 1977, when the UN adopted a mandatory embargo on arms sales to South Africa.

In 1974 a revolutionary movement overthrew the Portuguese dictatorship in Lisbon, and the former colonial territories of Angola and Mozambique demanded independence from Portugal. Their liberation movements-turned-Marxist governments were committed to the eradication of colonialism and racial discrimination throughout southern Africa. Following the 1980 independence of Zimbabwe, a nation now led by a socialist government opposed to apartheid, South Africa found itself surrounded by countries hostile to its policies and ready to give refuge to the exiled forces of the ANC and the PAC. Internal and external opposition to apartheid was fueled in 1976, when the Soweto uprising began with the protests of high-school students against the enforced use of Afrikaans—viewed by many Africans as the oppressor's language. The protests led to weeks of demonstrations, marches, and boycotts throughout South Africa. Violent clashes with police left more than 500 people dead, several thousand arrested, and thousands more seeking refuge outside South Africa, many with the exiled forces of the ANC and the PAC.

Fearful of growing instability in South Africa, many foreign investors began to withdraw their money or to move it into short-term rather than long-term investments; as a result, the economy became increasingly sluggish. In order to cope with labor unrest and to boost investor confidence, the government decided in 1979 to allow black workers to establish unions as a necessary step toward industrial peace. This decision was a crucial step in the growing perception that apartheid would have to end. It undercut a basic ideological premise of apartheid, that blacks were not really full citizens of South Africa and, therefore, were not entitled to any official representation. It also implied an acceptance by employers, many of whom had called for the change in policy, that in order for labor relations to operate effectively, disgruntled workers would have to be negotiated with, rather than subjected to arbitrary dismissal and police arrest, as in the past.

Pretending otherwise had already become increasingly difficult. A national census in 1980 showed that whites were declining as a proportion of South Africa's population. From more than 20 percent of the population at the beginning of the century, whites accounted for only about 16 percent of the population in 1980 and were likely to constitute less than 10 percent by the end of the century. By the end of the 1980s, almost one-half of black South Africans—according to apartheid theory, a rural people—would be living in cities and towns, accounting for nearly 60 percent of South Africa's urban dwellers. Demographic facts, alone, made it increasingly difficult to argue that South Africa was a white man's country.

In the early 1980s, NP reformers tinkered with the basic structure of apartheid. Concerned about demographic trends, Prime Minister P. W. Botha led his government in implementing a new constitutional arrangement, one that embraced the concept of multiracial government but, at the same time, perpetuated the concept of racial separation. The new constitution established three racially segregated houses of parliament, for whites, Asians, and coloureds, but excluded blacks from full citizenship. Botha and his allies hoped that such a change would bolster NP support among coloureds and Asians, and thereby give the party enough numerical strength to counter growing dissent.

The constitution implemented in 1984 only inflamed further opposition to apartheid. It was denounced inside and outside South Africa as anachronistic and reactionary. Opponents argued that by further institutionalizing the exclusion of the majority black population, the new constitution only extended apartheid and did not undercut it in any significant way. Within South Africa, protests against apartheid far exceeded earlier levels of opposition. In many black townships, police stations and other government buildings were destroyed, along with the homes of black policemen and town councilors, who were denounced as collaborators with the apartheid regime.

Newly legalized black trade unions took a leading role in the opposition, particularly by organizing strikes that combined economic and political complaints. The number of work days lost to strikes soared to more than 5.8 million in 1987. Armed members of the ANC and PAC infiltrated South Africa's borders from their bases in Angola, Mozambique, and Zimbabwe and carried out a campaign of urban terror. With South Africa on the verge of civil war, the government imposed a series of states of emergency, used the police and the army against opponents of apartheid, and dispatched military forces on armed raids into neighboring countries.

Although the government's repressive actions strengthened state control in the short term, they backfired in the long run. Police repression and brutality in South Africa, and military adventures elsewhere in southern Africa, only heightened South Africa's pariah status in world politics. As events in the country grabbed world headlines and politicians across the globe denounced apartheid, the costs for South Africa of such widespread condemnation were difficult to bear. Foreign investors withdrew; international banks called in their loans; the value of South African currency collapsed; the price of gold fell to less than one-half of the high of the 1970s; economic output declined; and inflation became chronic.

In the face of such developments, it was clear to most South African businessmen, and to a majority of NP party leaders, that apartheid itself had to undergo substantial reform if economic prosperity and political stability were to be regained. In 1989 a stroke precipitated Botha's resignation, and he was succeeded by F. W. de Klerk, formerly a hard-line supporter of apartheid but by the end of the 1980s the candidate of those who regarded themselves as moderates within the National Party.

De Klerk moved faster and farther to reform apartheid than any Afrikaner politician had done before him, although in many instances it seemed that events rather than individuals were forcing the pace and scale of change. De Klerk released Nelson Mandela from twenty-seven years of imprisonment in February 1990, and rescinded the banning orders on the ANC, the PAC, the SACP, and other previously illegal organizations. Reacting to demands from within and outside South Africa, de Klerk in 1990 and 1991 repealed the legislative underpinnings of apartheid: gone were the Reservation of Separate Amenities Act, which had enforced petty apartheid; the Natives Land Act, which had made it illegal for Africans to own land in urban areas; the Group Areas Act, which had segregated people by race; and the Population Registration Act, which had assigned every resident of South Africa to a specific racial group. The pace of change was so rapid that many within the Afrikaner community questioned the wisdom of de Klerk's moves, and he came under increasing attack from right-wing proponents of a return to apartheid. For most critics of apartheid, however, the pace of change was not fast enough. They wanted to see apartheid not reformed, but overthrown entirely. Indeed, once it had been accepted that black Africans were, in fact, South Africans, the real question for de Klerk and his allies was whether they could be incorporated into the country in any fashion short of giving them equal rights. The answer was no.

With this realization, from the end of 1991 onward, government negotiators met regularly with representatives from other political organizations to discuss ways in which some form of democracy could be introduced and the remaining structures of apartheid dismantled. Those involved called their forum the Convention for a Democratic South Africa (Codesa). The negotiations were neither clear-cut nor easy, in part because each participating group brought a different past and different demands to the bargaining table. An official commission of inquiry in 1990, for example, found evidence that de Klerk's government had turned a blind eye to clandestine death squads within the security forces that were responsible for the deaths of many opponents of apartheid. Moreover, elements within the government were found to have surreptitiously funded Zulu leader Buthelezi's Inkatha Freedom Party (IFP) and to have supplied weapons that were used to attack ANC members in KwaZulu and in a number of mining compounds.

The ANC's armed struggle against apartheid also lingered in popular memory during the negotiations. ANC leader Mandela raised fears among white businessmen with talk about the need for the nationalization of industries and for the redistribution of wealth to the victims of apartheid. Yet there was more common ground than difference in Codesa. De Klerk and Mandela and their respective supporters were united in the belief that continued violence would destroy all hope of economic recovery. Such a recovery was vital for the attainment of peace and prosperity. They were also united in their belief that there was no alternative to a negotiated settlement.

Codesa's negotiations were assisted by the decline of left- and right-wing alternatives to parliamentary democracy. The fall of communism in Eastern Europe and the failures of socialism in Africa essentially eliminated the likelihood of a socialist state in South Africa. Although radical redistribution of property had much support among black youth, there were few leaders in the antiapartheid forces who spoke for that point of view. Joe Slovo, the leader of the SACP, argued for compromise with the government rather than for the immediate introduction of a workers' state. Chris Hani, the charismatic general secretary of the SACP and the head of Umkhonto we Sizwe (Spear of the Nation)—the ANC's armed wing—was assassinated in April 1993. Winnie Mandela, long a proponent of more radical solutions to the problems of poverty and discrimination in South Africa, saw her influence decline as her marriage to Mandela fell apart. Nor did the PAC, long an adherent of the view that South Africa was a black man's country in which whites were merely guests, win much support for its continued support of armed struggle and its slogan, "One settler, one bullet."

The white right wing was weakened by a series of inept maneuvers that discredited the movement in the eyes of its most likely supporters in the police and in the defense forces. Two members of the Afrikaner Weerstandsbeweging (Afrikaner Resistance Movement—AWB) were quickly arrested and convicted of the murder of Chris Hani. Television cameras captured scenes of AWB leader Eugene Terreblanche leading an unruly band of armed followers in an attack on the building that housed the Codesa negotiations. The scenes broadcast were of crowd violence and anarchy, bringing to mind images of pre-World War II fascism. The final straw, and the one that caused leaders within the security establishment to disavow any links with white extremists, was the botched attempt by AWB members to reinstate Lucas Mangope as leader of the Bophuthatswana homeland in early 1993. Again television cameras were the right wing's undoing, as they broadcast worldwide the execution of several AWB mercenaries, lying beside their Mercedes Benz sedan, by professionally trained black soldiers. For South Africans, the telling image was not of blacks killing whites (although that was significant), but of the ineptness of the right.

The members of Codesa sped up the pace of negotiations and of plans to implement the interim constitution. South Africa was to have a federal system of regional legislatures, equal voting rights regardless of race, and a bicameral legislature headed by an executive president. The negotiators also agreed that the government elected in 1994 would serve for five years, and that a constitutional convention, sitting from 1994 onward and seeking input from all South Africans, would be responsible for drawing up a final constitution to be implemented in 1999.

The election in April 1994 was viewed by most participants as a remarkable success. Although several parties, especially the IFP, had threatened to boycott the election, in the end no significant groups refused to participate. The polling was extended to four days to allow for logistical and bureaucratic problems. In the end, it was carried out peacefully, for the most part, and there were few complaints of interference with anyone's right to vote. No political party got everything that it wanted. The ANC won nearly 62.6 percent of the vote, but it did not get the two-third's majority needed to change unilaterally the interim constitution, and it therefore had to work with other parties to shape the permanent constitution. The NP, as expected, no longer led the government, but it did succeed in winning the second largest share of votes, with 20.4 percent. The IFP did not do well nationally, but with a much stronger base of support in KwaZulu-Natal than most commentators expected, it came in third, with 10.5 percent, and won for Buthelezi control of the provincial government. The Freedom Front, a right-of-center, almost exclusively white party led by former members of the security establishment, got 2.2 percent of the votes; the PAC, appealing solely for the support of blacks, won 1.2 percent. On May 9, 1994, Nelson Mandela was unanimously elected president by the National Assembly, with Thabo Mbeki, deputy leader of the ANC and Mandela's likely successor, and F.W. de Klerk named deputy presidents. South Africa had made a peaceful political transition from an apartheid police state to a democratic republic.

As the new government is established in the mid-1990s, South Africa's leaders face the daunting challenges of meeting the expectations of black voters while fulfilling the economic potential of the country. Half a century of apartheid and a much longer period of legally enforced racial discrimination have left most black South Africans poor and undereducated. The reliance on a low-wage work force, especially in the country's mines but also in other areas of the economy, left South Africa without a significant consumer class among its black majority. Instead, nearly one-half of the population in the mid-1990s lives below internationally determined minimum-subsistence levels. Nearly fifty years of Verwoerdian "Bantu education" left the country short of skills and unable to generate the sort of labor force that could produce an "Asian miracle" along the lines of the skilled-labor-dependent industries of South Korea or Taiwan.

Demands for immediate economic improvements intensified in 1995 and 1996. Labor unions pressed demands on behalf of organized workers, many of whom feared that their interests would be ignored, lost amid the government's concerns for alleviating severe poverty and for bolstering investor confidence in a stable workforce. Many labor unions were also weakened, at least temporarily, by the loss of key leaders who were elected or appointed to government office.

After these chapters were completed in May 1996, the Constitutional Court approved the new ("final") constitution, intended to govern after the five-year transition. President Mandela signed the new constitution into law on December 10, 1996, and the government began phasing in provisions of the new document in February 1997. The final constitution contains a Bill of Rights, modeled on the chapter on fundamental rights in the interim constitution. It also ends the powersharing requirements that were the basis for the Government of National Unity under the interim constitution. NP deputy president de Klerk left office in June 1996, after legislators voted to forward the new constitution to the Constitutional Court, and the NP vacated its offices in the national and provincial executive branches, which had been based on the interim constitution's powersharing provisions. The NP in 1997 is attempting to establish a new political identity as an active participant in the national political debate; it will challenge ANC initiatives it opposes and compete with the ANC for political support among all racial groups.

South Africa conducted its first postapartheid census in October 1996. The process of enumeration proved even more difficult than expected, in part because provincial governments are still establishing their functions and authority, and administrative boundaries are still in dispute in a few areas. The final results—likely to reveal a population of more than 45 million—are not yet available as of April 1997.

The government has made substantial progress in expanding social services, health care, and education, but the backlog in demand for these services has been impossible to meet. These inadequacies continue to erode confidence in the new government, despite impressive progress in areas such as the provision of potable water and electricity, and the expansion of educational opportunities in previously underserved areas. The demand for housing is proving particularly difficult to meet; foreign construction firms are participating in the effort, and the pace of new home construction is expected to increase steadily during 1997 and 1998.

South Africa's culturally diverse society has not yet negotiated acceptable compromises for dealing with controversial aspects of individual behavior, such as women's rights to abortion or contraceptive use and behavior related to the spread of acquired immune deficiency syndrome (AIDS). ANC legislators successfully voted to liberalize public policy in many areas, most notably concerning abortion, despite strong opposition from some Christian and Muslim groups. The campaign against AIDS continues to be mired in political debate, funding controversies, and personal acrimony, as of 1997.

The Truth and Reconciliation Commission has heard more than 2,000 testimonials and received nearly 4,000 applications for amnesty for acts committed during the apartheid era. Grisly stories have emerged from the commission's hearings; a few lingering questions about apartheid-era deaths and disappearances have been answered, but others have arisen in response to allegations of official collusion in unrestrained violence. Commission chair Archbishop Desmond Tutu expressed confidence in early 1997 that the commission's long-term impact will be to further reconciliation among racial groups. Others, including survivors of victims, however, have expressed growing anger and stepped up demands for vengeance. Outside of the commission's purview, the courts have convicted a few former security officers and former freedom fighters for crimes committed before May 1994, although some of those found guilty in the courts may also apply for amnesty before the Truth and Reconciliation Commission.

Violence, both political and criminal, continues to plague the country. The newly organized South African Police Service has not yet eliminated the corruption and racial biases that characterized some segments of the police force during the apartheid era. Vigilante groups are emerging in response to popular demands for stricter law enforcement. The best-known of these, a Muslim-based coalition—People against Gangsterism and Drugs (PAGAD)—has attacked, and even killed, accused drug-dealers and others deemed to be outlaws, especially in Cape Town and surrounding areas of the Western Cape. Vigilantism is also increasing in crime-ridden areas around Johannesburg, and elsewhere.

The continuing violence and political uncertainty contributed to a steady decline in the value of the rand (for value of the rand—see Glossary) in late 1996 and early 1997. Levels of foreign investment have lagged behind that needed for economic growth, and the government is offering incentives to increase foreign participation in South Africa's business and manufacturing sectors. The Ministry of Finance outlined new economic strategies aimed at liberalizing foreign-exchange controls and imposing stricter fiscal discipline, in a framework document entitled *Growth, Employment and Redistribution*. The 1996 document describes investment incentives and steps toward restructuring the tax base to help stimulate new growth without substantially increasing public spending. It also outlines further steps toward the lifting of import tariffs and exchange controls to expand foreign trade.

As of April 1997, the most likely successor to President Mandela appears to be deputy president Thabo Mbeki; Mandela signaled his approval of this choice several times in the past year. A respected ANC diplomat and trained economist, Mbeki is expected to press for fiscal responsibility. Private-sector development, already a high priority, is likely to receive even greater emphasis in the early twenty-first century. At the same time, any new government will face the challenge of narrowing the gap between rich and poor, which will be crucial to furthering the goals of peace and reconciliation. Any new government also will face obstacles created by political extremists and economic opportunists hoping to reap their own gains in the new, post-apartheid South Africa.

April 2, 1997   William H. Worger and Rita M. Byrnes

Chapter 1. Historical Setting

Sheer cliffs overlooking the Valley of Desolation near Graaff-Reinet

HISTORY HAS A COMPELLING IMPORTANCE in South Africa. Political protagonists often refer to historical events and individuals in expounding their different points of view. The African National Congress (ANC), for example, has as one of its symbols the shield of Bambatha, a Zulu chief who died leading the last armed uprising of Africans against the British in 1906. Mangosuthu (Gatsha) Buthelezi, leader of the former KwaZulu homeland (see Glossary) and the Inkatha Freedom Party (IFP), often refers to Shaka Zulu, the first great monarch to arise in South Africa, who created a vast military state in the 1820s. Afrikaners (see Glossary) have frequently called themselves a "chosen people," ordained by God to rule in South Africa. They have argued that their ancestors settled the subcontinent before any African, but that for the past 200 years they have had to fight against the treachery of Africans and the oppression of British imperialists. The study of the history of South Africa, therefore, is a highly contentious arena marked by wide variations of interpretation and infused with politics.

South Africa did not exist as a unified self-governing state until 1910. Indeed, before the discovery of minerals—diamonds and gold—in the late nineteenth century, the emergence of such a country appeared unlikely because the early history of the subcontinent was marked by economic and political fragmentation. Black African settlement of southern Africa, which archaeologists have dated back to thousands of years before the arrival of whites, produced a great number of African societies that ruled much of what we now know as South Africa until the latter half of the nineteenth century. White settlement, beginning in the seventeenth century, was confined primarily to a small area of the southwestern coast throughout the eighteenth and the early nineteenth centuries. Slaves imported from outside southern Africa were the colonists' laborers. White settlers expanded into the interior and along the southeastern coast in the middle of the nineteenth century, but they usually skirted areas heavily populated by Africans. Moreover, the white settlers in the interior—Afrikaners, as they became known at the end of the nineteenth century—engaged in the same cattle-farming and hunting activities as their African neighbors. Although African and Afrikaner often competed—for pastureland and game—a balance of power prevented one from conquering the other.

Mineral discoveries in the 1860s and 1880s revolutionized the economic and political settings. Diamonds and gold fueled economic growth in southern Africa, creating both new market opportunities and a great demand for labor. To meet these labor needs, the British conquered most of the African peoples of the region in a rapid series of campaigns in the 1870s and 1880s and subjected the defeated people to controls that persisted practically to the present day: pass laws regulating the movement of people within urban areas and between urban and rural areas; discriminatory legal treatment of blacks compared with whites; and the establishment of "locations," for rural Africans, that were much smaller than the original landholdings of autonomous African societies in the nineteenth century. When the Union of South Africa was instituted in 1910, its constitutional provisions reflected a society in which whites had achieved a monopoly on wealth and power. .

The rise of an industrial economy also brought about conflict between English-speaking whites—primarily mine owners and industrialists, and Dutch-speaking whites—mostly farmers and impoverished urban workers, who competed for control over African land and labor and for access to the great mineral wealth of the country. Between 1910 and 1948, Afrikaner politicians organized and developed a powerful ethnic identity, portraying Africans as savage and threatening and building especially upon white fears of economic competition from cheaper black workers manipulated by unscrupulous English-speaking businessmen. In 1948 the Afrikaner nationalists won control of the government and implemented apartheid (apartness—see Glossary), a policy that reinforced existing segregationist practices securing white supremacy but that also aimed at ensuring Afrikaner domination of political power.

After 1948, black Africans, "coloureds" (mixed-race—see Glossary), and Asians fought against Afrikaner domination and white supremacy, denying the apartheid dictum that South Africa is a white man's country in which other races should find economic and political autonomy within their own geographically separated communities. Peaceful and violent protests alternated with periods of official repression, but during forty-five years of apartheid, the boundaries the Afrikaners had constructed to ensure their own survival proved intolerable for them as well as for other racial groups. Apartheid bred a climate of intolerance that was repugnant to many people of all races and a social system that turned out to be an economic disaster. The deliberately inferior living conditions and opportunities for a majority of citizens fueled frustration with government, deprived South Africa of a significant domestic market, and made it a pariah among civilized states. By the fourth decade of apartheid, the pressures for reform both from within South Africa and elsewhere, the growing realization that the system was intolerable, and the crumbling economy emboldened political leaders on all sides to take steps to dismantle apartheid.

Nelson (Rolihlahla) Mandela, South Africa's most popular anti-apartheid leader, had witnessed the rise and decline of apartheid firsthand. In the mid-1980s, after more than twenty years in prison for opposing apartheid, he assumed a central role in helping to end it. Government and opposition leaders met for talks—tentative ones at first, and then with greater confidence and amid more publicity—and they agreed on a general approach to political reform. Four years of difficult and uneven progress, amid escalating violence and competing political pressures, finally paid off in 1994, when South Africa held its first multiracial democratic elections. And while both sides could claim some of the success in achieving this historic goal, both sides also faced even greater challenges in trying to establish a stable multiracial society in the decades ahead.

Southern African Societies to ca. 1600

The Earliest South Africans

The oldest evidence in the world documenting the emergence of humankind has been found in South Africa; fossils of the earliest hominids (*Australopithecus africanus*) date back at least 2.5 million years, and remains linked to modern Homo sapiens date back more than 50,000 years. Roughly 20,000 years ago, South Africa, still in the grip of the world's last Ice Age, was occupied by people now known as San. Remnants of San communities still survive today as so-called Bushmen (now considered a pejorative term) in the Kalahari Desert. The San, who developed their society over thousands of years in isolation, speak a language that includes unique "click" consonants, are smaller statured, and have lighter skin pigmentation than the Bantu (see Glossary) speakers who later moved into southern Africa. However, older notions that such differences indicate that San are a distinct "race" of people have now been discredited and replaced by arguments that all the black inhabitants of South Africa are closely related, sharing a common gene pool, and that any physical differences among them can be attributed to geographical distribution and extent of contact rather than to race.

San obtained a livelihood from often difficult environments by gathering edible plants, berries, and shellfish; by hunting game; and by fishing. Gathering was primarily the task of women, who provided approximately 80 percent of the foodstuffs consumed by the hunter-gatherer communities. Men hunted, made tools and weapons from wood and stone, produced clothing from animal hides, and fashioned a remarkable array of musical instruments. San also created vast numbers of rock paintings—South Africa contains the bulk of the world's prehistoric art still extant—which express an extraordinary esthetic sensibility and document San hunting techniques and religious beliefs. The rock paintings also demonstrate that considerable interaction took place among hunter-gatherer communities throughout southern Africa.

The primary social unit among the San was the nuclear family. Families joined together to form hunter-gatherer bands of about twenty to fifty people. Men and women had equal status in these groups and there was no development of a hereditary chiefship, although the male head of the main family usually took a leading role in decision making. Such bands moved about the countryside seeking foodstuffs, sometimes remaining for long periods in particularly productive environments, sometimes splitting apart and joining other groups when food was scarce. Because they made such limited demands on their environment, San managed to provide a living for themselves for thousands of years. Population numbers did remain small, however, and settlement was generally sparse.

Approximately 2,500 years ago, some San in the northern parts of present-day Botswana acquired fat-tailed sheep and long-horned cattle, perhaps through trade with people from the north and the east, and became pastoralists. Their descendants, called "Hottentots" by early Dutch settlers, are now more accurately termed Khoikhoi, "men of men," or Khoi, in their own language. Although Europeans often considered San and Khoikhoi distinct races culturally and physically, scholars now think they are essentially the same people, distinguished only by their occupations. Differences in size—Khoikhoi are generally taller than San—are now attributed to the greater protein intake of pastoralists. Moreover, occupational status could often change in an individual's lifetime: San hunter-gatherers who found a particularly well-watered and fertile area might well acquire livestock through trade, settle down, and become relatively sedentary Khoikhoi pastoralists; pastoralists in times of drought or other ecological disaster might turn to hunting and gathering to survive.

Because the southern Cape is fertile and well-watered, many Khoikhoi settled along the coast between the Orange River and the Great Fish River. With the greater and more regular supplies of food that they derived from their herds, Khoikhoi lived in larger settlements than those of the San, often numbering several hundred people in a single community. Still, as pastoralists, Khoikhoi moved with the seasons among coasts, valleys, and mountains in search of pastureland. Such movement contributed to the fissiparous nature of Khoikhoi society, in which groups of people, usually in patrilineally related clans, periodically broke away and formed their own communities. The larger size of Khoikhoi communities as compared with those of the San did, however, lead to the development of more hierarchical political structures. A Khoikhoi group was generally presided over by a *khoeque* (rich man). The *khoeque* was not an autocrat, but rather could only exercise power in consultation with other male elders.

The Khoikhoi engaged in extensive trade with other peoples in southern Africa. In exchange for their sheep and cattle, they acquired copper from the north and iron from Bantu-speaking Africans in the east and fashioned these metals into tools, weapons, and ornaments. They also acquired *dagga* (cannabis) from the coast of what is modern-day Mozambique, cultivated it themselves, and traded it for other goods. With San, too, they bartered sheep and cattle products for game and hides.

By 1600 most of the Khoikhoi, numbering perhaps 50,000 people, lived along the southwest coast of the Cape. Most San, their numbers practically impossible to determine, lived in drier areas west of the 400-millimeter rainfall line (the limit for cultivation), including present-day Northern Cape province, Botswana, Namibia, and southern Angola (see fig. 2).

The Arrival of Bantu-Speaking Africans

Bantu-speaking Africans, whose descendants make up the overwhelming majority of the present-day inhabitants of South

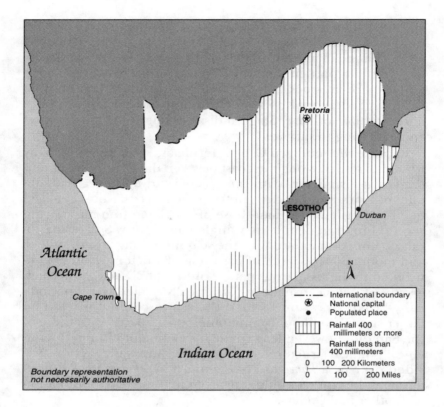

Figure 2. 400-millimeter Rainfall Line

Africa, had moved south of the Limpopo River by about 1,500 years ago. Farmers who combined knowledge of cattle-keeping and slash-and-burn (swidden) cultivation with expertise in metal-working, the Bantu speakers came from West Central Africa north of the Congo River near present-day Cameroon. Historians and archaeologists now argue that this movement took place not in any single great migration but rather in a slow southward shift of people throughout sub-Saharan Africa that resulted from the gradual drying up of the Sahara beginning about 8,000 years ago. The southward movement involved not the conquering hordes previously imagined but rather a moving frontier of farmers seeking new fields and pastures who interacted with pastoralists and hunter-gatherers, sometimes trading, sometimes incorporating people in client relationships, sometimes fighting for access to the same crucial resources. The farmers settled throughout southern Africa east of the 400-millimeter rainfall line and as far as the southwestern limits of cropping along the Great Kei River.

The Bantu-speaking farmers chose to minimize risks rather than to maximize production in their use of the environment. They kept large herds of cattle and invested these animals with great material and symbolic value. Cattle provided a means to acquire and to display considerable wealth, and they were used for significant social and political transactions, such as bridewealth compensation (*lobola*) and tribute demands. Cattle were also valued for their milk and for their hides, but they were seldom killed for their meat except on ceremonial occasions. Hunting of game continued to provide a major source of protein, while additional supplies came from domesticated goats and sheep. Bantu speakers also cultivated a range of indigenous crops, including millet, sorghum, beans, and melons along with other grains and vegetables. Those close to the sea collected shellfish and fished. By utilizing such a great range of food sources, the farmers spread their risks in a difficult ecological system constantly subject to drought, disease, and crop failure.

Still, the accumulation of large herds and the cultivation of extensive fields produced greater concentrations of population and considerably more stratification among Bantu speakers than among their San and Khoikhoi neighbors. Archaeologists have found evidence of settlements established more than 1,400 years ago comprising several thousand people each. Toutswe, in eastern Botswana, consisted of a series of communities built on large flat-topped hills with fields cultivated below and cattle pastured locally. The residents smelted iron and engaged in extensive trade with people as far east as the Indian Ocean. Similar large communities emerged at least 1,000 years ago just south of the Limpopo River where Bambandyanalo and then Mapungubwe arose as significant early states (both situated at the intersection of the present-day borders of Botswana, Zimbabwe, and South Africa). Cultivating extensive fields and holding large numbers of cattle, the residents of these states also produced finely worked gold and copper ornaments, hunted for ivory, and engaged in extensive long-distance trade. They were generally presided over by chiefs who held considerable—although never total—power; elders always had to be consulted about major decisions. Compared with the smaller-scale communities of San and Khoikhoi, the Bantu-speaking societies were marked by greater degrees of stratification: of old over young, men over women, rich over poor, and chiefs over commoners.

There were, however, significant differences between the settlement patterns and the degree of political centralization established by Bantu speakers who settled inland and by those who lived closer to the coast. The inland Bantu speakers, termed Sotho-Tswana on the basis of their dialects, concentrated in greater numbers around water sources and trading towns. By the late sixteenth century, a series of powerful hereditary chiefs ruled over the society known as the Rolong, whose capital was Taung. The capital and several other towns, centers of cultivation and livestock raising as well as major trading communities, had populations of 15,000 to 20,000. By contrast, the Bantu-speakers termed Nguni, who settled on the coastal plains between the Highveld (see Glossary) and the Indian Ocean, lived in much smaller communities and had less hierarchical political structures. Moving their cattle often in search of fresh pastureland, they lived in small communities scattered across the countryside. In many cases, a community identified itself on the basis of descent from some ancestral founder, as did the Zulu and the Xhosa. Such communities could sometimes grow to a few thousand people, as did the Xhosa, the Mpondo, the Mthethwa, and others, but they were usually far smaller.

By 1600 all of what is now South Africa had been settled: by Khoisan peoples in the west and the southwest, by Sotho-Tswana in the Highveld, and by Nguni along the coastal plains. Portuguese travelers and sailors shipwrecked along the coast in the seventeenth century reported seeing great concentrations of people living in apparent prosperity.

Early European Settlement

Origins of Settlement

Portuguese mariners explored the west coast of Africa throughout the latter half of the fifteenth century. Two ships under Bartholomeu Dias eventually rounded the Cape of Good Hope in 1488 and traveled more than 600 kilometers along the southwestern coast. In 1497 an expedition under Vasco da Gama rounded the Cape, sailed up the east African coast to the Arab port of Malindi (in present-day Kenya), and then crossed the Indian Ocean to India, thereby opening up a way for Euro-

Monument to Portuguese navigator Bartholemeu Dias, who sailed around the Cape of Good Hope in 1488
Courtesy Embassy of South Africa, Washington

peans to gain direct access to the spices of the East without having to go through Arab middlemen. The Portuguese dominated this trade route throughout the sixteenth century. They built forts and supply stations along the west and east African coasts, but they did not build south of present-day Angola and Mozambique because of the treacherous currents along the southern coast. At the end of the sixteenth century and in the early seventeenth century, English and Dutch merchants challenged the Portuguese monopoly in West Africa and Asia and saw the Cape peninsula as a source of fresh water, meat, and timber for masts, all of which they could obtain through trade with the local Khoikhoi. The English government refused its mariners' requests that it annex land there and establish a base, but in 1652 the Dutch East India Company (Verenigde Oostindische Compagnie—VOC) established a supply station in Table Bay on the Cape peninsula, instructing its station commander, Jan van Riebeeck, and his eighty company employees to build a fort and to obtain supplies of foodstuffs for the Dutch fleets.

Establishing a Slave Economy

The VOC's directors intended that the settlement at Table Bay should amount to no more than a small supply station able largely to pay for itself. European settlement was to be limited to VOC employees only, and their numbers were to be kept as small as possible. Company ships could stop to take on water, to get supplies of fresh fruit and vegetables grown by VOC employees, and to trade for fresh meat and milk from the local Khoikhoi. The Khoikhoi were also expected to supply the labor needs of the settlement—building wharves and warehouses, putting up offices, and laying out roads. Within its first half decade, however, the Cape Colony was growing in ways unforeseen at its establishment. Most Khoikhoi chose not to labor for the Dutch because of low wages and harsh conditions; and, although ready initially to trade with the Dutch, they became increasingly unwilling to sell their farm products at the prices offered by the VOC. As a result, three processes were set in motion in the 1650s that were to produce a rapidly expanding, racially stratified society. First, the VOC decided to import slaves to meet local labor needs, and it maintained that policy for more than 100 years. Second, the VOC decided to free some of its employees from their contracts and to allow them to establish farms of their own to supply the Dutch fleets, thereby giving rise to a local settler population. Third, to supply the needs of the fleets as well as of the growing local population, the Dutch expanded ever farther into the lands of the Khoikhoi, engaging in a series of wars that, together with the effects of imported diseases, decimated the indigenous population.

Van Riebeeck had concluded within two months of the establishment of the Cape settlement that slave labor would be needed for the hardest and dirtiest work. Some thought was given to enslaving Khoikhoi men, but the idea was rejected on the grounds that such a policy would be both costly and dangerous. With a European population that did not exceed 200 during the settlement's first five years, war against neighbors numbering more than 20,000 would have been foolhardy. Moreover, the Dutch feared that Khoikhoi people, if enslaved, could always escape into the local community, whereas foreigners would find it much more difficult to elude their "masters."

Between 1652 and 1657, a number of unsuccessful attempts were made to obtain men from the Dutch East Indies and from Mauritius. In 1658, however, the VOC landed two shiploads of slaves at the Cape, one containing more than 200 people brought from Dahomey (later Benin), the second with almost 200 people, most of them children, captured from a Portuguese slaver off the coast of Angola. Except for a few individuals, these were to be the only slaves ever brought to the Cape from West Africa. Thereafter, all the slaves imported into the Cape until the British stopped the trade in 1807 were from East Africa, Mozambique, Madagascar, and South and Southeast Asia. Large numbers were brought from India, Ceylon, and the Indonesian archipelago. Prisoners from other countries in the VOC's empire were also enslaved. The slave population, which exceeded that of the European settlers until the first quarter of the nineteenth century, was overwhelmingly male and was thus dependent on constant imports of new slaves to maintain and to augment its size.

Emergence of a Settler Society

In 1657 nine European men were released from the VOC's service, given the status of "free burghers," and granted blocks of land. They were exempted from taxation for twelve years, but the VOC held a mortgage on their lands. They were free to trade with Khoikhoi for sheep and cattle, but they were prohibited from paying higher prices for the stock than did the VOC, and they were told not to enslave the local pastoralists. They were encouraged to grow crops, especially grains, for sale to the VOC, but they were not allowed to produce anything already grown in the company's own gardens. By such measures, the VOC hoped not only to increase local production and thereby to pay the costs of the settlement, but also to prevent any private producers from undercutting the VOC's control over prices.

Conflict between Dutch farmers and Khoikhoi broke out once it became clear to the latter that the Dutch were there to stay and that they intended to encroach on the lands of the pastoralists. In 1659 Doman, a Khoikhoi who had worked as a translator for the Dutch and had even traveled to Java, led an armed attempt to expel the Dutch from the Cape peninsula. The attempt was a failure, although warfare dragged on until an inconclusive peace was established a year later. During the following decade, pressure on the Khoikhoi grew as more of the Dutch became free burghers, expanded their landholdings, and sought pastureland for their growing herds. War broke out again in 1673 and continued until 1677, when Khoikhoi resistance was destroyed by a combination of superior European weapons and Dutch manipulation of divisions among the local people. Thereafter, Khoikhoi society in the

western Cape disintegrated. Some people found jobs as shep-
herds on European farms; others rejected foreign rule and
moved away from the Cape. The final blow for most came in
1713 when a Dutch ship brought smallpox to the Cape. Hith-
erto unknown locally, the disease ravaged the remaining
Khoikhoi, killing 90 percent of the population.

The community at Table Bay grew larger and more diverse
throughout the late 1600s, particularly after the VOC decided
in 1679 that European settlement should be boosted in order
to expand agricultural production. German and Dutch settlers
were offered free farms if they would come to the Cape. In
1688 several hundred Huguenots fleeing persecution by the
French were offered free passage to the Cape and grants of
land. These settlers, all of whom soon assimilated Dutch culture and language, grew large crops of wheat as well as other
grains for sale to the VOC, although they found such crops
barely profitable. They also planted grapevines, so that they
could make wine and brandy—products much in demand for
Dutch sailors and capable of being exported to Europe, unlike
other, perishable items. The mainstay of most settlers, however,
was livestock farming, which required large areas of pastureland because the soil was generally poor. By the end of the century, pressures for land in and around the Cape peninsula had
become intense. There were approximately 1,500 Europeans in
the Cape settlement and a slightly larger number of slaves, and
the area of settlement had extended well beyond the original
base at Table Bay to include freehold farms reaching sixty kilometers inland.

The rise of an expanding settler society fueled tensions
between free burghers and the VOC. Free burghers criticized
the autocratic powers of the local VOC administration, in
which the governor had full control and the settlers had no
rights of representation. They denounced the economic policies of the VOC that fixed the prices at which settlers could sell
their agricultural products. They called attention to the cor-
rupt practices of VOC officers, who granted themselves prime
land and then sold their own crops at higher prices to the company. Above all, they complained about the VOC's failure—at
least in their eyes—to police the frontier boundaries and to
protect the settlers' crops and herds from Khoikhoi and San
raiders.

Trekboers (semi-migrant farmers of primarily Dutch, German, and French ancestry; more commonly known as Boers—

see Glossary) played a key role in the eighteenth century in the expansion of the settlement and in the growth of frontier conflict. With much of the better land close to the Cape in the hands of VOC officials and rich burghers, poorer whites sought to make a living beyond the boundaries of the settlement. Traveling by wagon inland and along the southwestern coast, individual farmers, along with their immediate families (if any), a few slaves, several Khoikhoi herdsmen, and small numbers of livestock, set out to establish farms on large tracts of land (averaging 2,500 hectares) granted on loan by the VOC (see fig. 3). Because much of this land was already occupied by Khoikhoi pastoralists near the coast and by San hunter-gatherers in the interior, considerable warfare resulted. Trekboers raided the herds of the Khoikhoi and seized control of the springs on which pastoralists and hunter-gatherers alike depended for water, while Khoikhoi and San counterraided the herds of the Trekboers.

In the face of burgher agitation, growing frontier conflict, and increasing overproduction of agricultural goods for the local market, the VOC in 1717 attempted to limit the growth of European settlement. It stopped all assisted immigration of Europeans and decided that thereafter only slaves should be used in the future development of the settlement. Moreover, it ended the granting of freehold title to land, although it did continue to make farms available on loan.

Such measures had only a limited impact on the growth of the settlement. Throughout the eighteenth century, the settlement continued to expand through internal growth of the European population and the continued importation of slaves. The approximately 3,000 Europeans and slaves at the Cape in 1700 had increased by the end of the century to nearly 20,000 Europeans, almost 25,000 slaves, and another 15,000 Khoikhoi and mixed-race people living within the boundaries of the settlement.

In the west, the economy was dominated by the bustling port at Table Bay and the wheat farms and vineyards of Stellenbosch and Swellendam, which depended almost totally on slave labor. Politically, the VOC governor continued to be in firm control, although a number of wealthy burghers exercised considerable informal influence. Socially, the community was marked by considerable stratification and diversity. Most wealth was concentrated in the hands of a few company officials and a minority of burghers. The majority of Europeans earned a living as

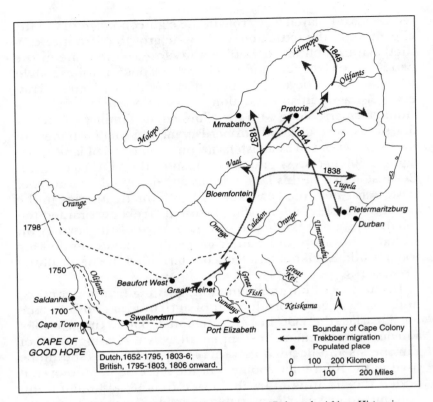

Source: Based on information from Michael Kwamena-Poh et al., *African History in
Maps*, Essex, United Kingdom, 1982, 26–27, 42–43; and Leonard Thompson,
A History of South Africa, New Haven, 1995, 89.

Figure 3. European Expansion, 1652–1848

artisans, traders, and innkeepers, although almost all whites
owned at least one or two slaves. A small community of mixed-
race people had also emerged, the offspring of relationships
among whites, Khoikhoi, Asians, and African slaves.

In the eastern areas of the Cape, beyond the Cape Colony
itself, Trekboers predominated with their extensive pastoral
economy. Most owned some slaves, but they depended more
on Khoikhoi and San to meet their labor needs. Although
nominally under the jurisdiction of the VOC, the Trekboers
largely ruled themselves. They did not believe that Khoikhoi
and San should be treated equally with Europeans in the
courts, and they established harsh labor regimes on their
farms. To deal with frontier problems, they periodically raised

armed bands of men to protect their herds and to carry out punitive expeditions against Khoikhoi and San. They developed a consciousness of themselves as a distinct community settled permanently in South Africa and, unlike the employees of the VOC, they did not plan to return to Europe.

By the last quarter of the eighteenth century, both western and eastern areas of the Cape were undergoing a period of stress. Continued overproduction for the local market in the west and resulting economic hardship led burghers to identify the VOC as the source of all their problems. The discontents of the Trekboers were even greater. Their continuing expansion was blocked by a number of barriers: by aridity 500 kilometers north of the Cape peninsula, by hunter-gatherer raiders in the northeast, and, most important, by large numbers of Bantu-speaking farmers (Xhosa) settled roughly 700 kilometers to the east of Cape Town and just south of the Great Fish River. Throughout much of the eighteenth century, Xhosa and Trekboers had peacefully traded with one another, with the Dutch exchanging glass beads, nails, and other manufactured items for African cattle and ivory. By the late 1770s, however, tensions rose as Xhosa farmers were expanding west of the Great Fish River at the same time that the Trekboers were moving eastward.

Demand for the same resources—land and water—brought Trekboers and Xhosa into conflict, and a series of frontier wars erupted in 1779 to 1781, and in 1793. In the second war, the Xhosa avenged their defeat in the first. Their capture of thousands of head of Boer cattle and their occupation of large areas of land previously claimed by the Dutch were officially recognized and accepted by a local representative of the VOC. Enraged by what they considered the treachery of the company, Trekboers in Graaff-Reinet rebelled in 1795, expelling the VOC magistrate and proclaiming an independent republic. This attempt at autonomy ended, however, with the British takeover of the Cape settlement in 1795.

Fearing that the strategic port at Table Bay might fall into the hands of Napoleon, the British seized the Cape to defend their sea route to India. They sent troops to the eastern Cape to prevent Boer insurrection and to establish order on the frontier, but they made no attempt to extend the boundaries of the settlement. Like the VOC before them, the British intended that the Cape settlement should remain as small as possible. Its value lay in its strategic position, not in its production. Moreover, the British had no wish to become embroiled in costly local struggles between European settlers and African farmers in the interior.

In 1802 the Treaty of Amiens, which ended a decade of upheaval in Europe, called for the return of the Cape Colony to Dutch control. This was accomplished in 1803, but the Dutch Batavian Republic in Europe had done little to implement this claim when the treaty began to break down in 1805. Britain again seized control of the Cape in 1806 and defied Dutch claims by occupying and expanding its presence in the Cape region. Finally, in 1814 the former Batavian Republic— the Kingdom of Holland—agreed to abandon its claim to the Cape in return for a grant of roughly 2 million British pounds.

The Rise of African States

By the eighteenth century, several groups of immigrants from the north, known for their skill in smelting iron and in metalworking, had occupied the mountains along the Limpopo River (see fig. 4). This heterogeneous population had coalesced into a number of chiefdoms, known as the Venda, or VaVenda. In the southern Highveld, the powerful Tswana-speaking kingdom known as the Rolong had split, giving rise to the Tlhaping (BaTlhaping) and the Taung. The Taung were named for a legendary military leader (Tau) among the Rolong.

One of several Khoisan-European populations in the interior in the eighteenth century was that of the Griqua, most of whom spoke Dutch as their first language and had adopted Christianity. A unique Griqua culture emerged, based on hunting, herding, and trade with both Africans and Europeans along the Orange River.

The Xhosa and related groups were the westernmost of the Nguni-speaking societies between the southern Highveld and the coast. Rivalries among Xhosa chiefs were common, however, and their society was weakened by repeated clashes with Europeans, especially over land between the Sundays River and the Great Fish River. By the late eighteenth century, the Ndwandwe, Mthethwa, and Ngwane were emerging as powerful kingdoms south of the Highveld. The Zulu were still a small group among the Mthethwa and had not yet begun the conquest and assimilation of neighboring groups that would characterize much of the early nineteenth century.

Background to the *Mfecane*

A combination of local factors—population growth, the depletion of natural resources, and devastating drought and famine—led to revolutionary changes in the political, economic, and social structure of Bantu-speaking communities in southern Africa in the first half of the nineteenth century. Thousands of people died because of ecological catastrophe and warfare; thousands more were displaced. Large centralized states of tens of thousands of people with standing armies of up to 40,000 men and autocratic leaders emerged where before there had been only small-scale political entities and no chief had had total power. This period of revolutionary change—known as the *mfecane* (or crushing—see Glossary) by the Zulu and the *difaqane* (see Glossary) by the Sotho—is also often referred to as "the time of troubles" (see fig. 5).

The causes of the *mfecane* were emerging by the end of the eighteenth century, when population levels increased rapidly, and ecological resources were sometimes scarce. Communities that previously had often spread across the countryside or had repeatedly divided and moved along the frontier became more settled and more concentrated. The introduction of corn from the Americas through the Portuguese in Mozambique was one major reason for this trend. Corn produced more food than indigenous grasses on the same land, and thus could sustain a larger population. Trade in ivory with the Portuguese in Delagoa Bay was another factor that induced people to settle just south of Mozambique. Moreover, possibilities for population movement had become much more limited by the end of the eighteenth century because land was in short supply. Bantu-speaking farmers had reached the margins of arable land on the edge of the Kalahari Desert in the northwest and in the mountains on the southern border of the Highveld, and people settling in the area found their access to water more and more limited.

Declining rainfall in the last decades of the eighteenth century, followed by a calamitous ten-year drought that began about 1800, caused massive disruption and suffering. The adoption of corn as a major staple gave this drought an even greater impact than those of the past because corn needed much more water than local grains in order to produce. When the rains failed, therefore, the effect was devastating. People fought one another for meager supplies of grain and cattle, hunted down whatever game they could find, and sought out

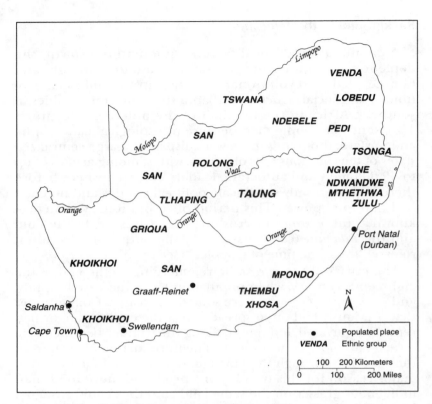

Source: Based on information from Kevin Shillington, *History of Southern Africa*,
London, 1987, 16; and Reader's Digest Association, *Reader's Digest Illustrated
History of South Africa*, Pleasantville, New York, 1989, 63.

Figure 4. Major African Ethnic Groups, Eighteenth Century

any remaining water supplies in a desperate attempt to survive.
Warfare erupted, and two kingdoms—the Ndwandwe under
the leadership of Zwide, and the Mthethwa under Dingiswayo—battled for control of resources. Both kingdoms
became more centralized and militarized, their young men
banded together in age regiments that became the basis for
standing armies, and their kings became more autocratic as
they fought for survival. The Ndwandwe appeared victorious in
1818 when Dingiswayo was killed and his forces scattered, but
they were soon overcome by Shaka, founder of the Zulu state.

Shaka and the Rise of the Zulu State

Shaka Zulu was born in 1787, the illegitimate son of Senzangakona, chief of the Zulu clan. An outcast as a child, Shaka was brought up among a number of neighboring groups, finally ending with the Mthethwa where he distinguished himself as a skilled warrior in Dingiswayo's army. Dingiswayo was so impressed by Shaka that in 1816 he helped him become chief of the Zulu upon the death of Senzangakona. Among the Zulu, Shaka consolidated a number of military innovations—some developed by Dingiswayo, some dating back to the eighteenth century—to produce a powerful military machine. All young men were incorporated into age regiments and given military training. A short stabbing spear was introduced in addition to the traditional long throwing spears, giving Shaka's army an advantage in close combat. Military strategies, such as the "horn" formation by which Zulu regiments encircled their enemies, were perfected. When Dingiswayo was killed, Shaka with his military machine avenged his mentor's death, destroying the Ndwandwe in battle (two of Zwide's generals, Shoshangane and Zwangendaba, fled north and established kingdoms in present-day Mozambique and southern Tanzania, respectively). Shaka then incorporated the Mthethwa under his rule, and established the Zulu state as the dominant power among the northern Nguni.

By the mid-1820s, Shaka ruled a kingdom of more than 100,000 people with a standing army of 40,000 men. He centralized power in the person of the king and his court, collected tribute from regional chiefs, and placed regiments throughout his state to ensure compliance with his orders. These regiments also looked after the royal herds and carried out public works. Women, too, were incorporated into their own age regiments, which were paired with male regiments to provide food and other services for the soldiers. Shaka forbade members of these regiments to marry, however, until they had completed their military service. For men this meant their late thirties, and for women their late twenties. Only after marriage could men and women leave their regiments and set up their own homesteads.

Shaka fostered a new national identity by stressing the Zuluness of the state. All subjects of the state became Zulu and owed the king their personal allegiance. Zulu traditions of origin became the national traditions of the state. Customary Nguni festivals, such as planting and harvest celebrations, became occasions on which Shaka gathered vast numbers of his people and extolled the virtues of the state. Through such

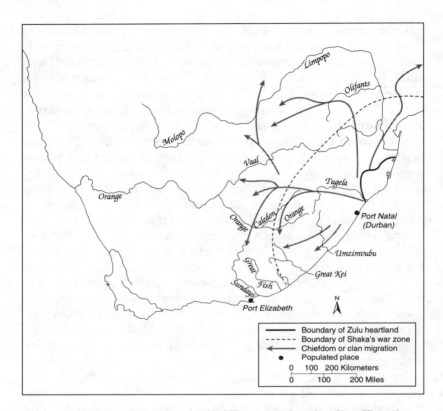

Source: Based on information from Michael Kwamena-Poh et al., *African History in
        Maps*, Essex, United Kingdom, 1982, 36–37; Leonard Thompson, *A History of
        South Africa*, New Haven, 1995, 82; and Reader's Digest Association, *Reader's
        Digest Illustrated History of South Africa*, Pleasantville, New York, 1989, 91.

Figure 5. The Mfecane, 1817–28

means, Shaka developed a Zulu consciousness that tran-
scended the original identities and lineages of the various peoples who were his subjects.

During most of the 1820s, Shaka consolidated his power
through a series of wars against neighboring peoples. His
armies raided for cattle and food; they attacked any who challenged the authority of the Zulu monarch; and they extended
the limits of Shaka's realm north to the borders of present-day
Mozambique, west across the Drakensberg Mountains, and
south to the margins of the area that would later become the
Transkei homeland. He also welcomed British traders to his
kingdom and sent diplomatic emissaries to the British king.

Shaka was assassinated at the height of his powers in 1828 and was succeeded by Dingane, his half-brother and one of the assassins. Dingane was a much less accomplished ruler than the founder of the Zulu state. His weak claim to the throne and his constant fear of assassination made him a despotic ruler. Dingane maintained the centralized and militarized organization of the Zulu state and sent his armies out on raiding missions. Victories, however, were few because of the growing strength of neighboring African kingdoms, and by the end of the 1830s Dingane's hold on power was being challenged by internal discontent and external threats.

Swazi, Sotho, and Ndebele States

Indeed, as a result of the *mfecane,* a series of states formed throughout southern Africa as people banded together to secure access to foodstuffs and to protect themselves from Zulu marauders. Sobhuza, leader of the Ngwane people to the north of the Zulu, built a defensive state that eventually took the name of his son and heir Mswati to form the basis of the modern Swazi nation, Swaziland. Sobhuza secured the boundaries of his state through a combination of diplomacy and force. He negotiated marriage alliances with Ndwandwe and later Zulu chiefs and cemented similar arrangements with his own chiefs. He paid tribute to the Zulu kings when he thought it necessary, but he also built a powerful army with which the Swazi were able to repel Dingane's incursions in the 1830s.

Moshoeshoe, another contemporary (b. 1786) of Shaka, forged a strong Sotho kingdom on the southern Highveld in the 1820s and 1830s. This kingdom became the foundation for the modern state of Lesotho. Moshoeshoe, seeking in the 1820s to protect his people from the worst ravages of the *difaqane,* fortified a large mesa, Thaba Bosiu, that proved impregnable to attack for decades thereafter. With this natural fortress as his base, he built a large kingdom, welcomed in particular refugees from famine and wars elsewhere, and provided them with food and shelter. These refugees, once incorporated into the state, were considered Sotho like their hosts; thus, as with the Zulu, ever larger numbers were integrated into a group with a consolidated ethnic identity, a practice that furthered the process of nation building. Moshoeshoe also sought to strengthen his kingdom militarily, especially by acquiring guns and horses from the Cape. A superb diplomat, he sought to maintain cordial relations with all his neighbors, even paying tribute on occasion to Shaka and seeking always to avoid war. Believing that they could act as emissaries on his behalf to the intruding European powers while also teaching his children to read and write, he welcomed French Protestant missionaries. By the mid-1830s, Moshoeshoe's kingdom comprised about 30,000 people and was the largest state on the southern Highveld.

A fourth major African state formed in South Africa during the 1820s and 1830s was the Ndebele state ruled by Mzilikazi. Mzilikazi had been a subject chief of Shaka, but in 1821 he had sought to demonstrate his independence by refusing to send tribute cattle to the king. Fleeing from a punitive force sent by Shaka, Mzilikazi and a few hundred followers crossed the Drakensberg Mountains and established a series of armed settlements on the Highveld. Raiding for cattle and grain and forcibly incorporating Sotho-Tswana people into his forces, Mzilikazi built a powerful kingdom in the 1830s near present-day Johannesburg and Pretoria.

Although the *mfecane* in many ways promoted the political development of southern Africa, it also caused great suffering. Thousands died because of famine and warfare, and thousands more were uprooted from their homes and were forced to travel great distances, many to become refugee laborers in the Cape who sought work at any wage. Perhaps the most significant result in terms of the future was that large areas of South Africa were temporarily depopulated, making it seem to Europeans that there were unclaimed lands in the interior into which they could expand.

The Expansion of European Settlement

British Colonialism

The British adopted contradictory policies in ruling their newly acquired Cape Colony in the first three decades of the nineteenth century. Having seized the Cape from the VOC in 1795, the British returned the colony to the Dutch government in 1803 when peace had been concluded with the French. In 1806, however, with the beginning of the Napoleonic Wars, the British again took the Cape in order to protect the sea route to their Asian empire. Like the VOC before them, the British tried to keep the costs low and the settlement small. Local officials continued the policy of relying on imported slave labor rather than encouraging European immigration with the latter's implication of permanent and expanding settlement. They also introduced racially discriminatory legislation to force Khoikhoi and other so-called "free" blacks to work for as little as possible. The Hottentot Code of 1809 required that all Khoikhoi and other free blacks carry passes stating where they lived and who their employers were. Persons without such passes could be forced into employment by white masters.

The British attempted to alleviate the land problems of Boers in the eastern Cape by sending imperial armies against the Xhosa of the Zuurveld (literally, "sour grassland," the southernmost area of Bantu-speaking settlement, located between the Sundays River and the Great Fish River). They attacked the Xhosa from 1799 to 1803, from 1811 to 1812, and again from 1818 to 1819, when at last, through ruthless warfare, they succeeded in expelling the Africans into the area north of the Great Fish River. Thereafter, the British sought to create a fixed frontier by settling 5,000 British-assisted immigrants on smallholder farms created out of land seized from the Xhosa south of the Great Fish River and by clearing all lands between the Great Fish River and the Keiskama River of all forms of African settlement.

But other policies and developments worked against these measures. In 1807 Parliament in London ordered an end to British participation in the slave trade everywhere in the world. This decision threatened the basis of the Cape's labor supply, for farmers in the eastern areas as well as in the west.

British missionaries, who were active in South Africa for the first time in the 1810s and who had a sympathetic audience in Britain, condemned the cruel labor practices often adopted by Trekboers against their slave and Khoikhoi workers and decried the discriminatory provisions of the Hottentot Code. Although British officials did not rescind the legislation, they did respond to this criticism by establishing a circuit court to monitor conditions in the western Cape. This court offended many Boer sensibilities by giving equal weight to the evidence of "servants" and "masters," black and white alike. The British also raised a force of colonial police, including Khoikhoi regulars, to enforce the court's authority. In 1815 a Dutch-speaking Afrikaner farmer who refused to answer a court summons for mistreating a Khoikhoi employee was shot dead while resisting arrest. Relatives and neighbors rose in what became known as the Slachter's Nek Rebellion, but their resistance was soon crushed, and the British hanged five of the rebels.

British policies on the eastern frontier also engendered growing Boer hostility. The attempt to close the frontier in 1819–20 following the defeat of the Xhosa and the importation of British immigrants only exacerbated land shortages. British settlers found that they could not make a living from small farms, and they competed with the Dutch pastoralists for the limited arable land available, thereby intensifying Boer-British tensions.

The British government, acting largely at the behest of the missionaries and their supporters in Britain in the 1820s, abolished the Hottentot Code. Ordinance 50 of 1828 stated that no Khoikhoi or free black had to carry a pass or could be forced to enter a labor contract. Five years later, the British Parliament decreed that slavery would no longer be permitted in any part of the empire. After a four-year period of "apprenticeship," all slaves would become free persons, able, because of Ordinance 50, to sell their labor for whatever the market would bear. Moreover, slaveowners were to receive no more than one-third of the value of their slaves in official compensation for the loss of this property. The Boers felt further threatened when, in 1834 and 1835, British forces, attempting to put a final stop to Boer-Xhosa frontier conflict, swept across the Keiskama River into Xhosa territory and annexed all the land up to the Keiskama River for white settlement. In 1836, however, the British government, partly in response to missionary criticism of the invasion, returned the newly annexed lands to the Xhosa and sought a peace treaty with their chiefs.

The Great Trek

Dutch speakers denounced these actions as striking at the heart of their labor and land needs. Those living in the eastern Cape, most of them among the poorer segment of the Dutch-speaking population, were particularly impassioned in their criticisms, and many decided to abandon their farms and to seek new lands beyond the reach of British rule.

Beginning in 1836, Boer families, together with large numbers of Khoikhoi and black servants, gathered up their belongings and traveled by ox-wagon up into the Highveld interior to the north of the eastern Cape frontier. (Travel farther east was blocked by the Xhosa.) All told, some 6,000 Boer men, women, and children, along with an equal number of blacks, participated in this movement in the late 1830s. Fewer Boer families migrated from the western Cape, where they were more pros-

Voortrekker monument overlooking Pretoria; its friezes depict the Great Trek and the Battle of Blood River.
Courtesy Embassy of South Africa, Washington

perous on their grain and wine farms and therefore less concerned about land shortages and frontier pressures. The exodus from the Cape was not organized in a single movement at the time, but it was later termed the Great Trek by nationalist historians, and its participants were called Voortrekkers (pioneers).

The first groups of Voortrekkers moved into the southern Highveld, skirted the powerful Lesotho kingdom of Moshoeshoe to the east, and pastured their herds on lands between the Orange River and the Vaal River. A large group moved farther north to the grasslands beyond the Vaal River into territory where Mzilikazi had recently established a powerful Ndebele state. Competing for the same resources—pasturelands, water, and game—the Voortrekkers and the Ndebele soon came into conflict. In 1836 the Voortrekkers fought off an Ndebele attempt to expel them from the Highveld. In the following year, the northern Voortrekkers allied with the Rolong and the Griqua, who were known for their fighting skills. This time the northern Voortrekkers succeeded in defeating Mzilikazi and forcing him and most of his followers to flee north into present-day Zimbabwe, where he conquered the Shona and established a new state.

The majority of Voortrekkers, however, neither settled between the Orange and the Vaal nor trekked to the north, but moved northeastward around Lesotho and traveled down toward the sea into Zulu-ruled areas of southeastern Africa. The leader of this group, Piet Retief, attempted to negotiate with Dingane for permission to settle in relatively sparsely populated areas south of the Tugela River. Dingane was at first receptive to Retief's entreaties, but then, apparently fearing that the introduction of European settlers would undermine his authority, he had Retief and seventy of his followers killed while they were at his capital in February 1838. Dingane then sent out Zulu regiments to eliminate all Voortrekkers in the area; they killed several hundred men, women, and children and captured more than 35,000 head of cattle and sheep.

Not all of the settlers were killed, however, and in December the survivors, reinforced by men from the Cape Colony, marched 500 strong to avenge the deaths of Retief and his followers. Commanded by Andries Pretorius, the Voortrekkers pledged that they would commemorate a victory as a sign of divine protection. They then met and defeated Dingane's army at the Battle of Blood River. Their victory is celebrated each year on December 16, the Day of the Vow.

The Zulu kingdom split into warring factions after this defeat. One group under Mpande, a half-brother of Shaka and Dingane, allied with Pretorius and the Voortrekkers, and together they succeeded in destroying Dingane's troops and in forcing him to flee to the lands of the Swazi, where he was killed. The Voortrekkers recognized Mpande as king of the Zulu north of the Tugela River, while he in turn acknowledged their suzerainty over both his kingdom and the state that they established south of the Tugela. The Voortrekker Republic of Natalia (the basis of later Natal Province) was established in 1839, and by 1842 there were approximately 6,000 people occupying vast areas of pastureland and living under a political system in which only white males had the right to vote.

The British, however, feeling that their security and authority were threatened, annexed the republic as Natal. They did not want the Dutch speakers to have independent access to the sea and thereby be able to negotiate political and economic agreements with other European powers. They also feared that harsh treatment meted out to Africans—such as Voortrekker attempts to clear the land by removing Africans from the Republic of Natalia—would eventually increase population pressures on the eastern Cape frontier. Although acquiescing in the annexation, the great majority of the Voortrekkers effectively abandoned Natal to the British and moved back to the Highveld in 1843. The British, having taken Natal for strategic purposes, then had to find a way to make the colony pay for its administration. After experimenting with several crops, they found that sugar grew well and could be exported without deteriorating. Attempts to force Africans to endure the onerous labor in the sugar fields failed, however, and in 1860 the British began importing indentured laborers from India to provide the basic work force. Between 1860 and 1866, 6,000 Indians (one-quarter of them women) were brought to the colony on five-year contracts.

The Voortrekker Republics and British Policies

The Voortrekkers established two states in the 1840s and the 1850s: the Orange Free State between the Orange and the Vaal rivers and the South African Republic (Zuid Afrikaansche Republiek, a union of four Boer republics founded by the Voortrekkers) to the north of the Vaal River in the area later constituting the Transvaal. Like the Africans among whom they settled, the Voortrekkers in both states made their living from a combination of extensive pastoralism and hunting. Ivory was the most important product at first, and the search for it engendered great competition between African and European hunters. In the 1860s, ostrich feathers also became an important export. All processed foods and manufactured goods were acquired by trading ivory, skins, and feathers to British merchants at the Cape.

Politically, the two states were republics, with constitutions modeled in part on that of the United States, each with a president, an elected legislature, and a franchise restricted to white males. Africans could not vote, or own land, or carry guns because the laws of both republics, unlike those of the British colonies, did not recognize racial equality before the law. By the end of the 1860s, there were approximately 50,000 whites settled in the two republics, practically all of them living in rural areas, although small capitals had been established at Bloemfontein in the Orange Free State and at Pretoria in the South African Republic.

Initially, the British attempted to strengthen their own position by extending colonial control beyond the Cape Colony's boundaries. In 1848, after the northern frontier was threatened by fighting between Voortrekkers and Griqua on the Orange River and by continued competition for resources among settlers and Africans, the governor of the Cape Colony, Sir Harry Smith, annexed all the land between the Orange and the Vaal rivers. This area, which the British called the Orange River Sovereignty, comprised large numbers of Voortrekker communities and practically all of the Sotho state, Lesotho. Smith, urged on by land-hungry white settlers, also annexed the Xhosa lands between the Keiskama and the Great Kei rivers that the British had first taken and then returned in 1835 and 1836. Moreover, he sought to win a decisive military victory over the Xhosa and to break forever the power of their chiefs by pursuing a ruthless war against them from 1850 to 1852.

The British had mixed success. Their attempts to tax the Orange River Voortrekkers produced almost no revenue. Claims to Sotho lands were met with opposition from Moshoeshoe, who in 1851 and 1852 successfully defeated British attempts to extend their authority into his lands. As a result of the Sotho resistance, the British decided to withdraw from the Highveld, but in so doing they recognized the primacy of European rather than African claims to the land. The Sand River Convention of 1852 and the Bloemfontein Convention of 1854 recognized the independence of the South African Republic and the Orange Free State, respectively, as Voortrekker republics so long as their residents agreed to acknowledge the ultimate sovereignty of the British government, agreed not to allow slavery in their territories, and agreed not to sell ammunition to Africans. It was not until 1868 that the British again attempted to extend their power onto the Highveld, and that was only when Lesotho's defeat by the Orange Free State was so complete that the total destruction of the Sotho people seemed likely.

On the eastern Cape frontier, however, British policies brought about enormous destruction for the Xhosa. Smith was recalled by the British government in 1852 for instigating conflict with the Xhosa, but the Colonial Office decided to pursue the war to victory nonetheless in 1853. Large areas of Xhosa land were annexed, and thousands of head of cattle were confiscated. Drought and disease further reduced the Xhosa's remaining herds. Defeated in war, their lands greatly reduced and food supplies in decline, the Xhosa turned for salvation to a young girl, Nongqawuse, who prophesied that if the people purified themselves through sacrifice—by destroying their cattle and their grain, and by not planting new crops—then their ancestors would return to aid them, the herds would reappear, and all the whites would be driven into the sea. Although not all Xhosa believed the prophecies, by 1857 more than 400,000 head of cattle had been killed and vast quantities of grain had been destroyed. As a result, 40,000 Xhosa died from starvation, and an equal number sought refuge in the Cape Colony, where most became impoverished farm laborers.

By the end of the 1860s, white settlement in South Africa was much more extensive than it had been at the beginning of the century. There were now two British colonies on the coast (Cape Colony and Natal) instead of one, and two Voortrekker republics on the southern and the northern Highveld (the Orange Free State and the South African Republic) (see fig. 6). The white population had also increased considerably, from the 20,000 or so Europeans resident in the Cape Colony in 1800 to 180,000 reported in the 1865 census. There were another 18,000 whites living in Natal and perhaps 50,000 more whites in the Voortrekker states.

Yet there were evident constraints to growth. Economically, South Africa was little different from what it had been when the British first arrived. The Cape produced wine, wheat, and wool, none of them particularly profitable items on the world market in the 1860s, especially because of competition from American, Argentine, and Australian farmers. Natal's sugar kept the colony going, but it was not an expanding industry. In the interior, the Voortrekkers engaged in the same economic activities as their African neighbors—pastoralism, limited cultivation of grain crops, and hunting—and whereas these provided a living for the people involved, they were not the basis on which an expanding economy could be built. Perhaps the best indicator of the limited attractions of South Africa's economy was the fact that fewer Europeans emigrated there than to the United States, Canada, Australia, or even New Zealand.

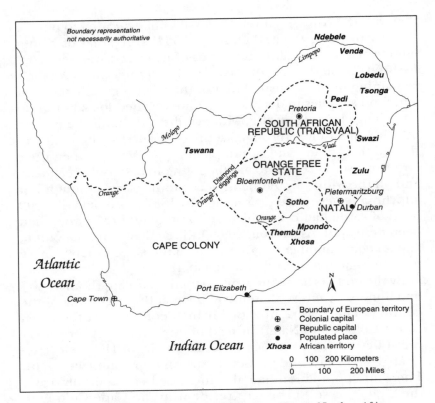

Source: Based on information from Kevin Shillington, *History of Southern Africa,*
London, 1987, 84.

Figure 6. Southern Africa, 1870

Moreover, areas of white and black settlement and political
control were largely separate. In 1865 the Cape contained
200,000 Khoikhoi and people of mixed ancestry (the basis of
today's coloured population), as well as 100,000 Bantu speakers. Several hundred thousand blacks lived in Natal and in the
Voortrekker republics. The vast majority of South Africa's black
inhabitants, however, continued to live in independent African
states ruled by their own kings and chiefs. In the 1860s,
Mpande's Zululand was a still powerful state in which most
Zulus lived. Moshoeshoe's Lesotho, although it had been
attacked by the Orange Free State and its borders contracted,
contained most of the Sotho people. To the northeast of the
South African Republic, the Pedi under their king Sekhukhune
had a well-armed state, and the Swazi kingdom continued to be

a powerful entity. Any observer traveling in South Africa in the late 1860s would have had little reason to assume that this balance of power between blacks and whites would change dramatically during the remainder of the nineteenth century.

Industrialization and Imperialism, 1870–1910

The Mineral Revolution

Mineral discoveries in the 1860s, the 1870s, and the 1880s had an enormous impact on southern Africa. Diamonds were initially identified in 1867 in an area adjoining the confluence of the Vaal and the Orange rivers, just north of the Cape Colony, although it was not until 1869 to 1870 that finds were sufficient to attract a "rush" of several thousand fortune hunters. The British government, attracted by the prospect of mineral wealth, quickly annexed the diamond fields, repudiating the claims of the Voortrekker republics to the area. Four mines were developed, and the town of Kimberley was established. The town grew quickly and became the largest urban society in the interior of southern Africa in the 1870s and the 1880s. Although the mines were worked initially by small-scale claimsholders, the economics of diamond production and marketing soon led to consolidation. Within two decades of the first diamond find, the industry was essentially controlled by one monopolistic company—Cecil Rhodes's De Beers Consolidated Mines.

The diamond industry became the key to the economic fortunes of the Cape Colony by providing the single largest source of export earnings, as well as by fueling development throughout the colony. Whereas the Cape's exports in 1870 had been worth little more than £2,000,000, with wool providing the bulk of earnings, by the end of the century the value of exports had risen to more than £15,000,000, with diamonds alone accounting for £4,000,000. There was also substantial growth in population, much of it from immigration. As a result, there were close to 400,000 resident Europeans in the Cape Colony by 1900, twice the number who had lived there in 1865.

Gold soon eclipsed diamonds in importance. Africans had mined gold for centuries at Mapungubwe (in South Africa, on the border with Zimbabwe) and later at the successor state of Great Zimbabwe, and they had traded with Arabs and Portuguese on the east coast of Africa. In the 1860s and the 1870s, Europeans made a number of small finds of their own, but the major development took place in 1886 when potentially enormous deposits of gold were found on the Witwatersrand (literally, "Ridge of White Waters" in Afrikaans, commonly shortened to Rand—see Glossary) near present-day Johannesburg. English-speaking businessmen who had made their fortunes in the diamond industry quickly bought up all the auriferous claims and established a series of large gold-mining companies that were to dominate the industry well into the twentieth century.

Rhodes, who had succeeded in monopolizing the diamond industry, was much less successful on the Rand, where his companies proved to be poorer producers than those of his competitors. In the 1890s, he sought to compensate for his lackluster performance by carving out a personal empire in present-day Zimbabwe, original site of the fifteenth-century gold industry of Great Zimbabwe. There he ruled the Ndebele and the Shona people through his British South Africa Company.

Although beset by a number of technological problems in its early days, gold mining on the Rand grew rapidly, with output increasing from £80,000 in 1887 to nearly £8,000,000, or one-fifth of the world's gold production, in 1895. By the end of the century, more than £60,000,000 of capital had been invested in the gold industry, most of it by European investors, who thereby continued the pattern developed at Kimberley that southern Africa received more foreign investment than the rest of Africa combined. The gold mines employed 100,000 African laborers, five times as many as did the diamond mines, and drew these men from throughout southern Africa, although most came from Portuguese-ruled areas of Mozambique. Johannesburg, the newly established hub of this industry, had a population of 75,000 Europeans by the end of the century, which made it the largest city in southern Africa.

Africans and Industrialization

African Enterprise

Africans participated actively in the new industrial economy. Thousands came to Kimberley in the early 1870s, some to obtain diamond claims, the majority to seek jobs in the mines and thereby to acquire the cash that would enable them to rebuild cattle herds depleted by drought, disease, and Boer raids. In the early 1870s, an average of 50,000 men a year migrated to work in the mines, usually for two to three months, returning home with guns purchased in Kimberley, as well as cattle and cash. Many who lived in the area of the diamond finds chose to sell agricultural surpluses, rather than their labor, and to invest their considerable profits in increasing production for the growing urban market. African farmers in British Basutoland (the British protectorate established in Lesotho), the Cape, and Natal also greatly expanded their production of foodstuffs to meet rising demand throughout southern Africa, and out of this development emerged a relatively prosperous peasantry supplying the new towns of the interior as well as the coastal ports. The growth of Kimberley and other towns also provided new economic opportunities for coloureds, many of whom were skilled tradesmen, and for Indians, who, once they had completed their contracts on the sugar plantations, established shops selling goods to African customers.

Extending European Control

Mineowners struggling to make a profit in the early days of the diamond industry sought, however, to undercut the bargaining strength of the Africans on whom they depended for labor. In 1872 Kimberley's white claimsholders persuaded the British colonial administration to introduce a pass law. This law, the foundation of the twentieth-century South African pass laws, required that all "servants" be in possession of passes that stated whether the holders were legally entitled to work in the city, whether or not they had completed their contractual obligations, and whether they could leave the city. The aim of this law, written in "color-blind" language but enforced against blacks only, was to limit the mobility of migrant workers, who frequently changed employers or left the diamond fields in a constant (and usually successful) attempt to bargain wages upward.

Other restrictions followed the pass law. These included the establishment of special courts to process pass law offenders as rapidly as possible (the basis of segregated courts in the twentieth century), the laying out of special "locations" or ghettos in Kimberley where urban blacks had to live (the basis of municipal segregation practices), and, finally, in 1886 the formation of "closed compounds," fenced and guarded institutions in which all black diamond mine workers had to live for the duration of their labor contracts.

The institutionalization of such discriminatory practices produced in Kimberley the highest rate of incarceration and the lowest living standards for urban blacks in the Cape Colony. It also marked a major turnabout in the British administration of law. The previous official policy that all people irrespective of color be treated equally, while still accepted in legal theory, was now largely ignored in judicial practice. South Africa's first industrial city thus developed into a community in which discrimination became entrenched in the economic and social order, not because of racial antipathies formed on the frontier, but because of the desire for cheap labor.

Because blacks would not put up with such conditions if they could maintain an autonomous existence on their own lands, the British embarked on a large-scale program of conquest in the 1870s and the 1880s. Mine owners argued that if they did not get cheap labor their industries would become unprofitable. White farmers, English- and Dutch-speaking alike, interested in expanding their own production for new urban markets, could not compete with the wages paid at the mines and demanded that blacks be forced to work for them. They argued that if blacks had to pay taxes in cash and that if most of their lands were confiscated, then they would have to seek work on the terms that white employers chose to offer. As a result of such pressures, the British fought wars against the Zulu, the Griqua, the Tswana, the Xhosa, the Pedi, and the Sotho, conquering all but the last. By the middle of the 1880s, the majority of the black African population of South Africa that had still been independent in 1870 had been defeated, the bulk of their lands had been confiscated and given to white settlers, and taxes had been imposed on the people, who were now forced to live on rural "locations." In order to acquire food to survive and to earn cash to pay taxes, blacks now had to migrate to work on the farms, in the mines, and in the towns of newly industrialized South Africa.

African Initiatives

The final quarter of the nineteenth century was marked also by the rise of new forms of political and religious organization as blacks struggled to attain some degree of autonomy in a world that was rapidly becoming colonized. Because the right to vote was based on ownership of property rather than on race in the Cape, blacks could participate in electoral politics, and this they did in increasing numbers in the 1870s and the 1880s, especially in the towns. In 1879 Africans in the eastern Cape formed the Native Educational Association (NEA), the purpose of which was to promote "the improvement and elevation of the native races." This was followed by the establishment of the more overtly political Imbumba Yama Nyama (literally, "hard, solid sinew"), formed in 1882 in Port Elizabeth, which sought to fight for "national rights" for Africans.

In 1884 John Tengo Jabavu, a mission-educated teacher and vice president of the NEA, founded his own newspaper, *Imvo Zabantsundu* (Native Opinion). Jabavu used the newspaper as a forum through which to express African grievances about the pass laws; "location" regulations; the unequal administration of justice; and what were considered "anti-native" laws, such as the one passed in 1887 by the Cape Parliament at Rhodes's behest that raised the property qualification for voters and struck 20,000 Africans off the rolls. Through these organizations and newspapers, and others like them established in the late nineteenth century, Africans protested their unequal treatment, pointing out in particular contradictions between the theory and practice of British colonialism. They called for the eradication of discrimination and for the incorporation of Africans into colonial society on an equal basis with Europeans. By the end of the nineteenth century, after property qualifications had again been raised in 1892, there were only about 8,000 Africans on the Cape's voting roll.

Africans sought to bypass what they considered the discriminatory practices of the established Christian churches (which often preached to segregated audiences and seldom promoted Africans within their ranks) by founding separate organizations of their own. Starting in 1884 with Nehemiah Tile, a Thembu (Tembu) Methodist preacher from the eastern Cape who left the Methodists and established the Tembu National Church, Africans built their own churches throughout South Africa. Many of these churches were termed "Ethiopian" by their founders, on the basis of the biblical prophecy "that Ethiopia shall soon stretch out her hands to God," and because for centuries an African-run independent Christian church had existed in Ethiopia. A strong influence on these churches in the 1890s and the early 1900s was the United States-based African Methodist Episcopal Church (AME), which sent missionaries to South Africa and trained many blacks from South Africa at its own institutions in the United States. Members of these independent churches called not so much for the elimination of racial discrimination and inequality as for an "Africa for the Africans," that is, a country ruled by blacks.

British Imperialism and the Afrikaners

Minerals and the Growth of Boer-British Antipathy

British pressures on the Dutch-speaking population of the South African Republic became intense in the aftermath of industrialization. In seizing the diamond fields in 1870, the British had swept aside many Boer land claims. In 1877, fearing a collapse of the South African Republic in the face of defeat by a Pedi army, the British had formally annexed the Boer state, as the Transvaal. They then set about destroying the Pedi to obtain laborers for the Kimberley mines, and they completed the task in 1879. In 1880, however, the Transvaalers rose, and at the Battle of Majuba Hill in 1881, they defeated a British army. The British then withdrew, leaving the Boers victorious in what they would later call their First War of Independence.

The discovery of gold on the Witwatersrand greatly increased Boer-British tensions. Here was vast mineral wealth beyond British control. Moreover, the president of the South African Republic, Paul Kruger, attempted to lessen his state's long-term dependence on Cape merchants by developing a rail link to Portuguese East Africa. Such a link threatened British commercial interests and revived old fears of the Boers' gaining direct access to the sea and thus to other European powers. At the same time, the mine owners were, without exception, English speakers who exhibited no loyalty to the South African Republic and who did not seek to reinvest their gold profits in the local community. Indeed, they complained bitterly about all attempts to tax the gold industry.

These economic tensions lay at the base of a political issue: the right of English speakers to have the vote. With the rise of the gold industry and the growth of Johannesburg, the South African Republic had been inundated by so many English-speaking immigrants (called *uitlanders* by the Boers), most of them skilled mine workers, that by the 1890s they constituted a majority of the white male population. The state's constitution limited the vote to males who had lived in the South African Republic for at least seven years, and Kruger feared that expanding the franchise would only enable mine owners to manipulate their workers and to thereby win political power.

British mine owners and officials constantly decried Kruger's refusal to extend the franchise. In December 1895, Cecil Rhodes took matters a step further by sending 500 armed men, employees of his British South Africa Company, into the South African Republic under the leadership of Dr. Leander Starr Jameson. Rhodes hoped that the *uitlanders* would rise and join the invaders to help overthrow Kruger's government. The invasion, however, was a fiasco: Boer commandos disarmed Jameson and his men with little resistance, and the *uitlanders* took no action. Rhodes resigned the premiership of the Cape Colony in disgrace. The British government denied having advance knowledge of the invasion and claimed that it had no expansionist plans of its own.

Distrusting the mine owners and the British government, Kruger sought to build his country's strength. He engaged in diplomatic relations with Germany, imported arms from Europe, and continued to deny the vote to *uitlanders*. He also cemented relations with the Orange Free State and sought support from Dutch speakers in the Cape. In these endeavors, he was assisted by a growing sense of Afrikaner identity that had developed in the last quarter of the nineteenth century. This nationalistic identity had emerged clearly in the early 1880s, after the victory of Majuba Hill, when S.J. du Toit, a Dutch Reformed minister in the Cape, had published a newspaper, *Die Afrikaanse Patriot* (The Afrikaner Patriot), and a book, *Die Geskiedenis van ons Land in die Taal van ons Volk* (The History of our Land in the Language of our People), which argued that Afrikaners were a distinct people with their own fatherland in South Africa and that they were fulfilling a special mission determined expressly by God. Du Toit had gone on to found a political party in the Cape, the Afrikanerbond, to represent the interests of Dutch speakers. The Jameson Raid and anti-Boer sentiments expressed by gold magnates and British officials further cemented an Afrikaner sense of distinctiveness, which in the 1890s reached across political boundaries to include Dutch speakers in the Cape and the citizens of the Orange Free State as well as the Transvaalers.

Rhodes, together with his fellow gold mining magnates and the British government (in the persons of Joseph Chamberlain, secretary of state for the colonies, and Alfred Milner, high commissioner in South Africa), continued to denounce Kruger and his government. Rhodes and his peers called attention to what they considered rampant official corruption while also complaining that taxes were too high and that black labor was too expensive (because of perceived favoritism by the government regarding the labor needs of Afrikaner farmers). Chamberlain had concluded by the second half of the 1890s that the British needed to take direct action to contain Afrikaner power, and he had at first used diplomatic channels to pressure Kruger, although with little success. Milner pointed out what he considered the appalling condition of British subjects in the South African Republic, where, without the vote, they were, he argued, "kept permanently in the position of helots." In 1899 Milner advised Chamberlain that he considered the case for British intervention "overwhelming." Ignoring attempts by Kruger to reach a compromise, Chamberlain in September 1899 issued an ultimatum requiring that Kruger enfranchise British residents of the South African Republic. At the same time, Chamberlain sent troop reinforcements from Britain to the Cape. Kruger, certain that the British were bent on war, took the initiative and, allied with the Orange Free State, declared war on the British in October 1899.

The South African War

The South African War (1899–1902), fought by the British to establish their hegemony in South Africa and by the Afrikaners to defend their autonomy, lasted three years and caused enormous suffering. Ninety thousand Afrikaners fought against a British army that eventually approached 500,000 men, most from Britain but including large numbers of volunteers also from Australia, New Zealand, and Canada. Approximately 30,000 Africans were also employed as soldiers by the British, while thousands more labored as transport workers. Kruger's forces, taking advantage of initial superiority in numbers (before the British regulars arrived) and of surprise, won a number of victories at the beginning of the war. In 1900, however, British forces overwhelmed the Boers, took Bloemfontein (capital of the Orange Free State), Johannesburg, and Pretoria (capital of the South African Republic), and forced Kruger into exile. Resistance continued, however, in the countryside, where the Boers fought a ferocious guerrilla war. The British ultimately succeeded in breaking this resistance, but only by adopting a scorched-earth policy. In 1901 and 1902, the British torched more than 30,000 farms in the South African Republic and the Orange Free State and placed all the Afrikaner women and children in concentration camps, where, because of over-

*Reproduction of painting by R. Caton Woodville of the ill-fated
Jameson Raid, 1895–96
Courtesy Prints and Photographs Division, Library of Congress*

crowding and unsanitary conditions, more than 25,000 perished.

Peace was finally concluded at the town of Vereeniging on May 21, 1902. Milner, who drew up the terms, intended that Afrikaner power should be broken forever. He required that the Boers hand over all their arms and agree to the incorporation of their territories into the British empire as the Orange River Colony and the Transvaal. However, he made one significant concession to Boer sentiments by agreeing that the franchise would not be extended to Africans throughout South Africa (they had no vote in the Boer republics) until the local white population could decide that issue themselves. Since Milner himself believed that "political equality" of blacks and whites was "impossible" and that South Africa was really a white man's country in which the role of blacks should essentially be limited to that of "well-treated" labor, the concession was not a large one for him to make.

Milner's Peace

Milner sought to consolidate the military victory by adopting three policies. He planned to encourage large numbers to emigrate from Britain so that English speakers would attain a numerical majority among South Africa's white population. He wanted to institute policies of denationalization and of anglicization so that Afrikaners would lose their sense of a separate identity and would assimilate into British culture. To ensure the successful implementation of both policies, he intended to rule South Africa directly without local representation.

Milner also believed that the successful development of a loyal colonial society rested above all on ensuring the profitability of the gold industry even if that meant great strains for the African population. To that end, he sought to address the postwar labor needs of the gold mines by strictly enforcing pass laws in the cities and by collecting taxes from Africans in the countryside.

Relations between Africans and Europeans were increasingly strained as Milner's policies were implemented. Pressures in Natal were particularly severe. Most of Zululand had been annexed to Natal in 1897, a decade after approximately one-third of Zululand had been incorporated into the South African Republic. These strains erupted into violence in 1905, when a Zulu chief, Bambatha, invoking the memory of King Shaka, led an armed uprising. British firepower was too great, however, and in 1906 Bambatha and several thousand of his followers were killed in central Natal. His was the last armed struggle against colonial rule.

Despite opposition from local whites, who feared the addition of yet another racial group to their community, Milner also supported the gold magnates' plans to import large numbers of indentured Chinese laborers to work in the mines. The first men arrived in 1904, and by 1906 there were 50,000 Chinese at work, comprising one-third of the gold mines' labor force.

Milner's belief expressed before the war that blacks and whites could never be recognized as equal in South Africa received official sanction in 1905 with the final report of the South African Native Affairs Commission (SANAC). The British had gone to war in 1899 stating their abhorrence of the racially discriminatory policies adopted in the Afrikaner republics and because of such sentiments had received the active support of thousands of Africans. Between 1903 and 1905, the SANAC commissioners looked into the question of developing a common "native policy" for all of South Africa. Despite the testimony of numerous members of the educated African elite decrying discriminatory policies, the commissioners concluded that there should be no political equality between blacks and whites, that separate voters' rolls should be established, and that territorial separation was advisable for the races.

Yet none of Milner's policies met with real success. The gold industry, burdened with the costs of rebuilding after the devastation of the war, produced only limited profits, and South Africa continued to be economically depressed for much of the first decade of the twentieth century. Few immigrants were attracted by such poor prospects, and fewer than 1,200 British settler families came, less than one-eighth of the number Milner had hoped for. His denationalization policy was a complete failure. Indeed, Afrikaners, already imbued with a sense of collective suffering by their nineteenth-century experiences at the hands of British imperialists, were even more united after the South African War (which they termed the Second War of Independence). They celebrated their language, Afrikaans, and demonstrated its beauty in an outpouring of poetry. They set up their own schools, insisting that their children should be taught in Afrikaans and not be limited to the English-only instruction of government schools. In addition, they established new political parties to push for self-government: Oranje Unie (Orange Union) formed by Abraham Fischer and General James "Barry" Munnik (J.B.M.) Hertzog in the Orange River Colony and Het Volk (The People) founded by General Louis Botha and Jan C. Smuts in the Transvaal. The greatest blow to Milner's plans, however, came in 1905 with the victory of the Liberal Party in the British general election and the formation of a government led by men who had opposed the scorched-earth policy in the South African War as no more than "methods of barbarism."

Formation of the Union of South Africa, 1910

Accepting the fact that English speakers would never constitute a majority in white South Africa, the Liberal government sought to come to terms with the Afrikaner majority. In 1907 the British granted limited self-government to both the Transvaal and the Orange River Colony, and in subsequent elections, Het Volk and the Oranje Unie swept to victory. In the following year, the South African Party (SAP), led by an English-speaking critic of British imperialism and dependent on the support of the Afrikaner Bond, came to power in the Cape Colony. Reassured by the readiness of Het Volk's leaders, Botha and Smuts, to assist the gold-mining industry in obtaining larger supplies of cheap black labor (although without the Chinese workers who were repatriated in 1908) and in repressing militant white miners (who protested conditions of labor and job competition from blacks), the British government encouraged negotiations in South Africa among white representatives of the four self-governing colonies with the aim of establishing a single state.

Negotiations held in 1908 and in 1909 produced a constitution that embodied three fundamental principles: South Africa would adopt the Westminster style of government and would become a unitary state in which political power would be won by a simple majority and in which parliament would be sovereign; the question of voting rights for blacks would be left up to each of the four self-governing colonies to decide for itself (the Cape and Natal based their franchise on a property qualification; the Orange River Colony and the Transvaal denied all blacks the vote); and both English and Dutch would be official languages. The constitution also provided for future incorporation of the British-governed territories of Southern Rhodesia, Bechuanaland (present-day Botswana), Basutoland (present-day Lesotho), and Swaziland into the union.

In May 1910, Louis Botha became the first prime minister of the newly established Union of South Africa, a dominion of the British Empire, and Jan Smuts became his deputy. Just eight years earlier, both men had been generals in Kruger's army; now, through the SAP, they governed a country of 4 million Africans, 500,000 coloureds, 150,000 Indians, and 1,275,000 whites.

Segregation, 1910–48

Building the Legal Structure of Racial Discrimination

Several pieces of legislation marked the establishment of the Union of South Africa as a state in which racial discrimination received official sanction. The Native Labour Regulation Act (No. 15) of 1911 made it a criminal offense for Africans, but not for whites, to break a labor contract. The Dutch Reformed Church Act of 1911 prohibited Africans from becoming full members of the church. The Mines and Works Act (No. 12) of 1911 legitimized the long-term mining practice by which whites monopolized skilled jobs by effectively restricting Africans to semi-skilled and unskilled labor in the mines. Most important, the Natives Land Act (No. 27) of 1913 separated South Africa into areas in which either blacks or whites could own freehold land: blacks, constituting two-thirds of the population, were restricted to 7.5 percent of the land; whites, making up one-fifth of the population, were given 92.5 percent. The act also stated that Africans could live outside their own lands only if employed as laborers by whites. In particular, it made illegal the common practice of having Africans work as sharecroppers on farms in the Transvaal and the Orange Free State.

Formation of the African National Congress, 1912

Milner's pro-white policies followed by the discriminatory legislation enacted by the Union of South Africa engendered considerable resistance from blacks and led to the formation and growth of new political bodies. In 1902 coloureds in Cape Town had formed the African Political Organisation to represent the interests of "educated . . . Coloured people." Abdullah Abdurahman, a Scottish-trained doctor, became president of the organization in 1904, and, by stressing the political discrimination to which coloureds were subjected, he had built it into a vital body with 20,000 members by 1910. Mohandas Gandhi began a passive resistance campaign against the pass laws in 1906, leading Indians in Natal and the Transvaal (they were legally prohibited from living in or entering the Orange Free State) in demonstrations and organizing stop-work protests that won the support of thousands of people. Numerous meetings were held by Africans, coloureds, and Indians to protest the whites-only nature of the constitutional discussions that took place in 1908 to 1909. These activities culminated in March 1909 in a South African Native Convention, which called for a constitution giving "full and equal rights" for all blacks, coloureds, and Indians.

But it was opposition to the Natives Land Act, preliminary drafts of which were debated in 1911, that led to the formation in 1912 of the most significant organization, the South African Native National Congress (renamed the African National Congress [ANC] in 1923). Several hundred members of South Africa's educated African elite met at Bloemfontein on January 8, 1912, and established a national organization to protest racial discrimination and to appeal for equal treatment before the law. The founding president was John L. Dube, a minister and schoolteacher who had studied in the United States and who had been strongly influenced by Booker T. Washington.

Pixley Ka Isaka Seme, a lawyer with degrees from Columbia University and Oxford University and a prime mover in organizing the meeting to establish the congress, was appointed treasurer. Solomon T. Plaatje, a court translator, author, and newspaper editor who had worked in Kimberley and Johannesburg, became secretary general. The meeting opened and closed with the singing of the hymn "Nkosi sikelel'i Afrika" ("God Bless Africa"), which had been composed at the end of the nineteenth century by a Xhosa poet.

The congress was moderate in composition, tone, and practice. Its founders were men who felt that British rule had brought considerable benefits, especially Christianity, education, and the rule of law, but who also considered that their careers as teachers, lawyers, and court translators were hindered by the racial discrimination so endemic in South Africa. They called not for an end to British rule but for respect for the concept of equality for all, irrespective of color. They respected "traditional" authorities in African societies and made chiefs and kings office-holders as of right within the congress. They believed that they could best achieve their aims by dialogue with the British. As John Dube said, the congress pursued a policy of "hopeful reliance on the sense of common justice and love of freedom so innate in the British character." Such reliance, however, proved unfounded. When the congress sent a deputation to London in 1914 to protest the Natives Land Act, the colonial secretary informed them that there was nothing that he could do. Members of another deputation that went to London in 1919 were received sympathetically by Prime Minister Lloyd George, but they were also told that their problems would have to be resolved in South Africa by the South African government.

World War I and Afrikaner Nationalism

In August 1914, Louis Botha and Jan Smuts, amid much controversy, took South Africa into World War I on the side of the British. Botha and Smuts considered that South Africa, as a British dominion, had no choice in the matter, and they sent troops to conquer the German protectorate of South-West Africa (present-day Namibia, mandated by the League of Nations to South Africa following World War I). More soldiers, including a corps of coloured volunteers, were later sent to fight in German East Africa and in France. Many Afrikaners felt no loyalty to Britain and opposed going to war with Germany, which had aided them during the South African War. An attempted coup against Botha's government in September was aborted when one of the leaders, an Afrikaner hero from the South African War, was killed by police. An armed uprising of nearly 10,000 men in the Orange Free State and the Transvaal later in the year, led by another war hero, was crushed by Botha's forces.

The political opposition to Botha's entry into the war was led by J.B.M. Hertzog and his newly formed National Party of South Africa (NP). Hertzog was a former close ally of Botha who had split with the SAP over three issues: he felt that the SAP worked too closely with English mine owners (whom he considered "fortune-hunters"); he thought that only lip-service was being given to the policy of making Dutch equal with English as an official language; and he wanted more done to separate blacks and whites. The National Party was established in January 1914 to take up these issues. Support for the party grew, especially with South African entry into the war, and by 1915 there were branches in the Transvaal and the Orange Free State led by Hertzog and by Tielman Roos, respectively, and in the Cape, where Daniel F. (D.F.) Malan edited the party's newspaper, *Die Burger* (*The Citizen*).

Hertzog and his allies took various steps to strengthen the basis of Afrikaner nationalism. They stressed the richness and importance of Afrikaans rather than Dutch, and supported publication of books and magazines in the former language. They also sought to alleviate the poverty that had become endemic among Afrikaners, many of whom had been driven off the land into the cities in the last decades of the nineteenth century and during the South African War. Because almost all commercial enterprises and banks were run by English speakers, these people had little success in obtaining jobs or loans from such institutions. Many found work as unskilled laborers in the mines, where their color alone assured that they got higher pay than blacks.

Using the concept of *helpmekaar* (mutual aid), initially adopted to assist the unsuccessful rebels of 1914 and their families, relatively wealthy Afrikaner wine farmers in the western Cape pooled their resources and in 1918 established the South African National Trust Company (Santam) and the South African National Life Assurance Company (Sanlam). These new companies, a credit institution and a life insurance business, respectively, acquired their capital from Afrikaners and invested their funds only with Afrikaners. Also in 1918, another exclusively Afrikaner organization was formed, the Afrikaner Broederbond (later the Broederbond, or Brotherhood—although this literal translation has never been used as a term of reference). This organization, which in 1921 became a secret society, was established by young professionals—teachers, clerks, and ministers in the Dutch Reformed Church—who believed that they, too, needed to act to protect and to celebrate Afrikaner culture.

Conflict in the 1920s

In 1922 the interaction of economic and ethnic factors produced armed conflict among whites. Strikes had been organized by white miners in 1907, 1913, and 1914 over the conditions of labor and the threat of black competition, with the result that mine owners had agreed to reserve some semiskilled work for whites. In addition, white miners split politically; many of the English-speaking mine workers joined the Labour Party (formed in 1909), while the Afrikaners supported the National Party. Some of the more radical workers left the Labour Party in 1915 to form the International Socialist League of South Africa, which in turn became the Communist Party of South Africa (CPSA) in 1921.

In the context of postwar depression, the mine owners proposed in 1922 that wages be reduced, that several thousand white semi-skilled and unskilled workers be dismissed, and that the statutory "colour bar" be lifted, thereby enabling the employers to increase the ratio of black workers to white. The white workers, supported by the Labour and National parties, went on strike. With militant Afrikaner nationalists taking a leading role and organizing commandos, the strikers marched through Johannesburg behind banners proclaiming "Workers of the World Unite, and Fight for a White South Africa," occupied fortified positions in the mines, and announced the establishment of a White Workers' Republic. Smuts, prime minister since Botha's death in 1919, struck back with 20,000 troops and with artillery, tanks, and bomber aircraft. In the ensuing conflict, seventy-six strikers were killed, 4,748 were arrested, and eighteen were sentenced to death, of whom only four were hanged.

Smuts won only a temporary victory because in the 1924 general election he was swept out of office by an alliance of the National and Labour parties and was replaced as prime minister by J.B.M. Hertzog. The new government took immediate steps to protect the privileged position of white labor by enacting the Industrial Conciliation Act of 1924 and the Wage Act of 1925. The former law gave legal recognition to white trade unions but not to black; the latter enabled the minister of labor to force employers to give preference to the hiring of white workers. In addition, the Mines and Works Amendment Act of 1926 reinforced the color bar in the mining industry. Together, these laws became the cornerstone of what Hertzog termed his "civilised labour" policy. Hertzog also introduced measures to provide whites with greater job opportunities by instituting higher protective tariffs to encourage local manufacturing; by opening up new overseas trade relations, especially with Germany; and by establishing the state-owned South African Iron and Steel Corporation (Iscor). He proposed as well a number of "native bills" to restrict the voting rights of Africans, removed the property qualification for all white voters, and enfranchised white women, thereby more than doubling the number of eligible white voters while reducing black voters to a negligible number. He also introduced legislation replacing Dutch with Afrikaans as an official language.

Black opposition to these measures took a variety of forms, the most important of which was the growth of the Industrial and Commercial Workers Union (ICU). The ICU had been established in 1919 as a trade union for coloured dockworkers in Cape Town by Clements Kadalie, a mission-educated African from Nyasaland (present-day Malawi). Kadalie's organization grew enormously in the 1920s, in rural as well as in urban areas, as it tapped the great discontent that blacks already felt for the segregationist policies of Botha and Smuts and their increased disturbance over Hertzog's "civilised labour" legislation. ICU organizers, often men with links to the independent African churches who had little time for the overly "moderate" policies of the ANC and who were strongly influenced by the back-to-Africa movement of Marcus Garvey, galvanized mass support with calls for an immediate end to discrimination and to colonial rule. By 1928 the ICU's claimed membership, predominantly rural-based, had grown to between 150,000 and 200,000 Africans, 15,000 coloureds, and 250 whites, making it a far larger political body than the ANC. Yet the organization soon collapsed, brought down by the contradiction between the near-millennial expectations of its followers and the refusal of Hertzog's government to offer any concessions, and by the inability of blacks to force the government to change any of its policies. By the end of the 1920s, only a few regional branches of the ICU remained, and Kadalie was no longer at the head of the organization.

The Great Depression and the 1930s

The onset of the Great Depression brought about considerable political change. Hertzog, whose National Party had won the 1929 election alone, after splitting with the Labour Party, received much of the blame for the devastating economic impact of the depression. Fearing electoral defeat in the next election (1934), he sought a partnership with his former opponent, Jan Smuts, and the latter's South African Party. In 1933 Hertzog and Smuts made an alliance, and in the following year they merged their two parties to form the United South African National Party, also known as the United Party (UP). Hertzog and Smuts then won the general election; Hertzog continued as prime minister and Smuts became his deputy. Many Afrikaners criticized Hertzog's move, especially because they considered Smuts to be an opponent of Afrikaner nationalism who was too closely allied with the English mine owners; under the leadership of D.F. Malan and the Broederbond, they split away to form their own political party, the Purified National Party.

Malan built his political appeal by stressing the particular sufferings of the Afrikaner people. Their economic problems had become especially evident during the depression, when the Carnegie Commission on Poor Whites had concluded in 1931 that nearly one-third of Afrikaners lived as paupers, whereas few English-speaking whites lived below the poverty line. To deal with this problem, Malan and his allies in the Broederbond encouraged the development of an Afrikaner economic movement. The Volkskas (People's Bank) was founded in 1934; and exclusively Afrikaner trade unions, which espoused a Christian-National ethic combining devout Calvinism with ethnic nationalism, were established at the same time. In subsequent years, the Broederbond worked closely with Sanlam/Santam to pool whatever wealth was available and to invest it in new economic opportunities for the *volk* (people). Malan and his allies also drew attention to the past sufferings of the Afrikaner people by organizing a commemorative reenactment in 1938 of the Great Trek. Ox-wagon parades through the country culminated in a festival held in Pretoria on December

Afrikaans Language Monument (Afrikaanse Taalmonument) at Paarl, Western Cape
Courtesy Embassy of South Africa, Washington

16, the exact day on which, 100 years earlier, the Zulu had been defeated at the Battle of Blood River. A massive Voortrekker Monument, replete with friezes depicting the heroism of the Voortrekkers and the treachery of the Africans, was officially opened while Malan made a speech in which he said that it was the duty of Afrikaners "to make South Africa a white man's land."

Hertzog and Smuts, while rejecting the ethnic nationalism of Malan, hardly differed with him in their policies toward blacks. In the mid-1930s, the United Party government introduced legislation to remove Africans from the common voters' roll in the Cape, to limit them to electing white representatives to Parliament, and to create a Natives Representative Council that had advisory powers only (Representation of Natives Act [No. 12] of 1936). The government increased the amount of land set aside for blacks from 7.5 percent to 13 percent of South Africa, but confirmed the policy that the country should always be segregated unequally by race (the Native Trust and Land Act [No. 18] of 1936) and enforced even stricter regulation of the pass laws (the Native Laws Amendment Act of 1937). In response to growing anti-Semitic sentiments among Afrikaners—usually directed at the mine owners, many of whom were Jewish—the government introduced legislation to prevent the immigration of Jews into South Africa (the Aliens Act [No. 1] of 1937). The same law also prohibited the entry of any immigrant who could not quickly assimilate into the white population.

Organized black responses to these measures were muted. The ANC, under the conservative leadership of Pixley Seme since 1930, concentrated on advising Africans to try to better themselves and to respect their chiefs rather than engaging in an active condemnation of Hertzog's policies. Membership in the congress fell to a few thousand. In December 1935, some ANC members, dissatisfied with this approach, together with representatives of Indian and coloured political organizations, met in Bloemfontein and formed the All-African Convention (AAC) to protest the proposed new laws as well as segregation in general. But even this organization, composed largely of members of the black professional class along with church leaders and students, avoided the confrontational approach of the ICU. The AAC leaders stressed their loyalty to South Africa and to Britain and called yet again for the British Parliament to intervene to ameliorate the condition of blacks.

The Impact of World War II

The outbreak of World War II in 1939 proved a divisive factor in the white community. Smuts favored entry into the war on the side of the British. Hertzog supported neutrality. Many of Malan's supporters wanted to enter the war on Germany's side. German National Socialism, with its emphasis on the racial superiority of Germanic peoples, its anti-Semitism, and its use of state socialism to benefit the "master race," had garnered many Afrikaner admirers in the 1930s. A neo-Nazi Greyshirt organization had been formed in 1933 that drew increasing support, especially among rural Afrikaners, in the late 1930s. In 1938 Afrikaners participating in the commemoration of the Great Trek had established the Ossewabrandwag (Oxwagon Sentinel) as a paramilitary organization aimed at inculcating a "love for fatherland" and at instituting, by armed force if necessary, an Afrikaner-controlled republic in South Africa. By the end of the decade, the Ossewabrandwag claimed a membership of 250,000 out of a total Afrikaner population of a little more than 1 million. Oswald Pirow, Hertzog's minister of defense until the end of 1939, formed a movement within the National Party called the New Order, a fascist program for remaking South African society along Nazi lines. Smuts prevailed, however, winning the support of a majority of the cabinet and becoming prime minister. Hertzog resigned and joined with Malan in forming the Herenigde (Reunited) National Party (HNP). South Africa sent troops to fight on the British side in North Africa and in Europe. In South Africa, several thousand members of the Ossewabrandwag, including a future prime minister, John Vorster, were interned for antiwar activities.

Economically and socially, the war had a profound effect. While gold continued to be the most important industry, providing two-thirds of South Africa's revenues and three-quarters of its export earnings, manufacturing grew enormously to meet wartime demands. Between 1939 and 1945, the number of people employed in manufacturing, many of them African women, rose 60 percent. Urbanization increased rapidly: the number of African town dwellers almost doubled. By 1946 there were more Africans in South Africa's towns and cities than there were whites. Many of these blacks lived in squatter communities established on the outskirts of major cities such as Cape Town and Johannesburg. Such developments, although necessary for war production, contradicted the segregationist ideology that blacks should live in their rural locations and not become permanent urban residents.

More unsettling still to the segregationists was the development of new black organizations that demanded official recognition of their existence and better treatment of their members. In Johannesburg, for example, James Mpanza proclaimed himself king of his Orlando squatter encampment, set up his own system of local government and taxation, and established the Sofasonke ("We shall all die together") Party. Urban black workers, demanding higher wages and better working conditions, also formed their own trade unions and engaged in a rash of strikes throughout the early 1940s. By 1946 the Council of Non-European Trade Unions (CNETU), formed in 1941, claimed 158,000 members organized in 119 unions. The most important of these new trade unions was the African Mineworkers Union (AMWU), which by 1944 claimed a membership of 25,000. In 1946 the AMWU struck for higher wages in the gold mines and succeeded in getting 60,000 men to stop work. The strike was crushed by police actions that left twelve dead, but it demonstrated the potential strength of organized black workers in challenging the cheap labor system.

The 1948 Election

Smuts's governing United Party and Malan's HNP went into

the 1948 general election campaign on opposing platforms. The United Party based its platform on the report of the Native Laws Commission chaired by Judge Henry Fagan. The Fagan commission argued that because of the influx of Africans into the cities and because of the impoverishment of the African reserves, total segregation was impossible. Although it did not recommend social or political integration, the commission suggested that African labor should be stabilized in the cities, where the needs of industrial and commercial operations were greatest. The HNP's platform, based on a report by Paul Sauer, argued to the contrary, that only total separation of the races would prevent a move toward equality and the eventual overwhelming of white society by black.

The HNP stated that Africans should be viewed as only temporary dwellers in the cities and should be forced periodically to return to the countryside to meet the labor needs of farmers (primarily Afrikaners). In addition, the HNP platform declared that Africans should develop political bodies in "their true fatherland," the African reserves, and should have no form of parliamentary representation in South Africa.

Malan also called for the prohibition of mixed marriages, for the banning of black trade unions, and for stricter enforcement of job reservation. Running on this platform of apartheid, as it was termed for the first time, Malan and the HNP, benefiting from the weight given to rural electorates, defeated Smuts and the United Party. The HNP won a majority of the seats contested but only a minority of the votes cast. The HNP became the government and, renamed the National Party (NP), ruled South Africa until 1994.

Apartheid, 1948–76

The Legislative Implementation of Apartheid

Malan and the National Party, fearing that they might lose office in the next election, immediately set about introducing laws to give apartheid a legislative reality that could not easily be overturned. Such laws aimed at separating whites and blacks, at instituting as a legal principle the theory that whites should be treated more favorably than blacks and that separate facilities need not be equal, and at providing the state with the powers deemed necessary to deal with any opposition.

Separating Black from White

The Population Registration Act (No. 30) of 1950 provided the basis for separating the population of South Africa into different races. Under the terms of this act, all residents of South Africa were to be classified as white, coloured, or native (later called Bantu) people. Indians, whom the HNP in 1948 had refused to recognize as permanent inhabitants of South Africa, were included under the category "Asian" in 1959. The act required that people be classified primarily on the basis of their "community acceptability"; later amendments placed greater stress on "appearance" in order to deal with the practice of light-colored blacks "passing" as whites. The act also provided for the compilation of a population register for the whole country and for the issuing of identity cards.

Other laws provided for geographic, social, and political separation. The Group Areas Act (No. 41) of 1950 extended the provisions of the Natives Land Act (No. 27) of 1913, and later laws divided South Africa into separate areas for whites and blacks (including coloureds), and gave the government the power to forcibly remove people from areas not designated for their particular racial group. The Tomlinson Commission in 1954 officially concluded that the areas set aside for Africans would support no more than two-thirds of the African population even under the best of conditions, but the government ignored its recommendation that more land be allocated to the reserves and began removing Africans from white areas.

The Prohibition of Mixed Marriages Act (No. 55) of 1949 made marriages between whites and members of other racial groups illegal. The Immorality Act (No. 21) of 1950 extended an earlier ban on sexual relations between whites and blacks (the Immorality Act [No. 5] of 1927) to a ban on sexual relations between whites and any non-whites. The Bantu Authorities Act (No. 68) of 1951 established Bantu tribal, regional, and territorial authorities in the regions set out for Africans under the Group Areas Act, and it abolished the Natives Representative Council. The Bantu authorities were to be dominated by chiefs and headmen appointed by the government. The government also sought in 1951 to remove coloured voters in the Cape from the common roll onto a separate roll and to require that they elect white representatives only (Separate Representation of Voters Act [No. 46] of 1951). The Supreme Court immediately declared the act invalid on constitutional grounds, but after a long struggle it was successfully reenacted (the Separate Representation of Voters Amendment Act [No. 30] of 1956).

Separate and Unequal

The concept of unequal allocation of resources was built into legislation on general facilities, education, and jobs. The Reservation of Separate Amenities Act (No. 49) of 1953 stated that all races should have separate amenities—such as toilets, parks, and beaches—and that these need not be of an equivalent quality. Under the provisions of this act, apartheid signs were erected throughout South Africa.

The Bantu Education Act (No. 47) of 1953 decreed that blacks should be provided with separate educational facilities under the control of the Ministry of Native Affairs, rather than the Ministry of Education. The pupils in these schools would be taught their Bantu cultural heritage and, in the words of Hendrik F. Verwoerd, minister of native affairs, would be trained "in accordance with their opportunities in life," which he considered did not reach "above the level of certain forms of labour." The act also removed state subsidies from denominational schools with the result that most of the mission-run African institutions (with the exception of some schools run by the Roman Catholic Church and the Seventh Day Adventists) were sold to the government or closed. The Extension of University Education Act (No. 45) of 1959 prohibited blacks from attending white institutions, with few exceptions, and established separate universities and colleges for Africans, coloureds, and Indians.

The Industrial Conciliation Act (No. 28) of 1956 enabled the minister of labour to reserve categories of work for members of specified racial groups. In effect, if the minister felt that white workers were being pressured by "unfair competition" from blacks, he could recategorize jobs for whites only and increase their rates of pay. Under the terms of the Native Laws Amendment Act (No. 54) of 1952, African women as well as men were made subject to influx control and the pass laws and, under Section 10 of the act, neither men nor women could remain in an urban area for longer than seventy-two hours without a special permit stating that they were legally employed. The Abolition of Passes and Co-ordination of Documents Act (No. 67) of 1952, which was designed to make the policy of pass restrictions easier, abolished the pass, replacing it with a document known as a "reference book." The act stated that all Africans had to carry a reference book containing their photograph, address, marital status, employment record, list of taxes paid, influx control endorsements, and rural district where officially resident; not having the reference book on one's person was a criminal offense punishable by a prison sentence.

Security Legislation

Whereas the above laws built largely on existing legislation, police powers underwent a much greater expansion. The Suppression of Communism Act (No. 44) of 1950 had declared the Communist Party and its ideology illegal. Among other features, the act defined communism as any scheme that aimed "at bringing about any political, industrial, social, or economic change within the Union by the promotion of disturbance or disorder" or that encouraged "feelings of hostility between the European and the non-European races of the Union the consequences of which are calculated to further . . ." disorder. The act allowed the minister of justice to list members of such organizations and to ban them, usually for five-year periods, from public office, from attending public meetings, or from being in any specified area of South Africa. The Public Safety Act (No. 3) of 1953 gave the British governor general power to suspend all laws and to proclaim a state of emergency. The Criminal Law Amendment Act (No. 8) of 1953 stated that anyone accompanying a person found guilty of offenses committed while "protest[ing], or in support of any campaign for the repeal or modification of any law," would also be presumed guilty and would have the burden of proving his or her innocence. The Native Administration Act (No. 42) of 1956 permitted the government to "banish" Africans, essentially exiling them to remote rural areas far from their homes. The Customs and Excise Act of 1955 and the Official Secrets Act (No. 16) of 1956 gave the government power to establish a Board of Censors to censor books, films, and other materials imported into or produced in South Africa. During the 1950s, enforcement of these various laws resulted in approximately 500,000 pass-law arrests annually, in the listing of more than 600 inhabitants as communists, in the banning of nearly 350 inhabitants, and in the banishment of more than 150 other inhabitants.

White Politics

The National Party's legislative program received increasing support from the white electorate. The NP won re-election in 1953 and in 1958, each time with increased majorities. Malan retired in 1955 and was replaced as prime minister by J.G. Strydom, leader of the Transvaal branch of the party. After Strydom's death in 1958, Hendrik F. Verwoerd, the Dutch-born minister of native affairs as well as a former professor of applied psychology and the preeminent proponent of apartheid, became prime minister. The United Party (UP) competed aggressively for white votes by adopting a pro-white platform, by rejecting government expenditures on acquiring more land for African reserves, and by supporting the removal of coloured voters from the common roll. In 1959 the more liberal members of the UP broke away to form the Progressive Federal Party (PFP) but with little impact. Practically all Afrikaners and increasing numbers of English-speaking whites voted for the National Party. In 1960 a majority of white voters, irritated by growing world condemnation of apartheid, especially by the newly independent Asian and African members of the British Commonwealth of Nations, supported Verwoerd's proposal to make South Africa a republic, whereupon it left the Commonwealth. In the 1961 general election, the NP won 105 seats, the UP forty-five, and the PFP only one.

Black Resistance in the 1950s

The Congress Youth League and the Programme of Action

In 1943, during World War II, young members of the ANC, critical of what they considered its passivity, formed their own organization, the Congress Youth League (CYL). Anton Lembede, president of the CYL from 1944 until his death in 1947, stressed that South Africa was "a black man's country," in which the concerns of Africans should take precedence. He argued that African society was socialistic, but, because he considered the conflict in South Africa to be primarily a racial rather than a class struggle, he repudiated any alliance with the Communist Party in bringing about "national liberation." After the war and Lembede's death, and faced by the implementation of apartheid, the CYL's leaders, Peter Mda, Jordan Ngubane, Nelson Mandela, Oliver Tambo, and Walter Sisulu, strove to take charge of the ANC. They called on the organization to adopt the use of strikes, boycotts, stay-at-homes, and various forms of civil disobedience and non-cooperation to make the apartheid system unworkable. Overcoming the opposition of ANC president Alfred Xuma, the CYL succeeded in 1949 in electing James Moroka to the presidency, in seating three CYL members (Sisulu, Tambo, and Mandela) on the party's national executive body, and in persuading the congress formally to adopt the program of action.

The ANC's new leaders formed a Joint Planning Council with leaders of the South African Indian Congress (SAIC) (unlike Lembede, the Mandela, Sisulu, and Tambo team believed strongly in working with other groups) and in February 1952 called on the government to repeal all unjust laws or face a Defiance Campaign starting on April 6, the tercentenary of Jan van Riebeeck's arrival at the Cape. Malan rejected the ultimatum. The ANC and the SAIC, led by Yusuf Dadoo, then organized mass rallies and stay-at-homes for April 6 and June 26. These actions drew the support of thousands of men and women. The government reacted by banning leaders and newspapers under the Suppression of Communism Act and by arresting participants in the demonstrations. By December 1952, approximately 8,500 people had been arrested, most of them in the Cape, and the Defiance Campaign had largely come to an end without bringing about any change in the laws. The ANC had grown enormously, however: its paid membership had increased from fewer than 7,000 at the beginning of 1952 to more than 100,000 by the end of the year. Its leadership had also changed: James Moroka had been dismissed in disgrace for having pleaded guilty to charges placed under the Suppression of Communism Act, and Albert Luthuli had been made president.

The Congress of the People and the Freedom Charter

House arrests, bannings, and other forms of government restriction limited the ability of ANC and SAIC leaders to organize publicly in 1953 and 1954, but in 1955, approximately 3,000 delegates met on June 25 and June 26 near Soweto in a Congress of the People. They represented black (the ANC), white (the Congress of Democrats), Indian (the SAIC), and coloured (the Coloured People's Congress) political organizations and the multiracial South African Congress of Trade Unions (SACTU). The congress was held to develop a new vision for a future South Africa, one that reached beyond protest politics. The prime document discussed was the Freedom Charter, which had been drafted several weeks before the congress met. The charter emphasized that South Africa should be a nonracial society with no particular group assumed to have special rights or privileges. The charter stated that all people should be treated equally before the law, that land should be "shared among those who work it," and that the people should "share in the country's wealth," a statement that has sometimes been interpreted to mean a call for nationalization. The congress delegates had ratified almost all the sections of the charter when the police surrounded the meeting, announced that they suspected treason was being committed, and recorded the names and addresses of all those in attendance.

The Pan-Africanist Congress and Sharpeville

Struggles over apartheid legislation continued through the remainder of the 1950s. In 1956 the police arrested 156 leaders, including Luthuli, Mandela, Tambo, Sisulu, and others, and put them on trial for treason in a court case that dragged on for five years. Mass resistance, however, continued in a variety of forms. Thousands of people participated in bus boycotts on the Rand, preferring to walk to work rather than to pay high fares to travel on substandard vehicles. Thousands of African women, organized by the newly formed Federation of South African Women (FSAW), protested the extension of the pass laws. In 1956, 20,000 of them marched on the Parliament buildings in Pretoria and presented a petition with the signatures of tens of thousands of people opposed to the pass laws. Yet these efforts had little effect on the Nationalist government, which was determined to implement apartheid.

The failure to achieve any real success caused a major split in black resistance in 1959. Critics within the ANC argued that its alliance with other political groups, particularly the white Congress of Democrats, caused their organization to make too many compromises and to fail to represent African interests. Influenced by the writings of Lembede, the Africanists, led by Robert Sobukwe, called on the ANC to look to African interests first and to take more action to challenge the government. They were, however, forced out of the ANC, and they formed their own organization, the Pan-Africanist Congress (PAC). In March 1960, the PAC began a national campaign against the pass laws and called on Africans to assemble outside police stations without their passes and to challenge the police to arrest them. One such demonstration outside the police station at Sharpeville, a "native" township in the industrial area of Vereeniging to the south of Johannesburg, ended in violence when the police fired on the demonstrators, killing at least sixty-seven of them and wounding 186. Most of the dead and wounded were shot in the back. Stoppages and demonstrations continued, including a peaceful march of 30,000 Africans on the Houses of Parliament in Cape Town. Verwoerd's government reacted by declaring a state of emergency, by arresting approximately 18,000 demonstrators, including the leaders of the ANC and the PAC, and by outlawing both organizations.

Consolidating Apartheid in the 1960s

The ANC and the PAC Turn to Violence

Prohibited from operating peacefully or even having a legal existence in South Africa, both the ANC and the PAC established underground organizations in 1961 to carry out their struggle against the government. The militant wing of the ANC, Umkhonto we Sizwe (MK—Spear of the Nation, also known as Umkhonto), targeted strategic places such as police stations and power plants but carefully avoided taking any human lives. Poqo (Blacks Only), the militant wing of the PAC, engaged in a campaign of terror, targeting in particular African chiefs and headmen believed to be collaborators with the government and killing them. Some young white students and professionals established their own organization, the antiapartheid African Resistance Movement, and carried out bomb attacks on strategic targets, including one at the Johannesburg railway station that killed at least one person.

By 1964 the police had succeeded in crushing all of these movements. Seventeen Umkhonto leaders, including Walter Sisulu, had been arrested at a farmhouse at Rivonia near Johannesburg in July 1963 and, along with Nelson Mandela— who had already been imprisoned on other charges—were tried for treason. Eight of them, including Mandela, were sent to prison for life. Albert Luthuli had been awarded the Nobel Peace Prize in 1960, but the government confined him to his rural home in Zululand until his death in 1967. Tambo escaped from South Africa and became president of the ANC in exile. Robert Sobukwe of Poqo was jailed on Robben Island until 1969 and then placed under a banning order and house arrest in Kimberley until his death in 1978. The Johannesburg railway station bomber, John Harris, was hanged. He marched to the gallows singing "We shall overcome."

The government campaign to crush internal resistance was orchestrated by John Vorster, then minister of justice, and by General Hendrik J. (H.J.) van den Bergh, head of the Bureau of State Security (BOSS). Both were former members of the Ossewabrandwag who had been interned for pro-Nazi activities during World War II. Vorster and van den Bergh used new security legislation to put down the resistance. In particular, the General Law Amendment Act of 1963 allowed the police to detain people for ninety days without charging them and without allowing them access to a lawyer. At the end of that period, the police could re-arrest and re-detain them for a further ninety days. During the period of detention, no court could order a person's release; only the minister of justice had that authority. Because of his success in defeating the ANC and the PAC, John Vorster became prime minister of South Africa in 1966 when Verwoerd was assassinated by a coloured parliamentary messenger.

Consolidating Apartheid

The government took several measures in the 1960s to make the theory of apartheid work in practice. The Nationalists wanted particularly to establish alternative political structures for Africans in the homelands or reserves (see Glossary), and to eliminate the squatter camps that had grown up around the major cities in the 1930s and the 1940s. In 1963 the Transkei homeland, poverty-stricken and overpopulated, was made self-governing, and in 1976 it was declared "independent," although no country except South Africa recognized the new state. Other homelands were even less economically viable. Bophuthatswana consisted of nineteen separate pieces of land spread hundreds of kilometers apart, and KwaZulu (formed out of Zululand and other parts of Natal in 1972) was divided into at least eleven fragments interspersed with white farms and coastal lands allocated to whites. The South African government, nonetheless, moved ahead with preparing them for independence.

Under the provisions of the Group Areas Act, urban and rural areas in South Africa were divided into zones in which members of only one racial group could live; all others had to move. In practice, it was blacks who had to move, often under the threat or use of force. Between 1963 and 1985, approximately 3.5 million blacks were removed from areas designated for whites and were sent to the homelands, where they added to the already critical problem of overpopulation. Still, even though the homeland population rose by 69 percent between 1970 and 1980, the numbers of blacks in the cities continued to rise through natural growth and evasion of influx control, so that by 1980, after twenty years of removals, there were twice as many blacks in South Africa's towns as there were whites.

South Africa enjoyed an economic boom in the 1960s. Foreign investors had withdrawn their funds and white immigration had come to a halt in the immediate aftermath of Sharpeville, but Vorster's harsh measures rebuilt confidence in the security of investments and the stability of the state, and money and people returned. Foreign investment in South Africa, attracted by rates of return on capital often running as high as 15 to 20 percent, more than doubled between 1963 and 1972, while high immigration levels helped the white population to increase by 50 percent during the same period. Investment and immigration fueled an impressive economic boom.

The Rise of Black Consciousness

Steve Biko and the South African Students' Organisation

With the ANC and the PAC banned and African political activity officially limited to government-appointed bodies in the homelands, young people sought alternative means to express their political aspirations. In the early 1960s, African university students looked to the multiracial National Union of South African Students (NUSAS) to represent their concerns, but, as this organization adopted an increasingly conservative stance after Vorster's crackdown, they decided to form their own movement. Led by Steve Biko, an African medical student at the University of Natal, a group of black students established the South African Students' Organisation (SASO) in 1969 with Biko as president. Biko, strongly influenced by the writings of Lembede and by the Black Power movement in the United States, argued that Africans had to run their own organizations; they could not rely on white liberals because such people would always ally in the last resort with other whites rather than with blacks. He argued that blacks often oppressed themselves by accepting the second-class status accorded them by the apartheid system, and he stressed that they had to liberate themselves mentally as well as physically. He rejected, however, the use of violence adopted by the ANC and the PAC in the early 1960s and emphasized that only nonviolent methods should be used in the struggle against apartheid.

Biko's message had an immediate appeal; SASO expanded enormously, and its members established black self-help projects, including workshops and medical clinics, in many parts of South Africa. In 1972 the Black Peoples' Convention (BPC) was set up to act as a political umbrella organization for the adherents of black consciousness. Although the government had at first welcomed the development of black consciousness because the philosophy fit in with the racial separation inherent in apartheid, it sought to restrict the activities of Biko and his organizations when these took a more overtly political turn. In 1972, SASO organized strikes on university campuses resulting in the arrest of more than 600 students. Rallies held by SASO and the BPC in 1974 to celebrate the overthrow of Portuguese colonialism in Angola and Mozambique resulted in the banning of Biko and other black consciousness leaders and their arraignment on charges of fomenting terrorism.

Soweto, 1976

In 1974 the newly appointed minister of Bantu education, Michael C. Botha, and his deputy, Andries Treurnicht, decided to enforce a previously ignored provision of the Bantu Education Act that required Afrikaans to be used on an equal basis with English as a medium of instruction. A shortage of Afrikaans teachers and a lack of suitable textbooks had resulted in English and African languages being used as the languages of instruction. Because Afrikaans was identified by Africans, especially by the young and by those sympathetic to black consciousness, as the language of the oppressor, opposition to this new policy grew throughout 1975 and into 1976. Some African school boards refused to enforce the policy and saw their members dismissed by the government. Students began to boycott classes.

On June 16, 1976, hundreds of high-school students in Soweto, the African township southwest of Johannesburg, marched in protest against having to use Afrikaans. The police responded with tear gas and then with gunfire that left at least three dead and a dozen injured. The demonstrators, joined by angry crowds of Soweto residents, reacted by attacking and burning down government buildings, including administrative offices and beer halls. The government sent in more police and troops and quelled the violence within a few days but at the cost of several hundred African lives.

Similar outbreaks occurred elsewhere in South Africa, and violence continued throughout the rest of 1976 and into 1977. By February 1977, official figures counted 494 Africans, seventy-five coloureds, one Indian, and five whites killed. In August of that year, Steve Biko, who had been held in indefinite detention, died from massive head injuries sustained during police interrogation. By that time, SASO and the BPC had been banned and open black resistance had been brought to a halt.

Government in Crisis, 1978–89

The Contradictions of Apartheid

By the middle of the 1970s, apartheid was clearly under strain. The popularity of black consciousness and the massive levels of participation in the Soweto demonstrations illustrated profound discontent among the black population, particularly the young, and an increasing readiness to challenge the system physically. Indeed, hundreds of young Africans slipped across South Africa's northern borders in the aftermath of Soweto and volunteered to fight as guerrilla soldiers for the ANC and the PAC. In the late 1970s, some of these people began to reenter South Africa secretly and to carry out sabotage attacks on various targets that were seen as symbols of apartheid.

Labor discontent had also grown. The combination of discriminatory legislation and employer reliance on the use of inexpensive labor meant that African workers were poorly paid and were subjected to an enormous number of restrictions (see Legal Restrictions, ch. 3). Economic recession in the early 1970s, followed by inflation and a contraction in the job market, resulted in a dramatic upsurge in labor unrest. In the first three months of 1973, some 160 strikes involving more than 60,000 workers took place in Durban; in the early 1970s, no more than 5,000 African workers had struck annually, and in the 1960s the average had been closer to 2,000. Labor unrest spread to East London and the Rand and continued. In addition to the high level of participation they engendered, the strikes were also noteworthy for other features. Fearing that the police would arrest any person who organized a strike, the workers chose not to form representative bodies or to elect a leadership. Rather than entering protracted negotiations, they also engaged in sudden "wildcat" strikes, thereby limiting the ability of employers and police to take preventive measures. Over time, an African union movement developed out of these strikes, but it did so on a factory-by-factory basis rather than through the establishment of a mass-based industrial movement as had been the case in the 1940s.

Urban-based African strikes drew attention to the fact that, despite the segregationist ambitions of apartheid, the South African economy depended on blacks living and working in supposedly white areas. Nearly three-quarters of South Africa's urban population in 1980 was black. Only half of the African population lived in the homelands, and even then the rural land available was so inadequate that population densities were far greater than they were in the rest of the country. At least four-fifths of the homeland dwellers lived in poverty.

Yet the South African government persisted in arguing that Africans were really rural dwellers and that they should exercise political rights only in the homelands. In 1976 the government proclaimed the Transkei an independent nation-state and followed this move by granting independence to Bophuthatswana in 1977, to Venda in 1979, and to Ciskei in 1981. Citizens of these states, including the half who lived outside their borders, were then deemed aliens in South Africa. Another six ethnically based homelands were granted limited self-government in preparation for eventual independence: they were KwaZulu, Lebowa, Gazankulu, QwaQwa, KaNgwane, and KwaNdebele (see System of Government, ch. 4). None of these states received international recognition.

Within South Africa, there was great opposition. Blacks viewed the homelands as a way for whites to perpetuate a form of "divide and rule." Mangosuthu (Gatsha) Buthelezi, the government-appointed head of the KwaZulu homeland, while building up an ethnically oriented power base with his Inkatha Freedom Party, argued that independence should not be accepted on the government's terms because that would mean Africans would be giving up claims to the bulk of South Africa forever. He proposed instead the development of a unified multiracial South African state (see The Interim Constitution, ch. 4).

South Africa's international borders also became much less secure. Until 1974 South Africa had been part of a largely white-ruled subcontinent, with the Portuguese still governing their empire in Angola and Mozambique, and Ian Smith and his white-settler regime controlling Southern Rhodesia (present-day Zimbabwe). Botswana had achieved independence soon after Lesotho in 1966 and Swaziland in 1968; however, they were surrounded by white-ruled areas, and their economies depended on that of South Africa.

The 1974 overthrow of the government of Premier Marcello Caetano in Portugal dramatically changed matters. Portugal withdrew from Angola and Mozambique in 1975, and both countries gained independence with governments that were avowedly Marxist and that strongly denounced apartheid. These events directly threatened South African control of South-West Africa (called Namibia by the United Nations [UN], which in 1969 had terminated South Africa's trusteeship over the territory and had demanded its return to the international organization). South African forces invaded Angola in 1975 but were forced to pull back by the arrival of Cuban troops. Seeking both to destabilize the Angolan government and to prevent infiltration of guerrilla fighters into Namibia where the South-West Africa People's Organisation (SWAPO) was fighting actively against South African forces, South Africa maintained a military force in southern Angola.

In Rhodesia, Africans fighting against Ian Smith's government began to turn the tide, and by 1979 Smith was forced to the negotiating table. In 1980 Robert Mugabe and his Zimbabwe African National Union-Patriotic Front (ZANU-PF) party won a landslide election victory and formed a government that, like those in Angola and Mozambique, was Marxist and antiapartheid. The South African government thereafter pursued a policy of occasional armed intervention in Zimbabwe and other frontline states and sent in strike teams periodically to destroy what it considered to be bases for guerrillas planning to infiltrate South Africa. South Africa also expanded military support for the Mozambican National Resistance movement (Resistência Nacional Moçambicana—MNR or Renamo), an organization originally formed by Ian Smith's security forces to destabilize the Mozambique government (see Relations with African States, ch. 4; Regional Issues, ch. 5).

Crackdowns on opposition groups in South Africa and the country's readiness to invade neighboring states led to increasing international condemnation of the apartheid regime. The administrations of United States presidents Richard Nixon and Gerald Ford, including United States secretary of state Henry Kissinger, had favored working with the National Party government. They saw South Africa as a key strategic ally in the Cold War and had both encouraged the invasion of Angola and promised United States military support. President Jimmy Carter, however, considered South Africa a liability for the West. His vice president, Walter Mondale, told John Vorster that the United States wanted South Africa to adopt a policy of one person, one vote, a principle that the ANC upheld but that no white group in South Africa, not even those opposed to apartheid, supported. Antiapartheid sentiments also grew in Britain and in Europe, while the UN, composed of a majority of Third World states, had in 1973 declared apartheid "a crime against humanity" and in 1977 had declared mandatory the existing embargo on the sale of arms to South Africa.

Such criticism had a considerable material impact. South Africa had to invest large sums in the development of its own armaments industry (see Arms Trade and the Defense Industry, ch. 5). Because of an embargo by the Organization of the Petroleum Exporting Countries (OPEC), it also had to pay more for oil and purchased most of its supplies from the shah of Iran until his overthrow in 1979. Foreign investment in South Africa, on which the country depended for much of its economic growth, also became increasingly expensive and uncertain in the second half of the 1970s. A growing sluggishness in the South African economy, coupled with concerns about the country's political stability in light of the Soweto demonstrations, caused most investors to seek out more attractive ventures for their capital in other countries. Foreign capital still flowed into South Africa, but it was primarily in the form of short-term loans rather than investments. In 1976, for example, two-thirds of the foreign funds entering South Africa were in short-term loans, usually of twelve months' duration (see External Debt, ch. 3).

Divisions in the White Community

Increasing economic and political pressures caused splits in the white political parties. In 1968 Vorster had dismissed three conservatives from his cabinet. One of these, Albert Hertzog, a son of J.B.M. Hertzog, founded the Reconstituted National Party (Herstigte Nasionale Party—HNP). Hertzog and the HNP argued that no concessions should be made in pursuing the full implementation of apartheid, whereas Vorster and his allies argued that compromise was necessary. The split was commonly labeled a division between the *verligtes* (the enlightened) and the *verkramptes* (the narrow-minded), although the differences often seemed to be primarily tactical rather than ideological. The HNP contested elections in 1970 and in 1974 but without winning a single seat from Vorster. In 1978, however, the unfolding of a major national scandal brought about Vorster's downfall. An official investigation determined that Vorster, together with a small group of supporters including the head of the Security Police, General H.J. van den Bergh, had secretly and illegally used government funds to manipulate the news media in South Africa and to try to purchase newspapers overseas, including the *Washington Star.* Vorster resigned his position as prime minister for the largely ceremonial post of president; his preferred successor, Connie Mulder, was purged from the National Party, and P.W. Botha, minister of defence since 1966, became prime minister.

Botha, strongly supported by Afrikaner businessmen and by the armed forces leaders, initiated a self-styled program of reform. He tried to do away with aspects of "petty" apartheid that many had come to regard as unnecessarily offensive to blacks and to world opinion, such as the allocation of separate public facilities and the use of racially discriminatory signs to designate who could use the facilities. Hoping to develop a black middle class that would be impervious to the socialist message of the ANC, Botha also accepted in large part the recommendations of two government commissions appointed to investigate the way labor and pass laws were applied to Africans.

The Commission of Inquiry into Labour Legislation (Wiehahn Commission), established in the aftermath of the strike wave of the early 1970s, argued that blacks should be allowed to register trade unions and to have them recognized as part of the official conciliation process. The commission also recommended the elimination of statutory job reservation. Legislation incorporating these recommendations was passed in 1979 and resulted in a huge growth in African trade unionism in the early 1980s.

The Commission of Inquiry into Legislation Affecting the Utilisation of Manpower (Riekert Commission), accepting the fact that poverty in the homelands would continue to push tens of thousands of Africans into the cities, recommended in 1979 that instead of using the pass laws to punish Africans who were illegally entering urban areas, the government should prosecute employers and landlords if they gave jobs or housing to blacks who lacked documentary proof of their right to live in the cities. Botha accepted this recommendation, although it was not until eight years and more than 1 million arrests later that he introduced legislation abolishing the pass laws.

At the same time, Botha pursued harsh measures against those he deemed his enemies in order to ensure the maintenance of white power. The late 1970s and early 1980s were marked by numerous military interventions in the states bordering South Africa and by an extensive military and political campaign to eliminate SWAPO in Namibia. Within South Africa, vigorous police action and strict enforcement of security legislation resulted in hundreds of arrests and bannings and an effective end to the ANC's stepped-up campaign of sabotage in the 1970s. Botha also continued to support the homeland policy, arguing as his predecessors had done that Africans should exercise political rights only within what were deemed to be their own communities, which in the 1980s continued to be as small and fragmented as they had been in the 1950s.

Yet one issue loomed ever larger in the eyes of apartheid's architects, and that was the matter of demographics. Whereas whites had accounted for 21 percent of South Africa's population in 1936, by 1980 they constituted only 16 percent. Future projections estimated that by 2010 the white proportion would be less than 10 percent and falling, while the African population would make up 83 percent of the total and would be increasing. In light of these projections, Botha's government proposed in 1983 that political power in South Africa be shared among whites, coloureds, and Indians, with separate houses of parliament to be established for each racial group. This proposal caused angry opposition among a number of National Party members, sixteen of whom, including Andries Treurnicht, were expelled when they refused to sign a motion of confidence in Botha's leadership.

Treurnicht formed the Conservative Party of South Africa (CP), bringing together old enemies of Botha such as Connie Mulder and supporters of the *verkrampte* faction of the NP. Botha proceeded with his plans, calling for a referendum in which only white voters would be asked whether or not they approved of the prime minister's plans for constitutional change. Some liberal opponents of the government, such as Frederik van Zyl Slabbert, leader of the Progressive Federal Party (PFP), and Harry Oppenheimer, head of the Anglo American Corporation, denounced Botha's plans because they would permanently exclude Africans from having any political role in South Africa. Many other politicians and businessmen, English- and Afrikaans-speaking alike, argued that any change in apartheid would be an improvement. Most white voters agreed, and two-thirds of those who participated in the referendum voted "yes."

Limited Reforms

The new constitution came into force in 1984. In place of the single House of Parliament, there were three constituent bodies: a 178-member (all-white) House of Assembly, an eighty-five-member (coloured) House of Representatives, and a forty-five-member (Indian) House of Delegates. Whites thus retained a majority in any joint session. Presiding over the three houses was the state president, a new office quite unlike the ceremonial position that it replaced. The state president was chosen by an eighty-eight-member electoral college that preserved the 4:2:1 ratio of whites:coloureds:Indians. The president could dissolve Parliament at any time and was authorized to allocate issues to each of the three houses (see System of Government, ch. 4). P.W. Botha became the first state president, occupying the position from the beginning of 1984 until late 1989.

Most blacks strongly condemned the new constitution. Rather than viewing it as a major step toward reform, they saw it as one more effort to bolster apartheid. It reinforced the apartheid notion that Africans were not, and could never be considered as, citizens of South Africa, despite the fact that they constituted 75 percent of the country's population and the vast bulk of its labor force. The constitution's negative impact was compounded by the fact that Africans could not buy land outside the homelands and that government services for blacks, especially in education, were deliberately inferior (see Education under Apartheid, ch. 2).

Indians and coloureds argued that the continued existence of a white majority in Parliament and effective white monopolization of the state presidency made their incorporation into the political process little more than window-dressing. Although the (coloured) Labour Party of Allan Hendrickse and the (Indian) National Peoples' Party of Amichand Rajbansi participated in elections in 1984 for the House of Representatives and the House of Delegates, only 30 percent of registered coloured voters and only 20 percent of registered Indian voters cast ballots.

Opposition to the government's plans consolidated. The United Democratic Front (UDF), which was formed in late 1983 as 1,000 delegates representing 575 organizations—ranging from trade unions to sporting bodies—aimed to use nonviolent means to persuade the government to withdraw its constitutional proposals, to do away with apartheid, and to create a new South Africa incorporating the homelands. In early 1984, the UDF claimed a membership of more than 600 organizations and 3 million individuals; and two respected religious leaders, Bishop Desmond Tutu and the Reverend Allan Boesak, emerged as its prime spokesmen.

Black trade unions, many formed after the Wiehahn Commission, took an increasingly prominent role in economic and political protests in the mid-1980s. They organized strikes in East London and on the Rand protesting economic conditions as well as the constitutional proposals. The National Union of Mineworkers (NUM), newly formed under the leadership of Cyril Ramaphosa, successfully enlisted the support of almost all African miners in bringing work to a stop in a dispute over wage increases. NUM also joined with thirty other nonracial unions in December 1985 to form the Congress of South African Trade Unions (COSATU), an umbrella organization that represented more than 500,000 trade union members and won new members almost every month. By the end of 1985, there had been more than 390 strikes involving 240,000 workers, and industrial unrest was increasing.

Conflict was even more intense in the townships, where residents attacked and burned government buildings and sought to destroy all elements of the apartheid administration. Numerous attacks were made on the homes of black policemen and town councillors, whose participation was necessary to the government's operation of township administration. Violence broke out in some of the homelands, particularly in Lebowa, KwaNdebele, and Bophuthatswana, involving struggles between supporters and opponents of homeland "independence." Sabotage also increased, including bombings of police stations, power installations, and—in one particularly dramatic instance in May 1983—the headquarters of the South African Air Force in Pretoria. Deaths from violence increased, many of them at the hands of the police. Whereas in 1984 there had been 174 fatalities linked to political unrest, in 1985 the number increased to 879, and it continued to rise after that.

International pressures on the South African government also intensified in the mid-1980s. Antiapartheid sentiment in the United States, fueled in large part by television coverage of the ongoing violence in South Africa, heightened demands for the removal of United States investments and for the imposition of official sanctions. In 1984 forty United States companies pulled out of South Africa, with another fifty following suit in 1985. In July 1985, Chase Manhattan Bank caused a major financial crisis in South Africa by refusing to roll over its short-term loans, a lead that was soon followed by most other international banks, fueling inflation and eroding South African living standards (see Historical Development, ch. 3). In October 1986, the United States Congress, overriding a presidential veto, passed legislation implementing mandatory sanctions against South Africa; these included the banning of all new investments and bank loans, the ending of air links between the United States and South Africa, and the banning of many South African imports.

President Botha activated security legislation to deal with these crises. In mid-1985 he imposed the first in a series of states of emergency in various troubled parts of South Africa; this was the first time such laws had been used since the Sharpeville violence in 1960. The state of emergency was extended throughout the nation the following year. The emergency regulations gave the police powers to arrest without warrants and to detain people indefinitely without charging them or even allowing lawyers or next of kin to be notified. It also gave the government even greater authority than the considerable powers it already possessed to censor radio, television, and newspaper coverage of the unrest. Botha deployed police and more than 5,000 troops in African townships to quell the spreading resistance. By February 1987, unofficial estimates claimed that at least 30,000 people had been detained, many for several months at a time.

South Africa's complex and fragmented society became increasingly polarized around antiapartheid groups, who expressed a growing sense of urgency in their demands for an end to the failed system of racial separation, and white conservative defenders of apartheid, who intensified their resistance to change. Facing mounting international disapproval and economic stagnation, the government tentatively began to signal its awareness that its plan for separate development by race would have to be substantially altered or abandoned.

In January 1986, President Botha shocked conservatives in the all-white House of Assembly with the statement that South Africa had "outgrown the outdated concept of apartheid." The government undertook tentative, incremental change, at a carefully controlled pace, and, as it began to yield to demands for racial equality, it severely limited the activities of antiapartheid agitators. The government tightened press restrictions, effectively banned the UDF and other activist organizations, and renewed a series of states of emergency throughout the rest of the 1980s.

As the inevitability of political change became apparent, conservative whites expressed new fears for the future. The CP swamped the PFP in parliamentary by-elections in May 1987, making the CP the official parliamentary opposition. Liberal whites and other opponents of apartheid reorganized to broaden their popular appeal, first as the National Democratic Movement (NDM) and later as a new United Party. This coalition tried unsuccessfully to win support from the progressive wing of the NP. Within the NP, progressives were outmaneuvered by conservatives, who bolted from the party to join the CP in an attempt to prolong apartheid. In early 1988, the government, seeking to stem the erosion of its NP support, tightened press restrictions and further restricted political activity by antiapartheid organizations. Still excluded from national politics, blacks sought new avenues for pressing their demands, and their demonstrations often erupted in violence. Supporters of the Zulu-dominated Inkatha Freedom Party (IFP) and the banned ANC clashed in an upsurge of "black-on-black" violence that would cause as many as 10,000 deaths by 1994.

President Botha suffered a stroke in January 1989. Choosing his successor almost split the NP, but when Botha resigned as party leader a month later, NP moderates managed to elect Minister of Education Frederik W. (F.W.) de Klerk to succeed him. A few weeks later, the NP elected de Klerk state president, too, but Botha stubbornly refused to step down for several months. Soon after he resigned under pressure on August 14, 1989, the electoral college named de Klerk to succeed him in a five-year term as president.

Dismantling Apartheid, 1990–94

President de Klerk recognized the urgent need to bring the black majority of South Africans into the political process, and most NP moderates agreed with him in principle. He had held secret talks with the imprisoned ANC leader Mandela to begin preparations for this major policy shift. De Klerk nonetheless surprised some supporters and critics alike when he announced on February 2, 1990, not only the impending release of Mandela, but also the unbanning of the ANC, the PAC, and the SACP, and the removal of restrictions on the UDF and other legal political organizations. De Klerk also lifted the four-year-old media restrictions, and he invited former liberation fighters to join the government at the negotiating table to prepare for a new multiracial constitution. De Klerk pledged that his government would investigate alleged human rights abuses by the security forces. He also sought improved relations with the rest of Africa by proposing joint regional development planning with neighboring states and by inviting other African leaders to increase trade with South Africa.

Widely hailed as historic, de Klerk's speech was nonetheless attacked by antiapartheid critics for what it lacked—it did not mention the two most despised legislative pillars of apartheid, the Population Registration Act and the Group Areas Act. It did not lift all of the security provisions that had been imposed under states of emergency. At the same time, CP leader Treurnicht, calling for de Klerk's resignation, said de Klerk lacked the authority to carry out such sweeping changes, and he accused de Klerk of helping to destroy the Afrikaner *volk*.

As Mandela was released on February 11, 1990, at age seventy-one after twenty-seven years in prison, South Africans poured into the streets in celebration. His first words were to assure his supporters in the ANC that his release was not part of a "deal" with the government, and to reassure whites that he intended to work toward reconciliation. He also quoted his well-known statement at the Rivonia trial in 1964, "I have fought against white domination, and I have fought against black domination. I have cherished the idea of a democratic and free society in which all persons live together in harmony and with equal opportunities. It is an ideal which I hope to live for and to achieve. But if needs be, it is an ideal for which I am prepared to die."

In the flurry of receptions and public statements that followed, Mandela enunciated other objectives that were less welcome in political and business circles. He reaffirmed ANC policies in favor of nationalization of major sectors of the economy. He refused to renounce the armed struggle immediately, refused to call for the lifting of international sanctions against

South Africa until further progress was achieved, and refused to accept an interim power-sharing arrangement proposed by the government. ANC officials elected Mandela deputy president in March 1990, giving him effective control over policy decisions in consultation with their ailing president, Oliver Tambo.

Despite the ANC's strong symbolic displays of unity, like other political organizations facing new challenges, it showed widening internal fractures. Blacks who had been unanimous in their demands for Mandela's release from prison, nonetheless differed sharply in the extent of their willingness to reconcile peacefully over past injustices. In addition, militant black consciousness leaders, especially in the Pan-Africanist Congress (PAC), rejected outright Mandela's proposals for multiracial government and demanded black control over future decision-making institutions. At PAC offices in Zimbabwe, PAC leader Zephania Mothopeng rejected appeals by Mandela and by Zimbabwe's President Robert Mugabe for the PAC leader to join Mandela in discussions in Pretoria.

Some of the ANC's estimated 40,000 exiles began returning to South Africa in the early 1990s, and as organizational leaders debated their future role, many militant former exiles and others rejected Mandela's conciliatory approach and insisted on continuing the armed struggle. Left-wing ANC factions pressed Mandela to demand the immediate nationalization of private-sector conglomerates. The ANC was also accused of abuse and brutality against dissidents during its nearly three decades of operating underground and outside South Africa—accusations Mandela acknowledged were based in fact. Old and young liberation fighters appeared capable of warring even against one another as the end of apartheid approached.

The Quest for Peace

Amid rising tensions and unrest, representatives of the government and the ANC—with strong misgivings—met in Cape Town in May 1990 to begin planning for constitutional negotiations. Even holding "talks about talks" was risky. The government had to grant immunity from prosecution to many formerly banned or exiled ANC members before they could safely appear in public. In a few antiapartheid strongholds, political moderates were attacked for being too conciliatory.

President de Klerk faced an increasingly divided constituency of his own. Conservatives intensified their demands for him to step down, while NP progressives pressured him to move more boldly toward multiracial government. Planning sessions for eventual negotiations were postponed repeatedly as Mandela and de Klerk had to reassure their constituencies of their determination to set aside the past and to work peacefully toward a broadly legitimate government.

De Klerk's credibility was low among his former opponents. The talks snarled over his insistence on defending what he termed the "rights of minorities"—a phrase the ANC viewed simply as a ploy to preserve white control. De Klerk's standing in the negotiations was further weakened in late 1990, when the government-appointed Commission of Inquiry into Certain Alleged Murders (Harms Commission), which he had established earlier that year, found evidence—but not "proof"—that clandestine death squads had operated within the security services. The commission's hearings were often marred by violence and by claims of witness intimidation.

The international response to change in South Africa was cautious. Several African countries, visited by Mandela within weeks of his release from prison, held to their pledge to await his signal of progress toward ending apartheid before they began to lift sanctions against South Africa. Several European countries, visited by de Klerk in May 1990, broke with European Community (EC—see Glossary) sanctions agreements and immediately lifted their bans on investment and travel to South Africa. International athletic teams were drawn into the controversy, as some sports organizations tried to adhere to international boycotts, while in South Africa, sports enthusiasts and athletes demanded readmission to world competitions. In late 1990, both de Klerk and Mandela again went abroad seeking political and financial support. De Klerk traveled to the United States in September 1990 and to Britain and the Netherlands in October; at about the same time, Mandela traveled to India, Japan, and other Asian countries.

Popular pressure for lifting sanctions increased in the United States. The US Comprehensive Antiapartheid Act of 1986 had specified that five conditions would have to be met before sanctions could be lifted. By late 1990, three of them had been accomplished—the government had entered into multiracial negotiations, had removed bans on multiracial political organizations, and had lifted the state of emergency in Natal. The remaining two conditions—freeing political prisoners and repealing the Group Areas Act and the Population Registration Act—were not met until 1991.

The climate of uncertainty spread to the homelands during 1990 and 1991. These arid patches of land were despised by many as symbols of the apartheid system. Several homeland leaders, who depended heavily on Pretoria for their legitimacy—and their budgets—faced growing dissent and demands for reincorporation into South Africa. Zulu residents of the wealthiest and most populous homeland, KwaZulu, increasingly feared that their interests and culture would be submerged in the groundswell of support for Mandela and the ANC, and that their past cooperation with the NP would be forgotten.

ANC and government leaders tried to find common ground for negotiating a new constitution, but they managed only incremental progress while they worked to rein in the extremist fringes of their respective constituencies. In June 1990, de Klerk and Mandela met officially for the first time to set the agenda for further talks. The two sides moved cautiously toward each other. In August Mandela announced the suspension of the ANC's thirty-year armed struggle. The government continued lifting apartheid restrictions, and in October—at de Klerk's prompting—the NP opened its ranks to all races. On October 15, 1990, parliament repealed the Reservation of Separate Amenities Act of 1953, which had sanctioned "petty apartheid" in public places such as beaches, libraries, and places of entertainment.

The talks were threatened by escalating violence throughout 1990, and in August Mandela accused the government of doing little to end it. De Klerk and Mandela continued their political tug-of-war. De Klerk sought domestic and international approval for the changes already under way, while Mandela pressed for change at a faster pace. A series of legislative decisions and political breakthroughs in 1990 moved South Africa closer to multiracial democracy, but at the end of the year, it was clear that many obstacles remained.

The ANC gradually accepted the notion of a coalition interim government, but ANC leaders insisted on determining the rules for forming that coalition. In early 1991, debates raged over various formulas for multiracial government, and over the allocation of powers between regional and national authorities, as political leaders on all sides realized that it was easier to define an illegitimate government than to construct a legitimate one. They agreed that an all-party congress would have responsibility for the most onerous organizational tasks: it would draw up broad principles on which a new constitution would rest, would determine the makeup of the constitution-making body, and would establish an interim government to oversee the transition itself.

In January 1991, Mandela met for the first time in nearly thirty years with Zulu leader Buthelezi in an effort to allay Zulu fears of ANC domination. This historic meeting did little to quell escalating ANC-IFP violence, however, and the weak police response only fueled ANC suspicions of covert police support for the IFP. Amid rising unrest, the government implemented a new security crackdown in the townships, dubbed "Operation Iron Fist." Mandela faced new demands from his militant younger generation of followers to abandon the negotiations entirely.

Finally, in February 1991, de Klerk and Mandela reached a compromise over efforts to reduce both violence and the smuggling of arms into South Africa, and to achieve the release of political prisoners. The ANC was anxious to repatriate its remaining exiles, many of whose skills were needed in the negotiations, but the logistical problems of returning refugees from countries that lacked diplomatic ties with South Africa seemed insurmountable until the United Nations High Commissioner for Refugees (UNHCR) was persuaded to intervene on behalf of the ANC.

On June 5, 1991, the government repealed two more legislative pillars of apartheid, the Land Act of 1913 (and 1936) and the Group Areas Act of 1950. The 1991 legislation gave all races equal rights to own property anywhere in the country, enabled some 300,000 black householders to convert ninety-nine-year leases to full ownership, enabled suburban residents of all races to set (racially nondiscriminatory) residency standards for their neighborhoods, authorized the establishment of new townships and the extension of services to their residents, and encouraged the development of farmland and rural communities. This legislation did not authorize compensation for blacks who had been displaced from their land in the preceding thirty years; instead, it left their complaints to be dealt with by a special court or commission to be established for that purpose.

On June 17, 1991, the government repealed the Population Registration Act of 1950, the most infamous pillar of apartheid, which had authorized the registration by race of newborn babies and immigrants. Its repeal was hailed as historic throughout the world, although critics pointed to related laws still on the books that permitted inequitable treatment in voting, in pensions, in social services, and in many other areas of public behavior.

The National Peace Accord of September 1991 was a critical step toward formal negotiations. The thirty-three-page accord, signed by representatives of twenty-seven political organizations and national and homeland governments, set codes of conduct for all parties to the process, including the police. The accord also established a network of "peace committees," to contain the violence that continued to plague the townships. Ironically, the most important results of the National Peace Accord turned out to be the establishment of networks of committed individuals, the opening of communications channels, and the trust that began to be sown through discussion. The accord itself failed to accomplish its immediate goal; the violence continued and increased sporadically throughout 1992.

"Irreversible Progress" Toward Democracy

Through dogged perseverance, amid claims and counterclaims of sabotage and brutality, key political leaders began formal constitutional negotiations on December 20, 1991. Calling themselves the Convention for a Democratic South Africa (Codesa), delegations from nineteen governmental and political organizations began planning the creation of a transitional government and a representative parliament. They established five working groups, each made up of thirty-eight delegates and thirty-eight advisers, to take the lead in creating a climate for free political activity; in determining basic constitutional principles; in establishing transitional procedures for the nominally independent homelands of Bophuthatswana, Ciskei, Transkei, and Venda; in setting and overseeing timetables for the transition; and in dealing with new problems that would arise during the transition itself.

International organizations and other countries were torn between recognizing South Africa's impressive accomplishments and encouraging further progress. Most international sanctions were lifted soon after the Population Registration Act, Group Areas Act, and Land Acts were repealed. In July 1991, the United States Congress lifted remaining sanctions under its Comprehensive Antiapartheid Act, although laws restricting commercial ties with South Africa remained on the books in many states and cities in the United States. The EC lifted most trade and investment bans in January 1992 and remaining restrictions on sporting, scientific, and cultural links three months later. On April 6, 1992, the EC lifted its oil embargo. Other countries gradually lifted a range of boycotts, and many African governments—under pressure from their own business communities—reestablished diplomatic ties with South Africa. The United Nations General Assembly would wait until late 1993 to lift remaining UN sanctions.

Much of de Klerk's effort in 1992 was directed toward appeasing and weakening his right-wing opponents—staunch defenders of apartheid who had broken with the NP during the 1980s. He first tried reassuring them about the future. Then, as conservative resistance hardened, he called for a referendum among white voters to test his mandate for change. The question posed in the March 17, 1992, referendum was carefully worded: "Do you support continuation of the reform process which the State President began on February 2, 1990, and which is aimed at a new constitution through negotiation?" The outcome was a resounding 68.6 percent "yes." Election analysts reported that support among Afrikaners was even slightly higher than among English speakers. Only one region of the country—the northern Transvaal (later Northern Province)—voted "no." A few militant defenders of apartheid boycotted the referendum.

Buoyed by the outcome, de Klerk presented Codesa with proposals for a two-phase transition, the first phase managed by transitional councils appointed by Codesa, and the second phase—the constitution-writing process—managed by an elected transitional government headed by a multiperson presidency and a bicameral legislature. The ANC's counterproposals called for a single-stage transition, a committee elected by proportional representation to draft the constitution, with a two-thirds majority needed to pass constitutional provisions. Negotiations were suspended as both sides sought to refine their proposals and to unify their constituencies.

In mid-1992 escalating violence, allegations of police brutality, and government financial scandals threatened to derail negotiations. After a particularly brutal attack on June 17, 1992, by IFP supporters on ANC sympathizers in Boipatong, a township near Johannesburg, the ANC suspended negotiations and threatened to withdraw entirely unless the government made greater efforts to end the violence and to curtail covert police support for the IFP. Mandela took his complaint to the Organization of African Unity (OAU) and the UN, where, on July 15, 1992, he accused the government of "a cold-blooded strategy of state terrorism." Finally, in September 1992, de Klerk and Mandela arrived at a Record of Understanding affirming police responsibility for protecting residents in workers' hostels, where support for the ANC was high. ANC fears lingered, however, especially in late 1992, when the Commission of Inquiry Regarding the Prevention of Public Violence and Intimidation (Goldstone Commission) released its findings of a "dirty tricks" campaign against the ANC, apparently sanctioned by senior figures within the South African Defence Forces (SADF).

In protest against the Record of Understanding, Zulu leader Buthelezi established an alternative to Codesa to include the leaders of groups disadvantaged by the ANC's strong lead in the Codesa forum—i.e., white conservatives and black homeland leaders, whose power bases were eroding. The resulting Concerned South Africans Group (Cosag) pressed for a federal constitution to preserve the rights of ethnic minorities, especially the Zulu and whites.

Negotiations resumed on March 5, 1993, but the fragile process was again threatened a month later, when Chris Hani, the popular general secretary of the South African Communist Party (SACP), was murdered. ANC leaders joined the government in trying to stem outbreaks of retaliatory violence, and several white extremists were arrested within weeks after the murder. With a new sense of urgency, political negotiators tried to speed the process and set the date for nationwide elections no later than April 27, 1994.

The draft constitution published on July 26, 1993, contained concessions to all sides—a federal system of regional legislatures, equal voting rights regardless of race, and a bicameral legislature. Negotiators were undeterred by the storm of protests that followed, and they went on to establish a Transitional Executive Council (TEC), a multiracial body that would share executive responsibilities with President de Klerk during election preparations. Cosag boycotted the TEC and formed the Freedom Alliance to demand equal status with the government and the ANC. Sensing new momentum, however, the government cracked down on right-wing violence and tried to reason with white extremists, without slowing the pace of election preparations.

Preparing for Elections

In November 1993, negotiators endorsed the draft of the interim constitution calling for a five-year transitional government, and the tricameral parliament endorsed the draft in December (see The Interim Constitution, ch. 4). The timetable for elections remained firm after that. Mandela and the ANC, sensing their imminent rise to power and to responsibility for the country's welfare, called for the immediate lifting of remaining international sanctions and sought new donors and investors for South Africa. But the ongoing violence, which was frightening away investors, also threatened to delay the April elections.

In December 1993, the multiracial TEC was installed as part of the executive branch of government—over the objections of the Freedom Alliance and the PAC. The TEC quickly established seven subcouncils with specific responsibilities during the transition. It also approved the formation of an eleven-member Independent Electoral Commission (IEC) to organize and to verify the planned elections, and it deployed police and army units to northern Natal to try to end the violence.

Other countries and international organizations began mobilizing support for South Africa's historic vote. The United Nations Observer Mission in South Africa (UNOMSA), which had deployed in small numbers to quell township violence in August 1992, expanded its mission to about 2,000 personnel to coordinate the teams of election observers that were being sent by the OAU, the European Union (EU—see Glossary), the British Commonwealth, and several individual countries.

The antielection Freedom Alliance began to unravel in early 1994. White conservatives stepped up their demands for a separate, whites-only homeland—dispelling any illusions of support for their Freedom Alliance partners. The government of Ciskei, a homeland where the ANC's popularity exceeded that of the appointed president, broke away from its alliance partners and declared its intention to permit homeland residents to vote. The government in Bophuthatswana—another Freedom Alliance partner facing strong popular opposition—sought armed support from the neo-Nazi Afrikaner Resistance Movement (Afrikaner Weerstandsbeweging—AWB), prompting the SADF to intervene and to remove Bophuthatswana President Lucas Mangope from office. With the Freedom Alliance severely weakened, PAC President Clarence Makwetu—another election holdout—announced that group's suspension of its armed struggle, thus opening the way for election participation by its members.

Violence continued, mostly between supporters of the IFP and the ANC, and the TEC authorized rapid training for a 10,000-member national peacekeeping force—an effort that eventually failed. The force was disbanded as the elections began. The Goldstone Commission found evidence of serious police complicity in the continuing unrest, and the government suspended several officers pending investigations. The country appeared poised to launch into violence-wracked balloting, when de Klerk imposed a state of emergency in Natal and KwaZulu on March 31, 1994, deploying 3,000 SADF troops to allow residents of the area to defy the IFP election boycott and to go to the polls.

On April 12, 1994, a team of international mediators headed by former British foreign secretary Lord Carrington and former United States secretary of state Henry Kissinger arrived to attempt to break the logjam that was keeping the IFP out of the elections. After two days of fruitless discussions, their effort was declared a failure, and the mediators left. Only days later, however, on April 19, Buthelezi—under intense pressure from trusted local and international figures—relented and agreed to allow the IFP to be placed on the ballot.

When the elections finally took place on schedule, beginning on April 26, 1994, the government and the ANC had several thousand security forces, with varying degrees of training and authority, in place to prevent serious outbreaks of violence. Remarkably, the violence subsided. A few "exceptional" votes were cast by voters who were disabled or were living outside South Africa on April 26. During the next two days, more than 22 million voters stood in line for hours at some 9,000 polling places to exercise their newly won right to vote. Balloting was extended through April 29. There was no voter registration list, so IEC officials marked voters' fingers with indelible ink to prevent fraud.

For days after the elections, tensions remained high, and some accusations of election fraud surfaced—especially in Natal. As the counting proceeded, the IEC prompted party leaders to negotiate agreements over disputed results that would allow the IEC to certify the elections as "substantially free and fair." The official results, released on May 6, 1994, gave the ANC 62.6 percent of the vote; the NP, 20.4 percent; and the IFP, 10.5 percent. Seven political parties won seats in the National Assembly (see table 17, Appendix). Three parties won the 5 percent of votes necessary to participate in the cabinet of the coalition government.

Mandela was unanimously elected president by the National Assembly on May 9, 1994, in Cape Town. His two deputy presidents, former ANC chairman Thabo Mbeki and former president de Klerk, stood with Mandela when he was inaugurated on May 10 at ceremonies in Pretoria. Representatives of 140 countries were present. Mandela's inaugural address stressed the need for reconciliation, both within South Africa and with other countries, and once again he quoted his own words at the Rivonia trial that had preceded his long imprisonment, and he reaffirmed his determination to forge a peaceful, nonracial society.

*   *   *

Two excellent histories of South Africa have recently been published. Leonard M. Thompson's *A History of South Africa* provides a well-written and scholarly survey by the foremost historian of the country. Reader's Digest's *An Illustrated History of South Africa: The Real Story* offers much more detailed coverage but without any sacrifice of scholarly quality. Useful chapters surveying the history of South Africa can also be found in the multi-volume *Cambridge History of Africa* and in the two-volume *Oxford History of South Africa*. Richard Elphick and Hermann Giliomee's *The Shaping of South African Society, 1652–1840* is essential reading on the early history of the Cape. Martin Hall's *Farmers, Kings, and Traders* provides an innovative study that shifts the focus of pre-1870 history away from the Cape and toward developments in southern Africa at large. T. Dunbar Moodie's *The Rise of Afrikanerdom: Power, Apartheid, and the Afrikaner Civil Religion* is still the basic text on Afrikaner nationalism. Willem A. de Klerk's *The Puritans in Africa: The Story of Afrikanerdom* is also interesting, in large part because it was written by the brother of the former president of South Africa.

Tom Lodge's *Black Politics in South Africa since 1945* provides a very detailed study of resistance movements up to the early 1980s, although for a thorough analysis of black consciousness the reader needs to consult Gail M. Gerhart's *Black Power in South Africa: The Evolution of an Ideology*. Three studies co-edited by Shula Marks and others bring together the most recent writings by "radical" authors who have dominated much of the scholarship produced on South Africa in the 1970s and the 1980s: *Economy and Society in Pre-Industrial South Africa; Industrialisation and Social Change in South Africa;* and *The Politics of Race, Class, and Nationalism in Twentieth Century South Africa.* Finally, Joseph Lelyveld's Pulitzer Prize-winning *Move Your Shadow: South Africa, Black and White* is the finest journalistic study ever written about South Africa. (For further information and complete citations, see Bibliography.)

Chapter 2. The Society and Its Environment

Farmhouse with familiar windmill beneath flat-topped ridges along the southern edge of the Great Karoo

SOCIETY IS STILL BEING FORMED in South Africa in the 1990s. The region's earliest cultures have long since been displaced, and most people living in South Africa today are descendants of Africans who came to the region in the first millennium A.D. These early populations did not remain in one place over the centuries, however. Instead, their settlement patterns changed as numerous small chiefdoms were thrown into upheaval by increasing conflicts over land, the arrival of European settlers after the seventeenth century, and nineteenth-century Zulu expansionism. During the twentieth century, several million South Africans were displaced by the government, especially after the country's system of apartheid (see Glossary) invalidated many of their land claims.

South Africa's turbulent social history should not obscure the fact that this region probably was home to some of the earliest humans on earth. Archaeological evidence suggests that human populations evolved in the broad region of south central and eastern Africa, perhaps as early as 2 million years ago, but at least 200,000 years ago. Fossil remains of Homo sapiens in eastern South Africa have been tentatively dated to 50,000 years ago, and other remains show evidence of iron smelting about 1,700 years ago in the area that became the northern Transvaal. The evolutionary links between the earliest inhabitants and twentieth-century African populations are not well known, but it is clear that San and Khoikhoi (also called Khoi) peoples have been in southern Africa longer than any other living population.

San hunters and gatherers and Khoikhoi herdsmen, known together as Khoisan because of cultural and linguistic similarities, were called "Bushmen" and "Hottentots" by early European settlers. Both of these terms are considered pejorative in the late twentieth century and are seldom used. Most of the nearly 3 million South Africans of mixed-race ancestry (so-called "coloureds") are descendants of Khoisan peoples and Europeans over the past three centuries.

Bantu language speakers who arrived in southern Africa from the north during the first millennium A.D. displaced or killed some Khoisan peoples they encountered, but they allowed many others to live among them peacefully. Most Bantu societies were organized into villages and chiefdoms, and their economies relied primarily on livestock and crop cultivation. Their early ethnic identities were fluid and shifted according to political and social demands. For example, the Nguni or Nguni speakers, one of the largest Bantu language groups, have been a diverse and expanding population for several centuries. When groups clashed with one another, or their communities became too large, their political identity could easily shift to emphasize their loyalty to a specific leader or descent from a specific forebear.

Historians believe that the ancestors of the Nguni-speaking Xhosa peoples were the first Bantu speakers to reach the southern tip of the continent. The Zulu, a related group of small chiefdoms, arrived soon after, and by the early nineteenth century they had evolved into a large, predatory kingdom. Zulu armies displaced or destroyed many small chiefdoms, and in the upheaval some of those who fled north probably retraced the pathways their ancestors had used centuries earlier as they moved into the region. Others were subjugated and assimilated into Zulu society, and a few—the forebears of today's Swazi and Sotho peoples—resisted Zulu advances and withdrew into mountainous regions that would later become independent nations.

European travelers and explorers visited southern Africa over the centuries and, after the mid-seventeenth century, began settling near the Cape of Good Hope. Dutch immigrants moved inland from the coast in search of farmland and independence, especially during the nineteenth century, when their migration became known as the "Great Trek." British merchants, farmers, and missionaries arrived in large numbers during the nineteenth century. Asians, including merchants and traders as well as laborers and slaves, arrived from India, China, Malaya, and the Indonesian archipelago. South Africa began to develop a multiethnic mercantile, trading, and financial class, based primarily on the country's mineral wealth after the discovery of diamonds and gold in the 1880s.

The South African War of 1899–1902, one of the Anglo-Boer Wars, hastened the process of assimilation that made South Africa one of the twentieth century's most diverse populations. After the war, East Europeans arrived in growing numbers, many of them fleeing religious or political persecution. South Africans of African descent were increasingly marginalized as the concept of racial separation became a central theme in political debate and a key factor in government strategies for economic development.

The mining industry fueled the development of the interior plateau region as the nation's industrial heartland. Agriculture was made possible in this relatively arid land scattered with rocky outcrops only by employing indigenous or imported laborers at low wages and by the extensive use of irrigation. These measures allowed rural whites to achieve living standards that would have been impossible elsewhere and contributed to the growth of flourishing urban centers. The earliest of these were Cape Town, where the relatively dry hinterland proved ideal for grain farming and vineyards, and Durban, where agricultural development centered around sugarcane, forestry, and a variety of food crops.

The government adopted elements of legally entrenched racial supremacy in the twentieth century that culminated in the legal separation of the races, or apartheid, after 1948. Some believed that apartheid would allow parallel development of all ethnic and racial groups, but it was soon clear to most South Africans and to others that apartheid was an intolerable system of racial privilege and subordination bolstered by the frequent use of force.

Until the mid-twentieth century, white South Africans' views on race were relatively consistent with those of other Western nations. But after World War II, when the rest of the world began working toward greater integration among races and nations, South Africa veered in the opposite direction. By the 1960s, white domination had become entrenched, even as colonial rule was ending in the rest of Africa and racial segregation was condemned throughout much of the world.

As a result, South Africa became increasingly marginalized within the international community. Apartheid became so repugnant to so many people worldwide that this wealthy nation faced mounting economic and political pressures to end it. South Africa's growing isolation, together with the disastrous effects of apartheid, convinced most whites that racial separation would, in the long run, not guarantee their safety or prosperity. The government began dismantling racial barriers in the early 1990s, but apartheid-era distinctions left lasting marks on South African society, and the new, multiracial government in the mid-1990s faced too many pressing needs to spend much time celebrating its country's newfound character.

*Cape Town set against Table Mountain, which rises more than 1,000
meters above sea level
Courtesy Embassy of South Africa, Washington*

Physical Setting

South Africa occupies the southern tip of the African continent, stretching from 22°S to 35°S latitude and from 17°E to 33°E longitude. The northeastern corner of the country lies within the tropics, astride the Tropic of Capricorn. South Africa covers 1.2 million square kilometers of land, one-seventh the area of the United States, or roughly twice the area of Texas. Nearly 4,900 kilometers of international boundaries separate South Africa from Namibia, Botswana, Zimbabwe, Mozambique, and Swaziland—from northwest to northeast—and South Africa completely surrounds the small nation of Lesotho. In addition, the 2,881-kilometer coastline borders the Atlantic Ocean on the west and the Indian Ocean on the south and east. South Africa's extraterritorial holdings include Robben Island, Dassen Island, and Bird Island in the Atlantic Ocean, and Prince Edward Island and Marion Island about 1,920 kilometers southeast of Cape Town in the Indian Ocean. Marion Island, at 46°S latitude, is the site of an important weather research station.

South Africa forms a distinct region, or subcontinent, divided from the rest of Africa by the rivers that mark its northern border. In the northwest, the Orange River cuts through the Namib Desert and divides South Africa from Namibia. In the east, the Limpopo River traverses large areas of arid grassland along the common border with Zimbabwe and southeastern Botswana. Between these two, the Molopo River winds through the southern basin of the Kalahari Desert, also dividing South Africa from Botswana. Populations have moved across these rivers almost continuously over the centuries, but, in general, the northern border region of South Africa is sparsely populated.

The geological substratum of the subcontinent was formed at least 3.8 billion years ago, according to geologists, and most of the country's natural features evolved into their present form more than 200 million years ago. Especially since the early twentieth-century writings of Alfred Wegener, geologists have hypothesized that South Africa was once part of a large land mass, now known as Gondwana, or Gondwanaland, that slowly fractured along the African coastline millions of years ago. Theories of such a supercontinent are bolstered by geological continuities and mineral similarities between South Africa and South America, by fossil similarities between South Africa and the Indian Ocean island of Madagascar, and by the sharp escarpments, or geological fractures, that encircle most of southern Africa near the coast.

The ancient rock substratum is overlain by sedimentary and volcanic rock formations. Because ground cover is sparse, only about 11 percent of the land in South Africa is arable. More than 20 percent of the land is too arid or the soil is too poor for any agricultural activity without irrigation; roughly 66 percent is suitable only for livestock grazing. Even the thin soil cover has been severely eroded, especially in the country's most overpopulated and impoverished rural areas. The relatively poor land conceals enormous wealth in minerals, however, including gold, diamonds, copper, platinum, asbestos, and coal.

Geographic Regions

Like much of the African continent, South Africa's landscape is dominated by a high plateau in the interior, surrounded by a narrow strip of coastal lowlands. Unlike most of Africa, however, the perimeter of South Africa's inland plateau rises abruptly to form a series of mountain ranges before dropping to sea level. These mountains, known as the Great Escarpment, vary between 2,000 meters and 3,300 meters in elevation. The coastline is fairly regular and has few natural harbors. Each of the dominant land features—the inland plateau, the encircling mountain ranges, and the coastal lowlands—exhibits a wide range of variation in topography and in natural resources (see fig. 7).

The interior plateau consists of a series of rolling grasslands ("veld," in Afrikaans), arising out of the Kalahari Desert in the north. The largest subregion in the plateau is the 1,200-meter to 1,800-meter-high central area known as the Highveld. The Highveld stretches from Western Cape province to the northeast, encompassing the entire Free State (formerly, Orange Free State). In the north, it rises into a series of rock formations known as the Witwatersrand (literally, "Ridge of White Waters" in Afrikaans, commonly shortened to Rand—see Glossary). The Rand is a ridge of gold-bearing rock, roughly 100 kilometers by thirty-seven kilometers, that serves as a watershed for numerous rivers and streams. It is also the site of the world's largest proven gold deposits and the country's leading industrial city, Johannesburg.

North of the Witwatersrand is a dry savanna subregion, known as the Bushveld, characterized by open grasslands with scattered trees and bushes. Elevation varies between 600 meters

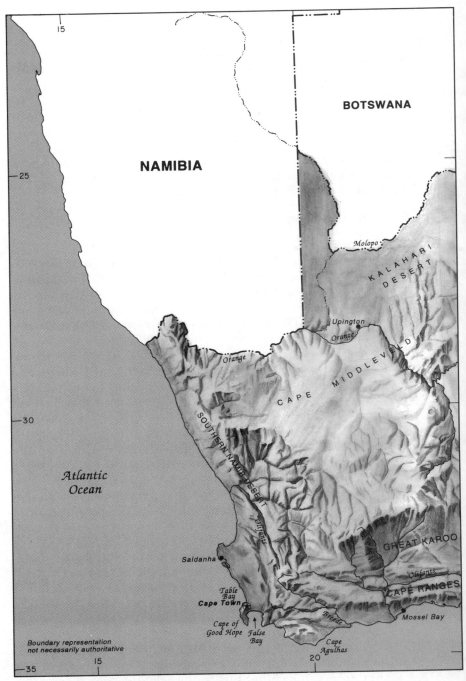

Figure 7. Topography and Drainage

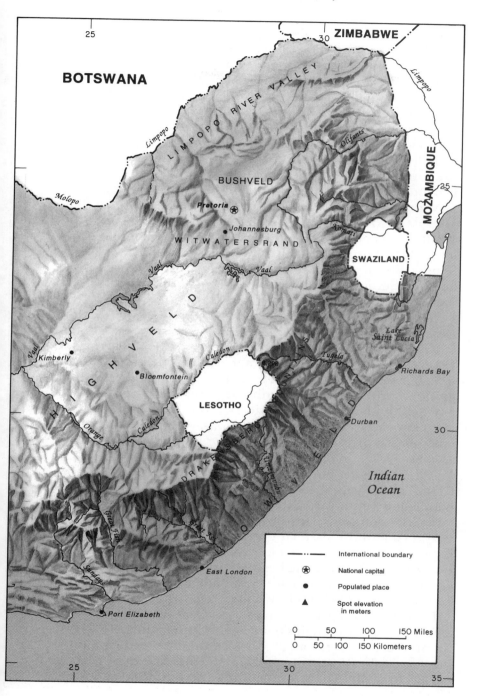

and about 900 meters above sea level. The Bushveld, like the Rand, houses a virtual treasure chest of minerals, one of the largest and best known layered igneous (volcanic) mineral complexes in the world. Covering an area roughly 350 kilometers by 150 kilometers, the Bushveld has extensive deposits of platinum and chromium and significant reserves of copper, fluorspar, gold, nickel, and iron.

Along the northern edge of the Bushveld, the plains rise to a series of high plateaus and low mountain ranges, which form the southern edge of the Limpopo River Valley in Northern Province. These mountains include the Waterberg and the Strypoortberg ranges, and, in the far north, the Soutpansberg Mountains. The Soutpansberg range reaches an elevation of 1,700 meters before dropping off into the Limpopo River Valley and the border between South Africa and Zimbabwe. The Kruger National Park, which is known for its diverse terrain and wildlife, abuts most of the north-south border with Mozambique.

West of the Bushveld is the southern basin of the Kalahari Desert, which borders Namibia and Botswana at an elevation of 600 meters to 900 meters. Farther south, the Southern Namib Desert stretches south from Namibia along the Atlantic coastline. Between these two deserts lies the Cape Middleveld subregion, an arid expanse of undulating plains that sometimes reaches an elevation of 900 meters. The Cape Middleveld is also characterized by large depressions, or "pans," where rainfall collects, providing sustenance for a variety of plants and animals.

The southern border of the Highveld rises to form the Great Escarpment, the semicircle of mountain ranges roughly paralleling South Africa's coastline. The Drakensberg Mountains, the country's largest mountain range, dominate the southern and the eastern border of the Highveld from the Eastern Cape province to the border with Swaziland. The highest peaks of the Drakensberg Mountains in KwaZulu-Natal exceed 3,300 meters and are even higher in Lesotho, which is known as the "Mountain Kingdom."

In the west and the southwest, the Cape Ranges, the country's only "fold mountains"—formed by the folding of the continental crust—form an "L," where the north-south ranges meet several east-west ranges. The north-south Cape Ranges, paralleling the Atlantic coastline, include the Cedarberg Mountains, the Witsenberg Mountains, and the Great Winterhoek Mountains, and have peaks close to 2,000 meters high. The east-west ranges, paralleling the southern coastline, include the Swartberg Mountains and the Langeberg Mountains, with peaks exceeding 2,200 meters.

The Cape Ranges are separated from the Highveld by a narrow strip of semidesert, known as the Great Karoo (Karoo is a Khoisan term for "land of thirst"). Lying between 450 meters and 750 meters above sea level, the Great Karoo is crossed by several rivers that have carved canyons and valleys in their southward descent from the Highveld into the ocean. Another narrow strip of arid savanna lies south of the Great Karoo, between the Swartberg Mountains and the Langeberg Mountains. This high plain, known as the Little Karoo, has a more temperate climate and more diverse flora and fauna than the Great Karoo.

The narrow coastal strip between the Great Escarpment and the ocean, called the Lowveld, varies in width from about sixty kilometers to more than 200 kilometers. Beyond the coastline, the continental shelf is narrow in the west but widens along the south coast, where exploitable deposits of oil and natural gas have been found. The south coast is also an important spawning ground for many species of fish that eventually migrate to the Atlantic Ocean fishing zones.

Lakes and Rivers

Water shortages are a chronic and severe problem in much of South Africa. The country has no commercially navigable rivers and no significant natural lakes. Along the coastline are several large lagoons and estuarine lakes, such as Lake Saint Lucia in KwaZulu-Natal. The government has created several artificial lakes, primarily for agricultural irrigation.

South Africa's largest river, the Orange River, rises in the Drakensberg Mountains and flows to the west and northwest, draining the highlands of Lesotho before being joined by the Caledon River between the Eastern Cape province and the Free State. The Orange River forms the border with Namibia before emptying into the Atlantic Ocean.

The major tributary of the Orange River, the Vaal ("foul"— for its murky cast) River, rises in the Drakensbergs and flows westward, joining the Orange River from the north in Northern Cape province. Together, the Orange and the Vaal rivers drain almost two-thirds of the interior plateau of South Africa. Other major rivers are the Breede River, the Komati River, the

Olifants River, the Tugela River, and the Umzimvubu River, which run fairly short distances from the interior plateau to the ocean, and the Limpopo and Molopo rivers along the northern border with Botswana and Zimbabwe.

Climate and Rainfall

Climatic conditions generally range from Mediterranean in the southwestern corner of the country to temperate in the interior plateau, and subtropical in the northeast. A small area in the northwest has a desert climate. Most of the country has warm, sunny days and cool nights. Rainfall generally occurs during summer (November through March), although in the southwest, around the Cape of Good Hope, rainfall often occurs in winter (June through August). Temperatures are influenced by variations in elevation, terrain, and ocean currents more than latitude.

Temperature and rainfall patterns vary in response to the movement of a high-pressure belt that circles the globe between 25° and 30° south latitude during the winter and low-pressure systems that occur during summer. There is very little difference in average temperatures from south to north, however, in part because the inland plateau rises slightly in the northeast. For example, the average annual temperature in Cape Town is 17°C, and in Pretoria, 17.5°C, although these cities are separated by almost ten degrees of latitude. Maximum temperatures often exceed 32°C in the summer, and reach 38°C in some areas of the far north. The country's highest recorded temperatures, close to 48°C, have occurred in both the Northern Cape and Mpumalanga (formerly Eastern Transvaal).

Frost occurs in high altitudes during the winter months. The coldest temperatures have been recorded about 250 kilometers northeast of Cape Town, where the average annual minimum temperature is –6.1°C. Record snowfalls (almost fifty centimeters) occurred in July 1994 in mountainous areas bordering Lesotho.

Climatic conditions vary noticeably between east and west, largely in response to the warm Agulhas ocean current, which sweeps southward along the Indian Ocean coastline in the east for several months of the year, and the cold Benguela current, which sweeps northward along the Atlantic Ocean coastline in the west. Air temperatures in Durban, on the Indian Ocean, average nearly 6°C warmer than temperatures at the same latitude on the Atlantic Ocean coast. The effects of these two currents can be seen even at the narrow peninsula of the Cape of Good Hope, where water temperatures average 4°C higher on the east side than on the west.

Rainfall varies considerably from west to east. In the northwest, annual rainfall often remains below 200 millimeters. Much of the eastern Highveld, in contrast, receives 500 millimeters to 900 millimeters of rainfall per year; occasionally, rainfall there exceeds 2,000 millimeters. A large area of the center of the country receives about 400 millimeters of rain, on average, and there are wide variations closer to the coast. The 400-millimeter "rainfall line" has been significant because land east of the rainfall line is generally suitable for growing crops, and land west of the rainfall line, only for livestock grazing or crop cultivation on irrigated land (see fig. 2).

Environmental Trends

South Africa has a wealth of natural resources, but also some severe environmental problems. The mainstay of the economy, the mining industry, has introduced environmental concerns, and mineowners have taken some steps in recent years to minimize the damage from this enterprise (see Environmental Protection and Tourism, ch. 3). Agriculture suffers from both land and water shortages, and commercial farming practices have taken a toll on the land. Energy production, too, has often contributed to environmental neglect.

Because of the generally steep grade of the Great Escarpment as it descends from the interior to the coastal lowlands, many of South Africa's rivers have an unusually high rate of runoff and contribute to serious soil erosion. In addition, water consumption needs and irrigation for agriculture have required building numerous dams. As of the mid-1990s, the country has 519 dams with a total capacity of 50 billion cubic meters. Water management engineers estimate that the Vaal River, which provides most of the water for the industrial hub around the Witwatersrand, has reached its maximum capacity for water utilization.

The Lesotho Highlands Water Project, the largest hydroelectric project ever undertaken in Africa, is a thirty-year joint endeavor between South Africa and Lesotho that is due for completion in the year 2020. Through a series of dams on the headwaters of the Orange River, it will alleviate water shortages in South Africa and is expected to provide enough electrical power to enable Lesotho to become virtually self-sufficient in energy.

Much of the land in South Africa has been seriously over-grazed and overcultivated. During the apartheid era, black African farmers were denied many government benefits, such as fertilizers, which were available to white farmers. Settlement patterns, too, have contributed to land degradation, particularly in overcrowded black homelands, and the inadequate and poorly administered homelands' budgets have allowed few improvements in land use.

The environmental impacts of the mining industry have been devastating to some areas of the Witwatersrand, the country's most densely populated region. Some of the gold deposits located here have been mined for more than a century. According to South African geographer Malcolm Lupton and South African urban planning expert Tony Wolfson, mine shafts—the deepest is 3,793 meters—have made hillsides and ridges less stable. Pumping water from subterranean aquifers has caused the natural water table to subside, and the resulting cavities within the dolomite rock formations that overlie many gold deposits sometimes collapse, causing sinkholes. Moreover, these impacts of the mining industry could worsen over time.

Industrial wastes and pollutants are another mining-related environmental hazard. Solid wastes produced by the separation of gold from ore are placed in dumps, and liquid wastes are collected in pits, called slimes dams. Both of these contain small amounts of radioactive uranium. Radon gas emitted by the uranium poses a health threat when inhaled and can contribute to lung cancer and other ailments. Furthermore, the dust from mine dumps can contribute to respiratory diseases, such as silicosis.

Acids and chemicals used to reduce the ore to gold also leave dangerous contaminants in the water table. Streams around Johannesburg townships, such as Soweto, have been found to contain uranium, sulfates, cyanide, and arsenic. Land near mining operations is sometimes rendered "sterile" or too contaminated for farming, and efforts to reclaim the land have often proved too costly for industry or government.

Air pollution is a serious problem in some areas. Most homes lack electricity in the mid-1990s, and coal is used for cooking and heating. Air-quality tests have revealed high levels of particulate pollution, as a result, especially during cold weather. The World Health Organization (WHO) reported in the early

1990s that air-quality measurements in Soweto and surrounding townships outside Johannesburg exceeded recommended levels of particulate pollution for at least three months of the year. Other studies suggest that air pollution contributes to child health problems, especially respiratory ailments, in densely populated areas.

Electricity for industrial and commercial use and for consumption in urban areas is often produced in coal-burning power stations. These electric power stations lack sulfur "scrubbers," and air-quality surveys have shown that they emit as much as 1.2 million tons of sulfur dioxide a year. A 1991 government-appointed panel of researchers reported that South Africa had contributed about 2 percent of the so-called greenhouse gases in the global environment.

Many government officials in 1995 had been among the strongest critics of earlier governments, and a frequent topic of criticism was environmental neglect. Preserving the environment, therefore, was important in the mid-1990s, but financial constraints were limiting the government's ability to enact or implement such measures. Economic development and improved living standards among the poor appeared likely to outweigh long-range environmental concerns for at least the remainder of the 1990s.

Population

Size and Growth

The first census of the Union of South Africa was taken in 1911, one year after its formation. Several enumerations occurred after that, but the black African population was not accurately counted in any of them. In 1950, when apartheid legislation officially restricted black peoples to approximately 13 percent of the land, the government declared that a national census would be taken at the beginning of each decade. After that, Africans were gradually assigned to live in these homelands (see Glossary), then called Bantustans. As the first four homelands were granted nominal independence in the 1970s and the early 1980s, their residents and others assigned to live there were excluded from the official census of South Africa.

Another problem with census measurements was that many black South Africans lived in informal settlements, or "squatter camps," close to cities where they worked or hoped to work, and squatters were often omitted from census counts. In addition, although all citizens were legally required to register births, deaths, marriages, and divorces, many people—especially urban blacks—avoided doing so, in part because of the stringency and complexity of the laws governing legal residency.

The 1980 census count was nearly 23.8 million; another 4.6 million were added to compensate for acknowledged undercounting, resulting in a nationwide population of 28.4 million. The figures excluded those living in the three homelands that were nominally independent in 1980—an estimated 2.7 million in Transkei, 1 million in Bophuthatswana, and about 350,000 in Venda. A fourth homeland, Ciskei, with a population of 678,000, became "independent" in 1981.

The next census, in 1991, took place amid unprecedented political violence. For the first time, the government used aerial photography and sample surveys to enumerate residents in eighty-eight "unrest" areas, which were otherwise inaccessible to government officials. After being adjusted for underenumeration, the 1991 census yielded a count of 30,986,920 citizens, excluding the four "independent" homelands. Residents of the other six non-independent ("self-governing") homelands—10,746,504 people—were included in the nationwide count.

In 1992 the United States Bureau of the Census estimated that 48 percent of all black South Africans, and about 1 percent of all other racial groups, lived in the ten homelands—which made up only about one-seventh of the total land area of the country. On this basis, the bureau estimated the total population of South Africa at 40.6 million.

In 1994 the South African government estimated the total nationwide population at 40.4 million, after all ten homelands had been reincorporated into South Africa (see table 2, Appendix). In that year, the United States Bureau of the Census estimated the total population of South Africa at 43.9 million. Relying on the South African government's enumeration and legal categories, the South African Institute of Race Relations estimated that the population was 76.4 percent black, 12.6 percent white, 8.5 percent coloured, and 2.5 percent Asian.

Population growth rates declined from about 2.9 percent per year in the early 1980s to 2.4 percent in 1995, according to the Development Bank of Southern Africa, a South African economic research and lending organization. Again, racial groups varied; population growth was about 2.6 percent per year for blacks, 2.2 percent for coloureds, 1.9 percent for Asians, and 1.0 percent for whites. The government estimated that the population would double by the year 2025.

Life expectancy at birth was 62.7 years for males and 68.3 years for females in 1996, placing South Africa just below the global median. These figures, too, varied considerably by race; for black males, life expectancy was about nine years less than for white males. About 50.5 percent of the population is female and 49.5 percent is male, according to the South African Central Statistical Service (see fig. 8). In some rural areas and the former homelands, labor policies that draw men into urban areas have resulted in strongly skewed gender ratios. For example, in the early 1990s, the population of QwaQwa was estimated to be 56 percent female; in KwaZulu, 54 percent female.

In 1995 overall fertility was 4.1 births per adult female, down from 5.6 a decade earlier. The crude birth rate was 27.1 births per 1,000 people, according to official estimates. Twelve percent of all births in the early 1990s were to women aged nineteen or younger. Infant mortality was estimated at 45.8 deaths within the first year, per 1,000 live births. The average annual death rate for the entire population was 7.6 per 1,000. Until 1994, these statistics had been reported by racial group, and both birth and death rates were higher among blacks than among whites.

The median age was 19.2 years in 1995, according to official estimates. Roughly 37 percent of all South Africans were fifteen years of age or younger. Nearly 13 percent were above the age of fifty. Racial disparities in age composition were large, however; for example, 52 percent of blacks and only 31 percent of whites were under age nineteen.

The age dependency ratio, or the ratio of the combined population of children and the aged (those less than fifteen years of age and those more than sixty-four years of age) compared to the number between age fifteen and sixty-four, was 70.6 percent in 1995. This measurement is often used to estimate the burden of "economic dependence" on the economically active population. Variations among provinces are great, in part because of the uneven job concentration across the country. For example, in the Northern Province, the age dependency ratio is more than 100; while in Gauteng, the age dependency ratio is less than 50.0, according to the Central Statistical Service.

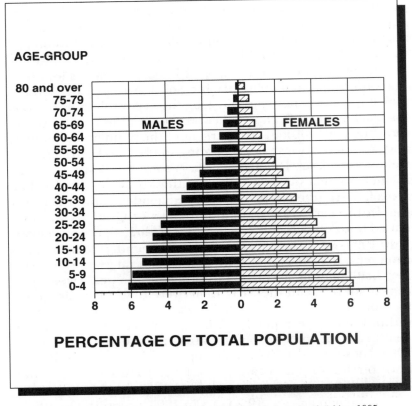

AGE-GROUP

PERCENTAGE OF TOTAL POPULATION

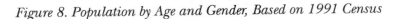

Source: Based on information from South Africa Foundation, *South Africa, 1995,* Johannesburg, 1995, 117.

Figure 8. Population by Age and Gender, Based on 1991 Census

Distribution

Population density averaged 34.4 persons per square kilometer in 1995, although distribution is uneven nationwide. The eastern half of the country is more densely populated than the western half, primarily because of the aridity of much of the west and the concentration of minerals in the east. The most densely populated areas of the country until 1994 were the homelands—where average densities sometimes exceeded 300 people per square kilometer—and Gauteng, which includes Pretoria, Johannesburg, and the mining region of Witwatersrand. More than 7 million people, nearly 17 percent of the population, live in Gauteng, which constitutes less than 2 percent of the land area of South Africa (see fig. 9). The population of Gauteng is expected to double by the year 2010.

Population distribution by racial group is also uneven. In 1995 black South Africans formed a majority in all provinces except the Western Cape, where they made up only 20 percent of the population. Cities were predominantly white, and the townships and squatter areas that ringed the cities were overwhelmingly black. The racial composition of cities and of formerly white neighborhoods began to change in the early 1990s as apartheid-related laws were rescinded or ignored, and the pace of change accelerated in the mid-1990s.

The Johannesburg-based Urban Foundation and other researchers have estimated that the urban population was approximately 57 percent of the total in 1995. Rates of urbanization varied widely by province. The most highly urbanized provinces were Gauteng (nearly 96 percent), Western Cape (86 percent), and Northern Cape (73 percent). The population of Northern Province, in contrast, was only about 9 percent urban, according to the Development Bank of Southern Africa.

Ethnic Groups and Language

South Africans represent a rich array of ethnic backgrounds, but the idea of ethnicity became highly explosive during the apartheid era, when the government used it for political and racial purposes. Whites in South Africa often attributed the recent centuries of warfare in the region to the varied origins of its peoples, rather than to the increasing economic pressures they had faced. Government officials, accordingly, imposed fairly rigid ethnic or tribal categories on a fluid social reality, giving each black African a tribal label, or identity, within a single racial classification.

Apartheid doctrines taught that each black population would eventually achieve maturity as a nation, just as the Afrikaner people, in their own view, had done. Officials, therefore, sometimes referred to the largest African ethnic groups as nations. The government established language areas for each of these and, during the 1950s and 1960s, assigned them separate residential areas according to perceived ethnic identity (see fig. 10). Over the next decade, portions of these language areas became Bantustans, and then self-governing homelands; finally, in the 1970s and the 1980s, four of the homelands—Transkei, Bophuthatswana, Venda, and Ciskei—were granted nominal "independence" (see fig. 11). Although the indepen-

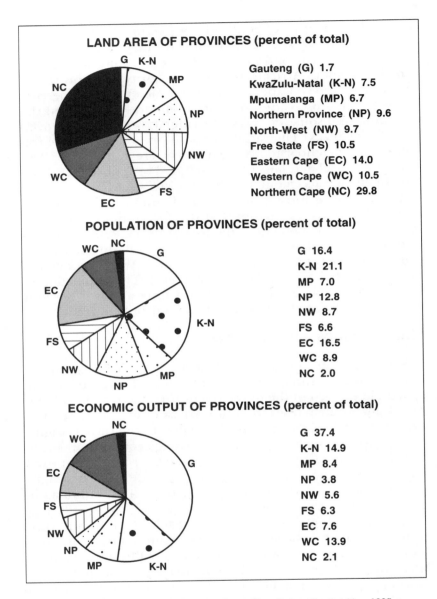

LAND AREA OF PROVINCES (percent of total)

Gauteng (G) 1.7
KwaZulu-Natal (K-N) 7.5
Mpumalanga (MP) 6.7
Northern Province (NP) 9.6
North-West (NW) 9.7
Free State (FS) 10.5
Eastern Cape (EC) 14.0
Western Cape (WC) 10.5
Northern Cape (NC) 29.8

POPULATION OF PROVINCES (percent of total)

G 16.4
K-N 21.1
MP 7.0
NP 12.8
NW 8.7
FS 6.6
EC 16.5
WC 8.9
NC 2.0

ECONOMIC OUTPUT OF PROVINCES (percent of total)

G 37.4
K-N 14.9
MP 8.4
NP 3.8
NW 5.6
FS 6.3
EC 7.6
WC 13.9
NC 2.1

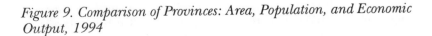

Source: Based on information from South Africa Foundation, *South Africa, 1995,* Johannesburg, 1995, 11, 19–23.

Figure 9. Comparison of Provinces: Area, Population, and Economic Output, 1994

dent homelands were not recognized as separate nations by any country other than South Africa, people assigned to live there were officially "noncitizens" of South Africa.

Apartheid policies also empowered the government to remove black Africans from cities and to preserve the "ethnic character"of neighborhoods in the African townships that were created, legally and illegally, around the cities. Many township neighborhoods were given specific "tribal" designations. Township residents generally ignored these labels, however, and reacted to the divisiveness of the government's racial policies by minimizing the importance of their ethnic heritage, or disavowing it entirely. A few South Africans embraced the notion that ethnicity was an outdated concept, a creation of governments and anthropologists, invoked primarily to create divisions among people of a particular class or region.

The word "tribe" assumed especially pejorative connotations during the apartheid era, in part because of the distortions that were introduced by applying this concept to society. Technically, no tribes had existed in South Africa for most of the twentieth century. The term "tribe," in anthropology, is often defined as a group of people sharing a similar culture—i.e., patterns of belief and behavior—settled in a common territory, and tracing their ancestry to a common—perhaps mythical—ancestor. But none of South Africa's black peoples shared a common, ancestral territory; they had been uprooted and relocated by warfare, by the search for new land, or by government action. Few rural residents could trace their descent from an ancestor shared with many of their neighbors.

Then in 1993 and 1994, as the country emerged from the apartheid era, many South Africans appeared to reclaim their ethnic heritage and to acknowledge pride in their ancestry. The new political leaders recognized the practical advantage of encouraging people to identify both with the nation and with a community that had a past older than the nation. So the interim constitution of 1993 reaffirmed the importance of ethnicity by elevating nine African languages to the status of official languages of the nation, along with English and Afrikaans.

Language Groups

The most widely spoken of South Africa's eleven official languages in the mid-1990s are Zulu (isiZulu), Xhosa (isiXhosa), Afrikaans, and English (for Bantu prefixes, see Glossary). The others—isiNdebele, sePedi (seSotho sa Leboa), seSotho,

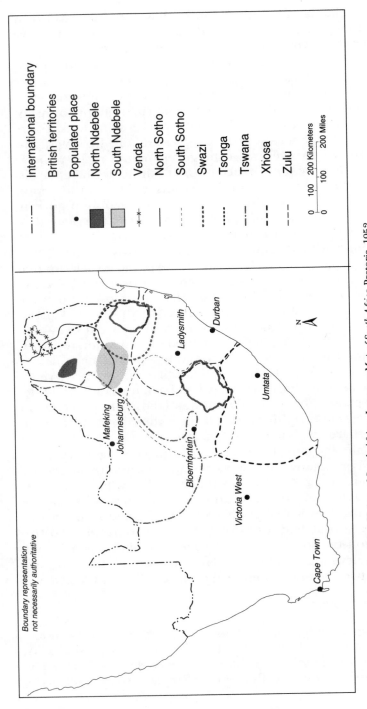

Source: Based on information from Union of South Africa, *Language Map of South Africa*, Pretoria, 1952.

Figure 10. Government-Demarcated Language Areas, 1952

seTswana, siSwati, tshiVenda (also referred to as luVenda), and xiTsonga—are spoken in large areas of the country (see fig. 12). Each of the eleven includes a number of regional dialects and variants.

Despite the diversity of these language groups, it is nonetheless possible to begin to understand this complex society by viewing language groupings as essentially the same as ethnic groupings. This is possible because, in general, most South Africans consider one of the eleven official languages, or a closely related tongue, to be their first language; and most people acquire their first language as part of a kinship group or an ethnically conscious population.

Nine of South Africa's official languages (all except Afrikaans and English) are Bantu languages. Bantu languages are a large branch of the Niger-Congo language family, which is represented throughout much of sub-Saharan Africa. Bantu languages are spoken by more than 100 million Africans in Central Africa, East Africa, and southern Africa. Four major subgroups of Bantu languages—Nguni, Sotho, Tsonga-Shangaan, and Venda—are represented in South Africa.

The largest group of closely related languages in South Africa is the Nguni. Nguni peoples in the country number at least 18 million. About 9 million Sotho (BaSotho) and 2 million Tswana (BaTswana) speak seSotho or a closely related language, seTswana. More than 2 million Tsonga and Shangaan peoples speak xiTsonga and related languages; at least 600,000 Venda (VaVenda) speak tshiVenda (luVenda).

Each of these language groups also extends across South Africa's boundaries into neighboring countries. For example, Nguni-speaking Swazi people make up almost the entire population of Swaziland. At least 1.3 million seSotho speakers live in Lesotho, and more than 1 million people in Botswana speak seTswana. Roughly 4 million speakers of xiTsonga and related languages live in Mozambique, and tshiVenda is spoken by several thousand people in southern Zimbabwe. Language boundaries are not rigid and fixed, however; regional dialects often assume characteristics of more than one language.

Nguni

The Nguni peoples are classified into three large subgroups, the Northern Nguni, the Southern Nguni, and the Ndebele. The Zulu and the Swazi are among the Northern Nguni. The Xhosa are the largest Southern Nguni society, but the neigh-

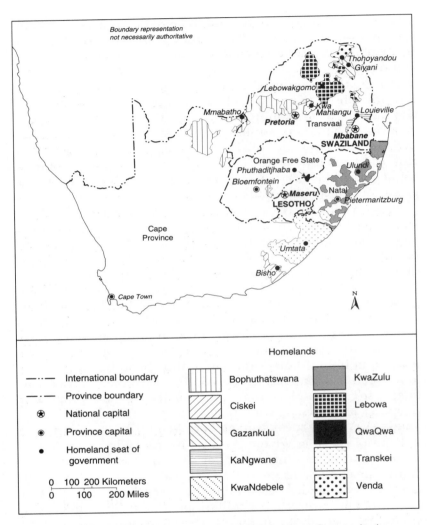

Source: Based on information from South Africa, South African Communication
Service, *South Africa Yearbook, 1994*, Pretoria, 1995, x.

Figure 11. Former African Homelands and Provinces, until 1994

boring Thembu and Mpondo are also well known Southern
Nguni societies, often described as subgroups of the Xhosa.
Each of these groups is a heterogeneous grouping of smaller
(also heterogeneous) ethnic groups.

Four of South Africa's official languages are Nguni languages; isiZulu, isiXhosa, siSwati, and isiNdebele are spoken

primarily by the Zulu, the Xhosa, the Swazi, and the Ndebele peoples, respectively. Each of these languages has regional variants and dialects, which are often mutually intelligible.

Before the nineteenth century, the dominant Nguni settlement pattern was that of dispersed households, as opposed to villages. The typical household was centered on a patrilineage; it also included other relatives through a variety of kinship ties, and people who had attached themselves to the household—often as indentured laborers who were rewarded in cattle. Cattle were central to most Nguni economies, which ranged from almost complete dependence on herding to mixed pastoralism and crop cultivation, often supplemented by hunting.

Nguni political organization generally consisted of small chiefdoms, sometimes only a few hundred people loyal to a person chosen by descent, achievement, or a combination of factors. Until the eighteenth century or later, historians believe, these chiefdoms were not united under a king or monarch. Each chiefdom typically included a group of related patrilineal clans, or descent groups united by common ancestry only a few generations deep, and others who had chosen to attach themselves to a particular chief. A chief could demand support and tribute (taxes) from his followers, could reward those he favored, could form political alliances, and could declare war against his enemies. A chief's followers, in turn, usually had the right to leave and to join another chiefdom, if they wished. Larger chiefdoms sometimes exercised limited control over smaller ones, but such hegemony generally did not last for more than a generation or two.

Zulu

An estimated 8 million South Africans consider themselves Zulu (amaZulu) or members of closely related ethnic groups in the 1990s. By the eighteenth century, Zulu society encompassed a number of Nguni-speaking chiefdoms north of the Tugela River (see fig. 4). The Zulu homestead (*imizi*) consisted of an extended polygynous (see Glossary) family and others attached to the household through social obligations. This social unit was largely self-sufficient, with responsibilities divided according to gender. Men were generally responsible for defending the homestead, caring for cattle, manufacturing and maintaining weapons and farm implements, and building dwellings. Women had domestic responsibilities and raised crops, usually grains, on land near the household.

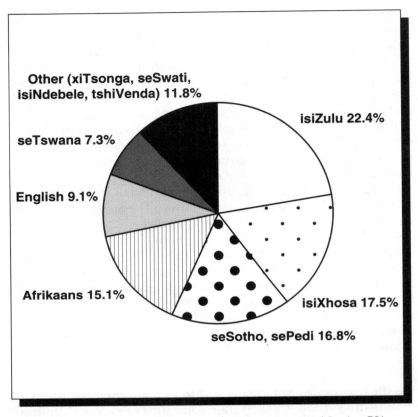

Source: Based on information from South Africa, Central Statistical Service, *RSA Statistics in Brief, 1994*, Pretoria, 1994, 2.9, 2.10.

Figure 12. Percentage of Population Using Each Official Language as First Language, 1994

Zulu chiefs demanded steadily increasing tribute or taxes from their subjects, acquired great wealth, commanded large armies, and, in many cases, subjugated neighboring chiefdoms. Military conquest allowed men to achieve status distinctions that had become increasingly important. In the early nineteenth century, the large and powerful Mthethwa chiefdom, led by Dingiswayo, dominated much of the region north of the Tugela River (see The Rise of African States, ch. 1). Shaka, a Zulu warrior who had won recognition in 1810 by skillfully subduing the leader of the warring Buthelezi chiefdom, took advantage of Dingiswayo's military defeat by the neighboring Ndwandwe armies to begin building the Zulu empire in 1817.

As king, Shaka Zulu (r. 1817–28) defied tradition by adopting new fighting strategies, by consolidating control over his military regiments, and by ruthlessly eliminating potential rivals for power. Shaka's warrior regiments (*impis*) eventually subjugated the powerful Ndwandwe, and decimated or drove from the area the armies of Shaka's rivals. Spreading warfare—exacerbated by pressures from Europeans—drove thousands of Africans north and west, and the ensuing upheaval spawned new conflicts throughout the region (see fig. 5).

The Zulu empire weakened after Shaka's death in 1828 and fragmented, especially following military defeats at the hands of the Afrikaners in 1839 and the British in 1879. Zululand, the area north of the Tugela River, was incorporated into the British colony, Natal, in 1887. The last Zulu uprising, a poll tax protest led by Chief Bambatha in 1906, was ruthlessly suppressed. The Zulu population remained fragmented during most of the twentieth century, although loyalty to the royal family continued to be strong in some areas. Leaders of Zulu cultural organizations and Zulu politicians were able to preserve a sense of ethnic identity through the symbolic recognition of Zulu history and through local-level politics.

Zulu men and women have made up a substantial portion of South Africa's urban work force throughout the twentieth century, especially in the gold and copper mines of the Witwatersrand. Zulu workers organized some of the first black labor unions in the country. For example, the Zulu Washermen's Guild, Amawasha, was active in Natal and the Witwatersrand even before the Union of South Africa was formed in 1910. The Zululand Planters' Union organized agricultural workers in Natal in the early twentieth century.

The KwaZulu homeland was carved out of several unconnected plots of land in Natal in the 1960s. In 1976 Mangosuthu (Gatsha) Buthelezi, a member of the Zulu royal family, was named chief minister of KwaZulu, and the government declared KwaZulu a self-governing territory a year later. Buthelezi established good relations with the National Party-dominated government and, in the process, severed his former close ties to the African National Congress (ANC).

During the 1980s, Buthelezi refused repeated government offers of homeland independence; he preferred to retain the self-governing status that allowed the roughly 4 million residents of KwaZulu to be citizens of South Africa. Zulu solidarity was enhanced by Buthelezi's intellectually powerful and dominant personality and by his leadership of the Zulu cultural organization, Inkatha Yenkululeko Yesizwe (National Cultural Liberation Movement—usually called Inkatha), which became the Inkatha Freedom Party (IFP) during the 1990s.

During the apartheid era, many people in areas officially designated as Zulu were descendants of nineteenth-century Zulu warriors or subjects of the Zulu royal family, who retained a strong ethnic consciousness and pride in their Zulu identity. Others in these areas, however, traced their descent to those who resisted Shaka's domination or celebrated his death at the hands of his own relatives in 1828. Some viewed their association with Zulu royalty as little more than an artificial political creation. A substantial minority within the diverse Zulu society in the 1980s and the 1990s supported the rival ANC.

Military prowess continued to be an important value in Zulu culture, and this emphasis fueled some of the political violence of the 1990s. Zulu people generally admire those with physical and mental agility, and those who can speak eloquently and hold a crowd's attention. These attributes strengthened Buthelezi's support among many Zulu, but his political rhetoric sometimes sparked attacks on political opponents and critics, even within Zulu society.

Buthelezi's nephew, Goodwill Zwelithini, is the Zulu monarch in the 1990s. Buthelezi and King Goodwill won the agreement of ANC negotiators just before the April 1994 elections that, with international mediation, the government would establish a special status for the Zulu Kingdom after the elections. Zulu leaders understood this special status to mean some degree of regional autonomy within the province of KwaZulu-Natal.

Buthelezi was appointed minister of home affairs in the first Government of National Unity in 1994. He led a walkout of Zulu delegates from the National Assembly in early 1995 and clashed repeatedly with newly elected President Nelson (Rolihlahla) Mandela. Buthelezi threatened to abandon the Government of National Unity entirely unless his Zulu constituency received greater recognition and autonomy from central government control.

Swazi

About 1.6 million Swazi people live in the region in the 1990s—almost 900,000 in Swaziland and the remainder in South Africa, especially in the area of the former homeland,

KaNgwane. Until the late eighteenth century, Swazi society consisted of a group of closely related Nguni chiefdoms organized around patrilineal descent groups. At that time, a powerful chief, Ngwane I, seized control over several smaller neighboring chiefdoms of Nguni and Sotho peoples to strengthen his own army's defense against the Mthethwa forces led by Dingiswayo. The greatest rival of the Mthethwa, the Ndwandwe, later subjugated the Mthethwa and killed Dingiswayo. Ngwane I, under pressure from the Ndwandwe, then withdrew into the mountainous territory that would later become Swaziland.

Ngwane I was able to resist incorporation into the Zulu empire during the reign of Shaka, and the Swazi maintained generally peaceful relations with Shaka's successors. Some Swazi clans were forced to move north, however, as regional upheaval spread, and together with displaced Zulu clans, they established aristocratic dynasties over herdsmen and farmers as far north as areas that would later become Malawi and Zambia.

In the twentieth century, the Swazi kingdom retained its autonomy, but not total independence, as the British protectorate of Swaziland in 1903 and as a British High Commission territory in 1907. In 1968 Swaziland became an independent nation led by King Sobhuza II. Swaziland has pressured Pretoria for the return of Swazi-occupied areas of South Africa since the 1960s. In 1982 Pretoria agreed, but that decision was reversed by the South African Supreme Court.

KaNgwane was carved out of land adjacent to Swaziland during the 1960s and was declared a "self-governing" territory with a population of about 400,000 in 1984. KaNgwane's Chief Minister Enos Mabuza tried to build an agricultural and industrial economy in the small, segmented territory, and he became the first homeland leader to grant full trade union rights to workers in his jurisdiction. Mabuza also led the fight against the incorporation of KaNgwane into Swaziland. During the late 1980s, he clashed with Pretoria by expressing strong support for the ANC, although many KaNgwane residents remained uninvolved in South African politics.

Xhosa

The Xhosa (amaXhosa) people in South Africa in the mid-1990s number roughly 6 million, according to official estimates, including the Pondo (Mpondo), Thembu, and several other small ethnic groups, which have been assimilated, to varying degrees, into Xhosa society over several centuries. Each of these is also a heterogeneous grouping of smaller populations.

Most Xhosa people speak English, and often several other languages, but they also take great pride in speaking Xhosa (isiXhosa), an Nguni language closely related to Zulu. Unlike most other African languages, Xhosa has more than a dozen "click" sounds, probably assimilated from Khoisan speakers over long periods of acculturation between Xhosa and Khoisan peoples.

Some ancestors of twentieth-century Xhosa arrived in the eastern Cape region from the north before the fifteenth century, and others moved into the area during the sixteenth and seventeenth centuries. Xhosa history tells of settlement east of the Sundays River by the early eighteenth century. The Xhosa eliminated or enslaved some of the Khoisan speakers they encountered, but many Khoikhoi were peacefully assimilated into Xhosa society. Khoikhoi workers were often entrusted with the care of cattle for a generation or two before being accepted as equal members of Xhosa society. The Xhosa generally incorporated newcomers who recognized the dominance of the Xhosa chief. In fact, until the twentieth century, the term Xhosa was often used to designate territorial affiliation rather than common descent. The resulting Xhosa society was extremely diverse.

Most Xhosa lived by cattle herding, crop cultivation, and hunting. Homesteads were normally built near the tops of the numerous ridges that overlook the rivers of the area, including the Fish River, the Keiskama River, the Buffalo River, and the Kei River. Cattle, serving as symbols of wealth, as well as means of exchange, pack animals, and transportation, were central to the economy. Crops such as corn, sorghum, and tobacco thrived in years with adequate rainfall. Woodworking and iron-working were important men's occupations.

Xhosa homesteads were organized around descent groups, with descent traced through male forebears. These lineages, and the large clans formed by groups of related lineages, provided the center of Xhosa social organization. These descent groups were responsible for preserving ancestral ties and for perpetuating the group through sacrifices to the ancestors, mutual assistance among the living, and carefully arranged marriages with neighboring clans or lineages. Political power was often described as control over land and water. A powerful chief may be praised in oral histories by the claim that he had power over the land close to a large river, and a lesser chief, by the claim that he had power over land near a smaller river or tributary.

Xhosa oral histories tell of installing a royal lineage, probably by the early seventeenth century. This family, the Tshawe, or amaTshawe (people of Tshawe), continued to dominate other Xhosa clans for more than a century; only the Tshawe could be recognized as chiefs over other Xhosa, according to historical accounts in *The House of Phalo: A History of the Xhosa People in the Day of Their Independence,* by Jeffrey B. Peires. The Xhosa also experienced a rapid increase in population, and they divided several times over six or seven generations. The resulting dominant chiefdoms, the Gcaleka and the Rharhabe (Rarabe), formed distinct sections of Xhosa society throughout the twentieth century.

Xhosa people had extensive contact with Europeans by the early nineteenth century, and they generally welcomed European missionaries and educators into their territory. A Xhosa grammar book—the first in a southern African language—was published in 1834. Their early and sustained contact with Christian missionaries and educators led the Xhosa to distinguish between "school people," who had accepted Western innovation, and "red people," who were identified with the traditional red ocher used to dye clothing and to decorate the body. By the twentieth century, the Xhosa school people formed the core of South Africa's emerging black professional class and included lawyers, physicians, and ministers.

The South African government recognized the split between the Gcaleka Xhosa and the Ngqika (a subgroup of Rharhabe) Xhosa in the twentieth century by establishing two Xhosa homelands. Transkei, a segmented territory in eastern Cape Province bordering Lesotho, was designated for the Gcaleka Xhosa, and Ciskei—just west of Transkei—was for the Ngqika Xhosa. Transkei became an independent homeland in 1976, and Ciskei, in 1981.

Xhosa language speakers also include the Thembu (Tembu), the eastern neighbors of the Xhosa during much of their history. The Thembu represent a number of clans that managed to exert their dominance over neighboring clans. The Thembu had long and varied contacts with the Xhosa. These were often peaceful and friendly—for example, Xhosa history says that the Great Wife of each chief was a Thembu—

but they sometimes erupted into war. The Thembu recognize their own royal clan, the Hala, who led many Thembu into battle against the Xhosa during the late eighteenth century.

Also closely related to the Xhosa are the Pondo (Mpondo), the eastern neighbors of the Thembu. The Pondo royal clan, the Nyawuza, struggled to establish and to preserve its dominance over neighboring clans well into the nineteenth century, when some of the Pondo and their neighbors were displaced and subjugated by the Zulu.

Another population often described as a Xhosa subgroup is the Mfengu, consisting of descendants of small remnants of clans and chiefdoms that were displaced during the early nineteenth-century upheaval of the *mfecane* (or crushing—see Glossary). Survivors of the *mfecane* attached themselves to Xhosa society, which was relatively stable, often in Xhosa villages located near Christian missions. After an initial period of clientship, or social inferiority that eroded as generations passed, the Mfengu were generally accepted as equals in the diverse Xhosa population.

Ndebele

The term Ndebele, or amaNdebele, in the 1990s refers primarily to about 800,000 South Africans whose forebears have inhabited areas of the northern Transvaal (now Northern Province) for more than a century. The Ndebele language, isiNdebele, is classified among the Nguni languages, although Sotho influences are strong enough in some areas that isiNdebele is sometimes also classified as a variant of seSotho.

Most Ndebele trace their ancestry to the area that became Natal Province, later KwaZulu-Natal. Some began moving northward well before the early nineteenth-century *mfecane*, and many of these settled in the northern Transvaal. Others, subjects of the Zulu leader Mzilikazi, fled north from Natal after his defeat by Shaka in 1817. Ndebele peoples throughout the region were forced to move several times after that, so that by the end of the nineteenth century, the Ndebele were dispersed throughout much of Natal, the Transvaal, and adjacent territory.

Many Ndebele became formidable warriors, often subjugating smaller chiefdoms and assimilating them into Ndebele society, and Ndebele clashed repeatedly with Voortrekker militias around Pretoria. The late nineteenth-century Afrikaner leader Paul Kruger jailed or executed many of their leaders, seized

Traditional murals decorate homesteads in former
KwaNdebele homeland.
Courtesy Lisowski Collection, Library of Congress

their land, and dispersed others to work for Afrikaner farmers as indentured servants. Some of the land was later returned to a few Ndebele, often as a reward for loyalty or recognition of status.

Under apartheid, many Ndebele living in the northern Transvaal were assigned to the predominantly seSotho-speaking homeland of Lebowa, which consisted of several segiments of land scattered across the northern Transvaal. Others, mostly southern Ndebele, who had retained more traditional elements of their culture and language, were assigned to KwaNdebele. KwaNdebele had been carved out of land that had been given to the son of Nyabela, a well-known Ndebele fighter in Kruger's time. The homeland was, therefore, prized by Ndebele traditionalists, who pressed for a KwaNdebele independence through the 1980s.

KwaNdebele was declared a "self-governing" territory in 1981. Very few of its 300,000 residents could find jobs in the homeland, however, so most worked in the industrial region of Pretoria and Johannesburg. At least 500,000 Ndebele people lived in urban centers throughout South Africa and in homelands other than KwaNdebele through the 1980s.

During the 1980s and the early 1990s, many Ndebele recognized a royal family, the Mahlangu family, and the capital of KwaNdebele was called KwaMahlangu. The royal family was divided, however, over economic issues and the question of "independence" for the homeland. These disputes were overridden by the dissolution of the homelands in 1994. At that time, in addition to the estimated 800,000 Ndebele people in South Africa, nearly 1.7 million Ndebele lived in Zimbabwe, where they constituted about one-sixth of the population and were known as Matabele; about 300,000 lived in Botswana.

Sotho

At least 7 million Sotho (also BaSotho) people who speak seSotho and related languages live in South Africa. Another 3 million Sotho and closely related people live in neighboring countries. The diverse Sotho population includes the Northern Sotho (Pedi), the Southern Sotho, and the Tswana (BaTswana), each of which is itself a heterogeneous grouping.

Ancestors of today's Sotho population migrated into the region in the fifteenth century, according to historians, probably from the area of the northern Transvaal. Like many neighboring Nguni peoples, the Sotho traditionally relied on a combination of livestock raising and crop cultivation for subsistence. Most Sotho were herders of cattle, goats, and sheep, and cultivators of grains and tobacco. In addition, the Sotho were skilled craftsmen, renowned for their metalworking, leatherworking, and wood and ivory carving.

Also like the Nguni, most Sotho lived in small chiefdoms, in which status was determined in part by relationship to the chief. Unlike the Nguni, Sotho homesteads were grouped together into villages, with economic responsibilities generally shared among village residents. Villages were divided into wards, or residential areas, often occupied by members of more than one patrilineal descent group.

The village chief—a hereditary position—generally appointed ward leaders, whose residences were clustered around the chief's residence. Sotho villages sometimes grew into large towns of several thousand people. Farmland was usually outside the village, not adjacent to the homestead. This village organization may have enabled the Sotho villagers to defend themselves more effectively than they could have with dispersed households, and it probably facilitated control over ward leaders and subjects by the chief and his family.

Sotho villages were also organized into age-sets, or groups of men or women who were close in age. Each age-set had specific responsibilities—men organized for warfare and herding, depending on age-set, and women for crop cultivation and religious responsibilities. An entire age-set generally graduated from one task to the next, and the village often celebrated this change with a series of rituals and, in some cases, an initiation ceremony.

Sotho descent rules were important, even though descent groups did not form discrete local groups. Clans were often totemic, or bound to specific natural objects or animal species by mystical relationships, sometimes involving taboos and prohibitions. Major Sotho clans included the Lion (Taung), Fish (Tlhaping), Elephant (Tloung), and Crocodile (Kwean) clans.

Both Nguni and Sotho peoples reckoned descent through patrilineal ties, but their marriage rules differed markedly. Sotho patrilineages were usually endogamous—i.e., the preferred marriage partner would be a person related through patrilineal descent ties. Nguni patrilineages, in contrast, were exogamous—marriage within the descent group was generally forbidden.

By the early twentieth century, Sotho villages were losing their claims to land, largely because of pressure from whites. Cattle raising became more difficult, and as Western economic pressures intensified, Sotho people living in Lesotho and in South Africa increasingly turned to the mines for work. By the early 1990s, an estimated 100,000 BaSotho worked in South Africa's mines, and many others were part of South Africa's urban work force throughout the country.

Northern Sotho

The heterogeneous Northern Sotho are often referred to as the Pedi (or BaPedi), because the Pedi make up the largest of their constituent groups. Their language is sePedi (also called seSotho sa Leboa or Northern Sotho). This society arose in the northern Transvaal, according to historians, as a confederation of small chiefdoms some time before the seventeenth century. A succession of strong Pedi chiefs claimed power over smaller chiefdoms and were able to dominate important trade routes between the interior plateau and the Indian Ocean coast for several generations. For this reason, some historians have credited the Pedi with the first monarchy in the region, although their reign was marked by population upheaval and occasional military defeat.

During the nineteenth century, Pedi armies were defeated by the Natal armies of Mzilikazi and were revived under the command of a Pedi chief, Sekwati. Afrikaner Voortrekkers in the Transvaal acquired some Pedi lands peacefully, but later clashed with them over further land claims. By the 1870s, the Voortrekker armies were sufficiently weakened from these clashes that they agreed to a confederation with the British colonies of Natal and the Cape that would eventually lead to the South African War in 1899.

The smaller Lobedu population makes up another subgroup among the Northern Sotho. The Lobedu are closely related to the Shona population, the largest ethnic group in Zimbabwe, but the Lobedu are classified among the Sotho primarily because of linguistic similarities. The Lobedu were studied extensively by the early twentieth-century anthropologist J.D. Krige, who described the unique magical powers attributed to a Lobedu female authority figure, known to outsiders as the rain queen.

The Northern Sotho homeland of Lebowa was declared a "self-governing" (not independent) territory in 1972, with a population of almost 2 million. Economic problems plagued the poverty-stricken homeland, however, and the population was not unified by strong ethnic solidarity. Lebowa's chief minister, Cedric Phatudi, struggled to maintain control over the increasingly disgruntled homeland population during the early 1980s; his death in 1985 opened new factional splits and occasioned calls for a new homeland government. Homeland politics were complicated by the demands of several ethnic minorities within Lebowa to have their land transferred to the jurisdiction of another homeland. At the same time, government efforts to consolidate homeland territory forced the transfer of several small tracts of land into Lebowa.

Southern Sotho

The Southern Sotho peoples are a diverse group that includes almost 2 million South Africans, many of whom live in the area surrounding Lesotho, and 1.6 million residents of Lesotho. The Southern Sotho were unified during the reign of King Moshoeshoe I in the 1830s. Moshoeshoe established control over several small groups of Sotho speakers and Nguni speakers, who had been displaced by the *mfecane*. Some of

Cooking hearth between family members' huts in a Northern Sotho
location near Pietersburg
Courtesy R. T. K. Scully

these communities had established ties to San peoples who lived just west of Moshoeshoe's territory. As a result, Southern Sotho speech, unlike that of Northern Sotho, incorporates a number of "click" sounds associated with Khoisan languages.

Southern Sotho peoples were assigned to the tiny homeland of QwaQwa, which borders Lesotho, during the apartheid era. QwaQwa was declared "self-governing" in 1974, but Chief Minister Kenneth Mopeli rejected independence on the grounds that the homeland did not have a viable economy. Only about 200,000 Sotho people lived in QwaQwa during the 1980s.

A community of more than 300,000 people, Botshabelo, was incorporated into QwaQwa in 1987. Officials in the homeland capital, Phuthaditjhaba, and many homeland residents objected to the move, and the South African Supreme Court returned Botshabelo to the jurisdiction of the Orange Free State a short time later. The homeland continued to be an overcrowded enclave of people with an inadequate economic base until the homelands were dissolved in 1994.

Tswana

The Tswana (BaTswana), sometimes referred to as the Western Sotho, are a heterogeneous group, including descendants of the once great Tlhaping and Rolong societies, as well as the Hurutshe, Kwena, and other small groups. Their language, seTswana, is closely related to seSotho, and the two are mutually intelligible in most areas. About 4 million Tswana people live in southern Africa—3 million in South Africa and 1 million in the nation of Botswana. In South Africa, many BaTswana live in the area that formed the numerous segments of the former homeland, Bophuthatswana, as well as neighboring areas of the North-West Province and the Northern Cape. Tswana people are also found in most urban areas throughout South Africa.

By the nineteenth century, several Tswana groups were politically independent, loosely affiliated chiefdoms that clashed repeatedly with Afrikaner farmers who claimed land in the northern Transvaal. In the late nineteenth century, Afrikaner and British officials seized almost all Tswana territory, dividing it among the Cape Colony, Afrikaner republics, and British territories. In 1910, when the Cape and the Transvaal were incorporated into the Union of South Africa, the Tswana chiefs lost most of their remaining power, and the Tswana people were forced to pay taxes to the British Crown. They gradually turned to migrant labor, especially in the mines, for their livelihood.

Tswana culture is similar to that of the related Sotho peoples, although some Tswana chiefdoms were more highly stratified than those of other Sotho or the Nguni. Tswana culture was distinguished for its complex legal system, involving a hierarchy of courts and mediators, and harsh punishments for those found guilty of crimes. Tswana farmers often formed close patron-client relationships with nearby Khoisan-speaking hunters and herdsmen; the Tswana generally received meat and animal pelts in return for cattle and, sometimes, dogs for herding cattle.

Bophuthatswana was declared "independent" in 1977, although no country other than South Africa recognized its independence. The homeland consisted primarily of seven disconnected enclaves near, or adjacent to, the border between South Africa and Botswana. Efforts to consolidate the territory and its population continued throughout the 1980s, as successive small land areas outside Bophuthatswana were incorporated into the homeland. Its population of about 1.8 million in the late 1980s was estimated to be 70 percent Tswana peoples; the remainder were other Sotho peoples, as well as Xhosa,

Zulu, and Shangaan. Another 1.5 million BaTswana lived elsewhere in South Africa.

Bophuthatswana's residents were overwhelmingly poor, despite the area's rich mineral wealth. Wages in the homeland's industrial sector were lower than those in South Africa, and most workers traveled to jobs outside the homeland each day. The poverty of homeland residents was especially evident in comparison with the world's wealthy tourists who visited Sun City, a gambling resort in Bophuthatswana.

The non-Tswana portion of the homeland population was denied the right to vote in local elections in 1987, and violence ensued. Further unrest erupted in early 1988, when members of the Botswana Defence Force tried to oust the unpopular homeland president, Lucas Mangope. Escalating violence after that led to the imposition of states of emergency and government crackdowns against ANC supporters in Bophuthatswana, who were often involved in anti-Mangope demonstrations. Mangope was ousted just before the April 1994 elections, and the homeland was officially dismantled after the elections.

Tsonga and Venda

Tsonga

The Tsonga are a diverse population, generally including the Shangaan, Thonga, Tonga (unrelated to another nearby Tonga population to the north), and several smaller ethnic groups. Together they number about 1.5 million in South Africa in the mid-1990s, and at least 4.5 million in southern Mozambique and Zimbabwe.

In the eighteenth century, the ancestors of the Tsonga lived in small, independent chiefdoms, sometimes numbering a few thousand people. Most Tsonga relied on fishing for subsistence, although goats, chickens, and crop cultivation were also important. Cattle were relatively rare in their economies, probably because their coastal lowland habitat was tsetse-fly infested. The Tsonga maintained a tradition of inheritance by brothers, in preference to sons, which is common in many Central African societies but not among other South Africans.

During the *mfecane* and ensuing upheaval of the nineteenth century, most Tsonga chiefdoms moved inland. Some successfully maintained their independence from the Zulu, while others were conquered by Zulu warriors even after they had fled (see The Rise of African States, ch. 1). One Zulu military leader, Soshangane, established his command over a large Tsonga population in the northern Transvaal in the mid-nineteenth century and continued his conquests farther north. The descendants of some of the conquered populations are known as the Shangaan, or Tsonga-Shangaan. Some Tsonga-Shangaan trace their ancestry to the Zulu warriors who subjugated the armies in the region, while others claim descent from the conquered chiefdoms. The Tsonga and the Zulu languages remain separate and are mutually unintelligible in some areas.

The Tsonga-Shangaan homeland, Gazankulu, was carved out of northern Transvaal Province during the 1960s and was granted self-governing status in 1973. The homeland economy depended largely on gold and on a small manufacturing sector. Only an estimated 500,000 people—less than half the Tsonga-Shangaan population of South Africa—ever lived there, however. Many others joined the throngs of township residents around urban centers, especially Johannesburg and Pretoria.

In the 1980s, the government of Gazankulu, led by Chief Minister Hudson Nsanwisi, established a 68-member legislative assembly, made up mostly of traditional chiefs. The chiefs opposed homeland independence but favored a federal arrangement with South Africa; they also opposed sanctions against South Africa on the grounds that the homeland economy would suffer. In areas of Gazankulu bordering the seSotho-speaking homeland of Lebowa, residents of the two poverty-stricken homelands clashed frequently over political and economic issues. These clashes were cited by South African officials as examples of the ethnic conflicts they claimed would engulf South Africa if apartheid ended.

Venda

The Venda (also VaVenda) population of about 600,000 people coalesced into an identifiable social unit in the area of the northern Transvaal and in Zimbabwe over several centuries. The Venda language, tshiVenda or luVenda, emerged as a distinct tongue in the sixteenth century, according to scholars. In the twentieth century, the tshiVenda vocabulary is similar to seSotho, but the grammar shares similarities with Shona dialects, which are spoken in Zimbabwe.

Venda culture is similarly eclectic; it appears to have incorporated a variety of East African, Central African, Nguni, and Sotho characteristics. For example, the Venda forbid the consumption of pork, a prohibition that is common along the East

African coast. They practice male circumcision, which is common among many Sotho, but not among most Nguni peoples.

Early Venda social organization consisted of small kinship groups, often dispersed among several households. These were organized into chiefdoms, and some were ruled by chiefly dynasties in the eighteenth century. Smaller chiefdoms often served as vassal states to larger and stronger chiefdoms, but they were neither entirely incorporated into them nor administered directly by a paramount chief. Venda traditional religious beliefs, like other aspects of culture, appear to have combined elements from several neighboring religious systems and Christianity.

The homeland of Venda became nominally independent in 1979 but was not recognized by any country except South Africa. Unlike other homelands, Venda actually drew most of the 700,000 people assigned to live there. Its economy depended on agriculture and small industry, and coal mining began in the late 1980s. Nearly 70 percent of the men worked elsewhere in South Africa, however, and at least 40 percent of the homeland's income was migrant labor wages. Facing economic collapse, Venda authorities applied for readmission into South Africa in 1991. Their petition was essentially overtaken by the political negotiations and constitutional reforms of the early 1990s, which led to the dissolution of the homelands in 1994.

Afrikaans Speakers

Afrikaners

Roughly 3 million people, or 7 percent of the people of South Africa, trace their roots to Dutch, German, Belgian, and French forebears (see Early European Settlement, ch. 1). Their language, Afrikaans, and membership in the Dutch Reformed Church are the most widespread common features of this population. Afrikaans, a seventeenth-century African variant of Dutch, differs from its parent language in that it has eliminated grammatical gender and many inflected verbs. Afrikaans was recognized as a separate language in the nineteenth century, after a significant literature began to develop.

Many of the Afrikaners' forebears arrived in southern Africa in search of independence from government oppression. They settled the region by fighting a series of wars, first with Khoikhoi and Xhosa peoples who had preceded them in the area, and then with Zulu and British armies, who also hoped to defend their territorial claims. The Afrikaners' defeat in the South African War was a crucial turning point in their history; their greatly outnumbered troops suffered a military defeat, and more than 26,000 Afrikaners—including many women and children—died in British concentration camps. The two formerly independent Afrikaner republics, the Orange Free State and the South African Republic (later the Transvaal), were incorporated into the Union of South Africa within the British empire in 1910.

The war left much of the Afrikaners' farm land devastated, the result of the British "scorched earth" policy. Farmers had also been hard hit by cyclical occurrences of drought and rinderpest fever. This desperate rural poverty drove many Afrikaners into urban areas for the first time, to seek jobs in the growing industrial sector and particularly the flourishing mining industry. But many Afrikaners lacked educational credentials and urban work experience, and they were threatened by competition from the large black population in the cities. Africans had, in some cases, become accustomed to the work and lifestyle changes that were new to Afrikaners at the time. Afrikaner mineworkers, nonetheless, demanded superior treatment over their black counterparts, and they organized to demand better wages and working conditions through the 1920s.

During the 1920s and the 1930s, Afrikaner cultural organizations were important vehicles for reasserting Afrikaners' pride in their cultural identity. The most important of these was the Afrikaner Broederbond, also known as the Broederband (Brotherhood), an association of educated elites. The Broederbond helped establish numerous other Afrikaner social and cultural organizations, such as the Federation of Afrikaner Cultural Organisations (Federasie van Afrikaanse Kultuurvereniginge—FAK), and a variety of Afrikaner social service organizations. Most of these groups represented people of different classes and political persuasions, but Afrikaner leaders worked hard in the 1930s and the 1940s to forge a sense of unity and pride among them.

By the 1940s, the National Party (NP) had gained widespread appeal among Afrikaners by emphasizing racial separation and Afrikaner nationalism. Its narrow election victory in 1948 brought apartheid into all areas of social and economic life in South Africa. The force of the government's commitment to apartheid, and the popularity of the Dutch Reformed Church among Afrikaners, contributed to the impression of Afrikaner unity during the decades of National Party rule. But numerous rifts divided the community, and heated debates ensued. Some believed that the basic assumptions of apartheid were flawed; others, that it was being applied poorly. A small number of Afrikaners worked to end apartheid almost as soon as it was imposed.

Most Afrikaners strongly supported the government's 1960s and 1970s campaign to stem the spread of communist influence in southern Africa—the Total Strategy—based in part on their suspicion of strong centralized government and on their religious beliefs. But many were critical of South Africa's military intervention in neighboring states during the 1980s, and of escalating military costs in the face of the receding threat of what had been called the communist "Total Onslaught." By the late 1980s, enforcing apartheid at home was expensive; the unbalanced education system was in disarray and could not produce the skilled labor force the country needed. Most Afrikaners then welcomed the government's decision to try to end apartheid as peacefully as possible.

"Coloureds"

Roughly 3.2 million South Africans of mixed-race (Khoikhoi and European or Asian) ancestry were known as "coloureds" in apartheid terminology. About 83 percent of them speak Afrikaans as their first language, and most of the remainder speak English as their first language. Almost 85 percent of coloureds live in Western Cape and Northern Cape provinces, and a sizable coloured community lives in KwaZulu-Natal.

The largest subgroup within the coloured population is the Griqua, a largely Afrikaner-Khoikhoi population that developed a distinct culture as early as the seventeenth century. Their community was centered just north of the area that later became the Orange Free State. Growing conflicts with Afrikaner farmers and, later, diamond diggers, prompted Griqua leaders to seek the protection of the British, and later, to relocate portions of their community to the eastern Cape Colony and Natal. Nineteenth- and twentieth-century demands for land and the implementation of apartheid forced Griqua communities to move repeatedly, and many eventually settled north of Cape Town. They number at least 300,000 in the 1990s. Most speak a variant of Afrikaans as their first language and are members of the Dutch Reformed Church.

Another large subgroup, the Cape Malays, number about 180,000, primarily in the Western Cape, in the 1990s. Most are descendants of Afrikaners, indigenous Khoikhoi, and slaves brought to South Africa from the Dutch East Indies. The Cape Malays have retained many cultural elements from their diverse origins, but they are recognized as a distinct community largely because most are Muslims.

The coloured population suffered many indignities under apartheid, such as eviction from homes and neighborhoods preferred by whites. But the limited political reforms of the 1980s gave them political rights that were denied blacks, such as a separate house of parliament in the tricameral legislature and the right to vote in national elections. Coloured politicians took advantage of their status to improve life for their constituents, but at the same time, many were active in the antiapartheid movement.

In April 1994, the coloured community in the Western Cape gave the NP its only provincial victory in the national elections. Coloured voters outnumbered black voters by three-to-one, and white voters by two-to-one, according to local estimates. The population voted for the NP by a large margin, in part out of fear that its interests would be sidelined by a provincial government dominated by the ANC, and in part because conservative members of the coloured community had distanced themselves from the ANC's revolutionary rhetoric over the years. Another important consideration for many was their desire to preserve their first language, which is Afrikaans.

English Speakers

"Europeans"

Although most of the English spoken in South Africa is spoken by nonwhites, the term "English speakers" is often used to identify non-Afrikaner whites in particular, largely because this group shares no other common cultural feature. Some of South Africa's roughly 2 million English-speaking whites trace their forebears to the large influx of British immigrants of the 1820s and the 1830s. Many more Europeans arrived in the late nineteenth century, after the discovery of gold and diamonds. Almost two-thirds of English speakers trace their ancestry to England, Scotland, Wales, or Ireland, but a few arrived from the Netherlands, Germany, or France and joined the English-speaking community in South Africa for a variety of social and political reasons. During the late 1930s and the 1940s, East Europeans arrived in substantial numbers. Unlike the Afrikaners, the English-speaking community has not worked to forge a common identity. During the apartheid era, non-Afrikaner whites held relatively little political power, but they maintained their superior wealth, in many cases, through their activities in commerce and business.

Also among South African whites are about 49,000 Portuguese immigrants, and 13,000 Greeks. South Africa's Jewish population of about 100,000 has been a relatively cohesive community, in comparison with other non-Afrikaner whites. Many South African Jews trace their ancestry to Eastern Europe or to the United Kingdom, and many others fled from Nazi Germany during the 1930s and the 1940s. In general, Jewish South Africans opposed apartheid, in part because of its emphasis on racial purity derived from National Socialist (Nazi) thought. Many Jews have also experienced religious discrimination in South Africa.

Asians

Of the roughly 1 million people of Asian descent in South Africa in the mid-1990s, all but about 20,000 are of Indian descent. Most speak English as their first language, although many also speak Tamil or Hindi, and some speak Afrikaans as a second or third language. Many South Africans of Indian descent trace their ancestry to indentured agricultural laborers brought to Natal in the nineteenth century to work on sugar plantations. But almost all Indians in South Africa in the 1990s were born there, because the South African government curtailed immigration from India in 1913.

Asians have endured racial and ethnic pressures throughout the past century. In the late nineteenth century, they were prohibited from living in the Orange Free State; a few settled in the Pretoria-Johannesburg area, but in the 1990s almost 90 percent of the Asian population live in KwaZulu-Natal—especially in Durban and other large urban centers. Only about 10 percent live in rural areas.

In the nineteenth century, Indians were divided by class, between those who had arrived as indentured laborers or slaves, and wealthier immigrants who had paid their own passage. The latter were given citizenship rights, in most cases, and were not bound by the labor laws applied to indentured workers. This class difference was reinforced by the origins of the immigrants—most of the wealthier Indian immigrants had arrived from northern and central India, and a substantial number were Muslims, while many indentured laborers were Hindus.

By the 1990s, these differences were narrowing; more than 60 percent of all Indians in South Africa are Hindus. About 20 percent are Muslims and 8 percent, Christians, and a few are members of other religions. Most are merchants or businessmen, but significant numbers are teachers or artisans. Caste differences based on Indian custom continue to have some influence over social behavior but are of decreasing importance.

Khoisan

Khoisan languages, characterized by "click" sounds not found elsewhere in Africa, have almost disappeared from South Africa in the 1990s. All remaining Khoisan speakers are believed to be San, living in the Kalahari Desert region in the Northern Cape and North-West Province. The government has no accurate count of their numbers, although it is generally believed that larger numbers of San live in Botswana and Namibia.

The closely related Khoikhoi, who were living in coastal areas of the southwest in the seventeenth century, have been entirely destroyed or assimilated into other cultures. No Khoikhoi peoples remain in South Africa in the 1990s, although many so-called coloureds and others can trace their ancestry through Khoikhoi and other lines of descent.

The San hunters and gatherers who occupied southern Africa for several thousand years organized their society into small kinship-based villages, often including fewer than fifty people. The San economy developed out of the efficient use of the environment; their diet included a wide array of birds, animals, plants, and, among coastal populations, fish and shellfish. The San espoused generally egalitarian values and recognized few leadership roles, except that of religious specialist, or diviner. The culture of the Khoikhoi was similar to that of the San, but the Khoikhoi acquired livestock—mainly cattle and sheep—probably from Bantu speakers who moved into the area from the north.

Some South Africans of mixed-race descent and Khoikhoi residents of Namibia have preserved Khoikhoi oral histories that tell of a time when their ancestors quarreled and split apart. Ancestors of the Namaqua (Nama) moved to the Atlantic Ocean coastline and south toward the Cape of Good Hope; other Khoikhoi moved toward the Kalahari and the Namib deserts and farther north. Seventeenth-century European immigrants enslaved hundreds of Khoikhoi around Cape Town, and many died in smallpox epidemics that swept southern Africa in 1713 and 1755. Others were absorbed into the dominant societies around them, both African and European, and into the populations of laborers who were brought from Malaya, China, and from other region of Africa.

Religion

Almost all South Africans profess some religious affiliation, according to the official census in 1991. Attitudes toward religion and religious beliefs vary widely, however. The government has actively encouraged specific Christian beliefs during much of the twentieth century, but South Africa has never had an official state religion nor any significant government prohibition regarding religious beliefs.

About 80 percent of all South Africans are Christians, and most are Protestants. More than 8 million South Africans are members of African Independent churches, which have at least 4,000 congregations. The denomination generally holds a combination of traditional African and Protestant beliefs. The other large Protestant denomination, the Dutch Reformed Church, has about 4 million members in several branches. Most are whites or people of mixed race.

Other Protestant denominations in the mid-1990s include at least 1.8 million Methodists, 1.2 million Anglicans, 800,000 Lutherans, 460,000 Presbyterians, and smaller numbers of Baptists, Congregationalists, Seventh Day Adventists, and members of the Assembly of God and the Apostolic Faith Mission of Southern Africa. More than 2.4 million South Africans are Roman Catholics; about 27,000 are Greek or Russian Orthodox. More than 7,000 are Mormons. Adherents of other world religions include at least 350,000 Hindus, perhaps 400,000 Muslims, more than 100,000 Jews, and smaller numbers of Buddhists, Confucians, and Baha'is.

Historical Background

African Religions

The earliest southern African religions, those of the Khoisan peoples, were more complex than early missionaries often recorded. Their beliefs and practices were substantially eroded by contacts with Europeans. Exceptional records of Khoisan rituals were made by a German linguist, Wilhelm Bleek, during the 1870s and the 1880s. Some traditional Khoisan beliefs have been preserved through oral histories, and some religious practices are still observed in remote areas of Botswana and Namibia.

Many Khoisan peoples believe in a supreme being who presides over daily life and controls elements of the environment. In some Khoisan belief systems, this god is worshiped through rituals or small sacrifices. A second, evil deity brings illness and misfortune to earth. This dualism between good and evil pervades other areas of Khoisan thought about the nature of the universe. Some Khoisan belief systems maintain that a person should never attempt to communicate with the beneficent deity, for fear of provoking his evil counterpart, and some believe that spiritual beings simply ignore humanity most of the time.

Traditional Khoisan religion also included numerous mythic tales of gods and ancestor-heroes, whose lives provided examples of ways to cope with social conflicts and personal problems. Also important was the use of dance and altered states of consciousness to gain knowledge for healing an individual or remedying a social evil. Healing dances are still among the most widely practiced religious rituals in South Africa, even in the 1990s, and are used in some African Independent churches to heal the sick or eradicate evil.

For many Khoisan peoples, the sun and the moon were gods, or aspects of a supreme deity. The cycle of religious observance was, therefore, carefully adjusted according to the cycles of the moon. Seventeenth- and eighteenth-century observers in the Cape Colony noted the importance of ritual dances and prayers during the full moon each month. Khoisan legends and myths also refer to a "trickster" god, who could transform himself into animal or human forms, and who could die and be reborn many times over. The praying mantis, a predatory insect with large eyes and other features characteristic of animal predators, figures in San myths and folktales in a role similar to the clever fox in European folktales. Khoisan herdboys still use mantises to "divine" the location of lost animals, and in Afrikaans, the mantis is referred to as "the Hottentot's god."

Bantu-speaking peoples brought an array of new religious practices and beliefs when they arrived in the first millennium A.D. Most believed in a supreme being, or high god, who could bestow blessings or bring misfortune to humans. More influential in their spiritual life, however, was a group of ancestral spirits—a different pantheon of spiritual beings in each community. These spirits could communicate with and influence the lives of the living, and they could sometimes be influenced by human entreaties. The male head of a homestead was usually the ritual leader, responsible for performing rituals, giving thanks, seeking a blessing, or healing the sick on behalf of his homestead. Rites of passage, or rituals marking major life-cycle changes such as birth, initiation, marriage, and death, were also important religious observances, and rituals were used for rainmaking, strengthening fertility, and enhancing military might.

Zulu and Xhosa religions generally sought to placate male ancestral spirits, often with libations of beer or offerings of meat, and to seek their guidance or intercession. Ancestral spirits were almost uniformly benevolent; evil was generally attributed to witches or sorcerers, who might overpower or bypass a spiritual protector or ancestor. Ancestral spirits occasionally caused minor illnesses, primarily as a warning against religious neglect or misdeeds.

Most Bantu religious systems had no priesthood, or officially recognized mediator between the material and the spiritual worlds. Rather, they believed that political leadership was accompanied by religious responsibility. For example, a chiefdom or kingdom relied on the chief or monarch for physical and spiritual survival. Particular importance was attached to the status of the diviner, or *sangoma*, however; the *sangoma* underwent rigorous training to acquire the extensive knowledge and skills necessary for divination and healing.

Bantu religions usually avoided any claim that rituals performed by human beings could influence the actions of the supreme deity, or high god; rituals were normally intended to honor or placate lesser spiritual beings, and sometimes to ask for their intervention. The high god was a remote, transcendent being possessing the power to create the Earth, but beyond human comprehension or manipulation. Ancestors, in contrast, were once human and had kinship ties with those on earth, and they were sometimes amenable to human entreaties.

Many Bantu societies have historical accounts or myths that explain the presence of human society on earth. In many cases, these myths affirm that human beings first emerged from a hole in the ground, that they were plucked from a field or a bed of reeds, or that they were fashioned from elemental substances through the efforts of a supreme deity. Death originated in the failure of human beings or their messengers, such as a chameleon who was sent to relay a divine message of immortality, but who delayed and was overtaken by the message of death.

Such widespread myths not only provide an account of the origins of the human condition, but they also describe appropriate behavior for coping with a complex world. For example, a Zulu myth tells of the creation of both black and white human beings, the assignment of the black people to the land and the white people to the sea, and the provision of spears for black people and guns for whites. Many of life's conflicts arise, it is believed, when people defy the divine plan.

Scholars have reported that during the rapid acculturation of the nineteenth century in southern Africa, new myths and legends arose, attributing greater and greater power to traditional gods. In this way, new events and displays of power were incorporated into existing belief systems. Others have suggested that the upheaval of the nineteenth century provided fertile ground for Christian and Muslim missionaries, whose teachings of a Supreme Being presiding over the entire world provided reassurance of a divine order in a changing environment. In this view, the new world religions drew converts based on their appeal as an explanation of changing circumstances.

The Arrival of Christianity

Religion and politics were inextricably interwoven as soon as the Portuguese navigator Bartholomeu Dias (Diaz) erected a limestone pillar and Christian cross at the Cape of Good Hope in the year A.D. 1488. Religious missionaries did not arrive in any significant numbers for more than a century, however. In 1652 the Dutch East India Company established a resupply station at the Cape, based largely on the experience of Jan van Riebeeck, who had survived a shipwreck off the coast of the Cape in 1648 and who later became the governor of the Cape

Man consulting a Shangaan herbalist, whose manipulation of cowrie shells, carved bones, and other ritual objects helps communicate her diagnosis
Courtesy R. T. K. Scully

Colony. Dutch Reformed Church missionaries reported in 1658 that Khoikhoi slaves in the area attended their mission services (and were rewarded with a glass of brandy after the sermon).

Religious reforms swept through the Netherlands in the early seventeenth century, and the Calvinist Synod ruled in 1618 that any slave who was baptized should be freed. In the Cape Colony, however, farmers who depended on their slaves refused repeated entreaties from the church authorities in Europe to free these slaves. Instead, the slaveowners banned religious instruction for slaves, so none could be baptized.

The London Missionary Society sent large numbers of missionaries to the Cape Colony in 1799, and soon after that, the Glasgow Missionary Society and the Wesleyan Methodist Missionary Society arrived, along with missionaries from the United States, France, Germany, and Scandinavia. Most missions placed a high priority on literacy and Biblical instruction, but as the Industrial Revolution swept through Europe and the United States, the evangelical message increasingly emphasized the spiritual benefits of productive labor. Missionaries also promoted European values and occupations as well as the possession of material goods unrelated to spiritual salvation, such as European clothing, houses, and tools.

Many Western missionaries mistakenly believed that southern Africans had no religion because of the differences in their faiths. Africans often denied the existence of a single, supreme being who could be influenced by prayer on behalf of humans. They appeared to confirm the missionaries' suspicions that they were "godless" by performing ritual oblations to lesser spiritual beings and ancestors. The absence of a priest or minister, or any type of church, was interpreted as further proof of the lack of spiritual beliefs, even among those who had strong beliefs in an array of spiritual beings and forces.

A few African leaders took advantage of the missionaries' presence to enhance or to reinforce their own political power. For example, the nineteenth-century Sotho King Moshoeshoe I claimed that Christian teachings only validated rules of behavior he had long advocated for his subjects. The Xhosa chief, Ngqika, rewarded local missionaries when their prayers appeared to bring much-needed rain. Sotho, Tswana, and others sought the protection of Christian missionaries during the *mfecane* and the related upheaval of the first part of the nineteenth century. The term Mfengu was originally applied to these displaced people who settled around Christian mission stations, but over time, the Mfengu came to be recognized as a relatively cohesive ethnic group.

The relationships among indigenous African leaders, missionaries, and European settlers and officials were always complex. Missionaries whose efforts were frustrated by local chiefs sometimes sought government intervention to weaken the chiefs' power. Government officials relied in part on the influence of missionaries in order to convince indigenous Africans of the validity of European customs. At times, however, missionaries objected to official policies that they considered harmful to their followers, and they were criticized by government officials, as a result, for interfering in official matters.

In the 1830s and the 1840s, British officials in the eastern Cape Colony tried to eliminate the Xhosa practice of witch hunts, which were increasing in response to the turmoil in the region and were spreading fear through many religious communities. The British also abolished traditional economic practices, such as the Xhosa custom of paying *lobola*, or bridewealth given by the family of a groom to that of his bride. But abolishing an element of traditional culture almost always resulted in an array of unforeseen cultural consequences, and this was especially true when the practices being eliminated were central to a group's social organization, as was the *lobola*.

By 1850, the Xhosa were enraged by the British presence. A leading Xhosa healer and diviner, Mlangeni, organized an army to confront the British and promised supernatural assistance in this effort, as long as the Xhosa people sacrificed all of their yellow and dun-colored cattle to counteract the evil spell that had engulfed them. A brutal frontier war ensued, and the rebellion was suppressed in 1853.

The Xhosa defeat was made even more bitter when a chiefly adviser, Mhlakaza, convinced many people of a prophecy brought by his niece, Nongqawuse, telling of an end to British domination and the redemption of the Xhosa if they would first kill all their remaining cattle and destroy their food stocks. In 1856 and 1857, thousands of Xhosa responded to the prophecy; more than 400,000 cattle were sacrificed. After the prophecy failed, more than 40,000 people died of starvation, and almost as many were forced to seek work in the colonial labor market.

Religion and Apartheid

Dutch Reformed Churches

Christianity became a powerful influence in South Africa, often uniting large numbers of people in a common faith. In the twentieth century, however, several Christian churches actively promoted racial divisions through the political philosophy of apartheid. The largest of these denominations was the Dutch Reformed Church (Nederduitse Gereformeerde Kerk— NGK), which came to be known as the "official religion" of the National Party during the apartheid era. Its four main branches had more than 3 million members in 1,263 congregations in the 1990s.

The Dutch Reformed Church arrived in South Africa in the seventeenth century, after Calvinist reforms in Europe had entrenched the idea of predestination, and the Synod of Dort in the Netherlands had proclaimed this church as the "community of the elect" in 1619. The church gained recognition as the state religion in 1651, and the Dutch East India Company, as an

extension of the state in southern Africa, established the first
Dutch Reformed Church at the Cape of Good Hope in 1652.

Church members in South Africa generally resisted liberal
trends that arose in Europe in the nineteenth century, but rifts
occurred in the church in 1853 with the formation of the
Nederduitsch Hervormde Kerk (also translated, the Dutch
Reformed Church), and in 1859, with the formation of the
Gereformeerde Kerk van Suid-Afrika (the Reformed Church of
South Africa). The NGK is generally referred to as the Dutch
Reformed Church, and these two newer churches are also
referred to as Dutch Reformed churches.

All of the Dutch Reformed churches share similar Calvinist
beliefs and presbyterial organization. Their doctrines assert
that God is eternal, infinite, wise, and just, and the Creator of
the universe. He has planned the life and the fate of each individual on earth; the "chosen" are saved, as long as they adhere
to the church's teachings. The Bible—both the Old Testament
and the New Testament—is the final authority on religious
matters.

The presbyterial organization of the Dutch Reformed
churches means that the functioning of each congregation is
governed, in part, by that community, whereas decisions concerning policy and discipline are generally handled by regional
synods. A general synod is responsible for the denomination as
a whole. In South Africa, a national synod and nine regional
synods oversee the operation of the Dutch Reformed congregations.

As black Africans and people of mixed race converted to the
religion, church members debated the question of racial separation. Pressures grew for racially separate congregations, and
the issue was complicated by the demands of some black
church members for their own churches and congregations. In
1881 the Dutch Reformed Mission Church (Sending Kerk)
established a separate coloured church. In 1910, when black
South Africans made up about 10 percent of the community,
the synods established the NGK in Afrika, as it became known,
for black Africans. (An Indian Dutch Reformed Church was
formed in 1951.)

Racial separation was only widely accepted in the church in
the early twentieth century, as many Afrikaners came to believe
that their own survival as a community was threatened, and as
the belief in racial separation was gaining acceptance among
white South Africans in general. Social and spiritual survival

became intertwined in church philosophy, influenced in part by the early twentieth-century persecution of the Afrikaners by the British (see British Imperialism and the Afrikaners, ch. 1). Church leaders refused to condemn Afrikaner rebellions against the British, and their followers gained strength by attributing divine origins to their struggle for survival.

As the system of apartheid was called into question throughout the country in the 1970s and the 1980s, church leaders were, in general, more committed to apartheid than many of their followers, and the church became an impediment to political reform. A few Dutch Reformed clergy opposed apartheid. The best known of these, Reverend Beyers Naude, left his whites-only church in the late 1970s and joined a black parish within the Dutch Reformed church. The efforts of other church leaders who worked to reduce the church's racist image were often constrained by the fact that parish finances were controlled by the church's highest authorities, who supported apartheid.

Other Religious Organizations

In the 1990s, black South Africans form a majority in all large Christian churches in South Africa, except the Dutch Reformed churches, and this was true throughout the apartheid era. In these churches, many people became involved in efforts to reverse or to ameliorate the effects of apartheid policies, but with varying degrees of militancy. Again, there were often significant differences between church leaders and their followers concerning race and politics. For example, senior officials within the Roman Catholic Church in South Africa opposed apartheid, but a group of Catholics formed the South African Catholic Defence League to condemn the church's political involvement and, in particular, to denounce school integration.

Leaders of the Church of the Province of South Africa, the Anglican Church, spoke out in opposition to apartheid, but church members disagreed about tactics for expressing their views. Some white Anglicans vigorously opposed their church's involvement in politics, while many black Anglicans became leaders in the antiapartheid movement. The Methodist Church, which was overwhelmingly black, adopted openly antiapartheid stands on many public issues, but its leaders' activism cost it support among those who feared public scrutiny on this politically sensitive issue.

Religious alliances provided a means of coordinating church opposition to apartheid while minimizing the public exposure of church leaders and parishioners. The South African Council of Churches (SACC) was the most active antiapartheid umbrella organization. The SACC not only opposed apartheid but also offered encouragement to those who contravened race laws. Under the leadership of Anglican Archbishop Desmond Tutu in the 1980s, the SACC also attempted to withhold cooperation with the state, as much as possible, in protest against apartheid. SACC leaders were outspoken in their political views, lodging frequent complaints with government officials and organizing numerous peaceful protests.

Countering the efforts of the antiapartheid community, the Christian League of Southern Africa rallied in support of the government's apartheid policies. The Christian League consisted of members of Dutch Reformed and other churches who believed apartheid could be justified on religious grounds. The group won little popular support, however, and was criticized both for its principles and for its tactic of bringing religious and political issues together in the same debate.

Zion Christian Church

The largest and fastest-growing of the African independent churches in the 1990s is the Zion Christian Church. Its members, estimated to number between 2 million and 6 million in more than 4,000 parishes, live primarily in urban townships and rural communities. The church is well known by the abbreviation, ZCC, pronounced "zed-say-say." The ZCC was established in 1910 by Engenas Lekganyane, a farm worker in a rural area that later became Zion City, in the Northern Province. Lekganyane was educated by Scottish Presbyterian missionaries, and the church reflects some elements of that religion. The ZCC took its name from Biblical references to the Mount of Zion in Jerusalem, based in part on the inspiration of a similar community in Zion, Illinois.

The highlight of the ZCC religious calendar is the Easter celebration, which has drawn more than 1 million church members for several days of religious services at Zion City. Zionist beliefs emphasize the healing power of religious faith, and for this reason ZCC leaders sometimes clash with the traditional healers, or *sangomas*, who are important in many belief systems. Despite occasional conflicts, however, the ZCC respects traditional African religious beliefs, in general, especially those con-

Nobel Peace Prize winner Archbishop Desmond Tutu in Milwaukee,
Wisconsin, May 1995
Permission of the Milwaukee Journal Sentinel;
photographer Ronald M. Overdahl

cerning the power of the ancestors to intercede on behalf of
humans.

ZCC beliefs are eclectic, but the church's practices are often
strict. The ZCC proscribes alcoholic beverages, smoking, and
eating pork. It condemns sexual promiscuity and violence. As a
result, church members have become known in the business
community for their honesty and dependability as employees.

The growth of the independent churches was spurred by the
antiapartheid movement. Nevertheless, because devout ZCC
members place their spiritual agenda ahead of earthly politics,
they generally avoided antiapartheid demonstrations and organizations. As a result, ZCC members were often shunned, and
some were even attacked, by antiapartheid militants. President
Mandela is popular among ZCC members in the 1990s, however, in part because of his political moderation and antiviolent
rhetoric.

Islam

South Africa's small Muslim community of about 400,000 is
gaining new members, especially among black South Africans,

in the 1990s. The majority of Muslims are of Indian descent, however, and a small minority are Pakistanis or people of mixed race. Most live in or near Cape Town, Durban, or Johannesburg. The Africa Muslim Party won 47,690 votes, less than 1 percent of the total vote, in the April 1994 nationwide elections.

Most South African Muslims are members of the Sunni branch of Islam, although a small Shia sect is becoming more vocal in the 1990s. The Muslim Youth Movement, the Muslim Student Association, and several other Islamic organizations have small branches in South African universities. Diplomats and other visitors from Iran, Saudi Arabia, and Kuwait have contributed to the building of mosques and other efforts to promote Islam. The desire to proselytize in the region was an important topic of discussion at the first southern African conference on Islam, which was held in Cape Town in April 1995.

Education

Schools in South Africa, as elsewhere, reflect society's political philosophy and goals. The earliest mission schools aimed to inculcate literacy and new social and religious values, and schools for European immigrants aimed to preserve the values of previous generations. In the twentieth century, the education system assumed economic importance as it prepared young Africans for low-wage labor and protected the privileged white minority from competition. From the 1950s to the mid-1990s, no other social institution reflected the government's racial philosophy of apartheid more clearly than the education system. Because the schools were required both to teach and to practice apartheid, they were especially vulnerable to the weaknesses of the system.

Many young people during the 1980s were committed to destroying the school system because of its identification with apartheid. Student strikes, vandalism, and violence seriously undermined the schools' ability to function. By the early 1990s, shortages of teachers, classrooms, and equipment had taken a further toll on education.

South Africa's industrial economy, with its strong reliance on capital-intensive development, provided relatively few prospects for employment for those who had only minimal educational credentials, or none at all. Nationwide literacy was less than 60 percent throughout the 1980s, and an estimated 500,000 unskilled and uneducated young people faced unemployment by the end of the decade, according to the respected Education Foundation. At the same time, job openings for highly skilled workers and managers far outpaced the number of qualified applicants. These problems were being addressed in the political reforms of the 1990s, but the legacies of apartheid—the insufficient education of the majority of the population and the backlog of deficiencies in the school system—promised to challenge future governments for decades, or perhaps generations.

Early Development

Many African societies placed strong emphasis on traditional forms of education well before the arrival of Europeans. Adults in Khoisan- and Bantu-speaking societies, for example, had extensive responsibilities for transmitting cultural values and skills within kinship-based groups and sometimes within larger organizations, villages, or districts. Education involved oral histories of the group, tales of heroism and treachery, and practice in the skills necessary for survival in a changing environment.

In many Nguni-speaking chiefdoms of southern Africa, highly regimented age-groups of young men acquired knowledge and skills vital to their survival and prestige under the instruction of respected military, religious, or political leaders. The socialization of women, although sometimes done within age-groups, was more often in small groups of siblings or cousins, and it emphasized domestic and agricultural skills necessary to the survival of the family. In all of these settings, the transmission of religious values was a vital element of education.

The socialization of African youth was sometimes interrupted by warfare or political upheaval. More serious disruptions occurred in the late nineteenth century and the twentieth century, when government policies drew large numbers of adult men away from their homes for long periods of employment in mines or urban industries. Women were heads of households for months or years at a time. And after apartheid became entrenched in the early 1950s, security forces sometimes removed entire villages from their land and relocated them to less desirable areas in the interest of white economic development.

The earliest European schools in South Africa were established in the Cape Colony in the late seventeenth century by

Dutch Reformed Church elders committed to biblical instruction, which was necessary for church confirmation (see Early European Settlement, ch. 1). In rural areas, itinerant teachers (*meesters*) taught basic literacy and math skills. British mission schools proliferated after 1799, when the first members of the London Missionary Society arrived in the Cape Colony.

Language soon became a sensitive issue in education. At least two dozen English-language schools operated in rural areas of the Cape Colony by 1827, but their presence rankled among devout Afrikaners, who considered the English language and curriculum irrelevant to rural life and Afrikaner values. Throughout the nineteenth century, Afrikaners resisted government policies aimed at the spread of the English language and British values, and many educated their children at home or in the churches.

After British colonial officials began encouraging families to emigrate from Britain to the Cape Colony in 1820, the Colonial Office screened applicants for immigration for background qualifications. They selected educated families, for the most part, to establish a British presence in the Cape Colony, and after their arrival, these parents placed a high priority on education. Throughout this time, most religious schools in the eastern Cape accepted Xhosa children who applied for admission, and in Natal many other Nguni-speaking groups sent their children to mission schools after the mid-nineteenth century. The government also financed teacher training classes for Africans as part of its pacification campaign throughout the nineteenth century.

By 1877 some 60 percent of school-age children in Natal were enrolled in school, as were 49 percent in the Cape Colony. In the Afrikaner republics, however, enrollments remained low—only 12 percent in the Orange Free State and 8 percent in the Transvaal—primarily the result of Afrikaner resistance to British education. Enrollments in these republics increased toward the end of the century, after the government agreed to the use of Afrikaans in the schools and to allow Afrikaner parents greater control over primary and secondary education.

By the late nineteenth century, three types of schools were receiving government assistance—ward schools, or small rural schools generally employing one teacher; district schools, providing primary-level education to several towns in an area; and a few secondary schools in larger cities. But during the last decades of that century, all four provinces virtually abolished

African enrollment in government schools. African children attended mission schools, for the most part, and were taught by clergy or by lay teachers, sometimes with government assistance.

Higher education was generally reserved for those who could travel to Europe, but in 1829 the government established the multiracial South African College, which later became the University of Cape Town. Religious seminaries accepted a few African applicants as early as 1841. In 1852 British officials in the Transvaal and the Orange Free State acknowledged the right of Afrikaners to establish their own institutions of higher learning, and based on this understanding, Britain's incoming governor—Sir George Grey—allocated small sums of money to help fund Afrikaner institutions. The government established Grey College—later the University of the Orange Free State— in Bloemfontein in 1855 and placed it under the supervision of the Dutch Reformed Church. The Grey Institute was established in Port Elizabeth in 1856; Graaff-Reinet College was founded in 1860. The Christian College was founded at Potchefstroom in 1869 and was later incorporated into the University of South Africa and renamed Potchefstroom University for Christian Higher Education.

Following the British victory in the South African War, the new representative of the Crown, Sir Alfred Milner, brought thousands of teachers from Britain, Canada, Australia, and New Zealand to instill the English language and British cultural values, especially in the two former Afrikaner republics. To counter the British influence, a group of Afrikaner churches proposed an education program, Christian National Education, to serve as the core of the school curriculum. The government initially refused to fund schools adopting this program, but Jan C. Smuts, the Transvaal leader who later became prime minister, was strongly committed to reconciliation between Afrikaners and English speakers, and he favored local control over many aspects of education. Provincial autonomy in education was strengthened in the early twentieth century, and all four provincial governments used government funds primarily to educate whites.

The National Party (NP) was able to capitalize on the fear of racial integration in the schools to build its support. The NP's narrow election victory in 1948 gave Afrikaans new standing in the schools, and after that, all high-school graduates were required to be proficient in both Afrikaans and English. The

NP government also reintroduced Christian National Education as the guiding philosophy of education.

Education under Apartheid

The Bantu Education Act

The Bantu Education Act (No. 47) of 1953 widened the gaps in educational opportunities for different racial groups. Two of the architects of Bantu education, Dr. W.M. Eiselen and Dr. Hendrik F. Verwoerd, had studied in Germany and had adopted many elements of National Socialist (Nazi) philosophy. The concept of racial "purity," in particular, provided a rationalization for keeping black education inferior. Verwoerd, then minister of native affairs, said black Africans "should be educated for their opportunities in life," and that there was no place for them "above the level of certain forms of labour." The government also tightened its control over religious high schools by eliminating almost all financial aid, forcing many churches to sell their schools to the government or close them entirely.

Christian National Education supported the NP program of apartheid by calling on educators to reinforce cultural diversity and to rely on "mother-tongue" instruction in the first years of primary school. This philosophy also espoused the idea that a person's social responsibilities and political opportunities are defined, in large part, by that person's ethnic identity. The government also gave strong management control to the school boards, who were elected by the parents in each district.

Official attitudes toward African education were paternalistic, based on trusteeship and segregation. Black education was not supposed to drain government resources away from white education. The number of schools for blacks increased during the 1960s, but their curriculum was designed to prepare children for menial jobs. Per-capita government spending on black education slipped to one-tenth of spending on whites in the 1970s. Black schools had inferior facilities, teachers, and textbooks.

Soweto and Its Aftermath

Tensions over language in education erupted into violence on June 16, 1976, when students took to the streets in the Johannesburg township of Soweto. Their action was prompted by the decision of Prime Minister Hendrik Verwoerd, the archi-

Children at play in schoolyard, KTC Township (Cape Town)

tect of the Bantu education system, to enforce a regulation requiring that one-half of all high-school classes must be taught in Afrikaans. A harsh police response resulted in the deaths of several children, some as young as eight or nine years old. In the violence that followed, more than 575 people died, at least 134 of them under the age of eighteen.

Youthful ANC supporters abandoned school in droves; some vowed to "make South Africa ungovernable" to protest against apartheid education. Others left the country for military training camps run by the ANC or other liberation armies, mostly in Angola, Tanzania, or Eastern Europe. "Liberation before education" became their battle cry.

The schools suffered further damage as a result of the unrest of 1976. Vandals and arsonists damaged or destroyed many schools and school property. Students who tried to attend school and their teachers were sometimes attacked, and administrators found it increasingly difficult to maintain normal school activities. Some teachers and administrators joined in the protests.

The National Policy for General Affairs Act (No. 76) of 1984 provided some improvements in black education but maintained the overall separation called for by the Bantu education system. This act gave the minister of national education authority to determine general policy for syllabuses, examinations, and certification qualifications in all institutions of formal and informal education. But responsibility for implementing these policies was divided among numerous government departments and offices, resulting in a bewildering array of educational authorities: For example, the Department of Education and Training was responsible for black education outside the homelands. Each of the three houses of parliament—for whites, coloureds, and Indians—had an education department for one racial group, and each of the ten homelands had its own education department. In addition, several other government departments managed specific aspects of education.

Education was compulsory for all racial groups, but at different ages, and the law was enforced differently. Whites were required to attend school between the ages of seven and sixteen. Black children were required to attend school from age seven until the equivalent of seventh grade or the age of sixteen, but this law was enforced only weakly, and not at all in areas where schools were unavailable. For Asians and coloured children, education was compulsory between the ages of seven and fifteen.

The discrepancies in education among racial groups were glaring. Teacher: pupil ratios in primary schools averaged 1:18 in white schools, 1:24 in Asian schools, 1:27 in coloured schools, and 1:39 in black schools. Moreover, whereas 96 percent of all teachers in white schools had teaching certificates, only 15 percent of teachers in black schools were certified. Secondary-school pass rates for black pupils in the nationwide, standardized high-school graduation exams were less than one-half the pass rate for whites.

As the government implemented the 1984 legislation, new violence flared up in response to the limited constitutional reforms that continued to exclude blacks (see Constitutional Change, ch. 4). Finally, the government began to signal its awareness that apartheid could not endure. By 1986 President P.W. Botha (1984–89) had stated that the concept of apartheid was "outdated," and behind-the-scenes negotiations had begun between government officials and imprisoned ANC leader Nelson Mandela. The gap between government spending on education for different racial groups slowly began to narrow, and penalties for defying apartheid rules in education began to ease.

The School System in the 1990s

Reorganizing education was one of the most daunting tasks the government faced as apartheid laws were being lifted in the 1990s. President Frederik W. (F.W.) de Klerk, in a speech to Parliament in January 1993, stressed the need for a nonracial school system, with enough flexibility to allow communities to preserve their religious and cultural values and their home language. De Klerk established the Education Co-ordination Service to manage education during the political transition of the 1990s, and he charged it with eliminating the bureaucratic duplication that had resulted from apartheid education.

In August 1993, de Klerk gathered together leading experts on education in the National Education and Training Forum to formulate a policy framework for restructuring education. Anticipating rising education costs, the government earmarked 23.5 percent of the national budget in fiscal year (FY—see Glossary) 1993–94 for education. It established new education offices and gave them specific responsibilities within the reorganization plan. When the new school year began in January

1995, all government-run primary and secondary schools were officially integrated, and the first stage of the transformation in education had begun almost without violence.

The new policies were difficult to implement, however, and many policy details remained to be worked out. Education was compulsory for all children between age seven and age sixteen, for example, but there had not been enough time or resources to provide adequate schools and teachers for the entire school-age population. The schools received government assistance for teachers' salaries only; they had to charge fees for equipment and supplies, but pupils who could not pay school fees could not be expelled from school.

In 1995 South Africa had a total of 20,780 primary and secondary schools. Of these, 20,303 belonged to the government, and 477 were private. In addition, 226 specialized schools were in operation for gifted pupils or students with special needs (see table 3, Appendix). More than 11 million pupils were enrolled, about 6.95 million in primary school and 4.12 million in secondary schools. The number of teachers in the regular primary and secondary schools was 344,083, of whom 226,900 were black. Of the white teachers, more than 60 percent were Afrikaners. Men teachers were paid substantially more than women; women's salaries averaged 83 percent of men's salaries for the same job with equal qualifications.

Higher Education

University-level education suffered under apartheid. When the NP came to power in 1948, there were ten government-subsidized institutions of higher learning—four with classes taught in English; four with classes taught in Afrikaans; one bilingual correspondence university; and the South African Native College at Fort Hare, in which most classes were taught in English but other languages were permitted. The four Afrikaans universities and one of the English-language universities (Rhodes University) admitted white students only. Students of all races attended the University of Cape Town, the University of the Witwatersrand, and the University of Natal, although some classes at these universities were segregated.

The Extension of University Education Act (No. 45) of 1959 prohibited established universities from accepting black students, except with the special permission of a cabinet minister. The government opened several new universities and colleges for black, coloured, and Indian students, and these students were allowed to attend a "white" university only if their "own" institutions became too overcrowded. The University of the North, established in 1959, for example, admitted students of Tsonga, Sotho, Venda, or Tswana descent only.

The 1959 law also gave the central government control over the South African Native College at Fort Hare (later the University of Fort Hare), and the government instituted a new policy of admitting Xhosa students only to that school. Several *technikons* (advanced-level technical schools) gave preference to students of one ethnic group. Overall, however, the 1959 legislation reduced opportunities for university education for blacks, and by 1978 only 20 percent of all university students in South Africa were black. During the 1980s, several university administrations, anticipating the dismal impact of the long-term racial biases in education, began admitting students from all racial groups.

As of the mid-1990s South Africa has twenty-one major universities, which are government-financed and open to students of all races. In addition, secondary-school graduates can attend one of fifteen *technikons*, 128 technical colleges, and seventy teacher-training colleges (which do not require high-school certificates for admission), or another in a wide array of teacher training institutions (see table 4, Appendix). Students in universities and teacher-training colleges numbered 362,000 in 1994, and the institutions themselves had 14,460 academic staff members. At technical colleges and *technikons*, students numbered 191,087, and teaching staff numbered 5,532.

Each university administration is headed by a government-appointed chancellor, the institution's senior authority; a vice chancellor; and a university council. The chancellor is often a civic leader or political figure whose primary function is to represent the university to the community. The university council, comprising members of the university and the community, names the vice chancellor or rector, who controls the administration of the institution. The vice chancellor generally holds office until age sixty-five.

The university senate manages academic and faculty affairs, under the vice chancellor's authority. Each university sets its own tuition costs and receives government funding based on student:faculty ratios and tuition receipts. The university academic year lasts thirty-six weeks; school terms and vacation periods are set by the university council. The government establishes general degree requirements, but the individual

university's council and administration set specific requirements for each campus.

A variety of adult education opportunities are available.
These include classes in basic literacy, in technical and vocational subjects, and in sports and leisure activities. Two universities, those of Cape Town and Witwatersrand, offer classes for
instructors in adult education, and Witwatersrand has a course
leading to a diploma for adult educators. Some of these programs are being reoriented in the 1990s to emphasize literacy
training for the more than 8 million adults who cannot read.

Health and Welfare

South Africa's population in general enjoys good health,
compared with other African countries in the 1990s. Rural
health care compares favorably with delivery systems in Kenya
and in Nigeria, for example. The system reflects the biases of
apartheid, in that superior care is available to wealthy urban
residents, most of whom were white as of 1995, and inferior services are available to the poor, who are black. These differences
began to narrow in the early 1990s, as apartheid was being dismantled. Under the government's 1994 blueprint for social
and economic development, the Reconstruction and Development Programme (RDP), R14 billion (for value of the rand—
see Glossary) was set aside for improvements in health care.

Incidence of Disease

Tuberculosis is the most prevalent disease reported to health
officials in the 1990s. European settlers probably introduced
this disease into southern Africa in the seventeenth or the eighteenth century, and it was perhaps reintroduced by nineteenth-
century gold and diamond miners from Europe or China. Miners of all races lived in unhealthy and unsanitary conditions
during the first decades of industrial development, and these
conditions contributed to the spread of the disease in the early
twentieth century. From the beginning, whites who became ill
received better treatment than others. In 1955 tuberculosis
reached epidemic proportions among black mineworkers,
which prompted the South African Chamber of Mines to
improve mineworkers' dwellings and health care services.

About 90 percent of tuberculosis cases reported after 1970
were among blacks. The rate of infection appeared to decline
between 1970 and 1985, and the government, citing this

Business students in a Pretoria technical college
Courtesy Embassy of South Africa, Washington

decline, ended compulsory tuberculosis vaccinations in 1987. Although tuberculosis among blacks increased after that, health officials believed other causes were important. Overcrowding in urban housing projects increased in the late 1980s, and many tuberculosis patients discontinued treatment after only a few weeks, rather than the prescribed year. The South African National Tuberculosis Association reported that its case load increased from 88,000 cases in 1985 to more than 124,000 in 1990 and continued to increase after that. More than 6,000 people died of tuberculosis and related effects each year in the early 1990s. More than 47,800 new cases of the disease were reported in 1994.

Malaria ranked second among reported diseases, again affecting whites less than other racial groups. This disease reached epidemic levels in the late nineteenth and the early twentieth century, especially in the northern Natal and the lowveld areas of the northern and eastern Transvaal. During the 1960s, there were 2.7 cases of malaria per 100,000 non-whites, compared with only 1.1 cases per 100,000 whites. As malaria increased during the 1970s and the 1980s, the gap between races widened and these rates rose to 40.5 cases per 100,000 among blacks, Asians, and people of mixed race, compared with six cases per 100,000 whites in the early 1990s. In 1994 health officials reported 4,194 cases of malaria nationwide.

Several factors probably contributed to the changing patterns in malaria incidence. The use of insecticides helped reduce the incidence of malaria temporarily in the 1950s. The 1972 worldwide ban on the insecticide, DDT, though only partially observed in South Africa, was followed by a steady increase in the incidence of malaria. At the same time, mosquitoes and other parasites became more resistant to chemicals and medicines. Residential patterns also changed, and several mosquito-infested areas of the country were permanently settled. For example, the black homelands of Venda, Gazankulu, and Lebowa were established in heavily malaria-infested areas of the northern Transvaal.

Most other diseases decreased between 1970 and 1990. In keeping with world trends, smallpox was virtually eradicated in South Africa by the 1970s. Diphtheria declined to almost negligible levels—fewer than 0.1 cases per 100,000 people—by 1990. Leprosy showed similar trends, diminishing to 0.5 cases per 100,000 in 1990.

Typhoid continues to appear in scattered areas of the country in the 1990s, and most typhoid cases are among blacks. In the early 1990s, between twenty-five and thirty-five cases of typhoid were reported per 100,000 blacks, per year, compared with fewer than eight cases per 100,000 whites, Indians, and coloureds. A total of 581 new cases were reported in 1994. Measles outbreaks remained fairly steady in the early 1990s, with thirty to seventy new cases per 100,000 whites, coloureds, and Indians, and sixty to 150 cases per 100,000 blacks, each year. In 1994 a total of 1,672 cases of measles were reported. Other common ailments, such as gastroenteritis, kill several hundred black South Africans each year, even though these diseases are easily treatable in South African hospitals.

Infectious and parasitic diseases cause roughly 12 percent of all deaths among blacks but only 2 percent of deaths among whites. Health officials attribute the high incidence of infectious diseases in poor areas to the lack of clean water and sewage disposal systems. As a result, these services are high priorities in the government's development plans for the late 1990s.

Heart disease and cancer, which are common in industrialized nations, affect whites more than other racial groups in South Africa. Heart disease accounts for about 38 percent of all deaths among whites in the 1990s, compared with only 13 percent of deaths among blacks. Cancerous tumors are responsible for 18 percent of deaths among whites, but for only 8 percent of deaths among blacks.

Acquired Immune Deficiency Syndrome (AIDS)

Although the incidence of sexually transmitted diseases had declined from 1966 through the 1980s, the overall rate of infection increased after 1990, and among these diseases, acquired immune deficiency syndrome (AIDS) raised the greatest fears. South Africa's first recorded death from AIDS occurred in 1982, although the risks of AIDS were not widely publicized at the time. In 1985 health officials began testing blood to prevent AIDS transmission through transfusion.

By early 1991, 613 cases of AIDS had been reported nationwide, and 270 people were known to have died from the disease. Officials at the South African Institute of Medical Research estimated at that time that 15,000 people were infected with human immunodeficiency virus (HIV). The World Health Organization (WHO) reported 1,123 cases of AIDS in South Africa in 1992. By March 1996, the number of reported AIDS cases had reached 10,351.

Some health researchers estimated that between 800,000 and 1 million South Africans were HIV-positive in the mid-1990s. More than 500—perhaps as many as 700—people were becoming infected each day, according to these estimates, and the rate of infection was likely to double every thirteen months in the late 1990s. These figures suggested that between 4 million and 8 million people would be HIV-positive by the year 2000. Estimates of the number of likely deaths from AIDS in the early twenty-first century ranged as high as 1 million.

As in most of Africa, AIDS is primarily an urban phenomenon in South Africa, but it has spread rapidly into rural areas and has affected a disproportionate number of people between the ages of fifteen and forty. Recognizing the potential impact on the country's economic output, the South African Chamber of Mines, the nation's largest employer, began an aggressive campaign to educate workers and to curtail the spread of AIDS in the 1980s, after the chamber's health adviser warned that AIDS could be the country's most serious health problem by the late 1990s. The industry already had established treatment and counseling services for workers afflicted with sexually transmitted diseases, so it used this network to promote its campaign against AIDS. The Chamber of Mines found an incidence of only 0.05 percent of HIV infection among more than 30,000 mine workers in a baseline study in 1986. It then initiated random blood testing on 2,000 to 3,000 workers each month and found that the rate of HIV infection had risen to 6 percent by 1992.

The government was able to build on the early efforts of the Chamber of Mines to help stem the spread of HIV and AIDS in the 1990s. Government officials, health specialists from the ANC, and others established the National AIDS Convention of South Africa to coordinate the nationwide campaign emphasizing public education. In 1993 the National AIDS Convention, working with the Chamber of Mines, WHO, and other international experts, received financial assistance from the European Union (EU—see Glossary) for its efforts. In 1994 and 1995, however, the campaign became embroiled in funding disputes and was slowed by partisan political debate.

Although health officials were concerned about the spread of AIDS, some were still more concerned about the incidence of tuberculosis in the mid-1990s. They argued that tuberculosis caused as many as thirty-six deaths each day, on average, compared with less than one death per day from AIDS. Moreover, methods for preventing the spread of tuberculosis were already well known and could help in the fight against AIDS. Health officials had reported that people infected with tuberculosis are more susceptible to HIV infection and more likely to develop AIDS symptoms in a shorter time after being infected, and that these AIDS sufferers are likely to die sooner than those free of tuberculosis.

Health Care Services

Until 1990 apartheid was practiced in most hospitals, to varying degrees. Some admitted patients of one racial group only, and others designated operating rooms and special care facilities for patients of certain racial groups. This practice often led to expensive and redundant services and organizations, and, at times, unnecessary neglect. A few medical personnel, nonetheless, ignored apartheid-related restrictions, especially in emergency rooms and public clinics. By the early 1990s, deliberate racial distinctions were beginning to disappear from hospital care in general. Health care services continued to reflect the status of the communities in which they were found, however; wealthier people had easier access to health care and generally received better care.

South Africa's health care facilities include hospitals, day hospitals, community health care centers, and clinics. In 1995 about 25,600 doctors as well as 24,500 supplementary health professionals, 160,000 nurses and nurses' auxiliaries, and more than 5,100 dentists and dental specialists were registered with the South African Medical and Dental Council (SAMDC) and the South African Nursing Council. In the early 1990s, only about 1,500 doctors, nationwide, were black. Wealthy white areas averaged one doctor per 1,200 people; the poorest black homelands, one doctor for 13,000 people.

Seven universities have medical schools, and six provide dental training. Nurses are trained at several universities, hospitals, and nursing schools. More than 300 hospitals are managed entirely or in part by provincial governments, and 255 hospitals are privately operated. There are an estimated 108,000 hospital beds nationwide, and almost 24,800 beds in psychiatric hospitals.

The South African Red Cross renders emergency, health, and community services, and operates ambulance services, senior citizens' homes, and air rescue services across the nation, but primarily in urban areas. Some areas also have twenty-four-hour-a-day poison control centers, child-assistance phone services, rape crisis centers, and suicide prevention programs.

One of the interim government's highest priorities in the mid-1990s is the prevention of childhood death and disease through nationwide immunization programs. The incidence of tetanus, measles, malaria, and other communicable diseases is high, especially in the former African homelands. For this reason, one of President Nelson Mandela's first actions after assuming office in May 1994 was to implement a program of free health care for children under the age of six. By early 1996, officials estimated that at least 75 percent of all infants had been immunized against polio and measles.

Malnutrition and starvation also occur in a few, especially rural, areas. These problems are being addressed through other elements of the government's RDP of the 1990s (see Postapartheid Reconstruction, ch. 3). Minister of Health Nkosazana Zuma noted in December 1994 that only 20 percent of South Africans have any form of health insurance. The government plans to institute a program of free universal primary health care, but health officials estimated in early 1996 that it might take ten years to implement the plan fully.

Social Welfare

Disabilities and the Aged

Social welfare services in the 1990s include care for the disabled and the aged, alcohol and drug-rehabilitation programs, previous offenders' programs, and child care services. At least 1,742 private welfare organizations and numerous government agencies administer these programs.

The National Welfare Act (No. 100) of 1978 established a coordinating council, the South African Welfare Council, to help manage these diverse programs. Amendments to the act in 1987 signaled the government's growing awareness of the need to narrow differences in social welfare among racial groups. In the early 1990s, the government spent about R1 billion per year on welfare programs, excluding old-age pensions. About one-half of that amount was spent on whites. Government spending under the RDP in the mid-1990s was geared toward improving social services for other racial groups.

About 3.5 million South Africans are physically disabled in the mid-1990s. The government's approach is to encourage independent, although sometimes assisted, living for them. Assistance is sometimes available through outpatient rehabilitation centers, counseling services, workshops, and sheltered employment centers. Families and church groups are still important in assisting the handicapped, especially the mentally and psychologically impaired, although government-funded services are available for the blind and the deaf. Substance abuse programs, especially for alcohol abuse or marijuana dependence, are also available in some communities.

The government administers about 1.8 million old-age (nonmilitary) pensions in the 1990s that represent a total of about R4 billion. The government began narrowing the gap in pensions for different racial groups in 1992 and pledged to elimi-

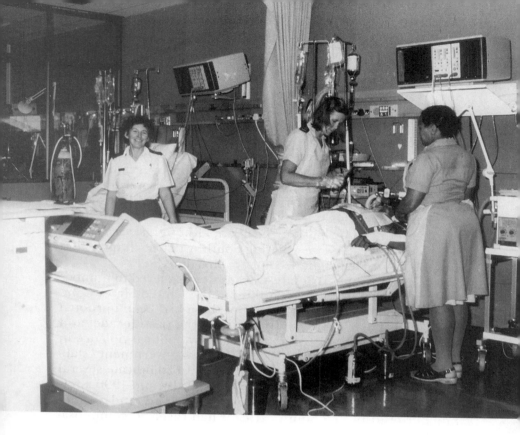

Intensive-care unit at Morningside Medi Clinic,
Bryanston (Johannesburg)
Courtesy Embassy of South Africa, Washington

nate such disparities. But elderly black and other citizens continued to claim that they were disadvantaged because of their racial identity in the mid-1990s. Government welfare agencies also provide veterans' benefits, adoption and foster care services, services for alcoholics and drug addicts, and services for abused and neglected children.

Refugees

Most refugees in South Africa in the 1980s and 1990s were from Mozambique, fleeing that country's civil war. Estimates of their number varied widely, in part because many other Mozambican migrant workers were in South Africa during that time. The number of refugees was particularly difficult to estimate because until 1993, South African officials sometimes

denied access to refugee camps for international observers trying to monitor the refugees' living conditions.

In early 1994, officials estimated that perhaps 1 million
Mozambicans were working in South Africa, legally or illegally,
and that perhaps as many as 500,000 were refugees. Although
only a few took advantage of a repatriation program implemented by the United Nations High Commissioner for Refugees (UNHCR) in April 1994, in early 1995 relief workers
estimated the number of refugees at about 200,000. This number was reduced by half during 1995, although several thousand Mozambicans were entering South Africa each month in
early 1995—some for the second or third time.

Internally displaced South Africans were believed to number
at least 500,000 in 1995, according to the United States Committee on Refugees (USCR). Most of these had been uprooted
by official apartheid-related policies in the past decade, and
perhaps 10,000 or more were displaced by political violence in
KwaZulu-Natal in the early 1990s. The new government established a Land Claims Court and planned to adjudicate several
thousand of such claims by the late 1990s. By mid-1996 a few
cases had been resolved by restoring lost land, and a small
number of displaced South Africans had received compensation for their losses.

Narcotics

After South Africa's international isolation ended and border trade increased in the early 1990s, problems associated
with narcotics trafficking and drug use increased dramatically,
according to the South African Police Service (SAPS). In 1994
South African authorities confiscated more than 2.4 million
ounces of cocaine; nearly 25,000 grams of heroin; more than
16,000 units of LSD; 27,000 ounces of hashish, and 7 million
kilograms of cannabis (marijuana), according to police
records, and most of these figures were expected to increase in
1995 and 1996. At the same time, officials at the National
Council on Alcoholism and Drug Dependence reported an
increase in problems related to substance abuse and addiction,
and police officials reported that narcotics dealers often were
involved in other forms of crime, such as arms smuggling, bur-
glaries, or car hijackings.

Women in Society

In general, all racial and ethnic groups in South Africa have long-standing beliefs concerning gender roles, and most are based on the premise that women are less important, or less deserving of power, than men. Most African traditional social organizations are male centered and male dominated. Even in the 1990s, in some rural areas of South Africa, for example, wives walk a few paces behind their husbands in keeping with traditional practices. Afrikaner religious beliefs, too, include a strong emphasis on the theoretically biblically based notion that women's contributions to society should normally be approved by, or be on behalf of, men.

Twentieth-century economic and political developments presented South African women with both new obstacles and new opportunities to wield influence. For example, labor force requirements in cities and mining areas have often drawn men away from their homes for months at a time, and, as a result, women have borne many traditionally male responsibilities in the village and home. Women have had to guarantee the day-to-day survival of their families and to carry out financial and legal transactions that otherwise would have been reserved for men.

Women and Apartheid

Apartheid imposed new restrictions on African women beginning in the 1950s. Many lived in squalor in the former homelands, where malnutrition, illness, and infant mortality were much higher than in urban areas. Other women who followed their husbands into cities or mining areas lived in inadequate, and often illegal, housing near industrial compounds. Women often left their own families to commute long distances to low-wage jobs in the domestic work force in white neighborhoods. Substantial numbers were temporary workers in agriculture; and a growing number of women joined the burgeoning industrial work force, as has been carefully researched in Iris Berger's *Threads of Solidarity: Women in South African Industry, 1900–1980.*

Women became the major source of resistance to many race-related restrictions during the apartheid era, especially the pass laws, which required Africans to carry documents permitting them to be in white-occupied areas. The Women's Defence of the Constitution League, later known as the Black Sash, was formed in 1954, first to demonstrate against such laws and later to assist pass-law violators. Black Sash established pass-law advice centers in many cities and helped reduce sentences or assist violators in other ways.

The African National Congress Women's League (ANCWL), formed in 1943, was able to organize more than 20,000 women to march on government buildings in Pretoria to protest against the pass laws and other apartheid restrictions in 1955. Their protests eventually failed, however. In the early 1960s, pass-law restrictions were extended to women and new legislation restricted black women without steady employment to stays of no more than seventy-two hours in any urban area. Also in 1964, many senior ANC leaders were arrested, and others fled from South Africa or went underground, and the ANCWL became almost defunct.

Women continued to join the urban work force, and by the late 1980s, women made up at least 90 percent of the domestic work force and 36 percent of the industrial work force, according to labor union estimates. Women's wages were lower than men's even for the same job, however. In addition, positions normally held by women had long hours and few benefits, such as sick leave; women often were dismissed without advance notice and without any type of termination pay.

Conservative Afrikaner women have organized in support of Afrikaner cultural preservation and apartheid since the 1970s. The Kappiekommando was established in the late 1970s to demand a return to traditional Afrikaner values. This organization was named for its distinctive Voortrekker dress, which caused some young Afrikaners and others to ridicule its members' appearance and their militancy. The Kappiekommando's militant opposition to political reforms eventually contributed to its marginalization, even among staunchly conservative Afrikaners.

The Afrikanervroue-Kenkrag (AVK), another Afrikaner women's organization, was formed in 1983 and worked primarily to oppose racial integration in schools and other public places. AVK membership grew to about 1,000 during the mid-1980s. The group published a monthly newsletter and cooperated with other Afrikaner organizations, but like the Kappiekommando, the AVK lost support when mainstream Afrikaner political leaders began working toward racial inclusiveness in the 1990s.

Women in the 1990s

The ANCWL was resurrected in 1990, after the ban on the

ANC was lifted, and women in more than 500 towns and cities organized to press for consideration of gender issues in the upcoming constitutional negotiations. At the insistence of its Women's League, the ANC accepted, in principle, the proposal that women should receive one-third of the political appointments in the new government. Other symbolic gains by the ANCWL have included strong policy stands on women's rights and protection against abuse and exploitation, but translating these standards into enforceable laws proved to be a difficult task.

Women are achieving new prominence in politics as a result of the sweeping political reforms of the 1990s. In 1994 women won election to eighty of the 400 seats in the National Assembly, the only directly elected house of parliament, and a woman, Frene Ginwala, was elected Speaker of the National Assembly. Women also were elected to almost one-third of the seats in the nine provincial assemblies.

President Mandela appointed two women cabinet ministers in May 1994, and a woman succeeded the late minister of housing, Joe Slovo, after his death in January 1995. Three women were deputy ministers in early 1995. One of these, President Mandela's former wife, Winnie Mandela, was appointed deputy minister of arts, culture, science, and technology.

Mrs. Mandela had been a courageous fighter for the rights of the downtrodden for more than two decades while her husband was in prison, and she had achieved high office within the ANC. But her association with violent elements of the ANC Youth League in the late 1980s and other accusations against her in the 1990s led many within the ANC to shun her. She was also outspoken in her criticism of the government in early 1995 for its failure to move more quickly to ease the extreme poverty of many citizens. Her defiance led to her removal from office in March of that year.

Eliminating violence against women and improving educational opportunities for women are almost universally supported goals in South Africa in the mid-1990s, but these goals receive only rhetorical support, in many cases. More urgent priorities are to eliminate the vestiges of apartheid legislation and to improve economic and social conditions for the very poor, for children, and for other groups that were especially disadvantaged in recent decades. Gender-related inequities appear likely to be decried, but relegated to secondary importance, well into the twenty-first century.

*　　*　　*

Studies of South Africa's rich cultural heritage begin with ethnographic classics by Hilda Kuper on the Swazi, Max Gluckman on the Zulu, Isaac Schapera on the Tswana, J. D. Krige on the Lobedu, John Marshall and Elizabeth Marshall Thomas on the San, and Monica Hunter Wilson on the Pondo. Their works are available in numerous monographs and collections of articles, especially in the International African Institute's Ethnographic Survey of Africa, which includes valuable field-work observations and initial analyses. More recent monographs include Jeffrey B. Peires's *The House of Phalo: A History of the Xhosa People in the Days of Their Independence* and Gerhard Maré's *Brothers Born of Warrior Blood: Politics and Ethnicity in South Africa* on the Zulu.

South Africa's complex society cannot be fully understood by analyzing specific cultures, however. Patrick J. Furlong's *Between Crown and Swastika: The Impact of the Radical Right on the Afrikaner Nationalist Movement in the Fascist Era* describes the growth of authoritarian politics in South Africa. Religious developments are presented in David Chidester's *Religions of South Africa.* Iris Berger's *Threads of Solidarity: Women in South African Industry, 1900–1980* describes women's role in the growth of the working class. Recent national developments are examined by Marina Ottaway in *South Africa: The Struggle for a New Order* and by a variety of authors in *South Africa: The Political Economy of Transformation* edited by Stephen John Stedman. The complexities of the rapid changes of the 1990s are documented by Timothy Sisk in *Democratization in South Africa.* Numerous articles in the *Journal of Southern African Studies* provide insights into political and social change under apartheid.

Available information on population, health, and education—although incomplete—has been carefully compiled each year by the South African Institute of Race Relations in its *Race Relations Survey.* The South African government's *South Africa Yearbook,* originally published as the *South Africa Official Yearbook,* and numerous reports by the Central Statistical Service include available data on many social issues. Urbanization and social change are surveyed from diverse points of view in *The Apartheid City and Beyond: Urbanization and Social Change in South Africa* edited by David M. Smith. Environmental concerns are outlined in Hamish Main and Stephen Wyn Williams's *Environ-*

ment and Housing in Third World Cities. (For further information and complete citations, see Bibliography.)

Chapter 3. The Economy

Sheep outnumber people in areas of the Great Karoo.

TRADING ON JOHANNESBURG'S financial markets reached a new all-time high on April 26, 1994, reflecting the buoyant mood of voters of all races who were about to participate in the country's first democratic elections. As South Africa emerged from the economic stagnation and international isolation of the apartheid era, the new government and its theme of economic reconstruction received international acclaim and encouragement. At the same time, however, it faced conflicting pressures to speed economic growth, to strengthen South Africa's standing among international investors and donors, and, at the same time, to improve living conditions for the majority of citizens.

South Africa's economy had been shaped over several centuries by its abundant natural resources and by the attempts of immigrant populations to dominate and to exploit those who had arrived before them. For most of the twentieth century, its mineral wealth had surpassed that of almost any other country in the world, except the Soviet Union. South Africa produced nearly half of the world's gold and ranked among the top ten producers of a dozen other valuable minerals, including diamonds and copper. The mining industries provided the foundation for the strongest economy on the continent, which, by the mid-twentieth century, included a comprehensive transportation system, an extensive electric power grid, and a significant manufacturing sector. South Africa's main resource deficiency is oil, and as a result, many industries rely on coal rather than on imported fuels.

By the mid-1980s, the economy was distorted by government policies designed to bolster the economic and political power of a small minority and to exclude many of South Africa's citizens, selected by race, from significant participation in the nation's wealth. Basic needs were unmet, resulting in hunger, malnutrition, and undereducation, especially in rural areas. Industrial development could not be sustained through domestic resources, and there was stagnation in some areas when foreign capital was reduced in the face of strong international pressures for political reform. Because the mining industry continued to dominate the economy, wide fluctuations—especially in the price of gold—eroded currency values and reduced the country's ability to import goods. At the same time, keeping black wages low, which was crucial to profits in all areas of the economy, perpetuated the discrimination that provoked widespread protests and condemnation.

By the early 1990s, the weaknesses in the economy were increasingly evident despite the country's dazzling mineral wealth. Some segments of the population were poorer, and living in more difficult circumstances, than many people in far less developed African countries. Moreover, a poorly educated, impoverished majority of the population could not provide the skills and the resources that the country's infrastructure and labor market required. The government cast off the constraints of apartheid (see Glossary) in the early 1990s, in part to confront the serious economic problems caused by that system. The new government in the mid-1990s faces the enormous challenges of improving living standards and managing the country's resources profitably.

Historical Development

Before South Africa's vast mineral wealth was discovered in the late nineteenth century, there was a general belief that southern Africa was almost devoid of the riches that had drawn Europeans to the rest of the continent. South Africa had no known gold deposits such as those the Portuguese had sought in West Africa in the fifteenth century. The region did not attract many slave traders, in part because local populations were sparsely settled. Valuable crops such as palm oil, rubber, and cocoa, which were found elsewhere on the continent, were absent. Although the local economy was rich in some areas—based on mixed farming and herding—only ivory was traded to any extent. Most local products were not sought for large-scale consumption in Europe.

Instead, Europeans first settled southern Africa to resupply their trading expeditions bound for other parts of the world (see Origins of Settlement, ch. 1). In 1652 the Dutch East India Company settled a few employees at a small fort at present-day Cape Town and ordered them to provide fresh food for the company's ships that rounded the Cape on their way to East Africa and Asia. This nucleus of European settlement quickly spread outward from the fort, first to trade with the local Khoikhoi hunting populations and later to seize their land for European farmers. Smallpox epidemics swept the area in the late eighteenth century, and Europeans who had come to rely on Khoikhoi labor enslaved many of the survivors of the epidemics.

By the early nineteenth century, when the Cape settlement came under British rule, 26,000 Dutch farmers had settled the area from Stellenbosch to the Great Fish River (see fig. 7). In 1820 the British government sponsored 5,000 more settlers who also established large cattle ranches, relying on African labor. But the European immigrants, like earlier arrivals in the area, engaged primarily in subsistence farming and produced little for export.

The discovery of diamonds in 1869 and of gold in 1886 revolutionized the economy. European investment flowed in; by the end of the nineteenth century, it was equivalent to all European investment in the rest of Africa. International banks and private lenders increased cash and credit available to local farmers, miners, and prospectors, and they, in turn, placed growing demands for land and labor on the local African populations. The Europeans resorted to violence to defend their economic interests, sometimes clashing with those who refused to relinquish their freedom or their land. Eventually, as the best land became scarce, groups of settlers clashed with one another, and rival Dutch and British populations fought for control over the land (see Industrialization and Imperialism, 1870–1910, ch. 1).

South Africa was drawn into the international economy through its exports, primarily diamonds and gold, and through its own increasing demand for a variety of agricultural imports. The cycle of economic growth was stimulated by the continual expansion of the mining industry, and with newfound wealth, consumer demand fueled higher levels of trade.

In the first half of the twentieth century, government economic policies were designed to meet local consumer demand and to reduce the nation's reliance on its mining sector by providing incentives for farming and for establishing manufacturing enterprises. But the government also saw its role as helping to defend white farmers and businessmen from African competition. In 1913 the Natives Land Act reserved most of the land for white ownership, forcing many black farmers to work as wage laborers on land they had previously owned. When the act was amended in 1936, black land ownership was restricted to 13 percent of the country, much of it heavily eroded.

White farmers received other privileges, such as loans from a government Land Bank (created in 1912), labor law protection, and crop subsidies. Marketing boards, which were established to stabilize production of many crops, paid more for produce from white farmers than for produce from black farmers. All farm activity suffered from the cyclical droughts that swept the subcontinent, but white farmers received greater government protection against economic losses.

During the 1920s, to encourage the fledgling manufacturing industries, the government established state corporations to provide inexpensive electricity and steel for industrial use, and it imposed import tariffs to protect local manufacturers. Again black entrepreneurs were discouraged, and new laws limited the rights of black workers, creating a large pool of low-cost industrial labor. By the end of the 1930s, the growing number of state-owned enterprises dominated the manufacturing sector, and black entrepreneurs continued to be pressured to remain outside the formal economy.

Manufacturing experienced new growth during and after World War II. Many of the conditions necessary for economic expansion had been present before the war—cities were growing, agriculture was being consolidated into large farms with greater emphasis on commercial production, and mine owners and shareholders had begun to diversify their investments into other sectors. As the war ended, local consumer demand rose to new highs, and with strong government support—and international competitors at bay—local agriculture and manufacturing began to expand.

The government increased its role in the economy, especially in manufacturing, during the 1950s and the 1960s. It also initiated large-scale programs to promote the commercial cultivation of corn and wheat. Government investments through the state-owned Industrial Development Corporation (IDC) helped to establish local textile and pulp and paper industries, as well as state corporations to produce fertilizers, chemicals, oil, and armaments. Both manufacturing and agricultural production expanded rapidly, and by 1970 manufacturing output exceeded that of mining.

Despite the appearance of self-sustaining economic growth during the postwar period, the country's economy continued to be susceptible to its historical limitations: recurrent drought, overreliance on gold exports, and the costs and consequences of the use of disenfranchised labor. While commercial agriculture developed into an important source of export revenue, production plummeted during two major droughts, from 1960 to 1966 and from 1981 to 1985. Gold continued to be the most important export and revenue earner; yet, as the price of gold fluctuated, especially during the 1980s, South Africa's exchange rate and ability to import goods suffered.

Manufacturing, in particular, was seriously affected by down-swings in the price of gold, in part because it relied on imported machinery and capital. Some capital-intensive industries were able to expand, but only with massive foreign loans. As a result, many industries were insulated from the rising labor militancy, especially among black workers, which sparked disputes and slowed productivity in the late 1980s. As black labor increasingly voiced its frustrations, and foreign banks cut short their loans because of mounting instability, even capital-intensive industries felt the impact of apartheid on profits.

The economy was in recession from March 1989 through most of 1993, largely in response to worldwide economic conditions and the long-term effects of apartheid. It registered only negligible, or negative, growth in most quarters. High inflation had become chronic, driving up costs in all sectors. Living standards of the majority of black citizens either fell or remained dangerously low, while those of many whites also began to decline. Economic growth continued to depend on decent world prices for gold and on the availability of foreign loans. Even as some sectors of the economy began to recover in late 1993, intense violence and political uncertainty in the face of reform slowed overall growth through 1994.

Postapartheid Reconstruction

As the African National Congress (ANC) shifted away from its liberation agenda toward a leadership role in government in the early 1990s, ANC economists, together with government and private-sector consultants, developed a blueprint for development in the late 1990s. This Reconstruction and Development Programme (RDP) analyzed nationwide living standards and proposed ways to improve government services and basic living conditions for the poor. The RDP detailed the extreme poverty of at least 17 million citizens who were living below internationally accepted minimum standards. The report estimated that 4.3 million families were without adequate housing, and some 12 million people lacked access to clean drinking water. Most homes, and many schools and hospitals, lacked electricity. An estimated 4.6 million adults were illiterate.

In May 1994, the new government adopted the RDP as the centerpiece of its economic policy, although President Nelson (Rolihlahla) Mandela was quick to reassure potential investors and donors that his government's social programs would be financed largely through cuts in existing government spending. He pledged that his government would avoid both dramatic increases in taxes and large-scale deficit spending to implement the much-needed welfare improvements.

The RDP envisioned sweeping government programs to raise living standards—to build houses and roads, to provide services, to upgrade education, and to create jobs to narrow the gap between rich and poor. By late 1994, the government had begun to implement its highest RDP priorities: a US$135 million school lunch program; a US$14 million program of free medical care for children and pregnant women; providing water and electricity to rural communities; and phasing in free, compulsory primary education for children of all races.

Government officials and ANC economists in the National Institute for Economic Policy estimated that RDP expenditures in fiscal year (FY—see Glossary) 1994–95 would amount to 2.5 billion rands (R; for value of the rand—see Glossary), or about 7 percent of government spending. They also estimated that RDP expenditures would double in FY 1995–96 and would increase by about R2.5 billion each year after that, to R12.5 billion—probably more than 25 percent of government spending—in FY 1998–99. The Development Bank of Southern Africa estimated costs approaching US$30 billion—US$19 billion in capital expenditures and US$11 billion in recurrent expenditures—by 1999. Government officials insisted that they would rely on increased trade and overall economic growth, as well as on international assistance and private-sector donations, for most of the additional revenue, and that reconstruction would be aided by a one-time, 5 percent levy on individuals and companies with taxable incomes of more than R50,000. They also predicted that the government would save money by increasing efficiency (in particular by eliminating the redundancy that had been necessary to provide services to separate racial groups under apartheid) and by reducing military expenditures.

To help finance the RDP, the government also undertook negotiations to sell some national assets to private citizens, despite the ANC's earlier opposition to privatization. Senior government officials, including the president, accepted salary

*Shopkeeper in a Lebowa township rewards his
young assistants with oranges.
Courtesy R. T. K. Scully*

cuts of between 10 percent and 20 percent to contribute to
social reconstruction. President Mandela also asked for con-
crete proposals and contributions from the business community—such as on-the-job training and employer subsidies of
housing, transportation, and education—to meet the urgent
needs defined in the RDP.

The new government launched worldwide appeals for new
trade and investment packages for South Africa, as it tried to
overcome more than a decade of international isolation. South
Africa began reentering world financial markets, establishing
new trading partners, and expanding formerly clandestine
trade ties that had long existed with many countries. International donors and investors responded cautiously at first, in
part because of the continuing high levels of urban and township violence.

After mid-1994 immigrants from other African countries arrived in large numbers—a total of perhaps a million in that year alone, according to some estimates—seeking jobs in postapartheid South Africa. Poorer neighboring states also intensified their requests for assistance from Pretoria, hoping South Africa's economic revival would increase output and trade throughout the region and that South Africa would become the region's new "engine of development."

Structure of the Economy

Gross Domestic Product

Historically, mining and agriculture contributed the most to national output. With government assistance during and after World War II, manufacturing grew to become the greatest contributor to overall gross domestic product (GDP—see Glossary), and overall economic growth in the 1960s rivaled that of Japan—averaging 5.9 percent per year in real terms (compared with the 4 percent annual average growth of the 1950s). During the 1970s, however, growth in both manufacturing and agriculture stagnated, and the services sector—especially the insurance industry, financial facilities, and transport services—became the fastest-growing economic sector (see table 5, Appendix).

The price of gold was allowed to float (relative to the rand) in the early 1970s, and by the end of the decade, high prices for gold and other export commodities sparked a brief economic recovery. Mining continued to be vital to the nation's economic future, because minerals, especially gold, dominated exports and influenced the growth of other major economic sectors, which relied on gold exports to bring in much-needed foreign exchange. Thus, even as the importance of gold in the GDP declined, it continued to affect the country's balance of payments. When gold prices (and export revenues) declined, local industries often were unable to obtain imports, such as machinery and other inputs necessary to maintain production; as a result, other exports also declined.

Economic growth slowed in the late 1970s and the early 1980s, not only because of declining gold revenues, but also because of rising prices for oil imports and increased international competition in other traditional export commodities. The first recession of this period occurred in 1976, following dramatic oil price hikes. Strong export growth based on higher gold prices helped the recovery from this recession, but the country was hit by a series of droughts in the 1980s, which seriously affected agricultural output. Further erratic changes in gold prices led to a series of booms and busts, reducing average annual GDP growth for the 1980s to only 1.5 percent.

Negligible growth in the 1980s led to an overall decline in living standards, as population growth far outpaced economic expansion. Per capita GDP declined by more than 10 percent during the decade, and for the average individual, real wealth in 1990 was no higher than it had been in 1970.

National economic stagnation continued in the early 1990s. GDP declined in 1991 and 1992, and registered only weak positive growth in 1993, according to the government's Central Statistical Service. Private consumption accounted for 57 percent of GDP in 1993, representing a minimal (0.4 percent) increase over 1992. Private consumption was constrained by high consumer indebtedness, however, and by concerns over violence and job security.

The recovery strengthened in 1994. In that year, GDP amounted to R432.8 billion (US$121.9 billion) representing 2.6 percent real growth over 1993 (see table 6, Appendix). Per capita GDP averaged about US$3,010, placing South Africa among the World Bank's (see Glossary) upper-middle-income developing countries. The recovery continued in 1995, and officials predicted GDP growth would exceed 4 percent in 1996 (see fig. 13; fig. 14).

National accounting procedures were adjusted in 1994 to incorporate the economies of the four former "independent" African homelands—Bophuthatswana, Ciskei, Transkei, and Venda. In addition, GDP measurements were adjusted upward by 5.6 percent to include a modest estimate of output in the informal sector, which had been omitted from national accounts until 1994. The informal sector constitutes a "parallel" economy, consisting primarily of unrecorded and untaxed wages, barter trade, and other unofficial receipts. For many rural families in South Africa, as in the rest of Africa, informal economic activity accounts for most of the household income.

South Africa's advanced industrial sector made it the twenty-fifth largest economy in the world, a giant among African countries in the 1990s. Per capita GDP, in 1994, compared with the rest of Africa, was topped only by the Seychelles, Réunion, and Gabon. With only about 7 percent of the population and 4 percent of the total land area of Africa, South Africa produced

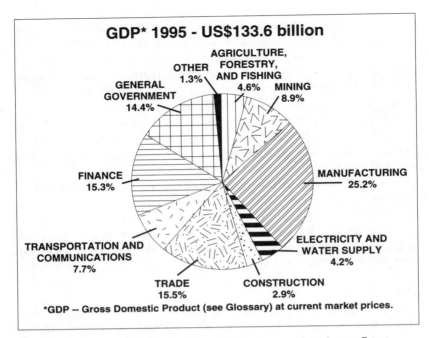

GDP* 1995 - US$133.6 billion

OTHER 1.3%

GENERAL GOVERNMENT 14.4%

AGRICULTURE, FORESTRY, AND FISHING 4.6%

MINING 8.9%

FINANCE 15.3%

MANUFACTURING 25.2%

TRANSPORTATION AND COMMUNICATIONS 7.7%

ELECTRICITY AND WATER SUPPLY 4.2%

TRADE 15.5%

CONSTRUCTION 2.9%

*GDP -- Gross Domestic Product (see Glossary) at current market prices.

Source: Based on information from Economist Intelligence Unit, *Country Report: South Africa*, No. 2, London, 1996, 3.

Figure 13. Origins of Gross Domestic Product, 1995

more than one-third of Africa's goods and services, and nearly 40 percent of its manufacturing output.

External Debt

Loan capital was readily available during the 1970s, and both the public and the private sectors borrowed heavily, often in the form of trade credits. Then in the early 1980s, foreign investments declined relative to the value of foreign loans needed to finance economic growth. As a result, equity capital dropped as a percentage of foreign debt from 60 percent in 1970 to less than 30 percent in 1984, while South Africa's loans grew from 40 percent to 70 percent of foreign debt. The government encouraged this trend by stepping in whenever foreign bankers hesitated to increase lending and stabilized indebtedness through gold swaps or by borrowing from the International Monetary Fund (IMF—see Glossary). As a result of these policies, South Africa's net indebtedness to the international banks increased sharply, and about two-thirds of its outstanding loans in 1984 had a maturity of one year or less. The banking sector was responsible for 44 percent of South Africa's foreign liabilities, and a further 16 percent had been incurred by the public sector. Only about 40 percent were private liabilities. Britain dominated foreign capital loans and investments, accounting for about 40 percent of foreign investment in 1985.

South Africa was hit with a major foreign debt crisis in 1985, when a group of banks, led by Chase Manhattan, withdrew substantial credit lines. The banks refused to roll over existing loans and called in many of the short-term loans. As a result, the value of the rand dropped precipitously, and the government temporarily closed its financial and foreign-exchange markets. Unable to meet debt obligations so suddenly, the government declared a standstill on repayments of approximately US$14 billion of South Africa's US$24 billion total external debt. Liabilities not included in the standstill were trade credits, loans from the IMF and central banks, and credits guaranteed by Paris Club (see Glossary) member governments. Publicly quoted issues of South African parastatals (state corporations) were also left out.

During the standstill, government officials met with representatives of creditor banks and drew up a rescheduling plan, which proposed extending the 1985 debt freeze until June 1987 and repaying 5 percent of the total outstanding by April 1987. An initial payment of US$420 million was made in mid-April 1986, but additional rescheduling agreements in 1987 and 1989 extended many of these loans. The 1989 agreement stipulated that the amount of debt remaining in those categories affected by the standstill, originally amounting to US$14 billion, would be reduced to roughly US$6 billion in four years.

A key problem in repaying its loans was the large, but undisclosed, portion of South Africa's debt that was denominated in hard nondollar currencies, but appreciated in dollar terms as the dollar weakened. South Africa nonetheless repaid between US$1.7 billion and US$1.9 billion of debt by 1990, and some foreign bankers were increasingly willing to refinance maturing South African credits. For example, US$300 million of US$900 million bearer bonds in deutsche marks and Swiss francs were rolled over or replaced in 1990.

There was almost no external borrowing by South Africa from 1985 to 1990, so even its slowed schedule of debt repayment made South Africa a net capital exporter during the late

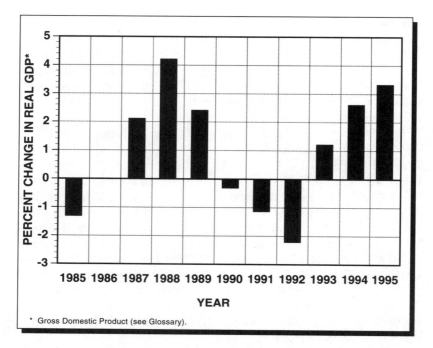

* Gross Domestic Product (see Glossary).

Source: Based on information from Nedcor Economic Unit, *South Africa's Statistical Profile, 1994*, Johannesburg, 1994, 3; and Economist Intelligence Unit, *Country Report: South Africa*, No. 1, London, 1996, 3.

Figure 14. Economic Growth, 1985–95

1980s. South Africa reduced its total disclosed foreign debt to less than US$20 billion in early 1992, down from nearly US$24 billion in 1985, according to the South African Reserve Bank. Currency fluctuations brought South Africa's international debt back to US$25.8 billion at the end of 1993, including rand-denominated foreign debt, and that figure continued to increase in 1994.

The government repaid about US$500 million in foreign debt in February 1994. At that time, South Africa was considered an under-borrower by conventional financial criteria, with a foreign debt/export ratio of about 60 percent and a foreign debt/GDP ratio of 15.1 percent, according to South African Reserve Bank figures. Overall, South Africa posted a net capital inflow of more than R8 billion in the second half of 1994. Foreign borrowing increased in 1995, when gross foreign debt rose to nearly 22 percent of GDP.

Inflation

Historically, South Africa's inflation rate was tied closely to that of its major trading partners. In the 1960s, annual inflation averaged about 3 percent. In line with world trends, it rose above 10 percent in 1974 and fluctuated between 11 and 14 percent through the early 1980s. During the late 1980s, however, South Africa's inflation rates did not decline along with those of its Western trading partners. Inflation reached a high of 18.6 percent in 1986, forcing a depreciation of the rand, and it continued in double-digit amounts after that. The erratic price of oil—a crucial import bought on the black market because of Organization of the Petroleum Exporting Countries (OPEC) sanctions—provided a consistent inflationary pressure.

Inflation continued to erode economic strength in the early 1990s, but declined to 9.1 percent in 1994. Inflation increased in early 1995 under pressure from new social spending, but declined to 8.7 percent by the end of the year. The lower rate of inflation resulted in part from a decline in food prices, the relative stability of the rand, and the lowering of import tariffs. Inflationary pressures persisted in the increase in credit purchases and strong labor demands.

Economic Distortions and Apartheid

National accounts in 1994 showed a sharp break with the past, as economic and legal data were reorganized to include citizens of all races and all jurisdictions, including former homelands. The interim constitution implemented in 1994 ended the use of racial categories to determine social and economic opportunity, but the economic system of the mid-1990s nonetheless continued to reflect some of the economic patterns that had developed during more than forty years of apartheid.

Creating the homelands and resettling people in them had drastically changed the country's population distribution and regional economic patterns in the 1970s and 1980s. Accounting for these anomalies caused confusion and obfuscation in economic data and analyses. Many homeland residents were barely able to support themselves, owing in part to the homelands' arid land, inferior roads and transportation, and overcrowding; some were therefore forced to travel great distances to work in "white" South Africa. Many of these workers were excluded from national accounts because they were not legal residents of South Africa.

It became increasingly clear in the 1980s that apartheid could not be implemented as decreed by law, and eventually many official and unofficial policies allowed some flexibility in its application. In 1986 the government called for "orderly urbanization," under which a limited numbers of blacks could live in officially "white" urban areas, as long as housing was available. Few black workers could afford to take advantage of this policy, however, and demographic trends did not change noticeably.

By the late 1980s, black poverty was so serious that the government began to take steps to alleviate some of the most dire impacts of apartheid. Government statistics then indicated that more than 16 million people were living below internationally determined minimum-subsistence levels. Using nutritional standards as an alternative measure, an estimated 2.3 million people were at severe risk from hunger and malnutrition. In 1988 the minister of national health and population development characterized the crisis as "worse than the Great Depression," and in response, the government initiated food programs and other social welfare initiatives (see Health and Welfare, ch. 2).

Role of the Government

South African economists in the 1980s described the national economy as a free-enterprise system in which the market, not the government, set most wages and prices. The reality was that the government played a major role in almost every facet of the economy, including production, consumption, and regulation. In fact, Soviet economists in the late 1980s noted that the state-owned portion of South Africa's industrial sector was greater than that in any country outside the communist bloc. The South African government owned and managed almost 40 percent of all wealth-producing assets, including iron and steel works, weapons manufacturing facilities, and energy-producing resources. Government-owned corporations and parastatals were also vital to the services sector. Marketing boards and tariff regulations intervened to influence consumer prices. Finally, a wide variety of laws governed economic activities at all levels based on race.

The government's main concern since the discovery of gold in 1886 had been balancing the growth of the mining industry against the need to diversify, in order to create sustained development and self-sufficiency. Successive governments had tried to encourage and to support local industries that could reduce imports, provide jobs, and create a multiplier effect by encouraging further industrial growth. Paul Kruger, who had led the Transvaal in the late nineteenth century, had granted monopoly concessions to industrialists; the 1920s governments of Jan C. Smuts and J.B.M. Hertzog had initiated state corporations, and the post-1948 National Party government had tried industrial decentralization (see Industrialization and Imperialism, 1870–1910; Segregation, 1910–48; and Apartheid, 1948–76, ch. 1).

Even after decades of policy shifts designed to spur development and diversification, however, South Africa's export economy in the 1980s still relied primarily on the gold-mining industry, and the government still protected import-substitution industries in order to keep them in operation. Furthermore, agriculture continued to be an uneven producer and therefore received substantial subsidies and other forms of government assistance. In the late 1980s, the government presented a blueprint for economic policy consistent with this history of economic struggle. Its central economic strategy advocated a shift toward strongly market-oriented policies, but left room for government intervention in response to social and political demands. The strategy increased the emphasis on local industrialization in order to cut imports and to create jobs. The only component of the central economic strategy that was really new was the effort to strengthen export industries, especially to increase value added through local processing of raw materials for export.

In 1994 the new Government of National Unity continued the economic policies of its predecessors, emphasizing a market orientation overall, but allowing government intervention when necessary, and maintaining import-substitution industries while trying to spur industrial development toward exports. International markets increasingly opened to South Africa, and trade flourished, especially with the new industrial giants of Asia. Senior government officials tried to downplay the ANC's longstanding commitment to nationalization of key industries in order to gain much-needed foreign investment. It was nonetheless clear that the debate over privatization would continue at least through the rest of the decade.

Legal Restrictions

Two legislative pillars of apartheid—the Natives Land Act (No. 27) of 1913 (and its amendment in 1936) and the Group Areas Act (No. 41) of 1950—limited African economic and business activities in both rural and urban areas (see The Legislative Implementation of Apartheid, ch. 1). These acts were repealed in 1991, but few blacks could yet afford to move into formerly white areas without financial assistance. Numerous other laws and regulations had restricted black economic activities and employment, especially the Mines and Works Act (No. 12) of 1911, the Native Labour Regulation Act (No. 15) of 1911, the Industrial Conciliation Act of 1924 and its amendments in 1937 and 1956, the Mines and Works Amendment Act of 1926, the Factories, Machinery, and Building Works Act (No. 22) of 1941, and the Bantu Labour Act (No. 67) of 1964. Public services and education opportunities were limited by the Bantu Education Act (No. 47) of 1953, the Reservation of Separate Amenities Act (No. 49) of 1953, and the National Policy for General Affairs Act (No. 76) of 1984.

In contrast to the government's control over domestic economic activity of South Africans, few legal restrictions were imposed on the economic activities of foreign nationals in South Africa, aside from stringent exchange controls on the repatriation of capital funds. Foreigners were welcome, even encouraged, to establish businesses in South Africa, and they could qualify for numerous government concessions and subsidies. During most of the apartheid era, those who wished to sell their South African assets, however, could do so only in financial rands (a currency control device), rather than the more commonly used commercial rands (see Currency, this ch.).

Financial rands could be sold only to a foreign buyer for capital investment inside the country, and the financial rand traded at a discount (15 percent in late 1994) compared with the commercial rand. Exchange restrictions did not apply to current earnings, however, and investors could transfer those funds, subject to taxation. In March 1995, as the financial rand strengthened, and under strong pressure from the business community, the government abolished the financial rand.

The new government in 1994 began to implement legislation intended to compensate some of the roughly 3.5 million black citizens who had been dispossessed of their land under apartheid. The Restitution of Land Act (No. 22) of 1994 provided for the creation of a Land Claims Court and a Commission on Restitution of Land Rights to arbitrate demands for restitution. Petitioners under the law were given three years to lodge their claims. White landowners who feared the loss of their land lobbied hard through the South African Agricultural Union, which represented 60,000 white farmers, and succeeded in weakening provisions in the new law that would have given land rights to many sharecroppers and labor tenants. The white landowners also won the right to appeal land-claim decisions and to receive legal aid services under the new legislation. By mid-1996, only a small number of land claims had been adjudicated.

Parastatals

The government's strong role in shaping the economy was especially evident in the large number of parastatals, or state corporations, that it established beginning in the 1920s. Its primary goal was to strengthen import-substitution industries, which had started to grow during World War I, by providing infrastructure improvements and basic materials. Among the first such enterprises were the Electricity Supply Commission (Eskom) and the South African Iron and Steel Corporation (Iscor), both founded in the 1920s, and the Industrial Development Corporation (IDC), established in 1940 to support other new industries. The IDC helped to establish many other state corporations, including the Phosphate Development Corporation (Foskor); the South African Coal, Oil, and Gas Corporation (SASOL); and the Southern Oil Exploration Corporation (Soekor). In addition, many state corporations also founded subsidiary companies in partnership with private firms, and many held controlling shares of stock in private firms.

Private individuals were allowed to purchase shares in many state-owned corporations. The government generally appointed a majority of corporate directors, but senior management made most personnel decisions independent of government control. The government's primary avenue of control over state corporations was by granting or withholding loans of state money. The electricity parastatal, Eskom, was always allowed to raise money publicly, but most other state corporations relied on government funds for capital financing.

The anticipated private-sector participation in these parastatals did not materialize, however. Investors showed little interest in purchasing parastatals' stock. Iscor suffered the embarrassment of an almost total public refusal of its stocks when they were offered for sale in 1929. In fact, most state corporation ventures were viewed as unprofitable and were funded by the government because of a lack of private interest. In 1979, however, after oil sales from Iran had been cut off, the synthetic fuel corporation, SASOL, offered shares to the public; investors eagerly bought all that were available and fully supported two more such issues.

In February 1988, President P. W. Botha announced plans to privatize several state-controlled industries, including Eskom, Foskor, and Iscor, as well as state-operated transport, postal, and telecommunications services. The reasons given for the privatization effort were that it would reduce public criticism of the government role in these enterprises and that these parastatals themselves were no longer profitable for the government. State corporations had been the major recipients of large foreign loans that were called in and cut off in 1985, leaving them with serious capital shortages. Sale of the corporations' assets could both ease the debt burden and provide the government with new revenue for much-needed social programs for the poor.

Iscor was the first major parastatal to be sold, in November 1989. Its sale raised R3 billion for the treasury. The government then scaled down its plans, and in the early 1990s the future of privatization was unclear. Officials estimated that the roughly R250 billion needed to finance the purchase of the largest state corporations probably could not be found inside the country. The argument for privatization was also weakened by the worsening investment climate as political negotiations stalled and violence increased. Government opponents, especially the ANC, vigorously opposed privatization—viewing it as a ploy to maintain white control in preparation for majority rule.

In 1995 the Government of National Unity began to develop its own privatization program. Late that year, Deputy President Thabo Mbeki announced that the government would seek equity partners in Telkom and in South African Airways and that it would sell several smaller parastatals outright. The announcement provoked strong protests from labor unions over the threat of job losses and over labor's exclusion from the policy decision-making process.

Budgets

The government enjoyed surplus budgets in most years during the 1970s and the early 1980s, until chronic high inflation and gold price fluctuations combined to diminish the business tax base in the mid-1980s. The severe decline in real gold prices reduced tax revenues to less than 2 percent of total revenues in FY 1990–91, compared with 25 percent of total revenues in the boom year a decade earlier (see table 7, Appendix).

The personal tax base had always been relatively narrow because of the limited income of the large black population (about 76 percent of the total population) and the relative affluence of most whites (about 13 percent of the population). Searching for additional revenue during the late 1980s, the government tried to avoid higher taxes on businesses and instead relied on deficit financing. For example, in FY 1987–88, the deficit was 5.8 percent of GDP as part of a deliberate fiscal stimulation of the economy. This pattern of spending continued, and the budget deficit rose to 9 percent of GDP in 1993.

The erratic price of gold during the 1980s led to other budget problems, fueling the cycle of reduced industrial revenue, currency devaluation, and high inflation. The government attempted to encourage business development through lenient tax policies, but average incomes continued to be low so this strategy failed to bring in the needed government revenues. The government tried to increase its revenues by "widening the net" of goods and services taxed in 1991, when it introduced a 10 percent value-added tax (VAT) to replace the former 13 percent general sales tax. Then, in an effort to encourage capital spending, businesses were exempted from paying the VAT on capital inputs. And to encourage investment, other forms of tax, such as corporate taxes, taxes on gold mines and gold companies, and import surcharges on capital goods, were reduced. By 1995 the VAT had been increased to 14 percent.

The FY 1994–95 budget projected revenues of R105.8 billion and expenditures of R135.1 billion, leaving a deficit of R29.3 billion, or about 6.2 percent of projected GDP (see table 8, Appendix). To raise revenues, the government planned to sell domestic stocks, increase foreign borrowing, and increase excise taxes on alcohol and tobacco products—expected to bring in an estimated R525 million. The government also levied a one-time, 5 percent "transition levy" on individuals and businesses with taxable incomes of more than R50,000, expecting to enhance its revenues by about R2.25 billion through this measure.

In March 1995, the ANC-led government's budget for FY 1995–96 estimated total revenues at roughly R123 billion and expenditures at R153.3 billion, with a budget deficit of R29.7 billion and a gross borrowing requirement (including interest on previous debt) of R38 billion. Government revenues were to be enhanced by higher taxes on alcohol, tobacco, and gasoline (and a higher, 43 percent maximum rate on individual incomes). The budget was well received overall, and the Johannesburg Stock Exchange generally held steady after it was presented.

The proposed government budget for FY 1996–97 projected revenues of roughly R145 billion and expenditures of R174 billion, with a projected deficit equivalent to 5.1 percent of GDP. Principal projected new revenues included taxes on monthly retirement income, while revenues from import tariffs would be reduced or eliminated. Proposed budget allocations included roughly R7.5 billion for salary increases and pay adjustments for government workers, intended to reduce the inequities of the apartheid era. The budget also envisioned expenditures of roughly R5.5 billion for education, R10.2 billion for military spending, and R9.8 billion for the police.

Foreign Trade and Investment

South Africa's foreign trade and investment were affected by sanctions and boycotts, especially during the 1980s and early 1990s. These measures included a voluntary arms embargo instituted by the United Nations (UN) in 1963, which was declared mandatory in 1977; the 1978 prohibition of loans from the United States Export-Import Bank; an oil embargo first instituted by OPEC in 1973 and strengthened in a similar move by Iran in 1979; a 1983 prohibition on IMF loans; a 1985 cutoff of most foreign loans by private banks; the United States 1986 Comprehensive Antiapartheid Act, which limited trade and discouraged United States investors; and the 1986 European Economic Community (EEC) ban on trade and investment. The Organization of African Unity (OAU) also discouraged trade with South Africa, although observers estimated that Africa's officially unreported trade with South Africa exceeded R10 billion per year in the late 1980s.

The most effective sanctions measure was the withdrawal of short-term credits in 1985 by a group of international banks. Immediate loan repayments took a heavy toll on the economy (see External Debt, this ch.). More than 350 foreign corpora-

Durban, historic port and multicultural city
Courtesy Embassy of South Africa, Washington

tions, at least 200 of which were United States owned, sold off their South African investments. In 1991 both the EEC and the United States lifted many official sanctions in view of measures taken by Pretoria to begin dismantling apartheid. Foreign investors were slow to return to South Africa, however; most banking institutions considered the country too unstable, and foreign corporations faced high labor costs and unrest if they tried to operate there.

In 1994 and 1995, many of the United States companies that had sold off shares or operations in South Africa in the past decade returned to do business there. By early 1996, at least 225 United States companies employed more than 45,000 South African workers.

Foreign Trade

Throughout the twentieth century, South Africa's economy

has depended heavily on foreign trade—a trend that continued even under pressure from international sanctions and recession. Gold dominated its exports to the point that the government occasionally intervened to promote nongold exports. During the 1970s and the 1980s, the price of gold directly affected the value of the rand and, therefore, the prices at which exports were sold overseas. As the gold price fluctuated, the exchange rate of the rand rose and fell, and export revenues responded accordingly. Under these uncertain conditions, few manufacturers were willing to risk large investments to increase their export capacity.

One of the 1970s programs that promoted nongold mineral exports was the development of new harbor facilities, railway lines, and mines, which helped to increase revenues from the export of metal ores at the impressive rate of nearly 18 percent per year, on average, during the 1980s. Also during the 1980s, the Board of Trade and Industry implemented structural adjustment programs for various industries and a General Export Incentive Scheme, which reduced import tariffs on raw materials to be used to manufacture goods for export, in proportion to their value and local content. One effect of these programs was to reduce the importance of gold in South African exports from 56 percent of revenues in 1980 to 36 percent in 1992, according to government statistics. Gold exports increased slightly in 1993 and 1994, as a fraction of export revenues, but remained below 40 percent of the total.

The government also took direct action to limit imports, in part to protect local industries. The government has the power to do so through tariffs, surcharges, and import licenses. Import tariffs provided some protection against dumping by foreign manufacturers. Import surcharges helped reduce import demand and raise government revenues. In August 1988, the surcharge on some items was raised as high as 60 percent in a bid to hold down imports, but in May 1989 the surcharge on capital goods was eased from 20 percent to 15 percent, and most import tariffs were being phased out in the 1990s.

Government pressures in the 1970s and the 1980s succeeded in reducing South Africa's import levels but did not succeed in changing the pattern of imports. By 1987, when total imports were down about 30 percent from their peak 1974 volume, industrial inputs continued to dominate imports. Machinery was the most important among these, followed by vehicles and transportation equipment, a variety of chemicals, and oil. After the OPEC boycott of 1973 and Iran's cutoff of oil to South Africa in 1979, however, official figures on oil trade were not available. Observers estimated that 1987 oil import costs reached US$1.75 billion.

The pattern of trade dominated by gold exports and industrial imports continued in the early 1990s (see table 9; table 10, Appendix). The government continued to promote exports and to limit imports in an effort to create the trade surplus (and foreign exchange reserve surplus) necessary for debt repayment. In 1993 exports were valued at roughly R79.5 billion (almost 35 percent of GDP) according to official estimates, and imports were valued at approximately R59 billion. In 1994 exports were valued at an estimated R89.1 billion, and imports, at R75.9 billion. In early 1995, imports began to outstrip exports, and South Africa's trade surplus declined at an uneven pace for the rest of the year. South African Reserve Bank estimates in early 1996 placed the value of exports in the previous year at R81 billion in merchandise and R20.2 billion in gold. Merchandise imports were about R98.5 billion, leading officials to predict that the trade balance could lapse into deficit. In early 1996, however, exporters took advantage of the sharp depreciation of the rand, and the trade surplus rose sharply. In dollar values, however, the trade balance remained almost flat as the benefits of the lower rand were offset by lower commodity prices

Foreign trade delegations began arriving in South Africa as international sanctions were being lifted in the early 1990s. Among its most dramatic turnabouts, South Africa sent a delegation to Moscow in mid-1991 to discuss strengthening trade ties, and for the first time, South African companies participated in a trade fair there.

South Africa's main trading partners in the mid-1990s are West European countries, the United States, and Japan. Members of the European Union (EU—see Glossary) receive roughly 40 percent of South African exports and provide one-third of South Africa's imports. In 1994 Switzerland, an important destination of South African diamonds, purchased the largest share of South African exports. Other markets for South African goods are the United Kingdom, the United States, Japan, and Germany, in that order. Leading sources of South African imports are Germany, the United States, the United Kingdom, Japan, and Italy.

The EU accorded South Africa duty-free entry on most of its industrial exports in early 1995, and the two were negotiating terms for the purchase of South Africa's agricultural products. In 1996 the EU granted South Africa a qualified membership in the Lomé Convention, to take effect in 1997. The Lomé Convention gives African, Pacific, and Caribbean countries preferential access to European markets.

South Africa's trade with the United States increased rapidly after 1994. In 1995 South Africa imported roughly US$2.75 billion worth of United States exports, mostly manufactured goods. This represented more than half of all United States exports to Africa. South Africa exported roughly US$2.21 billion worth of metals, alloys, and precious stones to the United States in that year, representing the only significant source of African products other than petroleum.

South Africa's trade with the rest of Africa, the natural market for its manufactured goods and agricultural products, was carried on both openly and clandestinely until the early 1990s, because of the OAU's long-standing trade ban. As commercial ties expanded in the 1990s, African countries purchased about 10 percent of South Africa's exports; Zimbabwe, Zambia, and Mozambique were the largest African markets. Only Zimbabwe supplied significant exports (primarily tobacco) to South Africa.

Official South African trade statistics include all members of the Southern African Customs Union (SACU). SACU arose out of a customs agreement between South Africa and the territories that became Botswana, Lesotho, and Swaziland, dating back even before the Union of South Africa was formed in 1910. SACU was formally established when the agreement was renegotiated in 1969, and Namibia joined the customs union when it became independent in 1990. Goods move freely among SACU member states, which share a common accounting procedure and impose a common tariff structure. Each country contributes to a shared fund and receives a fixed portion of revenues based on its approximate share of production and consumption. In the mid-1990s, South Africa was considering either dismantling SACU or restructuring its participation in the alliance.

Investment

During the 1960s, foreign investment in mining and manufacturing grew steadily, reaching over 60 percent of total foreign investment by 1970. After that, foreign investment in South Africa stagnated and in some cases declined, increasing the government's reliance on loans rather than on equity capital to finance development. In 1984 loans constituted over 70 percent of South Africa's foreign liabilities, as compared with only 27 percent from direct investments. As a result, when most loans were cut off in 1985, available investment capital dropped sharply, and the economy suffered. In 1989 a substantial proportion of gross investment—R39 billion out of R49 billion—represented depreciation.

Although international opposition to South Africa eased in the early 1990s and bans on investment were lifted, investment as registered on the Johannesburg Stock Exchange (JSE) continued to decline and South African share prices on the JSE and on the London Stock Exchange were low. Industrial shares fared better than other sectors, but even the industrial index showed only sluggish growth through 1991. The overall JSE index improved slightly in 1992, and this trend continued after that. In 1993 the index rose by nearly 50 percent, although the volume of trade continued to be low by international standards. By late 1995, foreign purchases on the JSE had risen to more than R4.5 billion.

Foreign purchases were primarily in portfolio investment rather than direct investment through the mid-1990s. Most foreign direct investment was in the form of joint ventures or buying into existing enterprises. There was very little foreign direct investment in new enterprises, a trend that hit hardest in the struggling black business sector in South Africa. United States direct investment in South Africa rose during this time, from about US$871 million in 1992 to more than US$1.34 billion in 1995.

South Africans invested heavily in other African countries, even during the years of declining investments in South Africa. Tourist facilities were a favorite target for South African investments during the sanctions era. South Africans invested in tourist parks in Madagascar, for example, and in hotel development in the Comoro Islands and in Mozambique in the early 1990s. South African tourists, banned from many other tourist locales at the time, then shared in the benefits of these developments.

Balance of Payments

Before the debt crisis of 1985, South Africa's current-account position traditionally mirrored its business cycle, showing alternate surpluses and deficits. Whenever the economy grew faster than about 3 percent a year, local demand for imports increased, and when the economy slowed, imports decreased. In times of growth, when current-account deficits became too large, the government implemented restrictive monetary and fiscal policies in order to slow demand. After the 1985 debt crisis, however, South Africa had no choice but to run continuous current-account surpluses to meet repayment commitments. By the early 1990s, South Africa had become a capital-exporting nation because creditors wanted repayment on loans, and almost no new capital inflows other than replacement or rollover trade credits were available.

South Africa's current-account surplus, which had averaged about 3 percent of GDP in the late 1980s, increased sharply to exceed R6 billion in 1991, before declining slightly in 1993, according to the Central Statistical Service. In 1994 and 1995, import growth forced the current account into a deficit for the first time in more than a decade and officials estimated that the current-account deficit could reach R10 billion by 1997.

South Africa's gold and foreign currency reserves were hit hard by the need to repay the nation's loans in 1985 and 1986. At that time, gold holdings were sufficient to cover only about ten weeks of imports, and by the end of 1988 the reserve position had deteriorated to little more than six weeks of import cover. Although the capital account started to improve in 1990, and total gold and other foreign reserves rose to US$2.39 billion, this amount was still equivalent to the cost of only about six weeks of imports of goods and services. Net foreign currency reserves were still very low in the mid-1990s, at about R15.7 billion (about two months of import cover) in late 1995, and R10 billion (only about one month's import cover) in mid-1996.

Employment and Labor

Labor Force

Agricultural employment in the formal economy declined beginning in the 1970s, reflecting the trends toward mechanization in agriculture and increasing urbanization. During that time, the government also changed its definition of agricultural employment to exclude many farmers who owned small plots of land and produced primarily for subsistence or for local markets. Impressive growth in the services sector—including trade, finance, insurance, restaurants, hotels, and other business and social services—accounted for most of the jobs created during the 1980s and the early 1990s. The services sector also included the country's large domestic work force, estimated at more than 800,000 in the early 1990s.

The distribution of labor continued to change in the 1990s, in response to global and regional market factors and political change in South Africa. For example, despite the importance of mining revenues throughout the twentieth century, the mining industry employed a dwindling share of the work force—only about 7 percent in 1995, down from nearly 10 percent a decade earlier. More than 200,000 mineworkers had been laid off between 1987 and 1993, according to the industrial umbrella organization, the South African Chamber of Mines (see table 11, Appendix).

In 1994 and 1995, officials revised employment statistics to incorporate into national accounts employment in the former black homelands—which were home to almost one-half of the black South African population. With these revisions, the government estimated the national work force in mid-1995 at 14.3 million people. Unemployment statistics also were being revised to incorporate workers outside the formal economy. In 1995 the government estimated unemployment at 32.6 percent. Unofficial estimates ranged to 40 percent or higher, and officials acknowledged that the rate was as high as 47 percent in some rural areas.

Labor and Politics

Even before apartheid restrictions were imposed during the 1950s, government policies, rather than market principles, determined many aspects of labor-management relations. From the 1950s until the early 1990s, black workers suffered systematic discrimination. Apartheid legislation authorized the "reservation" of many skilled jobs and managerial positions for whites; qualified blacks were legally excluded from most senior-level jobs, but black education standards were so inferior to those for whites that few blacks were qualified for well-paid jobs. Even in equivalent job categories, blacks received lower wages than whites. Although white workers were divided in their racial attitudes throughout the apartheid era, they often opposed benefits for black workers that could threaten their own economic standing.

Throughout South Africa's industrial history, workers of all races organized to demand better wages and working conditions, but through the early 1980s, almost all union leaders were white. This was true in part because some employers refused to negotiate with black representatives and because of legal restrictions on black labor organizations. The Industrial Conciliation Act of 1924, which governed many aspects of labor relations, redefined the term, *employee,* to exclude most blacks; the definition was amended by the Native Labour (Settlement of Disputes) Act (No. 48) of 1953 to exclude all blacks, thereby depriving them of any labor law protection.

A century of South African industrial development had relied on an abundance of low-wage labor in order to ensure profits. But as the economic and social problems associated with implementing apartheid emerged, and as new technologies were developed during the 1960s and the 1970s, many industries chose to increase their capital stock—investing in sophisticated machinery and employing a few skilled technicians—rather than adopt labor-intensive methods that would require training and managing a large work force. This trend toward capital-intensive operations probably resulted in lower labor costs and increased productivity. At the same time, it contributed to the country's soaring unemployment and spreading poverty, which fueled resentment and raised the costs to the government of preserving apartheid.

Increasing poverty among blacks, along with entrenched workplace discrimination and the marginalization of blacks from national politics, caused black workers' organizations to become increasingly politicized in the 1960s and the 1970s. They provided a legal arena in which political grievances could be aired. By the early 1970s, there were twenty-four African workers' organizations with a combined membership of nearly 60,000. Their increasing militance and a series of strikes that began in Durban in 1973 finally persuaded the government to begin reassessing its restrictions on black labor.

The government-appointed Commission of Inquiry into Labour Legislation (Wiehahn Commission) recommended the legal recognition of these fledgling unions, in part to exercise stronger control over black workers. As a result, Parliament enacted the Industrial Conciliation Amendment Act of 1979, recognizing black unions and extending labor law protection to them for the first time.

Adult labor often includes child-
care responsibilities: street
vendor's child plays beneath
urban kiosk.
Courtesy Embassy of South
Africa, Washington

A weaver's child accompanies
her to work.
Courtesy Sheila Ross

Under this legislation, many black workers had the legal right to bargain collectively with their employers in the 1980s, and, when legally required mediation procedures failed, they had the right to strike. They exercised these rights aggressively, using both legal and illegal labor actions to press their workplace demands and to protest against apartheid. Black union membership of about 500,000 in 1980 grew to more than 2.5 million in 1990. By the early 1990s, almost 70 percent of all union members in South Africa were black, and more than one-third of all employees in mining, industry, and commerce were union members.

The largest organizing effort among black workers resulted in the establishment of the Congress of South African Trade Unions (COSATU) in 1985. An umbrella organization of more than a dozen unions, COSATU had a total of 1.3 million members by 1990. COSATU affiliated with the African National Congress (ANC) and the South African Communist Party (SACP), both of which were banned. In addition to winning major financial concessions for its members, COSATU became the effective mobilizing arm of the ANC and the SACP. COSATU's two largest labor rivals were the National Council of Trade Unions (Nactu), a blacks-only confederation that rejected multiracial membership, and the United Workers' Union of South Africa (UWUSA), which was affiliated with the Zulu-based Inkatha Freedom Party (IFP).

Union militancy contributed to labor successes. Real wages for black manufacturing workers rose an average of 29 percent between 1985 and 1990. Overall wage increases, outside agriculture, rose by 11 percent during 1985 alone, and this annual rate of increase accelerated to 17 percent in 1990.

By the early 1990s, however, both labor and government leaders were alarmed over the violence that had erupted during some labor actions. Violence had been part of labor's history of confrontation; some employers used force to suppress labor militancy, and strikers often used violence against non-striking workers. But the scale of labor violence increased sharply, and the often-repressive police response also contributed to the destruction. In one of South Africa's most violent strikes—at a gold mine near Welkom, in the Orange Free State—more than eighty miners died in clashes between strikers and nonstrikers in 1991. Like many other violent strikes, this clash initially concerned economic issues, but it escalated because of political, ethnic, and racial grievances.

In the early 1990s, COSATU's largest and most militant unions were the National Union of Metalworkers of South Africa (NUMSA) and the National Union of Mineworkers (NUM), each with more than 300,000 members. NUMSA's actions cost automobile manufacturers and related industries more workdays than any other union in 1993 and 1994. NUMSA threatened even more costly labor actions in the future if auto workers' wage increases did not accelerate.

Three other large unions led the labor movement in the number of strikes called during the early 1990s. These were the National Education, Health, and Allied Workers' Union; the Transport and General Workers' Union; and the Food and Allied Workers' Union. Even workers in small companies were becoming more militant; during the early 1990s, more than 40 percent of all strikes involved 200 or fewer employees.

In 1994, with 194 legally recognized labor unions in the country, the government extended labor law protection to domestic workers for the first time. Initially, this meant recognizing their 70,000-member domestic workers' organization as a union and granting its members rights such as sick leave and on-the-job lunch breaks for the first time. Several COSATU-affiliated unions launched membership drives among domestic workers in 1995 and 1996, and they promised to work for the introduction of a legal minimum wage and access to literacy classes and other forms of vocational training for the large domestic work force.

Business and labor leaders agreed that confrontations with labor contributed to rising business costs during the 1980s and the early 1990s. The number of workdays lost to work stoppages rose from 175,000 in 1980 to 5.8 million in 1987. Lost workdays per year declined in the late 1980s, but labor actions still extracted high costs from business by slowing operations, by intimidating investors, and by destroying property. Among the most costly actions were those by transport workers, whose services were vital to all sectors of the economy. South Africa's ability to compete globally was also affected by labor militancy, in part because, officials estimated, a worker's cost to employers in 1994—including wages and benefits—averaged US$5 an hour in South Africa, or double the average labor costs in Mexico or Brazil and more than five times the average labor cost in China.

Education and Employment

The Bantu Education Act (No. 47) of 1953 helped pave the way for labor strife in the 1980s and the 1990s by institutionalizing a plan to restrict black workers to low-paid jobs through deliberately inferior education (see Education, ch. 2). During the 1960s and 1970s, per capita spending on white pupils was about ten times greater than educational spending on black pupils. By the early 1990s, the gap had been reduced by half, but in general, standards for teacher qualifications and facilities in black schools continued to be inferior to those in white schools.

The economic costs of implementing and enforcing apartheid sky-rocketed in the 1980s. Black poverty deprived South African businesses and manufacturers of a sizable domestic market. Even more ominous for the future, it became clear that South Africa lacked the necessary skilled personnel to maintain growth in its manufacturing enterprises, and millions of South African workers were unqualified for anything but the lowest-paid jobs.

South Africa's Education Foundation, a respected private research organization, estimated in 1991 that unemployment among unskilled and uneducated workers would increase during the 1990s, and that at least 500,000 skilled jobs and managerial positions were likely to remain unfilled, unless foreign workers were hired to fill them. The government's National Manpower Commission confirmed these bleak estimates in 1992, adding to the political pressure to end apartheid, especially in education.

The interlinked challenges of economic recovery and educational reorganization presented the new government with an intractable dilemma in 1994. Educational reform would require significant increased spending in an expanding economy, but, at the same time, economic growth would require a more highly skilled work force and educational reforms. The government approach to these challenges was deliberate and careful, and attempted with foreign donor assistance to convince those who were uneducated and unemployed that some of the benefits of ending apartheid would be seen during their lifetime. Officials sought international assistance in providing on-the-job training for workers in many industries and in speeding the pace of reforms, but by late 1995, only a few new programs were being implemented.

Women constituted only about 36 percent of the labor force in the formal economy in the mid-1990s, according to official estimates. Women of all races generally held lower-paid jobs than men, and they were paid less in comparable jobs. During the apartheid era, white women most often worked in service industries and clerical positions; a few white women held supervisory jobs or government offices. Black women dominated the large domestic work force; some worked in clerical positions or in temporary jobs, often in agriculture. Women managed most agricultural production in the former homelands and rural areas where men frequently left home to work in cities or in the mines.

Foreign workers have been an important segment of the industrial work force. In 1994 the government estimated that between 1 million and 1.2 million workers from Botswana, Lesotho, Malawi, Mozambique, and Swaziland were legally employed in South Africa—most on temporary contracts in the mines or urban industries. In addition, as many as 2 million foreign workers were believed to be self-employed or working illegally in South Africa in 1995, according to minister of home affairs Gatsha Buthelezi. Foreign workers were sometimes subject to immediate layoffs or discriminatory treatment at the hands of management or fellow employees, and in 1996, they faced the threat of new restrictions on their being hired.

Extractive Industries

South Africa's modern history has often been dated from the first commercial mining of diamonds and gold in the 1870s and the 1880s, when the region became a magnet for European investment. Mining in the region predated European arrivals by several centuries, however, as the new government recalled in its minerals policy statements in 1994 and 1995. Iron mining and smelting sites in the northeast were used as much as 1,700 years ago; copper was mined south of the Limpopo River more than 1,000 years ago; and historians describe early mining activities in the Witwatersrand (literally, "Ridge of White Waters" in Afrikaans, commonly shortened to Rand) area, which attracted miners from elsewhere in Africa as early as the thirteenth century.

Soon after the European rush for gold and diamonds in the late nineteenth century, mining operations expanded to include more than two dozen other minerals. By the mid-twentieth century, South Africa was the world's largest producer or second largest producer of gold, diamonds, platinum, chromium, manganese, and vanadium; and it ranked high among producers of coal, iron ore, uranium, copper, silver, fluorspar, asbestos, and limestone (see table 12, Appendix).

Clusters of minerals occur in five major mineral complexes—the Bushveld, Transvaal, Witwatersrand, Northern Cape, and Western Cape complexes (see fig. 15). Whereas most mines were originally funded and managed from European centers, by the 1970s most were managed by South Africa's large diversified corporations, which controlled assets around the world.

Despite its importance in export revenues, the mining industry contributes only about 9.6 percent of GDP in the mid-1990s, down from an average of nearly 15 percent during the 1980s. The mining sector had been gradually surpassed by manufacturing and financial services both in terms of national output and labor force participation. The mines still account

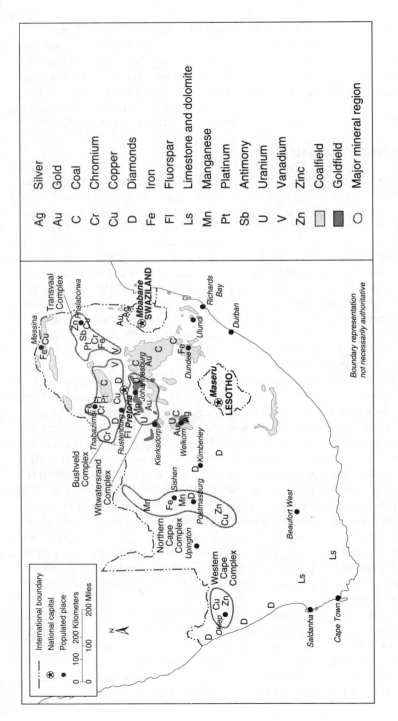

Figure 15. Minerals and Mining Activity, 1996

for a greater share of export revenues than any other single economic activity in the 1990s.

The mineowners' association, the South African Chamber of Mines, was formed in 1889 to represent the industry in dealings with the government. In the 1990s, the Chamber of Mines includes six major mining finance houses, with thirty-six gold mines, twenty-two coal mines, and sixteen diamond, platinum, antimony, asbestos, manganese, lead, and copper mines. Together they account for 85 percent of South Africa's mineral output. The Chamber of Mines negotiates labor concerns on behalf of mineowners, administers training programs for mineworkers, trains mineworkers in rescue and safety procedures, oversees pension and benefit funds, coordinates research programs, and refines and processes some minerals before sale.

Gold

Gold, first mined by Europeans in 1886 near Johannesburg, soon became the most important sector in the mining industry. South Africa has almost one-half of the world's known gold reserves, located primarily in the Rand in what was once a prehistoric lake. Gold is also mined in the Free State. Industry analysts estimated in the early 1990s that South Africa had produced more than 43,000 tons of gold in the past century, and that at least that amount remained in reserves.

Gold occurs in seams embedded in rock strata, sometimes more than a mile below the surface. Deep shafts must be sunk, large amounts of rock must be blasted and brought to the surface, and the rock must be crushed and chemically separated from the gold. Some gold mines then pump processed mine tailings underground to serve as backfill. Mining and processing are costly, especially in deposits where the gold seam is extremely thin compared with the surrounding rock. For example, in the early 1990s industry analysts estimated that only 5.6 grams of gold were extracted from each ton of ore excavated. Nevertheless, the industry has consistently earned high profits and has accounted for one-third to one-half of the world's gold production in the 1980s and 1990s. The country's fifty-seven operating gold mines produce between 600 and 620 tons of gold per year, representing almost 30 percent of the world production. Gold production in 1994 and 1995 fell below 600 tons for the first time since the 1960s.

Gold mining companies traditionally kept expenses to a minimum by paying low wages. Gold mines became known for their often exploitative labor policies, including the use of migrant workers on limited contracts, strict worker control in company compounds, and difficult working conditions. Labor costs were especially important in determining profits, because the price of gold was set at US$35 per ounce through the 1960s. After the price of gold was allowed to float in 1968, it gradually rose in response to market demand, and companies could afford to produce less and still earn even greater profits. They then began to expand operations into so-called low-grade-ore mines. The volume of South African gold production fell, and gold prices skyrocketed to an all-time high of US$613 per ounce in 1980.

During the 1980s, the dollar price of gold fluctuated widely, but because of devaluations of the rand, the rand price of gold generally advanced. When gold prices fell in 1989, the industry found that many of the low-grade-ore mines were no longer profitable. As the average value of the rand increased against the dollar, overall industry profits declined, and nearly half of the gold mines in operation were running at a loss. At least 40,000 gold mine workers were laid off in 1990, according to government estimates, and layoffs continued through 1993.

During 1994 all major gold mining houses except Johannesburg Consolidated Investments (JCI) were reporting lower profits as output fell in response to labor unrest and other factors. Randgold closed its Durban gold mine in mid-1994, owing primarily to poor grades of available ore, and other mines were threatening to close within the next few years unless profits improved.

In 1994 JCI began to "unbundle" its corporate structure by dividing into three separate companies. Anglo American, JCI's largest shareholder (with 48 percent), retained its platinum and some diamond interests in one company, Anglo American Platinum. JCI's gold mining and other industrial interests were separated into two companies, JCI Limited and Johnnies Industrial Corporation. Shares for these companies are being offered to the public, primarily as a vehicle for black investment and broadening participation in this sector of the economy.

Diamonds and Platinum

South Africa's diamond mining industry dates back to 1867, when diamonds were discovered near Kimberley, now in the Northern Cape. The Kimberley diamond fields, and later discoveries in Gauteng, the Free State, and along the Atlantic coast, emerged as major sources of gem-quality diamonds, securing South Africa's position as the world's leading producer in the mid-twentieth century. (Rough diamonds were produced in larger quantities in Australia, Zaire, Botswana, and Russia.) Through 1991 most of South Africa's diamonds were mined at only five locations, but a sixth mine, Venetia—in the Northern Cape—opened in 1992 and was expected to become a major diamond producer later in the decade.

The De Beers Consolidated Mines Company controlled most diamond mining in South Africa and influenced international trade through a diamond-producers' alliance, or cartel—the Central Selling Organisation. The cartel enabled diamond producers to control the number of gems put on the market and thereby to maintain high prices for gem-quality diamonds. The cartel was able to react to marketing efforts outside its control by temporarily flooding the market, and thereby driving down the price paid for an outsider's product.

Diamond prices fluctuated in the early 1980s, but the industry continued to expand even in the face of international recession and the discovery of the diamond-like cubic zirconia. Dollar prices for diamonds improved in 1985 but dropped again in 1987, requiring De Beers to support the market by withholding diamonds from dealers. Thus, annual production of more than 10 million carats in 1985 and in 1986 dropped to 9.1 million in the late 1980s. Gem and industrial diamond output in 1994 was 10.8 million carats, or roughly 11 percent of world production.

In 1990 the Soviet Union signed and openly acknowledged a contract to sell its diamonds (estimated at a value of about R13 billion over a five-year period) exclusively through De Beers. The action marked the first time in nearly thirty years that the Soviet Union had openly associated itself in commodity dealings with South Africa. Later that year, De Beers announced a loan of R2.63 million to the Soviet Union, against the security of an equivalent amount in diamonds.

Platinum group metals (platinum, palladium, ruthenium, rhodium, iridium, and osmium), which occur together in ore seams and are mined in one operation, were discovered in South Africa in 1924. Most of the estimated 59,000 tons of reserves are in the Bushveld complex of minerals; some concentrations are also found in the Transvaal and the Witwatersrand complexes. Platinum is used in automobile catalytic converters to reduce fuel emissions, as a catalyst in industrial processes, and in making jewelry.

South Africa is the world's leading producer of platinum. Its output of about ninety tons in 1993 accounted for almost 49 percent of world production. South Africa's platinum mines have profited, in particular, from the sale of rhodium, which sold for almost US$6,000 an ounce in the early 1990s, but world market prices fell after that.

Ferrous and Nonferrous Metals

South Africa has the world's largest known deposits of chromium, manganese, and vanadium, as well as significant deposits of iron ore, antimony, copper, nickel, lead, titanium, fluorspar, zinc, and zirconium. Most of these metals are exported unprocessed, with the exception of iron ore, which is also used in the local steel industry.

South Africa's chromium deposits contain about 72 percent of the world's reserves, most of it in the Bushveld complex of minerals. In 1993 its mines produced 2.8 million tons of chromium, or about 32 percent of world output—down from 4 million tons in 1989; production recovered, to roughly 3.6 million tons in 1994. Used primarily to produce stainless steel, chromium was one of South Africa's export successes in the 1980s; prices reached US$0.70 per pound but dropped sharply when producers tried to undercut each other in 1990. The government used various incentives, including export subsidies and power rebates to those who produced alloys for export, to encourage production. About one-third of chromium produced in 1993 was exported, much of it to the United States and Japan.

South Africa contains the largest known deposits of manganese ore in the world. Its reserves of at least 12.5 billion tons, mostly in the Northern Cape mineral complex, constitute 75 percent of the world total. Manganese is essential in the manufacture of iron and steel, and more than 90 percent of South Africa's manganese is used for this purpose. During the late 1980s, production fluctuated slightly, but it remained between 3 and 4 million tons per year, while prices generally rose, nearly doubling in 1989. By the end of 1991, however, South African producers were forced to reduce prices in response to a weak international market. In 1994 more than 2.8 million tons of manganese ore were produced, roughly 17 percent of world output.

South Africa produced between 25,000 tons and 30,000 tons of vanadium a year in the early 1990s, almost 45 percent of the world's supply. Its estimated 5.4 million tons constitute one-third of world reserves. The world's largest producer is a South African firm, Highveld Steel and Vanadium. The year 1989 set a record in terms of both production and exports for South Africa, but when world steel production declined, demand for vanadium dropped and prices plummeted, forcing one vanadium producer in South Africa to close down. Prices again surged in early 1995, and Highveld Steel and Vanadium expected earnings to more than double in 1995, compared with 1994. Vanadium is used in manufacturing steel, to provide tensile and torsional strength and resistance to abrasion.

South Africa is the largest producer of iron ore on the continent, with reserves estimated at more than 9.4 billion tons. Iron is mined in the Northern Cape, the Bushveld, and the Transvaal complexes, and in KwaZulu-Natal. More than 29.3 million tons of iron ore, roughly 3 percent of world output, were produced in 1993. Almost half of that amount was used in the steel industry. A record 19.6 million tons were exported in 1994, much of it to Japan.

Although small by world standards, South Africa's steel manufacturing industry is the largest on the continent (see Heavy Industry, this ch.). Steel production increased dramatically in the 1970s following the development of port facilities at Saldanha Bay and the associated rail line connecting it to the high-grade Sishen ore deposits in the Northern Cape. Projections for the use of steel in local construction were increasing as the government began to implement its Reconstruction and Development Programme in 1994. Government plans to implement stricter automobile emission standards promised another boost to the steel manufacturers, who produce stainless steel for use in catalytic converters.

South Africa has only about 2 percent of the world's known copper reserves, with the largest deposits in the Transvaal complex in the northeast. Copper is also mined in the Northern Cape and the Western Cape. Mining costs are high, because of the high concentration of other minerals in copper ore. At the country's largest copper mine, at Phalaborwa, production decreased in early 1993, in part because of flooding that brought work in the mine to a standstill. Later that year, the mine owners received government permission to institute a seven-day workweek, and the mine increased its work force to extend operations. Nationwide copper production, nonetheless, fell from more than 176,000 tons in 1992 to about 165,000 tons in 1994, and copper exports decreased steadily, to roughly 82,000 tons in 1994.

Energy Minerals and Petroleum

Fortunately for South Africa, it is well endowed with coal and uranium for energy production, because the country apparently has no significant petroleum reserves and was officially cut off from oil imports from 1979 to 1993. Oil accounted for about 20 percent of primary energy until the early 1970s, and the government had stockpiled an estimated 18 million tons of imported oil by 1979. Although unreported oil shipments continued during the sanctions era, many industries switched to the use of coal to power generators.

Imported crude oil is processed at four refineries—two in Durban, one near Cape Town, and one in Sasolburg, southwest of Johannesburg—with a combined distillation capacity of about 401,000 barrels per day, or 21.5 million tons per year. In 1994 the government invited international investment in oil and gas exploration for the first time since the 1960s. Minister of Mines and Energy Roelof "Pik" Botha announced the plan, saying that the government needed domestic energy sources for reconstruction and development. The state-owned Southern Oil Exploration Corporation (Soekor) also needed the investment capital to develop nine recently discovered small oilfields off the western Cape coast, and several other small wells near Mossel Bay.

South Africa's coal reserves, most located in the Witwatersrand and in northern KwaZulu-Natal, were estimated to be between 60 billion and 100 billion tons, enough to maintain early-1990s levels of domestic use and exports through much of the twenty-first century, according to industry analysts. The coal occurs in seams, often less than one hundred meters below the surface, and hence it is relatively easy and inexpensive to mine. Most coal used locally is burned in generators at electricity plants; it is also used for coking in the steel industry.

During the 1980s, Eskom, the government's electric power utility, was the coal industry's major customer. Eskom purchased about two-thirds of coal output, which fluctuated between 159 million and 176 million tons from 1984 to 1989. In the early 1990s, the coal industry produced more than 180 million tons of coal each year, of which at least 47 million tons

SASOL II oil-from-coal facility south of Johannesburg
Courtesy Embassy of South Africa, Washington

were exported. The industry employed more than 76,000 people. Eskom helped to finance coal mining operations and guaranteed coal prices to ensure the mining companies' return on investment.

International sanctions in the 1980s affected the coal industry in two ways. United States and European importers reduced their demand for South African coal exports, and South African homes and industries increased their use of coal in place of oil and other imported fuels. But in 1991 and 1992, as most sanctions were being lifted, the South African coal industry found itself facing stiff competition from emerging low-cost producers, such as Indonesia, Colombia, and Venezuela.

South Africa is ranked fifth in world uranium reserves in the 1990s with recoverable reserves estimated at nearly 180,000 tons. Uranium is produced as a by-product of gold in some mines of the Witwatersrand, and as a by-product of copper in the Phalaborwa mines of the far northeast of the country. Since 1968 all uranium produced in South Africa has been processed and marketed by the Nuclear Fuels Corporation of South Africa, a private company owned by the gold mines that produce uranium. Output declined in the late 1980s, as operating costs increased and uranium prices hit a thirteen-year low. Uranium output averaged nearly 2,000 tons a year in the early 1990s. Exports of uranium declined from roughly 1.3 percent of total export revenues in the 1980s to roughly 0.2 percent in the early 1990s.

South Africa produced substantial, but undisclosed, amounts of highly enriched uranium (HEU) in its nuclear weapons program, until that program was dismantled in the early 1990s. In 1994 the government, although a signatory to the Nuclear Nonproliferation Treaty (NPT), maintained stockpiles of HEU to produce industrial and medical isotopes, or to downgrade for use in power reactors.

The government has sponsored extensive research and development in the production of synthetic fuels, and South Africa became a pioneer in extracting oil and gas from coal in the 1960s and the 1970s. The South African Coal, Oil, and Gas Corporation (SASOL) established three facilities between 1950 and 1982 and is considering building a fourth plant in the late 1990s. After 1979, when SASOL shares were offered to the public, most of the corporation was run as a private company, with government assistance in constructing new facilities. Officials did not release production figures to the public, but the SASOL plants were believed to be supplying about 40 percent of South Africa's liquid fuel needs in the early 1990s. The corporation received tariff protection when the price of oil dropped below US$23 per barrel and paid into a fuel equalization fund when prices exceeded US$28.70 per barrel. In addition to liquid fuels, the company produces chemicals, fertilizers, and explosives.

Agriculture, Forestry, and Fishing

South Africa has a broad and well-developed agricultural sector and is a net food exporter in most years. Agricultural production, reflecting the sector's increased mechanization and commercialization, increased throughout the twentieth century. As mining and manufacturing industries expanded at a faster rate, however, agriculture's share of GDP declined from about 20 percent in the 1930s to about 12 percent in the 1960s and to less than 7 percent in the 1990s. The impressive range of crops—including almost every kind of food crop, as well as fibers, medicinal herbs, and components of cosmetic fragrances—reflects the country's diverse terrain, climate, and ecology. The agriculture sector provides for most domestic needs, and South Africa exports corn (maize), wool, sugar, peanuts (groundnuts), tobacco, and other farm products (see table 13, Appendix).

About 15 million hectares, or 12 percent of the land area, is under cultivation, and about 10 percent of this is under intensive irrigation. Agricultural production has suffered from cyclical droughts since the seventeenth century, and probably even earlier. Generally, the best rainfall is in the Western Cape and along the coast of KwaZulu-Natal. The rest of the country is relatively dry, and much of the arid Northern Cape is suitable only for grazing sheep (see fig. 16).

Under apartheid-era legislation until 1994, white farmers, who owned only 2 percent of the farms, controlled more than 80 percent of the arable land. White-owned farms averaged 1,300 hectares in size, whereas black farms averaged 5.2 hectares. Because nearly 80 percent of the population was restricted to less than 20 percent of the land, most black farmland was severely overused, leading to soil erosion and low productivity. As a result, many black farm families were supported by at least one person engaged in nonagricultural employment. The need for agrarian reform—broadening land ownership and increasing overall productivity—was one of the most serious issues facing the government in the mid-1990s as the inequities of apartheid were being reduced.

The government regulated both the production and the marketing phases of commercial agriculture through the early 1990s. Government-appointed marketing boards purchased important consumer crops—such as milk, corn, and most cereals—at fixed prices and sometimes subsidized consumer prices as well. Crops destined for further commercial processing—such as tobacco, wool, oilseeds, and dried fruit for export—also had to be sold through a marketing board, although producers generally received market value for these crops after the board sold the pooled national output. The only crops freely traded were fruits and vegetables sold at local markets. The government began to reduce the role of the marketing boards in the mid-1990s, and officials hoped to eliminate them entirely by the end of the decade.

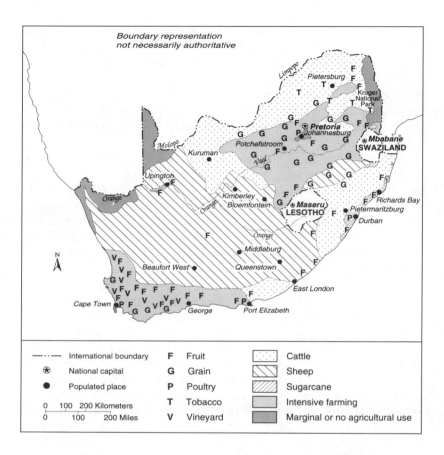

Figure 16. Major Agricultural Activity, 1996

Agriculture suffered serious effects from the chronic high inflation and debt that eroded other sectors of the economy in the early 1990s. Input costs (fertilizers, machinery, etc.) rose by 10 to 20 percent in some years; farm debt had reached R17 billion in 1992, more than four times the amount owed in 1980. Farmers also had witnessed deterioration in the terms of trade in farm products; for example, the amount of corn that had to be sold to buy a farm tractor increased from about 191 tons in 1984 to 347 tons in 1990. Moreover, South Africa faced reduced harvests as a result of severe drought in the early 1990s, forcing the government to spend vital foreign exchange on food imports.

Crops

Cereals and grains are South Africa's most important crops, occupying more than 60 percent of hectarage under cultivation in the 1990s. Corn, the country's most important crop, is a dietary staple, a source of livestock feed, and an export crop. Government programs, including generous loans and extension services, have been crucial to the country's self-sufficiency in this enterprise. Corn is grown commercially on large farms, and on more than 12,000 small farms, primarily in North-West, Mpumalanga (formerly, Eastern Transvaal), Free State (formerly, the Orange Free State), and KwaZulu-Natal provinces. Corn production generates at least 150,000 jobs in years with good rainfall and uses almost one-half of the inputs of the modern agricultural sector.

Corn production exceeds 10 million tons in good years; owing to regional drought in the early 1990s, however, production fell to just over 3 million tons in 1992, and roughly 5 million tons of corn were imported, at a cost of at least US$700 million. Both domestic and imported corn was shipped to neighboring countries to help ease the regional impacts of the drought. The drought eased in 1993, and officials estimated the 1994 harvest at approximately 12 million tons. Below-average rainfall in late 1994 again threatened to reduce corn output in 1995, and officials expected to import some 600,000 tons of corn in that year. Plentiful rain in late 1995 provided for a bumper crop in 1996.

Wheat production, which is concentrated in large, highly mechanized farms, also increased after World War II. Wheat cultivation spread from the western Cape where rainfall is fairly reliable, to the Orange Free State and the eastern Transvaal, primarily in response to rising consumer demand. But wheat harvest volumes vary widely; for example, roughly 2.1 million tons were produced in 1991 and only 1.3 million tons in 1992. Production in the early 1990s failed to meet local demand for about 2.2 million tons per year. Wheat imports in 1992, for example, cost more than US$5 million.

Other small grains are grown in localized areas of South Africa. For example, sorghum—which is native to southern Africa—is grown in parts of the Free State, as well as in the North-West and the Northern provinces, with yields often exceeding 200,000 tons. Sorghum has been used since prehistoric times for food and brewing purposes. Barley is also grown, primarily in the Western Cape. Nearly 300,000 tons of barley were produced in 1995.

South Africa produces peanuts, sunflower seeds, beans, and soybeans. Annual production of these crops varies significantly from year to year, although South Africa is usually able to meet domestic vegetable-oil needs and generate some exports. Plentiful rains in late 1995 meant increased harvests of these crops in 1996, compared to 1994 and 1995.

Fruits, including grapes for wine, earn as much as 40 percent of agricultural export earnings in some years. (Fresh fruit finds a good market in Europe because it matures during the northern hemisphere's winter.) Deciduous fruits, including apples, pears, and peaches, are grown primarily in areas of the Western Cape and the Eastern Cape, where cold winters and dry summers provide ideal conditions for these crops. Almost 1 million tons of deciduous fruits were sold fresh locally or were exported each year in the early 1990s.

Pineapples are grown, primarily in the Eastern Cape and KwaZulu-Natal. Tropical fruits—especially bananas, avocados, and mangoes—are also grown, especially in the northeast and some coastal areas. More than half of citrus production is exported in most years. South Africa exported 40 million cartons of citrus fruit in 1994, earning roughly R1.34 billion, according to industry sources.

More than 1.5 million tons of grapes are used domestically in South Africa's renowned wine industry, which dates back to the seventeenth-century vineyards introduced by French Huguenot immigrants. More than 100,000 hectares of land are planted in vineyards, centered primarily in the Western Cape. Smaller vineyards are also found in the Northern Cape, Free State, and Northern Province. One of the noticeable signs of the end of international sanctions against South Africa was a dramatic increase in worldwide demand for South African wines in 1994 and 1995.

Sugarcane is also an important export crop, and South Africa is the world's tenth largest sugar producer. Sugarcane was first cultivated in mid-nineteenth-century Natal. Production is still centered there, but sugar is also grown in Mpumalanga, where irrigation is used when rainfall is inadequate. Land under sugar cultivation has steadily increased, and the industry estimated that it produced more than 16 million tons of sugarcane in 1994.

Livestock

From the earliest times, livestock raising has been the backbone of South African agriculture. The large sheep herds of the Khoikhoi peoples on the Cape peninsula were admired and later appropriated by European settlers in the seventeenth century. The early Xhosa and Zulu societies were well known for the value they placed on cattle even before Europeans began cattle farming in the region in the seventeenth and the eighteenth centuries. The Europeans brought new breeds of sheep and cattle to southern Africa, and from these various stocks emerged a thriving commercial livestock sector. Cattle, estimated at more than 8 million head, are found in areas throughout the country; sheep (nearly 26 million) graze primarily in pastures stretching across the Northern Cape, Eastern Cape, western Free State, and Mpumalanga.

The livestock sector produces an estimated 900,000 tons of red meat each year. For example, the industry reported that nearly 2 million head of cattle were slaughtered in 1994. Poultry and pig farms are also found across the country, although most large commercial farms are near metropolitan areas. The industry estimates that farmers own roughly 1.2 million pigs. The poultry industry, with at least 11 million chickens, reportedly produced more than 500,000 tons of meat in 1994. In addition, a small but growing ostrich-raising industry produces plumes, skins, and meat.

Wool is an important agricultural export. South Africa became the world's fourth-largest exporter of wool by the late 1940s, and is consistently among the world's top ten wool producers, with an output of about 100,000 tons in most years. Approximately 60 percent of South African sheep are Merino, which produce high yields of fine wool. The newer, locally developed Afrino breed is a wool-mutton breed adapted to arid conditions. Most wool is exported, but the domestic wool-processing industry includes wool washing, combing, spinning, and weaving.

Dairy farming is found throughout the country, especially in the eastern half, and is sufficient to meet domestic needs, barring periods of extreme drought. The predominant dairy breeds are Holstein, Friesian, and Jersey cows. The milk price was deregulated in 1983, resulting in lower prices, but industry regulations continued to enforce strict health precautions. In a system dating to 1930, all wholesale milk buyers pay a compulsory levy to the National Milk Board. This money is pooled in a stabilization fund and used to subsidize dairies manufacturing butter, skim milk powder, and cheese when a surplus exists. Fresh-milk dairies objected in the early 1990s, however, and several of them were involved in litigation to have the levy lifted.

Forestry

South Africa's forests cover only about 1 percent of the country's total land area. The country never was heavily forested, and by the early twentieth century, humans had destroyed much of its natural wood resources. After World War I, the government began to establish forest plantations to grow trees for commercial use. Located primarily in the northeast and in KwaZulu-Natal, most timber plantations produce pine and eucalyptus trees. Although most wood is used for fuel, industrial uses include construction and mine props, paper products, and a variety of agricultural applications.

The country's pulp and paper industries expanded operations for export during the 1980s. About half of all commercial South African sawlogs came from state-owned plantations for use in the pulp and paper industries and in the mines. The two major paper manufacturers, Mondi (owned by Anglo American) and Sappi (owned by Gencor), spent approximately R3 billion to expand their operations during the 1980s, and in 1991 Sappi expanded even further by purchasing five specialty paper mills in Britain. Sappi was then ranked as the eleventh largest company in South Africa.

South Africa's forests produce more than 14.5 million cubic meters of unseasoned timber annually. Several hundred thousand people are employed on timber farms and in more than 240 wood-processing factories. Although South Africa could supply most of its own needs for wood and wood products, the timber industry faced problems on the export market in the early 1990s. The industry had relied on exports of pulp and paper, but falling world prices threatened profitability. In the mid-1990s, the government's Reconstruction and Development Programme calls for more than 1 million housing starts during the decade, and the timber industry is promoting the use of timber-frame houses to increase its domestic market share under this program.

Fishing

South Africa has a large commercial fishing industry. More than 4,500 commercial fishing vessels licensed by the Depart-

Tea plantation workers near Tzaneen, Northern Province
Courtesy Embassy of South Africa, Washington

ment of Environment Affairs work its nearly 3,000-kilometer coastline from Mozambique to Namibia. The industry employs more than 22,000 people. The principal species of shoal fish caught by coastal trawlers are anchovy, pilchard, and herring. Deep-sea trawlers bring in hake, barracuda, mackerel, monkfish, sole, and squid. The most important species caught by handline are tuna, cod, barracuda, silverfish, salmon, and yellowtail. Cape rock lobsters are harvested along the west coast, and several hundred other species, along the east and the south coastline. The total catch in the early 1990s was between 500,000 and 700,000 tons each year.

South Africa exports about 80 percent of its fish in most years. Much of the rest is consumed domestically or processed into fish meal and fish oil. The industry hit a peak in the 1960s, with a catch of more than 1 million tons in 1968, but declined after that, in part because local waters had been overfished and marine resources were severely depleted. Recorded fish harvests also declined in the early 1990s after South Africa relinquished control over its former fishing territory off the coast of Namibia.

The government enforces strict conservation measures, including fishing quotas and closed seasons, to prevent overfishing and to protect the fishing industry. Since 1977 it has enforced an exclusive South African fisheries zone of 200 nautical miles. In 1983 the government reduced foreign fishing quotas, and in the early 1990s it began scaling down the rights of five foreign countries still fishing in South African waters— Japan, Israel, Spain, Portugal, and the Republic of China (Taiwan).

Much of the fishing near large ports, such as Cape Town, Durban, Mossel Bay, and Port Elizabeth, is controlled by Portnet, the national port authority, in the mid-1990s. The provincial governments supervise some harbor facilities and provide marine conservation inspectors at official fishing harbors, including Saldanha Bay, Hout Bay, and at least ten others.

Manufacturing

Although agriculture and, later, mining historically have dominated South Africa's economy, manufacturing became the most productive sector in the early twentieth century. Until then, manufacturing industries—wine making, tanning, and tallow production—were entirely derived from agriculture and were intended primarily for the domestic market. Then as the mining sector expanded, new industries arose to meet growing urban demands for processed foods, clothing, and footwear. Until the 1920s, the country still depended heavily on imports, ranging from mining equipment to textiles and clothing. The government encouraged local manufacturing through the establishment of state corporations to produce electricity (in 1922) and steel (in 1928) for manufacturers' use and through tariffs designed to protect local industry.

From 1936 to 1946, manufacturing output grew by 6 percent per year, and growth jumped even more dramatically after 1948, when the government tightened its control over imports. Annual manufacturing output increased an average of 13.3 percent in the early 1950s. Since then, most growth in manufacturing has been in heavy industry, led by the local iron and steel industry, but by the early 1990s, the manufacturing sector as a whole was relatively diverse (see table 14, Appendix).

As manufacturing activity expanded, the sector became increasingly capital intensive despite the availability of a large labor pool in South Africa. The government encouraged capitalization through tax incentives and led such investment through the state corporations. During the 1970s, manufacturing enterprises steadily increased their fixed-capital stock, leading to surplus capacity by the mid-1980s. In particular, massive extensions at the government's power utility, Eskom, as well as the establishment of SASOL synthetic fuel plants and the Koeberg nuclear power station, represented significant capital intensification but only a minimum labor requirement. Furthermore, most private manufacturers moved toward machinery and technology to cut labor costs, both to keep up with foreign producers and to avoid confronting an increasingly militant, organized labor force. Nevertheless, by the mid-1980s the government recognized that much of the responsibility for creating jobs for new entrants to the labor market would necessarily rest on the manufacturing industries, and for this reason, government programs in the 1990s were beginning to encourage more labor-intensive manufacturing enterprises.

Because of the general economic downturn of the 1980s, chronic high inflation, and the debt crisis—which hit capital-intensive manufacturing especially hard—manufacturing output slumped during the decade from an overall annual increase of 3 percent in 1981 to a decline of 2.5 percent in 1991. The biggest decreases were in textiles, footwear, industrial chemicals, and nonferrous base-metal industries. The poor performance in these industries reflected a weakness in local demand and the drawing down of inventories because of higher interest rates. Furthermore, average labor productivity in nonagricultural sectors was only about 2 percent higher in 1990 than in 1980, despite a major increase in capital per worker during the decade. Manufacturing sales increased after 1990, largely the result of improved business and investor confidence, increased domestic and export sales, and a decline in stocks of finished goods. In the early 1990s, manufacturing contributed more than 22 percent of total economic output.

Manufacturing industries are heavily concentrated in urban areas—especially in the industrial region around Johannesburg, which accounted for more than 50 percent of industrial output in the early and mid-1990s. Other major industrial centers are Cape Town, Port Elizabeth, East London, and Durban. Smaller, but nonetheless important, industrial concentrations are at Kimberley, Bloemfontein, Queenstown, and Mossel Bay. Government incentives for manufacturers to move to rural areas and the black homelands during the 1980s were generally unsuccessful, in part because of logistical and transportation difficulties. The government then tried regional development projects, intended to bring manufacturing jobs to undeveloped areas by providing performance-based incentives and improving infrastructure, although these projects were difficult and costly to initiate.

Manufacturing industries registered sharp increases in capacity utilization in 1994 and 1995, exceeding 90 percent of capacity in the coal and nonferrous metal industries, as well as in furniture and footwear manufacturing. Investors judged South Africa's manufacturing competitiveness in the international arena to be fairly weak, however, largely because of the outdated facilities and physical plant in many industries.

Electric Power

The country's first electric power plants were developed to support the turn-of-the-century mining industry. Most mines used on-site electrical generators until 1909, when the Victoria Falls Power Company was established. In 1923 the electricity parastatal, Eskom, began providing electricity for the country's railroads and nonmining industries. Eskom bought out the Victoria Falls Power Company in 1948 and has been the country's major power producer since then. Eskom's sales increased faster than GDP growth after World War II, and the utility expanded steadily. From 1950 to 1982, sales grew at an average rate of 8 percent per year.

Despite Eskom's strong sales record, officials became increasingly concerned over the government's capital investments in Eskom's expansion efforts, which were estimated at R27 billion between 1983 and 1987. Eskom was one of the enterprises hit hardest by the cutoff in foreign loans in 1985. After that, it scaled down plans for further expansion. Eskom supplied more than 97 percent of the electricity used nationwide in the early 1990s, but a few mines and industries had power generators of their own. Only about 40 percent of the population had electricity in their homes, but the new government in 1994 placed a high priority on supplying power to rural areas.

Eskom derives nearly 90 percent of its power from coal-fired electric power stations, 8 percent from nuclear power plants, and the remainder from hydroelectric plants. Some energy analysts predict that the country's coal reserves (estimated to be between 60 billion and 100 billion tons) will begin to run out by the middle of the twenty-first century. Eskom officials estimate that the last coal-fired station will be commissioned before the year 2045. With about 14 percent of the world's uranium reserves in South Africa, Eskom then plans to switch to the use of nuclear power to produce electricity.

The Koeberg nuclear power station, commissioned in 1976 but subsequently damaged through sabotage, began operations using uranium as an energy source in 1984. In the mid-1990s, it is the only nuclear power plant in operation, but sites have been selected for at least two additional plants to be built early in the twenty-first century.

South Africa imported electricity from the Cahora Bassa hydroelectric facility in Mozambique during the early 1980s, but that source was cut off in 1983 as a result of sabotage by Mozambican rebels. South Africa, Mozambique, and Portugal agreed on reconstruction plans, begun in 1995, that were expected to reestablish power to South Africa by 1997.

Heavy Industry

Iron and steel production dominates South Africa's heavy industry, providing material for manufacturing structural goods, transport equipment, and machinery, and for the engineering industry. Large-scale production of iron and steel was begun in 1934 by the state-owned South African Iron and Steel Corporation (Iscor). Iscor began selling shares to the public in 1989. It operate plants at Pretoria, Vanderbijlpark (Gauteng), and Newcastle (KwaZulu-Natal) and owns numerous coal, iron ore, and other mines throughout the country. Most major companies in this sector, including Union Steel (Usco), African Metals (Amcor), and Vanderbijl Engineering (Vecor), were established with help from Iscor or are operated as subsidiaries of Iscor. Highveld Steel and Vanadium is owned by the Anglo American Corporation.

South Africa produced about 9 million tons of steel, on average, each year in the early 1990s, only about 1 percent of world production. This output was more than enough to meet domestic demand and to provide some steel for export. The industry plans to increase production in the late 1990s to meet domestic construction needs and to increase steel exports.

The first vehicle assembly plant was established by Ford in Port Elizabeth, and in 1960 the government began to promote the increased use of local parts in vehicle assembly. Phase One through Phase Five of the local-content encouragement program were based on the weight rather than the value of local components and tended to make South African vehicles relatively heavy and expensive. In 1989 the government introduced Phase Six, which shifted the determination of content to value rather than weight. The result was a reduction in the cost of vehicles as manufacturers turned to low-cost imported parts in order to increase the percentage of value represented by local products. The lowered cost of assembly was evidenced in June 1991 when the South African Motor Corporation (Samcor) announced that it had started exporting locally assembled Mazdas to Britain.

Vehicles are manufactured primarily in the industrial area around Johannesburg, in Mpumalanga, and in the Eastern and Western Cape provinces, using parts manufactured locally at more than 150 plants and some imported parts. In 1994 South African automakers assembled more than 225,000 passenger cars and more than 97,000 commercial vehicles, employing more than 91,000 workers. At that time, almost 6 million vehicles, including more than 3.5 million passenger cars, were licensed to operate in South Africa.

South Africa also has a significant heavy-engineering industry that meets many of the country's industrial and construction requirements. Many of the firms connected to Iscor produce structural steel, for use in construction, as well as machinery and mining equipment. Most advanced machinery, such as Eskom's generators or SASOL's plant, was still being imported in the 1990s. Nevertheless, when the production of all categories of heavy industry is combined—including steel and metal products, machinery, and vehicles—this subsector accounts for about one-fourth of manufacturing output by value.

Chemicals Industry

South Africa has a well-developed chemicals industry that dates back to the use of explosives in the late nineteenth-century mining industry. Miners imported dynamite from France and Germany until 1896, when the De Beers company succeeded in establishing a dynamite factory at Modderfontein in partnership with a British chemical manufacturer. In addition

*Robots on Nissan assembly line,
Rosslyn (Pretoria)
Courtesy Embassy of South
Africa, Washington*

to explosives, the African Explosives and Chemical Industries (AECI) plant produced a wide variety of industrial chemicals including insecticides, paints, varnishes, nitrogen compounds, sulfuric acid, and cyanide.

The government controls a significant segment of the chemical industry. Its largest investment is the SASOL operation, in which synthetic oil and gas are extracted from coal through a gasification process that also produces ammonia, pitch, alcohol, and paraffin. The government established the Phosphate Development Corporation (Foskor) in 1950 to produce phosphate concentrates for use in chemical fertilizers, and Foskor also produces zirconium and copper. Government involvement in the industry increased in 1967, when the IDC created a holding company to merge several small chemical companies in an effort to achieve greater economies of scale.

Many other chemicals are produced in South Africa, including plastics, resins, dyes, solvents, acids, alkalis, hydrogen peroxide, iodine, nitrates, and chemical materials for atomic reactors. Pharmaceutical products are also produced, primarily by subsidiaries of large international firms.

Consumer Goods

The single most productive subsector in manufacturing is

the food-processing industry, which produces canned fruits and vegetables, dried fruit, dairy products, baked goods, sugar, and meat and fish products. Dairy products and baked goods are sold exclusively on the local market, but dried fruit, canned foods, sugar, meat, and fish products are exported. In the early 1990s, South Africa produced about 400,000 tons of canned fruits and vegetables each year.

Clothing manufacturing and textile weaving are important consumer industries. The clothing industry predated local textile manufacturing; even at the end of the nineteenth century, clothing manufacturers relied on imported textiles to produce a variety of apparel. By the 1990s, the clothing industry not only met the country's needs but also exported its goods, aided in part by the government's elimination of import duties on cloth. It maintained a 30 to 35 percent import duty on most apparel through the early 1990s. Then, because clothing manufacturers increasingly relied on imported cloth, the domestic textile industry suffered from the increased competition, and as all import tariffs were being lifted in 1995 and 1996, both clothing and textile manufacturers were laying off workers.

The bread industry was subsidized by the government for decades in order to avoid high prices for basic foodstuffs; the government eliminated the bread subsidy in 1991 in an effort to encourage competition. A few large institutions then dominated the bread industry; six of them, representing about 85 percent of the local market, reached a marketing agreement, allocating sales by producer quotas and by regional distributor. The government in the mid-1990s decided to allow the companies to continue market-sharing but was debating whether to discourage such agreements in the future.

Transportation and Telecommunications

South Africa has a well-developed transportation system, the product of more than a century of government investment. The Ministry of Transport, formerly part of the Ministry of Transport, Posts, and Telecommunications, handles national transportation policy. The South African Railways and Harbours Administration, established in 1910, managed the operations of most of the nation's transportation network; in 1985 it became the South African Transport Services (SATS). In 1990 SATS reorganized as the public commercial company, Transnet.

Transnet has six business divisions—Spoornet to operate the railroads; Portnet to manage the country's extensive port system; Autonet, a comprehensive road transport service; South African Airways (SAA); Petronet to manage petroleum pipelines; and a parcel delivery service, known as "PX." With assets of nearly R35 billion, Transnet is one of the country's largest business enterprises, employing roughly 120,000 people in 1995. The government is the sole shareholder in Transnet but is considering the privatization of some sectors of transportation management by the end of the decade.

Railroads

When the Union of South Africa was formed in 1910, railroad authorities had to unify and to coordinate the operations of the four separate provincial railroad systems. Rail transport was already a critical element in economic development because it linked mining, agricultural, and urban areas and moved unprocessed raw materials (primarily minerals) to the coast for transport between South African ports and for export. The major axis of railroad transportation at the beginning of the twentieth century—linking Cape Town, Durban, and present-day Maputo in Mozambique, and running inland to the mining centers of Kimberley and Johannesburg—still forms the major axis of railroad transportation almost a century later (see fig. 17).

The national rail authority, Spoornet, manages a network of 21,303 kilometers of 1.067-meter, narrow-gauge (regional standard) rail lines throughout the country. An additional 314 kilometers of track are .610-meter gauge. In addition to hauling freight (roughly 164 million tons in 1993–94), intercity passenger trains carry more than 600 million passengers per year.

Rail transportation relied on steam power or steam-generated electricity as a result of the country's easy access to coal and its lack of petroleum resources. Some of the rail lines were electrified as early as 1926. In the 1970s, the railroads began phasing out the use of steam locomotives in favor of electricity in order to increase the carrying capacity and the speed of trains, especially those used to haul heavy mineral ores and coal for export. By the early 1990s, more than half of the rail network was electrified, and most rail traffic—both passenger and freight—was carried by electric locomotives.

Suburban commuter trains are important to many industrial and urban workers who live in the formerly segregated town-

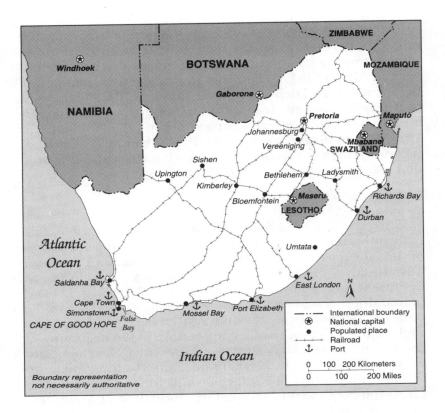

Figure 17. Transportation: Major Railroads and Ports, 1996

ships or rural areas, but the commuter lines are the least cost-effective rail service. The South African Rail Commuter Corporation (SARCC), relying on government subsidies of more than R600 million a year, manages these trains. Many trains are in poor condition, in part the result of the serious urban violence of the early 1990s, which often centered on the commuter rail lines as symbols of apartheid. The SARCC began refurbishing and modernizing rail coaches in 1994, at a cost of some US$180,000 per vehicle. Several private railroads also operate suburban commuter train service in several large cities.

Fast freight trains operate on eighteen routes nationwide, sometimes approaching speeds of 120 kilometers per hour, although the more common speed of rail travel is about sixty kilometers per hour. Railroad officials claimed a world record in 1989 when a 71,600-ton train ran at speeds of up to eighty kilometers per hour on the 861-kilometer Sishen-Saldanha ore line. Spoornet implemented a computerized operating information system in the early 1990s to manage high levels of rail traffic. In 1994 this system reported on more than 3,000 trains daily, often involving as many as 5,500 locomotives and 100,000 rail cars.

South Africa's luxury line, the Blue Train, travels the 1,600-kilometer route between Pretoria and Cape Town and is an important tourist attraction. Other well-known trains are the Trans-Oranj, which runs 2,088 kilometers between Durban and Cape Town; the Trans-Natal, which runs 721 kilometers between Johannesburg and Durban; the Diamond Express, which runs 563 kilometers between Pretoria and Kimberley; and the Limpopo, which runs 1,376 kilometers between Johannesburg and Harare, Zimbabwe. The Blue Train and the Trans-Karoo (between Johannesburg and Cape Town) have facilities for carrying passenger cars.

South Africa's railroads are also vital to the economies of several neighboring countries, especially landlocked Lesotho and Botswana, and Mozambique, where existing railroads have been sabotaged and destroyed through warfare. In 1990 the general managers from eight national railroads (South Africa, Botswana, Mozambique, Namibia, Swaziland, Zambia, Zimbabwe, and Zaire) formed a joint operations working group to integrate rail service in the region. In 1994 they began to coordinate timetables for scheduled freight service in order to speed transit of export commodities and perishables between countries. They also streamlined customs inspections and allowed trains to leave border stations with only partial loads of freight. As a result, during 1995, freight carried from Johannesburg to southern Zaire sometimes arrived in seven days, down from as much as forty days for the same journey in the past.

Ports and Shipping

South Africa has no commercially navigable rivers, but ocean shipping has long been a feature of its transportation network, capitalizing on the country's two-ocean frontage. The earliest nineteenth-century shipping firms began as coastal carriers for local commerce, traveling between southern African ports. After World War II, private investors initiated an international shipping service, and in 1946 the state corporation, South African Marine Corporation (Safmarine), assumed control over the private company. Safmarine operates container ships, general cargo vessels, and bulk carriers for mineral exports, and, since the 1980s, has offered expanded service to Europe, North America, South America, and Asia (South Korea, Hong Kong, and Taiwan). In 1992 it purchased the newest of its five container ships, *Oranje,* from Croatia at a cost of R100 million.

South Africa has six major commercial ports: Durban, Richards Bay, Cape Town, Saldanha Bay, Port Elizabeth, and East London. Portnet manages their facilities, including cargo-handling equipment, wharves, and container terminals, and provides services such as tugs, berthing, and cargo handling. Portnet also sets the standards for such services offered by private businesses. (In addition, Portnet manages forty-six lighthouses—eighteen operated by keepers and twenty-eight that are automatic.) Relying on containerization and automation to speed up service, Portnet handled more than 127 million tons of cargo on more than 12,900 seagoing vessels in 1994.

Each major port has traditionally played an important, specialized role in South Africa's export sector. For example, Durban handles general cargo, especially cereal exports; Cape Town specializes in exports of deciduous fruit, wine, and vegetables; and Saldanha Bay was built specifically to export mineral ores from the Northern Cape.

Durban's port encompasses 893 hectares of bay area. The port entrance channel is 12.7 meters deep at low tide. Durban has five deep-sea and two coastal container berths, and provides 15,195 meters of quayage for commercial ships. Durban also has repair facilities, including a floating dry dock. Through the 1980s, Durban was South Africa's busiest general cargo port, handling as much as 25 percent of the country's imports and exports in some years, but it was being surpassed by Richards Bay in the 1990s.

Richards Bay, a deep-water port 193 kilometers northeast of Durban, was commissioned in 1976 primarily to export coal from the eastern Transvaal, but by the early 1990s it was handling almost one-half of all cargo passing through South African ports. Port facilities can accommodate bulk carriers of up to 250,000 tons, with five berths for general and bulk cargo, and a coal berth.

Cape Town has one of the largest dry docks in the southern hemisphere, including five berths for container vessels and general cargo carriers, a pier for coastal traffic, and extensive ship repair facilities. The port at Cape Town has a water area of 112.7 hectares.

Port Elizabeth's enclosed water area of about 115 hectares has more than 3,400 meters of quayage for commercial shipping and a container terminal that has two berths. Vessels with a draught of up to twelve meters can use the harbor, and offshore anchorage is available for vessels of any draught. Facilities at Port Elizabeth include a mechanical ore-handling plant, which can process up to 1,500 tons per hour, and a precooling storage area with a capacity of 7,500 cubic meters.

Saldanha Bay, 110 kilometers northwest of Cape Town, is the largest port on the west coast of Africa and one of the best natural ports in the world. The facilities at Saldanha Bay provide anchorage in the lee of a breakwater where the minimum water depth is 14.6 meters. With a port area of about 5,000 hectares, Saldanha Bay is larger than the combined areas of the ports of Durban, Cape Town, Port Elizabeth, and East London. The ore-loading jetty can handle carriers of 350,000 tons.

South Africa's only river port, East London, is situated at the estuary of the Buffalo River in Eastern Cape province. Although East London is the smallest of the six major ports, it has a 75,000-ton capacity grain elevator—the largest in South Africa. East London handles agricultural exports and is the main outlet for copper exports from other African countries, such as Zambia and Zaire.

Two other coastal cities—Simonstown, south of Cape Town, and Mossel Bay, between Cape Town and Port Elizabeth—have substantial port facilities. Mossel Bay is a commercial fishing harbor between Cape Town and Port Elizabeth, and Simonstown is a naval base and training center (see Navy, ch. 5).

Road System and Transport

South Africa has an extensive national, provincial, and municipal road system covering the entire country (see fig. 18). As of 1996, the national routes include nearly 2,500 kilometers of limited-access freeways and 3,600 kilometers of highways with unlimited access. Roughly 60,000 kilometers of all-weather, paved roads and more than 100,000 kilometers of unpaved roads are maintained by the national and provincial governments.

More than 6 million vehicles are in operation nationwide, including about 3.5 million passenger vehicles, in 1996. Buses and private van services are also used by many workers who commute from townships and rural areas to urban workplaces. Several private bus companies run commuter lines, and municipal bus services operate within several cities.

South Africa has one of the highest road fatality rates in the world—more than 10,000 people, almost one-half of them pedestrians and bicyclists, were killed in more than 400,000 road accidents in 1992. The number of deaths was reduced slightly, to about 9,400, in 1993. The government has taken numerous measures to reduce accidents—for example, by implementing seat-belt laws and lowering speed limits. Nevertheless, in the mid-1990s, the government estimates that barely half of all automobile passengers wear seat belts, and traffic accidents continue to take a heavy toll.

Civil Aviation

The Chief Directorate of Civil Aviation, Ministry of Transport, is responsible for providing air traffic services at about twenty airports throughout the country and for issuing licenses to airline pilots, navigators, and flight engineers. This directorate also certifies the airworthiness of all registered craft, and approves maintenance schedules and flight manuals. In early 1996, more than 6,100 registered civil aviation aircraft operate in South Africa.

The Chief Directorate of Civil Aviation operates nine major airports. They are located at Bloemfontein, Cape Town, Durban, East London, Johannesburg, Kimberley, Port Elizabeth, George, and Upington. In the mid-1990s, the government changed the names of these and several other large airports from the Afrikaner heroes they had commemorated in the past, to the cities in which they are located. The airports at Johannesburg, Cape Town, and Durban are international airports and receive direct overseas flights. In addition, at least 300 landing strips throughout the country are used by private and commercial pilots.

South African Airways (SAA), the country's only national air carrier until the early 1990s, was established in 1934 by the South African Railways and Harbours Administration. After 1990 SAA was operated by the public company, Transnet. SAA has provided international service between Johannesburg and London since 1945 and has used jet passenger aircraft since 1953. In the mid-1990s, SAA operates a fleet of forty-eight aircraft, primarily Boeing 747s, Boeing 737s, and Airbus 300s, providing air service among all major cities in South Africa, with at least 687 domestic flights a week.

SAA was denied landing rights in most European and African countries and the United States in the 1980s and the early 1990s. A few African and Middle Eastern countries, such as Sudan, Congo, Saudi Arabia, Libya, and Morocco, also denied SAA overflight rights, forcing SAA pilots to fly longer routes to avoid prohibited air space. The airline nonetheless continued to operate flights to several European and African capitals throughout the sanctions era; then, as sanctions eased in the early 1990s, SAA reestablished and expanded its international flight routes to the rest of Africa, the United States, Europe, South America, the Middle East, and Asia.

After the government began deregulating airlines in 1990—legalizing competition with SAA on domestic and international routes—several new private airlines were established in South Africa, and the number of foreign air carriers flying to South Africa increased to more than fifty. Transnet assumed control of at least one former homeland airline and established Alliance Airlines as a joint venture between SAA and the national carriers of Tanzania and Uganda. In addition, at least fifteen independent feeder airlines operate more than 200 routes linking smaller towns to cities served by international air carriers.

Pipelines

Although South Africa has no significant petroleum reserves, it uses a nationwide network of pipelines to transport imported crude oil to refineries and to transport other petroleum products to industrial areas. At least 931 kilometers of crude-oil pipelines, 322 kilometers of natural gas pipelines, and 1,748 kilometers of pipelines for other petroleum products make up this network in the mid-1990s.

Telecommunications and Postal Service

Until 1990 the Department of Posts and Telecommunications regulated all nationwide communications networks. In 1991, in anticipation of possible privatization, the government formed two state-owned companies, the telecommunications corporation, Telkom, and the South African Post Office to deliver the mail. Telkom is the largest telecommunications system in Africa. It earned at least US$2.3 billion in 1993, providing telegraph, telex, telephone, radio, television, and data and facsimile transmissions. Telkom also holds a majority stake in

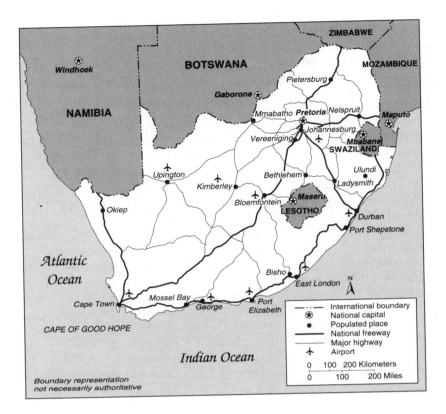

Figure 18. Transportation: Major Highways and Airports, 1996

one of the nation's two cellular phone networks that began operation in 1995.

The telephone system, which links all major cities and many small towns, encompasses roughly 5 million telephones in the mid-1990s, roughly 9.7 per 100 inhabitants. They are connected through more than 1,200 automatic exchanges. The telephone system includes a network of coaxial and fiber optic cable and radio-relay, three ground stations that communicate with satellites over the Atlantic Ocean and the Indian Ocean, and an undersea coaxial cable between South Africa and the Canary Islands that joins other cables linking Europe and South America.

Telephone service became a symbol of the racial disparities under apartheid, especially during the 1980s, when per capita access to telephone service in black communities was less than one-tenth that in white areas. For this reason, early-1990s plans for a cellular telephone network in rural and township areas assumed symbolic as well as economic importance as a means of black empowerment. In 1994 and 1995, this system extended telephone service into many rural areas for the first time and was assisting local entrepreneurs for whom communication had often been a major obstacle. Industry officials predicted that by the late 1990s, the cellular phone industry would create at least 4,500 jobs directly, and would contribute to the creation of perhaps 40,000 or more jobs in related industries.

The government began allowing the private sector to provide data transmission services in 1994. The plan was to allow companies to use Telkom facilities to provide customers with value-added services, such as the electronic transfer of funds and messages, management of corporate data networks, and the remote processing of corporate information. Telkom retained control over the independent telecommunications services, to continue the company's statutory monopoly overall and to regulate competition in the field. Private companies are able to lease facilities, such as data lines, from Telkom and charge customers only for value added to these services.

The South African Broadcasting Corporation (SABC) had a near-monopoly in television service in most of South Africa until the independent television company, M-Net, inaugurated service in January 1991. In 1993 the government placed SABC broadcasts under the supervision of the Independent Broadcasting Authority, as a step toward greater media independence from political control. Television service, which had been initiated in 1976, consisted of four channels broadcasting in English, Afrikaans, and five African languages. One of the English-Afrikaans stations was a subscription service, similar to cable television, owned by a syndicate of newspaper publishers. Until 1994 residents of some of the former black homelands, and those near the border with Swaziland, had received separate broadcasts from those areas. After that, television service in the former homelands was incorporated into the nationwide system. A reorganization of SABC was implemented in the mid-1990s to allow greater diversity in its broadcasts.

The SABC operates 300 frequency modulation (FM) and fourteen amplitude modulation (AM) radio stations. Programs were primarily in English and Afrikaans through the early 1990s, but several low-power FM stations broadcast in at least a dozen African languages, and the use of African languages was increasing. One short-wave external service, Radio RSA, broadcasts worldwide.

The South African Post Office provides postal and money-transfer services, as well as postal savings accounts. Its 1,580 post offices and other facilities handled more than 7 million items each workday in 1994, delivering mail to some 5 million addresses. In its first year in power (1994–95), the new Government of National Unity opened at least seventy new post offices and upgraded many others in previously ill-served areas. It also installed an estimated 700,000 new mail boxes at private addresses and in post-office box locations. Postal savings accounts are available to individuals with as little as R10 to deposit; interest payments in 1995 were reportedly as high as 5 percent on savings deposits and 11 percent on savings certificates. South Africa was readmitted to the Universal Postal Union in 1994, enabling it to participate in international technical assistance programs and accounting facilities within the union.

Environmental Protection and Tourism

Environmental Protection

South Africa has signed at least twenty-four major international agreements concerning environmental preservation, including the 1973 Convention on International Trade in Endangered Species of Wild Fauna and Flora (CITES) and the 1987 Protocol on Substances that Deplete the Ozone Layer, or Montreal Protocol. During the 1980s, the government enforced environmental legislation only weakly, however, and the Environment Conservation Act (No. 73) of 1989 further weakened existing practices. Based on this legislation, the government's Council on the Environment proposed a new approach, called Integrated Environmental Management, aimed at accommodating development concerns. As in other countries, many business and community leaders place infrastructure development far ahead of environmental issues, and many voters place a higher priority on alleviating poverty than preserving the environment.

The 1989 legislation and subsequent amendments set out the official objectives in environmental conservation—to preserve species and ecosystems, to maintain ecological processes, and to protect against land degradation and environmental deterioration resulting from human activities. The government requires environmental impact assessments for major development and construction projects, and it imposes fines on industrial polluters. Demographic researchers concluded in 1993, however, that the implications of rapid population growth are potentially devastating to the environmentalists' concerns— they estimate that the population is likely to double by the year 2025, and one-half of the population may then be living in "grinding poverty." As a result of these pronouncements, land preservation and population control became interlinked social causes in the 1990s.

Environmentalists argue that the country's advanced soil erosion and land degradation threaten future generations and will be worsened by overpopulation and overcultivation. Little more than one-tenth of the total land area is fit for cultivation; as much as 500 million tons of topsoil are lost each year through erosion caused by wind and water, and the problem is worsened by deforestation through uncontrolled tree harvesting. Environmentalists also note that industrial pollutants and raw sewage are allowed to seep into streams and lakes, and even into wells used for drinking water in some communities.

As the April 1994 elections approached, environmental activists persuaded ANC leaders to include a chapter on the environment in the Reconstruction and Development Programme (RDP), the blueprint for development in the 1990s. The ANC also commissioned an environmental study by the Canadian International Development Research Centre, and the new government gave strong lip service to environmental priorities when it assumed office in 1994.

Later that year, however, as some officials tried to maintain the priority on long-term environmental concerns, they faced strong opposition within the new, financially strapped government and from the business community. The government's Department of Environmental Affairs (formerly Department of Environment Affairs and Tourism) is in charge of coordinating environmental policy, but critics have argued that it is not pursuing this task very aggressively and that nongovernmental organizations lack the financial and political support to effect significant change.

South Africa has sought an exception to the 1973 CITES convention, which governs global trade in animals threatened with extinction. The convention aims to protect the dwindling African elephant population; it first banned trade in ivory products among signatory states and was amended in 1989 to outlaw commercial trade in all elephant parts. South Africa's request was based on local game officials' reports that elephants were not threatened with extinction in South Africa, and that animals being culled offered lucrative trade in hides and meat. By 1995 this petition, unlike earlier petitions from Pretoria, was being given serious consideration among CITES signatories, partly in recognition of the new government's post-apartheid needs.

Tourism

In the mid-1990s, control of the tourism industry was transferred from the Department of Environmental Affairs to the Department of Industry and Trade, partly to give a higher priority to tourist-industry development concerns. Through the new Department of Industry, Trade, and Tourism, the government operates National Tourist Bureaus throughout the country as well as the South African Tourism Board (Satour). Satour, established in 1983 to promote tourism from abroad, has been recognized internationally for its high-quality services.

Among South Africa's many tourist attractions are sixteen national parks and numerous provincial and local game parks, nature reserves, and wilderness areas. The National Parks Board employs more than 4,000 South Africans. Kruger National Park in Mpumalanga and Northern provinces is one of the most popular with visitors and is home to more than 140 species of mammals and 450 species of birds. The rare mountain zebra, which is unique to South Africa, is protected in the Mountain Zebra National Park in the Eastern Cape. The Augrabies Falls National Park, site of the fifty-six-meter- high Augrabies Falls on the Orange River near Upington, preserves plants and animals that have adapted to semi-desert conditions. The Kalahari Gemsbok National Park, in the Northern Cape bordering Namibia and Botswana, is known for its free-roaming gemsbok and springbok. In addition to game parks, nature reserves, and big-game hunting between May and July, the wine region of the Western Cape is a consistent tourist attraction.

South African tourism figures have risen since the late 1980s and exceeded 3.8 million in 1994 (see table 15, Appendix). More than half of the tourists in South Africa are from other African countries; most of the remainder are from the United Kingdom or Germany. South Africa is a member of the World

Tourism Organization and a participant in the Africa Travel Association, which promotes tourist attractions in Africa to the North American travel industry.

Banking and Currency

Banking

The heart of the banking system is the South African Reserve Bank, which is the primary monetary authority and custodian of the country's gold and foreign exchange reserves. The Reserve Bank is managed by a board of fourteen directors, seven representing major commercial and financial institutions, industry, and agriculture, and seven appointed by the government. Of the latter, one serves as governor, and three serve as deputy governors of the Reserve Bank.

The Reserve Bank's primary functions are to protect the value of the rand and to control inflation. The Reserve Bank regulates the money supply by influencing its cost—i.e., interest charged on loans to other institutions. It is technically independent of government control, but in practice it works closely with the Treasury and helps to formulate and to implement macroeconomic policy. The Reserve Bank issues banknotes and is responsible for the sale and purchase of foreign exchange for the government, as well as for the administration of the treasury-bill tender system. Its major customers are government agencies, private banks, and discount houses, although it also performs clearinghouse functions for private banks and assists banks that experience liquidity problems. Finally, the Reserve Bank is the authorized buyer of gold bullion, thereby acting as agent for the gold-mining industry in effecting sales on their behalf in the private market.

The Reserve Bank uses monetary policy to control inflation, primarily by adjusting the liquid-asset requirements of private banking institutions and by restricting bank credit in order to control consumer demand. Until 1975 the bank enforced fixed interest rates on long-term government securities, but thereafter it allowed transactions at market-related prices. Direct control over deposit interest rates quoted by banking institutions was abolished in 1980; nevertheless, the Reserve Bank still exercises considerable indirect control through its own bank rate.

The private banking sector was controlled by commercial banks until the 1950s when banking services began to diversify. Until then, commercial banks had avoided services such as personal loans, property leasing, and credit-card facilities. New institutions—including discount houses, merchant banks, and general banks—emerged to meet this demand, and in reaction to these changes in the banking sector, commercial banks increasingly entered into medium-term credit arrangements with commerce and industry and acquired interests in hire-purchase firms and leasing activities. In addition, they expanded their operations into insurance and even invested in manufacturing and commercial enterprises.

During the late 1980s, the "big five" commercial banks—First National Bank (formerly Barclays), Standard Bank of South Africa, Nedbank, Volkskas, and Trust Bank—were increasingly challenged by building societies, which had listed holding companies on the Johannesburg Stock Exchange (JSE) and had set up commercial and/or general banking arms. The Deposit Taking Institutions Act of 1991 formalized the overlapping of functions between the banks and the building societies that had existed for more than a decade. The act brought South Africa into line with internationally recognized standards for capital requirements.

In February 1991, four of the country's leading financial institutions—Allied Bank, United Bank, Volkskas, and Sage Banks—merged to create the largest banking group in the country, the Amalgamated Banks of South Africa (ABSA), with assets of R56 billion. ABSA, which merged with a fifth bank in 1992, is jointly controlled by the Rembrandt tobacco group and the South African National Life Assurance Company (Sanlam), the country's second-largest insurance group. The banking industry is undergoing further reorganization in the mid-1990s, in part to establish banking services in poor communities that were neglected under apartheid.

Currency

Until the late 1960s, South Africa had a fixed exchange rate for its currency; thereafter, the rand was pegged to major foreign currencies. In 1979 the government switched to a system that formally expressed parity against the dollar. The value of the rand followed changes in the balance of payments and moved roughly with sterling and other weaker currencies until 1985. The foreign-debt crisis of that year caused the rand to depreciate at an unprecedented rate, and it fell to an all-time low of less than US$0.40. The rand recovered somewhat in 1987, reaching US$0.43, but it declined steadily, with minor

The South African Reserve Bank (Pretoria) regulates money supply and monetary policy. Embassy of South Africa, Washington

adjustments, after that, dipping to about US$0.26 in late 1995. Between February 1 and May 1, 1996, the rand lost roughly 16 percent of its value, falling from R3.7 to R4.33 = US$1, or a value of about US$0.23.

A parallel currency, the financial rand, was used exclusively for the movement of nonresident capital during the 1980s and the early 1990s. Financial rands developed out of currency-exchange controls instituted in the early 1960s, known as the "blocked rand." The financial rand was available only to foreigners for investment in South Africa and was created by the sale of nonresidents' assets in the country. This two-tiered currency system insulated the country's foreign reserves from politically motivated capital flight, because all divestment by nonresidents was automatically met by new investment, and the price of the financial rand varied independently of the commercial rand. Financial rands invariably stood at a discount to commercial rands, but the size of the discount depended on South Africa's relative attraction as an investment destination. The discount stood at almost 40 percent during most of 1992, for example, but declined to about 20 percent in late 1993.

Reserve Bank governor Chris Stals, under pressure from the banking and business communities, said that the government would phase out the financial rand in 1994 or 1995, assuming that South Africa's foreign currency reserves reached at least R20 billion and that the discount between the financial and the commercial rands narrowed to about 10 percent. Foreign currency reserves were precariously low in early 1994 but, in a dramatic reversal of the capital outflow of 1993, increased steadily throughout 1994 and early 1995. In March 1995, with foreign reserves of only about R12 billion, the government abolished the financial rand. The newly unified currency traded well on international currency markets, marking a vote of confidence in South Africa's business potential.

Growth Trends and Potential

One sign of hope for South Africa's economic future in the mid-1990s is the black business sector, which struggled to survive during the 1980s but began to thrive in the postapartheid era. In 1994 the first major black-owned investment company to be listed on the Johannesburg Stock Exchange, New Africa Investment, Ltd., had 8,500 black shareholders. It holds a controlling stake in a major newspaper, a large life insurance company, and a cellular telephone company. These and other black-owned businesses plan to target rural communities and the poor for a substantial portion of their expansion. But they, like other enterprises in South Africa, must depend on a growing economy to finance new investment.

South Africa's businesses have been disappointed in the relatively slow increase in foreign investment since 1994, but they still hope that outside assistance will help ease the political and the economic transition of the 1990s. South Africa joined the African Development Bank (ADB) in 1995, in part because ADB membership offered the possibility of at least US$200 million in development aid by 1997, and because South African companies could bid for contracts on ADB-sponsored projects in other African countries. The value of these projects was estimated at US$3.5 billion in 1995.

South Africa's economic growth has always depended on increasing gold profits and foreign investments. In the mid-1990s, these continued to be important to the country's future, and both were directly linked to the ongoing dismantling of apartheid and political reconstruction. Yet profits were certain to drop if the government agreed to raise wages for industrial workers, as most labor leaders insisted. National earnings also would be reduced if the mining companies were to cut back on production. Thus, there were strong economic incentives for the government both to limit wages and to avoid serious outbreaks of labor unrest in order to attract much-needed foreign investment. But rising tensions in late 1994 and 1995 signaled the difficulty it faced in balancing these two goals. Neither manufacturing, which depended on foreign capital, nor agriculture, which produced erratically as a result of weather conditions, could provide sufficient independent growth to break this cycle. Furthermore, both of these sectors had long depended on low wage scales for labor and would experience the same difficulties as the mining sector in the 1990s.

In the long term, it appears doubtful that South Africa's economy can continue the same spectacular growth it experienced earlier in the twentieth century. But under a stable multiracial government, South Africa can gain access to many new export markets for manufactured goods throughout Africa and elsewhere, and, with labor's cooperation and barring serious unrest, it can attract the investments necessary to service those markets. The country is nonetheless likely to remain dependent on foreign capital and to suffer from erratic agricultural production into the twenty-first century.

*   *   *

There is a wealth of information available on South Africa's economy and its historical development. The South African government itself publishes the most useful information, and citations for numerous reports and other publications may be found in the annual *South Africa Yearbook*, formerly published as the *South Africa Official Yearbook*. *Source Material on the South African Economy: 1860–1970* by D. Hobart Houghton and Jenifer Dagut is a definitive guide to primary and secondary sources for the historical period.

Secondary sources on historical economic development are divided both on ideological grounds and by topic. The following are some of the best known: Colin Bundy, *The Rise and Fall of the South African Peasantry*; D. Hobart Houghton, *The South African Economy*; Frederick A. Johnstone, *Class, Race, and Gold: A Study of Class Relations and Racial Discrimination in South Africa*; Shula Marks and Anthony Atmore, eds., *Economy and Society in Pre-Industrial South Africa*; Shula Marks and Richard Rathbone, eds., *Industrialisation and Social Change in South Africa*; and Shula Marks and Stanley Trapido, eds., *The Politics of Race, Class, and Nationalism in Twentieth-Century South Africa*.

Initial analyses of economic change in the 1980s and the early 1990s are found in Merle Lipton and Charles Simkins's *State and Market in Post-Apartheid South Africa*. Excellent sources of current information are the South African Reserve Bank *Quarterly Bulletin*; *Financial Mail*; *Financial Times*; *Africa Economic Digest*; *Africa Research Bulletin: Economic, Financial, and Technical Series*; and the various publications of the Economist Intelligence Unit, in particular the quarterly *Country Report: South Africa* and the annual *Country Profile: South Africa*. (For further information and complete citations, see Bibliography.)

Chapter 4. Government and Politics

Steam engine wends its way past fields and homestead in hilly KwaZulu-Natal.

SOUTH AFRICA IN 1994 underwent the most radical and far-reaching political and constitutional transformation since the racially divisive South Africa Act provided the legal basis for the Union of South Africa in 1910. The latest sweeping transformation officially began with the April 26–29, 1994, national and provincial elections, and with the triumph of the previously banned African National Congress (ANC).

The country's main political antagonists, the ANC and the former ruling National Party (NP), had agreed in November 1993 on the composition of a multiparty Transitional Executive Council (TEC) to govern jointly until elections were held. They also agreed that, after the elections, a transitional Government of National Unity would be in power and that a transitional bicameral parliament would form a constitutional assembly to draft a final constitution. In addition, they agreed on an interim constitution that would guide the transition between the April 1994 elections and the adoption of the final constitution.

Domestic, regional, and international developments over the past decade had served to alter radically both Afrikaner (see Glossary) and black politics from the politics of repression and armed resistance to the politics of negotiation and participation. Since 1960 the banned ANC, ANC-allied South African Communist Party (SACP), and Pan-Africanist Congress (PAC) had waged an armed struggle from their bases in neighboring countries. The armed struggle intensified during the 1980s and expanded into a "people's war" involving mass demonstrations against the apartheid (see Glossary) state. International pressure in the form of economic and political sanctions, including diplomatic pressure by the United States, helped force the Afrikaner establishment—faced with a threat to its own economic well-being—to embark on a process that would ultimately result in sharing power, authority, and resources with the disenfranchised black majority.

A multiparty conference, the Convention for a Democratic South Africa (Codesa), met to formulate a new constitution on December 20, 1991, and, after talks foundered in 1992, resumed in March 1993 to plan the political transition. In April 1994, the nation's first nonracial provincial legislatures and the transitional National Assembly were democratically elected by universal suffrage. The 1994 elections were the culmination of a spectacular series of bilateral talks in which NP and ANC leaders agreed on a set of compromises concerning the interim period while formulating preliminary constitutional guidelines for a multiracial and majoritarian democratic society, based on the principle of "one person-one vote." Finally, the political conflict between the ANC and several recalcitrant parties that had boycotted the negotiations process—including the Inkatha Freedom Party (IFP, known as Inkatha), which demanded greater regional autonomy for its Zulu constituency, and the Freedom Front, a group committed to Afrikaner self-determination—was resolved only days before the April 1994 elections.

In the early 1990s, the right-wing Afrikaner parties, including neo-Nazi elements, had provided the main resistance to the transition to multiracial democracy. Their resistance took the form of legal political parties, extra-legal movements, and paramilitary organizations. Most of these groups were fragmented, particularly over ideology, and demoralized by their realization that accommodationist currents were running against them. Some of them splintered as they were being pushed to the margin of events by the pragmatism of President Frederik W. (F.W.) de Klerk.

Establishing a national consensus over the new nonracial, democratic political system was, therefore, the main task of the leaders of the NP and the ANC. Only a consensus could overcome the pressures of extremists on both sides, whose violence and racial antagonisms had been fueled by the authoritarianism, coercion, and distortions implicit in the apartheid system. The task facing the moderate leaders was complicated by the sharp increase in violent criminal activity throughout the country, as law and order broke down in many regions, even areas in which crime rates had been low in the past. Although officials estimated that at least 80 percent of all murders committed in the early 1990s were not politically motivated, political violence by extremist groups continuously threatened to undermine the country's fragile political stability as the elections approached.

The revolutionary changes sweeping South Africa in 1993 and 1994 were remarkable. It was almost unprecedented for a ruling group in a society that it so completely dominated, although it constituted an ethnic minority, to hand over power in a peaceful manner to the country's longstanding oppressed and banned opposition. South Africa's ruling party leaders did

Nelson Mandela addresses opening session of the Convention for a Democratic South Africa (Codesa), December 1991.
Courtesy Embassy of South Africa, Washington

so with the realization that the once-banned organizations represented the political will of the majority of citizens.

Many political leaders helped to shape the new political system. The two most instrumental in bridging the gap between the two sides were State President F.W. de Klerk, leader of the NP, which had ruled the country without effective electoral challenge since 1948, and Nelson (Rolihlahla) Mandela, president of the ANC, the foremost political leader among the black majority. A third player, Chief Mangosuthu (Gatsha) Buthelezi, leader of the Zulu-based IFP, also gave expression to black aspirations, particularly in the IFP stronghold of Natal Province's KwaZulu homeland (see Glossary). Other important players included supporters of the new regime, such as leaders of the coloured (mixed race—see Glossary) and the Indian communities, the largely English-speaking liberal white parties, and newly emerging leaders in the black homelands. In contrast were the virulent opponents of the postapartheid system, such as the Afrikaner extremists, who had split from the NP into several groups seeking to brake the slide toward political and social transformation in order to preserve a state based on the principles of apartheid.

As the country prepared to embark on full-scale democracy in the early 1990s, new challenges confronted the ANC. First, as a newly legalized party, the ANC had to demonstrate that it was no longer merely an extraparliamentary liberation movement, but a serious contender for the task of governing the country. It also had to balance the need to provide expression to a younger generation of black South Africans who had been radicalized by years of boycotts, jailings, suppression, and ethnic violence, against the need to attract new supporters not only from its black constituency, but from the white, the coloured, and the Indian communities as well.

Mandela, in order to succeed in the new political arena, had to gain the support of the more conservative, yet antiapartheid, ethnic leaders in the countryside and in the black homelands, while retaining the support of younger leaders and activists and while mobilizing the violence-prone majority in the townships. He also had to distance the party from the political and economic program of its longstanding ally, the SACP, even though a number of SACP leaders remained on the ANC's executive and working committees. To present a cohesive front, the ANC also had to join forces in one form or another with Inkatha Chief Buthelezi, although the tensions between the two black movements often erupted into violence over political turf, particularly in Natal and KwaZulu. Finally, the ANC had to fill the vacuum left by the loss of political and military support of previous state sponsors such as the former Soviet Union, which no longer provided material support to Third World liberation movements.

Similarly, NP leader de Klerk had to retain the party's traditional bases of support among Afrikaners while working to gain or to retain the support of coloured, Indian, and liberal white votes. Finally, de Klerk had to reach out to previously hostile black communities, a move that would invariably provoke white right-wing extremists, who had resorted to violence in the past and who were threatening antigovernment insurgency.

System of Government

The new political system was established by the interim constitution voted into law in late 1993 and officially implemented on April 27, 1994. The interim constitution provides for a Government of National Unity and for a five-year transition, during which the final constitution would be drafted by the Constitutional Assembly, consisting of the combined Senate and

National Assembly. To understand fully the revolutionary nature of the new government and the direction that the political transition is likely to take in the long term, it is necessary to examine the evolution of the political system that was based on the principles and practices of apartheid.

Historical Background

The Union of South Africa became a self-governing dominion within the British Commonwealth on May 31, 1910, when four British dependencies were merged under the South Africa Act passed by the British Parliament in 1909. Unification was interpreted differently by British and by Afrikaner leaders, however. To the British, uniting the four dependencies was central to their imperialist philosophy of consolidating the empire; to many Afrikaners, unity represented a step toward weakening British imperial influence. Ironically, however, this act failed to unite South Africa in a real sense because by excluding the black majority from political participation, it fueled the discontent and the conflict that characterized the country's politics throughout the twentieth century.

The South Africa Act served as the Union of South Africa's constitution until 1961. Although the country was formally ruled by a governor general representing the Crown, its government was granted almost total independence in internal affairs. Britain's 1931 Statute of Westminster removed many constitutional limitations on all British dominions, and South Africa's corresponding legislation, the Status of Union Act of 1934, declared that no act of the British parliament could apply to South Africa unless accepted by the Union parliament.

South Africa officially became the Republic of South Africa on May 31, 1961, following a national referendum among the country's white voters on October 5, 1960. The constitution of 1961 was based largely on the South Africa Act, but it severed ties with the British Commonwealth of Nations, replacing the words "king," "queen," and "crown" with "state." The state president replaced the British monarch and governor general.

The 1961 constitution provided for a president, a prime minister, and an executive council (cabinet) with offices at Pretoria (where most of the administrative bureaucracy was located). A bicameral legislature was situated at Cape Town. The independent judiciary was headquartered at Bloemfontein.

The 1961 constitution maintained white political domination through an electoral system that denied blacks, coloureds, and Asians the right to vote for national office holders. Coloureds and Asians, but not blacks, won limited participation in ethnic affairs through, respectively, a Coloured Persons' Representative Council established in 1964 and a South African Indian Council established in 1968. Since 1951 the Bantu Authorities Act had restricted black political participation to homelands (also referred to as Bantustans) set aside for Africans. During the 1970s and the 1980s, four of the ten homelands were declared "independent" black states, while the remaining six were known as "self-governing" territories.

Following intense debate and a series of legislative revisions in the early 1980s, the new Constitution of the Republic of South Africa Act (No. 110) of 1983 went into effect on September 22, 1984. It outlined a government led by a president, who served as head of state and chief executive, and a parliamentary system with increased coloured and Indian representation. The new, tricameral Parliament encompassed a (white) House of Assembly, a (coloured) House of Representatives, and an (Indian) House of Delegates. The president was selected by an eighty-eight-member electoral college consisting of fifty whites, twenty-five coloureds, and thirteen Indians, chosen by a majority vote in their respective houses of parliament. The president served for the duration of the parliament that selected him, normally a five-year term. The president could dissolve the parliament, or could extend it by up to six months beyond its five-year term.

The president shared executive authority with a cabinet, which he appointed from the tricameral parliament, and with a Ministers Council chosen by him from the majority in each house of parliament. In addition, the president relied on a sixty-member President's Council for advice on urgent matters and for resolution of differences among houses of parliament. The President's Council comprised twenty members from the House of Assembly, ten from the House of Representatives, five from the House of Delegates, fifteen nominated by the president, and ten nominated by opposition party leaders. The NP dominated the President's Council throughout the ten-year duration of the 1983 constitution.

The three-chambered parliament was based on a fundamental premise of the 1983 constitution, the distinction between a racial community's "own" affairs (encompassing education, health, housing, social welfare, local government, and some aspects of agriculture), and "general" affairs (encompassing defense, finance, foreign policy, justice, law and order, transport, commerce and industry, manpower, internal affairs, and overall agricultural policy). Thus, legislation "affecting the interests" of one community was deliberated upon by the appropriate house, but legislation on "general affairs" of importance to all races was handled by all three houses of parliament. Disagreements among houses of parliament on specific legislation could be resolved by the President's Council, giving the NP-dominated House of Assembly substantial weight in determining the outcome of all legislative debates. The president signed all legislation, and he also exercised administrative responsibility for black affairs.

The country was divided into four provinces—Cape of Good Hope Province (later, the Cape Province), Natal Province, the Transvaal, and the Orange Free State. The president appointed a provincial administrator for each province. Until the mid-1980s, the provincial administrator acted in consultation with a provincial council, which was elected by whites only. In July 1987, the provincial councils were replaced by eight multiracial regional services councils (RSCs)—four in the Transvaal, three in the Cape Province, and one in the Orange Free State. The RSCs were empowered to administer government regulations and to coordinate the provision of services to local communities.

Constitutional Change

The constitutional reforms of the early 1980s led to four phases of political change that, ultimately, irrevocably transformed the South African political system. First, the 1983 constitution's new political representation for coloureds and Indians made the glaring lack of participation by the country's black majority even more obvious. Even early discussions of the new constitution triggered widespread violent protests by anti-apartheid activists. The escalating violence prompted the government to impose a series of states of emergency and forced both the government and many citizens to realize that promising future political reform regarding black political participation would no longer suffice; sweeping political reforms would be necessary, and the need for such reforms was becoming increasingly urgent.

The second phase of change was a series of secret meetings between NP officials and imprisoned ANC leaders. These began in July 1984, after Minister of Justice Hendrik "Kobie" Coetsee (representing President P.W. Botha) paid several unpublicized visits to ANC leader Nelson Mandela, who was then serving the twenty-first year of a life prison sentence. The government formalized these visits in May 1988 by establishing a committee to handle government contacts with Mandela and with other imprisoned or exiled ANC leaders. On July 5, 1989, in response to Mandela's request for high-level discussions of a possible negotiated settlement to the ANC's armed struggle, Botha and Mandela held their first face-to-face talks.

Botha resigned from office, owing to ill health, in August 1989, and in December, Mandela suggested a "road map" for future negotiations to the new president, F.W. de Klerk. Mandela's proposal outlined a power-sharing plan for the NP and its political rivals and embraced the spirit of compromise that would be needed to weather the political turbulence that lay ahead.

These talks led to the third, and most transforming, phase in recent politics, beginning with de Klerk's historic speech of February 2, 1990, in which he legalized more than thirty anti-apartheid organizations; ordered the release of eight long-term political prisoners, including Mandela and ANC deputy president Walter Sisulu; removed many emergency regulations concerning the media and political detainees; and announced his intention to negotiate a new democratic constitution with his political opponents. In October of that year, the parliament took a symbolic step toward reform by repealing the Separate Amenities Act, an important legislative pillar of apartheid.

The fourth phase in the political transformation occurred as the NP government and the ANC leadership began to recognize their mutual dependence and the need for cooperation and compromise in embarking on constitutional negotiations. In this phase, their previously adversarial relationship was transformed through their discussions and their agreement on three accords—the Groote Schuur Minute (May 1990), the Pretoria Minute (August 1990), and the D.F. Malan Accord (February 1991). In these accords, ANC leaders pledged to suspend the armed struggle, the government agreed to release all political prisoners, and both sides agreed to pursue political reform through negotiation. On September 14, 1991, representatives of twenty-seven political parties, interest groups, and the national and homeland governments signed the National Peace Accord, agreeing to form a multiracial council, later called the Transitional Executive Council (TEC), to serve as temporary executive authority until democratic elections could be held.

Nearly three months after the signing of the historic peace accord, preliminary negotiations to agree on procedural rules began at the World Trade Center outside Johannesburg, as the Convention for a Democratic South Africa (Codesa). In September 1992, Mandela and de Klerk reached a Record of Understanding, formally committing both sides to accept a democratically elected, five-year interim Government of National Unity led by a political coalition. They also agreed that the center of government would remain in Pretoria and that the new state president would be chosen from the party winning the largest plurality of votes in nationwide nonracial elections. Any party that won at least 5 percent of the seats in parliament would be entitled to a place in the cabinet. The transitional, bicameral parliament was to be charged with drafting and adopting a new constitution. The ANC accepted the idea of sharing power with the NP during the transition. Assuming the ANC would win the elections, it would, as the majority party, exercise its prerogative on most matters, and the NP would serve as a junior partner in running the country.

These agreements on the transitional government represented important compromises by both the government and the ANC, and they helped to set new precedents for future negotiations. The NP won agreement on its refusal to give the new state president broad and extensive powers during the transition period. (Under the previous system, the president could override the views of minority parties.) At the same time, de Klerk compromised on his demand for a permanent consensus-style arrangement to be enshrined in any new constitution by agreeing to a five-year transitional government. The arrangement satisfied the NP demand for legally binding checks and balances to protect the country's white minority. The ANC, for its part, compromised on its earlier insistence on full and immediate majority rule, by agreeing to participate in a powersharing arrangement for at least five years. At the same time, many ANC leaders hoped that their party, as the dominant party in the transitional government, would win a sufficiently large majority to enable it to enact most of its policies, even without the consent of other parties.

Supporters on both sides viewed the Government of National Unity as the country's best hope for achieving long-term political and economic stability, for attracting much-needed foreign investment, and for limiting violence by both white and black extremists. One of the main criticisms of the proposed coalition government was that with the two major political rivals entering into a governing alliance, their small-party opponents would have little political maneuverability and would be forced into extraparliamentary protest.

By early 1994, a number of problems remained unresolved. The most crucial was the need to establish a broad consensus among the political parties over the basic principles to be embodied in a new constitution. The negotiators had yet to reach agreement on the powers and the functions of the three commissions responsible for overseeing the transition—the TEC, the Independent Electoral Commission (IEC), and the Independent Media Commission that would be charged with ensuring media fairness. Other problems concerned the operations of the interim government—such as joint ANC-NP control over the country's security forces and the integration of the ANC's and PAC's paramilitary wings into the new national army.

The ANC and Inkatha still had to resolve their civil war in Natal and KwaZulu, where more than 10,000 people had been killed in a decade of ethnic and political violence. The large Zulu population (of about 8 million) was split between supporters of the ANC and Inkatha, and Inkatha itself was split between the conflicting interests of IFP leader Buthelezi and the traditional Zulu monarch, King Goodwill Zwelithini.

The Interim Constitution

The interim constitution—The Constitution of the Republic of South Africa, 1993 (Act No. 200)—was ratified on December 22, 1993, and implemented on April 27, 1994. It provides a framework for governing for five years, while a new constitution, to be implemented by 1999, was drafted by the Constitutional Assembly. The final constitution had to comply with the principles embodied in the interim constitution, including a commitment to a multiparty democracy based on universal adult franchise, individual rights without discrimination, and separation of the powers of government.

The interim constitution consists of a preamble, fifteen chapters containing 251 sections, and seven attachments. It contains a chapter on fundamental rights, and it requires a constitutional court to invalidate any new law or government action that might unreasonably restrict these basic human freedoms. The guaranteed freedoms include the right to life and human dignity, freedom of religion, freedom of expression, the right of free association, language and cultural rights, and other internationally accepted human rights. Key provisions are proportional party representation in the legislature with representatives to be selected from lists of party delegates; a bicameral parliament comprising a 400-seat National Assembly and a Senate consisting of ten members chosen by each of the nine provinces; and a Constitutional Assembly made up of both houses of parliament. The interim constitution requires that the draft of the final constitution be prepared within two years and that the draft be approved by two-thirds of the legislators and by the Constitutional Court.

The interim constitution also defines the government's authority; reaffirms its sovereignty, the supremacy of the constitution, and existing national symbols; and defines the national executive (a president, at least two deputy presidents, and the cabinet), the judicial system (the Constitutional Court, the Supreme Court, and lower-level courts), the Office of the Public Protector, the Human Rights Commission, the Commission on Gender Equality, the Commission on Restitution of Land Rights, and the Public Service Commission. Further provisions relate to the police and security establishment; the continuation or repeal of existing laws and international agreements; and arrangements for legislative, executive, public service, legal, financial, and other administrative bodies. Schedules attached to the interim constitution describe the nation's nine new provinces, including areas still under contention; the electoral system; oaths and affirmations of office; the procedure for electing the president; and the authority of provincial legislatures.

Executive and Legislative Authority

The President

Under the interim constitution, executive authority is vested in the president, deputy presidents, and a cabinet chosen by the president in consultation with party leaders (see fig. 19). The executive offices are based in the administrative capital, Pretoria. The directly elected National Assembly elects the

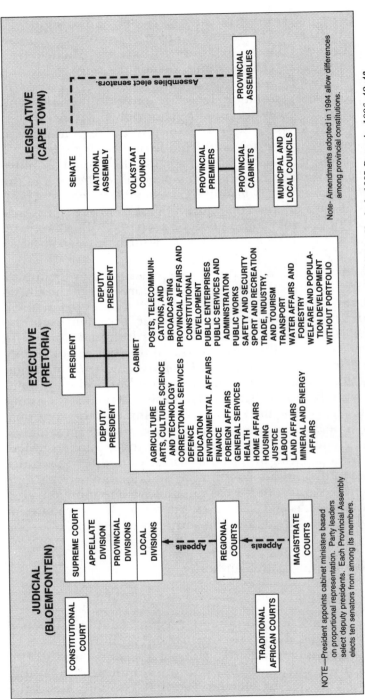

Figure 19. Structure of Government, 1996

Source: Based on information from South Africa, South African Communication Service, *South Africa Yearbook, 1995*, Pretoria, 1996, 42–43.

president from among its members and can remove the president from office by a vote of no-confidence or by impeachment. The president's primary responsibilities are to uphold, to defend, and to respect the constitution; to appoint cabinet members; to convene cabinet meetings; to refer bills back to the legislators or forward them to the Constitutional Court when constitutionality is in question; to summon the National Assembly for urgent matters; to appoint commissions of inquiry; to appoint ambassadors; and to accredit foreign diplomats.

According to the interim constitution, any party winning more than 20 percent of the popular vote is entitled to name a deputy president. If only one party or no party wins that percentage of votes, each of the two parties with the largest numbers of votes selects a deputy president. The deputy presidents' primary responsibilities are to assist the president in the duties of the executive and to succeed the president in the event of absence, incapacitation, or vacancy in that office. In 1994 the NP named outgoing president F. W. de Klerk and the ANC named Thabo Mbeki to serve as deputy presidents.

The Cabinet

The cabinet shares executive authority with the president and his deputies, and its members are appointed by the president in consultation with party leaders. Under the interim constitution, cabinet appointments reflect the relative strength of political parties; each party winning more than 5 percent of the popular vote is entitled to a proportional number of cabinet portfolios. In May 1994, the ANC was allocated seventeen cabinet portfolios, and a minister without portfolio was from the ANC. The NP was allocated six cabinet portfolios, and the IFP, three. After NP Minister of Finance Derek Keys resigned in July 1994, that post was designated "nonpartisan," and a new portfolio, General Services, was allocated to the NP in December 1994.

The president, in consultation with national party leaders, appoints a minister and deputy minister to manage each cabinet portfolio. In most ministries, a department staffed by government employees assists the ministry in the implementation of national policy. For example, the Department of Education, within the Ministry of Education, assists in implementing national educational policy. Each department is headed by a director general, who is generally a career government employee.

The cabinet customarily travels between the administrative capital, Pretoria, and the legislative capital, Cape Town, while the parliament is in session. The transitional cabinet's first session on May 23, 1994, took place in Cape Town. The president is required to consult with the cabinet and to gain the approval of two-thirds of the cabinet on issues of fundamental importance, but most cabinet decisions are reached by consensus.

The diversity represented in the new cabinet in 1994 was a major departure from earlier administrations (see table 16, Appendix). The ANC held key portfolios, such as foreign affairs, defense, safety and security, justice, and land affairs, and had strong deputy ministers in finance, home affairs, provincial affairs, and agriculture. The ANC appointees included older contemporaries of President Mandela, middle-aged former exiles, and younger antiapartheid activists of the 1980s. There were three women in the senior executive ranks—two women cabinet ministers and one woman deputy minister.

Other sharp breaks with the past were the reorganization and the renaming of several ministries. For example, in 1994 the Ministry of Law and Order became the Ministry of Safety and Security, and the Ministry of Information was subsumed under the Ministry of Posts, Telecommunications, and Broadcasting. In addition, the apartheid-based distinction between a racial community's "own" affairs and "general" affairs was abolished.

One of the new government's most controversial cabinet appointments was the minister of foreign affairs, Alfred Nzo, a veteran of the antiapartheid struggle who had little foreign affairs background. Nzo's deputy, Aziz Pahad, had been considered effective in managing the ANC foreign affairs department during the preelection period, and new Deputy President Mbeki planned to maintain close oversight of the foreign affairs portfolio. Another controversial ANC appointment was that of Winnie Mandela, President Mandela's estranged wife, as deputy minister of arts, culture, science, and technology. In March 1995, the president removed Mrs. Mandela from her post as deputy minister, citing insubordination as the cause for her dismissal. (After a legal challenge of his action, Mrs. Mandela resigned from the post.)

Cabinet ministers from the NP included some of the previous government's most experienced members. Important portfolios were assigned to Keys, who retained the finance portfolio until his resignation, and to constitutional negotiators Roelf Meyer (Ministry of Provincial Affairs and Constitutional Development) and Dawie de Villiers (Ministry of Environmental Affairs and Tourism). Veteran minister Roelof "Pik" Botha was appointed Minister of Mineral and Energy Affairs.

To appease and to accommodate Mandela's rival, the IFP leader, Zulu Chief Buthelezi, he was appointed minister of home affairs. His duties include managing elections and internal issues, several of which affect his IFP stronghold in KwaZulu-Natal. Buthelezi also shares responsibility for resolving the country's growing problem of illegal immigration from neighboring states.

Parliament

Under the interim constitution of 1993, legislative authority is vested in a bicameral parliament consisting of the National Assembly (lower house) and the Senate (upper house), based in the country's legislative capital, Cape Town. Members of the National Assembly are chosen by proportional representation: constitutionally, 200 of the 400 assembly delegates are chosen from party lists of national candidates, and 200 are chosen from lists of candidates representing specific provinces. The 200 selected from provincial party lists are allocated in the following proportions: Eastern Cape 28, Free State 14, Gauteng 44, KwaZulu-Natal 42, Mpumalanga 11, Northern Cape 4, Northern Province 25, North-West Province 12, and Western Cape 20.

In 1994 individual delegates could choose to run as national or provincial party delegates. Provincial party leaders submitted lists of delegates after elections or party caucuses in each province. A candidate nominated on a provincial list had to be a resident of that province, although exceptions were made for parties that listed only one nonresident candidate, or for cases in which fewer than 10 percent of the party's nominees lived outside the province. The assembly delegates elected a speaker and deputy speaker to preside over their deliberations. The speaker and the deputy speaker retained their parliamentary seats but could not vote, except in the case of a tie.

The Senate consists of ten members from each of the nine provinces, selected by the provincial legislature on the basis of proportional representation, to reflect party strength in each province. The president and the two deputy presidents preside over the Senate and are also members of the Senate. Although not granted a deliberative vote, they can vote in case of a tie.

The bicameral parliament is empowered not only to pass laws, but, in its additional role as the Constitutional Assembly, to draft and to adopt the final constitution, which had to be completed in 1996. Although intended to serve as the interim legislature for five years, parliament may be dissolved at any time by presidential decree, followed by new parliamentary elections.

The interim constitution requires ordinary bills introduced in either house of parliament to be voted on by both houses. If one house passes a bill and the other rejects it, the bill is referred to a joint committee from both houses. Both houses approve bills affecting the powers and the boundaries of provinces; the appropriate provincial legislature also must approve any bill affecting the powers and the boundaries of that province. Both houses deal with bills appropriating revenue or imposing taxes, and in case of a conflict between houses on any bill, the decision of the National Assembly prevails.

In accordance with the interim constitution, parliament generally convenes from January to June each year in Cape Town, although a briefer session may be called later in the year if needed. All members of the government plus many of the departmental secretaries and heads of other executive agencies reside in Cape Town when parliament is in session.

Reflecting the far-reaching changes in the new political system, the new parliament in 1994, unlike its predecessor, adopted an informal dress code—many new members dispensed with the conventional Western suit and instead wore kaftans or safari suits. For the first time as well, some speeches in parliament were delivered in African languages, with a bevy of translators assembled to render them in English or Afrikaans.

Volkstaat Council

In November 1994, the Volkstaat Council Act (No. 30) of 1994 established a Volkstaat Council within the legislative branch of the government to investigate the possibility of establishing an Afrikaner state within South Africa. The twenty members of the council were elected by a joint session of the National Assembly and the Senate. The functions of the council are to gather information concerning possible powers, boundaries, and structures of such a state; to study the feasibility of these; and to submit recommendations to the joint National Assembly and Senate. The Volkstaat Council began deliberations in early 1995. Its formal proposals had not been presented as of mid-1996.

Provincial and Local Government

Until 1994 South Africa was divided administratively into four provinces, the Cape Province, Natal Province, the Transvaal, and the Orange Free State; six "self-governing" homelands, Gazankulu, KaNgwane, KwaNdebele, KwaZulu, Lebowa, and QwaQwa; and four "independent" homelands or "sovereign independent states," Transkei, Bophuthatswana, Venda, and Ciskei (see fig. 11). The government estimated in the early 1990s that 44 percent of the country's total population resided in the ten homelands, which formed less than 14 percent of the total land area. A 1992 study by the Urban Foundation, a South African research organization, concluded that this high population density—several hundred persons per square kilometer in some areas—greatly exacerbated socioeconomic and political problems in the homelands.

To resolve these problems, government and ANC negotiators redrew the country's internal boundaries, dissolving the homeland boundaries and forming nine new provinces (see fig. 1). The demarcation process began in May 1993, when the Multiparty Negotiating Council appointed a 150-member Commission on the Demarcation of States/Provinces/Regions, with instructions to hold a public hearing and to submit recommendations to the council. After receiving 304 written reports and hearing eighty oral witnesses, the commission recommended the formation of nine provinces, with a few disputed borders to be reconsidered at a later date. These recommendations were incorporated into the interim constitution, and the homelands were officially dissolved on April 27, 1994.

The interim constitution assigns authority in each of the nine provinces to a provincial executive, or premier, and a legislative assembly. The premier, elected by the legislators, selects a council, or cabinet, based on proportional representation of political parties (see table 17, Appendix). Provincial legislatures have between thirty and 100 members, although within those limits, the size of the legislature is proportional to the number of votes cast in the province—i.e., the total is divided by 50,000, and that number is added to the base of thirty delegates (see table 18, Appendix). Thus, at both the provincial and the national levels, voters select a political party they wish to have represent them rather than a specific individual to serve as legislator. The legislators are chosen on the basis of proportional representation from lists of party representatives.

The capitals of the new provinces are Cape Town (Western Cape), Kimberley (Northern Cape), Bisho (Eastern Cape), Bloemfontein (Free State), Nelspruit (Mpumalanga), Pietersburg (Northern Province), Johannesburg (Gauteng), and Mmabatho (North-West Province). The capital of KwaZulu-Natal was not yet decided, between Ulundi and Pietermaritzburg, as of 1996.

As the 1994 elections approached, the government amended the interim constitution to strengthen the power of the provincial governments, largely in an attempt to appease Zulu and Afrikaner separatists. These new measures uphold the general principle of "self-determination," to the extent that people of a common culture are allowed to establish a "territorial homeland" where their language and traditions can be maintained. They also stipulate that the resulting homeland must have broad popular support within its boundaries and its policies may not be racially or ethnically discriminatory. The amendments also assign to the provincial authorities the power to levy taxes and to formulate a provincial constitution, as long as they do not violate constitutional provisions concerning fundamental rights. Furthermore, to satisfy Zulu aspirations, the negotiators adopted the name KwaZulu-Natal for the former Natal Province and agreed to allow the Zulu king to retain his honorary crown and to continue to receive his salary from the central government.

Although the new provincial administrations assumed power immediately after the April 1994 elections, many of them were unable to deliver government services to their constituents in the months following the elections. Provincial authority had not yet been fully defined, and many provincial and local-level offices and procedures continued to be under the control of apartheid-era civil servants. Throughout 1995, several provincial administrators demanded more autonomy and more financial support from the central government, and this issue delayed agreement on a draft of the final constitution in 1996.

One of the last steps in the creation of the new political system was the establishment of new local government institutions below the provincial level. The government planned for elections in 1995 to replace the existing all-white city councils with

Town meeting at chief's kraal *in Makushane location, Northern Province*
Courtesy R. T. K. Scully

nonracial, democratically chosen municipal governments and
to establish multiracial local councils in rural districts. The
Local Government Transition Act (No. 209) of 1993 required
40 percent of local government members to be elected by a system of proportional representation using a party list system,
and 60 percent to represent individual localities. The interim
constitution specified that the existing local governments in
1994 would continue in place until the new elections were
held.

On November 1, 1995, local government elections were held
in all areas of the country except KwaZulu-Natal and some
parts of the Western Cape. The elections put in place municipal and rural councils, replacing the bureaucratic infrastructure that had existed since the apartheid era. The elections
were successfully held in 686 constituencies, although only
about 52 percent of the registered electorate turned out to

vote. The ANC won seats on all 686 councils, and it won a majority of the seats on 387 councils. The NP won a majority of seats on forty-five councils. The Freedom Front won control over one local council. Independent or nonpartisan candidates won a majority of seats on at least forty-two councils. A few elections were finally decided in byelections held in early 1996. In KwaZulu-Natal and areas of the Western Cape, the local government elections were postponed until mid-1996.

Drafting a Final Constitution

On May 8, 1996, the Constitutional Assembly completed two years of work on a draft of a final constitution, intended to replace the interim constitution of 1993 by the year 1999. The draft embodied many of the provisions contained in the interim constitution, but some of the differences between them were controversial. In the final constitution, the Government of National Unity is replaced by a majoritarian government—an arrangement referred to by its critics as "winner-take-all" in national elections. Instead of requiring political parties to share executive power, the final constitution would enable the majority party to appoint cabinet members and other officials without necessarily consulting the minority parties that would be represented in the National Assembly.

The draft final constitution in 1996 also proposes changes in the country's legislative structure. The National Assembly would continue to be the country's only directly elected house of parliament, but the Senate would be replaced by a National Council of Provinces. Like its predecessor, the new council would consist of legislators chosen to represent each of the country's nine provinces. The new council would include some temporary delegates from each province, however, so some legislators would rotate between the National Council of Provinces and the provincial legislatures from which they were chosen.

Negotiators in the early 1990s had agreed that the 1996 draft constitution would be submitted to the Constitutional Court to ensure that it conformed to agreed-upon constitutional principles, such as the commitment to a multiparty democracy, based on universal franchise without discrimination. In May 1996, however, the Constitutional Court did not immediately approve the draft as received; instead, it referred the document back to the Constitutional Assembly for revision and clarification of specific provisions. Chief among its concerns were the need to clarify references to the powers that would devolve to the provincial legislatures and the rights of organized labor and management in an industrial dispute. The Constitutional Assembly was revising the draft constitution as of mid-1996.

Even before it was approved or implemented, the draft constitution had an immediate impact on the structure of government in 1996. Just one day after the draft had been completed by the Constitutional Assembly, the National Party declared its intention to resign from the Government of National Unity, effective June 30, 1996. In the weeks leading up to the NP's formal departure from the executive branch, NP leaders repeatedly tried to assure voters that the party would play a constructive role in politics as a loyal critic of the ANC-led government. President Mandela, too, accepted the NP departure as a sign of a "maturing democracy." NP legislators continued to serve in the National Assembly and in the Senate.

The Legal System

South Africa's legal system, like the rest of the political system, was radically transformed as the apartheid-based constitutional system was restructured during the early 1990s. Nevertheless, many laws unrelated to apartheid continued to be rooted in the old legal system. Thus, the justice system after 1994 reflected elements of both the apartheid-era system and nondiscriminatory reforms.

The Apartheid-Era Legal System

The principles embodied in the legal system were adapted from Roman-Dutch law with an admixture of English law introduced after 1806. The influence of English law is most pronounced in criminal legal procedures, in constitutional or statutory law, and in corporate and mercantile law. Roman-Dutch law predominates in private law—for example, the law of persons, of property, of succession, and the law of sale and lease. Despite the influence of these universally accepted laws, however, a prominent feature of the former legal system was the pervasive role of discriminatory apartheid-based laws, regulations, and codes (see The Legislative Implementation of Apartheid, ch. 1), and the extensive judicial apparatus required to enforce them.

Judicial authority is vested in the state, and the minister of justice is responsible for administering the justice system. The president appoints the attorneys general, who order public prosecutions on behalf of the state, and whose authority in the lower courts is delegated to public prosecutors. Similarly, the president also appoints judges from among members of the bar. Until the 1990s, all judges were white. The legal profession is divided broadly, as in Britain, into advocates (barristers) and attorneys (solicitors); only the former can plead a case in a higher court.

The judicial system is headed by the Supreme Court, the decisions and interpretations of which are considered an important source of the law. The Supreme Court comprises an Appellate Division and six provincial divisions. Each provincial division encompasses a judge president, three local divisions presided over by judges, and magisterial divisions presided over by magistrates. Separate traditional courts administer African traditional law and custom; they are presided over by traditional leaders, often chiefs or respected elders.

The Appellate Division of the Supreme Court is the highest court in the country and is seated in Bloemfontein, the country's judicial capital. The Appellate Division is composed of the chief justice and the judges of appeal, whose number varies, as determined by the president. Supreme Court members can be removed only on grounds of misbehavior or incapacity. The Appellate Division's decisions are binding on all lower courts, as are the decisions—within their areas of jurisdiction—of the provincial and the local divisions. Lower courts, which are presided over by civil service magistrates, have limited jurisdiction in civil and criminal cases. In 1995, there were 309 district magistrates' offices, presided over by 1,014 magistrates, 1,196 prosecutors, and 3,717 officers.

The Legal Aid Society, an independent statutory body, provides advice and assistance to indigent persons. Other programs offer aid or rehabilitation to prisoners. Until the mid-1990s, a few private voluntary organizations, such as Black Sash, offered legal assistance to people who faced legal problems arising out of the pass laws or other apartheid-era legislation.

The New Legal System

The postapartheid legal system introduced by the interim constitution of 1993 embodies the supreme law of the land and is binding on all judicial organs of the state. It establishes an independent judiciary, including a Constitutional Court with

Supreme Court in Bloemfontein
Courtesy Embassy of South Africa, Washington

the power to review and to abolish legislation inconsistent with the constitution. It includes provisions not found in apartheid-era laws, such as a prohibition on all forms of discrimination and an emphasis on individual rights. These rights include "equality before the law and equal protection of the law"; freedom of expression, assembly, demonstration, petition, and association; the right to "choose a place of residence anywhere in the national territory"; the right not to be deprived of citizenship without justification; full political rights; full access to the courts; and fair and lawful administrative justice mechanisms, including rights concerning detention, arrest, and accusation. Other provisions provide for specific rights in areas such as economic activity, labor relations, property, environment, children, language and culture, education, and conditions under which a state of emergency can be declared.

In 1994 the government established the new Constitutional Court, a Human Rights Commission, and a Judicial Services Commission that forwarded to the president its ten nominees to the Constitutional Court. Legislation in 1994 also set forth operating procedures for these bodies and established the Office of the Public Protector (public defender).

The new legal system also deals with the consequences of apartheid-related abuses and crimes, although it aims primarily to promote a spirit of national reconciliation and a new "culture of human rights," rather than to resolve long-standing grievances. In June 1994, the government announced that a Truth and Reconciliation Commission would investigate accusations of human rights abuses and political crimes by both supporters and opponents of apartheid, and that it would consider related issues such as amnesty and reparation to survivors and their dependents. The government established guidelines for the commission's operations in 1994 and 1995, and the Truth and Reconciliation Commission began hearing testimony by both victims and perpetrators of apartheid-era violence in early 1996 (see Human Rights and National Reconciliation, ch. 5).

Political Participation

The abolition of apartheid radically transformed political participation in South Africa in the 1990s. This change, in turn, had a major impact on the nature of the country's electoral system, political parties, and political elites.

The 1994 Elections

Until the nonracial elections in April 1994, the laws of apartheid governed elections. An elections administrator, or chief electoral officer, prepared a list based on the population registry of people who were qualified to register as voters. They had to be more than eighteen years of age and, under the 1983 constitution, to belong to one of the constituencies of the three racially based houses of parliament—white, coloured, and Indian (see Limited Reforms, ch. 1). In the 1989 parliamentary election, for example, only 2,176,481 votes were cast, out of 3,170,667 registered voters and a total population of almost 28 million.

In the April 1994 national and provincial elections, nineteen political parties, representing the country's diverse constituen-

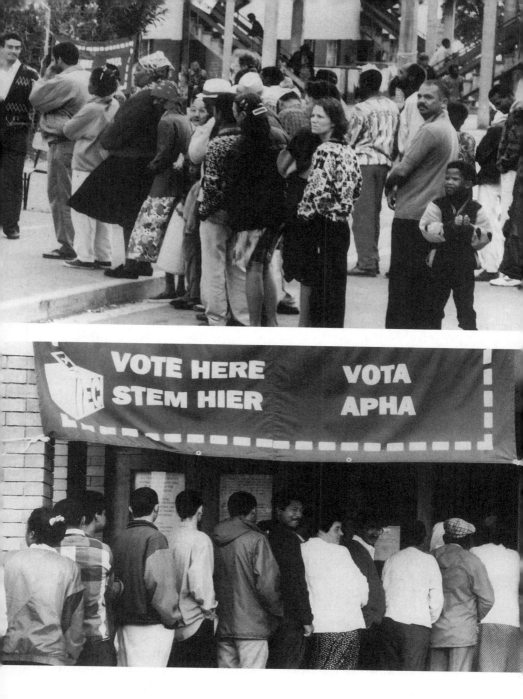

*Voters in Cape Town (above) and Durban (below)
in historic elections of April 1994
Courtesy James B. Parks*

cies, participated in the electoral process. Each voter received two ballots and cast two votes (enabling each voter to choose different parties at the national and the provincial levels). Voters selected a political party, not an individual candidate, to represent them in the National Assembly and in the provincial legislature. Each party had prepared ranked lists of delegates for the national and the provincial legislatures. Political parties gained seats in each body proportionally, according to the number of votes each party received, and party delegates became legislators based on their ranking on the appropriate list.

The number of eligible voters in 1994 was estimated at 21.7 million—about 16 million of whom had never voted before. In a radical departure from previous electoral practice, no formal voter register was prepared; instead, voters were asked to present identity books as proof of citizenship, and even this requirement was enforced with flexibility. Officials had determined before the elections that about 2.5 million people—mostly blacks—lacked identity books, and most of these were given temporary identity papers. For most residents of the homelands, valid travel documents were accepted as legal identification.

The Independent Electoral Commission (IEC) created a state electoral fund with an estimated 22 million rands (for value of the rand—see Glossary) to finance the April 1994 elections. Half of that amount was distributed among participating political parties before the election, and the balance afterward. The first payment was made in late March 1994 to nine parties that had submitted documentation of popular support.

During the campaign, political parties were hampered by several factors. One of the major challenges was the need to educate the electorate, particularly those who had never voted before, in basic elements of democracy and electoral procedures. For example, there was a great deal of skepticism about democratic practices—such as the secret ballot—particularly in rural areas where literacy rates are low, and where traditional leaders and white employers had often manipulated political participation in the past. In addition, the political violence leading up to the elections threatened to keep many potential first-time voters away from the polls. ANC voters felt especially vulnerable in KwaZulu, Bophuthatswana, and Ciskei, where the apartheid-era homeland leaders and security forces had harassed and intimidated ANC supporters. Similarly, in ANC-controlled areas, some of that party's activists intimidated IFP, NP, and even liberal Democratic Party (DP) organizers and disrupted their campaign rallies, despite ANC leaders' pleas for tolerance. Finally, the election posed a logistical nightmare for the IEC, which had to accommodate the IFP's last-minute decision to participate in the elections and add the party's name to the ballots. The IEC helped monitor the more-than-9,000 polling stations and was responsible for verifying the vote count before it was announced.

The IEC reported that it had counted 19,726,579 ballots and rejected 193,081 as invalid. The voting was declared generally free and fair. Observer missions from the United Nations (UN), British Commonwealth, European Union (EU—see Glossary), and Organization of African Unity (OAU) issued this statement: "South Africans' confidence in the secrecy of the ballot was manifest and they were able to participate freely in the elections. The outcome of the elections reflects the will of the people of South Africa."

Seven political parties won seats in the National Assembly, the ANC, 252 seats (representing 62.6 percent of the popular vote); the NP, 82 seats (20.4 percent); the IFP, 43 seats (10.5 percent); the Freedom Front (FF), 9 seats (2.2 percent); the DP, 7 seats (1.7 percent); the PAC, 5 seats (1.2 percent); and the African Christian Democratic Party (ACDP), 2 seats (0.5 percent). Twelve other parties received too few votes to be represented in the National Assembly. Each of the seven major parties also won representation in at least one of the nine provincial legislatures. The ANC won a majority in seven provincial legislatures. The NP won a majority in the Western Cape; and the IFP did so in KwaZulu-Natal (see table 18, Appendix).

Political Parties

South Africa's political party system underwent radical transformation in the early 1990s when previously illegal parties were unbanned and participated in the April 1994 elections. In what international observers called a "developing multiparty system," parties were challenged to become all-inclusive and not to limit their appeal to their traditional constituent groups. They also had to reorient themselves to participate in the bicameral multiracial legislature rather than the previous tricameral apartheid-based parliament. The most successful of the parties in the April 1994 elections (and the South African

Communist Party) are described below, in order of decreasing parliamentary strength.

African National Congress

The African National Congress (ANC) was founded in 1912 as the South African Native National Congress, under the leadership of Dr. Pixley Ka Isaka Seme, a Durban attorney. It was renamed the African National Congress in 1923. Although the ANC cooperated to some degree with the Communist Party of South Africa (CPSA—later, in 1953, the South African Communist Party, or SACP) in the early 1920s, cooperation ceased in 1927 when some traditional African leaders opposed white-led communist involvement in the black nationalist movement. In the 1930s, the ANC's influence declined, primarily because it was unsuccessful in representing black grievances and was weakened by factionalism and leadership disarray. The ANC's revival in the 1940s was largely the result of a dynamic group of young leaders—including Nelson Mandela, Walter Sisulu, Oliver Tambo, and Anton Lembede—who were influenced by a pan-African version of black nationalism. In 1943 they established the ANC Youth League to mobilize mass protest against racial discrimination. Following the rise to power of the NP in 1948 and its implementation of strict apartheid laws, the ANC, with many of the Youth League founders then in leadership positions, responded by launching a series of countrywide defiance campaigns. This activism invigorated the ANC and resulted in the movement's growth from 7,000 to some 100,000 dues-paying members in 1952.

In the mid-1950s, the ANC formed the Congress Alliance with other antiapartheid organizations to oppose the white state. On June 26, 1955, alliance members adopted the Freedom Charter, which advocated the creation of a nonsocialist multiracial society, but the debate over the charter widened an ideological rift in the ANC between Charterists and Africanists, concerning the question of multiracialism. A few activists opposed the ANC's inclusive policies and established the Pan-Africanist Congress (PAC) in 1959 to press for black political control.

The government declared the ANC an illegal organization on April 8, 1960, as part of a government crackdown and state of emergency following violent antiapartheid incidents at Sharpeville and Langa. The ANC went underground, many of its cadres left South Africa for exile in neighboring states, and its leaders adopted armed struggle as a means of achieving their goals. In 1961 ANC and SACP leaders created a joint military wing, Umkhonto we Sizwe ("Spear of the Nation," also known as Umkhonto, MK). The principle of armed struggle through guerrilla warfare to overthrow the South African regime superseded the goal of gaining political rights for all citizens. ANC sabotage and attacks between 1960 and 1962 led to the arrest of many party leaders. At the 1963 trial that became renowned as "the Rivonia trial," Mandela, Sisulu, Govan Mbeki, and others were convicted of treason and were sentenced to life terms in prison. Most ANC leaders fled the country, established ANC headquarters in Lusaka, Zambia, and continued their struggle against the Pretoria regime.

Over the years, the ANC built up a strong support network in many Western and Eastern-bloc states, in cooperation with overseas antiapartheid groups. Although certain Western states, particularly Scandinavian countries, provided financial support, the ANC's logistical support, including the supply of weapons, came from the Soviet Union and the German Democratic Republic (East Germany). The ANC also attained observer status at the UN and during the 1980s broadened its diplomatic ties with Western states.

The ANC's leadership structure consists of the president, deputy president, secretary general, deputy secretary general, and treasurer general. A ninety-member National Executive Committee (NEC) consults with senior officers and influences decisions on important issues. A twenty-six-member National Working Committee (NWC), chosen from the NEC, oversees day-to-day decision making and administration and manages the party's functional departments. The seven appointed members of the President's Committee serve as presidential advisers and assistants.

The ANC's annual national conference brings together more than 1,300 representatives, whose functions are to elect the NEC and to nominate delegates to the party's National Assembly, which meets every five years. At a working level, the party has nine national departments—Information and Research, Manpower and Development, Foreign Affairs, Youth, Political Education, Information and Publicity, Finance, Religious Affairs, and Women—as well as branches in each of the provinces.

In the early 1990s, the ANC took a number of steps to broaden its political base. It reactivated the ANC Youth League in order to bridge the generational gap between its older leaders and young members. In addition, propelled by the many politically active women in the organization, the ANC reactivated its Women's League in order to promote women's rights nationwide. The ANC Youth League and the ANC Women's League work in cooperation with the corresponding departments within the ANC.

Although the ANC primarily represents the interests of the majority black population, its membership is open to whites, coloureds, and Asians, as well. It had appealed to all races to join in 1969, and a substantial number of white liberals did join during the 1970s and the 1980s. In April 1991, five white members of parliament representing the Democratic Party left that party to join the ANC, giving the ANC official parliamentary representation for the first time in the all-white House of Assembly.

Until the ANC and the NP-led government entered into negotiations over the country's political future in 1991, the ANC's ideological platform for opposing apartheid ranged from Mohandas (Mahatma) Gandhi's strategy of passive resistance (in the early 1900s), to pan-Africanism (in the 1940s), to the Freedom Charter in 1955. In 1969 the ANC adopted an official policy advocating armed struggle to gain political control of the state, and in 1988 it promulgated the Constitutional Guidelines for a Democratic South Africa, derived from the Freedom Charter of the 1950s. These guidelines called for a nonracial democratic state based on universal franchise. In August 1989, the ANC adopted the Harare Declaration, advocating multiparty negotiations to arrive at a new form of government, giving strong emphasis to the concept of individual rights.

The ANC's major political partner throughout most of the apartheid era was the SACP. SACP leaders helped the ANC to secure the support of communist and socialist governments during its period of exile, played important roles in ANC policy formulation, and helped to consolidate support for the ANC in the labor movement. The SACP at times played a moderating role in the ANC, too; for example, in early 1993 SACP chair Joe Slovo drafted the ANC's proposals, couched in a "sunset clause," to compromise and to share power with the NP. Slovo's position was that compromise was necessary because the party was "not dealing with a defeated enemy," but with the NP as a minority party.

Although the ANC became the country's dominant political party in 1994, it still faced a number of long-term problems. The issue of political succession had yet to be resolved. President Mandela and other senior party leaders were members of the older generation, whose active leadership years were drawing to a close. Mandela had pledged he would not seek reelection in 1999. His most likely successors—Thabo Mbeki, the former ANC secretary for international affairs, and Cyril Ramaphosa, ANC secretary general since 1991—had not demonstrated the decades of practiced leadership of their seniors.

As the dominant party in the national unity government, the ANC had to balance the need to co-manage (along with the NP) the country's finances to facilitate economic growth against its long-standing affiliation with the Congress of South African Trade Unions (COSATU), the labor confederation known for vigorously defending workers' interests against those of the previous government. The ANC also had to overcome its image as a violator of human rights after its leaders acknowledged there had been instances of torture, execution, and abuse of dissidents in its exile camps and in some black townships during the antiapartheid struggle. In 1993 the party apologized for past abuses, but it refused to punish its human rights violators or to pay compensation to the victims or their families.

In 1994 the ANC proposed a number of controversial cabinet appointments, adding to the difficulties inherent in transforming itself from a former liberation movement into a broad-based political party. A notable case was that of Winnie Mandela, who had earlier been regarded as South Africa's "first lady of liberation." She had staged a political comeback after being stripped of her official posts in the ANC and after being shunned by many black leaders because of her 1991 conviction for her part in a kidnapping that had resulted in a death. Her five-year jail sentence was set aside for a fine, but she was subsequently removed from the ANC's NEC and as head of its Welfare Department.

Mrs. Mandela went on to organize an independent power base in the restive and impoverished squatter camps, where she was respected for her activism on behalf of the poor. In some communities, Mrs. Mandela was able to capitalize on the widespread distrust of government that extended even to black leaders like Nelson Mandela. During the preelection negotiations, she had criticized power-sharing proposals as a deal between "the elite of the oppressed and the oppressors" and had charged ANC leaders with "the distortion of a noble goal in favor of a short-cut route to parliament by a handful of individuals." But while she chided ANC leaders for their new-found "embourgeoisement," Mrs. Mandela continued to live in relative luxury in the Johannesburg township of Soweto. Even after she fell out of favor with the government led by her husband in 1994, she remained popular, especially among the poor and unemployed. Her defiance of the government led to her removal from office in March 1995.

South African Communist Party

In 1994 the South African Communist Party (SACP) was not an independent political entity, but a strong faction within the ANC, where its members held important leadership positions. Former party leaders, Joe Slovo and Chris Hani, for example, had both served as chief of staff of the ANC's military wing and on its most important committees. The SACP won strong representation in the National Assembly in 1994, not by participating openly in the April 1994 elections, but by having SACP members well represented among delegates from the ANC.

The SACP was originally founded as the Communist Party of South Africa (CPSA) in July 1921 in Cape Town. The CPSA was formed out of the merger of several leftist organizations, including the International Socialist League (ISL), the Social Democratic Federation, the Durban Marxist Club, the Cape Communist Party, and the Jewish Socialist Society. The CPSA affiliated with the Communist International (Comintern), headquartered in Moscow, which provided it with political direction, although some party factions opposed Moscow's intervention in South African affairs.

Although whites dominated the party in the 1920s, some CPSA leaders attempted to strengthen its reputation as an indigenous communist organization by increasing its African membership and orientation. David Ivon Jones and Sidney Percival Bunting, formerly of the ISL, translated the concept of social revolution into a struggle for a "black republic" and a "democratic native republic, with equal rights for all races." The major stumbling block they encountered was the belief, inherent in Marxist dogma, that all workers fundamentally share the same interests. In South Africa, white workers generally felt they had little in common with their black counterparts and feared that any improvements for black workers would reduce their own status and income.

Despite efforts at Africanization, the CPSA failed to establish strong ties with black political organizations, many of which were dominated by traditional tribal leaders. In 1928, for example, the ANC denounced the "fraternization" between the ANC and the CPSA. ANC President James T. Gumede was removed from office in 1930, after trying to educate ANC members about Marxism. Even as the CPSA gradually succeeded in recruiting more black members, its leadership continued to be white. For this reason, two ANC Youth League leaders in the 1940s—Nelson Mandela and Walter Sisulu—opposed any alliance between the ANC and the CPSA at that time.

CPSA members were divided over the increasing Comintern intervention in local affairs. Moscow urged the CPSA and all communist parties to continue to be small, revolutionary elite organizations, and to rid the party of alleged "rightist" elements. In 1931 a new Stalinist faction, led by Douglas Wolton, Molly Wolton, and Lazar Bach, assumed leadership roles in the CPSA and proceeded to purge the party of many white leaders. In the internal upheaval that followed, the party lost black support, too, and weakened its ties to labor. As its leadership ranks were "Stalinized" and leading party activists fled the country, CPSA membership dropped from an estimated 1,750 members in 1928 to about 150 in 1933. Racial divisions continued to exist between the predominantly white leadership and the largely black membership ranks.

At the outset of World War II, the CPSA opposed efforts to counter the Nazi threat, primarily because of the 1939 Nazi-Soviet Nonaggression Pact, which led to Soviet neutrality. Party members campaigned against military recruitment of blacks (and Indians) in South Africa, arguing that the "natives" should not be sacrificed to perpetuate their own exploitation. When Germany invaded the Soviet Union in 1941, the CPSA echoed Moscow's shift to support the anti-Nazi campaign, and the South African government responded by releasing some CPSA activists from detention and permitting political activities in support of the war effort.

By the mid-1940s, CPSA membership was increasing, and the party had gained influence after a few CPSA members (all white) won political office. After the 1948 NP election victory, however, the government quickly restricted black political activity and in 1950 banned the CPSA. The party went underground temporarily but also strengthened its ties to local nationalist organizations, such as the ANC. During the years it was banned, while the ANC continued to operate legally, the CPSA viewed the ANC as the primary expression of black aspirations for a multiracial socialist state under eventual communist leadership. The Comintern's Sixth Congress declared that "the CPSA could now play an active role in the ANC." The party re-emerged in 1953 under the leadership of Joe Slovo and his wife, Ruth First, and changed its name to the SACP.

The SACP and the ANC in the 1950s held similar views about policy and tactics as embodied in the ANC's Freedom Charter; in addition, they both advocated the use of guerrilla warfare against the apartheid regime in order to bring about the dual-phase revolution of political liberation followed by economic transformation. Party members reportedly persuaded the ANC to abandon African nationalism in favor of nonracialism, however, although the SACP, unlike the ANC, viewed the primary objective of the revolution as the creation of a socialist state. After many leaders of both organizations were arrested in 1963, both the SACP and the ANC shifted their political and military bases of operations to neighboring African states.

The close ties between the SACP and the ANC, particularly the predominance of SACP members in the ANC, have always been controversial, and in 1959 prompted a split by black nationalists from the ANC to form the militant Africanist, anti-communist PAC. The SACP-ANC relationship evolved into a symbiosis, derived in part from their dual memberships and overlapping leadership ranks. Throughout the 1980s, for example, the SACP was well represented on the ANC's NEC and in other key ANC positions, and in ANC-affiliated labor organizations, such as COSATU.

When the SACP was unbanned in February 1990, its strength was difficult to estimate because many party members had been underground for years. In July 1990, a party spokesman publicized the names of twenty-two SACP members who were prominent in national politics but said that the names of others would remain secret. In 1991 SACP leaders estimated that the party had 10,000 dues-paying members, but refused to publish the party's membership rolls.

SACP chairman Joe Slovo was the most prominent party member in government in 1994. Slovo was a trained lawyer and advocate, a member of the Johannesburg Bar, and one of the original members of MK, the ANC military wing. He served on the ANC's revolutionary council from 1969 until it was disbanded in 1983, became the first white member of the ANC's NEC in 1985, and served as MK chief of staff until April 1987. He was appointed SACP general secretary in 1986, following the death of Moses Madhiba, and continued in that post until 1991, when he became party chairman. Slovo was appointed minister of housing in the Government of National Unity in May 1994 and served in that post until his death in January 1995.

Slovo had been a hard-line communist, a Stalinist, when he joined the party in the 1940s, but along with others in the SACP had followed Moscow's 1980s reforms. By 1987 Slovo and his associates espoused the creation of a multiparty state with a mixed economy, and sought to broaden the party's membership base. This liberal philosophy might have explained the SACP's large representation among ANC leaders in the 1990s. The collapse of the Soviet system in the late 1980s had weakened the SACP's outside support and appeared to have weakened the appeal of the socialist ideals the party espoused for South Africa. Party activists believed, nonetheless, that the remaining economic disparities among racial groups provided fertile ground for SACP recruitment in the 1990s.

SACP leaders, considerably weakened by the murder of Chris Hani in 1993, debated the possibility that the party no longer represented a political asset to the ANC, as they prepared for the April 1994 elections. They realized that the SACP could do little to help the ANC broaden its popular support beyond its liberation allies, and public opinion polls gave the SACP, alone, strong support among only about 5 percent of voters. By including a large number of SACP members among the electoral delegates representing the ANC in the April 1994 elections, however, the SACP was able to gain significantly more representation in the national and provincial legislatures and more key posts in the government than it would have, had it run independently.

National Party

In the early 1990s, the National Party (NP), led by President de Klerk, led the white community in radically transforming the apartheid system and ushering in nonracial democracy. This process also served to transform the NP into a modern democratic party, while at the same time depriving it of the uninterrupted political dominance it had enjoyed for some forty-five years.

The present-day NP emerged out of Afrikaner organizations of the early 1900s. Founded by General J.B.M. Hertzog in January 1914 as an expression of Afrikaner ideology and ethnic nationalism, the NP sought to strengthen racial separation and to oppose British rule in South Africa. The NP, in alliance with the Labour Party—a white organization led by Colonel F.H.P. Creswell—defeated General Jan C. Smuts's ruling South African Party (SAP) in parliamentary elections in 1924. In 1933 the NP formed an alliance with the SAP, and the alliance was formalized in 1934 as the United South Africa National Party, or the United Party (UP). The merger prompted staunch segregationists from Cape Town to establish the Purified National Party under the leadership of Daniel F. (D.F.) Malan, to counteract the UP's relatively moderate positions on race. The UP ruled until it was unexpectedly defeated by Malan's party (then known as the Reunited National Party, owing to a reconciliation with a conservative faction of the UP) in parliamentary elections in May 1948. After the 1948 elections, the victorious alliance—again under the banner of the NP—ruled without interruption until April 1994.

The NP's dominance over political and security organizations gave it a vast patronage pool for its mostly Afrikaner constituency. Numerous cultural, social, economic, and religious organizations also furthered Afrikaner interests, including the Afrikaner Broederbond (later Broederbond, or Brotherhood), Nasionale Pers (National Press), South African National Life Assurance Company (Sanlam), the Voortrekkers (a scouting organization), the Federation of Afrikaner Cultural Organisations (Federasie van Afrikaanse Kultuurvereniginge—FAK), Helpmekaar (an Afrikaner social service organization, roughly translated "mutual aid"), and Volkskas (People's Bank).

Although the party did not publish membership figures, much was known about its organization—a federal structure divided into four provincial parties, linked through a Federal Council. At the lowest level were the party's local branches, consisting of 500 or fewer members. Local branches in rural areas reported to a District Council, which comprised a leader, a deputy leader, a secretary, and elected representatives from each local branch in the district. In addition, local branches elected Constituency Divisional Councils. Above each divisional council were a Head Council, a Provincial Congress that met annually, and a provincial leader. At the apex of the NP was the thirty-seven-member Federal Council that met at least once a year. The national leader of the NP, who until 1994 was also the state president, was elected by the party's parliamentary delegates in caucus.

Under P.W. Botha's leadership in the 1980s, the NP began to change directions, first to reform, and then to dismantle, apartheid. Although these reform initiatives led to a number of splits within the NP, the reformist wing (referred to in party parlance as *verligte*, or "enlightened") was sufficiently strong, its parliamentary delegation sufficiently disciplined, and its national leadership sufficiently cohesive to enable the party to remain in power as its members vigorously debated the question of reform. The NP quickly recovered after its conservative faction, led by Transvaal NP leader Andries Treurnicht, abandoned the party in February 1982 in protest against the proposed "power-sharing" constitution that established the tricameral parliament. Treurnicht launched the Conservative Party (CP), which gained immediate parliamentary representation through the conversion of seventeen NP members of parliament. The NP nonetheless retained its majority in the next elections in 1987.

The most dramatic changes in the NP began in 1989, when President Botha relinquished his party leadership following a stroke and was replaced by then Minister of Education F.W. de Klerk. De Klerk committed himself to establishing a new postapartheid South Africa, over the objections of Botha, who had retained his position as president. The NP's Federal Council in June 1989 went on to pass a five-year plan to reform apartheid. As de Klerk and Foreign Minister Roelof ("Pik") Botha prepared to discuss their planned political reforms with Zambian president Kenneth Kaunda later that year, President Botha objected to the pace of the proposed reforms, and he opposed any plan to hold discussions with Kaunda. In August 1989, his intransigence finally prompted the cabinet to ask him to resign. He did so in a televised broadcast, and de Klerk succeeded him as president. In national elections in September 1989, the NP under de Klerk's leadership remained in power both in the national House of Assembly and in the provincial legislatures, and de Klerk was confirmed as president for another five-year term.

The NP then spearheaded the reform process that paved the way for the postapartheid political system (see Constitutional

South Africa: A Country Study

Change, this ch.). The NP also sought to project a new party image. In 1990 it launched a nationwide recruitment drive for new members of all races, appointed a new management council and new regional secretaries to oversee its reforms, and established new training programs for party leaders, to emphasize racial tolerance. These changes broadened the party's parliamentary support. In May 1991, five MPs deserted the Labour Party, which since 1965 had represented the interests of the coloured community, to join the NP delegation. Their view that the new NP best represented the interests of their community was rejected by most of the Labour Party, but the NP continued to seek the support of the roughly 1.6 million voters in the coloured community.

As the April 1994 elections approached, the party tried new approaches to win support among the country's black majority. One of its campaign tactics was to emphasize its active role in dismantling apartheid and to portray itself as the liberator of the country's black population. The NP also portrayed the ANC as intolerant of political dissent.

The NP failed to gain many black votes in the April 1994 elections but nonetheless won the second-largest vote—20.4 percent of the total, gaining eighty-two seats in the National Assembly. The NP won a majority in the Western Cape, garnered the second-largest vote in seven provinces, and ranked third in KwaZulu-Natal. Despite its second-place performance in the elections, the NP—by virtue of its long-term political dominance—still exerts strong influence in the state bureaucracy and the country's security forces.

Inkatha Freedom Party

The Inkatha Freedom Party (IFP, also Inkatha) is a Zulu-based political party, based in its ethnic stronghold, KwaZulu-Natal. It is the ANC's main rival in the black community. Between 1970 and 1990, Inkatha portrayed itself as a moderate and democratic organization, contrasting its views with extremist positions within the ANC. But in the early 1990s, the IFP became increasingly intransigent in its efforts to preserve its traditional power base in KwaZulu, while the rest of the country was moving closer to nonracial democracy under the now moderate NP and ANC leadership.

Inkatha was originally established in 1922 as a cultural movement to promote the Zulu heritage. It was rejuvenated in 1928 by the Zulu king, Solomon ka Dinuzulu, as Inkatha ya kwa Zulu

(Organization of the Zulu). During this phase, controversy arose over the party's activities. For example, critics claimed that funds collected from Natal's impoverished black population were misused to pay for King Solomon's lavish life-style. Others suggested that the organization's 1928 constitution, written by a white lawyer from Durban at the urging of white businessmen in Natal, was intended to ensure that the party would express the interests of the traditional tribal elites, the conservative black petite bourgeoisie, and a few white power brokers. After a period of relative inactivity, and following an unsuccessful attempt to revive it in 1959, Inkatha ya kwa Zulu was reestablished as a political organization in March 1975 by KwaZulu's chief minister, Mangosuthu (Gatsha) Buthelezi. Buthelezi renamed the organization Inkatha Yenkululeko Yesizwe (National Cultural Liberation Movement). In August 1990, following the unbanning of antiapartheid organizations, Inkatha proclaimed itself a political party, the IFP, with membership open to all races.

From its primarily Zulu political base, Inkatha has played an important role in national politics. In 1977 it was the largest legal black movement in the country, having an estimated 120,000 members; by the late 1980s, its leaders estimated their membership at 1.5 million (considered highly inflated by the inclusion of the party's 600,000-member Youth Brigade and 500,000-member Women's Brigade). It has never managed to recruit many members outside the Zulu community, however.

The IFP in the 1990s is a tightly knit and authoritarian organization, dominated by Buthelezi. Its political structure consists of local branches organized into regions and provinces. The IFP's four provincial councils are led by the IFP National Council. Provincial delegates elect representatives to the annual general conference, where delegates to the National Council are elected each year. The IFP's power base is rooted in three sources—the former KwaZulu homeland bureaucracy, which the party controlled by virtue of its dominance over the local legislature and provincial government; the Zulu traditional leaders—i.e., chiefs and headmen; and the Zulu population, including the inhabitants of large squatter settlements near several cities, especially Johannesburg and Durban.

Although Inkatha and the ANC had close ties in the early 1970s, their relationship deteriorated after that. Inkatha became especially threatened by ANC organizing efforts among educated and urban Zulus. The ANC criticized

Buthelezi for becoming the leader of the KwaZulu homeland, and thereby accepting the government's demographic manipulation for apartheid purposes. The ANC pressed for a more militant antiapartheid campaign and waged a propaganda war against Buthelezi, demonizing him as a "stooge" of apartheid. In the late 1980s and early 1990s, this rivalry degenerated into violent conflict, spilling over into townships and rural areas, and claiming the lives of thousands of black South Africans.

Some Western observers and South African political leaders hoped that the IFP, rooted in Zulu tradition and Western in its outlook in support of a federalist democracy and free enterprise, would attract moderate South African blacks to its ranks. That prospect dimmed in the climate of escalating violence leading up to the 1994 elections. Buthelezi protested against his being sidelined by what he considered "ANC-NP collusion" in the negotiating process, and in early 1994 he announced that the IFP would boycott the country's first free elections.

The IFP ultimately participated in the elections, after the ANC and the NP agreed to consider international mediation on the issue of provincial autonomy and agreed to reinforce the status of Zulu King Goodwill Zwelithini and the Zulu homeland. The party's late entry cost it popular support at the polls, however. The IFP managed to win barely one-half of the vote in Natal and only 10.5 percent of the nationwide vote, with most of its support in KwaZulu and the area around Johannesburg.

The IFP's commitment to Zulu autonomy remained strong after the elections. In May 1994, at a caucus of the KwaZulu legislative assembly, Inkatha formed a new society called Iso Lesizwe, or Eye of the Nation, with Chief Buthelezi as its president. The new organization dedicated itself to pursuing Zulu autonomy "within the parameters of democratic and pluralistic forms of government and along with all the other peoples living in the ancestral territory of the Zulu nation." Debate over this issue intensified in 1995 and 1996.

Freedom Front

The Freedom Front (FF) is a right-wing Afrikaner political party established in March 1994, following a split among extremist organizations, to ensure a proapartheid presence in the April elections. It is a successor to the Afrikaner Volksfront (AVF), which was founded by General Constand Viljoen, who had also served as chief of the South African Defence Force (SADF) until November 1985. Viljoen emerged from retirement in 1991 to lead a group of right-wing former generals in forming an alliance of Afrikaner parties. As the AVF, the alliance included the White Protection Movement (Blanke Bevrydingsbeweging—BBB), the Boerestaat Party (Boer State Party, the military wing of which was known as the the Boer Resistance Movement, or the Boere Weerstandsbeweging—BWB), the Conservative Party of South Africa (CP), the Reconstituted National Party (Herstigte Nasionale Party—HNP), the Oranjewerkers (Orange Workers), and the Republic Unity Movement. The AVF's objective was to unify the extreme right and to advocate the formation of a *volkstaat*, an autonomous Afrikaner nation-state, in a postapartheid South Africa. However, even some AVF leaders were troubled by the violent racism and political extremism of some members of the front. Their refusal to participate in the nation's first nonracial elections weakened the movement, and in March 1994 General Viljoen and his allies broke away to form the FF.

Much of the support for the FF comes from farmers' organizations in the former Transvaal and the Free State. Among the FF's leaders are several former Conservative Party members of parliament, former high-ranking military officers, and a former chairman of the Broederbond.

In the 1994 elections, the FF received only 2.2 percent of the vote, gaining nine National Assembly seats. The party performed best in Gauteng, where some 40 percent of its votes were cast. Its participation in the elections helped to legitimize the electoral process and thus to neutralize the violent threat that the extremist right-wing extraparliamentary forces could have posed to the new political system. In doing so, it bolstered the standing of Viljoen and others who sought to preserve Afrikaner cultural autonomy through nonviolent means.

Other Political Parties

The Democratic Party (DP) was established in April 1989 as a liberal, centrist party. It was formed as an amalgamation of four liberal political groupings, the most important of which was the recently disbanded Progressive Federal Party (PFP), led by Zach de Beer. The coalition also included the Independent Party (IP), led by Dennis Worrall; the National Democratic Movement (NDM), led by Wynand Malan; and a group of reform-minded Afrikaners dubbed the "fourth force." The DP then became the primary left-of-center parliamentary opposition to the NP. It won 20 percent of white support in the 1989 general election, giving it thirty-three parliamentary seats.

The DP advocated the abolition of apartheid and the creation of a nonracial social democratic state through the protection of human rights, a government based on proportional party representation and universal suffrage, an independent judiciary, collective bargaining in industrial relations, and economic growth through individual entrepreneurship. Ironically, the NP adopted some of the DP's notions about reforming the apartheid state in 1989 and 1990, thus depriving the DP of some of its political base. A few DP leaders advocated an alliance with the ANC; others favored joining the NP; and the embattled center—led by the party's leader de Beer—sought to develop a distinctive, liberal, centrist image that would serve to mediate between the ANC and the NP. At the same time, the DP sought, without much success, to expand its support among all racial groups.

In preparation for the April 1994 elections, the DP's economic program gave top priority to creating jobs in a "free market economy with a social conscience," while rejecting the "nationalization of privately owned businesses and the expropriation of property for political purposes." The DP also opposed "economic populism," socialism, and the "politicization of education, housing, and social services." Its political program criticized the interim constitution for failing to eliminate laws that allowed detention without trial, and for failing to ensure the political independence of the media. The DP also opposed the antidefection clauses in the interim constitution, which made it difficult for members of parliament to break ranks and vote against the dictates of their party leaders. The DP called, instead, for a constitution based on individual rights, property rights, press freedom, women's rights, proportional representation within constituencies, federalism, devolution of federal powers to the provinces, and the direct election of senators by the provincial electorates.

In the 1994 elections, the DP's performance was considered disastrous, as it won only 1.7 percent of the vote and gained only seven seats in the National Assembly. The voting results revealed that it had failed to broaden its urban, middle-class, and English-speaking white base. It had won only about 3 percent of the coloured vote in the Western Cape, a comparable percentage of the Indian vote in KwaZulu-Natal, and no significant black support.

The Pan-Africanist Congress (PAC) was established in April 1959 by ANC dissidents who opposed that group's multiracial orientation and advocated black liberation within an exclusively black nationalist context. The party was founded in the black townships of Orlando and Soweto, outside Johannesburg, where it has received most of its support. The government declared the PAC an "unlawful" organization in 1960, because it advocated violent rebellion against the government. Like the ANC, the PAC was recognized by the United Nations (UN) and by the Organization of African Unity (OAU) as an official South African liberation movement. It was unbanned on February 2, 1990.

As advocates of the black liberation struggle, the PAC's founders criticized the ANC for diluting black nationalism by accepting white members (and Asians and coloureds). The PAC also opposed the ANC's alliance with the SACP because most PAC leaders rejected Marxist economic dogma (although the PAC had advocated some Maoist tenets in the late 1960s). Instead, the PAC advocated an indigenous form of African "communalism." It rejected the ANC's Freedom Charter because the charter sought to guarantee minority rights in a future postapartheid state, and issued instead the Azanian Manifesto in 1959. The manifesto promoted armed struggle by black South Africans as the only means of seizing power, overthrowing capitalism, and restoring their birthright of African landownership. Finally, unlike the ANC, which engaged in extensive political organizing through formal party structures, the PAC believed in the inevitability of national liberation through the spontaneous revolt of the masses.

From 1960 to 1990, the PAC's activities ranged from mass action campaigns, such as a campaign in 1960 to overcome what it termed "black psychological subservience to whites," to protests against the hated pass laws that required black South Africans to carry identity documents. One such demonstration in March 1960 led to at least sixty-seven deaths at police hands and more than 11,000 arrests in subsequent disturbances. The PAC's military wing, the Azanian People's Liberation Army (APLA)—then known by the name "Poqo" (loosely translated "blacks only")—also engaged in an underground armed struggle against white-dominated political and cultural institutions (see Consolidating Apartheid in the 1960s, ch. 1).

After the PAC was banned in 1960, the organization went underground, with headquarters located in Maseru, Lesotho.

It was led by an executive committee, the members of which had either evaded arrest or been released from prison. The PAC's senior leaders included its charismatic founder, Robert Sobukwe; acting president Potlako Leballo, who resigned under pressure in 1979; Vusumazi Make, who succeeded Leballo; John Pokela, who became leader in 1981; Johnson Mlambo, who succeeded Pokela as chairman in 1985; and Clarence Makwetu, who became president in 1990.

Following the PAC's unbanning in 1990, it reorganized as a legal political party, although its military wing continued to operate underground until 1994. Its internal organization consisted of a thirty-five-member National Executive Committee led by President Makwetu, first deputy president Johnson Mlambo, second deputy president Dikgang Moseneki, and general secretary Benny Alexander.

The PAC has eight working committees and a five-member National Coordinating Committee. Its members are organized into 105 local branches nationwide. Affiliated organizations include the Azanian National Youth Unity (Azanyu), a youth wing; the All African Student Committee (Aasac); the National Council of Trade Unions (Nactu); the African Organisation for Women (AOW); the Black Consciousness Movement (BCM); the Sobukwe Forum, a London-based faction; and the Pan-Africanist Students' Organisation (PASO), which has branches at several South African universities.

Although the PAC played little role in the multiparty negotiations during 1993 and early 1994, it formally suspended its armed struggle in early 1994 and agreed to participate in the April elections. It gained only 1.2 percent of the national vote, receiving five seats in the National Assembly, and it won one seat in each of three provincial legislatures—in Gauteng (then Pretoria-Witwatersrand-Vereeniging—PWV), KwaZulu-Natal, and the Eastern Cape.

Several other political parties participated in the 1994 elections, although, with the exception of the African Christian Democratic Party (which gained two seats in the National Assembly and seats in three of the nine provincial legislatures), none received more than 1 percent of the vote. These parties included the Sports Organisation for Collective Contributions and Equal Rights (SOCCER), the Keep It Straight and Simple Party (KISS), the Women's Rights Peace Party (WRPP), the Worker's List Party (WLP), the Ximoko Progressive Party (XPP), the Africa Muslim Party (AMP), the African Democratic

Movement (ADM), the African Moderates Congress Party (AMCP), the Dikwankwetla Party of South Africa (DPSA), the Federal Party (FP), the Luso-South Africa Party (LUSAP), and the Minority Front (MF).

Interest Groups

Interest groups have played a significant role in South African politics, although until apartheid was abolished the primary criterion for interest articulation was race, more often than economic issues. Interest groups work to achieve the goals of a particular ethnic community (Afrikaner, Xhosa, Zulu), racial group (white, black, coloured, or Indian), or other category of persons sharing a common goal. Leonard Thompson and Andrew Prior, in their book *South African Politics*, describe apartheid-era attempts by groups such as the Afrikaner Broederbond to win political influence in the parliament and the executive branch in order to maintain the status quo, while others, such as trade unions, sought to change labor relations and economic policy. Still other interest groups, such as the South African Media Council, had specific goals, in this case the establishment of a free and independent press. Finally, several organizations that were effectively banned from the political arena, such as the United Democratic Front (UDF) and the Mass Democratic Movement (MDM), continued to function as political interest groups during the apartheid era.

Within this system, the Afrikaner interest groups were the most influential, as they constituted an element in the country's ruling elite. After apartheid was abolished, however, interest-group politics began to change. Many organizations abandoned their ethnically based, secretive, extraparliamentary, or underground characteristics to meet the challenges of the new nonracial, open, and democratic political order.

Afrikaner Broederbond

The Afrikaner Broederbond (later Broederbond, or Brotherhood) was the most important apartheid-era interest group in South Africa. Functioning for almost sixty years as an elite, exclusively Afrikaner, secret society, the Broederbond gradually shifted its perspective on the future and supported the political reform process beginning in the early 1980s.

Founded in 1918, the Broederbond became a secret organization in 1921 and dedicated itself to advancing Afrikaner political, cultural, and economic interests. Membership was restricted to white Afrikaner males who passed a rigorous selection process. One of the group's primary goals was to place Afrikaner nationalists in key political positions and to establish other organizations to further Afrikaner interests. With members of the Broederbond in key leadership positions, the NP government often promoted the interests of the group.

The Broederbond's organizational structure and political strategy were first publicly disclosed in the late 1970s by Hennie Serfontein, an Afrikaner journalist who devoted much of his career to investigating the organization. According to internal Broederbond documents, in 1993 the society reportedly had 20,074 members—one of the highest figures in its history—organized into twelve regions and 1,392 branches, or cells. Branches varied in size from five to twenty members, and central committees in towns and cities coordinated branch activities. Branch cells selected representatives to regional councils, the next higher level of organization. Top policy-making authority was vested in the National Congress (Bondsraad), which met every two years and elected the organization's senior executive authorities, the Broederbond chairman and the Executive Council. The Executive Council served for two years; in 1993 it had eighteen members.

The Broederbond played an important role in transforming apartheid. Major governmental policy shifts in areas such as education and sports were first tested in Broederbond discussions before being aired in parliamentary debate. Then in November 1993, in preparation for the postapartheid political system, the Broederbond adopted a new constitution that radically transformed the previously clandestine organization. The Broederbond changed its name to the Afrikanerbond, removed its cloak of secrecy, and abolished its Afrikaner male exclusivity by permitting women and all racial groups to join. Some membership restrictions remained—new entrants had to speak Afrikaans, had to subscribe to the organization's constitution, and had to be approved by the other members. These restrictions helped to ensure the continued importance of Afrikaner interests and identity.

United Democratic Front

The United Democratic Front (UDF) was an extraparliamentary organization established in 1983, primarily in opposition to the government's constitutional proposals of that year. It served as an umbrella organization of antiapartheid groups.

Membership was open to any organization that endorsed the principles of the ANC's Freedom Charter. Affiliates of the UDF included the Congress of South African Trade Unions (COSATU), the South African National Student Congress (Sansco), the National Union of South African Students (NUSAS), and the Congress of South African Students (COSAS).

Following clashes with the government, the UDF was effectively banned—i.e., its political activities were proscribed—under the terms of the emergency regulations of February 24, 1988, and many of its affiliates were reorganized under the guise of a new political coalition. The UDF disbanded on August 20, 1991, declaring that its major objectives had been fulfilled.

Mass Democratic Movement

The Mass Democratic Movement (MDM) was the name of an informal coalition of antiapartheid groups during the 1970s and early 1980s. As a formal organization, the MDM was established as an antiapartheid successor to the UDF after the 1988 emergency restrictions effectively banned the UDF and several other opposition groups. Even after 1988, the MDM was a temporary loose coalition of antiapartheid activists with no permanent constitution, no official membership rolls, no national or regional governing body, and no officeholders. Like the UDF, the MDM drew much of its support from the black community; a condition for affiliation with the MDM was adherence to the provisions of the ANC's Freedom Charter.

The MDM gained prominence in 1989, when it organized a campaign of civil disobedience in anticipation of national elections scheduled to take place in September of that year. Defying the state-of-emergency regulations in effect at the time, several hundred black protesters entered "whites-only" hospitals and beaches. During that month, people of all races marched peacefully in several cities to protest against police brutality and repressive legislation. When the UDF was unbanned in February 1990, most MDM leaders and many members rejoined their former organizations.

Trade Unions

Labor activism dates back to the 1840s, when the first unions were formed. Most major industrial unions were organized after World War I either to support or to oppose racial privileges claimed by whites. Black and communist organizations formed antiapartheid unions to abolish racist policies in the workplace; most proapartheid unions were formed by government forces to support discriminatory labor practices. During the apartheid era, membership in most trade unions was based on race, and until 1979, the government did not recognize black unions or grant them labor law protection. In 1977, for example, out of 172 registered trade unions that were eligible to bargain collectively, eighty-three were white, forty-eight were coloured, and forty-one were open to whites, coloureds, and Asians. Among the proapartheid and all-white unions were the White Workers' Protection Association (Blankewerkersbeskermingsbond), the Mineworkers' Union, and larger coordinating bodies such as the South African Confederation of Labour.

The South African Congress of Trade Unions (SACTU), formed in the early 1950s, became the leader of the antiapartheid struggle in the labor movement. The government often arrested and harassed its leaders for political agitation. During the 1970s, however, the government recognized the need to exert greater control over labor activities and to improve government-union relations. In 1977 it established the Commission of Inquiry into Labour Legislation, headed by Professor Nicolas Wiehahn. The Wiehahn Commission recommended the legalization of black unions, in part to bring labor militants under government control. The government recognized black unions in 1979 and granted them limited collective bargaining rights. In the same year, the government established a National Manpower Commission, with representatives from labor, business, and government, to advise policy makers on labor issues.

During the 1980s, business owners and management organizations, such as the Afrikaner Trade Institute (Afrikaanse Handelsinstituut—AHI), which had represented Afrikaner commercial interests since the 1940s, were forced to negotiate with black labor leaders for the first time. To adapt to the new labor environment, they established the South African Employers' Consultative Committee on Labour Affairs (SACCOLA) to represent the owners in lobbying and collective bargaining sessions.

Black union membership soared during the 1980s. New labor confederations included the nonracial COSATU, which was affiliated with the ANC and the SACP; the PAC-affiliated National Council of Trade Unions (Nactu); and the IFP-affiliated United Workers Union of South Africa (UWUSA). By

1990 COSATU, the largest of these, had more than thirty union affiliates with more than 1 million members.

Efforts to begin dismantling apartheid during the early 1990s meant that union leaders were pressed to represent workers' interests more vigorously in the changing economic environment. Although the largest unions had been strong ANC supporters in the past—and were vital to ANC efforts to mobilize popular demonstrations against apartheid—they began to clash with ANC party officials and with government leaders in 1994 and 1995. Some union members feared that workers' interests would be overlooked in the effort to implement economic development plans in the postapartheid era.

Political Elites

Although change was evident at all levels of society as South Africa began to dismantle apartheid during the 1990s, particularly dramatic changes were occurring in the country's political and social leadership. Not only were new leaders emerging on the national level, but shifts were also occurring within political organizations, as new political expectations and aspirations arose and as new demands were placed on political leaders at all levels.

Since 1948 the country's governing class, the political elite, had been dominated by Afrikaners. Afrikaners held most high positions in government, including the legislature, the judiciary, the cabinet, and the senior ranks of the military and security services. Afrikaners also came to dominate the larger community of leaders, the power elite, by assuming important roles in the civil service bureaucracy, and to a lesser extent in business, the universities, and the media. Afrikaner dominance was reinforced by the rules of apartheid, in large part because the government's security and intelligence services helped to enforce the rules of apartheid through other institutions.

In general, during the apartheid era, English-speaking whites were less important in the political and power elites. They played only secondary roles in most areas of government. English speakers were, nevertheless, prominent in commerce and industry, where the Afrikaners' success had lagged behind their political achievements, as is explained by Thompson and Prior. By the 1980s, English-speaking whites also held important positions in universities and the media, and in a few areas of government.

In the early 1990s, these political and power elites were evolving, as is demonstrated in the authoritative survey of elites, *Who's Who in South African Politics*, by the South African writer Shelagh Gastrow. Gastrow divided South Africa's dominant political leaders into four major categories: political leaders within the Afrikaner community, most associated with the NP; an older generation of black opposition leaders, most within the ANC; a younger generation of leaders emerging from the Black Consciousness Movement; and a new group of labor leaders who had risen to prominence as the trade union movement strengthened during the 1970s and 1980s. A fifth category might be added—according to South African political scientist Roger Southall, who reviewed Gastrow's book—the small number of white political leaders who attempted to reshape white politics along nonracial, democratic lines.

A subsequent revised edition of Gastrow's book identified 118 individuals—110 men and only eight women—as constituting South Africa's evolving political elite in 1992. Among the obvious changes occurring at that time was the emergence of formerly imprisoned, exiled, or banned opposition leaders, who had been released from prison or had been legally recognized since early 1990. They could then be legally quoted in the country's media, and their ideas were being widely disseminated. In addition, new challengers arose to replace formerly entrenched leaders, especially conservative blacks, coloureds, and Indians who had gained office through various forms of state patronage in the black homelands or in other institutions of government.

Changes were also occurring within the senior ranks of the organizations from which the country's new leaders had emerged. As the ANC, for example, was forced to cooperate with former opponents, especially the NP, in pursuing national goals, new alliances and friendships were formed, shaped in part by a pragmatic appraisal of the political realities of the time. In addition, former opposition groups—especially the ANC—began to revise their rhetoric from that of guerrilla opponents of government, or "states in exile," to adapt to their new positions of responsibility. The ANC's best educated, skilled technocrats, capable of managing governmental and other bureaucracies, were gaining particular prominence.

At the same time, a greater distance was developing between these educated elites and the less educated rank-and-file within their own organizations. In particular, there was a growing dis-

Apartheid-era civil servant leaving location in Lebowa
Courtesy R. T. K. Scully

tance between the ANC and its radical youth wing in late 1994 and 1995. There was also a growing distance between the ANC leadership and their former ally, the South African Communist Party (SACP). Ties between these two organizations had not only been close in the past; their membership and leadership rolls had overlapped.

In some cases, the new elites appeared to have more in common with members of rival political organizations than with their organization's own members. Several new government leaders, for example, were drawn from traditional African elites—royal families, chiefs, and influential clans. President Mandela, while a university-trained lawyer, is also a descendant of a leading family among the Thembu (Tembu), a Xhosa sub-group. Like Mandela, the prominent Zulu leader and minister of home affairs, Mangosuthu (Gatsha) Buthelezi, is university-educated and the product of aristocratic origins. Buthelezi, a member of the Zulu royal family, is also a chief within the Buthelezi sub-group (also, "tribe") of the Zulu.

Other members of South Africa's new government also represent ethnic elites. For example, the minister of public enterprises in 1995, Stella Sigcau, is the daughter of a well-known Pondo paramount chief, Botha Sigcau. Stella Sigcau also had served as chief minister in the Transkei government during the early 1980s.

Many former ANC officials who were in government office in the mid-1990s had worked to overcome factional differences based on ethnicity during the apartheid era. Although the ANC is often stereotyped as "Xhosa-dominated," and a number of its officers are Xhosa, several ethnic groups have been represented in the ANC's senior ranks. Thomas Nkobi, treasurer general from 1973 through the early 1990s, represents a subgroup within the Zimbabwe-based Shona people. Former Secretary General Cyril Ramaphosa and National Working Committee member Sydney Mufamadi are Venda (VaVenda—see Ethnic Groups and Language, ch. 2). Ramaphosa's former deputy, Jacob Zuma, is one of several Zulu leaders who rose to prominence within the ANC. The ANC's former security and intelligence specialist, Patrick "Terror" Lekota, and former MK leader Joe Modise are Sotho (BaSotho). Several popular regional leaders are Tswana (BaTswana). In general, these leaders have rejected arguments that favored the use of ethnicity to define political factions.

Age differences appeared more divisive than ethnicity within the ANC during the early and the mid-1990s. There were heated debates over questions of political succession, as the ANC's aging leaders—many over the age of seventy—faced challenges from the generations below them. Nelson Mandela was seventy-five years old when he was elected president in 1994, and several other ANC leaders were more than seventy years of age. Their most likely successors—especially Mbeki, Ramaphosa, Zuma, and the ANC's former director of intelligence, "Mac" Maharaj—were roughly two decades younger. Some of the ANC's younger militants threatened revolt against senior party figures in the early months of the new government, as their demands for jobs, homes, and improved living standards continued to be unmet. Criticism of the "older generation" was fueled in late 1994 and early 1995, when the president's former wife, Winnie Mandela, clashed with the government and was ousted as a deputy minister, as she championed the grievances of the ANC's militant youth.

As the apartheid system was being dismantled, some members of the Afrikaner elite in government, the civil service, and the security services reacted with impressive flexibility. By adapting quickly to the new environment, many of them not only retained their valued positions in the bureaucracy but also won new respect from former adversaries. As the ANC assumed responsibility for the security establishment, the police, and the intelligence services, ANC leaders were often able to work closely and cooperatively with Afrikaners who had once been so effective in excluding blacks from the political process.

The shift in power and influence among the country's political elites had begun well before the April 1994 elections. An important arena in which this power shift occurred was that of the political negotiations concerning the interim constitution of 1993. During those negotiations, as difficult and unpromising as they sometimes appeared, then-governing whites began, some for the first time, to view their black counterparts as legitimate partners in the decision-making process. At the same time, many black leaders adjusted smoothly to the new climate of political tolerance.

Communications Media

South Africa's communications media were radically transformed by the political reforms sweeping the country in the 1990s. The most fundamental changes were the gradual easing of government censorship and its abolition in the interim constitution. In spite of frequent government censorship under apartheid, however, South Africans had received news reports through numerous publications and broadcasts.

Under apartheid, a vast array of legislation and regulations had imposed limits on the media. The South African Press Council, for example, had the power to fine newspaper editors for defying emergency regulations, which often barred coverage of political events. Under emergency regulations in the 1980s, journalists were forbidden to report on banned organizations and people; the media were prohibited from reporting events relating to "state security," such as protests and demonstrations. The public then had to rely on the government's Bureau of Information for official reports of political events. And for violating emergency regulations, some journalists were detained—even without being charged—and newspapers were temporarily suspended. Some editors and reporters were prosecuted, and foreign journalists were expelled or refused entry visas. Similarly, the Publications Control Board, under the Publications Act (No. 42) of 1974, censored certain books and movies, especially those dealing with race relations.

In the early 1990s as part of the government's pledge to reform apartheid, many of the emergency regulations relating to the media were removed. Thus, the Protection of Information Act of 1982, which imposed penalties on publications that violated national security, was repealed in February 1990 and less stringent guidelines for protecting sensitive information were established. Thereafter, the press, including numerous mainstream and alternative publications, was generally independent, criticizing both the government in power and the various opposition parties involved in the political transformation.

Radio and Television

South Africa has an estimated 12.1 million radio receivers and more than 3.5 million television sets in the mid-1990s. Radio and television broadcasting (with the exception of M-Net, a privately owned, subscriber-based cable television service) is controlled by the South African Broadcasting Corporation (SABC), a statutory body that obtains its revenue from licenses and advertising. It operates twenty-two domestic radio broadcasting services in eleven languages through SABC-Radio, one external radio broadcasting service in seven languages through Channel Africa Radio, and two television channels that broadcast in seven languages through SABC-Television. Although M-Net was the only privately owned television network (with more than 880,000 subscribers), there were at least six privately owned commercial radio stations by 1996.

The most fundamental change in the role of the media in the mid-1990s took place in the SABC, which had been controlled by NP-led governments and had generally expressed government views. In April 1993, a new twenty-five-member SABC board began to prepare the SABC for the postapartheid era as an independent, autonomous, and impartial broadcasting authority. President de Klerk relinquished the right to appoint its board members, and the members of the board were selected publicly for the first time, after an independent judicial panel had screened the nominees to ensure political neutrality. Ironically, however, as a reflection of the new bal-

Union Buildings house government offices and National Archives (Pretoria).
Courtesy Embassy of South Africa, Washington

ance of forces in the country, an estimated nineteen of the twenty-five new board members were ANC members or were generally believed to be ANC supporters, and new complaints of political bias in the media began to emerge.

Another major change in the broadcasting system was the establishment of the Independent Broadcasting Authority in January 1994, as authorized by the Independent Broadcasting Authority Act (No. 153) of 1993. The authority consists of a seven-member panel, appointed by the minister of home affairs after a period of public discussion and nominations. The authority in 1994 required all broadcasters to reapply for operating licenses. It issued temporary licenses to most, and it obtained court orders to close down a few broadcast stations that had not applied for licenses. Permanent licenses were issued in 1995, after five months of public hearings and debate over the rules of broadcasting in South Africa.

Newspapers, Magazines, and Journals

More than 5,000 newspapers, magazines, and journals were registered with the South African Department of Home Affairs by January 1994; sixty-six new ones registered in that year, and registration was no longer required after 1994. As in other nations, newspaper and magazine publishers are organized into corporate groupings. Major corporations include the Argus Printing and Publishing Company, Perskor, and Times Media. Newspapers are printed in English, Afrikaans, and several African languages. The country's two national newspapers, which are printed on Sundays, are the *Sunday Times* and *Rapport.* Both are printed in several cities, simultaneously. The *Sunday Times* had a circulation of about 524,164 in 1995, and *Rapport,* about 396,974. Other major newspapers (and 1995 circulation figures) are *City Press* (262,203), *The Sowetan* (204,219), and *The Star* (199,753) (see table 19, Appendix).

South Africa has more than 300 consumer magazines and 500 trade, technical, and professional publications. *Huisgenoot,* a weekly Afrikaans publication, sold more than 520,000 issues in 1995, while *You,* its English counterpart, sold nearly 300,000 issues. The leading business and political magazine is the weekly *Financial Mail,* with approximately 32,000 subscribers.

The South African Press Association (SAPA) is the country's national news agency. It is a forty-member nonprofit cooperative, engaged in foreign and domestic news-gathering and distribution. Foreign news agencies operating in South Africa include Agence France Presse, Associated Press, Reuters, and United Press International.

Foreign Relations

The Ministry of Foreign Affairs is responsible for South African foreign policy decisions. The Department of Foreign Affairs (DFA) within the Ministry of Foreign Affairs conducts liaison with foreign governments and international organizations on all matters affecting official relations. These relations are conducted through foreign government officials, through diplomats accredited to South Africa, and through South Africa's accredited embassies, consulates, and other missions abroad. Until the early 1990s, the DFA and the diplomatic corps competed against numerous counterestablishment "diplomatic services" run by antiapartheid organizations in exile, especially the ANC. The aim of these parallel communication channels was to isolate the South African government within the international community as a means of pressuring Pretoria to abolish apartheid.

After the abolition of apartheid and the inauguration of the democratically elected Government of National Unity, South Africa's foreign relations were dramatically transformed. The country's diplomatic isolation ended, and existing relations with other countries and with international organizations improved. South Africa reestablished diplomatic and trade relations with many countries, particularly in Africa, and established new relations with some former sanctions "hardliners," such as India, Pakistan, Bahrain, Malaysia, Jordan, Libya, and Cuba. Several regional and international organizations invited South Africa to join, or to reactivate its membership, including the Organization of African Unity (OAU), the Southern African Development Community (SADC), and the United Nations (UN). In addition, South Africa participated in international and bilateral sport, academic, and scientific activities, often for the first time in decades. Relations with the countries of the former Soviet Union, Eastern Europe, and Central Europe improved. South Africa had full diplomatic ties with thirty-nine countries in 1990; that number increased to sixty-nine in 1993, and to at least 147 in 1995.

After the April 1994 elections, President Mandela appointed two ANC members, Alfred Nzo and Aziz Pahad, as minister and deputy minister of foreign affairs. He refused to make immediate sweeping changes in the diplomatic corps. The pillars of South Africa's future foreign policy had been enunciated by Mandela in late 1993, in an article published in *Foreign Affairs*. These principles are the promotion of human rights and democracy; respect for justice and international law in interstate relations; the achievement of peace through "internationally agreed and nonviolent mechanisms, including effective arms-control regimes"; incorporation of African concerns and interests into foreign policy choices; and economic development based on "cooperation in an interdependent world." In southern Africa, Mandela denounced South Africa's earlier economic domination of the region and its deliberate destabilization of neighboring states. Instead, Mandela called for "cooperation in regional construction, infrastructure and resource development projects . . . in virtually every sector and area." Finally, Mandela advocated the full reintegration of South Africa into global trade networks.

These foreign policy principles were being implemented even before Mandela's inauguration. For example, in early 1994 de Klerk and Mandela, along with the presidents of Botswana and Zimbabwe, helped mediate an end to a military revolt in neighboring Lesotho. In mid-1994, South Africa provided its first assistance to a UN peacekeeping operation when it supplied hospital equipment for Rwanda. Also in 1994, President Mandela agreed to help resolve the intractable civil war in Angola, although he cautioned against unrealistically high expectations in this and other deep-rooted political and ethnic conflicts.

Relations with African States

Official delegations from almost every other African state visited Pretoria in 1992 or 1993 to discuss ways to strengthen bilateral ties. South Africa's estimated 100 assistance projects in twenty-two African countries in 1991 more than doubled by 1994 and provided technical aid and training in agriculture, wildlife conservation, education, and health care. The effects of the early-1990s drought in southern Africa would have been even more devastating to the region's agriculture and wildlife if South Africa had not provided transportation and food assistance to its neighbors.

The change in South Africa's regional standing was dramatically marked by its admission to the Southern African Development Community (SADC) in August 1994. The twelve-member organization (also including Angola, Botswana, Lesotho, Malawi, Mauritius, Mozambique, Namibia, Swaziland, Tanzania, Zambia, and Zimbabwe) aims to promote regional cooperation in economic development and security affairs. The SADC annual meeting of heads of state and government was held in Johannesburg on August 28, 1995. The assembled leaders agreed to create a regional common market with the elimination of all internal trade barriers by the year 2000. They also signed an agreement to share water resources among SADC member nations.

Almost all African countries had depended on South African trade even during the sanctions era, despite their strong rhetorical condemnation of the apartheid regime. In 1991 South Africa's trade with the rest of the continent was at least US$3.5

billion, and this figure increased steadily as apartheid was being dismantled.

For the five landlocked countries of southern Africa (Botswana, Lesotho, Swaziland, Zambia, and Malawi), South Africa's well-developed system of roads, railroads, and port facilities provides a vital trade link. The Southern African Customs Union (SACU), headquartered in South Africa, provides a common customs area, including Botswana, Lesotho, Swaziland, and Namibia (see Foreign Trade, ch. 3).

Botswana

Relations with Botswana were normalized in the early 1990s, after a period of strained ties in the 1980s. The most contentious issue between the two countries had been Botswana's willingness to provide safe haven for the ANC military wing, MK, and, to a lesser extent, for other opposition groups such as the Black Consciousness Movement of Azania (BCMA—the external wing of the Black Consciousness Movement). Although Botswana officially prohibited ANC use of its territory as a base for attacks against South Africa, the ANC violated this policy during the 1980s, provoking several small-scale raids by the South African Defence Forces (SADF) against ANC bases in Botswana. At the same time, although Botswana joined in the international condemnation of apartheid, its geographic and economic vulnerability deterred it from imposing economic sanctions against South Africa, with whom it maintained extensive but unpublicized trade relations.

Relations improved in the early 1990s, as apartheid was gradually dismantled. ANC camps in Botswana were closed in 1991 and 1992, as several hundred political exiles returned to South Africa under a program administered by the United Nations High Commissioner for Refugees (UNHCR).

Lesotho

Until the 1960s, several South African governments pressed for the incorporation of Lesotho, then a British protectorate, into the Union of South Africa. As a landlocked country completely surrounded by South Africa, Lesotho depended heavily on South Africa for its economic well-being. After Lesotho became independent in October 1966, South Africa played a major role in the country's internal affairs—for example, by supporting the new government led by Chief Leabua Jonathan.

Tensions between the two countries rose in the 1970s because of Lesotho's criticism of South Africa at the UN and at the OAU, its support for the ANC, its provision of safe haven to antiapartheid fighters such as MK, and its close ties to a number of socialist countries. Relations became severely strained in April 1983, when the Jonathan government announced that Lesotho was at war with South Africa, and again in 1984, when Lesotho refused to sign a nonaggression pact with South Africa. In response, South Africa impounded shipments of arms to Lesotho, threatened economic sanctions, and suspended talks concerning the Lesotho Highlands Water Project (a thirty-year cooperative engineering venture that would supply water to South Africa and provide electric power and financial compensation to Lesotho). Tensions eased in 1984, as some ANC forces withdrew from Lesotho, but in 1985 new tensions prompted Pretoria to step up security measures along the border between the two countrries.

In early 1986, South Africa backed a military coup in Maseru, bringing into power a government more sympathetic to Pretoria's security interests. Lesotho expelled several ANC members and technicians from the Democratic People's Republic of Korea (North Korea), whom Pretoria considered a menace, and relations between the two nations improved. Work on the Highlands Water Project resumed, and in 1987 they established a joint trade mission. Relations continued to improve after that, and the countries established full diplomatic ties in May 1992. Pretoria recognized the outcome of Lesotho's March 1993 elections, the first in twenty-two years.

In January 1994, Lesotho's democratically elected civilian government sought South African assistance in quelling an army mutiny over pay and conditions of service in the Lesotho Defence Forces. Pretoria refused to intervene directly, but threatened to seal off Lesotho's borders, which would have blocked vital commercial transportation to and from Maseru. De Klerk and Mandela, together with the presidents of Zimbabwe and Botswana, urged both sides to negotiate an end to the crisis, a move that represented the likely pattern of postapartheid diplomacy in southern Africa.

Swaziland

South Africa's relations with the Kingdom of Swaziland, one of Africa's smallest nations—which South Africa surrounds on the north, west, and south—were shaped by the kingdom's complete dependence on its powerful neighbor for its economic and political well-being. During the 1970s and early 1980s, although Swaziland claimed to be neutral in the East-West conflict, it was actually pro-Western and maintained strong relations with South Africa, including clandestine cooperation in economic and security matters. South Africa invested heavily in Swaziland's economy, and Swaziland joined the Pretoria-dominated SACU. During the 1980s, some South African businesses also used Swazi territory as a transshipment point in order to circumvent international sanctions on South Africa. Relying on a secret security agreement with South Africa in 1982, Swazi officials harassed ANC representatives in the capital, Mbabane, and eventually expelled them from Swaziland. South African security forces, operating undercover, also carried out operations against the ANC on Swazi territory. Throughout this time, part of the Swazi royal family quietly sought the reintegration of Swazi-occupied territory in South Africa into their kingdom.

In June 1993, South Africa and Swaziland signed a judicial agreement providing for South African judges, magistrates, and prosecutors to serve in Swaziland's courts. South Africa also agreed to provide training for Swazi court personnel. In August 1995, the two countries signed an agreement to cooperate in anti-crime and anti-smuggling efforts along their common border.

Zimbabwe

Bilateral relations between South Africa and Zimbabwe improved substantially as apartheid legally ended. In December 1993, the foreign ministers of both countries met for the first time to discuss ways to improve bilateral ties. Tensions between the two countries had been high since 1965, when South Africa demonstrated tacit support for the unilateral declaration of independence (UDI) by white-dominated Rhodesia (Southern Rhodesia), a former British colony. South Africa also had assisted the new regime led by Prime Minister Ian Smith for almost fourteen years, until it was brought down by a combination of guerrilla war and international pressure.

After Rhodesia's independence as Zimbabwe, the government in Harare supported mandatory sanctions against South Africa and provided political, diplomatic, and military support to the ANC in its armed struggle. Zimbabwe also provided military assistance, including troops, for Maputo's struggle against

South African-supported insurgents in the Mozambican National Resistance (Resistência Nacional Moçambicana—MNR or RENAMO). SADF troops retaliated against Harare, with two raids on alleged ANC bases in the capital in 1986 and 1987, and bomb explosions in Harare in October 1987 and in Bulawayo in January 1988.

Relations between the two countries began to stabilize in 1990, after Mandela was released from prison and South Africa moved toward constitutional reform. Even before international sanctions against South Africa were lifted, a number of unpublicized ministerial contacts took place to discuss matters of trade and transport. President de Klerk and Zimbabwean President Robert Mugabe met publicly for the first time on January 27, 1994, when de Klerk, Mandela, Mugabe, and Botswana's President Quett Masire joined together in urging a peaceful resolution to a military mutiny in Lesotho.

President Mandela visited Harare in early 1995. The two countries debated trade issues throughout the year, primarily centered around efforts to dismantle apartheid-era tariffs. In November 1995, a ceremony attended by presidents Mandela and Mugabe marked the opening of a new bridge linking the two countries, across the Limpopo River.

Namibia

South Africa's relations with Namibia (formerly South-West Africa) were normalized following the 1988 agreement that paved the way for the solution to the interlinked conflicts in Namibia and Angola. Prior to this agreement, Namibia had been under South Africa's control since 1919, when Pretoria received the League of Nations mandate over the territory then known as South-West Africa. In 1946 the UN refused South Africa's request to annex the territory. In 1964 South Africa introduced apartheid in South-West Africa (Pretoria had granted Europeans living there limited self-governing privileges since 1925).

The United Nations General Assembly in 1966 voted to revoke South Africa's mandate and to place the territory under direct UN administration. South Africa refused to recognize this UN resolution until 1985, when President Botha ceded administrative control to the territory's interim government. South Africa allowed a UN peacekeeping force and an administrator to implement United Nations Security Council Resolution 435 (1978), establishing the United Nations Transitional

Assistance Group (UNTAG) in Namibia. Finally, on December 22, 1988, South Africa signed an agreement linking its withdrawal from the disputed territory to an end to Soviet and Cuban involvement in the long civil war in neighboring Angola. Namibia's new government, led by the South-West Africa People's Organisation (SWAPO), was elected in a landslide victory in November 1989.

After Namibia's independence in March 1990, South Africa and Namibia established diplomatic ties, but relations between the two countries were uneasy, in part because many of Namibia's senior government officials had been leaders in the guerrilla war to oust South Africa from their country. Namibia nonetheless joined the Southern African Customs Union (SACU) and continued to be almost totally dependent on South Africa in trade and investment. In 1992, for example, 90 percent of Namibia's imports came from South Africa, and South Africa purchased 30 percent of Namibia's exports. Relations improved as apartheid was dismantled.

The two countries established a Joint Administrative Authority to manage the port facilities at Walvis Bay, Namibia's only deep-water port, which had remained under South African control after Namibian independence. Under pressure from the ANC, South Africa then agreed to transfer control over the port enclave to Windhoek before the 1994 elections. Namibia finally assumed control over Walvis Bay on March 1, 1994.

The prospects for multiracial democracy in South Africa prompted Namibia to sign a series of bilateral agreements with Pretoria in anticipation of the close ties they hoped to maintain through the rest of the 1990s. One of these, signed in 1992, pledged cooperation in supplying water to arid regions of both countries along their common border. In December 1994, President Mandela announced his government's decision to write off Namibia's debt, an estimated US$190 million owed to South Africa. He also transferred most South African state property in Namibia to Namibian government ownership.

Mozambique

After Mozambique's independence from Portugal in 1975, relations between South Africa and Mozambique were shaped by the rise to power of the revolutionary Front for the Liberation of Mozambique (Frente de Libertação de Moçambique—FRELIMO) government, and in particular, by FRELIMO's commitment to support regional liberation movements. South

Africa provided covert military assistance to the anti-FRELIMO insurgency, RENAMO. In an attempt to curtail South Africa's intervention, Maputo entered into negotiations with Pretoria in late 1983, resulting in a non-aggression pact, the Nkomati Accord, in 1984. This accord committed both countries to end their assistance to each other's opposition movements, and to establish a joint security commission to monitor implementation of the pact. South Africa continued to assist RENAMO, however, and relations between the two countries worsened.

After unsubstantiated allegations of South African involvement in the death (in a plane crash) of Mozambican president Samora Machel in October 1986, demonstrators attacked the South African trade mission in Maputo. Pretoria threatened to retaliate by banning Mozambican migrant laborers from South Africa's mines, but this plan was not implemented. Even after South African security forces raided ANC bases around Maputo in 1987, presidents Botha and Joaquim Chissano met to try to revive the Nkomati Accord. They agreed to establish a joint commission on cooperation and development, whereby South Africa would protect Mozambique's Cahora Bassa power lines, which had been targets of RENAMO sabotage, and would assist in improving Maputo's harbor as well as road and rail links with South Africa.

Relations continued to improve in 1989 following a South African initiative to help resolve Mozambique's civil war. Although both Chissano and RENAMO leader Afonso Dhlakama rejected Pretoria's proposal of United States mediation in Mozambique, Pretoria nonetheless played an important role in persuading the two men to pursue a negotiated peace. South African president de Klerk, Zimbabwe's president Mugabe, and other regional leaders urged Mozambique's warring parties to sign a peace agreement and, after they did so in October 1992, to prepare for democratic elections. In December 1992, the UN began deploying 7,500 troops for the UN Operation in Mozambique (UNOMOZ), and the date for Mozambique's first multiparty elections was finally set for October 1994.

In 1993 South Africa and Mozambique agreed to formalize their trade missions in each other's capitals and to upgrade diplomatic ties. Late that year, the two countries agreed to cooperate in repatriating more than 350,000 Mozambicans who had sought refuge in South Africa—some of the more than 800,000 Mozambican refugees scattered throughout the region. The

UNHCR reported that refugees continued returning to Mozambique throughout 1994 as the elections approached.

After South Africa's April 1994 elections, Deputy President Mbeki opened communication channels with RENAMO leaders, including Dhlakama, in an effort to help preserve the fragile peace in Mozambique. President Mandela made his first official state visit to the country on July 20, 1994, and he emphasized the challenges both countries faced in strengthening democratic institutions. The two governments signed agreements establishing a joint cooperation commission to pursue shared development goals in agriculture, security, transportation, and medicine.

In 1996 the two countries began to implement a South African proposal for a small group of South African farmers to settle and farm land in Mozambique. The proposal had originated in the desire of a few Afrikaner farmers to leave South Africa, and both governments viewed it as a possible means of improving the agricultural infrastructure in Mozambique and of providing jobs for farm laborers there. For Pretoria, the proposal held some promise of reducing the influx of farm workers into South Africa.

Zambia

South African-Zambian relations until 1990 were shaped by Zambia's support for antiapartheid movements inside South Africa, by its agreement to allow anti-South African SWAPO guerrillas to operate from Zambia's territory, and by its anti-RENAMO assistance to government forces in Mozambique. As one of the leaders of the frontline states against South Africa, Zambia provided safe haven for the ANC, which had its headquarters in Lusaka, prompting military reprisals by South Africa in the late 1980s. Relations between the two countries improved as apartheid was being dismantled in the early 1990s, leading to several visits by the two countries' leaders. Then-president Kaunda visited South Africa for the first time in February 1992, and the two countries established diplomatic ties and began to normalize trade relations later that year. (Zambia was already South Africa's second largest African trading partner.) President de Klerk visited Lusaka in mid-1993, the first visit by a South African head of state. In 1994 South Africa continued to be the most important source of Zambian imports— mostly machinery and manufactured goods—and the two

countries were exploring new avenues for trade during the rest
of the 1990s.

Angola

South Africa has long-standing geographic, commercial, and
political ties with Angola, which became independent from
Portugal in November 1975. Until the early 1990s, relations
between the two countries were strained, however, owing primarily to South Africa's extensive military support for the
insurgent movement in Angola. The National Union for the
Total Independence of Angola (União Nacional para a Independência Total de Angola—UNITA), led by Jonas Savimbi,
had waged a sixteen-year war against the Marxist-led government in Luanda. Pretoria became Savimbi's patron principally
because it feared the threat of Soviet and Cuban expansionism,
but by the late 1980s, a new geostrategic environment was
emerging in the region. The Cold War ended, accompanied by
the collapse of Angola's superpower patron, the former Soviet
Union; Cuban forces withdrew from Angola as part of the 1988
Angola-Namibia Accord, and the Angolan civil war ended tentatively, with a peace agreement in May 1991.

Angola's first democratic elections in September 1992 failed,
after Savimbi refused to accept his electoral defeat and the war
resumed. Pretoria then supported a negotiated outcome to the
festering civil war, although a few South Africans (said to be
operating outside Pretoria's control) continued their support
to Savimbi.

Relations between South Africa and Angola deteriorated
after Pretoria withdrew its diplomatic representation from
Luanda in late 1992. Early in 1993, however, both governments
again began working to normalize diplomatic ties, and Pretoria
promised to crack down on private channels of assistance from
South Africa to Savimbi. Although de Klerk announced that
South Africa would grant recognition only after a fully representative government had been installed in Luanda, Pretoria
reopened its offices in Luanda and upgraded diplomatic ties in
mid-1993. The two countries established full diplomatic relations on May 27, 1994, and Luanda appointed an ambassador
to South Africa later that year.

In June 1994, President Mandela agreed to requests by UN
Special Envoy to Angola, Alioune Blondin Beye, to attend talks
with Angolan President José Eduardo dos Santos and Savimbi
in an effort to end the fighting in Angola. Pretoria initially pro-

vided the venue for talks between dos Santos and President Mobutu Sese Seko of Zaire, as dos Santos sought an end to Zairian assistance to UNITA. Finally, in November 1994, Mandela witnessed an agreement between dos Santos and Savimbi to end the fighting in Angola and to begin rebuilding the country, and the slow process of disarming rebel fighters began in 1995.

Kenya

South Africa had long maintained relatively cordial relations with Kenya, one of Africa's leading pro-Western governments, although until 1990 these ties were mostly unpublicized and centered around trade. The nature of their relations changed in November 1990 when South Africa's minister of foreign affairs, Pik Botha, visited Kenya in the first publicized ministerial-level contact between the two countries since 1960. Relations were further consolidated when President de Klerk visited Kenya in June 1991, and Kenyan president Daniel Arap Moi visited Cape Town in June 1992—the first visit to South Africa by an African head of state.

In addition to strong trade ties in the mid-1990s, South Africa and Kenya share the desire to promote cooperation among countries of the Indian Ocean Rim (IOR). In March 1995, delegations from both countries, along with representatives of Australia, India, Oman, and Singapore, met in Mauritius to discuss ways to strengthen trade, investment, and economic cooperation among IOR member states.

Nigeria

Nigeria maintained a hostile attitude toward South Africa for more than thirty years until the early 1990s. Then the new political environment led to President de Klerk's visit to Nigeria in April 1992 to discuss bilateral issues, primarily trade. South Africa and Nigeria established diplomatic relations in mid-1994.

President Mandela was among the small number of world leaders who in late 1995 appealed to Nigeria's military head of state, General Sani Abacha, to spare the lives of the writer and environmental activist Ken Sarowiwa and eight others convicted of inciting violence that resulted in several deaths in Nigeria. After Sarowiwa and the others were executed on November 10, 1995, Mandela called for international sanctions against the Abacha government. South African officials later dropped this demand, deferring to the OAU, which was reluctant to impose sanctions against a member state.

Relations with Non-African States

Relations with non-African states focused mainly on the United States, Britain, and Western Europe through the 1980s. Commercial ties, often clandestine and subject to sanctions restrictions, were vital to the survival of many South African industries. As sanctions were lifted, commercial and diplomatic ties were immediately strengthened with the West, and at the same time, new alliances were being formed in the 1990s, especially in Asia and the Middle East.

United States

Although the United States joined the international community in 1986 in imposing economic sanctions against South Africa, earlier United States interests had been driven largely by the aim of reducing Soviet influence in southern Africa. United States officials had viewed South Africa as an important Western geostrategic bulwark in an unstable region. All United States administrations during the 1970s and the 1980s condemned apartheid, but they were generally opposed to broad economic sanctions, often arguing that the most severe impacts of such sanctions would be felt by the same segment of the population that was most disadvantaged by apartheid. The Carter administration (1977–81), however, adopted a tougher line toward Pretoria, viewing African nationalism as a driving force in the region that was compatible with United States interests.

The United States had imposed an arms embargo on Pretoria in 1964 and had joined the international consensus in refusing to recognize the "independence" of four of South Africa's black homelands between 1976 and 1984. The 1983 Gramm Amendment opposed the extension of International Monetary Fund (IMF—see Glossary) credits to "any country practicing apartheid." The 1985 Export Administration Amendment Act barred United States exports to South Africa's military and police, except for humanitarian supplies and medical equipment.

The United States maintained formal diplomatic relations with Pretoria throughout the apartheid era. The United States was still South Africa's second largest trading partner, with exports and imports valued at more than US$1.6 billion per year, during most of the sanctions years.

President Frederik W. de Klerk and President George Bush in
Washington, September 1990
Courtesy The White House

United States administrations tried to influence South African governments by working with them discreetly in a strategy called "constructive engagement" during the late 1970s and early 1980s. Guided primarily by Assistant Secretary of State for African Affairs Chester Crocker, the United States emphasized its common strategic interests with South Africa and insisted on unilateral rather than multilateral negotiations over South Africa's future (i.e., negotiations between the government and its opposition, as opposed to negotiations participated in by outside interests). One of the arguments against sweeping sanctions at the time was that United States officials hoped to maintain the small degree of influence they may have had in pressing for political reforms.

The United States also sought to bring about regional change through peaceful and democratic means and vigorously supported the negotiations for Namibian independence from South Africa. This policy approach ultimately paved the way for the 1988 agreement that linked the withdrawal of South African troops from Namibia with the withdrawal of Cuban troops from Angola, in a process that culminated in Namibia's first democratic elections in 1989 and independence in March 1990.

With the passage of the United States Comprehensive Anti-apartheid Act (CAAA) over a presidential veto in 1986, the United States Congress established an elaborate sanctions structure prohibiting future investments, bank loans, and some forms of trade with South Africa. More than 200 of the 280 United States companies in South Africa sold all, or part of, their operations there, and many of those remaining adhered to business principles intended to ameliorate the effects of apartheid. The CAAA called on the United States president to report to Congress each year on the state of apartheid in South Africa, in order to assess the need for further legislation. In 1987 the Intelligence Authorization Act prohibited intelligence sharing between the two countries. By 1990, twenty-seven state governments, ninety cities, and twenty-four counties had also imposed sanctions against South Africa or divestment measures on their own citizens' South African holdings.

In July 1991, United States President George Bush declared South Africa's progress toward democracy "irreversible," and the United States began to lift sanctions imposed under the 1986 CAAA. Most IMF and military-related bans remained in force until after the 1994 elections. A few city and county-level restrictions on dealings with South Africa remained on the books even after 1994.

In early 1994, Washington contributed US$10 million to assist the electoral process in South Africa, including election observers and technical assistance to parties participating in the elections. After the elections, the administration of President William J. Clinton announced a US$600 million, three-year aid, trade, and investment package for South Africa. The United States also promised to support the participation of international lending institutions, such as the IMF, in reconstructing the South African economy.

Minor strains emerged in South Africa's relations with the United States after the elections, however. President Mandela was critical of the United States on several fronts, including the level of economic assistance offered to help recover from apart-

President Nelson Mandela and President William J. Clinton in Washington, October 1994
Courtesy The White House

heid. Another source of tension arose out of a 1991 indictment by a United States court against South Africa's state-owned Armscor (Armaments Corporation of South Africa). The case concerned apparent violations of United States arms export controls during the 1980s. South African officials in 1994 requested that the indictment be dropped, noting that the target of sanctions—the apartheid regime—had been removed from power. United States officials refused to intervene in the judicial process, however, and the case was finally settled without public clamor in 1996.

Washington placed South Africa on a "trade watch" list in 1996, referring to apparent trademark violations that were being adjudicated in South African courts. These and other relatively minor disagreements might have been resolved fairly amicably, had they not taken place against the backdrop of anti-American rhetoric by South African officials on several occasions. For example, in his determination to maintain his government's sovereignty and freedom from outside interference, President Mandela repeatedly emphasized his loyalty and gratitude to countries that had staunchly opposed apartheid during the 1970s and 1980s. Among these countries were Cuba, Libya, and Iran, which the United States considered international outcasts or state sponsors of terrorism.

Pretoria has championed the cause of ending the thirty-year-old trade embargo against Cuba, in defiance of the United States, and South Africa hosted a conference to promote African-Cuban solidarity in October 1995. Pretoria also forged several new cooperation agreements with Iran in 1995 and 1996, and increased its oil purchases from Iran, over United States objections. President Mandela proclaimed South Africa's solidarity with Libya and welcomed that country's leader on a visit to South Africa in late 1995.

Despite these strains, South Africa and the United States are pursuing closer ties in many areas. More than 500 United States companies have more than US$5 billion in direct investments in South Africa in the mid-1990s, and trade between the two countries is increasing steadily. In March 1995, Washington and Pretoria established a United States-South Africa Binational Commission to improve communication and cooperation. (The United States has similar commissions with Egypt, Russia, and Mexico.) The commission is co-chaired by United States vice president Albert Gore and South African deputy president Thabo Mbeki. It has six committees to investigate avenues for cooperation in agriculture, business, environment and water resources, human resources and education, science and technology, and sustainable energy resources.

European Union

The twelve-member European Union (EU) was South Africa's leading trading partner in the early 1990s, purchasing almost 40 percent of its exports in most years. European (including British) direct investment in South Africa had reached US$17 billion, or 52 percent of all foreign investment in South Africa, by 1992. By the mid-1990s, the EU could promise South Africa one of the world's largest markets for South African exports. The EU also proposed a variety of loans and grants on preferential terms for South Africa in the 1990s, as well as a US$122 million aid program for priority needs such as education, health, job creation, and human rights.

South Africa's closest European ties have been with Britain, particularly with its Conservative Party-led governments. More than 800,000 white South Africans retained the right to live in Britain, although official ties weakened after South Africa left the British Commonwealth in 1961 (see Apartheid, 1948–76, ch. 1). Britain supported the 1977 Commonwealth decision to discourage sporting links with South Africa to register interna-

Deputy President Thabo Mbeki and Vice President Albert Gore
in Washington, March 1995
Courtesy The White House

tional disapproval of apartheid, but Britain's refusal to impose broader sanctions came under attack at subsequent Commonwealth heads of government meetings, especially in 1985, 1987, and 1989. In September 1994, British Prime Minister John Major, on a visit to Pretoria, promised a new investment protection treaty that would further strengthen commercial ties.

France played little role in South Africa before the 1990s. Trade between the two countries was increasing during the decade, however. South Africa imports roughly US$1 billion in French products a year, and at least 125 French companies operate in South Africa. French president François Mitterrand paid his first visit to South Africa on July 5, 1994, when the two nations signed an agreement aimed at strengthening commercial ties through long-term loans, subsidies, and technical assistance programs. Sectoral goals for these programs include strengthening cooperation between the private and public sectors, urban and rural development, financial reconstruction, and environmental protection.

Russian Federation

Pretoria severed diplomatic ties with the Soviet Union in 1956, largely because of Moscow's support for the SACP. In 1964 the Soviet Union began to deliver arms to ANC military training camps in Tanzania, and this support continued through the early 1980s. Then in 1986, Soviet president Mikhail Gorbachev denounced the idea of a revolutionary takeover in South Africa and advocated a negotiated settlement between Pretoria and its opponents. Officials from the two countries then sought improved commercial and diplomatic relations.

In July 1990, the South African mining conglomerate, De Beers Consolidated Mines, advanced a US$1-billion loan to the Soviet Union as part of an agreement for that company to serve as the exclusive exporter of Soviet rough diamonds. In August of that year, South Africa's minister of trade and industry, Kent Durr, visited Moscow to discuss possible South African assistance in the cleanup of the former Soviet nuclear site at Chernobyl. In early 1991, the two countries agreed to open interest sections in the Austrian embassies in each other's capitals, and Pretoria appointed its first trade representative to Russia a year later. Diplomatic ties were established in February 1992, and the first ambassador to South Africa of the new Russian Federation arrived in Pretoria in December 1992. At the time, the two countries hoped to develop trade ties, especially in military hardware, although they were competitors in some areas of international arms trade.

Iran

In early 1994, after a fifteen-year break, the Iranian Ministry of Foreign Affairs began preparing to reestablish formal ties by ending the oil embargo against South Africa. Iran had been South Africa's primary oil supplier until the fall of the shah in 1979, when open economic and political ties were suspended. Limited economic relations continued between the two countries, although at a discreet level. For example, the National Iranian Oil Company (NIOC) continued to maintain its 17.5 percent share in the Sasolburg refinery of the National Petroleum Refiners of South Africa, even after other ties between the two countries were suspended. In 1995 and 1996, South Africa pressed for closer ties to Iran, both to acquire oil imports on favorable terms and to demonstrate Pretoria's willingness and ability to defy United States pressures to shun Iran.

Israel

One of the most hidden but critical of South Africa's strategic relationships during the apartheid era was that with Israel, including both the Labor and the Likud governments. Israel officially opposed the apartheid system, but it also opposed broad international sanctions against Pretoria. For strategic reasons, much of the debate in Israeli government circles stressed coordinating ties to Pretoria within the framework of the tripartite relationship among Jerusalem, the United States (Israel's primary benefactor), and South Africa. Israel was also opposed to international embargoes in general, largely as a consequence of its own vulnerability to UN and other international sanctions.

South Africa and Israel had collaborated on military training, weapons development, and weapons production for years before broad sanctions were imposed in the late 1980s. Military cooperation continued despite the arms embargo and other trade restrictions imposed by the United States and much of Western Europe. Israel and several other countries discreetly traded with, and purchased enriched uranium from, South Africa throughout the 1980s. Romania's former president Nicolae Ceausescu, for example, used Israel as the "middleman" for exports to South Africa. In a few cases, joint ventures between Israel and South Africa helped to reduce the impact of sanctions on South African businesses.

The Israeli interest in South Africa sprang in part from the presence in South Africa of about 110,000 Jews, including at least 15,000 Israeli citizens. Israeli leaders sometimes justified trade with South Africa as support for the South African Jewish community, and South Africa provided a market for some of Israel's military exports. Israel's arms trade with South Africa was estimated at between US$400 million and US$800 million annually (see Arms Trade and the Defense Industry, ch. 5). In 1986 Israel also imported approximately US$181 million in goods, mainly coal, from South Africa, and exported to South Africa nonmilitary products worth about US$58.8 million.

In 1987 Israel took steps to reduce its military ties to South Africa to bring its policies in line with those of the United

States and Western Europe. Then Minister of Foreign Affairs Shimon Peres announced the Israeli plan to ban new military sales contracts with South Africa, to reduce cultural and tourism ties, to appoint a committee to study sanctions proposals, and to condemn apartheid—which Peres characterized as "a policy totally rejected by all human beings." Israel also established educational programs in Israel for black South Africans. Nevertheless, through the early 1990s, several secret treaties remained in force, continuing the military relationship between the two countries and their joint research in missile development and nuclear technology.

Relations with Other Countries

In the early 1990s, South Africa began establishing or reestablishing ties with many other countries. Algeria, Bulgaria, Italy, Libya, Mauritania, Mexico, Morocco, the Netherlands, Singapore, Sweden, Thailand, and Tunisia announced the end of trade sanctions against South Africa in 1991 and 1992, paving the way for full diplomatic relations. Representatives of 169 countries attended President Mandela's inauguration in May 1994; by 1995 South Africa had ties to at least 147 countries.

Among the many countries that were eager for closer ties to South Africa in the mid-1990s were the Republic of China (ROC) on Taiwan and the People's Republic of China (PRC). South Africa and the ROC had maintained ties during the apartheid era, partly because both were virtual outcasts from the international community. The PRC had been strongly critical of apartheid but had been cool toward the ANC (generally supporting the PAC). In the 1990s, President Mandela expressed South Africa's desire to maintain longstanding ties to the ROC and to establish diplomatic relations with the PRC. In response to PRC objections to proposals of dual recognition, Mandela suggested that the question of sovereignty should be decided between Taipei and Beijing, rather than being left to other countries to choose between them.

With one of the strongest economies in the world, the ROC has been an important source of investment, trade, and tourism for South Africa. Taiwanese investments in South Africa, for example, exceeded R1.4 billion in 1994, according to South African reports, and the ROC was then one of South Africa's six largest trading partners. In addition, Taipei made significant contributions to South Africa's Reconstruction and Development Programme and to other areas of development.

The PRC—with lower levels of investment, trade, and development assistance to South Africa—nonetheless represents a population of more than 1.2 billion people in the 1990s. In addition, Beijing holds a permanent seat on the United Nations Security Council and is recognized by most other countries as the legitimate representative of the Chinese people. With the expected transfer of control over Hong Kong to Beijing in 1997, some South African officials argued forcefully for strengthening ties between South Africa and the PRC, even at the expense of ties to the ROC. Opponents argued, in response, that Taiwan's record of commitment to South Africa and Beijing's record of disregard for international norms concerning human rights favored recognition of the ROC over the PRC, at least in the mid-1990s.

International Organizations

The year 1994 marked a watershed in South Africa's international relations, as it was welcomed into regional and international organizations, such as the UN, the Organization of African Unity (OAU), the Nonaligned Movement, and many others. The UN already had played an important role in South Africa's transition to democracy beginning in August 1992, when United Nations Security Council Resolution 772 authorized the United Nations Observer Mission in South Africa (UNOMSA) to help quell political violence. UNOMSA deployed thirty members in November of that year, and increased the number to 1,800 to oversee the April 1994 elections.

On May 25, 1994, the United Nations Security Council lifted the last of its punitive measures, the arms embargo of November 1977, known as Security Council Resolution 418 (strengthened in December 1984 as Security Council Resolution 558). Pretoria then refused to pay roughly US$100 million in dues and annual payments for the years its UN participation had been suspended. In 1995 the UN waived most of this amount, stating the Pretoria was not obliged to make back-payments on behalf of the apartheid regime.

President Mandela addressed the OAU summit in Tunis in June 1994, when South Africa assumed its seat in that organization for the first time. He emphasized his support for other African leaders and South Africa's solidarity with African interests. Also in June 1994, South Africa rejoined the British Commonwealth of Nations, which included fifty-one former British colonies. This action followed a thirty-three-year absence that had begun when South Africa declared itself a republic in 1961.

South Africa became the eleventh member of the Southern African Development Community (SADC) on August 29, 1994, when Deputy President Thabo Mbeki attended a SADC meeting at the organization's headquarters in Gaborone, Botswana. SADC's predecessor, the Southern African Development Coordination Conference (SADCC), had been established in 1979 to attempt to reduce regional economic dependence on South Africa. In 1992 SADCC's ten member states agreed to reorganize as SADC in order to strengthen regional ties and to work toward the formation of a regional common market.

On September 21, 1994, South Africa became the twenty-fourth member of the South Atlantic Peace and Cooperation Zone and attended that organization's meeting in Brasilia. South Africa also signed a declaration affirming the South Atlantic as a nuclear-weapons-free zone as well as agreements on trade and environmental protection in the region.

South African leaders in early 1996 were working to capitalize on the universal goodwill that had greeted their country's establishment of multiracial democracy in 1994 and its emergence from international pariah status. It was evident, at the same time, that some of the ANC's former staunch defenders in Africa were expecting concessions and assistance from the new government in Pretoria, in recognition of the decades of support South Africa's new leaders had received during their struggle to end apartheid.

*   *   *

Many excellent books, monographs, and articles are available concerning the South African political system. Valuable works include those of Robert M. Price, *The Apartheid State in Crisis: Political Transformation in South Africa, 1975–1990*; Donald L. Horowitz, *A Democratic South Africa? Constitutional Engineering in a Divided Society*; Allister Sparks, *The Mind of South Africa: The Story of the Rise and Fall of Apartheid*; Marina Ottaway, *South Africa: The Struggle for a New Order*; Kenneth W. Grundy, *South Africa: Domestic Crisis and Global Challenge*; Stephen John Stedman, ed. *South Africa: The Political Economy of Transformation*; John D. Brewer, *Restructuring South Africa*; John Kane-Berman, *Political Violence in South Africa*; and Timothy D. Sisk, *Democratization in South Africa: The Elusive Social Contract.*

Informative biographies of political leaders include two works by President Mandela: *The Struggle is My Life*, and *Long Walk to Freedom: The Autobiography of Nelson Mandela*; Willem de Klerk's biography of his brother, *F. W. de Klerk*; Gerhard Maré and Georgina Hamilton's *An Appetite for Power: Buthelezi's Inkatha and South Africa*; and David Ottaway's *Chained Together: Mandela, de Klerk, and the Struggle to Remake South Africa.* Analysis of political organizations is found in works by Edward Roux, *Time Longer than Rope: A History of the Black Man's Struggle for Freedom in South Africa*; Baruch Hirson, *Yours for the Union: Class and Community Struggles in South Africa, 1930–1947*; Anthony Marx, *Lessons of Struggle: South African Internal Opposition, 1960–1990*; Sheridan Johns and R. Hunt Davis, Jr., eds., *Mandela, Tambo, and the African National Congress: The Struggle Against Apartheid, 1948–1990*; Patrick J. Furlong, *Between Crown and Swastika: The Impact of the Radical Right on the Afrikaner Nationalist Movement in the Fascist Era*; and Vernon February, *The Afrikaners of South Africa.*

Outstanding analyses of the country's foreign relations include those of Pauline H. Baker, *The United States and South Africa: The Reagan Years*; Stephen Chan, *Exporting Apartheid: Foreign Policies in Southern Africa, 1978–1988*; George W. Shepherd, Jr., ed., *Effective Sanctions on South Africa: The Cutting Edge of Economic Intervention*; Gavin Maasdorp and Alan Whiteside, eds., *Towards a Post-Apartheid Future: Political and Economic Relations in Southern Africa*; and Chester A. Crocker, *High Noon in Southern Africa: Making Peace in a Rough Neighborhood.* (For further information and complete citations, see Bibliography.)

Chapter 5. National Security

Cape Point, outcroppings and coves typical of the southern coastline

SOUTH AFRICA'S NATIONAL SECURITY ORIENTATION, policies, and institutions were changing rapidly in the 1990s. South Africa had settled its protracted conflict with Angola and had negotiated independence for Namibia (formerly South-West Africa) after waging a twenty-two-year war to retain control over that country. South Africa signed nonaggression pacts with neighboring states and began working toward peaceful and constructive regional ties, while its first democratic constitution was being negotiated and implemented at home. Domestic security concerns shifted from the uncompromising suppression of dissent and the denial of political rights for a majority of citizens, first, to accommodation and negotiation with former adversaries, and, finally, in 1994 to a multiracial Government of National Unity.

South Africa had been the dominant military and economic power on the subcontinent for more than a century. Its military forces were not only capable of prevailing in any conceivable conventional conflict but also the only regional force capable of sustained military operations and of projecting national power beyond international borders. South Africa's real vulnerability until the 1990s was internal. Its governing philosophy and domination by a racial minority could not withstand the internal dissent generated during more than forty years of apartheid (see Glossary).

By the late 1980s, it was evident to many political leaders and others in South Africa that their impressive security establishment was functioning primarily to defend a failing system of apartheid against enemies within South Africa and elsewhere. Whites, with their monopoly over the national electoral process, were becoming increasingly polarized over tactics for dealing with the growing threat of antiapartheid dissidents. This polarization became evident in September 1989, when the largely Afrikaner (see Glossary) National Party (NP) suffered its worst electoral setback since it came to power in 1948. In the 1989 elections, the NP retained its majority in the all-white chamber of Parliament but lost ground to both the right-wing Conservative Party (CP) and the liberal Democratic Party (DP).

Whites who favored a stronger defense of apartheid became even more anxious about their own future after President Frederik W. (F.W.) de Klerk's historic February 2, 1990, speech announcing the legalization of black opposition groups and the release of political prisoners including African National Congress (ANC) leader Nelson (Rolihlahla) Mandela, and calling for multiracial constitutional negotiations. To those who supported political reform, the speech heralded new hope for domestic peace and improved relations with neighboring states, but, at the same time, it signaled the intensification of power struggles and an increase in violence in South Africa.

These unprecedented conditions emerged just as South Africa's external security environment became more benign. President de Klerk began to reduce the size and the power of the military in relation to other branches of government; concurrently, military commanders and their former adversaries, black liberation fighters, began to plan for the amalgamation of their organizations into a unified military. As the political negotiations over a new constitution proceeded haltingly during the early 1990s, a surprising degree of consensus emerged among senior military officers on all sides of the political debate. Even before the elections in April 1994, national and homeland military officers and former commanders of anti-apartheid fighters began the military reorganization that they hoped would ensure the country's future peace.

Historical Background

Precolonial Warfare

Bantu-speaking populations began moving into southern Africa from the center of the continent around A.D. 500 (see Southern African Societies to ca. 1600, ch. 1). In the process, they encountered the generally peaceful San and Khoikhoi populations who had preceded them in southern Africa by at least several centuries. Warfare and the desire for better land had been among the causes for the gradual southern migration, and some of these early chiefdoms routinely seized cattle from their neighbors. But warfare was not central to their culture or traditions. Most of southern Africa was sparsely settled, so fights over land were relatively rare. Ambitious men sought to control people, more than land. For example, during the seventeenth-century expansion of the Nguni-speaking Xhosa chiefdoms along the southern African coast, many Khoikhoi were peacefully incorporated into Xhosa society, and at least one Khoikhoi elder became a Xhosa chief.

The cultural emphasis on the value of cattle, which was strong among Nguni-speaking societies, prompted increasingly frequent cattle raids by the seventeenth and eighteenth centuries. In dry areas, such as the southern fringe of the Kalahari Desert, and in dry years, sporadic battles over land and water occurred. These clashes were generally limited in scope and were conducted under strict rules of engagement. Weapons were often spears (about two meters long) thrown at a distance, or knobkerries (wooden clubs) used in close combat. Bystanders sometimes cheered on the participants, and a battle often ended when one side admitted defeat but was not annihilated.

During the eighteenth century, Nguni-speaking Zulu warriors earned a reputation as the most fearsome fighters in the region. They sometimes defied tradition and fought in close combat with broken spears, or assegais; in this way, they inflicted unusually large numbers of casualties. The Zulu men's age-groups, close-knit fraternities organized primarily for social and religious purposes, provided armies when called on by their chiefs. By the late eighteenth century, these groups increasingly served as trained armed regiments to conduct raids and to fend off challenges from neighboring groups.

Under the leadership of Shaka Zulu (r. 1817–28), Zulu armies redefined military tradition, using new strategies, tactics, and formations. As Shaka's warriors became more skilled and ruthless, they overran their weaker neighbors and drew conquered clans into a confederacy under the Zulu monarchy. In the upheaval that followed, known as the *mfecane* (or crushing—see Glossary), thousands of Africans moved north and west, out of the expanding boundaries of the Zulu kingdom that was located in the area that would later become KwaZulu (see fig. 5).

Throughout the nineteenth century, European population growth and thirst for land added to the regional upheaval, in part because European immigrants sometimes forced African populations off land they had only recently settled and because Europeans sometimes used their superior weapons to annihilate or to subjugate indigenous populations. By the late nineteenth century, Zulu expansion had been halted. British forces eliminated the few remaining African leaders who defied them and finally subdued the Zulu army just before the outbreak of the most devastating in a series of Anglo-Boer (see Glossary) wars, the South African War of 1899–1902 (see Industrialization and Imperialism, 1870–1910, ch. 1). Military traditions and values continued to be central to the Zulu culture throughout the twentieth century and were reflected in Zulu political rhetoric of the 1990s.

Early Development of the South African Military

Ground Forces

The South African military evolved within the tradition of frontier warfare fought by popular militias and small commando forces, reinforced by the Afrikaners' historical distrust of large standing armies. Twentieth-century military developments were punctuated by mass mobilization for war and major crises. After the Union of South Africa was formed in 1910, General Jan C. Smuts, the union's first minister of defense, placed a high priority on creating a unified military out of the separate armies of the union's four provinces. The Defence Act (No. 13) of 1912 established a Union Defence Force (UDF) that included a Permanent Force—or standing army—of career soldiers, an active Citizen Force of temporary conscripts and volunteers, and a Cadet organization. The 1912 law also obligated all white males between seventeen and sixty years of age to serve in the military, but the law was not strictly enforced as long as there were enough volunteers to fill the military ranks. In 1913 and 1914, the new 23,400-member Citizen Force was called on to suppress several industrial strikes on the Witwatersrand (literally, "Ridge of White Waters" in Afrikaans, commonly shortened to Rand—see Glossary).

In September 1914, the union's troops supported Britain's declaration of war against Germany, despite strong objections from Afrikaner nationalists still resentful of Britain's treatment of them during the South African War. More than 146,000 whites, 83,000 Africans, and 2,500 people of mixed race ("coloureds") and Asians volunteered or were conscripted for service in World War I. At Britain's request, UDF forces commanded by General Louis Botha invaded the neighboring German colony of South-West Africa by land and sea, forcing German troops stationed there to surrender in July 1915. In 1920 South Africa received the League of Nations mandate to govern the former German colony and to prepare it for independence within a few years.

In East Africa, more than 20,000 South African troops fought under General Smuts's command when he directed the

British campaign against the Germans in 1915. South Africans also saw action with the Cape Corps in Palestine and with the First Brigade in Europe. By the end of World War I, 12,452 South Africans had died—more than 4,600 in the European theater alone.

Wartime casualties and postwar demobilization weakened the UDF. New legislation in 1922 reestablished conscription for white males over the age of twenty-one, for four years of military training and service. UDF troops assumed internal security tasks in South Africa and quelled numerous revolts against foreign domination in South-West Africa. South Africans suffered high casualties, especially in 1922, when an independent group of Khoikhoi—known as the Bondelswart-Herero for the black bands they wore into battle—led one of numerous revolts; in 1925, when a mixed-race population—the Basters—demanded cultural autonomy and political independence; and in 1932, when the Ovambo (Vambo) population along the border with Angola demanded an end to South African domination.

The UDF increased its active-duty forces to 56,000 by the late 1930s, and 100,000 men belonged to the National Riflemen's Reserve, which provided weapons training and practice. South Africa again joined the allies against Germany in World War II, despite growing protests by Afrikaners who objected to any alliance with Britain. South Africa, nonetheless, raised three divisions—334,000 volunteers, including some 211,000 whites, 77,000 blacks, and 46,000 coloureds and Asians. Nearly 9,000 South Africans were killed in action in campaigns in Ethiopia, North Africa, Italy, and Madagascar during World War II.

Wartime expansion was again followed by rapid demobilization after World War II. By then, a century of Anglo-Boer clashes followed by decades of growing British influence in South Africa had fueled Afrikaner resentment. Resurgent Afrikaner nationalism was an important factor in the growth of the NP as the 1948 elections approached. The system of apartheid was intended both to bolster Afrikaner pride and to compensate the Afrikaners for the suffering they had endured.

After the narrow election victory by the NP in 1948, the government began the steady Afrikanerization of the military; it expanded military service obligations and enforced conscription laws more strictly. Most UDF conscripts underwent three months of Citizen Force training in their first year of service, and an additional three weeks of training each year for four years after that. The Defence Act (No. 44) of 1957 renamed the

UDF the South African Defence Force (SADF) and established within it some quick-reaction units, or Commandos, to respond to localized threats. The SADF, numbering about 20,000 in 1958, would grow to almost 80,000 in the next two decades.

The 1960s ushered in a new era in military history. South Africa's growing international isolation and the intensified black resistance to apartheid prompted the government to increase military service obligations repeatedly and to extend periods of active duty. The Defence Act (No. 12) of 1961 authorized the minister of defense to deploy Citizen Force troops and Commandos for riot control, often to quell antiapartheid demonstrations. The Defence Act (No. 85) of 1967 also expanded military obligations, requiring white male citizens to perform national service, including an initial period of training, a period of active duty, and several years in reserve status, subject to immediate call-up.

As the military expanded during the 1970s, the SADF staff was organized into six divisions—to manage finance, intelligence, logistics, operations, personnel, and planning; and the South African Medical Service (SAMS) was made co-equal with the South African Army, the South African Navy, and the South African Air Force. Also during the 1970s, the SADF began accepting nonwhites and women into the military as career soldiers, not only as temporary volunteers or reservists, but it did not assign women to combat roles. By the end of the 1970s, the army had become the principal defender of the apartheid regime against the rising tide of African nationalism in South Africa and the region.

During the 1980s, the legal requirements for national service were to register for service at age sixteen and to report for duty when called up, which occurred at some time after a man's eighteenth birthday. National service obligations could be fulfilled by volunteering for active-duty military service for two years and by serving in the reserves, generally for ten or twelve years. Reservists generally underwent fifty days per year of active duty or training, after their initial period of service. The requirements for national service changed several times during the 1980s and the early 1990s in response to national security needs, and they were suspended in 1993.

Air and Naval Forces

The origin of the South African Air Force (SAAF) dates to the Defence Act (No. 13) of 1912, which established the South

Army troops on parade
Courtesy Embassy of South
Africa, Washington

African Aviation Corps (SAAC) as part of the army's Citizen Force. The SAAC's first aircraft were deployed against German forces in South-West Africa in January 1915. Before that, a few SAAC pilots had volunteered for service in Britain, where they joined the Royal Flying Corps (RFC). South African pilots in the RFC saw action over France in late 1914 and in East Africa in 1915. By the end of World War I, nearly 3,000 South African pilots had served in RFC squadrons.

The SAAF became a separate branch of the armed services in 1920 and was soon put to the test in suppressing one of a series of miners' strikes in the Rand, near Johannesburg, as well as rebellions in South-West Africa. World War II saw the SAAF grow from a small force of ten officers, thirty-five officer cadets, 1,600 men of other ranks, and 100 aircraft in 1939 to a force of 31,204 servicemen, including nearly 1,000 pilots and at least 1,700 aircraft, in 1941. By 1945, the SAAF had more than 45,000 personnel in thirty-five operational squadrons. More than 10,000 women served in the Women's Auxiliary Air Force during the war.

The air force established a Joint Air Training Scheme (JATS) in 1940. The JATS brought British and other Allied air and ground crews to South Africa for training and achieved impressive training records. By 1945 thirty-eight JATS training programs had turned out more than 33,300 air crew and 7,800 pilots, including 12,200 SAAF personnel.

In addition to protecting Allied shipping along South Africa's coastlines, SAAF combat and support units served in West Africa, East Africa, North Africa, Madagascar, the Middle East, Italy, the Balkans, and elsewhere in the European and the Mediterranean theaters. In North Africa alone, the SAAF's eleven squadrons flew nearly 34,000 missions and destroyed 342 enemy aircraft between April 1941 and May 1943. The SAAF's 17,000-man contingent in the Italian campaign played the dominant role in Allied air operations there. In all of World War II, the SAAF flew more than 82,000 missions and lost at least 2,227 SAAF members.

The SAAF's contributions to Western causes also included missions during the Berlin airlift of the late 1940s; SAAF crews flew 1,240 missions carrying 4,133 tons of supplies to West Berlin in 1948 and 1949. During the Korean War (1950–53), the SAAF's Second Squadron (the Flying Cheetahs) flew more than 12,000 missions, establishing a strong record of success. During that time, the SAAF reportedly lost only thirty-four pilots and seventy-eight aircraft.

By the end of the 1950s, South Africa faced increasing international isolation and the eruptions of internal and regional conflicts, which it confronted largely without the assistance of allies. SAAF pilots acquired the ability to fly at least twenty-six types of aircraft on a wide range of missions. In the escalating conflict in South-West Africa, the SAAF carried out long-range casualty evacuations, visual and photo reconnaissance missions, close air support, and air strikes, most often flying helicopters or light attack aircraft. The SAAF also developed both impressive early-warning equipment and maneuvering tactics to outsmart superior technology. SAAF mechanics were skilled repairmen; some aging SAAF aircraft were used through the 1980s and were not retired until the Namibian (South-West African) conflict wound down at the end of the decade.

The South African Navy (SAN) traces its origins back more than a century to the UDF's seagoing vessels, and to a naval volunteer unit formed in Durban in 1885. The British Royal Naval Volunteer Reserve established a division in South Africa in 1912. The navy's modern antecedent was the Seaward Defence Force (SDF), established in 1940 with fifteen small ships and several shore bases. The SDF soon grew into a force of several escort groups and minesweeping flotillas, some of which served

French-manufactured Puma helicopter used by South African Air Force
Courtesy Embassy of South Africa, Washington

in the Mediterranean in World War II. Many SDF personnel saw active service in British Royal Navy vessels.

The SDF was renamed the South African Naval Force in 1947 and the South African Navy in 1951. Its main assignments were to guard naval installations and harbors at Richards Bay, Durban, East London, Port Elizabeth, and Cape Town. The navy's small, elite Marine Corps branch had major responsibilities in this area until it was disbanded in 1957. The Marine Corps was reestablished in 1979, with a force of about 900 marines, who trained at several installations in western Cape Province.

Naval acquisitions were seriously impaired by international embargoes of the late 1970s and 1980s. Navy personnel were reduced from almost 9,000 to half that number by 1990, and the navy bore the brunt of the military retrenchment, or downsizing, of the early 1990s. The SAN closed some facilities at Richards Bay, East London, Port Elizabeth, and Durban, and reduced armaments depots and stores at its base at Simonstown, south of Cape Town.

Rise of the Security Establishment

Senior government officials became convinced in the 1970s that their country faced a serious threat of insurgency orches-

trated by communist world powers and carried out by their sur-
rogates in southern Africa. To emphasize the comprehensive
nature of this threat, they referred to it as a "Total Onslaught,"
and to counter it, they developed a "Total Strategy," which
called for mobilizing military, political, educational, economic,
and psychological resources. The SADF emerged as the key
participant in the Total Strategy, as the centerpiece of an elaborate national security apparatus encompassing the defense
establishment, the paramilitary South African Police (SAP),
numerous intelligence agencies, defense-oriented parastatal
and private organizations, and—by the late 1970s—a growing
number of government agencies with security concerns. The
SADF's expanded role increased its influence in policy decision
making and in resource allocation. By the end of the 1970s, the
military was at the center of the country's domestic and foreign
policy, implementing its Total Strategy to outmaneuver external and internal enemies of the state.

National Security Management System

Security concerns were foremost in the policies of P. W.
Botha, who became prime minister in 1978, following twelve
years as minister of defense. Botha and the new minister of
defense, General Magnus Malan, overhauled, consolidated,
and streamlined much of the government, subordinating its
other functions to their security concerns. To manage this cum-
bersome bureaucratic arrangement, Botha, Malan, and a few
key advisers created the National Security Management System
(NSMS) and consolidated the preeminence of the Directorate
of Military Intelligence within the government's information-
gathering community.

The NSMS subsumed and co-opted existing structures, both
public and private, in a comprehensive security apparatus.
Some critics of government viewed the NSMS as a shadow or
parallel government, or even a covert infrastructure for de
facto military rule. Its mission was based upon a classical counterinsurgency strategy—to identify and to neutralize antigovernment activists and to strengthen public support ("Winning
the hearts and minds"—WHAM) for security-related activities.

At the apex of the NSMS was the State Security Council
(SSC). The SSC had been established in 1972 as one of twenty
cabinet committees with advisory responsibilities to the executive branch of government. In 1979 it became the most important and most powerful of the four remaining cabinet

committees. Botha chaired the enlarged SSC, which also included the minister of defense, the minister of foreign affairs, the minister of justice, and the minister of law and order; the chief of the SADF; the chiefs of the military and the intelligence services; the commissioner of police; the chief of the security police; and other senior government officials by invitation.

The SSC functioned as a national command center, evaluating current intelligence, formulating policy, and directing a nationwide organizational network dedicated to implementing the Total Strategy. The scope of its responsibilities, size, organizational complexity, and budget far exceeded that of any other cabinet committee, past or present. The SSC was supported by a Work Committee and by the State Security Secretariat staff. The Work Committee met weekly to review and to coordinate the activities of more than a dozen interdepartmental committees and to refine issues to be put before the entire council. The secretariat staff of about ninety consisted primarily of military and intelligence personnel.

Internally, the SSC was organized into four branches. These had responsibility for security strategy—developing strategic options and monitoring overall government policy; for national intelligence—reviewing, evaluating, and interpreting information produced by other agencies; for strategic communication—considering problems associated with the government's psychological and public-relations campaigns; and for administration.

Below this national command center was a hierarchy of Joint Management Centers (JMCs), generally corresponding to SADF area commands. Twelve JMCs were operating in 1986; these were later reduced to nine to coincide with the government's newly designated economic development areas. Headquartered in major cities, the JMCs were chaired by military or police brigadiers (between colonel and major general), each directing fifty to fifty-five officials and security officers. JMC officials also directed the activities of sub-JMCs, or subcenters composed of officials from city government, police, and military in the area. At the bottom of the security apparatus pyramid were approximately 448 minicenters, directed by municipal officials, postmasters, fire chiefs, local defense officials, and other community leaders. JMC authorities at each level were assisted by three advisory committees specializing in communications; in intelligence; and in constitutional, economic, and social affairs.

In the mid-1980s, the government established the Military Area Radio Network (MARNET), a twenty-four-hour very-high-frequency system designed to link farmers in rural locations with police and military forces in the area. The radio network was intended to help protect civilians in emergencies, such as an armed uprising or terrorist attack, especially in the far northern Transvaal. Other civilian defense measures included weapons training, fire-fighting, and first-aid classes provided by the military.

As internal dissent escalated in the mid-1980s, the government again raised minimum national service requirements, and new legislation extended military service obligations to foreign residents of South Africa. By 1989 the SADF had grown to an estimated 103,000 active-duty and 455,000 reserve-duty troops. Growing civilian opposition, in the meantime, prompted an activist End Conscription Campaign to urge civilians to resist military service. The number of men who avoided conscription each year rose steadily, and the government debated instituting a system of conscientious objection (and alternative service) to allow a small number of conscripts to avoid military service legally, based on their religious beliefs. But by the time such a system became law in 1992, several thousand men each year had refused to be conscripted for military service, and a small number were prosecuted and were jailed or fined for this offense.

Regional tensions began to ease in the late 1980s. The government was reevaluating its commitment to apartheid, and expectations of political change were becoming evident in South Africa and throughout the region. Moreover, as the fighting in Angola began to subside, South African troops withdrew from Namibia, and the government began to seek contacts among former opponents to negotiate a way out of the political and economic impasse created by apartheid. National Service obligations were scaled back; for example, in 1991 the initial mandatory period of military service was reduced to one year.

Specialized Forces

The SADF increasingly assumed internal security functions during the 1970s and 1980s and was deployed to urban areas of South Africa, often referred to as the second front, to combat sabotage. In these nontraditional military functions, senior officers relied on specialized military and paramilitary units, some with unpublicized areas of responsibility.

The Special Forces were assigned sensitive missions and operations inside and outside South Africa, which were often closed to public scrutiny. The Special Forces consisted of five or six reconnaissance (recce) regiments during most of the apartheid era. Other specialized units were sometimes involved in clandestine operations, but were not technically included among the Special Forces. The reconnaissance regiments' commanders had the authority to initiate operations subject only to the approval of the military chief of staff for operations. The commanding general of all Special Forces reported directly to the SADF chief.

The oldest of the Special Forces, the First Reconnaissance Regiment, known as "One Recce," was formed in 1972 and was headquartered in Durban. It was responsible for the initial training of all Special Forces members from the mid-1970s on. The other reconnaissance units were formed in the late 1970s or early 1980s.

The Second Reconnaissance Regiment was headquartered in Pretoria and was deployed largely in that area. Little public information exists about the Third Reconnaissance Regiment, which reportedly was disbanded during the 1980s. The Fourth Reconnaissance Regiment, based at Langebaan, near Saldanha Bay, specialized in seaborne operations and saw extensive service in Angola during the early and mid-1980s.

The Fifth Reconnaissance Regiment, based at Phalaborwa, in the northeast, operated primarily in Mozambique in support of the Mozambican National Resistance (Resistencia Nacional Moçambicana—MNR or Renamo), but saw additional action in South Africa and Angola. The Sixth Reconnaissance Regiment also saw action in Mozambique. Members of the reconnaissance regiments were recruited in Zimbabwe (until 1980, Rhodesia), Angola, and Mozambique, and among South Africans who opposed the antiapartheid struggle or the ANC, in particular, for a variety of political and personal reasons.

Several other specialized military units provided clandestine and open support for the government and its apartheid policies. For example, the South-West Africa Territorial Force (SWATF), the Forty-Fourth Parachute Brigade, the Thirty-Second Battalion, and the Koevoet ("crowbar," in Afrikaans) counterinsurgency force had specific responsibilities for preserving the status quo or for defending the government. Some of these units—which often included members of all races but were usually commanded by whites—earned reputations for particular brutality in carrying out their missions.

Before Namibian independence in 1990, whites in that disputed territory had the same compulsory military service as in South Africa, and they sometimes served in SADF units in Namibia. In August 1980, the SADF established SWATF to counter the growing South-West Africa People's Organisation (SWAPO) insurgency, which had been fighting for independence since the 1960s. SWATF included some SADF units and local recruits; its commander, an SADF general, was both South-West Africa secretary of defense and general officer commanding South African army forces in the territory.

By 1987 SWATF was a 22,000-member militia, with a reaction force element and an area force. The reaction force had a motorized brigade composed of three infantry battalions and an armored car regiment, and a standing force of six light infantry battalions with supporting units recruited and trained for service in specific regions, or among specific ethnic groups. The area force comprised twenty-six multiracial counterinsurgency forces. Additional specialized units of SWATF included engineers, signals personnel, mounted troops, a parachute battalion, and a commando squadron. Several other multiracial units performed territory-wide functions in South-West Africa.

The Forty-Fourth Parachute Brigade, headquartered at Murray Hill near Pretoria, was the SADF's best-qualified rapid deployment force. The First Paratroop Battalion, its only standing battalion, was based at Tempe, outside Bloemfontein. These forces were used extensively in South-West Africa and in Angola during the late 1970s, and after 1980 were joined by paratroopers from the former Rhodesian army.

The Thirty-Second Battalion, a black multinational light infantry force, was formed in 1976 from remnants of Angolan rebel units that had been defeated in that country's civil war. It was primarily involved in anti-SWAPO operations in Namibia. The Thirty-Second Battalion worked closely with several reconnaissance units of the SADF. In April 1989, it moved to Pomfret, in the northern Cape Province, from which it was deployed to quell violence in black townships in several urban areas.

During the 1980s, the 3,000-strong Koevoet counterinsurgency force, composed mostly of Ovambo fighters commanded by white SADF officers, conducted anti-SWAPO operations in Namibia and earned a reputation for ruthlessness and brutality. Koevoet was largely disbanded after the territory achieved independence in 1990, and some of its members were transferred to the Namibian police force. Former Koevoet members are widely despised by citizens and, in particular, by former SWAPO members who have also joined the country's new police force.

Several other specialized military units were not part of the Special Forces, but their particular missions were defined in part by legally established racial boundaries. The South African Cape Corps (SACC), for example, traced its origins to a small force of coloured soldiers who had fought together during World War II. In 1965 Cape Corps personnel were permanently assigned to the navy, and later some were transferred to air force maintenance units. An Indian Corps was set up in 1974 to train Asian volunteers, primarily for the navy. During the 1980s, these volunteers were trained at the Indian Training Centre at Durban for service in the navy or the Marine Corps.

Until the early 1990s, the military's Catering Corps was responsible for enforcing aspects of apartheid related to food and dining. As a general rule, caterers in any of the military services could serve food only to members of their own racial group. They prepared different rations for soldiers of different racial identities and for those whose religions enforced food prohibitions. The caterers also served special rations to the crews of maritime aircraft, ships, and submarines, and to prisoners of war.

The State President's Guard, established as an elite, specially trained unit in May 1967, was disbanded in October 1990. It performed both protective and ceremonial functions. As a home guard, it protected and staffed the president's homes in Cape Town, Pretoria, Durban, and Bloemfontein while the president was in residence. It also served as a ceremonial honor guard at important events such as presidential inaugurations and funerals, state visits, and VIP visits. Over the course of its twenty-three-year history, it was successively attached to the Army Gymnasium in Pretoria, the South African Medical Service Training Centre at Heidelberg (southeast of Johannesburg), the Fourth Provost Company in Wonderboom (northeast of Bloemfontein), the Second Signal Regiment in Pretoria, and the South African Army College (near Pretoria). During the 1980s, a few presidential guard units were deployed to border areas for ten to twelve months, in part because their superior training enabled them to serve longer than the normal three-month rotation to those regions.

Homeland Militaries

Each of the four nominally independent homelands (see Glossary)—Bophuthatswana, Ciskei, Transkei, and Venda—maintained small defense forces that were effectively under SADF control, despite each government's claim to national sovereignty. (No country except South Africa recognized these homelands as independent countries.) The homelands were dissolved when the April 1994 elections took place, and their military forces were integrated into the new national military establishment in 1995 and 1996.

Bophuthatswana, with a population of 2.4 million, was declared "independent" in 1977. The homeland consisted of several scattered enclaves near the border with Botswana. Bophuthatswana's military, the 3,100-member Bophuthatswana Defence Force (BDF), was organized into six military regions. Its ground forces included two infantry battalions, possessing two armored personnel carriers. The BDF air wing of 150 personnel possessed three combat aircraft and two armed helicopters.

The BDF was deployed several times in the late 1980s and early 1990s to quell popular demonstrations by residents of what had been South African territory bordering the homeland, when their residential areas were incorporated into Bophuthatswana for administrative purposes. South African security forces intervened to suppress these demonstrations and at least one coup attempt against the unpopular regime of President Lucas Mangope, who had been appointed by Pretoria.

Mangope was removed from office in April 1994, after BDF troops had killed at least forty people and had injured 150 more who were insisting on the right to vote in South Africa's upcoming elections, a demand that Mangope refused. Members of South African right-wing white extremist organizations arrived to support Mangope and clashed with some members of the BDF who had sided with the civilian demonstrators. The clash led to the highly publicized executions of two whites by the homeland military. The unrest ended when SADF troops arrived and placed Bophuthatswana under the control of

South Africa's interim executive authority until the elections took place.

Ciskei and Transkei were largely Xhosa-speaking homelands in the southern coastal region that became the Eastern Cape province in 1994. Ciskei, with a population of only 1 million, became "independent" in 1981. The Ciskei Defence Force (CDF), consisting of about 1,000 troops, was organized into two infantry battalions, possessing one armored personnel carrier, and an air wing company with five light aircraft and four helicopters.

Ciskei's president in the early 1980s, Lennox Sebe, established an elaborate security apparatus to protect his government, but members of his family and his army, nonetheless, tried on several occasions to overthrow him. Sebe was ousted in a military coup in March 1990 and was replaced by a military council led by Brigadier Joshua Gqozo. Tensions rose as the new Ciskei government debated the reincorporation of the homeland into South Africa, and the Gqozo government was ousted in early 1994, only weeks before the historic South African national elections and the dissolution of the homelands.

Transkei, the second Xhosa-speaking homeland, was declared "independent" in 1976. It had a population of about 4.4 million. The Transkei Defence Force (TDF) numbered about 2,000, including one infantry battalion and an air wing with two light transports and two helicopters. The Transkei government of the 1980s had a strained relationship with South Africa, largely because of the existence of armed strongholds of the ANC and other antiapartheid organizations in the homeland (which included within its territory the birthplace of ANC leader Nelson Mandela).

In 1987 Major General Bantu Holomisa—a staunch ANC activist—led a bloodless coup against the Transkei government; he then suspended the civilian constitution and refused South Africa's repeated demands for a return to civilian rule, insisting that a civilian government would be a puppet controlled by Pretoria. When the homeland was dissolved in 1994, Holomisa was named deputy minister of housing in President Mandela's cabinet.

Venda, a tiny homeland in the northern Transvaal, had a population of about 665,000 and was declared "independent" in 1979. Venda's 900-member military force consisted of two infantry battalions with one armored personnel carrier, one engineering unit, and an air wing with three helicopters. These forces and their equipment were incorporated into the national military in 1995.

Women in the Military

South African women have a long history of service in the military. Women served in auxiliary roles in the SADF in World War I and World War II, and were assigned to active, non-combat duties after 1970. The army established a volunteer nursing service in 1914 and sent 328 nurses to serve with South African troops in Europe and East Africa in World War I. The Women's Auxiliary Army Service began accepting women recruits in 1916. Officials estimated that women volunteers relieved 12,000 men for combat in World War I by assuming clerical and other duties. During World War II, South Africa had five service organizations for women—the South African Military Nursing Service, and women's auxiliaries attached to the army, the navy, the air force, and the military police.

In 1970 the SADF began to accept women volunteers into the Permanent Force, and to assign them to duties that would release men for combat and operational duties. One year later, the South African Army Women's College initiated women's military training programs for jobs in military finance, personnel, intelligence, and medical units. No women were trained for combat. Women were not assigned to duties that presented a high risk of capture by foreign enemies.

During the late 1970s and 1980s, women were active in civil defense organizations and were being trained as part of the country's general mobilization against possible terrorist attacks. In 1989, for example, the Johannesburg Civil Defence Program provided training for 800 civil defense volunteers, about one-half of whom were women. These classes included such subjects as weapons training for self-defense, antiriot procedures, traffic and crowd control, first aid, and fire-fighting. An unreported number of women also received instruction in counterinsurgency techniques and commando operations. Women also served in military elements of liberation militias in the 1970s and the 1980s, and women were accepted into the ANC's military wing, Umkhonto we Sizwe (Spear of the Nation, also known as Umkhonto—MK), throughout the antiapartheid struggle.

In 1995 women of all races were being incorporated into the South African National Defence Force (SANDF), and a woman officer, Brigadier Jackie Sedibe, was appointed to oversee the implementation of new SANDF policies concerning the treatment of women. Women had been promoted as high as warrant officers and brigadiers in the Permanent Force by the early 1990s, but only ten women were SADF colonels in 1994. In 1996 Brigadier Sedibe became the first woman in the military to be promoted to the rank of major general. Widespread cultural attitudes in the 1990s still oppose the idea of women in combat, but officials are debating ways to assign women an equitable share of the leadership positions in the military.

Global and Regional Issues

Since the arrival of seafaring European powers in the fifteenth century, South Africa has never been isolated in a strategic sense. The Cape of Good Hope initially served as a reprovisioning depot for Portuguese, English, and Dutch traders on their way to and from the Orient (see Southern African Societies to ca. 1600, ch. 1). After the mid-seventeenth century, southern Africa attracted Dutch and French Huguenot traders and settlers, whose troops engaged in a series of wars with indigenous Africans. In the late eighteenth century, the region was caught up in the Napoleonic wars and passed to British imperial control. An influx of Indian laborers and traders in the nineteenth century added an Asian dimension to South Africa's increasingly complex multicultural society. During the twentieth century, South Africa fought on the side of the victorious allies in the two world wars and in the Korean War; after that, it was caught up in the global strategic contest between the United States and the Soviet Union.

Despite the strong international presence over several centuries, South Africa's strategic position has been peripheral rather than central. World powers have sought access to, or control of, its remote subcontinental location and its mineral resources as a means of furthering their own global or imperial designs. Their arrivals and departures in southern Africa paralleled their countries' rise and fall in the international political and economic hierarchy.

After World War II, international interest in South Africa centered on its mineral wealth and its location along southern trade routes and lines of communication between the Eastern and the Western hemispheres. South Africa's potential international importance was nonetheless limited because domestic conditions, specifically its apartheid policies, made it the object of international scorn. Its diplomatic isolation was compounded by international embargoes and by a wide range of Western economic sanctions during the 1980s. Paradoxically, this nation with a long history of trade, with a strategic location, with overwhelming military and economic power in the region, with strong cultural roots on three continents, and with hard-earned international stature, became a pariah. Then as East-West and United States-Soviet tensions eased, southern African regional conflicts ended and domestic political reforms reduced Pretoria's isolation. In the early 1990s, South Africans negotiated a peaceful end to apartheid and began to build new ties to the region and to the rest of the international community.

Arms Trade and the Defense Industry

Growth of the Defense Industry

South Africa's domestic arms industry originated in 1940 with the appointment of an Advisory Committee on Defence Force Requirements to study and to assess the country's military-industrial potential. Relying on its recommendations, the government, with British assistance, established six factories to produce or to assemble ammunition, bombs, howitzers, mortars, armored vehicles, and electronic equipment. A number of private companies also produced weapons during World War II. Most weapons factories were dismantled in the late 1940s.

Seeking long-term military research and development capabilities, the government in 1945 established the Council for Scientific and Industrial Research (CSIR) to study the country's overall industrial potential. The Board of Defence Resources, established in 1949, and the Munitions Production Office, established in 1951, oversaw policy planning concerning armaments. In 1953 the first rifle factory was established, and the Lyttleton Engineering Works, formerly the Defence Ordnance Workshop, collected technical data and information on manufacturing methods. In 1954 the government established the National Institute for Defence Research (NIDR) to assess and to improve the fledgling defense industry.

In 1960 the increasingly security-conscious National Party (NP) government stepped up programs to improve the arsenal of the armed forces. Pretoria raised arms production levels, sought new foreign sources of weapons, and began to acquire new defense technology systems. These efforts intensified after the 1963 United Nations (UN) Security Council resolution

restricting the sale of arms, ammunition, or military vehicles to South Africa. The Armaments Act (No. 87) of 1964 established an Armaments Production Board to manage the Lyttleton Engineering Works and a state-owned ammunition plant. The board assumed responsibility for coordinating arms purchases among government, military, and private agencies.

The Armaments Development and Production Act (No. 57) of 1968 established a special production unit, the Armaments Development and Production Corporation (Armscor), to consolidate and to manage public and private arms manufacturing. Through Armscor's efforts, South Africa soon achieved self-sufficiency in the production of small arms, military vehicles, optical devices, and ammunition. During the mid-1970s, Armscor reorganized as the Armaments Corporation of South Africa (still Armscor), expanded existing arms industries, and assumed control over most research and development done by NIDR. Before the voluntary UN arms embargo was declared mandatory in 1977, South Africa received military technology through licensing agreements, primarily with West Germany, Italy, Israel, France, Belgium, and Canada. Licensing and coproduction agreements in the 1970s and 1980s made it difficult to distinguish between fully indigenous military manufactures and those that relied on foreign manufacturing capabilities.

During the 1980s, Armscor was a central feature of South Africa's military-industrial complex, a state corporation that depended on private industry for specific processes and components. Armscor's financial autonomy was evident in its access to the capital market for loans, but at the same time, many of its functions were closely tied to the government. Armscor executives reported directly to the minister of defense. Armscor's ten-member corporate board had overlapping membership with the ministry's Defence Planning Committee and included leading businessmen, financiers, and scientists, as well as the government's director general of finance and the chief of the SADF. In addition, Armscor was represented on the government's high-level military planning and policy bodies.

Armscor's marketing and sales department, Nimrod, undertook an aggressive arms export promotion campaign in the 1980s. It participated in international arms exhibitions, in Greece in 1982, in Chile each year from 1984 through the end of the decade, and in Turkey in 1989 (displaying its G–5 howitzer and Rooikat armored vehicle). Armscor also displayed its manufactures at numerous demonstrations and trade fairs in South Africa. Despite the UN ban on arms sales to Pretoria and a 1984 UN ban on the purchase of arms from South Africa, Armscor's business flourished. The corporation did not disclose export figures or customers during the 1980s, but the United States government estimated South Africa's arms sales at US$273 million (in constant 1989 dollars) over the five-year period from 1984 to 1988. The best year was 1985, when it earned roughly US$102 million.

Armscor did experience the effect of the cutback in weapons sales in the late 1980s. Its work force had increased from 10,000 to 33,000 between 1974 and 1984, but had declined to about 20,000 by 1989. At that time, Armscor purchased most of its manufacturing components from twelve subsidiary companies and an estimated 3,000 private contractors and subcontractors, representing a total work force of more than 80,000 employees. The government began to privatize parts of the arms industry in the early 1990s. Under a major restructuring that began in April 1992, a segment of Armscor and several of its manufacturing subsidiaries were reorganized as an independent weapons manufacturing company, Denel. Denel and several other manufacturers produced equipment on contract with Armscor, which retained overall responsibility for military acquisitions. Armscor also acted as the agent of the state, regulating military imports and exports, issuing marketing certificates, and ensuring adherence to international agreements.

Defying International Embargoes

Despite the numerous international embargoes against arms trade with South Africa in the 1970s and 1980s, it nonetheless developed the most advanced military-industrial base on the continent. In the late 1970s, it ranked behind Brazil and Israel, among developing-country arms suppliers. The reasons for this apparent irony are evident in South Africa's defense production infrastructure, which had developed even before the first UN embargo in 1963; in the incremental, haphazard, and inconsistent ways in which the arms embargoes were imposed and enforced; in the deliberate refusal by several countries to comply with the embargoes; in Pretoria's use of clever and covert circumvention techniques; and in its ability to develop and to exploit advanced commercial and "dual-use" technologies for military applications. By the late 1960s, South Africa had acquired at least 127 foreign production licenses for arms, ammunition, and military vehicles. South Africa had purchased fighter aircraft, tanks, naval vessels, naval armaments, and maritime patrol aircraft, primarily from Britain. After that, military equipment was carefully maintained, upgraded, and often reverse-engineered or copied, after the embargo made it difficult to obtain replacements or replacement parts.

During the 1970s, South Africa expanded and refined its ability to acquire foreign assistance for domestic military production. Its broad-based industrial growth enabled it to shift imports from finished products to technology and components that could be incorporated into locally designed or copied military systems. Through this maneuver, multinational firms and banks became major sources of technology and capital for South Africa's defense industry, even during the embargo era. Dual-use equipment and technology—such as electronics, computers, communications, machine tools, and industrial equipment—and manufacturing techniques were not subject to embargo and were easy to exploit for military applications. South African engineers also were able to modify, to redesign, to retrofit, and to upgrade a wide range of weapons using foreign technology and systems.

South Africa also invested in strategic foreign industries; recruited foreign technicians to design, to develop, and to manufacture weapons; rented and leased technical services, including computers; and resorted to cover companies, deceptive practices, third-country shipments, and outright smuggling and piracy to meet its defense needs. By the 1980s, the defense industry, as extensive as it was, was nonetheless incapable of designing and producing some advanced military systems, such as high-performance combat aircraft, tanks, and aerospace electronics.

Even as Pretoria's diplomatic isolation increased in the 1980s, as many as fifty countries—including several in Africa—purchased Armscor's relatively simple, dependable, battle-tested arms for their own defense needs. The Johannesburg *Weekly Mail,* citing government documents, disclosed arms shipments in the mid-1980s to Iraq, Gabon, Malawi, Chile, France, Belgium, and Spain. Morocco and Zaire obtained Ratel armored vehicles from Pretoria, and South Africa's mobile razor-wire barrier, used for area protection and crowd control, was exported to at least fifteen countries, including several in Africa, and to United States forces in West Germany.

Reports of the Iran-Iraq conflict of the 1980s and of the Persian Gulf War of early 1991 highlighted Pretoria's previous sales to several countries in the Middle East. Armscor had sold G–5 towed howitzers to both Iran and Iraq, and G–6 self-propelled howitzers to the United Arab Emirates. South Africa also provided vaccines to Israel, for that country's use as a precaution against the possible Iraqi use of biological weapons. Numerous other reports of South African arms sales to the Middle East, to Peru, to several leaders of breakaway Yugoslav republics, and to other countries indicated the international awareness of the strength of South Africa's arms industry. The London-based humanitarian organization, Oxfam, criticized South Africa in 1992 for having sold automatic rifles, machine guns, grenade launchers, and ammunition to war-torn Rwanda. Military sales to Rwanda continued in the mid-1990s, even after that country's genocidal outbreak of violence in 1994.

The new Government of National Unity in 1994 faced the dilemma of whether to dismantle the defense industry many of its leaders had reviled for two decades or to preserve a lucrative export industry that still employed tens of thousands of South Africans. After some debate, President Mandela and Minister of Defence Joe Modise decided to maintain a high level of defense manufacturing and to increase military exports in the late 1990s. The industry, they argued, would benefit civil society in areas such as mass transportation, medical care, mobile services, information management, and other areas of infrastructure development. Increasing defense exports, they maintained, would bolster foreign currency reserves and would help reduce unemployment. Moreover, they pledged that military exports to other countries would require cabinet approval and verification by Armscor; and, they promised, arms would not be sold to countries that threatened war with their neighbors.

Nuclear, Chemical, and Biological Weapons

The international fear of nuclear proliferation made South Africa the focus of intense concern during the 1980s. Although Pretoria initially would not confirm it was developing, or possessed, nuclear weapons, it had large natural deposits of uranium, as well as uranium enrichment facilities and the necessary technological infrastructure. In addition, until the late 1980s South Africa had the deeply entrenched fear of its adversaries and the insecurity about its borders that were important incentives in other nations' nuclear programs. After 1981 South Africa was able to produce annually about fifty kilograms of highly enriched uranium, enough to make two or three twenty-kiloton nuclear bombs each year. With the cooperation of Israel—another technologically advanced, militarily powerful, nuclear-capable nation surrounded by hostile neighbors—South Africa developed at least six nuclear warheads, which it later acknowledged, along with a variety of missiles and other conventional weapons.

In 1987 President Botha announced that South Africa was considering signing the 1968 Nuclear Nonproliferation Treaty (NPT) and would begin discussions with other countries toward that end. In September 1990, Pretoria agreed to sign the NPT, but only "in the context of an equal commitment by other states in the Southern African region." After intensive diplomatic efforts, especially by the United States and the Soviet Union, Tanzania and Zambia agreed to sign the treaty. South Africa signed the NPT in July 1991, and an International Atomic Energy Agency (IAEA) safeguards agreement in September of that year. In addition, the government banned any further development, manufacture, marketing, import, or export of nuclear weapons or explosives, as required by the NPT. The IAEA declared it had completed its inspection in late

1994 and that South Africa's nuclear weapons facilities had been dismantled.

South Africa's nuclear parastatal, the Atomic Energy Corporation (AEC), which changed its emphasis from nuclear deterrents to industrial and economic needs, assists in the marketing of more than 150 products and services in the mid-1990s. These products have applications in mining and aerospace development, food production, transportation, and environmental preservation. Some examples are air filters for motor vehicles, a measuring device for minerals industry flotation processes, radio-isotopes for medical and industrial use, and a biogas unit to recover methane from refuse for use as vehicle fuel. These sales generated more than US$28 million between March 1993 and March 1994, according to official reports.

Although these developments represented a dramatic breakthrough in the international campaign to curb the spread of nuclear weapons, and a marked change in South Africa's own position, they did not permanently foreclose Pretoria's nuclear options. Pretoria could withdraw from its treaty obligations—NPT signatories may do so on ninety days' notice simply by citing "supreme interests." Moreover, South Africa could resume the production of weapons-grade uranium, although this product would be under IAEA safeguards and could not be used for nuclear explosives as long as South Africa chose to abide by the NPT.

South Africa's Council for Nuclear Safety, a statutory body set up to safeguard citizens and property against nuclear hazards, announced on September 27, 1994, an agreement between South Africa and the United States to exchange information about nuclear safety. This agreement, the first of its kind for South Africa—the twenty-ninth for the United States—enables signatory governments to remain abreast of the latest research information in the field of nuclear safety.

South Africa developed the ability to produce and to deploy chemical and biological weapons during the mid-1980s, although Pretoria then acknowledged only that it was developing defensive countermeasures against such weapons. Military officials then believed that chemical or biological weapons were being used by Angolan government forces in that country's festering civil war. In 1993, after South Africa's involvement in that war had ended, President de Klerk ordered the destruction of any remaining chemical and biological substances. His government also joined more than forty other African nations in signing the international Convention on Chemical Weapons. In October 1994, South Africa hosted the first conference in Africa on the implementation of the Convention on Chemical Weapons.

Regional Issues

South Africa was increasingly isolated, diplomatically and politically, after the early 1960s. Its system of apartheid, constructed to exclude blacks and to subordinate their concerns to white interests, made it a pariah on the continent. It was the only African country to be excluded from the Organization of African Unity (OAU); it became the target of a campaign intended to punish, to isolate, and to overthrow the government in Pretoria. A few OAU members tried unsuccessfully to mobilize a pan-African military force, which, they had hoped, would oust the NP government and would install the ANC in power in South Africa.

The climate of regional hostility intensified against a changing background of African politics in the 1960s and 1970s. Several dozen former European colonies and protectorates became independent African countries. After 1972 South African police units tried to bolster the illegal Rhodesian regime of Ian Smith against Zimbabwean national liberation armies, but by 1980 the new nation of Zimbabwe had achieved a new government with international legitimacy. Pretoria also assisted the Portuguese in their unsuccessful struggles against liberation movements in Angola and Mozambique; these two countries won independence from Portugal in 1975. In South-West Africa, the only other white-minority stronghold in the region, the South-West Africa People's Organisation (SWAPO) continued its independence struggle, which had begun in 1966.

By the early 1980s, Pretoria's former regional "buffer zone" against an enemy onslaught had become a hostile region of "front-line states" opposing Pretoria. South Africa's neighbors welcomed its dissidents, giving them political sanctuary and asylum, organizational headquarters, and military training facilities. South Africa found itself the lone white-ruled state in an unstable region. Civil wars in Angola and Mozambique, exacerbated by large-scale foreign intervention, drew Pretoria into protracted regional conflicts. It confronted an influx of Soviet, Warsaw Pact, and Cuban armed forces and weaponry into the region, and saw mounting dissent within its own borders.

Despite the regional animosities, no African army posed a serious or immediate challenge to South Africa's military might during this time, and its domestic enemies were not well enough organized or equipped to confront the power of the state. But the government in Pretoria often failed to distinguish between external and internal enemies. It saw itself as besieged, caught in a pernicious cycle of low-intensity, unconventional warfare from within and without—a Total Onslaught against which only a Total Strategy could ensure survival. This strategy required military and economic self-sufficiency; small, mobile, offensive-oriented armed forces; air superiority and at least a modest naval capability, backed by a large reserve force; a military doctrine of deterrence, including the use of preemptive and retaliatory force, as well as large-scale interventions in neighboring states; and an extensive intelligence and security network, both inside and outside South Africa.

South Africa's four-pronged strategy of alliance, accommodation, deterrence through defense, and counterthreat has been outlined by David Albright, a specialist in international security affairs. Pretoria's de facto alliances with Angola and Mozambique ended with their independence in 1975, and its informal cooperation pact with Southern Rhodesia (later, Rhodesia) ended soon after that. Then, lacking the option of forging open security alliances with neighboring states, Pretoria still tried to lessen regional tensions through nonaggression pacts, such as its agreements with Swaziland in 1982 and with Mozambique and Angola in 1984. It sought accommodation with regional states that were small, weak, or geographically remote, such as Malawi, Botswana, Lesotho, Swaziland, Madagascar, and—to a lesser degree—Zambia.

Two elements of South Africa's regional strategy, deterrence and counterthreat, which were increasingly important after the regional "buffer zone" had been eliminated, were only possible because South Africa had engaged in a massive security buildup over two decades. Beginning in the 1960s, Pretoria had extended military obligations for white males, had enlarged its permanent and reserve military forces, had increased its defense spending, had invested heavily in military industrialization, and had expanded and diversified its military arsenals.

Pretoria's most aggressive and open intervention in a neighboring state, in Angola in the mid-1970s, was believed to be necessary to avoid a communist onslaught in South-West Africa and, eventually, perhaps in South Africa. South African officials also estimated that competing Angolan nationalist armies would continue their power struggle after Portugal granted Angola independence in November 1975. Therefore, as Portuguese forces withdrew from the region, SADF troops intervened directly and continued to be engaged there until a United States-brokered peace accord was signed in December 1988 (see Relations with African States, ch. 4). During this time, Pretoria launched periodic cross-border military operations in Angola against the Soviet- and Cuban-backed Popular Movement for the Liberation of Angola (Movimento Popular de Libertação de Angola—MPLA) regime in Luanda. In addition, it launched frequent air and ground attacks on operational centers and training camps of liberation movements that supported the MPLA, including the ANC and SWAPO.

To counter the ANC threat, South Africa abducted and assassinated ANC exiles in neighboring states, in some instances. It also launched attacks into Mozambique in 1980, 1981, 1983, and 1987; into Lesotho in 1982 and 1985; into Botswana in 1985, 1986, and 1988; into Zambia in 1986 and 1987; and into Zimbabwe in 1982 and 1986. On one day, May 19, 1986, South African forces attacked alleged ANC bases in Botswana, Zambia, and Zimbabwe—all members of the British Commonwealth of Nations—souring relations with Commonwealth leaders who had tried to block international sanctions efforts against Pretoria.

Lesotho became the target of numerous South African counterinsurgency operations. Completely surrounded by South Africa, Lesotho was a natural haven for antiapartheid militants. South Africa applied economic and military pressure to quell criticism of Pretoria by Lesotho's prime minister, Chief Leabua Jonathan. A series of armed raids against alleged ANC strongholds around Maseru in the early 1980s prompted Chief Jonathan to declare a virtual state of war with South Africa in 1983. Finally, in January 1986, Pretoria provided covert support for a military coup that ousted Chief Jonathan and installed a military government led by Major General Justin Lekhanya; then, Lekhanya's government was pressured to prevent any ANC activity within its territory.

South Africa also furnished covert aid to opposition parties and to rebel organizations as part of an effort to destabilize hostile neighboring governments. For example, it supplied extensive aid to the Angolan rebel movement, the National

Union for the Total Independence of Angola (União Nacional para a Independência Total de Angola—UNITA). South Africa also supplied military assistance in the form of sanctuary, supplies, logistical support, training, and arms to the Mozambican National Resistance (Resistência Nacional Moçambicana— MNR or Renamo) during the early 1980s. Assistance to both UNITA and Renamo declined in the late 1980s (see Relations with African States, ch. 4).

Also during the 1980s, South Africa enforced border controls against illegal refugees and guerrilla infiltration by installing electrified fences, especially along its northeastern border. In 1985, for example, it installed 2,800-volt fences along portions of its borders with Zimbabwe, Mozambique, and Lesotho, and with the homelands of Bophuthatswana, Transkei, and Venda. During 1988, the first year of available records, at least seventy people were electrocuted on these fences.

Regional tensions began to ease by the end of the 1980s, and in southern Africa, as elsewhere on the globe, the year 1989 marked a turning point in political and security relationships. The agreement signed in December 1988 linked Namibia's independence from South Africa with the cessation of foreign military involvement in Angola, and set in motion a series of other changes that contributed to dramatically improved prospects for peace. The Soviet Union slowed, and eventually halted, arms shipments to Angolan and Mozambican forces and played an active role in seeking political settlements to those conflicts. South Africa recognized the reduced regional threat by cautiously beginning domestic political reforms, by reducing the military's domestic security role, by drawing down military personnel, and by reducing military spending in areas related to external operations.

Namibia held national elections in 1989 and achieved formal independence in March 1990; Pretoria's former nemesis, SWAPO, won control over the new government in Windhoek. SWAPO leader Sam Nujoma took a conciliatory line toward Pretoria, however, and both countries recognized Namibia's continued economic dependence on South Africa. In March 1991, South African and Namibian officials began negotiations aimed at transferring to Windhoek control over Namibia's only deep-water port, Walvis Bay, as well as the Penguin Islands. South Africa's last military battalion was removed from Walvis Bay later that year, and that enclave and the islands formally became part of Namibia on March 1, 1994.

A number of events in the early 1990s helped to solidify South Africa's view of its future leadership role in southern Africa. During a serious drought and famine that swept most of the region, South Africa was credited with saving thousands of lives by shipping domestic and imported corn to neighboring states and by providing other forms of drought assistance. The government also eased border restrictions, in part to facilitate the use of South Africa's developed transportation infrastructure by neighboring countries.

The rest of Africa began to open up formerly covert trade relations with South Africa and to welcome it into diplomatic circles. President de Klerk paid his first visit to Nigeria in April 1992, and his warm welcome by President Ibrahim Babangida sent a strong signal of acceptance to other African leaders. Within weeks, Zambia, Kenya, and Lesotho began preparations for establishing formal diplomatic relations.

While ties with the rest of Africa were being strengthened, South Africa's relationship with Angola continued to be uncertain. Hopes for peace in Angola rose and fell; the signing of the Bicesse Accord in May 1991 paved the way for national elections in September 1992. After a brief lull, the country returned to civil war. In 1994 the MPLA government employed military trainers from South Africa—former SADF fighters, including some who had fought against the MPLA during the 1980s—to help it recapture UNITA-held towns. Another peace agreement, signed in Zambia in late 1994, gave some hope of a UN-monitored peace and of elections in 1995 or 1996. As of mid-1996, however, rebel troops were still being disarmed, and a date for Angolan elections had not been set.

The 1980s power struggle in Lesotho had never really ended; when violence flared in 1994, Pretoria's response provided an indication of the regional role that the new Government of National Unity envisioned for itself for the next few years. The Lesotho military had forced the country's reigning monarch, King Moshoeshoe II, into exile in 1990, and in 1993 Lesotho had held its first nationwide elections in twenty-seven years. The former monarch was allowed to return, but the new prime minister, Ntsu Mokhehle, had allowed his own strained relationship with the army to deteriorate to the point that South African troops were posted to guard the border between the two countries in 1993 and in 1994. In 1994 South African officials helped to mediate a compromise between Lesotho's government and military, but President Mandela encouraged

Zimbabwe's President Robert Mugabe to take a leading role in regional peacemaking, while South Africa worked to reorganize and train its new National Defence Force.

Constitutional and Legal Framework

South Africa's 1984 constitution, the Republic of South Africa Constitution Act (No. 110) of 1983, which remained in effect through 1993, affirmed the provisions of the Defence Act (No. 44) of 1957 establishing the missions of the armed forces. These missions were, and continue to be, to defend the country; to fulfill South Africa's international treaty obligations; to prevent terrorism and domestic disorder; to protect life, health, and property; and to help maintain essential services. The president had the power to declare war, martial law, and states of emergency, and to establish peace. The minister of defence, under the overall direction of the president and with the consent of the State Security Council (SSC), bore responsibility for formulating and for executing defense policy. During the late 1980s, the military was frequently assigned domestic duties as part of the constitutional requirement to help the police and local authorities to maintain essential services and domestic order in times of emergency.

The 1994 interim constitution, the Constitution of the Republic of South Africa (No. 200) of 1993, reiterates the provisions of the 1957 Defence Act that make the president commander in chief of the armed forces. The constitution reserves specific powers related to national security for the president, who may, with parliamentary approval, declare a "state of national defence." This is, in effect, a state of national emergency, but the framers of the constitution emphasize their reluctance to undertake any offensive military action against neighboring states. The constitution also authorizes the president to establish a national defense force to fulfill the responsibilities formerly assigned to the SADF. It empowers the president to employ the military in accordance with constitutional principles to defend the sovereignty and the territorial integrity of the republic; to fulfill South Africa's international obligations; to preserve life, health, and property; to provide or to maintain essential services; to uphold law and order in cooperation with the police; and to support the general social and economic improvement of the population.

The interim constitution states that the new military organization, the South African National Defence Force (SANDF), will include former members of the SADF, the ANC's Umkhonto we Sizwe (MK), and the militias of the former homelands of Transkei, Bophuthatswana, Venda, and Ciskei. Former members of other militias, such as the Inkatha Freedom Party's Self-Protection Units, were admitted to the SANDF after the 1994 constitution was implemented.

In May 1996, the National Assembly and the Senate, in joint session as the Constitutional Assembly, completed a draft of the final constitution, to be implemented by the end of the formal political transition. Like the interim document that preceded it, the 1996 draft constitution calls for civilian control over the military. The draft makes no mention of the State Security Council or similar overarching security apparatus reminiscent of the 1980s. It reaffirms the missions of the armed forces as outlined in the Defence Act of 1957 and the role of the president to serve as commander in chief of the SANDF. As of mid-1996, the draft was being reviewed by the Constitutional Court, and after some revisions, was expected to be implemented in phases, beginning in 1997.

Military Organization

Four armed services—the South African Army, the South African Air Force, the South African Navy, and the South African Medical Service—make up the SANDF, also referred to as the National Defence Force. SANDF headquarters are in Pretoria. The SANDF is commanded by the chief of the armed forces, who is appointed by the president from one of the four branches of the military (see fig. 20). The SANDF chief is accountable to the minister of defence, who is a civilian.

The SANDF chief consults with members of several councils and committees and chairs the Defence Command Council (DCC), which oversees the defense budget. On the DCC are the four service chiefs, the chief of the National Defence Force staff, the military inspector general, the chiefs of defence headquarters staff divisions, and other key defense officials. Headquarters responsibilities are allocated among six staff divisions—the Finance Division, the Intelligence Division, the Logistics Division, the Operations Division, the Personnel Division, and the Planning Division.

Army

The army in the 1990s continues to rely on a small Perma-

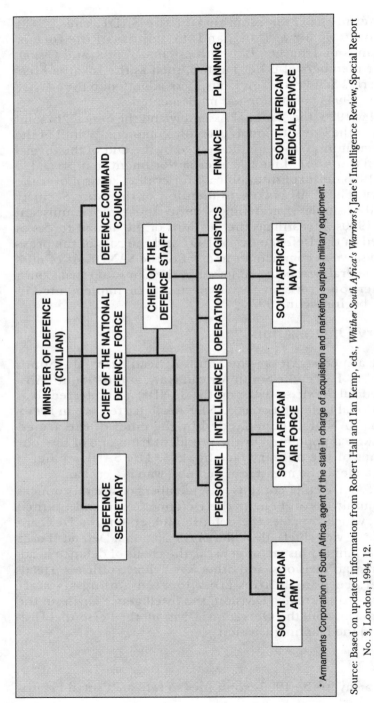

* Armaments Corporation of South Africa, agent of the state in charge of acquisition and marketing surplus military equipment.

Source: Based on updated information from Robert Hall and Ian Kemp, eds., *Whither South Africa's Warriors?*, Jane's Intelligence Review, Special Report No. 3, London, 1994, 12.

Figure 20. Command Structure of the South African National Defence Force (SANDF), 1996

nent Force of professional soldiers and a large Citizen Force. The Citizen Force consists of volunteers serving an initial period of training and active duty, followed by several years of reserve status. Reservists rotate into active duty when called upon. Volunteers can apply to transfer from the Citizen Force to the Permanent Force if they wish to become professional, career soldiers.

The sweeping changes of the mid-1990s allowed varying assessments of the strength of the army. The government's *South Africa Yearbook, 1995* indicated that roughly 95,000 active-duty members of the SADF and of the former homeland militaries, as well as about 27,000 former liberation fighters, made up the army in 1995. Many of the active-duty troops were in various stages of training or retraining for at least one year after that. After the integration of these forces into the SANDF was completed, officials planned to reduce army ranks, to a force of about 91,000 by the year 1998. Officials were also considering further reductions, perhaps to a force of about 75,000 active-duty troops, by the year 2000. The number of military reservists, in a wide variety of reserve duty statuses, was estimated at more than 360,000 in late 1995. The government's *South Africa Yearbook, 1995* indicated that more than 500,000 troops were on part-time or reserve status (see table 20, Appendix).

The chief of the army, who holds the rank of lieutenant general, commands all army forces. He is assisted by his general staff at the army headquarters in Pretoria. He also is responsible for the Army Battle School at Lohatla in the Northern Cape, the Defence College (formerly the South African Military College) at Pretoria, and various corps schools, such as the Artillery School at Potchefstroom (North-West Province), the Infantry School at Oudtshoorn (Western Cape), and the Intelligence School at Kimberley.

The army is organized into territorial forces and conventional forces, both commanded by the chief of the army through different command structures (see fig. 21). This division reflects the army's dual mission—to ensure internal security and to defend the country against external threats. The territorial forces are organized by region and are primarily responsible for internal security tasks, such as helping the police ensure law and order, combating terrorism, patrolling national borders, protecting strategic sites, providing emergency and disaster relief, and administering military reserve

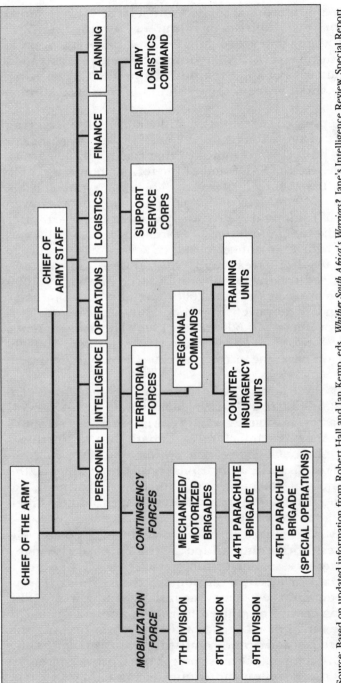

Source: Based on updated information from Robert Hall and Ian Kemp, eds., *Whither South Africa's Warriors?*, Jane's Intelligence Review, Special Report No. 3, London, 1994, 12.

Figure 21. Organization of the South African Army, 1996

forces within their region. In 1996 most members of the former homeland military forces were being incorporated into the territorial forces.

The ten regional military commands are headquartered at Cape Town, Port Elizabeth, Johannesburg, Kimberley, Durban, Bloemfontein, Pretoria, Potchefstroom, Nelspruit, and Pietersburg. In 1996 the boundaries of the military regions were being changed to conform more closely to the country's new administrative regions.

Like the territorial forces, the army's conventional forces are stationed throughout the country, but their training and organization are separate from the territorial forces. The conventional forces fall under the operational control of the army headquarters in Pretoria, not under the regional commanders. The conventional forces are trained to confront traditional security threats, such as a foreign enemy.

The conventional forces are organized into contingency forces and a mobilization force. As of the early and mid-1990s, the contingency forces consisted of one mechanized/motorized brigade and two parachute brigades—the Forty-fourth Parachute Brigade and the Forty-fifth Parachute Brigade. The mobilization force was organized into three mechanized divisions—the Seventh Division, the Eighth Division, and the Ninth Division.

Functionally, the army also distinguishes between combat corps and support service corps. The combat corps include infantry, artillery, antiaircraft, and armored corps. The infantry is the largest of the combat corps and has both mechanized and airborne units. The artillery corps uses indirect fire guns, howitzers, field guns, and multiple rocket launchers, generally coordinating operations with the antiaircraft corps to protect ground forces. The armored corps relies largely on tanks with 105-millimeter guns and on a variety of other armored vehicles.

The support service corps include engineers, signals specialists, and others trained in ordnance, technical services, intelligence, personnel, and finance, as well as musicians, caterers, and the military police. Service units maintain, repair, and recondition all equipment, except communications equipment. The military police serve as the army's internal police force and control traffic to and from operational areas.

The Commandos are formally under the authority of the regional commands of the army but are organized and deployed in a tradition similar to that of the National Guard in the United States. Originally volunteers trained for quick-response to local emergencies, they were used to quell unrest during the apartheid era; in the 1990s, Commando units are assigned to guard important installations, such as industrial plants, oil refineries, communication centers, and transportation facilities.

Commandos generally serve a total of 1,000 active-duty days over a ten- or twelve-year period. In emergencies, the period of active duty is increased in increments of fifty days. Urban Commando units are generally organized into a single urban battalion. Rural Commando units are sometimes organized into a regional battalion.

The army's ground forces in the mid-1990s can field an imposing array of equipment, most of it produced in South Africa. Their arsenal includes tanks, armored reconnaissance vehicles, infantry fighting vehicles, and armored personnel carriers (see table 21, Appendix). The army also has a wide array of artillery pieces, including towed and self-propelled heavy artillery, multiple-rocket-launcher systems, as well as mortars and antitank and air defense weapons.

Integrating Armies in the 1990s

The military's massive reorganization began a year before the historic April 1994 elections and was scheduled to be completed by late 1996. The process began with the creation of a multiservice Joint Military Coordinating Council (JMCC) by the Transitional Executive Council (TEC)—the country's interim executive authority. The TEC also established a Subcouncil on Defence to supervise the planning phase of the reorganization. The JMCC and the subcouncil worked together to set program goals, and in late 1993 the JMCC formed five working groups to address specific problems associated with finance, intelligence, logistics, operations, and personnel. These working groups presented their recommendations to the JMCC and the subcouncil in early 1994.

At that time, the major security challenge for South Africa was the need to end the township violence that threatened to derail the April 1994 elections. Officials hastily formed a multiracial National Peacekeeping Force (NPKF), including about 3,500 members of existing military organizations—primarily the SADF and MK. In February 1994, the NPKF was deployed to several townships around Johannesburg, but its troops, with widely varying military backgrounds and training, could not adequately coordinate their operations and standards of behavior. NPKF units encountered morale and disciplinary problems, and, in at least one instance, civilians were killed in gunfire between military and paramilitary personnel. The NPKF was disbanded soon after the April 1994 elections.

The failure of the NPKF did not delay the military reorganization, however, and other efforts already underway in early 1994 were more successful. SADF officials and a British Military Advisory and Training Team (BMATT) assembled members of the former homeland armies and former MK and Azanian People's Liberation Army (APLA—the military wing of the Pan-Africanist Congress) liberation fighters at locations near Johannesburg, Cape Town, and Bloemfontein to evaluate applicants for the new army. The SANDF accepted into its ranks most senior officers from both homeland and liberation armies without extensive testing. In addition, members of the homeland armies who had been trained by SADF instructors were generally accepted immediately into the new organization.

Finally, MK and APLA members were considered for admission on an individual basis, but these cases proved more difficult. Some of the liberation fighters could not meet minimal formal education requirements. Many had received uneven or inadequate training that left them ill-prepared for either combat or organizational responsibilities. Some had been trained in languages other than English or Afrikaans. A few were disqualified because of bureaucratic problems, such as lost files, or because they were overage. The SADF and BMATT personnel provided three to six months of basic training for many former liberation fighters, in order to rectify gaps in background qualifications or experience. For some of the new SANDF soldiers, training continued through 1996.

The New Face of the Army

As the military reorganization proceeded, a multiracial officer corps emerged. By early 1996, more than 1,300 former members of homeland or liberation armies held officer ranks of lieutenant or above. At least eleven black South Africans had been promoted to the rank of major general or above.

As of 1996, military officials had no plans to reinstate conscription as long as there were enough qualified volunteers to meet national security needs. They planned, instead, to transfer some soldiers into the police and others into service brigades. The latter would act as civic-action teams to work on road construction and other infrastructure development projects. Military officials chose this tactic over large-scale dismissals in order to avoid flooding the civilian work force and to provide some work-related training and job skills for former guerrilla fighters. Funds were allocated for this training in late 1994, and the first three- and six-month training courses began in early 1995.

Military officials were working to maintain continuity in SANDF military training, and, at the same time, to inculcate a sense of the changing responsibilities of the army in the 1990s. Military trainers were preparing for new border control problems, as the threat of political infiltration by antiapartheid dissidents gave way to a tide of political and economic refugees hoping to prosper in the new South Africa. Officials also were concerned about increased smuggling and other forms of border fraud. One of their greatest challenges was the dramatic increase in cross-border narcotics trafficking that threatened to bring South Africa into the global spotlight as an important transshipment point in the late 1990s. Finally, the military continued to prepare for the possibility of cross-border hostilities with a neighboring state, although this possibility appeared remote as of 1996.

Air Force

The South African Air Force (SAAF) includes about 7,000 career active-duty troops and 3,000 active-duty volunteers who are fulfilling their national service obligations, as of 1996. About 400 air force personnel are women. In addition, about 20,000 reservists are available to be rotated into active duty as ground support personnel; reservists are also assigned to tactical air units and to units charged with safeguarding SAAF facilities (see fig. 22).

The air force is under the overall command of the chief of the air force, a lieutenant general, who is assisted by the chief of the air force staff and the air force inspector general. The air force's headquarters organization reflects the same six-division administrative structure as the entire military establishment, with divisions handling finance, intelligence, logistics, operations, personnel, and planning.

All regional commands and functional commands are answerable to air force headquarters in Pretoria for all air operations. Until 1993, there were two regional commands, the Western Command and the Southern Command. The Western

Command was dismantled in preparation for South Africa's relinquishing control over Walvis Bay in early 1994. The Southern Command, located at Simonstown, has responsibility for several territorial command posts and bases in the southern coastal area. Air force bases not under the direct control of the Southern Command fall under air force headquarters at Pretoria.

The air force has two functional commands, the Training Command and the Air Logistics Command. The Training Command, headquartered in Pretoria, oversees programs in basic training, flying, navigation, logistics training, and other instruction, and controls most major training facilities. The Air Logistics Command controls several air force units, including airfield maintenance units, repair depots, and supply depots. It also provides complete matériel procurement and engineering services, including aircraft management and ground systems support.

Two other functional commands, the Air Space Control Command and the Tactical Support Command, were dismantled in the early 1990s as part of the overall military downsizing. The Air Space Control Command had been responsible for air defenses and control of airspace, in conjunction with civil authorities. The Tactical Support Command had conducted formal operational command and control training, as well as instruction in other air force operations. These responsibilities were assumed by other commands and by headquarters personnel.

In addition to regional and functional commands, the air force has several command posts, which are subordinate to commands. One of these, the Main Threat Area Command Post, is co-located with the air force headquarters at Pretoria. The Main Threat Area Command Post oversees the operations of several air bases, air defense radar sites, and other installations throughout the region. The Southern Command Post, headquartered at Cape Town, oversees operations of bases near Cape Town and Port Elizabeth, and is responsible for air force maritime and other operations in these coastal areas.

The air force operates an estimated 400 aircraft. The fleet includes Cheetah, Mirage, and Impala fighter aircraft, Cessna light reconnaissance aircraft, and Oryx and Alouette III helicopters (see table 22, Appendix). The air force in early 1996 was awaiting the delivery of fifty to sixty Pilatus PC–7 basic training aircraft from Switzerland and planned to purchase sev-

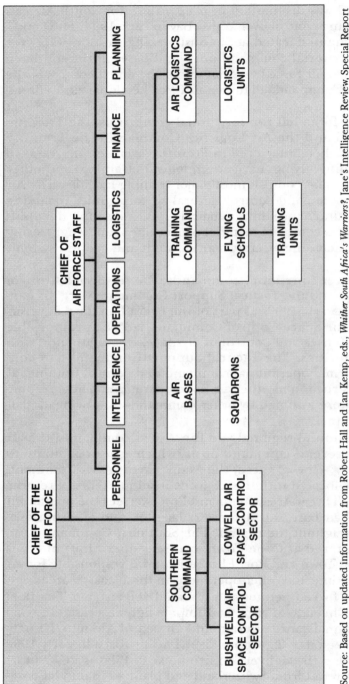

Source: Based on updated information from Robert Hall and Ian Kemp, eds., *Whither South Africa's Warriors?*, Jane's Intelligence Review, Special Report No. 3, London, 1994, 17.

Figure 22. Organization of the South African Air Force, 1996

eral locally manufactured Rooivalk combat helicopters. The air force is also upgrading its Cheetah fighter aircraft and is developing plans to produce short- and medium-range air-to-air missiles for this purpose.

Navy

In the mid-1990s, the South African Navy (SAN) is a 4,500-person uniformed force, including 300 women. The navy is commanded by a vice admiral, the chief of the navy. The chief of the navy is assisted by a chief of naval operations and a chief of naval support; the latter two positions are filled by rear admirals. Naval headquarters are at Pretoria, although most important elements of the navy are at the navy's two bases at Simonstown and on Salisbury Island, near Durban. In addition to the headquarters organization and bases, the command structure includes seven naval units, flotillas, and independent ships (see fig. 23). Naval units are stationed in Johannesburg and Pretoria and at several of South Africa's major ports.

Naval officer training is provided at the South African Naval College in Gordon's Bay, near Simonstown. Basic training is provided at the nearby South African Naval Staff College and on the SAS *Saldanha*. Technical naval training is provided on the SAS *Wingfield*, and advanced combat and other nontechnical specialist training is provided on the SAS *Simonsberg*. After completing an initial period of service with the navy, voluntary service personnel separating from active duty are assigned to one of the seven reserve naval units.

The navy is organized into a submarine flotilla, which possesses three Daphne-class submarines, a surface-strike flotilla with nine Minister-class 450-ton missile craft, and a mine countermeasure flotilla with four River-class mine hunters and four Ton-class minesweepers. The navy's plans for upgrading and expansion include the purchase of four corvette hulls, to be fitted with a locally manufactured combat system. These are expected to be commissioned by the year 1999. The navy also plans to acquire six 800- to 1200-ton strike craft by the year 2003 and four new submarines by the year 2005, and is considering the decommissioning of its nine well-worn Minister-class missile craft (see table 23, Appendix).

The navy helped to celebrate South Africa's return to the international community in the mid-1990s, when a growing number of foreign ships docked at South African ports. The January 1994 visit to Simonstown by the HMS *Norfolk* was the

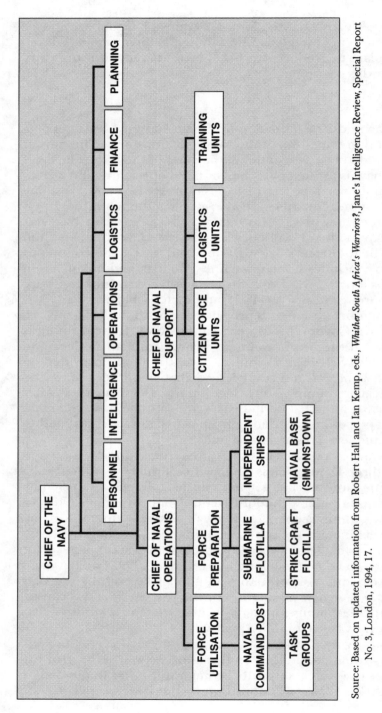

Source: Based on updated information from Robert Hall and Ian Kemp, eds., *Whither South Africa's Warriors?*, Jane's Intelligence Review, Special Report No. 3, London, 1994, 17.

Figure 23. Organization of the South African Navy, 1996

first British Royal Navy visit in twenty-seven years. A month later, the French frigate FNS *Germinal* made the first official visit by a French vessel in nineteen years. In November 1994, two United States vessels, the USS *Gettysburg* and the USS *Halyburton*, received a twenty-one-gun salute in Simonstown in the first call by United States Navy ships in twenty-seven years.

South African ships also participated in joint naval exercises in 1994, the first in twenty years. In June 1994, a 6,000-ton fleet replenishment ship, the SAS *Drakensberg*, took part in exercises with the British Royal Navy and the Royal Air Force. The South African Navy also carried out joint exercises with the Argentine, Brazilian, and Uruguayan navies in May 1995. In addition, maritime training involved ships and aircraft from the United States, Britain, Canada, France, Germany, Italy, the Netherlands, Norway, and Spain.

The navy has performed coast guard duties and search-and-rescue missions throughout its history, and is preparing for increased responsibilities during the late 1990s, primarily to protect the country's 200-nautical-mile exclusive economic zone (EEZ) and to combat smuggling and maritime narcotics trafficking. South Africa's navy is also in demand by other African governments; in the early 1990s, for example, South African personnel performed naval facility repairs for Zaire, marine surveys for Mozambique, and relief-supply transport to Kenya for shipment to Somalia and Rwanda.

Medical Service

The South African Medical Service (SAMS) was established as a full service branch of the SADF in 1979 to consolidate the medical services of the army, the navy, and the air force. The SAMS includes full-time army medical personnel, civilian employees of the Ministry of Defence, and (until the mid-1990s) qualified national service personnel on active duty. Reservists from the Citizen Force and from the Commandos are sometimes assigned to short-term active duty in the SAMS, as well. The military employs roughly 400 medical doctors, and private medical specialists are sometimes appointed to supplement the staff of the SAMS.

The surgeon general heads the SAMS and has the rank of lieutenant general. The SAMS operational units include three hospitals—the First Military Hospital near Pretoria, the Second Military Hospital at Cape Town, and the Third Military Hospital at Bloemfontein. There are also three specialized institutes—the Institute for Aviation Medicine, the Institute for Maritime Medicine, and the Military Psychological Institute. They provide comprehensive medical care for military personnel and their dependents, as well as the police and employees of other security-related government departments, and occasionally to neighboring countries. The SAMS also provides occasional veterinary services for animals (mainly horses and dogs) used by the security services. The Institute for Aviation Medicine and the Institute for Maritime Medicine screen pilot candidates for the air force and for civilian aviation certification, as well as divers and submariners for the navy. The military's medical services also include general medical and dental care, and specialized rehabilitation services.

The SAMS is organized into regional medical commands, corresponding to the army's regional commands, as well as a Medical Logistics Command and a Medical Training Command. The regional commands support military units, military base hospitals, and military unit sickbays in their region. The Medical Logistics Command is responsible for medical logistics only, as each service provides for its own logistics support. In addition, the Medical Training Command supervises the South African Medical Service College, the South African Medical Service Nursing College, and the South African Medical Service Training Centre, as well as the military hospitals' training programs. The nursing college, in Pretoria, grants a four-year nursing diploma in association with the University of South Africa. Specialized, in-service training courses for nurses and for nursing assistants are also available.

The SAMS implemented several retrenchment measures in the early 1990s. It consolidated all quartermaster stores in the Cape Town and the Bloemfontein areas, relocated the SAMS training center from Potchefstroom to Pretoria, closed several medical supply depots, consolidated computer centers and systems, rationalized procedures for procuring medicine and medical equipment, discontinued survival training, and reduced or closed sickbays and military medical clinics that served other armed services affected by retrenchments.

Uniforms, Ranks, and Insignia

The SADF has been recognized internationally for its emphasis on appearance and strict observance of dress-code regulations, and SANDF officers in the mid-1990s indicated their determination to maintain these high standards. SANDF uniforms are generally functional in design. The army's service uniform consists of a brown jacket and tie, and light brown shirt and trousers. In warm weather, an open-collared, short-sleeved khaki shirt or light jacket replaces the jacket and tie. Senior officers' service uniforms are distinguished by poppy-red lapel tabs. The army's field uniforms—required for work details, for training, and for field exercises—include a brown shirt, fatigue trousers, a webbed utility belt, and boots. Camouflage battle dress is authorized for selected units. A peaked cap or beret is worn on selected occasions with service uniforms and field uniforms. Some combat units are distinguished by the color of their berets. Bush hats are also worn in the field, but not in public.

Air force uniforms are steel blue. Like the army and the navy, the air force permits open-collared shirts in warm weather and shorts and knee socks on occasion.

The navy wears dark blue uniforms in winter and white, in summer. Enlisted ranks in the navy wear jacket-and-tie uniforms in cool weather and white jackets with a high collar in summer.

Military rank is indicated by shoulder or sleeve insignia (see fig. 24 and fig. 25). Officer insignia are worn on the shoulder, with the exception of naval officers' cool-weather uniforms, which display the insignia on the sleeve. Enlisted rank insignia are worn on the sleeve. Some military insignia were changed in the mid-1990s. For example, the Castle of Good Hope, in several army and air force insignia, was replaced by a nine-pointed star, symbolic of the nine provinces of the new South Africa.

Military awards recognize several categories of service and accomplishments. As of the mid-1990s, South Africa's highest decoration is the Castle of Good Hope, which is reserved for exceptional heroism on the battlefield. The Honoris Crux, conferred in four classes, is awarded for valor. The Order of the Star of South Africa, conferred in two classes, is restricted to general officers who perform meritorious service in promoting the efficiency and the preparedness of the armed forces. Other ranks are eligible for the Southern Cross and the Pro Merito decoration, and various medals are given in recognition of outstanding service and devotion to duty.

Military Intelligence and Intelligence Coordination

The military has a long history of intelligence gathering and evaluation, but military intelligence agencies were virtually

	2D LIEUTENANT	LIEUTENANT	CAPTAIN	MAJOR	LIEUTENANT COLONEL	COLONEL	BRIGADIER	MAJOR GENERAL	LIEUTENANT GENERAL	GENERAL
SOUTH AFRICAN RANK (ENGLISH)	2D LIEUTENANT	LIEUTENANT	CAPTAIN	MAJOR	LIEUTENANT COLONEL	COLONEL	BRIGADIER	MAJOR GENERAL	LIEUTENANT GENERAL	GENERAL
SOUTH AFRICAN RANK (AFRIKAANS)	TWEEDE LUITENANT	LUITENANT	KAPTEIN	MAJOOR	LUITENANT KOLONEL	KOLONEL	BRIGADIER	MAJOOR GENERAAL	LUITENANT GENERAAL	GENERAAL
ARMY AND AIR FORCE										
U.S. RANK TITLES	2D LIEUTENANT	1ST LIEUTENANT	CAPTAIN	MAJOR	LIEUTENANT COLONEL	COLONEL	BRIGADIER GENERAL	MAJOR GENERAL	LIEUTENANT GENERAL	GENERAL
SOUTH AFRICAN RANK (ENGLISH)	ENSIGN	SUBLIEUTENANT	LIEUTENANT	LIEUTENANT COMMANDER	COMMANDER	CAPTAIN	COMMODORE	REAR ADMIRAL	VICE ADMIRAL	ADMIRAL
SOUTH AFRICAN RANK (AFRIKAANS)	VAANDRIG	ONDER-LUITENANT	LUITENANT	LUITENANT KOMMANDEUR	KOMMANDEUR	KAPTEIN	KOMMODOOR	SKOUT ADMIRAAL	VISE ADMIRAAL	ADMIRAAL
NAVY										
U.S. RANK TITLES	ENSIGN	LIEUTENANT JUNIOR GRADE	LIEUTENANT	LIEUTENANT COMMANDER	COMMANDER	CAPTAIN	REAR ADMIRAL LOWER HALF	REAR ADMIRAL UPPER HALF	VICE ADMIRAL	ADMIRAL

Figure 24. Officer Ranks and Insignia, 1996

ARMY

	PRIVATE	LANCE CORPORAL	CORPORAL	SERGEANT	STAFF SERGEANT	WARRANT OFFICER CLASS 2	WARRANT OFFICER CLASS 1
SOUTH AFRICAN RANK (ENGLISH)	PRIVATE	LANCE CORPORAL	CORPORAL	SERGEANT	STAFF SERGEANT	WARRANT OFFICER CLASS 2	WARRANT OFFICER CLASS 1
SOUTH AFRICAN RANK (AFRIKAANS)	SKUTTER/WEERMAN	ONDER-KORPORAAL	KORPORAAL	SERSANT	STAFSERSANT	ADJUDANT OFFISIER KLAS 2	ADJUDANT OFFISIER KLAS 1
	NO INSIGNIA						
U.S. RANK TITLES	BASIC PRIVATE / PRIVATE	PRIVATE 1ST CLASS	CORPORAL / SPECIALIST	SERGEANT	STAFF SERGEANT	SERGEANT 1ST CLASS	MASTER SERGEANT / FIRST SERGEANT — SERGEANT MAJOR / COMMAND SERGEANT MAJOR

AIR FORCE

	PRIVATE	LANCE CORPORAL	CORPORAL	SERGEANT	FLIGHT SERGEANT	WARRANT OFFICER CLASS 2	WARRANT OFFICER CLASS 1
SOUTH AFRICAN RANK (ENGLISH)	PRIVATE	LANCE CORPORAL	CORPORAL	SERGEANT	FLIGHT SERGEANT	WARRANT OFFICER CLASS 2	WARRANT OFFICER CLASS 1
SOUTH AFRICAN RANK (AFRIKAANS)	WEERMAN	ONDERKORPORAAL	KORPORAAL	SERSANT	VLUGSERSANT	ADJUDANT OFFISIER KLAS 2	ADJUDANT OFFISIER KLAS 1
	NO INSIGNIA						
U.S. RANK TITLES	AIRMAN BASIC / AIRMAN / AIRMAN 1ST CLASS		SENIOR AIRMAN / SERGEANT	STAFF SERGEANT	TECHNICAL SERGEANT	MASTER SERGEANT	SENIOR MASTER SERGEANT — CHIEF MASTER SERGEANT

NAVY

		SEAMAN	ABLE SEAMAN	LEADING SEAMAN	PETTY OFFICER	CHIEF PETTY OFFICER	WARRANT OFFICER CLASS 2	WARRANT OFFICER CLASS 1
SOUTH AFRICAN RANK (ENGLISH)	NO RANK	SEAMAN	ABLE SEAMAN	LEADING SEAMAN	PETTY OFFICER	CHIEF PETTY OFFICER	WARRANT OFFICER CLASS 2	WARRANT OFFICER CLASS 1
SOUTH AFRICAN RANK (AFRIKAANS)	NO RANK	SEEMAN	BEVARE-SEEMAN	BAASSEEMAN	BOOTSMAN	EERSTE-BOOTSMAN	ADJUDANT OFFISIER KLAS 2	ADJUDANT OFFISIER KLAS 1
U.S. RANK TITLES	SEAMAN RECRUIT / SEAMAN APPRENTICE	SEAMAN	PETTY OFFICER 3D CLASS	PETTY OFFICER 2D CLASS / PETTY OFFICER 1ST CLASS	CHIEF PETTY OFFICER	SENIOR CHIEF PETTY OFFICER	MASTER CHIEF PETTY OFFICER	

Figure 25. Enlisted Ranks and Insignia, 1996

independent of each other and of other government agencies for much of this history. In 1962 the Directorate of Military Intelligence was established to coordinate the collection and the management of defense-related information among the military services. In 1969 the government established the Bureau of State Security (BOSS) to coordinate military, domestic, and economic intelligence. During the 1970s, BOSS became embroiled in several unethical projects and government scandals that seriously undermined its credibility. In 1978 President P. W. Botha established the Department of National Security to strengthen his control over the intelligence community and to incorporate it into his Total Strategy against opposition to the state. Botha himself held the cabinet portfolio on national intelligence and continually stressed the need for community-wide coordination.

In 1981 the Department of National Security, renamed the Directorate of National Intelligence, increased the emphasis on military intelligence and military access to all other forms of intelligence. The directorate worked closely with the military, coordinating efforts among intelligence agencies, and using directorate analyses and recommendations to formulate security policy.

In the uneasy atmosphere of the mid-1980s, the definition of "enemies of the state" expanded rapidly, extending the role of the intelligence community. Various intelligence services engaged in operations involving harassment, assault, disappearance, and sometimes the murder of antiapartheid activists.

In the early 1990s, the government began reorganizing the country's intelligence-gathering network. The Intelligence Services Act (No. 38) of 1994, the National Strategic Intelligence Act (No. 39) of 1994, and the Parliamentary Committee on Intelligence Act (No. 40) of 1994 established a National Intelligence Coordinating Committee (NICC) to present coordinated intelligence analyses to the president and the cabinet.

The NICC oversees the operations of the four arms of the intelligence community. These are the National Intelligence Agency (NIA), which is responsible for domestic intelligence gathering; the South African Secret Service (SASS), which manages foreign intelligence; the military intelligence agencies, and the police intelligence unit. The NICC is chaired by the deputy minister of intelligence services, who is appointed by the president and who reports directly to the president. (There is no minister in charge of intelligence activities.)

The 1994 legislation also authorizes military intelligence units to collect foreign intelligence and, under specific, limited circumstances, to collect domestic intelligence. It does not authorize any military intelligence agency to conduct domestic intelligence gathering on a routine basis.

One overriding concern among senior government officials in the postapartheid era is guaranteeing the protection of the individual against interference by the agencies under their control. To help protect citizens against such abuse, the president appoints an inspector general for the NIA and for the SASS. The two inspectors general report to the Joint Committee on Defence, which includes members of both houses of Parliament, appointed jointly by the president and the speaker of the National Assembly. This committee must report to both houses of Parliament at least once each year concerning the state of intelligence gathering nationwide.

Defense Budget

South Africa's defense budget grew almost tenfold in nominal terms between 1975 and 1989, from R1 billion to R9.4 billion (for value of the rand—see Glossary). In constant dollar value, however, the increase was modest—from US$3 billion per year in the early 1980s to US$3.43 billion per year in the last half of that decade, based on 1988 prices. Defense spending averaged 16.4 percent of government budgets in the 1980s; it ranged from a high of 22.7 percent in 1982 to 13.7 percent in 1987, but rose to 15.7 percent of government spending in 1989.

Although South Africa's defense spending was high in comparison with economic output in the 1980s, the "trend toward militarization" in that decade, which was noted by many observers in analyzing South Africa's apartheid-era spending, was not evident in global comparisons. Out of 144 countries surveyed by the United States Arms Control and Disarmament Agency in 1989, South Africa ranked thirtieth in total military expenditures, forty-fourth in military spending as a percentage of gross national product (GNP—see Glossary), and sixty-third in military spending as a percentage of total government spending. South Africa also ranked forty-ninth in the size of its armed forces and 103d in the size of the armed forces in relation to population.

By the mid-1990s, defense spending had been reduced to less than 3 percent of gross domestic product (GDP—see Glossary), and less than 10 percent of total government spending (see table 8; table 24, Appendix). Military salaries consumed more than half of defense spending, in part the result of the military reorganization. Spending on armaments and equipment had declined, as a portion of defense spending, from 44 percent in the 1980s to 28 percent in 1994, according to newly appointed SANDF chief General George Meiring. Meiring and other defense officials in 1995 expressed concern about military preparedness, noting the reduced production and acquisition of armored vehicles, the decline in antiaircraft capability, the reduction of civil service positions from 144,000 to about 100,000, the closure of military bases, and the reduction in military training courses. Deputy Minister of Defence Ronnie Kasrils said in 1995 that the government's planned cuts in defense spending could also result in the loss of as many as 90,000 jobs in defense-related industries.

The budget for military intelligence in 1994 was R163 million, and of this, R37 million was allocated for clandestine military intelligence gathering, according to a senior military intelligence officer reporting to the Joint Committee on Defence in October 1994. Spending on clandestine military intelligence was about 1 percent of the total military budget, according to the 1994 report.

Internal Security

Police

Early Development

The South African Police Service (SAPS) traces its origin to the Dutch Watch, a paramilitary organization formed by settlers in the Cape in 1655, initially to protect (white) civilians against attack and later to maintain law and order. In 1795 British officials assumed control over the Dutch Watch, and in 1825 they organized the Cape Constabulary, which became the Cape Town Police Force in 1840. The Durban Police Force, established in 1846, became the Natal Mounted Police in 1861, and gradually assumed increasing paramilitary functions as South Africa endured the last in a series of frontier wars that had continued for more than a century.

In 1913 a number of police forces consolidated into the Mounted Riflemen's Association, and some members of this association established a separate organization, which they

Officer of the South African
Police Service
Courtesy Embassy of South
Africa, Washington

called the South African Police (SAP). Four years later, the
Mounted Riflemen's Association relinquished its civilian
responsibilities to the SAP as most of the riflemen left to serve
in World War I. The SAP and the military maintained their
close relationship even after the SAP assumed permanent
responsibility for domestic law and order in 1926. Police officials often called on the army for support in emergencies. In
World War II, one SAP brigade served with the Second Infantry
Division of the South African Army in North Africa.

When the National Party (NP) edged out its more liberal
opponents in nationwide elections in 1948, the new government enacted legislation strengthening the relationship
between the police and the military. The police were heavily
armed after that, especially when facing unruly or hostile
crowds. The Police Act (No. 7) of 1958 broadened the mission
of the SAP beyond conventional police functions, such as maintaining law and order and investigating and preventing crime,
and gave the police extraordinary powers to quell unrest and
to conduct counterinsurgency activities. The Police Amendment Act (No. 70) of 1965 empowered the police to search
without warrant any person, receptacle, vehicle, aircraft, or
premise within two kilometers of any national border, and to
seize anything found during such a search. This search-and-

seize zone was extended to within ten kilometers of any border in 1979, and to the entire country in 1983.

The Police Reserve, established in 1973, enabled the government to recall former police personnel for active duty for thirty to ninety days each year, and for additional service in times of emergency. Another reserve (volunteer) force was established in 1981, consisting of unpaid civilians willing to perform limited police duties. A youth wing of this reserve force reported that it had inducted almost 3,000 students and young people to assist the police during the late 1980s.

The police increased the use of part-time, specialized personnel, such as the special constables (*kitskonstabels*), to help quell the growing violence in the 1980s. In 1987, for example, the police recruited almost 9,000 *kitskonstabels* and gave them an intensive six-week training course. These "instant" police assistants were then armed and assigned to areas of unrest, which were often the most turbulent townships. Even with training courses extended to three months, the *kitskonstabels'* often brutal and inept performance contributed to the growing hostility between the police and the public by the late 1980s.

Although the mission of the SAP grew well beyond conventional policing responsibilities during the 1970s, the size of the police force declined relative to population. In 1981 the police force of roughly 48,991 represented a ratio of less than 1.5 police per 1,000 people, down from 1.67 per 1,000 people in the 1960s. Alarmed by the increased political violence and crime in the mid-1980s and by the lack of adequate police support, officials then increased the size of the police force to 93,600—a ratio of 2.7 per 1,000 people—by 1991.

The police are authorized to act on behalf of other government officials when called upon. For example, in rural areas and small towns, where there may be no public prosecutor available, police personnel can institute criminal proceedings. The police can legally serve as wardens, court clerks, and messengers, as well as immigration, health, and revenue officials. In some circumstances, the police are also authorized to serve as vehicle inspectors, postal agents, and local court personnel.

The Police in the 1990s

After President de Klerk lifted the ban on black political organizations and released leading dissidents from prison in 1990, he met with the police and ordered them help end apartheid, to demonstrate greater political tolerance, and to improve their standing in black communities. The police accepted these orders, but did so much more slowly and reluctantly than the military. White police personnel were, in general, ambivalent about the changes taking place and divided over strategies for implementing them. For decades the police force had been organized around the authoritarian ideal of maintaining apartheid. With wide-ranging powers, the police had operated without strong institutional checks and balances and without serious external scrutiny. For many, the government's new policies represented an abrupt reversal in the orientation of the police.

Through the early 1990s, police units were sometimes integrated, but most police recruits had been trained in single-race classes, sometimes in institutions designated for one racial group. For example, most black police personnel had trained at Hammanskraal, near Pretoria; most whites, in Pretoria; most coloureds, at Lavis Bay, near Cape Town; and Asians at Wentworth, near Durban. As the apartheid era ended, these programs were restructured to emphasize racial tolerance and respect for basic human rights. The police also increased recruitment among black youth and hired international police training experts to advise them on ways to improve race relations in the service.

The basic police training regimen includes courses in criminal investigation procedures, self-defense, weapons handling, drills, inspections, public relations, and law. Specialized courses include crowd and riot control, detective skills, horsemanship and veterinary training, and advanced-level management skills. Since 1990, South Africa also has provided training for police from Lesotho, Swaziland, Malawi, and Zaire.

Police officers on duty generally carry a pistol or revolver and a truncheon. To quell disturbances, police use a variety of arms, including 37-millimeter stopper guns, which can shoot tear gas, rubber bullets, or signal colors; twelve-gauge Browning semiautomatic and Beretta pump shotguns; and R–1 semiautomatic rifles. Through the early 1990s, the police were also equipped with smoke and tear-gas dispensing vehicles, tank trucks with water cannons, vehicles that dispensed barbed wire or razor wire to cordon off areas rapidly, and a small number of helicopters capable of dropping "water bombs" on crowds of demonstrators. Riot-control forces deployed in specially designed buses or Casspir armored personal carriers.

The climate of escalating violence in the early 1990s often posed even greater challenges to the police than they had faced in the 1980s, as violence shifted from antigovernment activity to a mosaic of political rivalries and factional clashes. At the same time, many South Africans feared that the police were causing some of the criminal and political violence, and they demanded immediate changes in the police force to mark the end of apartheid-era injustices.

To meet the new challenges, the 91,000 active police personnel in 1991, including administrative and support personnel, were increased to more than 110,000 by 1993 and 140,000 by 1995. Throughout this time, police reserves numbered at least 37,000. In 1996 the combined active and reserve police represented a police-to-population ratio of almost 4.0 per 1,000.

As part of the overall reorganization of the police, the government merged the formerly dreaded Criminal Investigation Department (CID) and the police security branch to form a Crime Combatting and Investigation (CCI) Division. The new CCI, with responsibility for reversing the rising crime rate, combined the intelligence and operational resources of the security police with the anticrime capabilities of the CID.

Minister of Law and Order Hernus Kriel in 1991 also appointed an ombudsman to investigate allegations of police misconduct. He increased the recruitment of black police personnel, formed a civilian riot-control unit that was separate from the SAP but worked with it, developed a code of police conduct agreed upon by a number of political parties and communities, and substantially increased police training facilities. In 1992 Kriel began restructuring the SAP into a three-tiered force consisting of a national police, primarily responsible for internal security and for serious crime; autonomous regional forces, responsible for crime prevention and for matters of general law and order; and municipal police, responsible for local law enforcement and for minor criminal matters. He also established police/community forums in almost every police station.

By the time the April 1994 elections were held, the SAP had undergone a significant transformation, in keeping with the nation's sweeping political reforms. It was a more representative force, with greater dedication to protecting citizens' rights. The SAP was renamed the South African Police Service (SAPS), and the Ministry of Law and Order was renamed the Ministry of Safety and Security, in keeping with these symbolic reforms. The new minister of safety and security, Sydney Mufamadi, obtained police training assistance from Zimbabwe, Britain, and Canada, and proclaimed that racial tolerance and human rights would be central to police training programs in the future. By the end of 1995, the SAPS had incorporated the ten police agencies from the former homelands and had reorganized at both the national level and at the level of South Africa's nine new provinces.

The SAPS headquarters in Pretoria is organized into six divisions. These are the Crime Combatting and Investigation Division, the Visible Policing Division, the Internal Stability Division, the Community Relations Division, the Supporting Services Division, and the Human Resource Management Division.

The Crime Combatting and Investigation Division holds overall responsibility for coordinating information about crime and investigative procedures. It administers the SAPS Criminal Record Center, the SAPS Commercial Crime Unit, the SAPS Diamond and Gold Branch, the South African Narcotics Bureau, the Stock Theft Unit, the Inspectorate for Explosives, murder and robbery units located in each major city, and vehicle theft units throughout the country. In addition, the division manages the National Bureau of Missing Persons, which was established in late 1994.

The Visible Policing Division manages highly public police operations, such as guarding senior government officials and dignitaries. Most government residences are guarded by members of the division's Special Guard Unit. The division's all-volunteer Special Task Force handles hostage situations and other high-risk activities. The Internal Stability Division is responsible for preventing and quelling internal unrest, and for assisting other divisions in combatting crime. The Community Relations Division consults with all police divisions concerning accountability and respect for human rights. The Supporting Services Division manages financial, legal, and administrative aspects of the SAPS. The Human Resource Management Division helps to hire, to train, and to maintain a competent work force for the SAPS.

Three police unions are active in bargaining on behalf of police personnel and in protecting the interests of the work force, as of 1996. These are the Police and Prisons Civil Rights Union (Popcru), which has about 15,000 members; the South African Police Union (SAPU), which has about 35,000 members; and the Public Service Association (PSA), which has about 4,000 members.

Crime and Violence

Patterns of crime and violence in South Africa have often reflected political developments, especially since the 1950s. Crime surged to alarming proportions after a new constitution was implemented in 1984, granting limited parliamentary representation to coloureds and to Asians, but not to blacks. The number of reported murders in South Africa rose to 10,000 in 1989 and to 11,000 in 1990. The incidence of assault, rape, and armed robbery showed similar increases. Police estimated that 22,000 people died in crime-related violence in the fifteen months ending in February 1991. By 1992 South Africa had one of the world's highest crime rates, on a per capita basis.

Waves of serious violence swept through many townships around Johannesburg and in Natal Province, where the rivalry between the Inkatha Freedom Party (IFP) and the African National Congress (ANC) resulted in several hundred—some estimated more than 1,000—deaths each year in the late 1980s and the early 1990s. Officials estimated that 12,000 citizens (and 2,000 SADF troops) were involved in ANC-IFP clashes in the early 1990s.

White right-wing terrorists added to the crime rate as they were increasingly marginalized from the political process. Groups such as the White Liberation Army, the White Republican Army, the Boer Republican Army, the White Wolves, and the Order of the Boer Nation claimed responsibility for more than thirty-five bombings. Some of these groups formed an alliance known as the White People's Front in 1992 and threatened further violence as the political transition continued.

Community Response

Dealing with rising levels of crime and violence became a major public preoccupation in the 1990s and resulted in a variety of ad hoc security arrangements and alliances. For example, many organizations and a few individuals hired private security guards for protection. Civilians volunteered to monitor street crime in several turbulent townships. The ANC, after initially opposing these groups as "vigilantes," formed its own Self-Defense Units to help protect ANC supporters in the townships. Their political rivals in IFP strongholds responded by forming Zulu Self-Protection Units, especially in and around workers' hostels.

During the apartheid era, black South Africans had been legally barred from owning guns, but many whites considered gun ownership a normal defensive measure and a cherished right. Gun owners were legally required to register their weapons with the police, and a record 123,000 firearms were registered in 1990. By 1992 more than 2.5 million firearms had been registered nationwide. Police officials estimated that one-half of all white families owned at least one firearm, and at least 100,000 white households owned more than five registered weapons. Many more people were arming themselves illegally, according to police estimates.

Weapons thefts were extremely common. More than 7,700 firearms were reported stolen during 1990 alone. More than 5,000 guns were turned in to the police during a six-week amnesty in late 1990, and another 1,900, during a second amnesty in 1992. Although firearms and explosives were the cause of more than one-half of the deaths in the early 1990s, spears, knives, and axes—so-called Zulu traditional weapons, which were legal—were responsible for about 20 percent of violent deaths.

Government Response

Under strong pressure to end the township violence of the early 1990s, the police undertook numerous security sweeps through townships and squatter camps. During one of the largest of these, Operation Iron Fist, in late 1990, some 1,500 SAP and several hundred SADF troops swept through workers' hostels around Johannesburg and recovered several thousand illegal weapons. More than 30,000 SAP and SADF personnel conducted routine crime sweeps after that, and they made 337 arrests in one operation alone in 1991. By 1993 more than 10,000 people had been arrested, and large quantities of illegal drugs and weapons had been confiscated.

President de Klerk's credibility was severely damaged in July 1991, when official documents leaked to the public confirmed long-standing rumors of police support for the Zulu-dominated IFP in its rivalry with the ANC. A burst of publicity, dubbed "Inkathagate" by the press, threatened to derail constitutional negotiations after evidence linked senior government and police officials with funds secretly channeled to the IFP's labor activities and membership drives, which many believed had fueled the violence. Public anger rose, both because of the politicization of the police and because the government then appeared incapable of halting the violence as the scandal intensified.

The September 1991 National Peace Accord marked a desperate effort by both the government and the ANC to end the killing and to ease anxiety about official involvement in it. The accord, signed by more than two dozen leaders of government and political organizations, established committees and channels of communication at national, regional, and community levels to try to avert bloodshed arising out of political disagreements. Under this accord, the government established the Commission of Inquiry Regarding the Prevention of Public Violence and Intimidation, chaired by a respected jurist, Richard Goldstone, to investigate the causes of the violence. The Goldstone Commission's interim report in early 1992 attributed most of the killing to the political battle between supporters of the ANC and the IFP, but it also confirmed suspicions that elements of the security forces, especially the police, had contributed to the unrest.

Then ANC leader Mandela, who was vocal in his criticism of the government for its failure to quell the unrest of the early 1990s, insisted that international attention be given to the issue of state-sponsored violence. In June 1992, Mandela, Foreign Minister Roelof "Pik" Botha, and IFP leader Mangosuthu (Gatsha) Buthelezi addressed the United Nations concerning this issue. After that, other countries increased their involvement in South Africa's political reform. In August of that year, former United States Secretary of State Cyrus Vance went to South Africa as United Nations special envoy. Acting on his suggestion, the United Nations sent political monitors to South Africa to demonstrate international support for the institutions that had arisen out of the National Peace Accord. At the same time, South Africa's political leaders implemented another of Vance's recommendations—to speed up the pace of progress toward nationwide elections.

Then, in late 1992, the Goldstone Commission concluded that secret cells within the police force had, with the cooperation of military intelligence officials, "waged a war" on the ANC, primarily because of its commitment to armed struggle to end apartheid and its association with the South African Communist Party (SACP). The commission's report also implied that elements in the security forces were continuing to provoke or commit violent acts. In response to rising pressures, President de Klerk persuaded twenty-three senior military officers to retire, including the heads of the SADF and military intelligence.

Despite significant progress, there were at least 4,300 politically motivated deaths in 1993, according to the South African Institute of Race Relations, and each new round of violence brought a new sense of urgency to the task of preparing for elections. More than 2,000 murders were in Zulu-inhabited areas of KwaZulu and Natal Province. The Goldstone Commission later concluded that some of the weapons used in the violence against ANC supporters had been supplied by the police.

The police arrested a few whites who advocated violence to block the elections, including Afrikaner Resistance Movement (Afrikaner Weerstandsbeweging—AWB) leader Eugene Terreblanche. In most cases, the accused were fined for their activities or were granted immunity in return for information about their organizations and activities. White extremists were arrested for the April 1993 murder of a popular SACP leader, Chris Hani, and two were sentenced to death for that crime. (The death penalty was abolished before their sentences were carried out.)

Prison System

In the mid-1990s, South Africa's Department of Correctional Services operates 234 prisons. Of these, 226 are primarily or solely for male prisoners, and 119 of these have separate women's sections. The department also operates twenty prison farms.

There were roughly 114,000 prisoners nationwide—nearly 92,000 serving prison sentences and about 22,000 not yet sentenced—as of 1995. Some 70 percent of prisoners were black, 25 percent were coloured, 4 percent were white, and less than 1 percent were Asian. This prison population constituted roughly 130 percent of prison capacity. More than 400,000 people were jailed at some time during 1995, most for periods ranging from a few days to several months. Nearly 26,000 people per day were on parole.

The Department of Correctional Services has roughly 22,500 employees, at least 4,500 fewer than its workload requires, according to official estimates. Severe staff shortages are sometimes ameliorated by employing some of the 1,500 members of the Prisons Service Reserve Force (mostly retired prison staff) and as many as 1,000 military reservists.

Four categories of prisoners are held: unsentenced prisoners, most of whom are detained pending a hearing or sentencing; short-term prisoners, who are serving terms of less than two years; long-term prisoners; and juvenile prisoners, who are under twenty-one years of age. Through 1994 women made up about 4 percent of the prison population, but late that year, the new government granted an amnesty to all female prisoners with children under the age of twelve, if they had been convicted of nonviolent crimes. In late 1994, 250 prisoners over the age of sixty also had their sentences remitted and were released from prison.

In 1995 the prison population included 1,278 children under the age of eighteen, half of them awaiting trial, according to the Department of Correctional Services. The number represented less than half the number of juveniles in prison in 1992. A small, but unknown, number of children under age fourteen were among the juveniles in prison, according to international human rights observers.

Literacy training and vocational courses are offered in some prisons. Parole supervision is generally strict, and parole violators are returned to prison, where they must serve out their original terms and sometimes additional periods of incarceration. Some jurisdictions instituted a system of correctional supervision as an alternative to prison sentences in the early 1990s, partly in response to prison overcrowding. Correctional supervision entails community service, victim compensation, house arrest, treatment sessions, a prohibition of alcohol consumption, or a combination of these programs. The department also established correctional boards in 1992 to provide a communication link between its officials and residents of local communities. In addition, the department established a National Advisory Board on Correctional Services to advise prison authorities on legal and policy concerns. The National Advisory Board is chaired by a Supreme Court judge, and its members include specialists from the court system and the police, as well as social welfare authorities, and business and community representatives.

Penal Code

South Africa's courts are empowered to impose punishments of death (through early 1995), imprisonment, periodic impris-

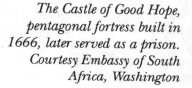
*The Castle of Good Hope,
pentagonal fortress built in
1666, later served as a prison.
Courtesy Embassy of South
Africa, Washington*

onment for a total of between 100 and 2,000 hours over a
period of weeks or months, being declared a "habitual criminal," commitment to an institution other than prison, fines,
and whipping. Those convicted of lesser crimes are often given
a choice of punishment—for example, a fine or imprisonment.
During the apartheid era, the courts imposed prison terms of
several days to several weeks for pass law violations, and ten to
twenty years for membership in the ANC or the SACP, which
were banned organizations until 1990. Other typical prison
sentences are terms of two to ten years for robbery; up to
twenty years for assault or rape; ten to fifteen years for possessing an illegal firearm; ten to twenty years for attempted murder; and twenty years to life in prison for murder.

Murder and treason were capital crimes through the 1980s,
although whites often received light sentences for crimes
against black people, and they were almost never sentenced to
death for murdering blacks. All executions were suspended in
early 1990, and although more than 240 people were sentenced to death between 1990 and early 1995, no one was executed during that time. Parliament abolished the death penalty
in early 1995.

Whipping is frequently used to punish juveniles for public
misbehavior, but may only be imposed on male offenders
under the age of thirty. The punishment may not exceed seven

strokes of a cane. Whipping is done in private, although the parents of a juvenile can be present. This punishment was imposed on more than 30,000 juveniles and young men each year in the early 1990s.

Human Rights and National Reconciliation

South Africa's record on human rights came under frequent attack during the apartheid era, and improving it became a high priority for achieving national reconciliation and international legitimacy in the 1990s. South Africa had more than 2,500 political prisoners in 1990, according to the UN Human Rights Commission. Responding to criticism on this sensitive subject during the early 1990s negotiations, then President de Klerk agreed to review all cases of crimes against state security, and as a result, the government released 933 political prisoners by April 1991. It rejected 364 appeals for release because of the nature of the crimes involved. In September 1992, based on special requests by ANC leader Nelson Mandela, and through the intervention of UN special representative, former United States Secretary of State Cyrus Vance, the government released an additional 400 political prisoners as a further step toward successful negotiations. Officials went ahead with election preparations even though the issue of political prisoners was not fully resolved, and the new government in mid-1994 released from prison several hundred people who had been convicted of nonviolent crimes. Among them were an unreported number whose offenses were considered political.

The ANC faced its own internal accusations of human rights violations during the early 1990s. Former detainees from ANC prison camps alleged that they had been held in harsh conditions in Angola, Kenya, Tanzania, Uganda, or Zambia. Human rights monitors confirmed that prisoners in these camps had sometimes been tortured and, in a few cases, had been executed. Moreover, they alleged that some of the camps continued to be in operation, even after the ANC had announced the suspension of its armed struggle against apartheid. Mandela promised to investigate and to end these practices, but would not agree to air the allegations in public.

The interim constitution's chapter on fundamental rights guarantees freedom of speech, the press, assembly, association, and religion, as well as the freedom to travel and to live where one chooses, and the protection of minority rights. The interim constitution repealed Section 29 of the Internal Security Act, which had allowed the government to detain individuals for indefinite periods without charging them with a crime. Subsequent legislation established an independent Human Rights Commission and Office of the Public Protector, both to be appointed by the parliament. The public protector is charged with investigating allegations of abuse or incompetence against members of the government, including the police.

Despite obvious improvements in human rights policies and practices in the mid-1990s, several forms of human rights abuse continued at unacceptable levels and appeared to involve high-level police officials. Thirty-one unexplained deaths occurred in police custody in 1994, according to the private South African Human Rights Committee. This number was eight fewer than in 1993, and fifty-six fewer than in 1990. Pathologists' reports confirmed instances of police abuse in some of the 1994 deaths, and a team of international human rights monitors and independent experts uncovered a pattern of torture of detainees by some police personnel in the Johannesburg area.

The Goldstone Commission's investigations had unearthed prima facie evidence implicating senior police officials in supplying weapons to the Zulu-based IFP in 1993 and 1994, and had noted that some of these weapons had surfaced at the scene of IFP attacks on political opponents. These conclusions had resulted in the retirement of several senior police officers; one police training unit commander was charged with murder and later sentenced to life in prison.

Soon after the new government was in office in 1994, it began investigating allegations of "hit squads" within the KwaZulu police (predominantly IFP supporters) and launched an investigation into ANC-instigated violence in KwaZulu-Natal. Despite some initial reluctance, the provincial government cooperated with the international human rights monitors and allowed them access to prisons and detainees.

Violence against women continued to occur with regularity through the mid-1990s. The Department of Justice issued chilling statistics in 1994: more than one-half of all women who were murdered had died at the hands of their male partners. About 43 percent of women questioned in one study said they had been the victim of marital rape or assault. The police received reports of more than 25,200 rapes between January 1 and October 31, 1994—a 17 percent increase over the same period in 1993—but estimated that most such incidents were not reported and only about 25 percent of reported rapes resulted in convictions. Numerous laws were passed, both before and after the April 1994 elections, aimed at protecting women against abuse, but these laws were often ignored or bypassed. The new government pledged stricter legislation and stronger efforts to establish fair treatment for women.

The new government's promises of an improved human rights record and of security forces that are accountable to the population helped to set the tone for democratic reforms in 1994 and 1995. But the security forces faced even greater challenges than the political leaders in trying to implement these reforms. Members of the police, in particular, had to abandon their apartheid-related agendas—enforcing or opposing the old order—while, at the same time, upholding the changing laws that apply to the entire population. They had to establish "instant legitimacy," as several South African scholars observed, in the midst of change.

Legislation in 1995 established a Truth and Reconciliation Commission to deal with grievances arising out of human rights violations of the apartheid era. The commission's goals are to establish the truth about such crimes, to identify victims and determine their fate, to recommend reparation for victims and survivors, and to recommend to the president amnesty or indemnity under limited circumstances. Any grant of amnesty initially applied only to politically motivated acts committed before October 8, 1990, and subsequent legislation extended the cut-off date to May 10, 1994.

President Mandela appointed Anglican Archbishop Desmond Tutu to chair the Truth and Reconciliation Commission and a respected jurist, Alex Boraine, as his deputy. The commission began hearing testimony in March 1996, and it scheduled hearings in each province to enable South Africans from all regions to testify or to apply for amnesty. By mid-1996 several hundred testimonies had been heard, most of them concerning brutality or other mistreatment by the former security forces.

With less than one-half of its hearings completed in mid-1996, the commission was generally viewed as a positive step toward national reconciliation. A few outspoken critics disagreed, however, and charged the commission with impeding justice. Among these were relatives of ANC activists who had been killed by the security forces; some survivors criticized the commission for even considering amnesty applications from those who might otherwise have been brought to justice in the courts. Some former members of the security forces, for their part, criticized the commission for its apparent willingness to accept allegations against them. A few others who had testified before the commission complained that they had received little or no compensation for their losses, although most requests for compensation had not yet been acted upon by mid-1996. Despite these complaints, it appeared likely that the hearings would contribute to a broader public understanding of the violence that had bolstered the implementation of apartheid.

*　　*　　*

South Africa has an extensive military history literature. Official accounts are available in numerous publications by Neil D. Orpen, such as *The History of the Transvaal Horse Artillery, 1904–1974; The Cape Town Rifles: The 'Duke,' 1856–1984; War in the Desert; East African and Abyssinian Campaigns*; and *Prince Alfred's Guard, 1856–1966*. Helmoed-Römer Heitman's *The South African War Machine, South African Arms and Armour,* and *War in Angola: The Final South African Phase* also cover important areas of military history. Different historical viewpoints are found in A. N. Porter's *The Origins of the South African War: Joseph Chamberlain and the Diplomacy of Imperialism, 1895–1899* and Carman Miller's *Painting the Map Red: Canada and the South African War, 1899–1902*. An interesting comparative perspective is found in James O. Gump's *The Dust Rose like Smoke: The Subjugation of the Zulu and the Sioux*. Jacklyn Cock's *Women and War in South Africa* presents a gender-related view of the subject.

The climate of domestic violence of the 1980s is analyzed in publications of the South African Institute of Race Relations, such as the annual *Race Relations Survey,* and in John Kane-Berman's *Political Violence in South Africa. Political Violence and the Struggle in South Africa,* edited by N. Chabani Manganyi and André du Toit; *Policing the Conflict in South Africa,* edited by Mary L. Mathews, Philip B. Heymann, and Anthony S. Mathews; and *Policing South Africa: The South African Police and the Transition from Apartheid,* by Gavin Cawthra, are also valuable.

South Africa's regional security policies since the early 1980s are discussed in numerous periodicals and monographs. *High Noon in Southern Africa: Making Peace in a Rough Neighborhood* by

Chester A. Crocker, and *Toward Peace and Security in Southern Africa*, edited by Harvey Glickman, discuss Western points of view on that era. *The New Is Not Yet Born: Conflict Resolution in Southern Africa* by Thomas Ohlson and Stephen John Stedman with Robert Davies reviews regional clashes and peacemaking efforts in recent decades.

The changing security situation in the mid-1990s is outlined in the *Stockholm International Peace Research Institute (SIPRI) Yearbook, 1995*; "Prospects for Security and Stability in the New South Africa" by Carole Birch in *Brassey's Defence Yearbook*; and "Current Trends in South Africa's Security Establishment" by Annette Seegers in *Armed Forces and Society*. Jane's Information Group's special report of July 1994, *Whither South Africa's Warriors?*, is a valuable contribution. The South African National Defence Force periodical, *Salut*, conveys brief insights into military concerns in the mid-1990s. (For further information and complete citations, see Bibliography.)

Appendix

Table 1. Metric Conversion Coefficients and Factors

When you know	Multiply by	To find
Millimeters........................	0.04	inches
Centimeters.......................	0.39	inches
Meters............................	3.3	feet
Kilometers........................	0.62	miles
Hectares..........................	2.47	acres
Square kilometers..................	0.39	square miles
Cubic meters......................	35.3	cubic feet
Liters	0.26	gallons
Kilograms.........................	2.2	pounds
Metric tons.......................	0.98	long tons
....	1.1	short tons
....	2,204	pounds
Degrees Celsius (Centigrade).........	1.8 and add 32	degrees Fahrenheit

Table 2. Population by Province, 1994

Province	Population[1]	Density[2]
Eastern Cape	6,665,400	38.2
Free State.........................	2,804,600	21.5
Gauteng	6,847,000	374.7
KwaZulu-Natal	8,549,000	94.5
Mpumalanga	2,838,500	38.4
Northern Cape	763,900	2.1
Northern Province	5,120,600	43.8
North-West Province.................	3,506,800	28.8
Western Cape......................	3,620,200	28.8

[1] Estimated.
[2] Persons per square kilometer.

Source: Based on information from South Africa, South African Communication Service, *South Africa Yearbook, 1995*, Pretoria, 1996, 5–21.

Table 3. *Number of Pupils and Teachers by Province, 1995*

Province	Pupils		Teachers
	Primary (six years)	Secondary (six years)	
Eastern Cape..............	1,583,261	741,962	58,254
Free State.................	414,826	283,573	23,521
Gauteng..................	787,599	621,036	46,335
KwaZulu-Natal.............	1,628,679	948,588	63,283
Mpumalanga	545,312	368,363	23,521
Northern Cape	110,223	62,333	7,222
Northern Province	1,050,594	866,428	52,061
North-West Province........	545,841	369,588	30,740
Western Cape	504,967	331,602	31,716
TOTAL	7,171,302	4,593,473	336,653

Source: Based on information from Jacob P. Strauss, Hendrik van der Linde, et al., *Education and Manpower Development, 1995*, Bloemfontein, 1996, 6–10.

Table 4. Major Institutions of Higher Learning and Research, 1995

Institution	Enrollment	Location	Date Founded
Universities			
Medical University of South Africa	3,497	Pretoria	n.a.[1]
Potchefstroom University for Christian Higher Education	10,408	Potchefstroom	1869
Rand Afrikaans University	20,145	Auckland Park	1966
Rhodes University.	4,594	Grahamstown	1904
University of Cape Town	14,672	Cape Town	1829
University of Durban-Westville.	10,626	Durban	1961
University of Fort Hare	5,200	Alice	1916
University of Natal	14,093	Durban/Pietermaritzburg	1910
University of North-West	4,918	Mmabatho	1979
University of Port Elizabeth	5,600	Port Elizabeth	1964
University of Pretoria	24,435	Pretoria	1908
University of South Africa (correspondence)	130,350	Pretoria	1873
University of Stellenbosch	14,608	Stellenbosch	1918
University of the North	19,012	Turfloop	1959
. . . .		Witzieshoek	
. . . .		Giyani	
. . . .		Phuthaditjhaba	
University of the Orange Free State	9,446	Bloemfontein	1855
University of the Western Cape	14,650	Bellville	1960
University of the Witwatersrand	17,428	Johannesburg	1922
University of Transkei	7,325	Eastern Cape	1976
University of Venda.	7,166	Sibasa	n.a.
University of Zululand	7,997	KwaDlangezwa	1960
Vista University (correspondence)	34,014	Pretoria	1982
Technikons[2]			
Border Technikon	1,366	East London	n.a.
Cape Technikon	9,360	Cape Town	1979
Mangosuthu Technikon.	4,648	Umlazi	1978
M.L. Sultan Technikon	6,359	Durban	1946
Peninsula Technikon	6,773	Bellville	1967
Technikon Natal.	7,551	Durban	1907
Technikon Northern Transvaal.	6,764	Pretoria	1979
Technikon Orange Free State	5,895	Bloemfontein	1981
Technikon Port Elizabeth	7,864	Port Elizabeth	1925
Technikon Pretoria	16,509	Pretoria	1906

Table 4. (Continued) Major Institutions of Higher Learning and Research, 1995

Institution	Enrollment	Location	Date Founded
Technikon SA......................	83,741	Florida	1980
Technikon Setlogalo	1,958	Rosslyn	n.a.
Technikon Witwatersrand...........	10,976	Doornfontein	1925
Transkei Technikon.................	2,181	Butterworth	n.a.
Vaal Triangle Technikon.............	7,856	Vanderbijlpark	1966
Research organizations			
Agricultural Research Council	—[3]	Pretoria	1992
Atomic Energy Corporation of South Africa....................	—	Pretoria	1982
Council for Geoscience..............	—	Pretoria	1912
Council for Scientific and Industrial Research	—	Pretoria	1945
Hartebeesthoek Radio Astronomy Observatory....................	—	Krugersdorp	1961
Human Sciences Research Council	—	Pretoria	1969
Institute for the Study of Man in Africa.......................	—	Johannesburg	1960
MINTEK[4]	—	Randburg	1934
Municipal Botanic Gardens...........	—	Durban	1849
National Zoological Gardens of South Africa....................	—	Pretoria	1899
South African Institute for Medical Research	—	Johannesburg	1912
Learned societies			
Africa Institute of South Africa........	—	Pretoria	1960
Classical Association of South Africa.........................	—	Bloemfontein	1956
Economic Society of South Africa	—	Pretoria	1925
Foundation for Education, Science and Technology.................	—	Pretoria	1950
Genealogical Society of South Africa ...	—	Kelvin	1963
Heraldry Society of Southern Africa ...	—	Cape Town	1953
Royal Society of South Africa	—	Cape Town	1877
South Africa Foundation.............	—	Johannesburg	1959
South Africa Institute of International Affairs.........................	—	Johannesburg	1934
South African Academy of Science and Arts......................	—	Pretoria	1909
South African Archaeological Society......................	—	Vlaeberg	1945
South African Association of the Arts...........................	—	Pretoria	1945
South African Geographical Society....	—	Witwatersrand	1917
South African Institute for Librarianship and Information Science	—	Pretoria	1930

Table 4. (Continued) Major Institutions of Higher Learning and Research, 1995

Institution	Enrollment	Location	Date Founded
South African Institute of Race Relations...............	—	Johannesburg	1929
South African Museums Association................	—	Sunnyside	1936
Van Riebeeck Society.............	—	Cape Town	1918

[1] n.a.—not available.
[2] Postsecondary technical training.
[3] —not applicable.
[4] Mineral science and mining technology.

Source: Based on information from *The World of Learning, 1995*, London, 1995, 1348–75; and South Africa, Department of Education, *Annual Report, June 1994–December 1995*, Pretoria, 1996, Appendix.

Table 5. Real Gross Domestic Product by Sector, Selected Years, 1948–93
(in millions of rands) [1]

Year	Primary Sector[2]	Secondary Sector[3]	Tertiary Sector[4]	Total[5]
1948.......	14,463	10,738	26,151	51,352
1953.......	17,197	15,007	30,966	63,169
1958.......	22,536	19,534	37,844	79,914
1963.......	30,094	26,042	45,412	101,548
1968.......	34,588	40,094	60,974	135,656
1973.......	33,410	58,125	78,418	169,953
1978.......	35,155	66,887	91,812	193,853
1983.......	33,205	77,164	110,029	220,399
1988.......	36,745	82,033	124,447	243,225
1993.......	36,451	76,895	128,655	242,001

[1] For value of the rand—see Glossary. Figures at factor cost and in constant 1990 prices.
[2] Includes agriculture, forestry, fishing, mining, and quarrying.
[3] Includes construction, electricity, gas, manufacturing, and water.
[4] Includes accommodations, business services, catering, communications, community services, finance, insurance, real estate, social and personal services, storage, transport, and wholesale and retail trade.
[5] Figures may not add to totals because of rounding.

Source: Based on information from South African Institute of Race Relations, *Race Relations Survey, 1994–95*, Johannesburg, 1995, 379–80.

Table 6. Key Economic Indicators, 1991–95
(in billions of United States dollars unless otherwise indicated)

	1991	1992	1993	1994	1995
Gross domestic product (GDP)[1]	310.1	341.0	383.1	432.8	485.9
Real GDP growth[2]	–1.0	–2.2	1.3	2.7	3.3
Consumer price inflation[2]	15.3	13.9	9.7	9.1	8.7
Gross domestic fixed investment[3]	50.1	47.5	45.9	50.1	55.2
Exports, f.o.b.[4]	23.3	23.6	24.1	25.1	27.9
Imports, c.i.f.[5]	18.9	19.8	20.0	23.4	29.4
Current account balance	2.2	1.4	1.8	–0.6	–3.1
Gross reserves[6]	3.0	3.0	2.7	3.1	4.4
External debt	25.6	27.2	25.5	27.9	30.8
Exchange rate[7]	2.76	2.85	3.26	3.55	3.64
Population[8]	38.0	38.6	39.5	40.4	41.2

[1] In billions of rands at current market prices; for value of the rand—see Glossary.
[2] In percentages.
[3] In billions of rands at constant 1990 prices.
[4] f.o.b.—free on board.
[5] c.i.f.—cost, insurance, and freight.
[6] Includes gold.
[7] In rands per United States dollar; annual average.
[8] In millions.

Source: Based on information from Economist Intelligence Unit, *Country Report: South Africa* [London], No. 1, 1996, 3, 5.

Table 7. Sources of Government Revenue, 1994, 1995, and 1996[1]
(in millions of rands)[2]

	1994	1995	1996[3]
Income taxes: individuals	37,786	44,763	49,755
Income taxes: companies	11,917	15,502	17,368
Value-added tax	25,425	28,975	32,750
Customs and excise duties	18,074	19,124	20,446
(Less payment to Southern African Customs Union)	–3,089	–3,250	–3,890
Other taxes and revenues	6,741	6,436	6,562
TOTAL	96,854	111,550	122,991

[1] For years ending March 31.
[2] For value of the rand—see Glossary.
[3] Estimated.

Source: Based on information from South Africa, South African Communication Service, *South Africa Yearbook, 1995*, Pretoria, 1996, 239.

Table 8. *Government Expenditures, 1995 and 1996*[1]

	1995		1996	
	Value[2]	Percentage	Value[2]	Percentage
Economic services				
Agriculture, forestry, and fishing...................	3,645	2.5	2,764	1.8
Fuel and energy..............	433	0.3	138	0.1
Manufacturing...............	802	0.5	621	0.4
Mining......................	223	0.2	208	0.1
Regional development.........	817	0.6	937	0.6
Transportation and communication................	6,701	4.5	6,357	4.1
Water projects...............	1,208	0.8	1,309	0.8
Export promotion and tourism...................	3,947	2.6	3,321	2.2
Total economic services	17,776	12.0	15,655	10.2
General government services				
Foreign affairs...............	1,320	0.9	1,321	0.9
General research	506	0.3	510	0.3
Administration and other	11,321	7.6	8,816	5.7
Total general government services	13,147	8.9	10,647	6.9
Security services				
Defense.....................	12,908	8.7	11,025	7.2
Judiciary....................	1,601	1.1	1,705	1.1
Police.......................	10,168	6.9	11,614	7.5
Prisons......................	2,584	1.7	2,862	1.9
Total security services	27,261	18.4	27,206	17.6
Social services				
Education	31,428	21.2	32,616	21.2
Health	15,565	10.5	16,885	11.0
Housing.....................	1,648	1.1	4,226	2.7
Community development[3]......	2,192	1.5	785	0.5
Recreation and culture	668	0.5	833	0.5
Social security and welfare......	13,672	9.2	16,713	10.8
Total social services	65,173	44.0	72,058	46.7
Interest.......................	24,863	16.8	28,604	18.6
Government enterprises..........	9	0.0	7	0.0
TOTAL......................	148,229	100.0	154,177	100.0

[1] For years ending March 31. Figures may not add to totals because of rounding.
[2] In millions of rands; for value of the rand—see Glossary.
[3] Includes sewage and sanitation services.

Source: Based on information from South Africa, South African Communication Service, *South Africa Yearbook, 1995*, Pretoria, 1996, 238.

Table 9. Major Imports, 1992, 1993, and 1994
(in millions of rands) [1]

Commodity	1992	1993	1994[2]
Machinery and appliances....................	15,010	17,131	24,805
Vehicles and transportation equipment........	6,619	8,916	11,284
Chemicals..............................	5,789	6,599	8,292
Base metals and articles.....................	2,502	2,606	3,399
Professional and scientific equipment..........	2,243	2,716	3,299
Textiles.................................	2,437	2,654	3,295
Plastics and rubber articles..................	2,250	2,639	3,256
Paper products..........................	1,463	1,740	2,183
Precious and semiprecious stones and precious metals........................	351	1,467	1,847
Vegetable products........................	2,570	1,928	1,365

[1] For value of the rand—see Glossary.
[2] Preliminary figures.

Source: Based on information from South Africa, South African Communication Service, *South Africa Yearbook, 1995*, Pretoria, 1996, 224; and *Africa South of the Sahara, 1997*, London, 1996, 908.

Table 10. Major Exports, 1992, 1993, and 1994
(in millions of rands) [1]

Commodity	1992	1993	1994[2]
Base metals and articles.....................	9,484	9,905	11,853
Precious stones and precious metals...........	7,160	10,138	10,213
Mineral products.........................	7,083	8,444	7,712
Chemicals and plastics.....................	3,221	3,378	4,757
Vegetable products........................	2,291	2,437	4,197
Prepared foodstuffs and tobacco..............	1,857	1,813	2,826
Machinery and appliances...................	2,151	2,811	2,567
Vehicles and transportation equipment........	2,329	2,701	2,265
Paper and paper products..................	1,896	1,937	2,042
Textiles.................................	1,809	1,812	1,923

[1] For value of the rand—see Glossary.
[2] Preliminary figures.

Source: Based on information from South Africa, South African Communication Service, *South Africa Yearbook, 1995*, Pretoria, 1996, 223; and *Africa South of the Sahara, 1997*, London, 1996, 908.

Table 11. Distribution of Employment in the Formal Economy, 1994
(in percentages)

Economic Activity	Regular Employment[1]	Casual Employment
Agriculture, forestry, and fishing	12.2	8.3
Armed forces	2.3	0.2
Construction	5.6	12.6
Domestic services	8.5	26.6
Education	7.8	2.8
Electricity and water services	1.9	1.6
Finance	4.2	1.6
Legal services	2.0	0.3
Manufacturing	16.6	9.8
Medical services	5.6	1.6
Mining	7.3	0.7
Hotels and restaurants	2.6	6.4
Transportation and communications	6.7	4.2
Wholesale and retail trade	10.9	16.7
Other	5.8	6.6
TOTAL	100.0	100.0

[1] Total labor force estimated at 12.5 million, excluding agriculture, forestry, and fishing.

Source: Based on information from South African Institute of Race Relations, *Race Relations Survey, 1994–95,* Johannesburg, 1995, 473.

Table 12. *Selected Mining Production, 1992, 1993, and 1994*
(in thousands of tons unless otherwise indicated)

Mineral	1992	1993	1994
Iron ore	28,226	28,912	32,321
Diamonds[1]	10,177	10,324	10,812
Manganese ore	2,462	2,504	2,851
Chrome ore	3,000	2,563	3,590
Gold[2]	611	616	580
Copper	167	157	165.2
Asbestos	124	97	92.1
Platinum[2]	69	90	164.8
Lead	75.4	100.2	95.8
Silver[2]	172	195	n.a.[3]
Uranium oxide[2]	2,222	2,008	1,913
Coal	174,072	182,262	190,672

[1] In thousands of carats.
[2] In tons.
[3] n.a.—not available.

Source: Based on information from South Africa, South African Communication Service, *South Africa Yearbook, 1994*, Pretoria, 1995, 59; and South Africa, South African Communication Service, *South Africa Yearbook, 1995*, Pretoria, 1996, 122, 125.

Table 13. *Selected Agricultural Production, 1992, 1993, and 1994*
(in thousands of tons)

Commodity	1992	1993	1994[1]
Barley	265	230	275
Corn	3,125	9,668	12,143
Grapes	1,450	1,249	1,284
Potatoes	1,215	1,127	1,306
Sorghum	98	478	520
Sugarcane	12,955	11,244	15,683
Wheat	1,269	1,984	1,782
Wool	124	111	106

[1] Initial estimates.

Source: Based on information from South Africa, South African Communication Service, *South Africa Yearbook, 1995*, Pretoria, 1996, 108; and *Africa South of the Sahara, 1997*, London, 1996, 905.

Table 14. Selected Industrial Production, 1992–95

Product	1992	1993	1994	1995
Automobiles, assembled	206,600	227,700	227,000	228,400
Cement[1]	5,850	6,135	7,065	7,437
Cigarettes[2]	35,563	34,499	n.a.[3]	n.a.
Electrical energy[4]	154,083	159,505	165,985	171,301
Petroleum products[5]				
Gasoline	7,234	8,113	8,720	8,947
Kerosene	703	916	980	935
Distillates.	5,893	5,915	5,736	6,551
Rubber tires[6]	7,333	7,676	8,111	8,947
Steel, crude[7]	9,061	8,610	8,300	8,000
Sugar, refined[7].	1,316	1,098	1,246	n.a.
Wheat flour[7]	1,833	1,867	1,872	n.a.
Wine[8]	3,779	3,647	2,150	n.a.

[1] In millions of tons.
[2] In millions of cigarettes.
[3] n.a.—not available.
[4] In millions of kilowatt-hours.
[5] In millions of liters.
[6] In thousands.
[7] In thousands of tons.
[8] In thousands of hectoliters.

Source: Based on information from South Africa, South African Communication Service, *South Africa Yearbook, 1995*, Pretoria, 1996, 124; and *Africa South of the Sahara, 1997*, London, 1996, 906.

Table 15. Foreign Tourist Arrivals, 1991–95

Region of Origin	1991	1992	1993	1994	1995
Africa	1,193,700	2,328,000	2,698,100	3,125,958	3,452,164
Europe	367,600	395,300	429,900	463,477	721,878
North America and					
South America . .	67,100	75,000	91,700	115,621	160,473
Asia	59,300	67,500	87,500	113,724	158,463
Oceania	20,000	24,800	30,100	36,658	61,085
Other	2,300	2,200	32,500	41,109	130,001
TOTAL.	1,710,000	2,892,800	3,369,800	3,896,547	4,684,064

Source: Based on information from *Africa South of the Sahara, 1996*, London, 1995, 882.

Table 16. Political Party Representation in National Government, 1995

Political Party	Executive			Legislature	
	President	Deputy Presidents	Cabinet[1]	National Assembly	Senate
African National Congress . .	1	1	18	252	60
National Party	—	1	6	82	17
Inkatha Freedom Party.	—	—	3	43	5
Freedom Front	—	—	—	9	5
Democratic Party	—	—	—	7	3
Pan-Africanist Congress	—	—	—	5	—
African Christian Democratic Party	—	—	—	2	—

[1] Plus one nonpartisan portfolio.

Table 17. Political Party Representation in Provincial Government: Executive Officials, 1995

Province	Premier	Executive Council			
		ANC[1]	NP[2]	IFP[3]	FF[4]
Eastern Cape	ANC	9	1	—	—
Free State	ANC	9	1	—	—
Gauteng	ANC	7	3	—	—
KwaZulu-Natal	IFP	3	1	6	—
Mpumalanga	ANC	9	1	—	—
Northern Cape	ANC	5	4	—	1
Northern Province	ANC	9	—	—	1
North-West Province	ANC	9	1	—	—
Western Cape	NP	4	6	—	—

[1] African National Congress.
[2] National Party.
[3] Inkatha Freedom Party.
[4] Freedom Front.

Table 18. Political Party Representation in Provincial Government: Legislative Assemblies, 1995

Province	Political Party								Total
	ANC[1]	NP[2]	IFP[3]	FF[4]	DP[5]	PAC[6]	ACDP[7]	Min[8]	
Eastern Cape...............	48	6	—	1	—	1	—	—	56
Free State	24	4	—	2	—	—	—	—	30
Gauteng...............	50	21	3	5	5	1	1	—	86
KwaZulu-Natal...............	26	9	41	—	2	1	1	1	81
Mpumalanga...............	25	3	—	2	—	—	—	—	30
Northern Cape...............	15	12	—	2	1	—	—	—	30
Northern Province...............	38	1	—	1	—	—	—	—	40
North-West	26	3	—	1	—	—	—	—	30
Western Cape...............	14	23	—	1	3	—	1	—	42

[1] African National Congress.
[2] National Party.
[3] Inkatha Freedom Party.
[4] Freedom Front.
[5] Democratic Party.
[6] Pan-Africanist Congress.
[7] African Christian Democratic Party.
[8] Minority Front.

Table 19. Major Newspapers, 1995

Newspaper	Place of Publication	Frequency	Language	Circulation
The Argus	Cape Town	Daily	English	82,774
Beeld (Image)	Johannesburg	Daily	Afrikaans	111,958
Die Burger (The Citizen)	Cape Town	Daily	Afrikaans	94,193
Business Day	Johannesburg	Daily	English	37,085
The Cape Times	Cape Town	Daily	English	48,685
The Citizen	Johannesburg	Daily	English	136,848
City Press	Johannesburg	Weekly	English	261,057
Daily Dispatch	East London	Daily	English	37,485
The Daily News	Durban	Daily	English	75,960
Diamond Fields Advertiser	Kimberley	Daily	English	8,000
EP Herald	Port Elizabeth	Daily	English	30,484
Evening Post	Port Elizabeth	Daily	English	16,827
Ilanga (The Sun)	Durban	Biweekly	Zulu[1]	125,761
Imvo Zabantsundu (Voice of the Black People)	King William's Town	Weekly	Xhosa[1]	14,401
The Natal Mercury	Durban	Daily	English	42,690
The Natal Witness	Pietermaritz-burg	Daily	English	27,500
Post (Natal)	Durban	Weekly	English	47,667
The Pretoria News	Pretoria	Daily	English	23,006
Rapport (Dispatch)	Johannesburg	Weekly	Afrikaans	375,723
Sowetan	Johannesburg	Daily	English	207,849
The Star.	Johannesburg	Daily	English	165,171
Sunday Nation	Johannesburg	Weekly	English	49,300
Sunday Times	Johannesburg	Weekly	English	467,745
Sunday Tribune	Durban	Weekly	English	115,418
Umafrika	Marianhill	Weekly	Zulu	40,500
Die Volksblad (The People's Paper)	Bloemfontein	Daily	Afrikaans	21,453
Weekly Mail.	Johannesburg	Weekly	English	28,220

[1] Some articles are in English.

Source: Based on information from South Africa, South African Communication Service, *South Africa Yearbook, 1995*, Pretoria, 1996, 296; and *Financial Mail* [Johannesburg], February 23, 1996, 85.

Table 20. Composition of South African National Defence Force, 1996[1]

Service	Active Duty	Reserve
Army...........................	118,000	377,000[2]
Air Force	8,400	20,000
Navy	5,500	1,700
Medical Service	6,000	n.a.[3]
TOTAL.........................	137,900	398,700

[1] Reorganization incomplete.
[2] Excluding Commandos (estimated 76,000).
[3] n.a.—not available.

Source: Based on information from *The Military Balance, 1996–1997*, London, 1996, 264–65.

Table 21. *Major Army Equipment, 1996*

Type and Description	Country of Origin	In Inventory
Main battle tanks		
Olifant 1A and 1B[1]	South Africa	Approximately 250
Tank technology demonstrator	South Africa	Being developed
Armored reconnaissance vehicles		
Eland–60 and –90	South Africa	1,100
Rooikat–76	South Africa	160
Armored infantry fighting vehicles		
Ratel–20, –60, and –90	South Africa	1,500
Armored personnel carriers		
Buffel, Casspir	South Africa	1,500
Mamba	South Africa	160+
Towed artillery		
G–1 (88mm)	South Africa	30
G–2 (140mm)	South Africa	75
G–4 (155mm)	South Africa	n.a.[2]
G–5 (155mm howitzer)	South Africa	75
Self-propelled artillery		
G–6 (155mm howitzer)	South Africa	20
Multiple rocket launchers		
Bataleur (127mm, 40-tube)	South Africa	120
Valkiri–22 (self-propelled, 24-tube)	South Africa	60
Valkiri–5 (towed)	South Africa	n.a.
Mortars		
M3 (81mm)	South Africa	4,000
Brandt (120mm)	South Africa	120+
Antitank guided weapons		
ZT–3 Swift	South Africa	n.a.
Milan	South Africa	n.a.
Rocket launchers		
FT–5 (92mm)	n.a.	n.a.
Recoilless launchers		
M–40A1 (106mm)	n.a.	n.a.
Air defense guns		
20mm, self-propelled	n.a.	600
23mm, self-propelled	n.a.	36
35mm	South Africa	150
Surface-to-air missiles		
SA–7 and SA–14	Soviet Union[3]	n.a.

[1] Olifant 1A and 1B manufactured in South Africa; derived from Centurion (Britain).
[2] n.a.—not available.
[3] Some captured in regional conflicts.

Source: Based on information from *The Military Balance, 1996–1997*, London, 1996, 264; and *Jane's Defence Weekly* [London], 23, No. 17, April 29, 1995, 23–41.

Table 22. *Major Air Force Equipment, 1996*

Type and Description	Country of Origin	In Inventory
Fighters, ground attack		
Mirage F–1AZ	France	20
Impala II	South Africa	75
Cheetah C	South Africa	38[1]
Cheetah E	South Africa	11
Fighters		
Mirage F–1CZ	France	11
Tanker/early warning		
Boeing 707–320	Israel	5
Transport aircraft		
C–130B	United States	7
HS–125 and –400B	Britain	3
Super King Air 200	United States	2
Citation	United States	1
C–47	United States	19
Liaison/fighter aircraft		
Cessna 185	United States	24
Helicopters		
SA–316/–319 (some armed)	France	63
SA–330 C/H/L Puma	France	63
BK–117	—[2]	19
CSH–2 Rooivalk	South Africa	12[1]
Training aircraft		
C–47TP	United States	12
Cheetah D	South Africa	14
T–6G Harvard IIA/III	United States	130
Impala I	South Africa	114
Pilatus PC–7	Switzerland	60
SA–316/–330 helicopters	France	37
Unmanned aerial vehicles		
Seeker	n.a.[3]	n.a.
Scout	n.a.	n.a.
Missiles		
Air-to-surface		
AS–11/–20/–30	n.a.	n.a.
Air-to-air		
R–530	n.a.	n.a.
R–550 Magic	n.a.	n.a.
V–3C Darter	n.a.	n.a.
V–3A/B Kukri	n.a.	n.a.
AIM–9 Sidewinder	n.a.	n.a.
Python 3	n.a.	n.a.

Table 22. (Continued) Major Air Force Equipment, 1996

Type and Description	Country of Origin	In Inventory
Ground equipment		
Armored personnel carriers (Rhino)........	South Africa	n.a.
Radar		
Fixed................................	n.a.	3
Mobile..............................	n.a.	Several
Surface-to-air missiles		
Cactus (Crotale).......................	n.a.	20
SA–8/–9/–13	n.a.	n.a.

[1] Some on order.
[2] Some acquired from former "independent" homelands.
[3] n.a.—not available.

Source: Based on information from *The Military Balance, 1996–1997*, London, 1996, 241, 265; and A.D. Baker, comp., *Combat Fleets of the World, 1995: Their Ships, Aircraft, and Armament*, Annapolis, Maryland, 1995, 676–79.

Table 23. *Major Naval Equipment, 1996*

Type and Description	Country of Origin	In Inventory
Submarines		
Daphné class......................... (550mm torpedo tube)[1]	France	3
Missile craft		
Minister class.........................	Israel	9
Inshore patrol craft		
Hydrofoils......................... (Coastguard T2212 class)	n.a.[2]	3
Harbor craft .... (Namicurra class)	n.a.	28
Mine warfare ships		
Coastal minesweepers.................. (Ton class)	Britain[1]	4
Minehunters......................... (River class)	n.a.	4
Support and miscellaneous		
Combat/logistic support vessels		
(Drakensberg)......................	South Africa	1
(Outeniqua).......................	Ukraine	1
Hydrographic survey vessel............	n.a.	1
Diving support vessel.................	n.a.	1
Antarctic transport with two helicopters.......................	n.a.	1
Tugs	n.a.	3
Frigates		
(1,500-ton to 1,800-ton).................	South Africa	4[3]

[1] Modified.
[2] n.a.—not available.
[3] Construction to begin late 1990s.

Source: Based on information from *The Military Balance, 1996–1997*, London, 1996, 264–65.

Table 24. Defense Budget, 1995 and 1996[1]
(in millions of rands)[2]

Budget Allocation	1995	1996
Ground defense	3,687	3,095
Air defense	1,633	1,777
Maritime defense	649	686
Medical services	857	720
Command and control...................	397	420
General support	320	323
Special defense account.................	3,093	3,514
TOTAL	10,636	10,535
Percentage of GDP[3]	3.4	2.2

[1] Years ending March 31.
[2] For value of the rand—see Glossary.
[3] GDP—gross domestic product.

Source: Based on information from Helmoed-Römer Heitman, "R2.9b Defence Budget Marks End to Decline," *Jane's Defence Weekly* [London], 23, No. 12, March 25, 1995, 5.

Bibliography

Chapter 1

Adam, Heribert, and Kogila Moodley. *The Negotiated Revolution: Society and Politics in Post-Apartheid South Africa.* Johannesburg: Ball, 1993.

Beinart, William. *Twentieth-Century South Africa.* New York: Oxford University Press, 1994.

Berger, Nathan. *Chapters from South African History, Jewish and General.* Johannesburg: Kayor, 1982.

Berger, Peter L., and Bobby Godsell, eds. *A Future South Africa: Visions, Strategies, and Realities.* Boulder, Colorado: Westview Press, 1988.

Bergh, J.S., and J.C. Visagie. *The Eastern Cape Frontier Zone, 1660–1980: A Cartographic Guide for Historical Research.* Durban: Butterworths, 1985.

Beukes, Piet. *The Religious Smuts.* Cape Town: Human and Rousseau, 1994.

Bickford-Smith, Vivian. "South African Urban History, Racial Segregation and the 'Unique' Case of Cape Town?" *Journal of Southern African Studies* [Oxford], 21, No. 1, March 1995, 63–78.

Bonner, Philip L. *Kings, Commoners, and Concessionaires: The Evolution and Dissolution of the Nineteenth-Century Swazi State.* New York: Cambridge University Press, 1983.

Bouch, Richard. "Glen Grey Before Cecil Rhodes: How a Crisis of Local Colonial Authority Led to the Glen Grey Act of 1894," *Canadian Journal of African Studies* [Toronto], 27, No. 1, Winter 1993, 1–24.

Bradford, Helen. *A Taste of Freedom: The ICU in Rural South Africa, 1924–1930.* New Haven: Yale University Press, 1987.

Bradford, Mary, and Richard Bradford, eds. *An American Family on the African Frontier: The Burnham Family Letters, 1893–1896.* Niwot, Colorado: Roberts Rinehart, 1993.

Bradlow, Frank R. *Francis Masson's Account of Three Journeys at the Cape of Good Hope, 1772–1775.* Cape Town: Tablecloth Press, 1994.

Breytenbach, Cloete. *The New South Africa: The Zulu Factor.* Montagu, South Africa: Luga, 1991.

Bundy, Colin. *The Rise and Fall of the South African Peasantry.* Berkeley: University of California Press, 1979.

Castle, Ian, and Ian Knight. *Fearful Hard Times: The Siege of and Relief of Eshowe, Anglo-Zulu War, 1879.* Harrisburg, Pennsylvania: Stackpole Books, 1994.

Cohen, Robin, Yvonne Muthien, and Abede Zegeye, eds. *Repression and Resistance: Insiders' Accounts of Apartheid.* London: Zell, for the Centre for Modern African Studies, 1990.

Cope, Nicholas. *To Bind the Nation: Solomon Kadinuzulu and Zulu Nationalism, 1913–1933.* Pietermaritzburg: University of Natal Press, 1993.

Dalby, David, ed. *Language and History in Africa.* London: Cass, 1970.

de Klerk, Willem A. *The Puritans in Africa: The Story of Afrikanerdom.* London: Collings, 1975.

Eilersen, Gillian Stead. "Historical Roots and Rural African Culture as Part of Bessie Head's Frame of Reference." Pages 173–83 in Raoul Granqvist, ed., *Culture in Africa: An Appeal for Pluralism.* Seminar Proceedings, No. 29. Uppsala, Sweden: Scandinavian Institute of African Studies, 1993.

Eldredge, Elizabeth A. "Sources of Conflict in Southern Africa, ca. 1800–1830: The 'Mfecane' Reconsidered," *Journal of African History* [Cambridge], 33, April 1992, 1–35.

Eldredge, Elizabeth A. *A South African Kingdom: The Pursuit of Security in Nineteenth Century Lesotho.* African Studies Series, No. 78. Cambridge: Cambridge University Press, 1993.

Elliott, Aubrey. *Zulu: Heritage of a Nation.* Cape Town: Struik, 1991.

Elphick, Richard. *Kraal and Castle: Khoikhoi and the Founding of White South Africa.* New Haven: Yale University Press, 1977.

Elphick, Richard, and Hermann B. Giliomee, eds. *The Shaping of South African Society, 1652–1840.* Middletown, Connecticut: Wesleyan University Press, 1989.

Engels, Dagmar, and Shula Marks, eds. *Contesting Colonial Hegemony: State and Society in Africa and India.* New York: Tauris, 1994.

Fage, John D., and Roland Oliver, eds. *The Cambridge History of Africa.* 8 vols. New York: Cambridge University Press, 1975–1986.

February, Vernon. *The Afrikaners of South Africa.* New York: Paul International, 1991.

Gerhart, Gail M. *Black Power in South Africa: The Evolution of an Ideology.* Berkeley: University of California Press, 1978.

Golan, Daphna. *Inventing Shaka: Using History in the Construction of Zulu Nationalism.* Boulder, Colorado: Lynne Rienner, 1994.

Granqvist, Raoul, ed. *Culture in Africa: An Appeal for Pluralism.* Seminar Proceedings, No. 29. Uppsala, Sweden: Scandinavian Institute of African Studies, 1993.

Guelke, Leonard, and Robert Shell. "Landscape of Conquest: Frontier Water Alienation and Khoikhoi Strategies of Survival, 1652–1780," *Journal of Southern African Studies* [Oxford], 18, No. 4, December 1992, 803–24.

Gutteridge, William F., ed., with contributions by Deon Geldenhuys and David Simon. *South Africa: From Apartheid to National Unity, 1981–1994.* Brookfield, Vermont: Dartmouth, 1995.

Guy, Jeffrey. *The Destruction of the Zulu Kingdom: The Civil War in Zululand, 1879–1884.* London: Longman, 1979.

Hall, Martin. *Farmers, Kings, and Traders: The Peopling of Southern Africa, 200–1860.* Chicago: University of Chicago Press, 1990.

Hallencreutz, Carl F. "Thomas Mofolo and Nelson Mandela on King Shaka and Dingane." Pages 185–93 in Raoul Granqvist, ed., *Culture in Africa: An Appeal for Pluralism.* Seminar Proceedings, No. 29. Uppsala, Sweden: Scandinavian Institute of African Studies, 1993.

Hallencreutz, Carl F., and Mai Palmberg, eds. *Religion and Politics in Southern Africa.* Uppsala, Sweden: Scandinavian Institute of African Studies, 1991.

Hamill, James. "South Africa and the Commonwealth: The Years of Acrimony," *Contemporary Review* [Surrey], 267, No. 1554, July 1995, 13–22.

Hanlon, Joseph. *Apartheid's Second Front: South Africa's War Against Its Neighbours.* New York: Penguin, 1986.

Head, Bessie. *Tales of Tenderness and Power.* London: Heinemann International, 1990.

Hill, Iris Tillman, and Alex Harris, eds. *Beyond the Barricades: Popular Resistance in South Africa.* New York: Aperture, 1989.

Horrell, Muriel, comp. *Laws Affecting Race Relations in South Africa.* Johannesburg: South African Institute of Race Relations, 1978.

Houghton, D. Hobart, and Jenifer Dagut. *Source Material on the South African Economy, 1860–1970.* 3 vols. New York: Oxford University Press, 1972–73.

Human Rights Watch/Africa. *South Africa: Impunity for Human Rights Abuses in Two Homelands: Reports on KwaZulu and Bophuthatswana.* New York: 1994.

Inskeep, R. R. *The Peopling of Southern Africa.* New York: Barnes and Noble, 1979.

Johns, Sheridan, and R. Hunt Davis, eds. *Mandela, Tambo, and the African National Congress: The Struggle Against Apartheid, 1948–1990: A Documentary Survey.* New York: Oxford University Press, 1991.

Johnston, Alexander. "South Africa: The Election and the Transition Process: Five Contradictions in Search of a Resolution," *Third World Quarterly* [London], 15, No. 2, June 1994, 187–204.

Juckes, Tim J. *Opposition in South Africa: The Leadership of Z. K. Matthews, Nelson Mandela, and Stephen Biko.* Westport, Connecticut: Praeger, 1995.

Kaarsholm, Preben, ed. *Cultural Struggle and Development in Southern Africa.* Harare, Zimbabwe: Baobab Books, 1991.

Karis, Thomas, and Gwendolen M. Carter. *From Protest to Challenge: A Documentary History of African Politics in South Africa, 1882–1964.* 4 vols. Stanford: Hoover Institution Press, 1972–1977.

Knight, Ian. *The Anatomy of the Zulu Army: From Shaka to Cetshwayo, 1818–1879.* Mechanicsburg, Pennsylvania: Stackpole Books, 1995.

Knight, Ian. *Zulu: The Study of a Nation Built on War.* New York: Sterling, 1994.

Kwamena-Poh, Michael A., et al. *African History in Maps.* Essex, United Kingdom: Longman, 1982.

Labour and Community Resources Project. *Freedom from Below: The Struggle for Trade Unions in South Africa.* Braamfontein: Skotaville Educational, 1989.

Lelyveld, Joseph. *Move Your Shadow: South Africa, Black and White.* New York: Time Books, 1985.

Lock, Ron. *Blood on the Painted Mountain: Zulu Victory and Defeat, Hlobane, and Kambula, 1879.* Mechanicsburg, Pennsylvania: Stackpole Books, 1995.

Lodge, Tom. *Black Politics in South Africa since 1945.* London: Longman, 1983.

McCracken, J.L. *New Light at the Cape of Good Hope: William Porter, the Father of Cape Liberalism.* Belfast: Ulster Historical Foundation, 1993.

MacMillan, Hugh. "Return to the Malungwana Drift—Max Gluckman, the Zulu Nation, and the Common Society," *African Affairs* [London], 94, No. 374, January 1995, 39–65.

Makhura, Tlou John. "Another Road to the Raid: The Neglected Role of the Boer-Bagananwa as a Factor in the Coming of the Jameson Raid, 1894–1895," *Journal of Southern African Studies* [Oxford], 21, No. 2, June 1995, 257–68.

Mandela, Nelson. *How Far We Slaves Have Come! South Africa and Cuba in Today's World.* New York: Pathfinder, 1991.

Mandela, Nelson. *Long Walk to Freedom: The Autobiography of Nelson Mandela.* Boston: Little, Brown, 1994.

Mandela, Nelson. *The Struggle Is My Life.* 3d ed. New York: Pathfinder, 1990.

Mandela, Nelson, et al. *Voices from Robben Island.* Jurgen Schadeberg, comp. Randburg: Ravan Press, 1994.

Marks, Shula. *The Ambiguities of Dependence in South Africa: Class, Nationalism, and the State in Twentieth-Century Natal.* Johannesburg: Ravan Press, 1986.

Marks, Shula, and Anthony Atmore. "The Problem of the Nguni: An Examination of the Ethnic and Linguistic Situation in South Africa Before the Mfecane." Pages 120–32 in David Dalby, ed., *Language and History in Africa.* London: Cass, 1970.

Marks, Shula, and Anthony Atmore, eds. *Economy and Society in Pre-Industrial South Africa.* London: Longman, 1980.

Marks, Shula, and Richard Rathbone, eds. *Industrialisation and Social Change in South Africa: African Class Formation, Culture, and Consciousness, 1870–1930.* New York: Longman, 1982.

Marks, Shula, and Stanley Trapido, eds. *The Politics of Race, Class, and Nationalism in Twentieth-Century South Africa.* New York: Longman, 1982.

Maylam, Paul. *A History of the African People of South Africa: From the Early Iron Age to the 1970s.* New York: St. Martin's Press, 1986.

Meli, Francis. *A History of the ANC: South Africa Belongs to Us.* Bloomington: Indiana University Press, 1988.

Miller, Carman. *Painting the Map Red: Canada and the South African War, 1899–1902.* Canadian War Museum Historical Publication No. 28. Montreal: Canadian War Museum and McGill-Queen's University Press, 1993.

Moleah, Alfred Tokollo. *South Africa: Colonialism, Apartheid, and African Dispossession.* Wilmington, Delaware: Disa Press, 1993.

Moodie, T. Dunbar. *The Rise of Afrikanerdom: Power, Apartheid, and the Afrikaner Civil Religion.* Berkeley: University of California Press, 1975.

Morris, Donald R. *The Washing of the Spears: A History of the Rise of the Zulu Nation under Shaka and Its Fall in the Zulu War of 1879.* New York: Simon and Schuster, 1965.

Mutunhu, Tendai. "Lobengula and the Matebele Nation: His Monarchial Rise and Relations with Missionaries, Boers, and the British," *Journal of Southern African Affairs,* 5, No. 1, January 1980, 5–22.

Nzuwah, Mariyawanda, ed. *The OAU on Southern Africa: Resolutions and Declarations of the Organization of African Unity on Southern Africa.* Washington: Southern Africa Technologies, 1980.

Odendaal, André. *Black Protest Politics in South Africa to 1912.* Totowa, New Jersey: Barnes and Noble, 1984.

O'Meara, Dan. *Volkskapitalisme: Class, Capital, and Ideology in the Development of Afrikaner Nationalism, 1934–1948.* New York: Cambridge University Press, 1983.

Omer-Cooper, John D. *History of Southern Africa.* 2d ed. London and Portsmouth, New Hampshire: Currey and Heinemann, 1994.

Omer-Cooper, John D. *The Zulu Aftermath: A Nineteenth-Century Revolution in Bantu Africa.* London: Longman, 1966.

Ottaway, David. *Chained Together: Mandela, De Klerk, and the Struggle to Remake South Africa.* New York: Time Books, 1993.

Ottaway, Marina. *South Africa: The Struggle for a New Order.* Washington: Brookings Institution, 1993.

Peires, Jeffrey B. *The Dead Will Arise: Nongqawuse and the Great Xhosa Cattle-Killing Movement of 1856–7.* Bloomington: Indiana University Press, 1989.

Peires, Jeffrey B. *The House of Phalo: A History of the Xhosa People in the Days of Their Independence.* Perspectives on Southern Africa, No. 32. Berkeley: University of California Press, 1982.

Price, Robert M. *The Apartheid State in Crisis: Political Transformation in South Africa: 1975–1990.* New York: Oxford University Press, 1991.

Rasmussen, R. Kent. *Migrant Kingdom: Mzilikazi's Ndebele in South Africa.* Cape Town: Philip, 1978.

Reader's Digest Association. *Illustrated History of South Africa: The Real Story.* Pleasantville, New York: 1989.

Roberts, Jack. *Nelson Mandela: Determined to Be Free.* Brookfield, Connecticut: Millbrook Press, 1995.

Roux, Edward. *Time Longer Than Rope: A History of the Black Man's Struggle for Freedom in South Africa.* London: Gollancz, 1948. Reprint. Madison: University of Wisconsin Press, 1964.

Saunders, Christopher C., ed. *An Illustrated Dictionary of South African History.* Sandton, South Africa: Ibis Books and Editorial Services, 1994.

Saunders, Frederick. *Mafeking Memories.* Ed., Phillip Thurmond Smith. Cranbury, New Jersey: Associated University Presses, 1996.

Schneidman, Witney W. *Postapartheid South Africa: Steps Taken, the Path Ahead.* CSIS Africa Notes, No. 156. Washington: Center for Strategic and International Studies, January 1994.

Shillington, Kevin. *History of Southern Africa.* Burnt Mill, United Kingdom: Longman, 1987.

Sparks, Allister. *The Mind of South Africa: The Story of the Rise and Fall of Apartheid.* New York: Knopf, 1990.

Stanley, Diane, and Peter Vennema. *Shaka: King of the Zulus.* New York: Mulberry Books, 1994.

Stock, Robert. *Africa South of the Sahara: A Geographical Interpretation.* New York: Guilford Press, 1995.

Tamarkin, Michael. *Cecil Rhodes and the Cape Afrikaners: The Imperial Colossus and the Colonial Parish Pump.* Portland, Oregon: Cass, 1995.

Taylor, Stephen. *Shaka's Children: A History of the Zulu People.* London: Harper Collins, 1994.

Thompson, Leonard M. *A History of South Africa.* Rev. ed. New Haven: Yale University Press, 1995.

Thompson, Leonard M. *The Political Mythology of Apartheid.* New Haven: Yale University Press, 1985.

Thompson, Leonard M. *Survival in Two Worlds: Moshoeshoe of Lesotho, 1786–1870.* New York: Oxford University Press, 1975.

United States Institute of Peace. *South Africa: The National Peace Accord.* Special Report, September 24, 1993. Washington: September, 1993.

van der Merwe, Petrus J. *The Migrant Farmer in the History of the Cape Colony, 1657–1842.* Trans., Roger B. Beck. Athens: Ohio University Press, 1995.

von der Ropp, Klaus. "'Outbreak of Peace' in South Africa?" *Aussenpolitik* [English ed.] [Hamburg], 45, No. 4, December 1994, 383–91.

Walker, Eric. *A History of Southern Africa.* London: Longman, 1962.

Walshe, Peter. *The Rise of African Nationalism in South Africa: The African National Congress, 1912–1952.* Berkeley: University of California Press, 1971.

Wilson, Francis. *Labour in the South African Gold Mines, 1911–1969.* Cambridge: Cambridge University Press, 1972.

Wilson, Monica Hunter, and Leonard M. Thompson, eds. *The Oxford History of South Africa.* 2 vols. New York: Oxford University Press, 1969, 1971.

Worden, Nigel. *The Making of Modern South Africa: Conquest, Segregation, and Apartheid.* 2d ed. Cambridge, Massachusetts: Blackwell, 1995.

Worden, Nigel. *Slavery in Dutch South Africa.* African Studies Series, No. 44. New York: Cambridge University Press, 1985.

Worger, William H. *South Africa's City of Diamonds: Mine Workers and Monopoly Capitalism in Kimberley, 1867–1895.* New Haven: Yale University Press, 1987.

(Various issues of the following periodicals were also used in preparation of this chapter: *Canadian Journal of African Studies* [Toronto]; *Christian Science Monitor; Economist* [London]; *Financial Mail* [London]; *Johannesburg Mail* [Johannesburg]; *Journal of Southern African Affairs; Journal of Southern African Studies*

[Oxford]; *Keesing's Record of World Events* [London]; *New York Times*; and *Washington Post.*)

Chapter 2

Adam, Heribert. "The Politics of Ethnic Identity: Comparing South Africa," *Ethnic and Racial Studies* [London], 18, No. 3, July 1995, 457–75.

Adam, Heribert, and Hermann Giliomee. *Ethnic Power Mobilized: Can South Africa Change?* New Haven: Yale University Press, 1979.

Adam, Heribert, and Kogila Moodley. *The Negotiated Revolution: Society and Politics in Post-Apartheid South Africa.* Johannesburg: Ball, 1993.

Africa South of the Sahara, 1994. 23d ed. London: Europa, 1993.

Africa South of the Sahara, 1995. 24th ed. London: Europa, 1994.

Alberti, Ludwig. *Account of the Tribal Life and Customs of the Xhosa in 1807.* Trans., William Fehr. Cape Town: Balkema, 1968.

Amnesty International. *Amnesty International Report, 1994.* New York: 1994.

Amnesty International. *Amnesty International Report, 1995.* New York: 1995.

Antle, John M., and Gregg Heidebrink. "Environment and Development: Theory and International Evidence," *Economic Development and Cultural Change,* 43, No. 3, April 1995, 603–25.

Arnold, Guy. *South Africa: Crossing the Rubicon.* New York: St. Martin's Press, 1992.

Atkinson, Simon, ed. *Magnificent South Africa: In Praise of a Beautiful Land.* Cape Town: Struik, 1994.

Balandier, Georges, and Jacques Maquet, eds. *Dictionary of Black African Civilization.* New York: Amiel, 1974.

Behr, Abraham L. *Education in South Africa: Origins, Issues, and Trends: 1652–1988.* Cape Town: Academica, 1988.

Behrens, R., and Vanessa Watson. "Inward Development: Solutions to Urban Sprawl," *Indicator South Africa* [Durban], 9, No. 3, Winter 1992, 51–54.

Benatar, Solomon R., and H.C.J. Van Rensburg. "Health Care Services in a New South Africa," *Hastings Center Report,* 25, July–August 1995, 16–21.

Berger, Iris. *Threads of Solidarity: Women in South African Industry, 1900–1980.* Bloomington: Indiana University Press, 1992.

Biehl, Amy. "Dislodging the Boulder: South African Women and Democratic Transformation." Pages 85–107 in Stephen John Stedman, ed., *South Africa: The Political Economy of Transformation.* Boulder, Colorado: Lynne Rienner, 1994.

Boonzaier, Emile, and John Sharp, eds. *South African Keywords: The Uses and Abuses of Political Concepts.* Cape Town: Philip, 1988.

Borchert, Peter. *This Is South Africa.* Cape Town: Struik, 1993.

Breytenbach, Cloete. *The New South Africa: The Zulu Factor.* Montagu, South Africa: Luga, 1991.

Bullwinkle, Davis A., comp. *African Women: A General Bibliography, 1976–1985.* Westport, Connecticut: Greenwood Press, 1989.

Burman, Sandra, and Pamela Reynolds, eds. *Growing Up in a Divided Society: The Contexts of Childhood in South Africa.* Johannesburg: Ravan Press, 1986. Reprint. Evanston, Illinois: Northwestern University Press, 1990.

Butterfield, Paul H. "South Africa." Pages 1104–14 in George Thomas Kurian, ed., *World Education Encyclopedia,* 2. New York: Facts on File, 1988.

Campbell, Catherine. "Learning to Kill? Masculinity, the Family, and Violence in Natal," *Journal of Southern African Studies* [Oxford], 18, No. 3, September 1992, 614–28.

Campbell, Catherine, Gerhard Maré, and Cherryl Walker. "Evidence for an Ethnic Identity in the Life Histories of Zulu-speaking Durban Township Residents," *Journal of Southern African Studies* [Oxford], 21, No. 2, June 1995, 287–302.

Cashmore, Ellis. *Dictionary of Race and Ethnic Relations.* 3d ed. London and New York: Routledge, 1994.

Chidester, David. *Religions of South Africa.* New York: Routledge, 1992.

Chikane, Frank. "Children in Turmoil: The Effects of Unrest on Township Children." Pages 333–44 in Sandra Burman and Pamela Reynolds, eds., *Growing Up in a Divided Society: Context of Childhood in South Africa.* Johannesburg: Ravan Press, 1986. Reprint. Evanston, Illinois: Northwestern University Press, 1990.

Clarke, James. "The Insane Experiment: Tampering with the Atmosphere." Pages 139–57 in Jacklyn Cock and Eddie Koch, eds., *Going Green: People, Politics, and the Environment in South Africa*. Cape Town: Oxford University Press, 1991.

Cock, Jacklyn. *Women and War in South Africa*. Cleveland, Ohio: Pilgrim Press, 1993.

Cock, Jacklyn, and Eddie Koch, eds. *Going Green: People, Politics, and the Environment in South Africa*. Cape Town: Oxford University Press, 1991.

Colclough, Christopher, and Keith Lewin. *Educating All the Children: Strategies for Primary Schooling in the South*. Oxford: Clarendon Press, 1993.

Constitution of the Republic of South Africa, Act 200 of 1993. Pretoria: Government Printer, 1994.

Cooper, Saths. "Political Violence in South Africa: The Role of the Youth," *Issue: A Journal of Opinion*, 22, No. 2, Summer 1994, 27–29.

Courtney-Clarke, Margaret. *Ndebele: The Art of an African Tribe*. New York: Rizzoli International, 1986.

Cronin, Duggan M. *The Bantu-speaking Tribes of South Africa*. Cambridge: Cambridge University Press, 1939.

Cross, Catherine, Simon Bekker, and Craig Clark. "People on the Move," *Indicator South Africa* [Durban], 9, No. 3, Winter 1992, 41–46.

Dafnah, Golan. *Investing Shaka: Using History in the Construction of Zulu Nationalism*. Boulder, Colorado: Lynne Rienner, 1994.

Davidson, Basil. *The Search for Africa: History, Culture, Politics*. New York: Random House, 1994.

Davies, Susan. *The South African Book of Lists*. Rivonia, South Africa: Waterman, 1993.

Development Bank of Southern Africa. *South Africa: An Inter-regional Profile*. Midrand: 1992.

Donaldson, Andrew R. "Basic Needs and Social Policy: The Role of the State in Education, Health, and Welfare." Pages 271–320 in Merle Lipton and Charles Simkins, eds., *State and Market in Post Apartheid South Africa*. Boulder, Colorado: Westview Press, 1993.

Dugard, John. "South Africa's 'Independent' Homelands: An Exercise in Denationalization," *Denver Journal of International Law and Policy*, 10, No. 1, Fall 1980, 11–36.

Duncan, Sheena. "Women and Democracy: 'We Have Avoided Entrenching Inequality'," *Journal of Theology for Southern Africa* [Cape Town], No. 86, March 1994, 67–71.

Du Pré, Roy H. *Separate But Unequal: The 'Coloured' People of South Africa, a Political History.* Johannesburg: Ball, 1994.

Durning, Alan B. *Apartheid's Environmental Toll.* Worldwatch Paper, No. 95. Washington: Worldwatch Institute, 1990.

El-Bakry, Zeinab B. "Enhancing the Capacity of the African Woman Entrepreneur." Pages 138–47 in Sadig Rashid and David Fasholé Luke, eds., *Development Management in Africa: Toward Dynamism, Empowerment, and Entrepreneurship.* Boulder, Colorado: Westview Press, 1995.

Eldredge, Elizabeth A. *A South African Kingdom: The Pursuit of Security in Nineteenth-Century Lesotho.* African Studies Series, No. 78. Cambridge: Cambridge University Press, 1993.

Elliott, Arthur. *A Cape Camera: The Architectural Beauty of the Old Cape.* Johannesburg: Donker, 1993.

Elliott, Aubrey. *The Magic World of the Xhosa.* New York: Scribner, 1970.

Engelbrecht, S.W.H., and F.J. Nieuwenhuis. "Educational Strategies for the Future." Pages 145–69 in H.C. Marais, ed., *South Africa: Perspectives on the Future.* Pinetown, South Africa: Burgess, 1988.

Esman, Milton J. *Ethnic Politics.* Ithaca: Cornell University Press, 1994.

"Ethnicity and Identity in Southern Africa," *Journal of Southern African Studies* [Oxford], 20, No. 3, Special Issue, September 1994.

Everatt, David, ed. *Creating a Future: Youth Policy for South Africa.* Johannesburg: Ravan Press, 1994.

Fage, John D. *A History of Africa.* 2d ed. Boston: Unwin Hyman, 1988.

Fallon, Peter, and Luis Pereira da Silva. *South Africa: Economic Performance and Policies.* Washington: World Bank, 1994.

Faure, Véronique. "De la communauté des convertis *amakholwa* à la naissance de l'Inkatha," *Cahiers d'Études Africaines* [Paris], 35, No. 1, January 1995, 133–61.

February, Vernon A. *The Afrikaners of South Africa.* New York: Paul International, 1991.

Fenton, Thomas P., and Mary J. Heffron, comps. and eds. *Third World Resource Directory, 1994–1995: An Annotated Guide to Print and Audiovisual Resources from and about Africa, Asia and Pacific, Latin America and Caribbean, and the Middle East.* Maryknoll, New York: Orbis, 1994.

Foote, Karen A., Kenneth H. Hill, and Linda G. Martin, eds. *Demographic Change in Sub-Saharan Africa.* Washington: National Academy Press, 1993.

Forde, Daryll, ed. *African Worlds.* New York: Oxford University Press, 1954.

Fortes, Meyer, and E.E. Evans-Pritchard, eds. *African Political Systems.* New York: Oxford University Press, 1940.

Fortes, Meyer, and S. Patterson, eds. *Studies in African Social Anthropology.* London: Academic Press, 1975.

Frederikse, Julie. *All Schools for All Children: Lessons for South Africa from Zimbabwe's Open Schools.* Cape Town: Oxford University Press, 1992.

Frederikse, Julie. *South Africa: A Different Kind of War.* Boston: Beacon Press, 1986.

Freund, Bill. "Indian Women and the Changing Character of the Working Class Indian Household in Natal 1860–1990," *Journal of Natal, Southern African Studies* [Oxford], 17, No. 3, September 1991, 414–29.

Furlong, Patrick J. *Between Crown and Swastika: The Impact of the Radical Right on the Afrikaner Nationalist Movement in the Fascist Era.* Hanover, New Hampshire: Wesleyan University Press, 1991.

Gerwel, Jakes. "Education in South Africa: Means and Ends." Pages 82–93 in John E. Spence, ed., *Change in South Africa.* New York: Council on Foreign Relations Press for the Royal Institute of International Affairs, 1994.

Gill, Stephen J. *A Short History of Lesotho from the Late Stone Age until the 1993 Elections.* Lesotho: Morija Museum and Archives, 1993.

Gluckman, Max. *Custom and Conflict in Africa.* Oxford: Blackwell, 1956.

Gluckman, Max. "Kinship and Marriage Among the Lozi of Northern Rhodesia and the Zulu of Natal." Pages 166–206 in Alfred R. Radcliffe-Brown and Daryll Forde, eds., *African Sys-*

tems of Kinship and Marriage. New York: Oxford University Press, 1950.

Goldblatt, David, Margaret Courtney-Clarke, and John Kench. *Cape Dutch Homesteads.* Cape Town: Struik, 1981.

Goodwin, June, and Ben Schiff. *Heart of Whiteness: Afrikaners Face Black Rule in the New South Africa.* New York: Scribner, 1995.

Gordimer, Nadine. *Some Monday for Sure.* London: Heinemann Educational, 1976.

Granqvist, Raoul, ed. *Culture in Africa: An Appeal for Pluralism.* Seminar Proceedings, No. 29. Uppsala, Sweden: Scandinavian Institute of African Studies, 1993.

Greenstein, Ran. "The Study of South African Society: Towards a New Agenda for Comparative Historical Inquiry," *Journal of Southern African Studies* [Oxford], 20, No. 4, December 1994, 641–61.

Grundy, Kenneth W. "The Politics of South Africa's National Arts Festival: Small Engagements in the Bigger Campaign," *African Affairs* [London], 93, No. 372, July 1994, 387–409.

Gump, James O. *The Dust Rose like Smoke: The Subjugation of the Zulu and the Sioux.* Lincoln: University of Nebraska Press, 1994.

Gurr, Ted Robert, with Barbara Hanff, Monty G. Marshall, and James R. Scarritt. *Minorities at Risk: A Global View of Ethnopolitical Conflicts.* Washington: United States Institute of Peace Press, 1993.

Haffajee, Ferial. "No Streets Paved with Gold in Egoli," *Weekly Mail* [Johannesburg], May 7–13, 1993, 17.

Hall, James. *Sangoma: My Odyssey into the Spirit World of Africa.* New York: Simon and Schuster, 1995.

Haskins, Jim, and Joann Biondi. *From Afar to Zulu: A Dictionary of African Cultures.* New York: Walker, 1995.

Hawthorne, Peter, and Barry Bristow. *Historic Schools of South Africa: An Ethos of Excellence.* Cape Town: Pachyderm Press, 1993.

Heese, Chris, and Dirk Badenhorst. *South Africa, the Education Equation: Problems, Perspectives, and Prospects.* Pretoria: Van Schaik, 1992.

Herselman, Stephen. "Towards More Effective Patient Care: The Role of the Nurse as Culture Broker," *South African Journal of Ethnology* [Pretoria], 17, No. 3, September 1994, 83–87.

Heywood, Donald. *Vanishing Faces of Southern Africa.* Cape Town: Human and Rousseau, 1994.

Hodgson, Janet. *Ntsikana's Great Hymn.* Cape Town: Centre for African Studies, University of Cape Town, 1982.

Horwitz, Frank M. "South Africa." Pages 86–101 in M. Afzalur Rahim and Albert A. Blum, eds., *Global Perspectives on Organizational Conflict.* Westport, Connecticut: Praeger, 1994.

Human Sciences Research Council. *The South African Society: Realities and Future Prospects.* Westport, Connecticut: Greenwood Press, 1987.

Huntley, Brian, Roy Siegfried, and Clem Sunter. *South African Environments into the Twenty-First Century.* Cape Town: Human and Rousseau, 1989.

Innes, Duncan. *Disqualified: A Study of the Effects of Uprooting the Coloured People of South Africa.* Studies in the Mass Removal of Population in South Africa, No. 5. London: Africa Publications Trust, 1975.

Johnson, R.W. "Myths of the New Nation: Soviet/South Africa Parallels," *Indicator South Africa* [Durban], 9, No. 3, Winter 1992, 7-10.

Joyce, Peter. *Traveller's Guide to South Africa.* Cape Town: Struik, 1993.

Junod, Henri A. *The Life of a South African Tribe.* Neuchâtel: Imprimerie Attinger Frères, 1912.

Kairos Theologians. *The Kairos Document: Challenge to the Church: A Theological Comment on the Political Crisis in South Africa.* 2d rev. ed. Grand Rapids, Michigan: Eerdmans, 1986.

Keller, Bill. "A Surprising Silent Majority in South Africa," *New York Times Magazine,* April 17, 1994, 34–41, 54, 72, 78, 83.

Kentridge, Matthew. *An Unofficial War: Inside the Conflict in Pietermaritzburg.* Cape Town: Philip, 1990.

Khan, Farieda. "Rewriting South Africa's Conservation History: The Role of the Native Farmers Association," *Journal of Southern African Studies* [Oxford], 20, No. 4, December 1994, 499–516.

Khumalo, Bongi. "The Power of Women on April 27," *Southern Africa Political and Economic Monthly* [Harare, Zimbabwe], 7, No. 7, April 1994, 6–7.

Knight, Ian. *Zulu: The Story of a Nation Built on War.* New York: Sterling, 1994.

Krige, Dulcie, Sandy Cairns, Bulelwa Makalima, and Di Scott. *The Education Atlas of South Africa.* Durban: Education Foundation, 1994.

Krige, E. *The Social System of the Zulus.* London: Longmans, 1936.

Krige, Jacob D. *The Realm of the Rain Queen: A Study of the Pattern of Lovedu Society.* London: Oxford University Press, 1943.

Kuckertz, Heinz. *Creating Order: The Image of the Homestead in Mpondo Social Life.* Johannesburg: Witwatersrand University Press, 1990.

Kuper, Hilda. "Kinship among the Swazi." Pages 86–110 in Alfred R. Radcliffe-Brown and Daryll Forde, eds., *African Systems of Kinship and Marriage.* New York: Oxford University Press, 1950.

Kuper, Hilda. *The Swazi.* Ethnographic Survey of Africa, Southern Africa, Pt. 1. London: International African Institute, 1952.

Kuper, Leo, and M.G. Smith. *Pluralism in Africa.* Berkeley: University of California Press, 1969.

Kurian, George Thomas, ed. *Encyclopedia of the Third World.* 4th ed. New York: Facts on File, 1992.

Larson, Ann. "The Social Epidemiology of Africa's AIDS Epidemic," *African Affairs* [London], 89, No. 354, January 1990, 5–25.

Lave, Tamara Rice. "A Nation at Prayer, a Nation in Hate: Apartheid in South Africa," *Stanford Journal of International Law,* 30, No. 2, Summer 1994, 483–524.

Lelyveld, Joseph. *Move Your Shadow: South Africa, Black and White.* New York: Time Books, 1985.

Le Roux, Johann, ed. *The Black Child in Crisis: A Socio-Educational Perspective.* 2 vols. Pretoria: Van Schaik, 1993.

Leroux, Vincent, ed. *Secret Southern Africa: Wonderful Places You've Probably Never Seen.* Cape Town: AA, The Motorist, 1994.

Lewis, Gavin. *Between the Wire and the Wall: A History of South African 'Coloured' Politics.* New York: St. Martin's Press, 1987.

Liebenberg, Ian. "A Research Report: South African Youth and Politics, 1987–1992," *Politeia,* 13, No. 1, March 1994, 97–117.

Lipton, Merle, and Charles Simkins, eds. *State and Market in Post Apartheid South Africa.* Boulder, Colorado: Westview Press, 1993.

Lupton, Malcolm, and Tony Wolfson. "Low-Income Housing, the Environment and Mining on the Witwatersrand, South Africa." Pages 107–24 in Hamish Main and Stephen Wyn Williams, eds., *Environment and Housing in Third World Cities.* New York: Wiley and Sons, 1994.

Lurie, David. *Life in the Liberated Zone.* Text by Rian Malan. Rivonia, South Africa: Waterman, 1994.

Maasdorp, Gavin, and Alan Whiteside, eds. *Towards a Post-Apartheid Future: Political and Economic Relations in Southern Africa.* New York: St. Martin's Press, 1992.

Mabin, Alan. "Dispossession, Exploitation, and Struggle: An Historical Overview of South African Urbanization." Pages 13–24 in David M. Smith, ed., *The Apartheid City and Beyond: Urbanization and Social Change in South Africa.* New York: Routledge, Chapman, and Hall, 1992.

McCaul, Coleen. *No Easy Ride: Rise and Future of the Black Taxi Industry.* Johannesburg: South African Institute of Race Relations, 1990.

Macmillan, Hugh. "Return to the Malungwana Drift: Max Gluckman, the Zulu Nation, and the Common Society," *African Affairs* [London], 94, No. 374, January 1995, 39–65.

Macmillan, Hugh, and Shula Marks, eds. *Africa and Empire: W.M. Macmillan, Historian and Social Critic.* London: Institute of Commonwealth Studies, 1989.

Mahlasela, Benjamin E. N. *A General Survey of Xhosa Literature from Its Early Beginnings in the 1800s to the Present.* Working Paper No. 2. Grahamstown, South Africa: Rhodes University, Department of African Languages, 1973.

Main, Hamish, and Stephen Wyn Williams, eds. *Environment and Housing in Third World Cities.* New York: Wiley and Sons, 1994.

Mair, Lucy, ed. *Methods of Study of Culture Contact in Africa.* London: International African Institute, 1938.

Makan, Amita. "Power for Women and Men: Towards a Gendered Approach to Domestic Energy Policy and Planning in South Africa," *Third World Planning Review* [Liverpool], 17, No. 2, May 1995, 183–98.

Malan, Rian. *My Traitor's Heart: A South African Exile Returns to Face His Country, His Tribe, and His Conscience.* New York: Atlantic Monthly Press, 1990.

Manby, Bronwen. "South Africa: Minority Conflict and the Legacy of Minority Rule," *Fletcher Forum of World Affairs*, 19, Winter/Spring 1995, 27–52.

Mandela, Nelson. *Long Walk to Freedom: The Autobiography of Nelson Mandela.* Boston: Little, Brown, 1994.

Manganyi, N. Chabani, and André du Toit, eds. *Political Violence and the Struggle in South Africa.* New York: St. Martin's Press, 1990.

Maphai, Vincent, ed. *South Africa: The Challenge of Change.* Harare, Zimbabwe: Southern Africa Printing, 1994.

Marais, H.C., ed. *South Africa: Perspectives on the Future.* Pinetown, South Africa: Burgess, 1988.

Maré, Gerhard. *Brothers Born of Warrior Blood: Politics and Ethnicity in South Africa.* Johannesburg: Ravan Press, 1992.

Marks, Shula. *Divided Sisterhood: Race, Class, and Gender in the South African Nursing Profession.* New York: St. Martin's Press, 1994.

Mashabela, Harry. *Townships of the Pretoria-Witwatersrand-Vereeniging.* Johannesburg: South African Institute Race of Relations, 1988.

Meer, Fatima. *Black-Woman-Worker.* Durban: Madiba Publishers for the Institute for Black Research, 1990.

Meer, Fatima, ed. *Poverty in the 1990s: The Responses of Urban Women.* Paris: UNESCO and the International Social Science Council, 1994.

Moodie, T. Dunbar. "Ethnic Violence in South African Gold Mines," *Journal of Southern African Studies* [Oxford], 18, No. 3, September 1992, 584–613.

Moon, Bernard P., and George F. Dardis. *The Geomorphology of Southern Africa.* Johannesburg: Southern Book, 1988.

Morris, Donald R. *Washing the Spears: The Rise and Fall of the Zulu Nation.* New York: Simon and Schuster, 1986.

Mosalakae, Kenosi. *Introspection of an African.* New York: Vantage Press, 1994.

Mostert, W.P., J.L. Van Tonder, and B.E. Hofmeyr. "Demographic Trends in South Africa." Pages 59–86 in H.C. Marais, ed., *South Africa: Perspectives on the Future.* Pinetown, South Africa: Burgess, 1988.

Moulder, James. *Facing the Education Crisis: A Practical Approach.* Johannesburg: Heinemann, 1991.

Mountain, Edgar D. *The Geology of Southern Africa.* Cape Town: Books of Africa, 1968.

Moya, Lily Patience. *Not Either an Experimental Doll: The Separate Worlds of Three South African Women.* Bloomington: Indiana University Press, 1988.

Mungazi, Dickson A. *The Challenge of Educational Innovation and National Development in Southern Africa.* American University Studies, Series on Education, No. 36. New York: Lang, 1991.

Nader, Laura, ed. *Law and Culture in Society.* Chicago: Aldine, 1969.

Newman, James L. *The Peopling of Africa: A Geographic Interpretation.* New Haven: Yale University Press, 1995.

Norment, Lynn. "The Women of the New South Africa," *Ebony,* 44, No. 10, Special Issue on South Africa, August 1994, 98–108.

O'Dowd, M. *Education and Growth.* Keynote Address to the Conference on Education for Growth, March 27, 1992. Johannesburg: South African Institute of Race Relations, 1992.

Oliver, Roland, and Anthony Atmore. *Africa since 1800.* 4th ed. New York: Cambridge University Press, 1994.

Oliver, Roland, and Michael Crowder, eds. *The Cambridge Encyclopedia of Africa.* Cambridge: Cambridge University Press, 1981.

Ottaway, Marina. *Democratization and Ethnic Nationalism: African and Eastern European Experiences.* Policy Essay No. 14. Washington: Overseas Development Council, 1994.

Ottaway, Marina. *South Africa: The Struggle for a New Order.* Washington: Brookings Institution, 1993.

Packard, Randall M. *White Plague, Black Labour: Tuberculosis and the Political Economy of Health and Disease in South Africa.* Berkeley: University of California Press, 1989.

Peires, Jeffrey B. *The House of Phalo: A History of the Xhosa People in the Days of Their Independence.* Perspectives on Southern Africa, No. 32. Berkeley: University of California Press, 1982.

Phillipson, David W. *African Archaeology.* New York: Cambridge University Press, 1985.

Phinney, Jean S., and Mary Jane Rotheram, eds. *Children's Ethnic Socialization: Pluralism and Development.* Newbury Park, California: Sage, 1987.

Pieterse, Hendrik J.C., ed. *Desmond Tutu's Message: A Qualitative Analysis.* Kampen, The Netherlands: Kok Pharos, 1995.

Platsky, Laurine, and Cherryl Walker. *The Surplus People: Forced Removals in South Africa.* Johannesburg: Ravan Press, 1985.

Potts, Deborah. "Urban Environmental Controls and Low-Income Housing in Southern Africa." Pages 207–23 in Hamish Main and Stephen Wyn Williams, eds., *Environment and Housing in Third World Cities.* New York: Wiley and Sons, 1994.

Preston-Whyte, Robert A. "The Politics of Ecology: Dredge-Mining in South Africa," *Environmental Conservation,* 22, Summer 1995, 151–56.

Professors World Peace Academy. *Foreign Policy Issues in a Democratic South Africa: Papers from a Conference of Professors World Peace Academy.* Johannesburg: 1993.

Race Relations Survey: 1992–1993. Johannesburg: South African Institute of Race Relations, 1993.

Race Relations Survey: 1993–1994. Johannesburg: South African Institute of Race Relations, 1994.

Radcliffe-Brown, Alfred R., and Daryll Forde, eds. *African Systems of Kinship and Marriage.* New York: Oxford University Press, 1950.

Ramphele, Mamphela. *A Bed Called Home.* Cape Town: Philip, 1992.

Raper, Peter E. *Dictionary of Southern African Place Names.* Johannesburg: Lowry, 1987.

Rashid, Sadig, and David Fasholé Luke, eds. *Development Management in Africa: Toward Dynamism, Empowerment, and Entrepreneurship.* Boulder, Colorado: Westview Press, 1995.

Rasmussen, R. Kent. *Migrant Kingdom: Mzilikazi's Ndebele in South Africa.* Cape Town: Philip, 1978.

Rich, Paul B. *Hope and Despair: English-speaking Intellectuals and South African Politics.* New York: British Academic Press, 1993.

Robbins, David. *Driving South.* Halfway House, South Africa: Southern Book, 1993.

Robertson, Claire, and Iris Berger, eds. *Women and Class in Africa.* New York: Africana, 1986.

Røgilds, Flemming. *In the Land of the Elephant Bird: Voices of South Africa.* Brookfield, Vermont: Ashgate, 1994.

Rosen, Andreas. *Apartheid, Widerstand, und politische Gewalt in KwaZulu/Natal.* Hamburg: Münster, 1993.

Russell, Charmane. "The AIDS Crisis: A Mining Industry Perspective," *Mining Survey* [Johannesburg], No. 2, April 1991, 20–31.

Savage, Michael, and Olive Shisana. "Health Provision in a Future South Africa." Pages 94–111 in John E. Spence, ed., *Change in South Africa.* New York: Council on Foreign Relations Press, 1994.

Schapera, Isaac. "The Political Organization of the Ngwato of Bechuanaland Protectorate." Pages 56–82 in Meyer Fortes and E.E. Evans-Pritchard, eds., *African Political Systems.* New York: Oxford University Press, 1940.

Schapera, Isaac. *The Tswana.* Ethnographic Survey of Africa, Southern Africa, Pt. 3. London: International African Institute, 1968.

Segar, Julia. *Transkei.* Cape Town: Anthropos, 1988.

September, P.E. "Promoting Information Literacy in Developing Countries: the Case of South Africa," *African Journal of Library, Archives, and Information Science* [Ibadan, Nigeria], 3, No. 1, April 1993, 11–22.

Shillington, Kevin. *A History of Southern Africa.* Burnt Mill, United Kingdom: Longman, 1987.

Smith, David M., ed. *The Apartheid City and Beyond: Urbanization and Social Change in South Africa.* New York: Routledge, Chapman, and Hall, 1992.

South Africa. Central Statistical Service. *1991 Census Results.* Pretoria: 1991.

South Africa, Central Statistical Service. *RSA Statistics in Brief, 1994.* Pretoria: 1994.

South Africa. Department of Education. *Annual Report, June 1994–December 1995.* Pretoria: 1996.

South Africa. Department of Environment Affairs. *Building the Foundation for Sustainable Development in South Africa.* National Report to the United Nations Conference on Environment and Development (UNCED), March 1992. Pretoria: 1992.

South Africa. President's Council. *Report of the Three Committees of the President's Council on a National Environmental Management System.* Cape Town: 1991.

South Africa. South African Communication Service. *South Africa, 1993: Official Yearbook of the Republic of South Africa.* 19th ed. Pretoria: 1994.

South Africa. South African Communication Service. *South Africa Yearbook, 1994.* 1st ed. Originally published as *South Africa Official Yearbook, 1994.* Pretoria: 1995.

South Africa. South African Communication Service. *South Africa Yearbook, 1995.* 2d ed. Pretoria: 1996.

"South Africa." Pages 1348–75 in *The World of Learning, 1995.* 45th ed. London: Europa, 1994.

South Africa Foundation. *South Africa, 1995.* Johannesburg: 1995.

South African Institute of Race Relations. *Fast Facts: The Population Dissected.* Johannesburg: 1993.

South African Institute of Race Relations. *Race Relations Survey 1992–93.* Johannesburg: 1993.

South African Institute of Race Relations. *Race Relations Survey 1993–94.* Johannesburg: 1994.

South African Institute of Race Relations. *Race Relations Survey 1994–95.* Johannesburg: 1995.

Sparks, Allister. *The Mind of South Africa.* New York: Knopf, 1990.

Sparks, Allister. *Tomorrow Is Another Country: The Inside Story of South Africa's Road to Change.* New York: Hill and Wang, 1995.

Spence, John E., ed. *Change in South Africa.* New York: Council on Foreign Relations Press, 1994.

Stedman, Stephen John, ed. *South Africa: The Political Economy of Transformation.* Boulder, Colorado: Lynne Rienner, 1994.

Stevenson, Robert F. *Population and Political Systems in Tropical Africa.* New York: Columbia University Press, 1968.

Stock, Robert. *Africa South of the Sahara: A Geographical Interpretation.* New York: Guilford Press, 1995.

Stoto, Michael A. "Models of the Demographic Effect of AIDS." Pages 350–79 in Karen A. Foote, Kenneth H. Hill, and Linda G. Martin, eds., *Demographic Change in Sub-Saharan Africa.* Washington: National Academy Press, 1993.

Strauss, Jacob P., Hendrik J. van der Linde, S.J. Plekker and J.W.W. Strauss. *Education and Manpower Development, 1995.* Bloemfontein: Research Institute for Education Planning, 1996.

Swanepoel, Hennie, and Frik de Beer. "Training of Racially Mixed Groups in South Africa," *Community Development Journal: An International Forum* [Oxford], 30, No. 3, July 1995, 296–303.

Swartz, Leslie, and Ann Levett. "Political Oppression and Children in South Africa: The Social Construction of Damaging Effects." Pages 265–86 in N. Chabani Manganyi and André du Toit, eds., *Political Violence and the Struggle in South Africa.* New York: St. Martin's Press, 1990.

Switzer, Les. *Power and Resistance in an African Society: The Ciskei Xhosa and the Making of South Africa.* Madison: University of Wisconsin Press, 1993.

Szeftel, Morris. "Ethnicity and Democratization in South Africa," *Review of African Political Economy* [London], No. 60, July 1994, 185–99.

Tamarkin, Michael. *Cecil Rhodes and the Cape Afrikaners: The Imperial Colossus and the Colonial Parish Pump.* Portland, Oregon: Cass, 1995.

Tarver, James D. *The Demography of Africa.* Westport, Connecticut: Praeger, 1995.

Tomlinson, Richard. *Informal Sector Employment.* Johannesburg: Development Bank of Southern Africa, 1993.

Tutu, Desmond. *The Rainbow People of God: The Making of a Peaceful Revolution.* New York: Doubleday, 1994.

United Nations Development Programme. *Human Development Report, 1995.* New York: Oxford University Press, 1995.

United Nations Economic Commission for Africa. *African Population Profile: A Chartbook.* 3d ed. Addis Ababa, Ethiopia: 1994.

University of the Witwatersrand. *Report of the Vice Chancellor, 1992.* Johannesburg: 1992.

Urban Foundation. *Population Trends: Demographic Projections Model.* Johannesburg: 1990.

Vail, Leroy, and Landeg White. *Power and the Praise Poem: Southern African Voices in History.* Charlottesville: University Press of Virginia, 1991.

Vail, Leroy, ed. *The Creation of Tribalism in Southern Africa.* Berkeley: University of California Press, 1989.

Van der Ross, R.E. *The Rise and Decline of Apartheid: A Study of Political Movements among the Coloured People of South Africa, 1880–1985.* Cape Town: Tafelberg, 1986.

Van Zyl, C. *The de Lange Report: 10 Years On.* Pretoria: Human Sciences Research Council, 1991.

Wade, Michael. *White on Black in South Africa.* New York: St. Martin's Press, 1993.

Walker, Cherryl, ed. *Women and Gender in Southern Africa to 1945.* Cape Town: Philip, 1990.

Whiteside, Alan. "Labour Flows, Refugees, AIDS, and the Environment." Pages 155–73 in Gavin Maasdorp and Alan Whiteside, eds., *Towards a Post-Apartheid Future.* New York: St. Martin's Press, 1992.

Wilson, Frances, and Mamphela Ramphele. *Uprooting Poverty: The South African Challenge.* New York: Norton, 1989.

Wilson, Monica Hunter. *Reaction to Conquest: Effects of Contact with Europeans on the Pondo of South Africa.* Cape Town: Philip, 1979.

Wilson, Monica Hunter. "The Sotho, Venda, and Tsonga." Pages 131–82 in Monica Wilson and Leonard Thompson, eds., *The Oxford History of South Africa*, 1. Oxford: Clarendon Press, 1969.

Wilson, Monica Hunter, and Leonard M. Thompson, eds. *The Oxford History of South Africa*, 2 vols. New York: Oxford University Press, 1969, 1971.

Wolpe, Harold. *Race, Class, and the Apartheid State.* London: Currey, 1988.

The World of Learning, 1995. 45th ed. London: Europa, 1994.

World Resources Institute. *World Resources, 1990–91.* Oxford: Oxford University Press, 1990.

(Various issues of the following periodicals were also used in preparation of this chapter: *Argus* [Cape Town]; *Beeld* [Johannesburg]; *British Medical Journal* [London]; *Citizen* [Johannesburg]; *Economist* [London]; *Facts and Reports* [Amsterdam]; *Geographic Journal* [Cambridge]; *Journal of Southern African Stud-*

ies [Oxford]; *Politikon* [Pietermaritzburg]; *South African Journal of African Affairs* [Pretoria]; *South African Journal of Cultural History* [Pretoria]; *South African Journal of Education* [Pretoria]; *South African Journal of Higher Education* [Pretoria]; *Sowetan* [Johannesburg]; and *Star* [Johannesburg].)

Chapter 3

Africa South of the Sahara, 1997. 26th ed. London: Europa, 1996.

Akeroyd, Anne V. "HIV/AIDS in Eastern and Southern Africa," *Review of African Political Economy* [London], 61, June 1994, 173–84.

Ally, Russell. *Gold and Empire: The Bank of England and South Africa's Gold Producers, 1886–1926.* Johannesburg: Witwatersrand University, 1994.

Arndt, E.H.D. *Banking and Currency Development in South Africa (1652–1927).* Cape Town: Juta, 1928.

Baker, Pauline H., Alex Boraine, and Warren Krafchik, eds. *South Africa and the World Economy in the 1990s.* Washington: Brookings Institution, 1993.

Behr, Abraham L. *Education in South Africa: Origins, Issues, and Trends, 1652–1988.* Cape Town: Academica, 1988.

Behrens, R., and Vanessa Watson. "Inward Development: Solutions to Urban Sprawl," *Indicator South Africa* [Durban], 9, No. 3, Winter 1992, 51–54.

Beinart, William. *Twentieth-Century South Africa.* New York: Oxford University Press, 1994.

Bendix, Sonia. *Industrial Relations in the New South Africa.* 3d ed. Kenwyn, South Africa: Juta, 1996.

Berger, Iris. *Threads of Solidarity: Women in South African Industry, 1900–1980.* Bloomington: Indiana University Press, 1992.

Bosman, G.C.R. *The Industrialization of South Africa.* Rotterdam: G.W. den Boer, 1938.

Bozzoli, Belinda. "Capital and the State in South Africa," *Review of African Political Economy* [London], No. 11, January–April 1978, 40–50.

Branaman, Brenda. "South Africa: Politics, Economic Development, U.S. Assistance." Library of Congress, Congressional Research Service, 95–414F. Washington: February 14, 1995.

Brent, R. Stephen. "South Africa: Tough Road to Prosperity," *Foreign Affairs*, 75, March–April 1996, 113–26.

Brewer, John D., ed. *Can South Africa Survive? Five Minutes to Midnight*. New York: St. Martin's Press, 1989.

Buckle, Tony. "'Ndihlala e London' ("I Live in London")," *Third World Planning Review* [Liverpool], 17, No. 1, February 1995, 97–109.

Bundy, Colin. *The Rise and Fall of the South African Peasantry*. Berkeley: University of California Press, 1979.

Caldwell, Don. *No More Martyrs Now: Capitalism, Democracy, and Ordinary People*. Johannesburg: Conrad Business Books, 1992.

Cartwright, Alan Patrick. *The Corner House: The Early History of Johannesburg*. Johannesburg: Purnell, 1965.

Cartwright, Alan Patrick. *The Dynamite Company: The Story of African Explosives and Chemical Industries Limited*. Cape Town: Purnell, 1964.

Christie, Pam. *The Right to Learn: The Struggle for Education in South Africa*. Braamfontein, South Africa: Ravan Press, 1985.

Christie, Renfrew. *Electricity, Industry, and Class in South Africa*. Albany: State University of New York Press, 1984.

Clark, Nancy L. *Manufacturing Apartheid: State Corporations in South Africa*. New Haven: Yale University Press, 1994.

Cock, Jacklyn, and Eddie Koch. *Going Green: People, Politics, and the Environment in South Africa*. Cape Town: Oxford University Press, 1991.

Commonwealth Observer Mission to South Africa. *South Africa in Transition: The Report of the Commonwealth Observer Mission to South Africa: Phase III, August–December 1993*. London: Commonwealth Secretariat, 1994.

Coupe, Stuart. "Divisions of Labour: Racist Trade Unionism in the Iron, Steel, Engineering, and Metallurgical Industries of Post-War South Africa," *Journal of Southern African Studies* [Oxford], 21, No. 3, September 1995, 451–71.

Cramer, Christopher. "Rebuilding South Africa," *Current History*, 93, No. 583, May 1994, 208–12.

Davies, Robert H. *Capital, State, and White Labour in South Africa, 1900-1960: An Historical Materialist Analysis of Class Formation and Class Relations*. Atlantic Highlands, New Jersey: Humanities Press, 1979.

Davis, Graham A. *South African Managed Trade Policy: The Wasting of a Mineral Endowment.* Westport, Connecticut: Praeger, 1994.

De Kock, Gerhard. *A History of the South African Reserve Bank.* Pretoria: Van Schaik, 1954.

Deng, Lual A., and Elling N. Tjonneland, eds. *South Africa: Wealth, Poverty, and Reconstruction.* Pretoria: Centre for Southern African Studies, 1996.

De Wet, C. "Resettlement and Land Reform in South Africa," *Review of African Political Economy* [London], 21, 1994, 359–73.

Doxey, G.V. *The Industrial Colour Bar in South Africa.* Cape Town: Oxford University Press, 1961.

Du Toit, Bettie. *Ukubamba Amadolo: Workers' Struggles in the South African Textile Industry.* London: Onyx Press, 1978.

Economist Intelligence Unit. *South Africa: Country Profile, 1994–95.* London: 1995.

Economist Intelligence Unit. *South Africa: Country Report, Issues 1994–1995.* London: 1994–1995.

Economist Intelligence Unit. *South Africa to 1990: Growing to Survive.* London: 1986.

Edgar, Robert E., ed. *Sanctioning Apartheid.* Trenton, New Jersey: Africa World Press, 1990.

Esterhuysen, Peter, Denis Fair, and Erich Leistner. *South Africa in Subequatorial Africa: Economic Interaction.* Pretoria: Africa Institute of South Africa, 1994.

Falkena, H.B., L.J. Fourie, and W.J. Kok, eds. *The Mechanics of the South African Financial System: Financial Institutions, Instruments, and Markets.* Johannesburg: Macmillan, South Africa, 1984.

Floor, Bernal C. *The History of National Roads in South Africa.* Stellenbosch, South Africa: Floor, 1985.

Franzsen, D.G. *Economic Growth and Stability in a Developing Economy: Some Aspects of the Union's Postwar Experience.* Pretoria: Van Schaik, 1960.

Freund, Bill. *The African Worker.* African Society Today Series. Cambridge: Cambridge University Press, 1988.

Friedman, Steven. *Building Tomorrow Today: African Workers in Trade Unions, 1970–1984.* Johannesburg: Ravan Press, 1987.

Greenberg, Stanley B. *Race and State in Capitalist Development: Comparative Perspectives.* New Haven: Yale University Press, 1980.

Greenberg, Stanley B. *Legitimating the Illegitimate: State, Markets, and Resistance in South Africa.* Berkeley: University of California Press, 1987.

Grundy, Kenneth W. "South Africa: Putting Democracy to Work," *Current History,* 94, No. 591, 172–76.

Guest, Bill, and John M. Sellers, eds. *Receded Tides of Empire: Aspects of the Economic and Social History of Natal and Zululand since 1910.* Pietermaritzburg: University of Natal Press, 1994.

Hanke, Steve H. "The New Apartheid," *Forbes,* 155, No. 9, April 24, 1995, 64.

Hart, Gillian Patricia. *Some Socio-Economic Aspects of African Entrepreneurship with Particular Reference to the Transkei and Ciskei.* Grahamstown, South Africa: Rhodes University, Institute of Social and Economic Research, 1972.

Hauck, David. *Black Trade Unions in South Africa.* Washington: Investor Responsibility Research Center, 1982.

Hawkins, Tony. *Country Risk Profiles with Specific Reference to Southern Africa.* Pretoria: Institute for Strategic Studies, University of Pretoria, 1996.

Hengeveld, Richard, and Jaap Rodenburg. *Embargo: Apartheid's Oil Secrets Revealed.* Amsterdam: Amsterdam University Press, 1995.

Henning, Cosmo G. *The Indentured Indian in Natal, 1860–1917.* New Delhi: Promilla, 1993.

Holden, Merle. "GATT Trade Policy Review—South Africa: 1993," *World Economy,* 18, Special Issue, 1995, 121–33.

Horwitz, Robert B. "The Uneasy Relation Between Political and Economic Reform in South Africa: The Case of Telecommunications," *African Affairs* [London], 93, No. 372, July 1994, 361–85.

Houghton, D. Hobart. *The South African Economy.* Cape Town: Oxford University Press, 1973.

Houghton, D. Hobart, and Jenifer Dagut. *Source Material on the South African Economy, 1860–1970.* 3 vols. New York: Oxford University Press, 1972–73.

Innes, Duncan. *Anglo American and the Rise of Modern South Africa.* New York: Monthly Review Press, 1984.

International Bank for Reconstruction and Development. *World Development Report, 1994.* New York: Oxford University Press, 1994.

International Energy Agency. *Energy Policies of South Africa: 1996 Survey.* Paris: Organisation for Economic Co-operation and Development, 1996.

Jeeves, Alan H. *Migrant Labour in South Africa's Mining Economy: The Struggle for the Gold Mines' Labour Supply, 1870–1920.* Kingston, Ontario: McGill-Queen's University Press, 1985.

Johnstone, Frederick A. *Class, Race, and Gold: A Study of Class Relations and Racial Discrimination in South Africa.* London: Routledge and Paul, 1976.

Keegan, Timothy J. *Rural Transformations in Industrializing South Africa: The Southern Highveld to 1914.* Braamfontein, South Africa: Ravan Press, 1986.

Lemon, Anthony, and Gillian P. Cook. "South Africa." Pages 315–41 in James D. Tarver, ed., *Urbanization in Africa.* Westport, Connecticut: Greenwood Press, 1994.

Lewis, Jon. *Industrialisation and Trade Union Organisation in South Africa, 1924–55: The Rise and Fall of the South African Trades and Labour Council.* New York: Cambridge University Press, 1984.

Lewis, Stephen R., Jr. *The Economics of Apartheid.* New York: Council on Foreign Relations Press, 1990.

Lieberman, Evan S., ed. *Beyond a Political Solution to Apartheid: Economic and Social Policy Proposals for a Postapartheid South Africa.* Princeton, New Jersey: Center of International Studies, 1993.

Lipton, Merle. *Capitalism and Apartheid: South Africa, 1910–84.* Totowa, New Jersey: Rowman and Allanheld, 1985.

Lipton, Merle, and Charles Simkins, eds. *State and Market in Post Apartheid South Africa.* Boulder, Colorado: Westview Press, 1993.

Maasdorp, Gavin, and Alan Whiteside, eds. *Towards a Post-Apartheid Future: Political and Economic Relations in Southern Africa.* New York: St. Martin's Press, 1992.

McGregor, Robin. *McGregor's Who Owns Whom.* Somerset West, South Africa: Purdey, 1984.

Macro-Economic Research Group (MERG). *Making Democracy Work: A Framework for Macroeconomic Policy in South Africa.* Cape Town: African National Congress, 1993.

Magubane, Bernard M. *The Political Economy of Race and Class in South Africa.* New York: Monthly Review Press, 1979.

Manning, Claudia. *Informal Manufacturing in the South African Economy.* Durban, South Africa: University of Natal, Centre for Social and Development Studies, 1993.

Marks, Shula, and Anthony Atmore, eds. *Economy and Society in Pre-Industrial South Africa.* London: Longman, 1980.

Marks, Shula, and Richard Rathbone, eds. *Industrialisation and Social Change in South Africa: African Class Formation, Culture, and Consciousness, 1870–1930.* New York: Longman, 1982.

Marks, Shula, and Stanley Trapido, eds. *The Politics of Race, Class, and Nationalism in Twentieth-Century South Africa.* London: Longman, 1987.

Marsh, J.H. *South African Transport Service (SATS), 1910–1985, and the Story of Transport in Southern Africa.* Johannesburg: Travel and Trade Promotions, 1985.

Martins, J.H. *Household Expenditure in South Africa by Area, Population Group, and Product, 1993.* Pretoria: University of South Africa, Bureau of Market Research, 1994.

Martins, J.H. *Socio-Economic Profile of the Nine Provinces of South Africa, 1994.* Pretoria: University of South Africa, Bureau of Market Research, 1994.

Marx, Anthony W. *Lessons of Struggle: South African Internal Opposition, 1960–1990.* New York: Oxford University Press, 1992.

Masisela, Calvin, and Daniel Weiner. "Resettlement Planning in Zimbabwe and South Africa's Rural Land Reform Discourse," *Third World Planning Review* [Liverpool], 18, No. 1, February 1996, 23–43.

Morrell, Robert, ed. *White But Poor: Essays on the History of Poor Whites in Southern Africa, 1880–1940.* Pretoria: University of South Africa, 1992.

Murray, Colin. "Structural Unemployment, Small Towns and Agrarian Change in South Africa," *African Affairs* [London], 94, No. 374, January 1995, 5–22.

Nattrass, Jill. *The South African Economy: Its Growth and Change.* Cape Town: Oxford University Press, 1981.

Nattrass, Nicoli. "Politics and Economics in African National Congress Economic Policy," *African Affairs* [London], 93, No. 372, July 1994, 343–59.

Nowels, Larry. "South Africa Aid: U.S. Assistance Package for FY 1994–1996." Library of Congress, Congressional Research Service, 94–851F. Washington: October 28, 1994.

O'Meara, Dan. *Volkskapitalisme: Class, Capital, and Ideology in the Development of Afrikaner Nationalism, 1934–1938.* New York: Cambridge University Press, 1983.

Post-apartheid Population and Income Trends: A New Analysis. Johannesburg: Centre for Development and Enterprise, 1995.

Preston-Whyte, Robert A. "The Politics of Ecology: Dredge-Mining in South Africa," *Environmental Conservation*, 22, Summer 1995, 151–56.

Price, Robert M. *The Apartheid State in Crisis: Political Transformation in South Africa, 1975–1990.* New York: Oxford University Press, 1991.

Schrire, Robert, ed. *Wealth and Poverty: Critical Choices for South Africa.* New York: Oxford University Press, 1993.

Seidman, Ann, K.W. Mwanza, N. Simelane, and D. Weiner, eds. *Transforming Southern African Agriculture.* Trenton, New Jersey: Africa World Press, 1992.

Seidman, Gay W. "From Trade Union to Working-Class Mobilization: The Politicization of South Africa's Non-Racial Labor Unions." Pages 223–56 in Robert E. Mazur, ed., *Breaking the Links: Development Theory and Practice in Southern Africa.* Trenton, New Jersey: Africa World Press, 1990.

Seidman, Gay W. *Manufacturing Militance: Workers' Movements in Brazil and South Africa, 1970–1985.* Berkeley: University of California Press, 1994.

Simamba, B.H. *An African Preferential Trade Area: The Institutions, Law, and Operations.* Lusaka: University of Zambia Press, 1993.

Simkins, Charles. "The South African Economy: Problems and Prospects." Pages 65–81 in John E. Spence, ed., *Change in South Africa.* New York: Council on Foreign Relations Press, 1994.

Smith, David M., ed. *The Apartheid City and Beyond: Urbanization and Social Change in South Africa.* New York: Routledge, Chapman, and Hall, 1992.

South Africa. Central Statistical Service. *Report of the Commission of Inquiry into the Export Trade of South Africa.* Pretoria: 1972.

South Africa. Central Statistical Service. *Report of the Commission of Inquiry into Labour Legislation.* Pretoria: 1979.

South Africa. Central Statistical Service. *Report of the Commission of Inquiry into Legislation Affecting the Utilsation of Manpower.* Pretoria: 1979.

South Africa. Central Statistical Service. *Report of the Commission of Inquiry into Policy Relating to the Protection of Industry.* Pretoria: 1958.

South Africa. Central Statistical Service. *Report of the Industrial Legislation Commission.* Pretoria: 1951.

South Africa. Central Statistical Service. *Report of the National Manpower Commission for 1983.* Pretoria: 1983.

South Africa. South African Communication Service. *South Africa, 1993: Official Yearbook of the Republic of South Africa.* 19th ed. Pretoria: 1994.

South Africa. South African Communication Service. *South Africa Yearbook, 1994.* 1st ed. Originally published as *South Africa Official Yearbook, 1994.* Pretoria: 1995.

South Africa. South African Communication Service. *South Africa Yearbook, 1995.* 2d ed. Pretoria: 1996.

"South Africa," *World Link* [London], January–February 1995, 289–99.

South Africa Foundation. *South Africa, 1995.* Johannesburg: 1995.

South African Institute of Race Relations. *Race Relations Survey, 1994–95.* Johannesburg: 1995.

Sparks, Allister. *The Mind of South Africa: The Story of the Rise and Fall of Apartheid.* New York: Knopf, 1990.

Spence, John E., ed. *Change in South Africa.* New York: Council on Foreign Relations Press, 1994.

Stedman, Stephen John, ed. *South Africa: The Political Economy of Transformation.* Boulder, Colorado: Lynne Rienner, 1994.

United States. Congress. 104th, 1st Session. House of Representatives. *Agreement for Cooperation Between the United States of*

America and the Republic of South Africa Concerning Peaceful Uses of Nuclear Energy. No. 104–21. Washington: GPO, 1995.

Van Ameringen, Marc. *Building a New South Africa, 1. Economic Policy.* Ottawa, Canada: International Development Research Centre, 1995.

Van Ameringen, Marc. *Building a New South Africa, 2. Urban Policy.* Ottawa, Canada: International Development Research Centre, 1995.

Van Ameringen, Marc. *Building a New South Africa, 3. Science and Technology Policy.* Ottawa, Canada: International Development Research Centre, 1995.

Van Ameringen, Marc. *Building a New South Africa, 4. Environment, Reconstruction, and Development.* Ottawa, Canada: International Development Research Centre, 1995.

Van Wyk, H. de J. *The Economic Importance and Growth of Selected Districts in South Africa, 1995.* Pretoria: Bureau of Market Research, University of South Africa, 1994.

Voorhes, Meg, ed. *Challenges and Opportunities for Business in Post-Apartheid South Africa.* Washington: Investor Responsibility Research Center, 1994.

Webster, Eddie. *Cast in a Racial Mould: Labour Process and Trade Unionism in the Foundries.* Johannesburg: Ravan Press, 1985.

Weiland, Heribert, and Matthew Braham, eds. *Towards a New South African Economy: Comparative Perspectives.* Papers from a workshop, "Economic Concepts and Strategies: Comparative Experiences in View of a New South Africa," organized by the Arnold Bergstraesser Institute and the Friedrich Ebert Foundation, October 20–24, 1991. Freiburg, Germany: Arnold Bergstraesser Institute, 1992.

Williams, R.C. *Income Tax in South Africa: Cases and Materials.* Durban: Butterworths, 1995.

Wilson, Francis, Alide Kooy, and Delia Hendrie, eds. *Farm Labour in South Africa.* Cape Town: Philip, 1977.

Wolpe, Harold. "Capitalism and Cheap Labour-Power in South Africa: From Segregation to Apartheid," *Economy and Society,* 1, No. 4, November 1972, 425–56.

World Bank. *Key Indicators of Poverty in South Africa.* Cape Town: Reconstruction and Development Program, Office of the President, 1995.

World Bank. *Reducing Poverty in South Africa: Options for Equitable and Sustainable Growth.* Washington: 1994.

Yudelman, David. *The Emergence of Modern South Africa: State, Capital, and the Incorporation of Organized Labour on the South African Gold Fields, 1902–1939.* Westport, Connecticut: Greenwood Press, 1983.

Zucchini, W. *The Occurrence and Severity of Droughts in South Africa.* Stellenbosch, South Africa: University of Stellenbosch, 1984.

(Various issues of the following publications were also used in the preparation of this chapter: *Africa Economic Digest* [London]; *Africa Report; Africa Research Bulletin* (Economic, Financial, and Technical Series) [Oxford]; *African Business* [London]; *Bulletin of Statistics* [Pretoria]; *Business Day* [Johannesburg]; *Christian Science Monitor; The Citizen* [Johannesburg]; *Economist* [London]; *Financial Mail* [Johannesburg]; *Financial Times* [London]; Foreign Broadcast Information Service, *Daily Report: Sub-Saharan Africa;* International Monetary Fund, *International Financial Statistics;* Investor Responsibility Research Center, *South Africa Investor; Journal of Peasant Studies* [London] (see Special Issue on South Africa, January 1996); *Marchés Tropicaux et Méditerranéens* [Paris]; Nedcor Economic Unit, *Guide to the Economy* [Johannesburg]; *New York Times;* South African Chamber of Mines, *Newsletter* and *Mining Survey* [Johannesburg]; *South African Labour Bulletin* [Braamfontein]; South African Reserve Bank, *Quarterly Bulletin; Southern African Economist* [Harare]; *Southern Africa Political and Economic Monthly* [Harare]; *The Star* [Johannesburg]; *and Wall Street Journal.*)

Chapter 4

African National Congress. Department of Information and Publicity. *Regional Policy: Policy Guide.* Marshalltown, South Africa: 1993.

Akenson, Donald H. *God's Peoples: Covenant and Land in South Africa, Israel, and Ulster.* Ithaca: Cornell University Press, 1992.

Amato, Rob. *Understanding the New Constitution: Everyone's Guide to the Development and Implications of the New South African Constitution.* Cape Town: Struik, 1994.

Arnold, Guy. *South Africa: Crossing the Rubicon.* New York: St. Martin's Press, 1992.

Baker, Pauline H. *The United States and South Africa: The Reagan Years.* New York: Ford Foundation and Foreign Policy Association, 1989.

Banks, Arthur S. *Political Handbook of the World 1993.* Binghamton, New York: State University of New York, Center for Social Analysis, 1994.

Benson, Mary. *Nelson Mandela.* New York: Penguin, 1986.

Boraine, Alex, Janet Levy, and Ronel Scheffer, eds. *Dealing with the Past: Truth and Reconciliation in South Africa.* Cape Town: Institute for a Democratic Alternative for South Africa, 1994.

Borstelmann, Thomas. *Apartheid's Reluctant Uncle: The United States and South Africa in the Early Cold War.* New York: Oxford University Press, 1992.

Bray, Grantland. *Rebel with a Cause: Letters to the Editor, or A Neo-Conservative Agenda for a Post-Apartheid South Africa.* Johannesburg: Thorold's Africana Books, 1993.

Brewer, John D. *Restructuring South Africa.* New York: St. Martin's Press, 1994.

Breytenbach, Breyten. *Return to Paradise.* New York: Harcourt Brace, 1993.

Callinicos, Luli. *Working Life, 1886–1940.* Johannesburg: Ravan Press, 1987.

Cameron, Trewhella. *Jan Smuts: An Illustrated Biography.* Cape Town: Human and Rousseau, 1994.

Cefkin, J. Leo. "Israel and South Africa: Reconciling Pragmatism and Principle," *Middle East Review,* 21, Winter 1988–89, 29–40.

Chan, Stephen. *Exporting Apartheid: Foreign Policies in Southern Africa, 1978–1988.* New York: St. Martin's Press, 1990.

Clark, Steve, ed. *Nelson Mandela Speaks: Forging a Democratic, Nonracial South Africa.* New York: Pathfinder Press, 1993.

Commonwealth Secretariat. *The End of Apartheid: The Report of the Commonwealth Observer Group to the South Africa Elections, April 26–29, 1994.* London: 1994.

Copson, Raymond W. *South Africa: Political Situation, Constitutional Negotiations, U.S. Policy.* CRS Report 96–308F, April 5, 1996. Washington: Library of Congress, Congressional Research Service, 1996.

Corder, Hugh. "Towards a South African Constitution," *Modern Law Review* [London], 56, No. 4, July 1994, 491–533.

Crocker, Chester A. *High Noon in Southern Africa: Making Peace in a Rough Neighborhood.* New York: Norton, 1992.

Dale, Richard. *Botswana's Search for Autonomy in Southern Africa.* Westport, Connecticut: Greenwood Press, 1995.

Davis, R. Hunt, Jr., ed. *Apartheid Unravels.* Gainesville: University of Florida Press, Center for African Studies, 1991.

Davis, Stephen M. *Apartheid's Rebels: Inside South Africa's Hidden War.* New Haven: Yale University Press, 1987.

de Klerk, Willem. *F.W. de Klerk: The Man in His Time.* Parklands, South Africa: Ball, 1991.

de Ville, Jacques, and Nico Steytler, eds. *Voting in 1999: Choosing an Electoral System.* Durban: Butterworths, 1996.

Du Toit, Pierre van der P. *State Building and Democracy in Southern Africa: Botswana, Zimbabwe, and South Africa.* Washington: United States Institute of Peace Press, 1995.

Dyzenhaus, David. *Hard Cases in Wicked Legal Systems: South African Law in the Perspective of Legal Philosophy.* New York: Oxford University Press, 1991.

Ellis, Stephen. "Mbokodo: Security in ANC Camps, 1961–1990," *African Affairs* [London], 93, No. 371, April 1994, 279–98.

Etherington, Norman, ed. *Peace, Politics, and Violence in the New South Africa.* London: Zell, 1992.

Falk, Pamela, and Kurt N. Campbell. *The United States, Soviet Union, Cuba, and South Africa in Angola: The Quagmire of Four Party Negotiations, 1981–88.* Pew Case Studies in International Affairs, No. 429. Washington: Georgetown University, Institute for the Study of Diplomacy, 1988.

February, Vernon. *The Afrikaners of South Africa.* New York: Paul International, 1991.

Friedman, Steven, ed. *The Long Journey: South Africa's Quest for a Negotiated Settlement.* Johannesburg: Ravan Press, 1993.

Friedman, Steven, and Doreen Atkinson, eds. *The Small Miracle: South Africa's Negotiated Settlement.* Athens, Ohio: Raven Press, 1994.

Furlong, Patrick J. *Between Crown and Swastika: The Impact of the Radical Right on the Afrikaner Nationalist Movement in the Fascist*

Era. Hanover, New Hampshire: Wesleyan University Press, 1991.

Gastrow, Shelagh. *Who's Who in South African Politics.* 4th ed. New York: Zell, 1992.

Geldenhuys, Deon. *South Africa and the China Question: A Case for Dual Recognition.* East Asia Project Working Paper Series. Witwatersrand: University of the Witwatersrand, 1995.

Gevisser, Mark. *Portraits of Power: Profiles in a Changing South Africa.* Claremont, South Africa: Philip, 1996.

Gilbey, Emma. *The Lady: The Life and Times of Winnie Mandela.* London: Vintage, 1994.

Giliomee, Hermann. "Democratization in South Africa," *Political Science Quarterly,* 110, Spring 1995, 83–104.

Giliomee, Hermann. "The Non-Racial Franchise and Afrikaner and Coloured Identities, 1910–1994," *African Affairs* [London], 94, No. 375, April 1995, 199–225.

Giliomee, Hermann, and Lawrence Schlemmer, eds. *The Bold Experiment: South Africa's New Democracy.* Halfway House, South Africa: Southern Book, 1994.

Glanz, L.W., P. Mostert, and B.E. Hofmeyr. *An Analysis of South African Crime Statistics: Convictions for the Period 1956–1988.* Pretoria: Human Sciences Research Council, 1992.

Goodwin, June. *Heart of Whiteness: Afrikaners Face Black Rule in the New South Africa.* New York: Scribner, 1995.

Greenstein, Ran. *Genealogies of Conflict: Class, Identity, and State in Palestine/Israel and South Africa.* Hanover, New Hampshire: University Press of New England, 1995.

Grotpeter, John J. *Historical Dictionary of Namibia.* Metuchen, New Jersey: Scarecrow Press, 1994.

Grundy, Kenneth W. *South Africa: Domestic Crisis and Global Challenge.* Boulder, Colorado: Westview Press, 1991.

Grundy, Kenneth W. "South Africa: Putting Democracy to Work," *Current History,* 94, No. 591, April 1995, 172–76.

Guelke, Adrian. *Interdependence and Transition: The Cases of South Africa and Northern Ireland.* Johannesburg: South African Institute of International Affairs, 1993.

Haapiseva-Hunter, Jane. *Undercutting Sanctions: Israel, the U.S., and South Africa.* Washington: Middle East Associates, 1987.

Hadland, Adrian, comp. *Business Day Directory of Politics and Business in South Africa.* Sandton, South Africa: Struik, 1995.

Hamill, James. "The Crossing of the Rubicon: South Africa's Post-Apartheid Political Process, 1990–1992," *International Relations* [London], 12, No. 3, December 1994, 9–37.

Hanlon, Joseph. *Beggar Your Neighbours: Apartheid Power in Southern Africa.* Bloomington: Indiana University Press, 1986.

Harber, Anton, and Barbara Ludman, eds. *The A-Z of South African Politics: The Essential Handbook.* Rev. ed. New York: Penguin, 1995.

Harbeson, John W., and Donald Rothchild, eds. *Africa in World Politics: Post-Cold War Challenges.* 2d ed. Boulder, Colorado: Westview Press, 1995.

Harris, Mari. "Attitudes and Behaviour of the 'New' South African Electorate: An Empirical Assessment," *International Social Science Journal* [Paris], 47, No. 4, December 1995, 567–82.

Hatchard, John, and Peter Slinn. "The Path Towards a New Order in South Africa," *International Relations* [London], 12, No. 4, April 1995, 1–26.

Herbst, Jeffrey. "South Africa and Southern Africa after Apartheid." Pages 147–62 in John W. Harbeson and Donald Rothchild, eds., *Africa in World Politics: Post-Cold War Challenges.* 2d ed. Boulder, Colorado: Westview Press, 1995.

Hirson, Baruch. *Yours for the Union: Class and Community Struggles in South Africa, 1930–1947.* Atlantic Highlands, New Jersey: Zed Books, 1990.

Horowitz, Donald L. *A Democratic South Africa? Constitutional Engineering in a Divided Society.* Berkeley: University of California Press, 1991.

Horrell, Muriel, comp. *Race Relations as Regulated by Law in South Africa, 1948–1979.* Johannesburg: South African Institute of Race Relations, 1982.

Horwitz, Robert B. "The Uneasy Relation Between Political and Economic Reform in South Africa: The Case of Telecommunications," *African Affairs* [London], 93, 372, July 1994, 361–85.

Human Rights Watch/Africa. *South Africa: Impunity for Human Rights Abuses in Two Homelands: Reports on KwaZulu and Bophuthatswana.* New York: 1994.

Huntington, Samuel P. "Reform and Stability in South Africa," *International Security*, 6, No. 4, Spring 1982, 3–25.

International Republican Institute. *South Africa: Campaign and Election Report, April 26–29, 1994.* Washington: 1994.

Jackson, Gordon S. *Breaking Story: The South African Press.* Boulder, Colorado: Westview Press, 1993.

Jaster, Robert S. *South Africa's Other Whites: Voices for Change.* New York: St. Martin's Press, 1993.

Johns, Sheridan, and R. Hunt Davis, Jr., eds. *Mandela, Tambo, and the African National Congress: The Struggle Against Apartheid, 1948–1990.* New York: Oxford University Press, 1991.

Johnston, Alexander. "South Africa: The Election and the Transition Process: Five Contradictions in Search of a Resolution," *Third World Quarterly* [London], 15, No. 2, June 1994, 187–204.

Johnston, Alexander, Sipho Shezi, and Gavin Bradshaw. *Constitution-making in the New South Africa.* London: Leicester University Press, 1993.

Juckes, Tim J. *Opposition in South Africa: The Leadership of Z.K. Matthews, Nelson Mandela, and Stephen Biko.* Westport, Connecticut: Praeger, 1995.

Kane-Berman, John. *The New Liberals.* Johannesburg: South African Institute of Race Relations, 1993.

Kane-Berman, John. *Political Violence in South Africa.* Johannesburg: South African Institute of Race Relations, 1993.

Kibble, Steve, Paul Goodison, and Balefi Tsie. "The Uneasy Triangle—South Africa, Southern Africa, and Europe in the Post-Apartheid Era," *International Relations* [London], 12, No. 4, April 1995, 41–61.

Kitchen, Helen. *A Conversation with F. W. de Klerk.* Africa Notes, No. 167. Washington: Center for Strategic and International Studies, 1994.

Kitchen, Helen, and J. Coleman Kitchen, eds. *South Africa: Twelve Perspectives on the Transition.* Washington Papers, No. 165. Westport, Connecticut: Praeger, with the Center for Strategic and International Studies, Washington, 1994.

Kossler, Reinhart, and Henning Melber. *The Concept of Civil Society and the Process of Nation-Building in African States.* Windhoek, Namibia: Namibian Economic Policy Research Unit, 1994.

Kotzè, Hennie, and Anneke Greyling. *Political Organisations in South Africa, A-Z.* Cape Town: Tafelberg, 1991.

Lazarson, Joshua N. *Against The Tide: Whites in the Struggle Against Apartheid.* Boulder, Colorado: Westview Press, 1994.

Lelyveld, Joseph. *Move Your Shadow: South Africa, Black and White.* New York: Time Books, 1985.

Leys, Colin, and John S. Saul. *Namibia's Liberation Struggle: The Two-Edged Sword.* Athens: Ohio University Press, 1995.

Lijphart, Arend. *Democracy in Plural Societies: A Comparative Exploration.* New Haven: Yale University Press, 1977.

Lijphart, Arend. *Power-Sharing in South Africa.* Policy Papers in International Affairs, No. 24. Berkeley: University of California Press, Institute of International Studies, 1985.

Lipton, Merle. *Capitalism and Apartheid: South Africa 1910–1986.* Reprint of *Capitalism and Apartheid: South Africa, 1910–84,* with new Epilogue. Aldershot, United Kingdom: Wildwood House, 1986.

Lodge, Tom. *The African National Congress Comes Home.* African Study Seminar, Paper No. 317. Johannesburg: University of the Witwatersrand, 1992.

Lodge, Tom. *The ANC After Nkomati.* Johannesburg: South African Institute of Race Relations, 1985.

Lyman, Princeton N. "South Africa's Promise," *Foreign Policy,* 102, Spring 1996, 105–19.

Maasdorp, Gavin, and Alan Whiteside, eds. *Towards a Post-Apartheid Future: Political and Economic Relations in Southern Africa.* New York: St. Martin's Press, 1992.

McCarthy, Stephen. *Africa: The Challenge of Transformation.* New York: Tauris, distributed by St. Martin's Press, 1994.

McCaul, Coleen. *No Easy Ride: Rise and Future of the Black Taxi Industry.* Johannesburg: South African Institute of Race Relations, 1990.

MacDonald, Michael. "The Siren's Song: The Political Logic of Power-Sharing in South Africa," *Journal of Southern African Studies* [Oxford], 18, No. 4, December 1992, 709–25.

Mandela, Nelson. *Long Walk to Freedom: The Autobiography of Nelson Mandela.* Boston: Little, Brown, 1994.

Mandela, Nelson. *Report on the 49th ANC National Conference, Bloemfontein, December 1994.* Marshalltown, South Africa: African National Congress, Department of Information and Publicity, 1994.

Mandela, Nelson. *The Struggle is My Life.* London: Canon Collins House, 1978. Reprint. New York: Pathfinder Press, 1990.

Mandela, Nelson, et al. Jurgen Schadeberg, comp. *Voices from Robben Island.* Randburg, South Africa: Ravan Press, 1994.

Manzo, Kathryn A. *Domination, Resistance, and Social Change in South Africa: The Local Effects of Global Power.* Westport, Connecticut: Praeger, 1992.

Maphai, Vincent. "Prospects for a Democratic South Africa," *International Affairs* [London], 69, No. 2, April 1993, 223–37.

Maphai, Vincent, ed. *South Africa: The Challenge of Change.* Harare, Zimbabwe: Southern Africa Printing and Publishing House, 1994.

Marais, H.C., ed. *South Africa: Perspectives on the Future.* Pinetown, South Africa: Burgess, 1988.

Maré, Gerhard, and Georgina Hamilton. *An Appetite for Power: Buthelezi's Inkatha and South Africa.* Bloomington: Indiana University Press, 1987.

Marx, Anthony W. *Lessons of Struggle: South African Internal Opposition, 1960–1990.* New York: Oxford University Press, 1992.

Meer, Fatima. *The Codesa File: An Institute for Black Research Institute Project.* Durban: Madiba, 1993.

Meer, Fatima. *Higher than Hope: The Authorized Biography of Nelson Mandela.* New York: Harper and Row, 1988.

Meredith, Martin. *A Guide to South Africa's 1994 Election.* London: Mandarin, 1994.

Meredith, Martin. *In the Name of Apartheid: South Africa in the Post War Period.* New York: Harper and Row, 1988.

Meyer, Roelf P. *Lessons from the Government of National Unity for a Future South Africa.* Institute for Strategic Studies, University of Pretoria (ISSUP) Bulletin. Pretoria: ISSUP, 1995.

Mills, Greg, ed. *From Parish to Participants: South Africa's Evolving Foreign Relations, 1990–1994.* Johannesburg: South African Institute of International Affairs, 1994.

Mills, Greg. *South Africa's Foreign Policy Priorities: A 1996 Update.* Washington: Center for Strategic and International Studies, 1996.

Minter, William. *Apartheid's Contras: An Inquiry into the Roots of War in Angola and Mozambique.* Atlantic Highlands, New Jersey: Zed Press, 1994.

Motala, Ziyad. *Constitutional Options for a Democratic South Africa.* Washington: Howard University Press, 1994.

Murray, Martin J. *Revolution Deferred: The Painful Birth of Post-Apartheid South Africa.* New York: Verso, 1994.

Muthien, Yvonne G. *State and Resistance in South Africa, 1939–1965.* Brookfield, Vermont: Ashgate, 1994.

Muthien, Yvonne G., and Meshack M. Khosa. "'The Kingdom, the Folksstaat, and the New South Africa': Drawing South Africa's New Regional Boundaries," *Journal of Southern African Studies* [Oxford], 21, No. 2, June 1995, 303–22.

National Democratic Institute for International Affairs. *Nation Building: The U.N. and Namibia.* Washington: 1990.

Nel, Philip. "Transition Through Erosion: Comparing South Africa's Democratisation," *Aussenpolitik* [English ed.] [Hamburg], 46, No. 1, January 1995, 71–93.

Nelson, Daniel N. *After Authoritarianism: Democracy or Disorder?* Westport, Connecticut: Greenwood Press, 1995.

Nolutshungu, Sam C. *Southern Africa in a Global Context: Towards a Southern African Security Community.* Occasional Papers Series, No. 6. Harare, Zimbabwe: Southern Africa Political Economy Series (SAPES), 1994.

Ohlson, Thomas, Stephen John Stedman, with Robert Davies. *The New Is Not Yet Born: Conflict Resolution in Southern Africa.* Washington: Brookings Institution, 1994.

O'Meara, Patrick, and N. Brian Winchester. "Political Change in South Africa," *Fletcher Forum of World Affairs,* 15, No. 1, Winter 1991, 37–44.

Orkin, Mark. "Building Democracy in the New South Africa: Civil Society, Citizenship, and Political Ideology," *Review of African Political Economy* [London], 22, June 1995, 525–37.

Ottaway, David. *Chained Together: Mandela, de Klerk, and the Struggle to Remake South Africa.* New York: Time Books, 1993.

Ottaway, Marina. *Democratization and Ethnic Nationalism: African and Eastern European Experiences.* Policy Essay No. 14. Washington: Overseas Development Council, 1994.

Ottaway, Marina. *South Africa: The Struggle for a New Order.* Washington: Brookings Institution, 1993.

Payne, Richard J. *The Nonsuperpowers and South Africa: Implications for U.S. Policy.* Bloomington: Indiana University Press, 1990.

Podbrey, Pauline. *White Girl in Search of the Party.* Pietermaritzburg: Hadeda Books, 1993.

Price, Robert M. *The Apartheid State in Crisis: Political Transformation in South Africa, 1975–1990.* New York: Oxford University Press, 1991.

Race Relations Survey, 1993/1994. Johannesburg: South African Institute of Race Relations, 1994.

Race Relations Survey, 1994/1995. Johannesburg: South African Institute of Race Relations, 1995.

Ramamurthi, T.G., ed. *South Africa-India: Partnership in Freedom and Development.* New Delhi: Indian Council for Cultural Relations and New Age International, 1995.

Reader's Digest Association. *Illustrated History of South Africa: The Real Story.* Pleasantville, New York: 1989.

Reynolds, Andrew, ed. *Election '94 South Africa: The Campaigns, Results, and Future Prospects.* New York: St. Martin's Press, 1994.

Rhoodie, Eschel. *P W Botha: The Last Betrayal.* Melville, South Africa: S.A. Politics, 1989.

Rich, Paul B. *State Power and Black Politics in South Africa, 1912–51.* New York: St. Martin's Press, 1995.

Riley, Eileen. *Major Political Events in South Africa, 1948–1990.* New York: Facts on File, 1991.

Roux, Edward. *Time Longer than Rope: A History of the Black Man's Struggle for Freedom in South Africa.* London: Gollancz, 1948.

Schlemmer, Lawrence, and Ian Hirschfeld, eds. *Founding Democracy and the New South African Voter.* Pretoria: Human Sciences Research Council, 1994.

Schlemmer, Lawrence, and R. Lee. *South Africa: Transition to Democracy.* Oxford: Oxford University Press, 1991.

Schneidman, Witney W. *Postapartheid South Africa: Steps Taken, the Path Ahead.* CSIS Africa Notes, No. 156. Washington: Center for Strategic and International Studies, January 1994.

Schoeman, Elna, Jacquelin A. Kalley, and Naomi Muskier, comps. *Mandela's Five Years of Freedom: South African Politics, Economics, and Social Issues, 1990–1995.* Bibliographical Series, No. 29. Johannesburg: South African Institute of International Affairs, 1996.

463

Schrire, Robert, ed. *Leadership in the Apartheid State: From Malan to de Klerk.* Cape Town: Oxford University Press, 1994.

Sejaname, Mafa, ed. *From Destabilisation to Regional Cooperation in Southern Africa.* Maseru, Lesotho: National University of Lesotho, Institute of Southern African Studies, 1994.

Shepherd, George W., Jr., ed. *Effective Sanctions on South Africa: The Cutting Edge of Economic Intervention.* New York: Greenwood Press, 1991.

Sisk, Timothy D. *Democratization in South Africa: The Elusive Social Contract.* Princeton: Princeton University Press, 1995.

Slabbert, Frederik van Zyl. *The Last White Parliament.* London: Sidgwick and Jackson, 1985.

Slovo, Joe. *Has Socialism Failed?* Umsebenzi Discussion Pamphlet. London: Inkululeko, 1990.

South Africa. *Constitution of the Republic of South Africa, 1993.* Pretoria: 1994.

South Africa. Department of Regional and Land Affairs. *New Provinces: Maps and Figures.* Pretoria: 1994.

South Africa. *Government Gazette* [Cape Town], 343, No. 15466, January 28, 1994.

South Africa. Ministry of Foreign Affairs. *A Brief Outline of the Transitional Constitution for South Africa Which Will Come into Force on April 27, 1994.* Pretoria: 1994.

"South Africa." Pages 796–806 in Arthur S. Banks, ed., *Political Handbook of the World, 1994–1995.* Binghamton, New York: CSA, 1995.

South Africa. Parliament (1994). Constitutional Assembly. *Minutes of the Proceedings of the Constitutional Assembly, Republic of South Africa, 1994,* No. 1, May 24, 1994.

South Africa. Senate. *Debates of the Senate.* First Session, First Parliament, 1, May 20–27, 1994. Cape Town: Government Printer, 1994.

South Africa. South African Communication Service. *South Africa Yearbook, 1994.* 1st ed. Originally published as *South Africa Official Yearbook, 1994.* Pretoria: 1995.

South Africa. South African Communication Service. *South African Yearbook, 1995.* 2d ed. Pretoria: 1996.

South Africa. Volkstaat Council. *Broadening Democracy for Stability. First Interim Report of the Volkstaat Council.* Pretoria: 1995.

South African Institute of International Affairs (SAIIA) Research Group, eds. *South Africa and the Two Chinas Dilemma.* Johannesburg: SAIIA and Foundation for Global Dialogue, 1995.

South African Yearbook of International Law, 1993–1994, 19. Pretoria: University of South Africa, VerLoren van Themaat Centre for Public Law Studies, 1995.

South African Yearbook of International Law, 1995, 20. Pretoria: University of South Africa, VerLoren van Themaat Centre for Public Law Studies, 1996.

Southall, Roger. "The Development and Delivery of 'Northern' Worker Solidarity to South African Trade Unions in the 1970s and 1980s," *Journal of Commonwealth and Comparative Politics* [London], 32, No. 2, July 1994, 166–99.

Southall, Roger. Review of Shelagh Gastrow, ed., "Who's Who in South African Politics," *Journal of Southern African Studies* [Oxford], 18, No. 4, December 1992, 850–51.

Southall, Roger. "The South African Elections of 1994: The Remaking of a Dominant-Party State," *Journal of Modern African Studies* [London], 32, No. 4, September 1994, 629–55.

Spanger, Hans-Joachim, and Peter Vale, eds. *Bridges to the Future: Prospects for Peace and Security in Southern Africa.* Boulder, Colorado: Westview Press, 1995.

Sparks, Allister. *The Mind of South Africa: The Story of the Rise and Fall of Apartheid.* New York: Knopf, 1990.

Sparks, Allister. *Tomorrow Is Another Country: The Inside Story of South Africa's Road to Change.* Sandton, South Africa: Struik, 1995.

Spence, John E. "'Everybody Has Won, So All Must Have Prizes': Reflections on the South African General Election," *Government and Opposition* [London], 29, No. 4, Autumn 1994, 431–44.

Stedman, Stephen John, ed. *South Africa: The Political Economy of Transformation.* Boulder, Colorado: Lynne Rienner, 1994.

Steenkamp, Anton J. "The South African Constitution of 1993 and the Bill of Rights: An Evaluation in Light of International Human Rights Norms," *Human Rights Quarterly,* 17, No. 1, February 1995, 101–26.

Stockholm International Peace Research Institute (SIPRI). *SIPRI Yearbook, 1995: Armanents, Disarmament, and National Security.* New York: Oxford University Press, 1995.

Switzer, Les. *Power and Resistance in an African Society: The Ciskei Xhosa and the Making of South Africa.* Madison: University of Wisconsin Press, 1993.

Thompson, Leonard. *A History of South Africa.* Rev. ed. New Haven: Yale University Press, 1995.

Thompson, Leonard, and Andrew Prior. *South African Politics.* New Haven: Yale University Press, 1982.

Treverton, Gregory F., and Pamela Varley. *The United States and South Africa: The 1985 Sanctions Debate.* Pew Case Studies in International Affairs, No. 443. Washington: Georgetown University, Institute for the Study of Diplomacy, 1992.

United Nations. Department of Public Information. *The United Nations and Apartheid, 1948–1994.* New York: 1995.

United Nations. Institute for Disarmament Research. *Small Arms Management and Peacekeeping in Southern Africa.* New York: 1996.

United States. Department of State. *South Africa: The New South African Cabinet.* Background Paper. Washington: 1994.

University of Pretoria. Institute for Strategic Studies. *Lessons from the Government of National Unity for a Future South Africa.* Pretoria: 1994.

Van Aardt, Carel. *The Future South Africa: Issues, Options, and Prospects.* Pretoria: Van Schaik, 1994.

Van den Broek, Mark H. "South Africa, Southern Africa, and the Southern African Development Community: Contemplating the Future," *Politeia* [Pretoria], 13, No. 1, March 1994, 51–61.

Van Zyl, Slabbert. *The Quest for Democracy: South Africa in Transition.* London: Penguin, 1992.

Verwey, E.J., ed. *New Dictionary of South African Biography.* Pretoria: Human Sciences Research Council, 1995.

von der Ropp, Klaus. "'Outbreak of Peace' in South Africa?" *Aussenpolitik* [English ed.] [Hamburg], 45, No. 4, December 1994, 383–91.

Walshe, Peter. *Prophetic Christianity and the Liberation Movement in South Africa.* Pietermaritzburg: Cluster, 1995.

Woods, Donald. *Biko.* London: Paddington Press, 1978.

(Various issues of the following periodicals were also used in the preparation of this chapter: *Africa Confidential* [London]; *Africa Research Bulletin* (Political, Social, and Cultural Series) [Oxford]; *Canadian Journal of African Studies* [Toronto]; *Christian Science Monitor, Citizen* [Johannesburg]; *Current History, Facts and Reports* [Amsterdam]; *Foreign Report* [New Delhi]; *Guardian* [London]; *Journal of African Law* [Oxford]; *Journal of Modern African Studies* [London]; *Manchester Guardian Weekly* [London]; *New York Times, Opinion Analysis,* by United States Information Agency, Office of Research and Media Reaction; *Sunday Times* [Johannesburg]; *Third World Quarterly* [Abingdon, United Kingdom]; and *Washington Post.*)

Chapter 5

Adler, Fritz Baumann, A.E. Lorch, and H.H. Curson. *The South African Field Artillery in German East Africa and Palestine, 1915– 1919.* Pretoria: Van Schaik, 1958.

Alao, Abiodun. *Brothers at War: Dissident and Rebel Activities in Southern Africa.* London: Tauris, 1994.

Albright, David E. "South Africa's Changing Threat Perceptions and Strategic Response," *In Depth,* 1, Spring 1991, 114– 215.

Albright, David E. *Soviet Policy Toward Africa Revisited.* Significant Issues Series, 9, No. 6. Washington: Center for Strategic and International Studies, 1987.

Alden, Chris. *Apartheid's Last Stand: The Rise and Fall of the South African Security State, 1978–90.* New York: St. Martin's Press, 1995.

Alhadeff, Vic. *South Africa in Two World Wars: A Newspaper History.* Cape Town: Nelson, 1979.

Amnesty International. *Human Rights and United States Security Assistance.* New York: 1995.

Amnesty International. *South Africa: State of Fear.* New York: 1992.

Amnesty International. *South Africa: Torture, Ill-Treatment, and Executions in African National Congress Camps.* New York: 1992.

Amnesty International Report, 1994. New York: Amnesty International, 1994.

Amnesty International Report, 1995. New York: Amnesty International, 1995.

Anderson, Ken. *Nine Flames.* Cape Town: Purnell and Sons, 1964.

Andrade, John. *World Police and Paramilitary Forces.* New York: Stockton, 1985.

Arnold, Guy. *South Africa: Crossing the Rubicon.* New York: St. Martin's Press, 1988.

Arthur, Paul. "Some Thoughts on Transition: A Comparative View of the Peace Processes in South Africa and Northern Ireland," *Government and Opposition* [London], 30, No. 1, Winter 1995, 48–59.

Bagshawe, Peter. *Warriors of the Sky: Springbok Air Heroes in Combat.* Johannesburg: Ashanti, 1990.

Baker, A.D., comp. *Combat Fleets of the World, 1995: Their Ships, Aircraft, and Armament.* Annapolis, Maryland: U.S. Naval Institute Press, 1995.

Baker, Pauline H. "South Africa: Old Myths and New Realities," *Current History*, 90, No. 556, May 1991, 197–200, 232–33.

Barber, James. "BOSS [Bureau of State Security] in Britain," *African Affairs* [London], 82, July 1983, 311–28.

Barber, Simon. "South Africa Beyond Apartheid," *Optima* [Johannesburg], 35, No. 3, September 1987, 118–25.

Baynham, Simon. "Defence and Security Issues in a Transitional South Africa," *International Affairs Bulletin*, 14, No. 3, July–September 1990, 4–14.

Baynham, Simon, ed. *Military Power and Politics in Black Africa.* New York: St. Martin's Press, 1986.

Becker, Dave. *On Wings of Eagles: South Africa's Military Aviation History.* Durban: Walker-Ramus Trading Company, 1993.

Bennet, Mark, and Deborah Quin. *Political Conflict in South Africa: Data Trends, 1984–1988.* Indicator Project South Africa. Durban: University of Natal, Center for Social and Development Studies, 1991.

Berger, Peter L., and Bobby Godsell, eds. *A Future South Africa: Visions, Strategies, and Realities.* Cape Town: Tafelberg, 1988.

Bernstein, B.L. *The Tide Turned at Alamein: Impressions of the Desert War with the South African Division and the Eighth Army, June 1941–January 1943.* Cape Town: Cape Times, ca. 1944.

Berridge, G.R. *South Africa, the Colonial Powers, and 'African Defence.'* New York: St. Martin's Press, 1993.

Birch, Carole. "Prospects for Security and Stability in the New South Africa." Pages 300–22 in King's College London, Centre for Defence Studies, ed., *Brassey's Defence Yearbook, 1995.* London, Washington: Brassey's, 1995.

Birkby, C. *The Saga of the Transvaal Scottish Regiment, 1932–1950.* Cape Town: Timmins, 1950.

Boister, Neil B., and Kevin Ferguson-Brown, eds. *South African Human Rights Yearbook, 1992, 3.* New York: Oxford University Press, 1994.

Boraine, Alex, and Janet Levy, eds. *The Healing of a Nation?* Cape Town: Justice in Transition, 1995.

Bouwer, J.S., and M.N. Louw. *The SAAF at War, 1940–1984: A Pictorial Appraisal.* Johannesburg: Van Rensburg, 1989.

Brewer, John D. *Black and Blue: Policing in South Africa.* New York: Oxford University Press, 1994.

Brogden, Mike, and Clifford Shearing. *Policing for a New South Africa.* London and New York: Routledge, 1993.

Brzoska, Michael. *Arms and Warfare: Escalation, De-escalation, and Negotiation.* Columbia: University of South Carolina Press, 1994.

Brzoska, Michael. "South Africa: Evading the Embargo." Pages 193–214 in Michael Brzoska and Thomas Ohlson, eds., *Arms Production in the Third World.* Philadelphia: Taylor and Francis, 1986.

Buchan, John. *The South African Forces in France.* London: Imperial War Museum, 1992.

Butts, Kent Hughes, and Steven Metz. *Armies and Democracy in the New Africa: Lessons from Nigeria and South Africa.* Carlisle Barracks, Pennsylvania: United States Army War College, Strategic Studies Institute, 1996.

Campbell, Alexander. *Smuts and Swastika.* London: Gollancz, 1943.

Carpenter, Gretchen, and Henk Botha. *The Possible Conflict of Military Call-ups with the Equal Treatment Provision in the Constitution.* Institute for Strategic Studies, University of Pretoria (ISSUP) Bulletin. Pretoria: ISSUP, 1994.

Cawthra, Gavin. *Brutal Force: Apartheid War Machine.* London: International Defence and Aid Fund for Southern Africa, 1986.

Cawthra, Gavin. *Policing South Africa: The South African Police and the Transition from Apartheid.* London and Atlantic Highlands, New Jersey: Zed Books, 1993.

Cilliers, Jakkie, and Bill Sass, eds. *Mailed Fist: Developments in Modern Armour.* Institute for Defence Policy (IDP) Monograph Series, 2. Halfway House, South Africa: IDP, 1996.

Citino, Robert. *Germany and the Union of South Africa in the Nazi Period.* New York and London: Greenwood Press, 1991.

Clothier, Norman. *Black Valour: The South African Native Labour Contingent, 1916–1918, and the Sinking of the Mendi.* Pietermaritzburg: University of Natal Press, 1987.

Cock, Jacklyn. *Women and War in South Africa.* Cleveland, Ohio: Pilgrim Press, 1993. Originally published as *Colonels and Cadres: War and Gender in South Africa.* Cape Town: Oxford University Press, 1991.

Cohen, Herman J. "Political and Military Security." Pages 278–310 in John W. Harbeson and Donald Rothchild, eds., *Africa in World Politics: Post-Cold War Challenges.* 2d ed. Boulder, Colorado: Westview Press, 1995.

Coleman, Fancis L. *The Kaffrarian Rifles, 1876–1986.* East London: Kaffrarian Rifles Association, 1988.

Collyer, John Johnston. *The South Africans with General Smuts in German East Africa, 1916.* Pretoria: Government Printer, 1939.

Conteh-Morgan, Earl. "The Military and Human Rights in a Post-Cold War Africa," *Armed Forces and Society,* 21, No. 1, Fall 1994, 69–87.

Cooper, F.H. *Khaki Crusaders: With the South African Artillery in Egypt and Palestine.* Cape Town: Central News Agency, 1919.

Cooper, Frederick W. *The Police Brigade: 6th S.A. Infantry Brigade, 1939–45.* Cape Town: Constantia, 1972.

Copley, Gregory R., ed. *Defense and Foreign Affairs Handbook, 1994.* London: International Media, 1994.

Crais, Clifton C. *The Making of the Colonial Order: White Supremacy and Black Resistance in the Eastern Cape, 1770–1865.* Johannesburg: Witwatersrand University, 1992.

Crocker, Chester A. *High Noon in Southern Africa: Making Peace in a Rough Neighborhood.* New York: Norton, 1992.

Davis, Dennis, and Mana Slabbert. *Crime and Power in South Africa.* London: Global Book Resources; and Johannesburg: Philip, 1985.

Davis, R. Hunt, Jr., ed. *Apartheid Unravels.* Gainesville: University of Florida Press, Center for African Studies, 1991.

de Villiers, Jacobus W., Roger Jardine, and Mitchell Reiss. "Why South Africa Gave Up the Bomb," *Foreign Affairs,* 72, No. 5, November–December, 1993, 98–109.

Dodd, Norman L. "The South African Army in 1986," *Armed Forces,* 5, July 1986, 318–23.

Douglas, William S. *Regimental History of the Cape Town Highlanders, September 1939–February 1943.* Cairo: Schindler, 1944.

Douwes-Dekker, Loet, Abel Majola, Philip Visser, and David Bremner. *Community Conflict: The Challenge Facing South Africa.* Cape Town: Juta, 1995.

Du Pisani, André. *Beyond the Barracks: Reflections on the Role of the SADF in the Region.* Johannesburg: South African Institute of International Affairs, 1988.

Dupuy, Trevor N., ed. *International Military and Defense Encyclopedia, 5.* Washington: Brassey's, 1993.

Du Toit, Allan Kendall. *Ships of the South African Navy.* Cape Town: S.A. Boating, 1976.

Ellis, Stephen. "Mbokodo: Security in ANC Camps, 1961–1990," *African Affairs* [London], 93, No. 371, April 1994, 279–98.

Elphick, Richard, and Hermann B. Giliomee, eds. *The Making of South African Society, 1652–1840.* Middletown, Connecticut: Wesleyan University Press, 1989.

Etherington, Norman, ed. *Peace, Politics, and Violence in the New South Africa.* London: Zell, 1992.

Ewing, John. "South Africa in the 1914–18 War." Pages 739–62 in Eric A. Walker, ed., *The Cambridge History of the British Empire, 8.* 2d ed. Cambridge: Cambridge University Press, 1963.

Farwell, Byron. *The Great Anglo-Boer War.* New York: Harper and Row, 1976.

Frankel, Philip H. *Pretoria's Praetorians: Civil-Military Relations in South Africa.* Cambridge: Cambridge University Press, 1984.

Frankel, Philip H., Noam Pines, and Mark Swilling, eds. *State, Resistance, and Change in South Africa.* Kent, United Kingdom: Helm, 1988.

Fulghum, David A. "South Africa Tackles International Role," *Aviation Week and Space Technology,* 143, July 3, 1995, 52–55, 57–58, 60–69.

Furlong, Patrick J. *Between Crown and Swastika: The Impact of the Radical Right on the Afrikaner Nationalist Movement in the Fascist Era.* Hanover, New Hampshire: Wesleyan University Press, 1991.

Gann, Lewis H., and Peter J. Duignan. *Hope for South Africa.* Stanford: Hoover Institution Press, 1991.

Garson, N.G. "South Africa and World War I," *Journal of Imperial and Commonwealth History* [London], 8, No. 1, October 1979, 68–85.

Geldenhuys, Deon, and William Gutteridge. *Instability and Conflict in Southern Africa: South Africa's Role in Regional Security.* Conflict Studies, No. 148. London: Institute for the Study of Conflict, 1983.

Gibbs, Peter. *The History of the British South Africa Police.* 2 vols. Salisbury, Rhodesia: British South Africa Police, 1972, 1974.

Gleeson, Ian. *The Unknown Force: Black, Indian, and Coloured Soldiers Through Two World Wars.* Rivonia: Ashanti, 1994.

Glickman, Harvey, ed. *Toward Peace and Security in Southern Africa.* New York and London: Gordon and Breach Science, 1990.

Graaff, De Villiers. *Div Looks Back: The Memoirs of Sir De Villiers Graaff.* Cape Town: Human and Rousseau, 1993.

Griffiths, Robert J. "South African Civil-Military Relations in Transition: Issues and Influences," *Armed Forces and Society,* 21, Spring 1995, 395–410.

Grotpeter, John J. *Historical Dictionary of Namibia.* African Historical Dictionaries, 57. Metuchen, New Jersey: Scarecrow Press, 1994.

Grové, W. *The Drug Trade as a National and International Security Threat: Where Do We Stand?* Institute for Strategic Studies, University of Pretoria (ISSUP) Bulletin. Pretoria: ISSUP, 1994.

Grundlingh, Albert M. "Black Men in White Man's War: The Impact of the First World War on South African Blacks," *War and Society*, 3, No. 1, May 1985, 55–82.

Grundlingh, Albert M. *Fighting Their Own War: South African Blacks and the First World War.* Johannesburg: Ravan Press, 1987.

Grundlingh, Louis W.F. "Aspects of the Impact of the Second World War on the Lives of Black South African and British Colonial Soldiers," *Transafrican Journal of History* [Nairobi], 21, 1992, 19–35.

Grundlingh, Louis W.F. "The Recruitment of South African Blacks for Participation in the Second World War." Pages 181–203 in David Killingray and Richard Rathbone, eds., *Africa and the Second World War.* New York: St. Martin's Press, 1986.

Grundy, Kenneth W. *Confrontation and Accommodation in Southern Africa: The Limits of Independence.* Berkeley: University of California Press, 1973.

Grundy, Kenneth W. *The Militarization of South African Politics.* Bloomington: Indiana University Press, 1986.

Grundy, Kenneth W. "Some Thoughts on the Demilitarization of South and Southern Africa." Pages 57–71 in Harvey Glickman, ed., *Toward Peace and Security in Southern Africa.* New York and London: Gordon and Breach Science, 1990.

Gump, James O. *The Dust Rose like Smoke: The Subjugation of the Zulu and the Sioux.* Lincoln: University of Nebraska Press, 1994.

Gutteridge, William F. "The Military in South African Politics: Champions of National Unity?" *Conflict Studies* [London], No. 271, June 1994, 1–29.

Gutteridge, William F. *South Africa: From Apartheid to National Unity, 1981–1994.* Brookfield, Vermont: Dartmouth, 1995.

Gutteridge, William F. "South Africa's Defence and Security Forces: The Next Decade." Pages 50–64 in John E. Spence, ed., *Change in South Africa.* New York: Council on Foreign Relations Press, for the Royal Institute of International Affairs, 1994.

Hale, Terrel D., comp. *United States Sanctions and South Africa: A Selected Legal Bibliography.* Bibliographies and Indexes in Law and Political Science, No. 18. Westport, Connecticut: Greenwood Press, 1993.

Hall, Robert, and Ian Kemp, eds. *Whither South Africa's Warriors?* Jane's Intelligence Review, Special Report No. 3. London: Jane's Information Group, 1994.

Hanlon, Joseph. *Apartheid's Second Front: South Africa's War Against Its Neighbors.* New York: Penguin, 1986.

Harbeson, John W., and Donald Rothchild, eds. *Africa in World Politics: Post-Cold War Challenges.* 2d ed. Boulder, Colorado: Westview Press, 1995.

Heitman, Helmoed-Römer. "R2b Defence Budget Marks End to Decline," *Jane's Defence Weekly* [London], 23, No. 12, March 25, 1995, 5.

Heitman, Helmoed-Römer. *South African Arms and Armour.* Cape Town: Struik, 1988.

Heitman, Helmoed-Römer. *The South African War Machine.* Greenwich, Connecticut: Bison Books, 1985.

Heitman, Helmoed-Römer. "South Africa's Arsenal," *Military Technology* [Bonn], 18, No. 11, December 1994, 10–32.

Henderson, Robert D. "South African Intelligence under de Klerk," *International Journal of Intelligence and Counterintelligence*, 8, Spring 1995, 51–89.

Hewitt, G. *Womanhood at War: The Story of the SAWAS* [South African Women's Auxiliary Service]. Johannesburg: Frier and Munro, 1947.

Hough, Michael. *National Security in the RSA: The Strategic Importance of South and Southern Africa: The Pretoria View.* Pretoria: University of Pretoria, Institute for Strategic Studies, 1981.

Hough, Michael, and A. du Plessis, eds. *The Future Application of Air Power with Specific Reference to Southern Africa.* Institute for Strategic Studies, University of Pretoria (ISSUP), Ad Hoc Publication No. 32. Pretoria: ISSUP, 1995.

Howe, Herbert M. "The SADF Revisited." Pages 78–92 in Helen Kitchen and J. Coleman Kitchen, eds., *South Africa: Twelve Perspectives on the Transition.* Washington Papers, No. 165. Westport, Connecticut: Praeger, with Center for Strategic and International Studies, Washington, 1994.

Howe, Herbert M. "The South African Defence Force and Political Reform," *Journal of Modern African Studies* [London], 32, No. 1, March 1994, 29–51.

Howlett, Darryl, and John Simpson. "Nuclearisation and Denuclearisation in South Africa," *Survival* [London], 35, No. 3, Autumn 1993, 154–73.

Human Rights Commission (South Africa). *Political Imprisonment in South Africa.* Pretoria: 1991.

Human Rights Watch/Africa. *The Killings in South Africa: The Role of the Security Forces and the Response of the State.* New York: 1991.

Human Rights Watch/Africa. *Prison Conditions in South Africa.* New York: 1994.

Human Rights Watch/Africa. *South Africa: Impunity for Human Rights Abuses in Two Homelands: Reports on KwaZulu and Bophuthatswana.* New York: 1994.

Human Rights Watch/Africa. *Violence Against Women in South Africa: The State Response to Domestic Violence and Rape.* New York: Human Rights Watch, 1995.

James, Wilmot G., ed. *The State of Apartheid.* Boulder, Colorado: Lynne Rienner, 1987.

Jane's Fighting Ships, 1993–94. London: Jane's Information Group, 1993.

Jaster, Robert S. *South Africa in Namibia: The Botha Strategy.* Lanham, Maryland: University Press of America, 1985.

Jaster, Robert S. "The South African Military Reassesses Its Priorities." Pages 66–77 in Helen Kitchen and J. Coleman Kitchen, eds., *South Africa: Twelve Perspectives on the Transition.* Washington Papers, No. 165. Westport, Connecticut: Praeger, with Center for Strategic and International Studies, Washington, 1994.

Kane-Berman, John. *Political Violence in South Africa.* Johannesburg: South African Institute of Race Relations, 1993.

Kasrils, Ronnie. "The Reality of Democracy," *Military Technology* [Bonn], 18, No. 11, December 1994, 34–35.

Kasrils, Ronnie. "South Africa and Its Defence Industry," *Military Technology* [Bonn], 18, No. 11, December 1994, 36.

Kauppi, Mark Veblen. "The Republic of South Africa." Pages 476–519 in Douglas J. Murray and Paul R. Viotti, eds., *The Defense Policies of Nations: A Comparative Study.* 2d ed. Baltimore: Johns Hopkins University Press, 1989.

Keller, Bill. "Island of Fear: Inside a Soweto Hostel," *New York Times Magazine,* September 20, 1992, 32–37, 48–49.

Kempton, Daniel R. *Lessening Political Violence in South Africa: The CODESA Decision.* Pew Case Studies in International Affairs, No. 366. Washington: Georgetown University, Institute for the Study of Diplomacy, 1994.

Khadiagala, Gilbert M. "The Front Line States, Regional Interstate Relations, and Institution Building in Southern Africa." Pages 131–61 in Harvey Glickman, ed., *Toward Peace and Security in Southern Africa.* London and New York: Gordon and Breach Science, 1990.

Kitchen, Helen, and J. Coleman Kitchen, eds. *South Africa: Twelve Perspectives on the Transition.* Washington Papers, No. 165. Westport, Connecticut: Praeger, with Center for Strategic and International Studies, Washington, 1994.

Klein, Harry. *Springboks in Armour.* Cape Town: Purnell and Sons, 1965.

Knight, Ian. *The Anatomy of the Zulu Army: From Shaka to Cetshwayo, 1818–1879.* Mechanicsburg, Pennsylvania: Stackpole Books, 1995.

Landgren, Signe. *Embargo Disimplemented: South Africa's Military Industry.* New York: Oxford University Press, 1989.

Lulat, Y.G.M. *U.S. Relations with South Africa: An Annotated Bibliography, 1.* Boulder, Colorado: Westview Press, 1991.

McCarthy, Shaun. *Intelligence Services for a Democratic South Africa: Ensuring Parliamentary Control.* Conflict Studies, No. 286. London: Research Institute for the Study of Conflict and Terrorism, 1996.

McDougall, Gay J. *South Africa's Death Squads.* South Africa Project. Washington: Lawyers' Committee for Civil Rights under Law, 1990.

Mackinnon, James P., and Sydney H. Shadbolt. *The South African Campaign of 1879.* Mechanicsburg, Pennsylvania: Stackpole Books, 1995.

McWilliams, James P. *Armscor, South Africa's Arms Merchant.* London: Brassey's, 1989.

Mallaby, Sebastian. *After Apartheid: The Future of South Africa.* New York: Random House, 1992.

Mandela, Nelson. *Nelson Mandela: The Struggle Is My Life.* Bellville, South Africa: Mayibuye Books, 1994.

Manganyi, N. Chabani, and André du Toit, eds. *Political Violence and the Struggle in South Africa.* New York: St. Martin's Press, 1990.

Maré, Gerhard. *Brothers Born of Warrior Blood: Politics and Ethnicity in South Africa.* Johannesburg: Ravan Press, 1992.

Marsh, John H. *South Africa and the War at Sea in Word and Picture.* Cape Town: Stewart Printing, 1945.

Martin, A.C. *The Durban Light Infantry, 1854–1960.* 2 vols. Durban: Regimental Association, 1969.

Martin, Henry James, and Neil D. Orpen. *Eagles Victorious: The Operations of South African Forces over the Mediterranean and Europe, in Italy, the Balkans, and the Aegean, and from Gibraltar to West Africa.* Cape Town: Purnell and Sons, 1977.

Martin, Henry James, and Neil D. Orpen. *Salute the Sappers.* 2 vols. Johannesburg: Sappers Association, 1981–1982.

Martin, Henry James, and Neil D. Orpen. *South Africa at War: Military and Industrial Organisation and Operations in Connection with the Conduct of the War, 1939–1945.* Cape Town: Purnell and Sons, 1979.

Mathews, Anthony S. *Freedom, State Security, and the Rule of Law: Dilemmas of the Apartheid Society.* Cape Town: Juta, 1986.

Mathews, Anthony S. "South African Security Law and the Growth of Local and Regional Violence." Pages 18–32 in R. Hunt Davis, Jr., ed., *Apartheid Unravels.* Gainesville: University of Florida Press, 1991.

Mathews, Mary L., Philip B. Heymann, and A.S. Mathews, eds. *Policing the Conflict in South Africa.* Gainesville: University Press of Florida, 1993.

Maurice, F. *History of the War in South Africa.* 4 vols. London: Hurst and Blackett, 1906–8.

The Military Balance, 1995–1996. London: International Institute for Strategic Studies, 1995.

The Military Balance, 1996–1997. London: International Institute for Strategic Studies, 1996.

Miller, Carman. *Painting the Map Red: Canada and the South African War, 1899–1902.* Canadian War Museum Historical Publication No. 28. Montreal: Canadian War Museum and McGill-Queen's University Press, 1993.

Mills, Greg. "Armed Forces in Post-Apartheid South Africa," *Survival* [London], 35, No. 3, Autumn 1993, 78–96.

Mills, Greg, and Glenn Oosthuysen. "South Africa and Arms Control in Africa." Pages 111–40 in James Brown, ed. *Arms Control in a Multi-Polar World.* Amsterdam, The Netherlands: VU University Press, 1996.

Milton, John. *The Edges of War: A History of Frontier Wars, 1702–1878.* Cape Town: Juta, 1983.

Moleah, Alfred T. "South Africa under Siege: The Ever-Deepening Crisis of Apartheid," *Without Prejudice,* 1, Fall 1987, 58–84.

Moorcraft, Paul L. *African Nemesis: War and Revolution in Southern Africa, 1945–2010.* London: Brassey's, 1990.

Morris, Donald R. *The Washing of the Spears: A History of the Zulu Nation under Shaka and Its Fall in the Zulu War of 1879.* New York: Simon and Schuster, 1965.

Mostert, Noel. *Frontiers: The Epic of South Africa's Creation and the Tragedy of the Xhosa People.* New York: Knopf, 1992.

Murray, Douglas J., and Paul R. Viotti, eds. *The Defense Policies of Nations: A Comparative Study.* 3d ed. Baltimore: Johns Hopkins University Press, 1994.

Murray, Lionel Garner. *First City-Cape Town Highlanders in the Italian Campaign: A Short History, 1943–1945.* Cape Town: Privately printed, 1945.

Nasson, Bill. "War Opinion in South Africa, 1914," *Journal of Imperial and Commonwealth History* [London], 23, No. 2, May, 1995, 248–76.

Navias, Martin. "The Future of South Africa's Arms Trade and Defence Industries," *Jane's Intelligence Review* [London], 16, No. 11, November 1994, 522–24.

Nhlanhla, Joe. *Challenges Facing the Intelligence Community in South Africa.* Institute for Strategic Studies, University of Pretoria (ISSUP) Bulletin. Pretoria: ISSUP, 1995.

Norton, Conrad, and Uys Krige. *Vanguard of Victory: A Short Review of the South African Victories in East Africa, 1940–1941.* Pretoria: Government Printer, 1941.

Ohlson, Thomas. "South Africa: From Apartheid to Multi-Party Democracy." Pages 117–45 in *Stockholm International Peace Research Institute (SIPRI) Yearbook, 1995.* London: Oxford University Press, 1995.

Ohlson, Thomas, and Stephen John Stedman, with Robert Davies. *The New Is Not Yet Born: Conflict Resolution in Southern Africa.* Washington: Brookings Institution, 1994.

Orpen, Neil D. *The Cape Town Highlanders, 1885–1970.* Cape Town: Cape Town Highlanders History Committee, 1970.

Orpen, Neil D. *The Cape Town Rifles: The 'Dukes,' 1856–1984.* Cape Town: Cape Town Dukes Regimental Council, 1984.

Orpen, Neil D. *East African and Abyssinian Campaigns.* Cape Town: Purnell and Sons, 1968.

Orpen, Neil D. *The History of the Transvaal Horse Artillery, 1904–1974.* Johannesburg: Transvaal Horse Artillery Regimental Council, 1975.

Orpen, Neil D. *Prince Alfred's Guard, 1856–1966.* Port Elizabeth: Books of Africa, in conjunction with the Regiment, 1967.

Orpen, Neil D. *Total Defence: The Role of the Commandos in the Armed Forces of South Africa.* Cape Town: Nasionale Boekhandel, 1967.

Orpen, Neil D. *Victory in Italy: South African Forces in World War II,* 5. Cape Town: Purnell and Sons, 1975.

Orpen, Neil D. *War in the Desert.* Cape Town and Johannesburg: Purnell and Sons, 1971.

Pakenham, Thomas. *The Boer War.* New York: Random House, 1979.

Pande, Savita. "Politics of Nuclearisation and Denuclearisation in South Africa," *Strategic Analysis* [New Delhi], 16, No. 11, February 1994, 1457–73.

Peires, Jeffrey B. *The House of Phalo: A History of the Xhosa People in the Days of Their Independence.* Berkeley: University of California Press, 1982.

Peregrino, F.Z.S. *His Majesty's Black Labourers: A Treatise on the Camp Life of the South African Native Labour Corps.* Cape Town: Cape Times, 1918.

Pheko, S.E.M. *The Land Is Ours: The Political Legacy of Mangaliso Sobukwe.* New York: Pheko and Associates, 1994.

Pollock, A.M. *Pienaar of Alamein: The Life Story of a Great South African Soldier.* Pretoria: Bureau of Information, 1943.

Porter, Andrew N. *The Origins of the South African War: Joseph Chamberlain and the Diplomacy of Imperialism, 1895–1899.* New York: St. Martin's Press, 1980.

Rabert, Bernhard. "South Africa's Nuclear Weapons: A Defused Time Bomb?" *Aussenpolitik* [English ed.] [Hamburg], 44, No. 3, July 1993, 232–42.

Rake, Alan. "Great South Africans." Pages 95–139 in *100 Great Africans.* Metuchen, New Jersey: Scarecrow Press, 1994.

Rich, Paul B. *State Power and Black Politics in South Africa, 1912– 51.* New York: St. Martin's Press, 1995.

Roherty, James M. *State Security in South Africa. Civil-Military Relations under P.W. Botha.* Armonk, New York: Sharpe, 1992.

Rotberg, Robert I., ed. *South Africa and Its Neighbors: Regional Security and Self-Interest.* Lexington, Massachusetts: Heath, 1985.

Sampson, Philip J. *The Capture of De Wet: The South African Rebellion, 1914.* London: Arnold, 1915.

Saunders, Christopher C. *Historical Dictionary of South Africa.* African Historical Dictionaries, No. 37. Metuchen, New Jersey: Scarecrow Press, 1983.

Saunders, Christopher C. *An Illustrated Dictionary of South African History.* Sandton, South Africa: Ibis Press, 1994.

Saunders, Frederick S. *Mafeking Memories.* Cranbury, New Jersey: Associated University Presses, 1996.

Seegers, Annette. "Current Trends in South Africa's Security Establishment," *Armed Forces and Society,* 18, No. 2, Winter 1992, 159–74.

Seegers, Annette. "The Military in South Africa: A Comparison and Critique," *South Africa International* [Johannesburg], 16, No. 4, April 1986, 192–200.

Shackleton, Charles Walter. *East African Experiences, 1916: From the Diary of a South African Infantryman in the German East African Campaign.* Durban: Knox, 1940.

Shillington, Kevin. *A History of Southern Africa.* Burnt Mill, United Kingdom: Longman, 1987.

Simpkins, B.G. *Rand Light Infantry.* Cape Town: Timmins, 1965.

Simpson, J.S.M. *South Africa Fights.* London: Hodder and Stoughton, 1941.

Singh, Ravinder Pal, and Pieter D. Wezeman. "South Africa's Arms Production and Exports." Pages 569–82 in *Stockholm International Peace Research Institute (SIPRI) Yearbook, 1995.* London: Oxford University Press, 1995.

Smaldone, Joseph P. "The Security Crisis in South Africa: Crime, Violence, and the Security Establishment." Paper presented at the 35th Annual Conference of the African Studies Association, Seattle, Washington, November 20–23, 1992.

Smith, Iain R. *The Origins of the South African War, 1899–1902.* New York: Longman, 1996.

Smithers, Alan J. *The Kaffir Wars.* London: Cooper, 1973.

Smuts, Jan C. *Memoirs of the Boer War.* Johannesburg: Ball, 1994.

South Africa. Military (Union Defence Force) General Staff. *The Union of South Africa and the Great War, 1914–1918: Official History.* Pretoria: Government Printer, 1924.

South Africa. Prime Minister's Department. Union War Histories Section. *Crisis in the Desert, May–July 1942.* Cape Town: Oxford University Press, 1952.

South Africa. South African Communication Service. *South Africa, 1993: Official Yearbook of the Republic of South Africa.* 19th ed. Pretoria: 1994.

South Africa. South African Communication Service. *South Africa Yearbook, 1994.* Originally published as *South Africa Official Yearbook, 1994.* 1st ed. Pretoria: 1995.

South Africa. South African Communication Service. *South Africa Yearbook, 1995.* 2d ed. Pretoria: 1996.

"South Africa." Pages 490–93 in *Jane's Fighting Ships 1990–91.* London: Jane's Information Group, 1990.

Spence, John E. "South Africa's Military Relations with Its Neighbors." Pages 291–316 in Simon Baynham, ed., *Military Power and Politics in Black Africa.* New York: St. Martin's Press, 1986.

Stockholm International Peace Research Institute (SIPRI). *SIPRI Yearbook, 1995: Armaments, Disarmament, and National Security.* New York: Oxford University Press, 1995.

Switzer, Les. *Power and Resistance in an African Society: The Ciskei Xhosa and the Making of South Africa.* Madison: University of Wisconsin Press, 1993.

Thompson, Leonard. *A History of South Africa.* Rev. ed. New Haven: Yale University Press, 1995.

Tylden, G. *The Armed Forces of South Africa.* Johannesburg: Afrikana Museum, 1954.

United States Arms Control and Disarmament Agency. *World Military Expenditures and Arms Transfers*. Washington: GPO, 1994.

United States. Congress. 104th, 1st Session. House of Representatives. *Agreement for Cooperation Between the United States of America and the Republic of South Africa Concerning Peaceful Uses of Nuclear Energy*. No. 104–121. Washington: GPO, 1995.

United States. Department of State. *Country Reports on Human Rights Practices for 1994*. Report submitted to United States Congress, 104th, 1st Session, House of Representatives, Committee on International Relations, and Senate, Committee on Foreign Relations. Washington: GPO, 1995.

United States Institute of Peace. *South Africa: The National Peace Accord and the International Community*. Special Report. Washington: September 24, 1993.

Uys, Ian. *Bushman Soldiers: Their Alpha and Omega*. Germiston, South Africa: Fortress, 1994.

Uys, Ian. *Delville Wood*. Rensburg, South Africa: Uys, 1983.

Uys, Ian. *South African Military Who's Who, 1452–1992*. Germiston, South Africa: Fortress, 1992.

Vale, Peter. "The Search for Southern Africa's Security," *International Affairs*, 67, No. 4, October 1991, 697–708.

Van Niekerk, Fred. *Last But Not Least: The Wartime Story of 30 Squadron, South African Air Force*. Johannesburg: 30 Squadron Veterans' Association, 1984.

Van Rooyen, Johann. *Hard Right: The New White Power in South Africa*. New York: Tauris, 1994.

Venter, Al J. *The Chopper Boys: Helicopter Warfare in Africa*. Halfway House, South Africa: Southern Book, 1994.

Warwick, George William. *We Band of Brothers: Reminiscences from the 1st S.A. Infantry Brigade in the 1914–18 War*. Cape Town: Timmins, 1962.

Webb, H.S. *The Causes of the Rebellion in South Africa, 1914*. Pretoria: Northern Printing Press, 1915.

Weitzer, Ronald. "Policing." Pages 71–89 in John D. Brewer, ed., *Restructuring South Africa*. New York: St. Martin's Press, 1994.

Willett, Susan. "The Legacy of a Pariah State: South Africa's Arms Trade in the 1990s," *Review of African Political Economy* [London], 22, June 1995, 151–66.

(Various issues of the following periodicals, annual publications, and newspapers were also used in the preparation of this chapter: *Africa Analysis* [London]; *Africa Confidential* [London]; *Africa Contemporary Record*; *Africa Events* [London]; *Africa Report*; *Africa Research Bulletin* (Political, Social, and Cultural Series) [Oxford]; *Africa South of the Sahara* [London]; *African Affairs* [London]; *African Armed Forces Journal* (formerly *Armed Forces Journal*) [Pretoria]; *African Defence Journal* [Paris]; *Cape Times* [Cape Town]; *Christian Science Monitor*, *Commando* [Pretoria]; *Daily Telegraph* [London]; *Facts and Reports* [Amsterdam]; *Focus on Africa* [London]; Foreign Broadcast Information Service, *Daily Report: Sub-Saharan Africa*; *Guardian* [Manchester]; *Indian Ocean Newsletter* [Paris]; *Jane's Defence Weekly* [London]; *Journal of African History* [London]; *Journal of Imperial and Commonwealth History* [London]; *Journal of Modern African Studies* [London]; *Journal of Southern African Affairs*; *Journal of Southern African Studies* [Oxford]; *Keesing's Record of World Events* [London]; *Militaria* [Pretoria]; *Military Balance* [London]; *Military History Journal* [Johannesburg]; *Military Technology* [Bonn]; *New York Times*; *Paratus* [Pretoria]; *Rand Daily Mail* [Johannesburg]; *Salut* [Pretoria]; *Servamus* [Pretoria]; *Star* [Johannesburg]; *Times* [London]; *Strategic Review for Southern Africa* [Pretoria]; *Vlootnuus Navy News* [Simonstown]; and *Washington Post*.)

Glossary

Afrikaner—South African of Dutch ancestry, often with German, French, or other European forebears; member of white community tracing its roots to the seventeenth-century Dutch settlers at the Cape of Good Hope.

apartheid—"Separateness," (Afrikaans, Dutch); policy implemented by National Party government (1948–94) to maintain separate development of government-demarcated racial groups; also referred to as "separate development," and later "multinational development"; abolished by Constitution of the Republic of South Africa of 1993.

Bantu—Literally, "human beings," in more than 300 Bantu languages of equatorial and southern Africa. Bantu languages are classified within the central branch of the Niger-Congo language family; characterized by a system of noun classes marked by prefixes, so that each dependent word in a sentence carries a prefix of the same class. Outsiders often simplify by omitting prefix; for example, the amaZulu (people) are known as the Zulu; their language, isiZulu, is also referred to as Zulu. Speakers of seSotho, the BaSotho, are often referred to simply as Sotho peoples. Four major subgroups of Bantu languages—Nguni, Sotho, Tsonga-Shangaan, and Venda—are widely represented in South Africa. They include nine of South Africa's official languages—isiXhosa, isiZulu, isiNdebele, sePedi, seSotho, seTswana, siSwati, tshiVenda (also luVenda), and xiTsonga. During the apartheid era, the term *Bantu* was often used in government regulations, official statements, and sometimes in conversation to designate people of black African descent. Because this group was particularly disadvantaged by apartheid, the term *Bantu* assumed pejorative connotations in many apartheid-era contexts.

Bantustan—An area reserved for an officially designated Bantu-speaking ethnic group during the apartheid era; a term generally supplanted by "homeland," national state, or self-governing state during the 1970s and 1980s.

Boer—Farmer (Afrikaans); generally used in eighteenth and nineteenth century to refer to white South African settlers of Dutch, German, and French Huguenot origin; generally supplanted by the term *Afrikaner* (*q.v.*) in the twentieth century. *See also* Trekboer.

coloureds—Those "of mixed race," in apartheid terminology; usually referred to people with African and Dutch ancestry.

European Community (EC)—*See* European Union (EU).

European Union (EU)—Formerly, the European Community (EC), established as the EU by the Treaty on European Union, November 1, 1993. The EU comprises three communities: the European Coal and Steel Community (ECSC), the European Economic Community (EEC), and the European Atomic Energy Community (Euratom). Each community is legally distinct, but since 1967 the three bodies have shared common governing institutions. The EU forms more than a framework for free trade and economic cooperation: EU signatories have agreed in principle to integrate their economies and ultimately to form a political union. EU members in early 1996 were Austria, Belgium, Britain, Denmark, Finland, France, Germany, Greece, Ireland, Italy, Luxembourg, the Netherlands, Portugal, Spain and Sweden.

fiscal year (FY)—In South Africa, April 1–March 31. For example, FY 1997–98 includes the period from April 1, 1997, to March 31, 1998.

gross domestic product (GDP)—A measure of the total value of goods and services produced by a domestic national economy during a given period, usually one year. Obtained by adding the value contributed by each sector of the economy in the form of profits, compensation to employees, and depreciation (consumption of capital). Only domestic production is included, not income arising from investments and possessions owned abroad, hence the use of the word *domestic* to distinguish GDP from the gross national product (GNP—*q.v.*). Real GDP is the value of GDP when inflation has been taken into account.

gross national product (GNP)—The total market value of all final goods and services produced by an economy during a year. Obtained by adding gross domestic product (GDP—*q.v.*) and the income received from abroad by residents and then subtracting payments remitted abroad to nonresidents. Real GNP is the value of GNP when inflation has been taken into account.

Highveld—High-altitude grassland, generally between 1,200 meters and 1,800 meters above sea level.

homeland or reserve—A primarily residential area set aside for a single officially designated black ethnic group during the apartheid era. Some of the ten homelands in the 1980s consisted of more than a dozen discrete segments of land. Homeland boundaries shifted as the government assigned additional groups of people to the often crowded homelands or as neighboring jurisdictions successfully pressed claims to territory within a homeland's boundary.

import substitution—An economic development strategy that emphasizes the growth of domestic industries, often by import protection using tariff and nontariff measures. Proponents favor the export of industrial goods over primary products.

International Monetary Fund (IMF)—Established along with the World Bank (*q.v.*) in 1945, the IMF is a specialized agency, affiliated with the United Nations, that is responsible for stabilizing international exchange rates and payments. The main business of the IMF is the provision of loans to its members (including industrialized and developing countries) when they experience balance of payments difficulties. These loans frequently carry conditions that require substantial internal economic adjustments by the recipients, most of which are developing countries.

lineage—A group, the members of which are descended through males from a common male ancestor (patrilineage) or through females from a common female ancestor (matrilineage). Such descent can in principle be traced.

mfecane—"Crushing" or "hammering" (isiZulu); refers to early nineteenth-century upheaval in southeastern Africa caused by expansion of Zulu society under the military leadership of Shaka and combined economic and population pressures throughout the region; *difeqane,* in seSotho.

parastatal—A semi-autonomous, quasi-governmental, state-owned enterprise.

Paris Club—Informal name for a consortium of Western creditor countries (Belgium, Britain, Canada, France, Germany, Italy, Japan, the Netherlands, Sweden, Switzerland, and the United States) that have made loans, or have guaranteed export credits, to developing nations and that meet in Paris to discuss borrowers' ability to repay debts. Paris Club deliberations often result in the tendering of emergency loans to countries in economic difficulty or in the rescheduling of debts. Formed in October 1962, the organization has no formal or institutional existence. Its secretariat is run by the French treasury. It has a close relationship with the International Monetary Fund (*q.v.*), to which all of its members except Switzerland belong, as well as with the World Bank (*q.v.*), and the United Nations Conference on Trade and Development (UNCTAD). The Paris Club is also known as the Group of Ten (G–10).

polygynous—having more than one wife at the same time; polygynous marriages are allowed by tradition in many African societies.

rand (R)—Unit of currency. A decimal currency of 100 cents, the rand replaced the South African pound in 1961. The official exchange rate of the rand against the United States dollar was R1=US$1.40 until December 1971, and from September 1975 to January 1979, R1=US$1.15. From 1972 to 1975, and after 1979, the government allowed market forces to determine the value of the rand. The exchange rate averaged R3.55=US$1 in 1994 and R3.64=US$1 in 1995. On April 30, 1996, R4.34=US$1; conversely, R1= US$.23. Financial rands were issued only to foreign buyers for capital investment inside South Africa. They were available periodically until 1983 and again in September 1985, but were abolished in March 1995.

Rand—Local contraction of Witwatersrand (*q.v.*).

Trekboer—Migrant farmer, in Afrikaans; signifies participation in nineteenth-century population migrations eastward from the Cape of Good Hope. *See also* Boer.

Witwatersrand—Literally, "Ridge of White Waters" (Afrikaans), often shortened to Rand; mining region south of Johannesburg known primarily for rich deposits of gold and other minerals.

World Bank—Informal name used to designate a group of four affiliated international institutions that provide advice and assistance on long-term finance and policy issues to developing countries: the International Bank for Reconstruction and Development (IBRD), the International Development Association (IDA), the International Finance Corporation (IFC), and the Multilateral Investment Guarantee Agency (MIGA). The IBRD, established in 1945, has as its primary purpose the provision of loans at market-related rates of interest to developing countries at more advanced stages of development. The IDA, a legally separate loan fund administered by the staff of the

IBRD, was set up in 1960 to furnish credits to the poorest developing countries on much easier terms than those of conventional IBRD loans. The IFC, founded in 1956, supplements the activities of the IBRD through loans and assistance designed specifically to encourage the growth of productive private enterprises in the less developed countries. The president and certain senior officers of the IBRD hold the same positions in the IFC. The MIGA, which began operating in June 1988, insures private foreign investment in developing countries against such noncommercial risks as expropriation, civil strife, and nonconvertibility of currency. The four institutions are owned by the governments of the countries that subscribe their capital. To participate in the World Bank, member states must first belong to the International Monetary Fund (*q.v.*).

Index

AAC. *See* All-African Convention

Aasac. *See* All African Student Committee

Abacha, Sani, 315

Abdurahman, Abdullah, 45

Abolition of Passes and Co-ordination of Documents Act (No. 67) (1952), 56

abortion, lxiii

ABSA. *See* Amalgamated Banks of South Africa

acquired immune deficiency syndrome (AIDS), lxiii–lxiv, 159–60; deaths from, 159; education campaign, lxiii–lxiv, 159–60; number of cases of, 159

Advisory Committee on Defence Force Requirements, 350

Africa Muslim Party, 146, 292

African Christian Democratic Party: in elections, 275, 292; in National Assembly, 275

African Democratic Movement, 292–93

African Development Bank, 245

African Explosives and Chemical Industries, 227

African Independent churches, 135; healing dances of, 136; theology of, 135, 136–37

African languages: as languages of instruction, 64; newspapers in, 304; as official languages, 109–111, 114; radio broadcasts in, 237–38; television broadcasts in, 237

African Metals (Amcor), 225

African Methodist Episcopal Church (AME), 37

African Mineworkers Union (AMWU), 53; membership of, 53; strikes by, 53

African Moderates Congress Party, 293

African National Congress (ANC) (*see also* South African Native National Congress), lii, 202, 276–80; armed forces campaign against, 82, 359; armed struggle of, lvi, lviii, 61–62, 65, 76, 78, 81, 84, 175, 249, 277; banned, xlvii, lv, 61, 276; cabinet appoint-

ments, 261, 262, 279; conflict of, with Inkatha, lx, 257, 274, 275, 287–88, 388–89; in Congress of the People, 59; cooperation of, with Communist Party, 276, 277, 278, 280, 281, 282, 299; cooperation of, with National Party, 298; crackdown on, lvi, 70; defiance campaigns of, liv–lv, 59, 276; economists of, 177; in elections, xlvii, lxi–lxii, 84, 249, 275; ethnic distribution in, 300; foreign relations by, 305; formation of, 45–46, 276; generation gap in, 298–99, 300–301; in House of Assembly, 278; human rights violations by, 279, 394; in government, 177, 268, 279; and labor unions, 297; leaders of, 59, 276; matériel for, 277; members of, liii, 276; military wing, 277; in National Assembly, 275; national conference of, 277; organization of, 277; platform of, 52, 75–76, 252, 278; political succession in, lxv, 279; recruitment for, 277–78; schism in, 76; secret meetings of, with National Party, 256; supporters of, 116, 274, 277; symbols of, 3; transition proposals by, 81, 256, 257; transition talks, lix–lx, 250; unbanned, lix, 75, 332; in United Nations, 277; violence by, 395

African National Congress Women's League, 166–67; reactivated, 278

African National Congress Youth League, 281, 298–99; founded, 276; reactivated, 277–78

African Organisation for Women (AOW), 292

African Political Organisation, 45

African Resistance Movement, 61

Africans. *See* blacks

Africa Travel Association, 241

Afrikaanse Handelsinstituut. *See* Afrikaner Trade Institute

Afrikaanse Patriot, Die (The Afrikaner Patriot), 39

Afrikaans language, 129; as language of

491

members of, 135
anglicization, 42; failure of, 43
Anglo American Corporation, 70, 208, 220, 225
Anglo American Platinum, 208
Anglo-Boer Wars. *See* South African War; War of Independence
Angola, 66–67; civil war in, 306, 343, 356, 357, 360; Cuban troops in, 67, 318, 357; elections in, 314; independence for, lvi–lvii, 67, 357; intervention in, 306, 357, 358–59, 360; invasion of, 67, 343; relations with, 314–15, 331, 361; in Southern African Development Community, 306
Angola-Namibia Accord (1988), 314
antiapartheid resistance (*see also* political violence), 4–5, 58, 61, 255, 332; crackdowns on, lv, 62, 67, 70, 380; groups promoting, 294–95, 305
antimony, 210
AOW. *See* African Organisation for Women
apartheid, 54–65, 297; arrests under, lv, 57, 60, 61, 62, 70, 73; bannings under, 57, 61, 64, 65, 70; consolidation of, 62–63; costs of, 131, 173–74, 176–77, 185–86, 203–4; dismantling of, 5, 74–85, 285; economic problems under, 5, 185–86; education under, 56, 131, 146, 150–53; elections under, 272; employment under, 199; geographic distribution under, 63, 66, 107, 109; health care under, 156, 160–61; human rights violations under, 394; implementation of, liii, 4, 54–58, 91, 130–31, 335; international reaction to, 5, 67–68, 80, 91; and labor unions, 296; legal system under, 269–70; opposition to, liv–lv, lvi, lvii, lviii, 4–5, 58, 61, 131, 133, 146, 165, 166, 255, 276, 296; origins of, 90–91; principles of, 150; and religion, 133, 135, 141–44, 145; signs for segregation, 56; in South-West Africa, 310; support for, 128, 131, 141, 144, 150, 166, 296, 331, 336, 345, 368; telecommunications under, 236–37; tribes imposed under, 107; universities under, 154; and women, 56, 165–66
apartheid reform (*see also* Reconstruction and Development Programme), lviii, 69–71, 73–74, 153, 174, 177, 285;

Afrikaner participation in, 294; international reaction to, 173; National Party in, 285–86; opposition to, 84, 250, 251, 285, 385, 396; police under, 385, 396; problems in, 257; support for, 251, 257, 285; talks for, lix–lx, 250, 251
APLA. *See* Azanian People's Liberation Army
Apostolic Faith Mission of Southern Africa Church: members of, 135
Arabs: trade with, 33
Arap Moi, Daniel, 315
archaeological research, 5, 9, 89; art in, 6, 9
Argentina: joint military exercises with, 375
Argus Printing and Publishing Company, 304
Armaments Act (No. 87) (1964), 351
Armaments Corporation of South Africa (Armscor), 319, 351; board of, 352; employees, 352; marking department, 352; privatization of, 352; product exhibitions, 352; restructuring of, 352
Armaments Development and Production Act (No. 57) (1968), 351
Armaments Development and Production Corporation (Armscor), 351,
Armaments Production Board, 351
armed forces (*see also* paramilitary organizations; Union Defence Force): Afrikanerization of, 335; apartheid defended by, lviii, 331, 336, 345, 368; buildup of, 358; Cadet organization, 334; campaign of, against African National Congress, lviii, 82, 359; Catering Corps, 345; Citizen Force, 334, 335, 337, 365; civic-action role of, 362, 369–70; clandestine death squads of, 77; commander in chief, 363; Commandos, 336; conscription in, 335, 369; under constitutions, 362–63; decorations of, 377; demobilization of, 335; ethnic distribution in, 334, 336, 344, 345; headquarters of, 343, 363; history of, 334–39; homeland, 346–48; integration of, 257, 332, 334, 362–63, 365, 367, 368–69; internal security by, 335, 337, 340, 342–43; invasion of Angola by, 67, 331; invasion of Mozambique by, 359; invasion of

58, 59, 60, 276, 295

climate, 100–101; Marion Island weather station, 94; rainfall, 100–101, 215; rainfall line, 101; snowfall, 100; temperature, 100

Clinton, William J., 318

CNETU. *See* Council of Non-European Trade Unions

coal, 95, 212–13; effect of sanctions on, 213; exports of, 213; production of, 205, 212; reliance on, 173; reserves, 212, 225

coastline, 95

Codesa. *See* Convention for a Democratic South Africa

Coetsee, Hendrik "Kobie," 256

Coloured People's Congress: in Congress of the People, 59

Coloured Persons' Representative Council, 254

coloureds, 131–32; ancestors of, 89, 134; classification of, liii, 55; conflict of, with Afrikaners, liii, 4; discrimination against, liii, 45; and disease, 158; geographic distribution of, 131; histories of, 135; languages of, 131, 132; occupations of, 35; in police force, 385; origins of, 16; political affiliations of, 59; political representation for, lviii, 70, 71, 254; population of, 32, 44; population growth of, 105; religions of, 132, 135, 142, 146; revolt by, 335; rights of, 132; schools for, liv, 56; students, 154–55; voting by, xlvii, 55, 132, 254

Comintern. *See* Communist International

Commission of Inquiry into Certain Alleged Murders (Harms Commission), 77

Commission of Inquiry into Labour Legislation (Wiehahn Commission), 69, 200, 296

Commission of Inquiry into Legislation Affecting the Utilisation of Manpower (Riekert Commission), 69

Commission of Inquiry Regarding the Prevention of Public Violence and Intimidation (Goldstone Commission), 82, 84, 390–91; report of, 390–91, 395

Commission on Gender Equality, 259

Commission on Restitution of Land

Rights, 189, 259

Commission on the Demarcation of States/Provinces/Regions, 265

communications. *See* telecommunications

communism: apartheid definition of, liv, 57; campaign against, 131, 340; and labor unions, 296

Communist International (Comintern), 280

Communist Party of South Africa (CPSA) (*see also* International Socialist League of South Africa; South African Communist Party), 48; banned, liv, 281–82; cooperation of, with African National Congress, 276, 277, 281, 282; founded, 280; members of, 281; military wing, 277; name changed, 282; outlawed, 57; purged, 281; Stalinist faction, 281

Comoro Islands: investment in, 197

concentration camps, British: Boers in, 40–41, 130; deaths in, 41, 130

Concerned South Africans Group (Cosag), 82

Confucians, 135

Congregationalist Church: members of, 135

Congress Alliance, 276

Congress of Democrats: in Congress of the People, 59

Congress of South African Students (COSAS), 295

Congress of South African Trade Unions (COSATU), 72, 201–2, 279, 295; established, 201; members of, 201–2, 296

Congress of the People, 59–60; constituency of, 59

Congress Youth League, 58–59; formed, 58; leaders of, 58; platform of, 58

Conservative Party of South Africa (CP), 70, 285, 289; in elections, 74, 331

Constitutional Assembly, 252–53; under constitution of 1993, 259

Constitutional Court: under constitution of 1993, 259, 270–71; established, 272; proposed constitution submitted to, lxii–lxiii, 268, 363

Constitutional Guidelines for a Democratic South Africa, 278

constitution of 1909. *See* South Africa Act

constitution of 1961, 253–54; executive

204; and religion, 147; segregation of, 56, 131; spending on, 150, 192, 203; subsidies, 179; teacher:pupil ratios in, 153; for whites, 152, 203

Education Co-ordination Service, 153

Education Foundation, 147, 204

EEC. *See* European Economic Community

Eiselen, W.M., 150

elections: under apartheid, 272; of 1924, 284; of 1948, liii, 53–54, 130–31, 284, 335; of 1953, 58; of 1958, 58; of 1961, 58; of 1970, 69; of 1974, 69; of 1983 (reform referendum), 70–71; of 1984, 71; of 1987, 74, 127; of 1989, 272, 285, 331; of 1992 (reform referendum), 81; voter turnout in, 71

elections of 1994, xlvii, lxi, 5, 84–85, 249, 250, 272–75; accusations of fraud in, 84; African Christian Democratic Party in, 275, 292; African National Congress in, lxi–lxii, 249, 275; campaign for, 274, 286; coloureds in, 132; Democratic Party in, 275, 290; ethnic distribution in, xlvii; Freedom Front in, lxii, 275, 289; Inkatha Freedom Party in, lxii, 275, 288; Muslims in, 146; National Party in, lxii, 132, 249, 275, 286; observers for, 83, 275; Pan-Africanist Congress in, lxii, 275, 292; participation in, 84; political parties in, 292; preparations for, 83–84, 274–75; procedures for, 272–74, 275; united States assistance for, 318; voter turnout in, xlvii

Electricity Supply Commission (Eskom), 189, 223, 224–25; capital investment in, 224; coal used by, 212; imports by, 226; privatization of, 190

electric power, 173, 224–25; coal for, 212, 224; distribution of, lxiii, 177, 178; generation, 103; in homes, 224; hydro, 101–2, 225; imported, 225; nuclear, 223, 224; parastatals for, 176, 222, 223; in rural areas, 224

employment, 198–205; in agriculture, 91, 198–99, 217; under apartheid, 199; of blacks, li–lii, 199, 203; of domestic workers, 199; and education, 203–5; in fishing, 221; in homelands, 199; and job creation, 178, 223; in manufacturing, 53; in mining, 199; in prisons,

391–92; restrictions on, li–lii, 65, 69; in services sector, 199; in telecommunications, 237; in tourism, 240; by United States companies, 193; of whites, li–lii, 199

End Conscription Campaign, 342

energy production (*see also under individual energy sources*), 212–14; environmental problems caused by, 101; minerals for, 212–14

English language: as language of instruction, 43, 64, 148, 149; newspapers in, 304; as official language, 109; radio broadcasts in, 237–38; speakers of, 118, 131, 132–34; television broadcasts in, 237

English speakers (*see also* Asians, Europeans), xlvii, 297

environment, 101–3, 238–40; air pollution, 102–3; effect of population on, 239; impact assessments, 239; opposition to protection of, 239; problems in, 101, 102; protection of, 238–39; studies of, 239; and uranium, 356; water pollution, 102, 239

Environment Conservation Act (No. 73) (1989), 238

Eskom. *See* Electricity Supply Commission

ethnic identity: and language, 111

ethnicity: reaction to, 109; of Xhosa people, 117–18

EU. *See* European Union

Europe: opposition of, to apartheid, 68; in World War I, 335

Europe, Central: relations with, 305

Europe, Eastern: relations with, 305; settlers from, 90, 133

European Community (EC): sanctions of, 81, 350

European Economic Community (EEC): sanctions of, 192, 193, 350

Europeans, 132–33; ancestors of, 132–33; exploration by, 90; investment by, 175; and missionaries, 140; population of, 14, 15, 132; settlement by, xlix, 10–18, 24–33, 90, 135, 174, 333; trade with, 19, 33; violence by, 175

European Union (EU): election observers from, 83, 275; financial assistance from, 160; investment by, 320; relations with, 320–22; trade with, 195,

France: arms shipments to, 354; immigrants from, xlix, 129, 133, 349; matériel licensing agreements with, 351; missionaries from, 24, 139; relations with, 321–22; trade with, 321

Freedom Alliance, 82; decline of, 83; opposition by, 83

Freedom Charter (1955), lv, 59–60, 276, 291

Freedom Front, 250, 288–89; in elections, lxii, 275, 289; formed, 289; in government, 268, 275; support for, 289

Free State: agriculture in, 217, 218; capital of, 266; diamonds in, 209; gold in, 207; livestock in, 219; representation of, in parliament, 263; topography of, 95

FRELIMO. *See* Front for the Liberation of Mozambique

Frente de Libertação de Moçambique. *See* Front for the Liberation of Mozambique

Front for the Liberation of Mozambique (Frente de Libertação de Moçambique—FRELIMO), 311–12

fruit, 218

FSAW. *See* Federation of South African Women

Gabon: arms shipments to, 354

Gandhi, Mohandas: passive resistance campaigns, 45

Garvey, Marcus, 49

gas, natural: deposits, 99; exploration, 212; synthetic, 214, 227

Gastrow, Shelagh, 298

Gauteng: age dependency ratio in, 105; capital of, 266; diamonds in, 209; population of, 106–7; population density of, 106–7; representation of, in parliament, 263; urbanization rate in, 107

Gazankulu homeland, 128, 265; economy of, 128; government of, 128; malaria in, 158; population of, 128; self-government for, 66, 254; violence in, 128

Gcaleka Xhosa: chiefdom of, 119; homeland of, 119

GDP. *See* gross domestic product

Gencor, 220

General Export Incentive Scheme, 194

General Law Amendment Act (1963), 62

geographic regions, 95–99; rainfall line, 101

geology, 94–95

George: airport at, 234

George, Lloyd, 46

geostrategic situation, 349

Gereformeerde Kerk van Suid-Afrika (Reformed Church of South Africa), 142

German Democratic Republic (East Germany): matériel from, 277

Germany: immigration from, xlix, 14, 129, 133; missionaries from, 139; relations of, with Republic of South Africa, 39; relations of, with Union of South Africa, 49; trade with, 195

Germany, Federal Republic of (West Germany): matériel licensing agreements with, 351; trade with, 354

Geskiedenis van ons Land in die Taal van ons Volk (du Toit), 39

ghettos, li; in Kimberly, 35

Ginwala, Frene, 167

Glasgow Missionary Society, 139

GNP. *See* gross national product

gold, 95, 98, 207–8; deposits, 95, 207; discovery of, 1, 4, 34, 90, 175, 205; distribution of, 33, 34; export of, 53, 175, 176, 180, 187, 194; importance of, 33, 42, 173, 176, 245; mining of, 33, 34, 102, 128, 207; price of, lix, 173, 177, 180, 181, 191, 194, 208; profits, 207, 208; production, 34, 205, 207; reserves, 198, 207; revenues from, 53, 194

gold industry, 42; importance of, 187; protections for, 42; and Reserve Bank, 241; taxes on, 191; wages in, 245

Goldstone, Richard, 390

Goldstone Commission. *See* Commission of Inquiry Regarding the Prevention of Public Violence and Intimidation

Goodwill Zwelithini, King, 116, 257, 266, 288

Gorbachev, Mikhail, 322

Gore, Albert, 320

government: controls on industry, 227; ethnic distribution in, 297; loans by, 189; role of, in economy, 186–92

government, interim. *See* Government of

resignation of, 52
Hertzog (J.B.M.) government: "civilised labour" policy of, 49; discrimination under, 49, 51–52; parastatals under, 187
Het Volk (The People) party, 43; formed, 43
Highveld, 95; climate in, 101; elevation of, 95
Highveld Steel and Vanadium, 211, 225
Hindi, 133
Hindus, 134; number of, 135
history: anthropological, 5; importance of, 3
History of our Land in the Language of our People (du Toit), 39
HNP. *See* Herenigde (Reunited) National Party; Reconstituted National Party
Holland, Kingdom of, 18
Holomisa, Bantu, 347
homelands: armed forces of, 346–48, 365, 369; blacks removed to, 62–63, 103, 121, 185; citizenship in, 109; and economy, 186–86; employment in, 199; establishment of, li, liii–liv, 62; ethnic distribution in, 107; geographic distribution of, lv–lvi; independence for, 62, 66, 107–9, 126, 254; land degradation in, 102; manufacturing in, 224; opposition to, 66; population of, 63, 66; population density of, 66, 104, 106, 265; poverty in, 66, 185; self-government for, 66, 121, 254; support for, 70; television in, 237; transition of, from apartheid, 80, 265; violence in, 72, 78
Homo sapiens: fossils of, 89
Hottentot Code (1809), 25; abolished, 26
Hottentots. *See* Khoikhoi
House of Assembly (white), 71, 254; African National Congress representatives in, 278
House of Delegates (Asian), 71, 254
House of Phalo: A History of the Xhosa People in the Day of Their Independence (Peires), 119
House of Representatives (coloured), 71, 254
housing: construction, 178, 220; demand for, lxiii; subsidies, 179

Hout Bay: fishing in, 222
Huguenots: immigration of, 14, 218
Huisgenoot, 304
human rights, 272; abuses, 279, 394, 395, 396; under apartheid, 394, 395; and national reconciliation, 394–97; by police, 395; reparations, 396
Human Rights Commission, 259, 395; established, 272
hunter-gatherers, 6
hunting: by Africans, 31, 118; by Nguni, 113; by Voortrekkers, 29, 31
Hurutshe people, 126
hydroelectric projects, 101–2

ICU. *See* Industrial and Commercial Workers Union
IEC. *See* Independent Electoral Commission
IFP. *See* Inkatha Freedom Party
Imbumba Yama Nyama, 37
IMF. *See* International Monetary Fund
immigration, 1, 33, 43, 90; from African countries, 180; encouragement of, lvi, 148, 175; illegal, 263, 360; restrictions on, 15, 133; by whites, 1, 63, 175
Immorality Act (No. 5) (1927), 55
Immorality Act (No. 21) (1950), 55
imperialism, 33–44
imports: of agricultural products, 175; dependence on, 222; of food, 216, 217; industrial, 194–95, 226; of oil, 180, 185, 195; pattern of, 194–95; restrictions on, 194; tariffs on, 176, 191, 192, 194; value of, 195
Imvo Zabantsundu (Native Opinion), 37
income: from gold, 53
indentured laborers: from China, 42; from India, 29; number of, 42
Independent Broadcasting Authority, 237, 303–4
Independent Broadcasting Authority Act (No. 153) (1993), 303–4
Independent Electoral Commission (IEC), 83, 257, 274; administration of 1994 elections by, 274–75; electoral fund, 274; voter education by, 274
Independent Media Commission, 257
Independent Party, 289
India: immigrants from, 90, 349; indentured laborers from, 29, 90, 349; Man-

South Africa: A Country Study

isiZulu. *See* Zulu language
Islam, 145–46
Iso Lesizwe (Eye of the Nation), 288
Israel: arms shipments to, 354; fishing
rights of, 222; military cooperation
with, 323, 351; relations with, 323–24;
trade with, 323
Italy: matériel licensing agreements with,
351; relations with, 324; trade with,
195; in World War II, 335, 338
ivory: of Voortrekkers, 29; trade in, 19,
174

Jabavu, John Tengo, 37
Jameson, Leander Starr, 39
Jameson Raid (1895), 39
Japan: fishing rights of, 222; Mandela's
visit to, 77; trade with, 195, 210
JCI Limited, 208
Jewish Socialist Society, 280
Jews: discrimination against, lii, 51, 52,
133; population of, 133, 135, 323
Johannesburg, 266; airport at, 234;
crime in, lxiv; ethnic groups in, 133;
gold mining in, 34, 95; manufacturing
in, 223, 226; military headquarters in,
367; Muslims in, 146; population of,
34; squatter communities near, 53
Johannesburg Civil Defence program,
348
Johannesburg Consolidated Invest-
ments, 208
Johannesburg Stock Exchange, 192, 242;
foreign purchases on, 197; trading on,
173, 197, 244
Johannesburg *Weekly Mail*, 354
Johnnies Industrial Corporation, 208
Joint Air Training Scheme, 337–38
Joint Committee on Defence, 381
Joint Management Centers, 341–42;
advisory committees, 341–42; hierar-
chy of, 341
Joint Military Coordinating Council, 368
Joint Planning Council, 59; Defiance
Campaign of, 59; formed, 59
Jonathan, Leabua, 307, 359; ousted, 359
Jones, David Ivon, 280
Jordan: relations with, 305
journalists: detention of, 301–2
judges: appointment of, 270; sent to Swa-
ziland, 309

Judicial Services Commission: established, 272
judiciary: under constitution of 1961,
253

Kadalie, Clements, 49, 50
Kalahari Desert, 98; elevation of, 98; resi-
dents of, 5, 134
Kalahari Gemsbok National Park, 240
KaNgwane homeland, 265; self-govern-
ment for, 66, 254; and Swaziland, 117;
Swazi population of, 116–17
Kappiekommando, 166
Kaunda, Kenneth, 285, 313
Keep It Straight and Simple Party
(KISS), 292
Kenya: military cooperation with, 375;
relations with, 315, 361
Keys, Derek, 261, 263
Khoi people. *See* Khoikhoi people
Khoikhoi people, 6–7; extermination of,
12, 134, 135; geographic distribution
of, 7, 118; in Great Trek, 26; histories
of, 135; labor by, 16, 25; migrations of,
13–14; occupations of, 6; origins of,
89; population of, 7, 32; religion of,
139; settlements of, 7; as slaves, 135,
139, 174; social structure of, 7; trade
by, 7, 11, 12, 174; wars of, xlix, l, 12,
13, 15, 129–30, 335, 349
Khoisan languages, 134–35
Khoisan people, 89; descendants of, 89;
education of, 147; geographic distribution of, 10; religion of, 136
Kimberly, 266; airport at, 234; diamonds
in, 208; established, 33; locations
(ghettos) in, 35; manufacturing in,
224; migration to, for work, 34; military headquarters in, 367; racial dis-
crimination in, 35–36
KISS. *See* Keep It Straight and Simple
Party
Kissinger, Henry, 67–68, 84
Koeberg nuclear power station, 223, 225
Koevoet counterinsurgency force, 344–
45
Komati River, 99
Korean War, 338, 349
Kriel, Hernus, 386
Krige, J.D., 124
Kruger, Paul, 38, 39; assaults by, on Afri-

embargo on, lvi, 68, 192, 316, 325, 350, 353, 354; from France, 351; from Germany, 351; from Israel, 323, 351; from Italy, 351; licensing agreements, 351, 353; nuclear, 214, 355–57; police, 385; sales of, 354–55; self-sufficiency in, 351

Mauritania: relations with, 324

Mauritius: in Southern African Development Community, 306

Mbeki, Govan, 277, 320

Mbeki, Thabo, 326; as deputy president, lxii, 85, 190, 261; as successor to Mandela, lxv, 279

Mda, Peter, 58

MDM. *See* Mass Democratic Movement

media: censored, 301–2; ethnic distribution in, 297; removal of restrictions on, 75

Meiring, George, 382

men: circumcision of, 129; life expectancy of, 105; migration of, for work, 147; Nguni, 147; San, 6; status of, 6; wages of, 154; Zulu, 113, 333

Methodist Church: and apartheid, 143; members of, 135; missionaries from, 139

Mexico: relations with, 324

Meyer, Roelf, 263

mfecane ("crushing"): background to, 19–20; causes of, 19; missionaries in, 140; outcomes of, 20–24, 127; refugees from, 24, 120, 124, 140, 333

Mfengu people, 120, 140

Mhlakaza, 141

migration: by blacks, xlviii, xlix, li, 3, 8–9, 332; caused by *mfecane*, 24, 333; qualifications for, 148; restrictions on, 19, 56; by whites, xlix, l, 3, 63, 148

Military Area Radio Network (MARNET), 342

military assistance: from Britain, 350

military conscription, 335, 369

military cooperation: with Israel, 323; on technology, 351

military intelligence, 340, 377–81, 380, 381; budget for, 382

military officers, 369; from homeland armies, 369; from liberation armies, 369

military police: women in, 348

Military Psychological Institute, 376

military strategy: under Shaka, 21, 115, 333

military training, 370

Milner, Alfred, 39–40, 149

Milner's Peace, 41–43; failures of, 43

minerals, 95, 98; discovery of, 1, 4, 33–34; economic importance of, 173; export of, 194, 207, 210, 211, 214

miners: Sotho, 123; strikes by, 48, 337; Zulu, 115

mines: closing of, 208; development of, 194; geographic distribution of, 205, 210, 211, 212; migration to, for work, l, li, 34–35, 129, 147; number of, 207; taxes on, 191

Mines and Works Act (No. 12) (1911), li–lii, 44, 188

Mines and Works Amendment Act (1926), 49, 188

Mineworkers' Union, 296

mining: of copper, 205; of coal, 212–13; of diamonds, 95, 205; foreign investment in, 175, 196–97; of gold, 33, 34, 95, 180, 205; of iron, 205; as percentage of gross domestic product, 180, 205; of platinum, 95, 98; procedures, 207; of uranium, 214, 356

mining industry, 173, 205–14; color bar in, 48, 49, 130; electricity for, 224; employment in, 199, 213; environmental problems caused by, 101, 102; expansion of, 175, 205; importance of, 91, 175, 245; revenues of, 207; wages in, 207

Ministers' Council, 254

Ministry of Foreign Affairs, 304; Department of Foreign Affairs, 304

Ministry of Information, 262

Ministry of Law and Order, 262, 386

Ministry of Native Affairs, 56

Ministry of Posts, Telecommunications, and Broadcasting, 262

Ministry of Safety and Security, 262, 386

Ministry of Transport, 228, 234; Chief Directorate of Civil Aviation, 234

Ministry of Transport, Posts, and Telecommunications, 228

Minority Front, 293

missionaries, 119, 138; American, 139; British, 25, 139; Dutch, 139; French, 24, 139; German, 139; message of, 139–40; and *mfecane*, 140; Muslim,

Nguni, 113; of Voortrekkers, 29, 31
patron-client relationship: of Tswana, 126
peace committees, 80
Pedi language (sePedi, seSotho sa Leboa), 123; as official language, 109
Pedi people (*see also* Sotho people), 122, 123–24
Pedi state, 32; wars of, 36, 124
Peires, Jeffrey B., 119
penal code, 392–94
Penguin Islands, 360
People against Gangsterism and Drugs, lxiv
Peres, Shimon, 324
periodicals, 304
Perskor, 304
Peru: arms shipments to, 354
petroleum (*see also* oil), 212–14; imports of, 212; pipelines, 229; processing of, 212; reserves, 212
Petronet, 229
PFP. *See* Progressive Federal Party
Phatudi, Cedric, 124
Phosphate Development Corporation (Foskor), 189, 227; privatization of, 190
Phuthaditjhaba, 125
Pietersburg, 266; military headquarters in, 367
pipelines, 229, 235
Pirow, Oswald, 52
Plaatje, Solomon T., 46
platinum, 95, 98, 209–10; discovery of, 209; geographic distribution of, 209; production of, 205; reserves of, 209
Pokela, John, 292
police, 164, 340, 382–388; and apartheid reform, lviii, lxiv, 385, 396; attacks on, lviii, 72; under British, 25; brutality, 384, 395; complicity in violence, 84, 395; ethnic distribution in, 25, 385; headquarters, 387; history of, 382–84; intelligence, 380; matériel of, 385; military support for, lviii, 383; misconduct by, lxiv, 386; municipal, 386; national, 386; number of personnel in, 384, 386; organization of, 387; powers of, liv, 383–84; recruitment for, 386; regional, 386; reorganization of, 386; reserves, 384, 386; special constables, 384; spending on, 192; supplemental

duties of, 384; support by, for Inkatha Freedom Party, 82, 84, 389–91, 395; training, 385, 387; unions, 387–88; youth wing, 384
Police Act (No. 7) (1958), 383
Police Amendment Act (No. 70) (1965), 383
Police and Prisons Civil Rights Union (Popcru), 387
Police Reserve, 384
political crimes, 272
political demonstrations, 174; against apartheid, lviii, 255, 276, 368; against pass laws, 60
political elites, 297–301; Afrikaner, 297, 298, 301; black, 298, 299; evolving, 298; from labor, 298; white, 298
political harassment, 274
political parties (*see also under individual parties*), 275–93; Afrikaner, 250, 288–89; fourth force, 289; neo-Nazi, 250; reorientation of, 275; unbanned, lix, 275, 332
political reform, 69, 70, 332; coloureds under, 132; international pressure for, 5; negotiations for, 5; opposition to, 70, 72; reaction to, 75, 77
political repression, 4; of journalists, 301–2
political sanctions, 249, 350
political violence (*see also* violence), lxiv, 78, 81, 83, 177, 250; by African National Congress, lvi, lviii, 395; among blacks, 74, 386; attempts to contain, 80, 368; deaths from, 72, 74, 391; in homelands, 72, 127, 128; by Pan-Africanist Congress, lvi, lviii; police complicity in, 84, 395; and press censorship, 301–2; by students, 146; in townships, 72, 368–69
Pondo (Mpondo) people, 117, 120
Popcru. *See* Police and Prisons Civil Rights Union
Popular Movement for the Liberation of Angola (Movimento Popular de Libertação de Angola—MPLA), lvi–lvii, 359
population, 103–7; age distribution in, 105; density, 66, 104, 106, 265; distribution of, 106–7, 185; environmental impact of, 239; growth, 1, 15, 33, 63, 104–5, 239
population counts: of Africans, 44, 103;

60, 207

South African Coal, Oil, and Gas Corporation (SASOL), 189, 223; government investment in, 227; imports by, 226; stock offerings of, 190; and synthetic fuels, 214, 227

South African College (*see also* University of Cape Town), 149

South African Communist Party (SACP), liv, 82, 202, 276, 277, 280–83; armed struggle of, 249; cooperation of, with African National Congress, 278, 280, 282, 299; founded, 280; members, 282; in National Assembly, 280, 283; racial distribution in, 280; support for, 283; unbanned, lix, 75, 282, 332

South African Confederation of Labour, 296

South African Congress of Trade Unions (SACTU), 59, 296

South African Council of Churches, 144

South African Defence Forces (SADF). *See* armed forces

South African Employers' Consultative Committee on Labour Affairs, 296

South African Human Rights Committee, 395

South African Indian Congress (SAIC), 59; in Congress of the People, 59

South African Indian Council, 254

South African Institute of Medical Research, 159

South African Institute of Race Relations, 104, 391

South African Iron and Steel Corporation (Iscor), 49, 189, 225; privatization of, 190; stock offering of, 189–90, 225

South African Marine Corporation (Safmarine), 231–32

South African Media Council, 293

South African Medical and Dental Council, 161

South African Medical Service, 336, 375–76; organization of, 376; retrenchment of, 376; veterinary services of, 376

South African Medical Service College, 376

South African Medical Service Nursing College, 376

South African Medical Service Training Centre, 376

South African Military College, 365

South African Military Nursing Service, 348

South African Motor Corporation (Samcor), 226

South African National Defence Force. *See* armed forces

South African National Life Assurance Company (Sanlam), 47, 50, 242, 284

South African National Student Congress (Sansco), 295

South African National Trust Company (Santam), 47, 50

South African National Tuberculosis Association, 157

South African Native Affairs Commission (SANAC), 42

South African Native College at Fort Hare (*see also* University of Fort Hare), 154, 155

South African Native Convention (1909), 45

South African Native National Congress (*see also* African National Congress): formed, 45, 276

South African Naval College, 373

South African Naval Staff College, 373

South African Nursing Council, 161

South African Party (SAP), 43, 284; merged with National Party, 50, 284

South African Police. *See* police

South African Police Service. *See* police

South African Police Union (SAPU), 387

South African Politics (Thompson and Prior), 293

South African Press Association, 304

South African Press Council, 301

South African Rail Commuter Corporation, 230

South African Railways and Harbours Administration, 228, 234

South African Red Cross, 161

South African Republic (Zuid Afrikaansche Republiek), 29; annexed by the British, 38, 130; established, 29; independence of, 30; political organization of, 29; populations of, 30; relations of, with Germany, 39; relations of, with Orange Free State, 39; Rhodes's invasion of, 39; suffrage in, 38–39, 40

South African Reserve Bank, 241; directors of, 241; functions of, 241; and gold-mining industry, 241; policies of, 241

South African Secret Service (SASS), 380, 381

South African Students' Organisation (SASO), 63–64; banned, 65; established, 63; platform of, 63–64

South African Tourism Board (Satour), 240

South African Transport Services (*see also* Transnet), 228

South African War (1899–1902), li, 40–41, 43, 90, 333; consequences of, 130, 149; origins of, 124

South African Welfare Council, 162

South Atlantic Peace and Cooperation Zone, 326

Southern African Customs Union, 196, 307, 309, 311

Southern African Development Community: members of, 306; membership in, 305, 306, 326

Southern African Development Coordination Conference, 326

Southern Namib Desert, 98

Southern Oil Exploration Corporation (Soekor), 189, 212

Southern Rhodesia (*see also* Rhodesia; Zimbabwe), 67, 358; independence of, 309, 357; relations with, 309

South-West Africa (*see also* Namibia): apartheid in, 310; invasion of, 334, 337, 358–59; South African control of, 67, 310, 335, 357; war in, 338

South-West Africa People's Organisation (SWAPO), 67, 70, 311, 344, 357, 359, 360

South-West Africa Territorial Force, 343, 344; number of personnel in, 344; organization of, 344

Soutpansberg Mountains, 98

Soviet Union (*see also* Russian Federation): matériel from, 277, 360; relations of, with De Beers, 209, 322; relations with, 322; trade with, 195

Sowetan, The, 304

Soweto: pollution in, 103; uprising (1976), lvii, 64–65, 150–52

Spain: arms shipments to, 354; fishing rights of, 222

Spear of the Nation. *See* Umkhonto we

Sizwe

Special Forces, 343; ethnic distribution in, 344–45; missions of, 343–45; organization of, 343, 344, 345

Spoornet (railroad authority), 229

Sports Organisation for Collective Contributions and Equal Rights (SOCCER), 292

squatter communities, xlviii, li, 53, 103–4, 279; attempts to eliminate, 62; ethnic distribution in, 107; security sweeps in, 389

Stals, Chris, 244

Standard Bank of South Africa, 242

Star, The, 304

state of emergency: of 1985, lviii, 73; of 1994, 84

State Security Council, 340–41; members of, 341; organization of, 341; role of, 341; secretariat, 341; work committee, 341

Status of Union Act (1934), 253

Statute of Westminster (1931), 253

steel industry, 176, 211, 222, 226; production, 225

Stellenbosch: agriculture in, 15

strikes, 65–66, 202; by blacks, 72, 200, 202; costs of, 203; deaths in, 202; by miners, 48, 53, 72, 337; by students, 64, 146; suppression of, 334, 337

structural adjustment program, 194

Strydom, J.G.: as prime minister, 58

Strypoortberg mountain range, 98

student associations (*see also* South African Students' Organisation), 64; strikes of, 64

students: percentage of black, 155; segregation of, 154–55; strikes by, 64, 146

Subcouncil on Defence, 368

subsidies: for agriculture, 176, 187; for bread, 228

suffrage. *See* voting

sugar, 29, 31, 91, 218; export of, 215

Sunday Times, 304

Suppression of Communism Act (No. 44) (1950), liv, 57

Supreme Court, 259; decisions of, 55; divisions of, 270; judges in, 270

Sun City, 127

SWAPO. *See* South-West Africa People's Organisation

Swartberg Mountains, 99

Contributors

Rita M. Byrnes is Senior Analyst, African Studies, Federal Research Division, Library of Congress.

Nancy L. Clark is Associate Professor of History, California Polytechnic State University, San Luis Obispo, California.

Joshua Sinai is Senior Analyst, International and Security Studies, Federal Research Division, Library of Congress.

Joseph P. Smaldone is Chief, Weapons and Technology Control Division, U.S. Arms Control and Disarmament Agency, and adjunct professor, Georgetown University and University of Maryland.

Robert Thornton is Professor and Chairman of the Department of Anthropology, University of the Witwatersrand, Johannesburg, South Africa.

William H. Worger is Associate Professor of History, University of California, Los Angeles.

Published Country Studies

(Area Handbook Series)

550–41	Korea, South	550–37	Rwanda and Burundi
550–58	Laos	550–51	Saudi Arabia
550–24	Lebanon	550–70	Senegal
550–38	Liberia	550–180	Sierra Leone
550–85	Libya	550–184	Singapore
550–172	Malawi	550–86	Somalia
550–45	Malaysia	550–93	South Africa
550–161	Mauritania	550–95	Soviet Union
550–79	Mexico	550–179	Spain
550–76	Mongolia	550–96	Sri Lanka
550–49	Morocco	550–27	Sudan
550–64	Mozambique	550–47	Syria
550–35	Nepal and Bhutan	550–62	Tanzania
550–88	Nicaragua	550–53	Thailand
550–157	Nigeria	550–89	Tunisia
550–94	Oceania	550–80	Turkey
550–48	Pakistan	550–74	Uganda
550–46	Panama	550–97	Uruguay
550–156	Paraguay	550–71	Venezuela
550–185	Persian Gulf States	550–32	Vietnam
550–42	Peru	550–183	Yemens, The
550–72	Philippines	550–99	Yugoslavia
550–162	Poland	550–67	Zaire
550–181	Portugal	550–75	Zambia
550–160	Romania	550–171	Zimbabwe